Praise for This Book

"In a life laden with honors, Bill Gould has worked to lighten the burden of workers unjustly and illegally cut off from fully reaping the fruits of their labor. He cut his teeth in labor law at the United Auto Workers headquarters in Detroit, the first steps in a soaring career that has garnered national and international respect. This memoir is an expedition through some of the thorniest issues in labor law, and through a rich family history only three generations removed from slavery. And, of necessity, it is also a chronicle of a Boston native's fanatical and sometimes painful, though ultimately rewarding, devotion to the Red Sox."

—*Edward J. Boyer,* Los Angeles Times *(Retired)*

"Professor William B. Gould IV presents not only his own extraordinary story but the epic American story of the William Goulds who preceded him. At a time when our communities experience so much division, Professor Gould unites generations, working men and women with academics, and people of different races. He demonstrates that you don't have to be a Professor Kingsfield to have a long-lasting impact on your students. This book is essential reading for law students training to enter the profession, high school ethnic studies students seeking a better understanding of themselves and those around them, and for anyone wanting to join the fight against discrimination, overcome obstacles, expand opportunities, and make contributions to improve society."

—*John Trasvina, President Obama's HUD Assistant Secretary for Fair Housing & Equal Opportunity and, in the Clinton administration, headed the only federal government office devoted solely to immigrant workplace rights.*

"Bill Gould, one of the nation's leading labor lawyers and a lifelong Boston Red Sox fan, has made a huge impact on the game he loves: Major League Baseball. As chairman of the NLRB, he arbitrated player salary negotiations when club owners were on the verge of starting a new season with replacement players, after a general players' strike cancelled nearly half of the 1994 season, including the World Series, and threatened the 1995 season. He actually saved baseball as we know it. Following Gould's efforts, (then) Judge Sonia Sotomayor ordered the baseball training camps open and the season commenced with only a three-week delay. MLB and its Players Association would be wise to consult Bill Gould when its collective bargaining agreement comes up for renewal in 2026."

—*Joe Castiglione, Boston Red Sox Broadcaster 1983–2024 and Red Sox Hall of Famer, 2024 recipient of the National Baseball Hall of Fame Ford C. Frick Award*

"I first met Bill Gould as a 2nd-year Stanford Law School student in his introductory labor law class. His passion for working people and ability to give real world meaning to the labor laws were eye-opening and inspired me to a career in labor law and fighting for working people as he has. His memoir eloquently chronicles his extraordinary life and trailblazing careers in the courts, academia, and public service. For scholars and historians, his memoir is the story of labor and employment law in the US and parts of the world from the mid-20th century to the present. Other readers will be inspired to follow in his footsteps and fight for the causes to which he has devoted his life."

—*Mark Brewer, General Counsel, Michigan AFL-CIO and former Chair, Michigan Democratic Party*

"In over fifty years as a labor law professor at Stanford Law School, William B. Gould IV has written a lot about workers' rights and the efforts to maintain fair employment practices in the workplace. The range of this book is truly impressive. With great detail and research, it runs the gamut from his great grandfather's escape from slavery in 1862 and joining the US Navy to the author's many travels in the 1970s to 1990s to South Africa to help resolve industrial strife, lecture, teach about labor law reform, and to help win freedom from apartheid. He describes his meetings with leaders of the anti-apartheid movement, including Winnie and Nelson Mandela.

"The book also has a series of vignettes on his court room arguments for Black workers to obtain seniority rights in US factories and workplaces, his nomination and confirmation as the first Black Chair of the NLRB and his work as a salary arbitrator for Major League Baseball, whose players earn far more than the workers he normally dealt with. His great passion for baseball is portrayed in the report on his Stanford sports law class, where he invited Willie Mays, the fabulous center fielder of the San Francisco Giants to talk about the sport and his work in it. A fielder's glove from Mays is a proud remembrance for Gould of that visit. Can you imagine being a student in that class session?!

"This very thorough book should be read by anyone interested in workplace fairness issues and Gould's efforts to advance the opportunities for Blacks at work."

—*Joel A. D'Alba, former Chair, American Bar Association Section of Labor and Employment Law*

"Bill has been at the center of every major labor and employment law issue in the US over the last six decades including the development of collective bargaining, employment discrimination, and arbitration. He has also met most key players involved in those developments including JFK, Reuther, Clinton, RBG, Dusty, Mays, among many others. His memoir, which chronicles his life as a labor lawyer, law professor, arbitrator, politico, and chair of the NLRB and the Agricultural Labor Relations Board, is essential reading for anyone seeking to understand the capacity (and limits) of the law in promoting the well-being of workers."

—*Rafael Gely J.D., Ph.D., James E. Campbell Missouri Endowed Professor of Law, University of Missouri School of Law*

Those Who Travail and Are Heavy Laden

Other Books by William B. Gould IV

Black Workers in White Unions: Job Discrimination in the United States, Cornell University Press, 1977

A Primer on American Labor Law, MIT Press, 1982, 1986, 1993, 2004; Cambridge University Press, 2013, 2019

Japan's Reshaping of American Labor Law, MIT Press, 1984

Strikes, Dispute Procedures, and Arbitration: Essays on Labor Law, Greenwood Press, 1985

Labor Relations in Professional Sports (with Robert C. Berry et al.), Auburn House Publishing, 1986

Agenda for Reform: The Future of Employment Relationships and the Law, MIT Press, 1993

Labored Relations: Law, Politics, and the NLRB – A Memoir, MIT Press, 2000

Diary of a Contraband: The Civil War Passage of a Black Sailor, Stanford University Press, 2002

International Labor Standards: Globalization, Trade, and Public Policy, Stanford University Press, 2003

Bargaining with Baseball: Labor Relations in an Age of Prosperous Turmoil, McFarland & Company, 2011

For Labor to Build Upon: Wars, Depression and Pandemic, Cambridge University Press, 2022

Those Who Travail and Are Heavy Laden

Memoir of a Labor Lawyer

William B. Gould IV

Worcester Polytechnic Institute Press
Worcester, Massachusetts

Copyright © 2025 William B. Gould IV
First edition published 2025 by The WPI Press

The WPI Press
100 Institute Road
Worcester, MA 01609

Cataloging-in-Publication Data
Name: Gould, William B., IV, author.
Title: Those Who Travail and Are Heavy Laden: Memoir of a Labor Lawyer / William B. Gould IV.
Description: Worcester, MA : The WPI Press, 2025. | Includes Index.
Identifiers: ISBN: 978-1-965358-06-1 (paperback) | ISBN: 978-1-965358-08-5 (PDF) | ISBN: 978-1-965358-07-8 (epub)
Subjects: BIOGRAPHY & AUTOBIOGRAPHY / African American & Black | HISTORY / African American & Black | LAW / Labor & Employment |

This memoir is dedicated to my wife, Hilda Elizabeth Gould. It understates the matter to say that I am grateful to her for her love and patience, through thick and thin over many years.

CONTENTS

Preface	*xiii*
Acknowledgments	*xxxi*

Chapter 1: Song for My Father: The Goulds I Knew and Discovered — 1
My Father's Early Life — 1
My Mother and Our Early Boston Years — 7
A Move to New Jersey — 8
Family Visits — 19
Uncovering My Great-Grandfather's Story — 25

Chapter 2: My Path to Labor Law: McCarthyism, Civil Rights, and *Brown v. Board of Education* — 43
New Deal Democrats and the 1952 Election — 43
Joe McCarthy's Rise and Fall — 45
A Momentous Ruling, Race, and Values — 47
At the University of Rhode Island — 54
Momentum Toward the Law — 57
Cornell Law School — 58
Workplace Fairness Legislation — 62
Remarks Given at Stanford Law School — 65

Chapter 3: Detroit and United Auto Workers: My Labor Law Beginnings — 73
- My Summer Clerkship Begins — 74
- My Final Year at Cornell Law — 79
- Return to UAW — 83
- Exploring New Territory — 94
- Into the Home Stretch in Detroit — 99
- "In Memory of Walter Philip Reuther" — 103

Chapter 4: "Too Much Labor Law": The LSE and a Labour Party Perspective — 111
- Memories of Wartime — 112
- Arrival in London — 114
- Adjustments and Contrasts — 116
- Comparing Labor Issues — 118
- Classes, Meetings, and New Acquaintances — 119
- Travels Abroad, a Cold Winter, and a Life-Changing Debate — 122
- Musings: Where Next? — 125
- Home Again — 129

Chapter 5: Arbitration and Mediation: Labor Disputes in Washington, DC, and New York City — 131
- Off to Washington — 131
- At NLRB: Consequential Cases, Writing, and Constraints — 133
- New York: Answering to Three Lawyers — 135
- The EEOC and Title VII — 143
- Arbitration on My Own — 149
- U.S. Industries, and a Detroit Reunion — 155
- Wrapping Up in New York — 157

Chapter 6: Back to Detroit: Wayne State, Public Employees, and Detroit Edison — 169

Jumping into Teaching — 169
Public Education Arbitration — 171
Writing and Publishing — 173
Constitutional Law Issues — 176
Detroit Edison: Running Afoul of Title VII — 178
A Year at Harvard Begins — 183
Edison: Advances and Disappointments — 184

Chapter 7: Go West (and East), Young Man: Teaching, Affirmative Action, Politics, Travel — 207

Visiting Stanford — 208
Campus Life and Strife — 210
Arbitration — 215
Building Relationships — 216
Title VII Reverberations — 218
Back into Politics — 228
A Sojourn in Cambridge — 236
Travels and Research Abroad — 237

Chapter 8: Promoting Labor Rights and Standards Abroad: South Africa, Latin America, and Eastern Europe — 245

South Africa: Apartheid, Labor, Struggle — 246
Travels Beyond South Africa — 275

Chapter 9: Baseball Comes to Stanford Law: Salary Arbitration and a New Course in Sports Law — 283

Losing My Father — 283
ABA Assignments in France, Britain, Australia — 285

Challenging Assumptions in American Labor Law ... 290
Academic Ups and Downs ... 296
My Roots in Baseball ... 298
Teaching and Writing about Sports Law ... 319
Law School Committee Work ... 322
Baseball and Race Relations ... 325
Remembering Alvin Attles Jr. (1936–2024) ... 328

Chapter 10: Mr. Gould Goes to Washington: The Politics of the Confirmation Process ... 333
The Wheels Turn Slowly ... 336
The Rumor Mill Cranks Up ... 349
Many Meetings ... 351
The Hearing ... 356
The Opposition Ramps Up ... 361
The Vote ... 369

Chapter 11: Chairman of the Board: The Baseball Strike and the NLRB ... 373
Challenges from the Start ... 374
Reforms ... 377
Ups and Downs ... 378
The Baseball Strike ... 380
Adversaries and Allies ... 392
Departures and Disruption ... 400
The Home Stretch ... 407

Chapter 12: Return to California: Writers, Bus Drivers, Farm Workers, and More ... 419
The 2003 Writers Guild Election Dispute ... 420
The FirstGroup Independent Monitor Program ... 422
Protection of Construction Workers' Standards ... 440
The Agricultural Labor Relations Board ... 441

CONTENTS　　XI

    The City of San Francisco: Labor and Employment
    Discrimination Issues　　455
    The San Francisco Independent Reviewer 2021　　457

Epilogue　　467

Appendix 1　　475
  William B. Gould IV, introduction of Rev. Jesse Jackson,
  January 15, 1987 at Stanford University　　475

Appendix 2　　479
  "Fair Winds and Following Seas," Remarks Given at
  Memorial Service for Eugene P. Angrist, November 5,
  2005 in Washington, DC　　479

Appendix 3　　483
  William B. Gould IV, "Always and Forever, a Red Sox
  Devotee," **Red Sox Magazine**, 2008　　483

Appendix 4　　487
  William B. Gould IV, "My Fifty Years in Baseball: Ways
  in Which the Game Has Changed and Stayed the Same,"
  As the Inaugural Speaker of the Annual Hughie Jennings
  Memorial Lecture Series, April 1, 1996 at University of
  Maryland Law School　　487

Appendix 5　　501
  William B. Gould IV, "The Curse of the Bambino," S
  peech Delivered at "Baseball and the 'Sultan of SWAT'":
  A Conference Commemorating the 100th Birthday of
  Babe Ruth, April 27, 1995 at Hofstra University　　501

Appendix 6　　511
  William B. Gould IV, "Symposium on Sports and the Law:
  Introduction," Reproduction of Speech Delivered at
  Leonard Koppett's Memorial Service in Los Altos, CA, July 7,
  2003, **Stanford Law and Policy Review** 1 (2004)　　511

Appendix 7   519
William B. Gould IV, "Prospects for Labor Law Reform After the 2008 Election – Law Perspective," Speech Given at the 61st Annual Meeting Labor and Employment Relations Association, January 4, 2009 in Oakland, California   519

Appendix 8   527
William B. Gould IV, Remarks Given at Wilmington River Walk Watermen Sign Dedication, October 21, 2003 in Wilmington, North Carolina   527

Appendix 9   529
William B. Gould IV, Remarks Given at the Dedication of William B. Gould Park in East Dedham, Massachusetts, September 23, 2021   529

Appendix 10   537
William B. Gould IV, Remarks Given at the Unveiling of the Statue of William B. Gould at Gould Park in Dedham, Massachusetts, 169 Cong. Rec. E551-52, May 28, 2023   537

Index   *543*
About the Author   *563*

PREFACE

Come unto me all that travail and are heavy laden, and I will refresh you.   Matthew 11:28

In 2021, the citizens of Dedham, Massachusetts named a park in honor of my great-grandfather, William B. Gould. In 2023, one hundred years after his death, some of those same citizens unveiled his statue in William B. Gould Memorial Park. They brought back to public attention a man who had made a daring escape from slavery in 1862 and gone on to a distinguished career that included serving in the United States Navy and as a commander of the Grand Army of the Republic, founding Dedham's Episcopal Church of the Good Shepherd, and working for many years as a tradesman, plasterer, and mason of outstanding integrity.

One of the most remarkable gifts that my great-grandfather left behind is a diary, which he kept daily during his Navy service. It is filled with observations about the war and descriptions of battles in which he participated. The diary, discovered in 1958 by my father, William B. Gould III, reveals my great-grandfather's passionate belief in the objectives of the Civil War, "the holiest of all causes, Liberty and Union."[i] It also reveals his unwavering allegiance to "Uncle Samuel"—his name for Uncle Sam. When I read the diary myself, as a grown man, it moved me deeply: As I explain in chapter 1, I spent thirty years uncovering the rest of my great-grandfather's story and contemplating its impacts on my own life and choices.

WILLIAM JEFFERSON CLINTON

October 19, 2023

William B. Gould IV
Charles A. Beardsley Professor of Law, Emeritus
Stanford Law School
Crown Quadrangle
Room 238
Stanford, California 94305

Dear Bill:

I'm delighted to join your family, friends, colleagues, and many admirers in congratulating you as you celebrate 50 years on the faculty of Stanford Law School.

Throughout your legendary tenure, you've dramatically advanced the study and practice of labor and discrimination law, helping to make our nation fairer and stronger. Along the way, you have earned the respect of all who know you for your passion for the law, your academic scholarship, and your generous mentorship of countless students.

Of course, I will always be grateful I could convince you to spend four years in Washington as Chairman of the National Labor Relations Board. Your outstanding service brought new vision and purpose to the NLRB at a time of momentous economic and social change, and millions are better off today because of it. And perhaps most important of all—you saved baseball!

Thank you for all you've done throughout your life and career to move America forward. You have my very best wishes for many more years of health, happiness, and fulfillment.

Sincerely,

Bill Clinton

Figure 0.1: Letter from President Clinton to the author at the celebration of the 50th anniversary of appointment as professor of law at Stanford Law School.

Figure 0.2: Statue of William B. Gould, Unveiling at Dedham, Massachusetts, May 28, 2023.

Like the Comfortable Words[ii] that begin this preface, my great-grandfather's life, work, and words have given me strength as well as comfort in challenging periods of trial. In this past century, three generations removed from slavery, I was named as the first Black professor at Stanford Law School and the first Black chairman of the National Labor Relations Board in Washington. Truly, as I hope this book makes clear, I stand on the strong shoulders of William B. Gould and all the William B. Goulds who have gone before me.

I have been lucky in life. From the beginning of my involvement in law, I have had good fortune.

My labor–management relations work in Detroit and New York (chapters 3, 5, and 6) gave me the practical firsthand experience too infrequently possessed in the academic world of which I was to become a part. This experience supplemented my direct exposure to the world of manual work, which I had encountered as a teenager and young man. In essence, these two layers of experience prepared me for the work upon which I subsequently embarked.

I have been lucky to participate in and contribute to most of the important labor policy issues of my lifetime. Doors closed to my forebears opened for me, at least partially, as the cities burned in the 1960s. I have had a front row seat and more, in and outside of government, as observer, witness, chronicler, and teacher, during this past half century plus.

Though I have taken some excursions into the related fields of constitutional law,[iii] the overwhelming bulk of my work has been in the labor law field, that is, the relationship between unions as well as individual employees and employers, and the rapidly growing subcategory of employment discrimination or job bias discrimination.

In 1960, during the beginning of my United Auto Workers' Detroit experience (chapter 3), I recall the rather surprised reaction of a friend when I told her that I had three overriding objectives: (1) to litigate in the courts and administrative agencies on behalf of the labor movement and workers; (2) to write about labor law (though I was really thinking of articles of both the legal and nonlegal variety, not books); and (3) to be involved in the political process. "You want to be a trailblazer," she said—and I suppose that I did, and that I do now.

Examining the Seattle Building Trades court order, the first comprehensive relief against employment discrimination in the construction industry, in the early 1970s,[iv] I queried the lead union lawyer: "How is the decree working?"

"Wonderful," came the immediate reply.

"Oh, are many Blacks getting jobs?" I asked.

"No," came the prompt and satisfied reply.

Figure 0.3: My writing had begun in the 1950s and, along with a book review for the *Cornell Law Quarterly* (Volume 45, 1959), my very first publication appeared in *The New Republic* on September 21, 1959 (discussed further in chapter 8). This is the check for payment.

This was the reality hiding behind the law's substance. Throughout most of my life in labor and law, I have attempted to examine and sort out that reality.

For more than six decades my work has been known in the labor and employment arenas, initially attributable primarily to my role in job discrimination litigation. But my writings were always involved, bringing me to the attention of the Equal Employment Opportunity Commission (EEOC),[v] a development which plunged me headlong into the Black–white seniority dispute. My leading case was *Stamps v. Detroit Edison*[vi] (chapter 6), to which I devoted much of an entire decade, enduring airplanes and hotels as I engaged in research, writing, and oral argument in aspects of courtroom combat. The framed congratulatory letter from Legal Director Mel Wulf of the ACLU (which funded a number of my cases) hangs proudly on my Stanford office wall.

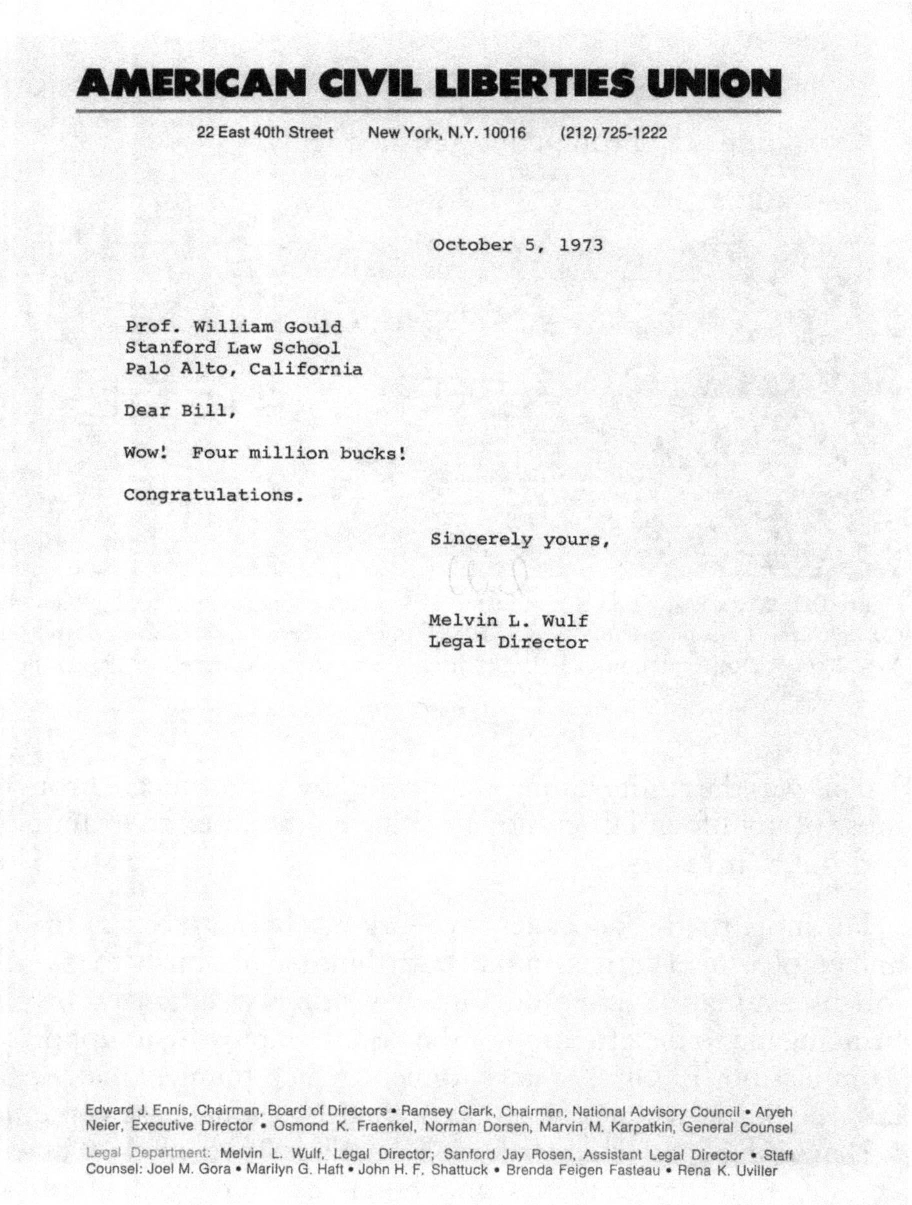

AMERICAN CIVIL LIBERTIES UNION

22 East 40th Street New York, N.Y. 10016 (212) 725-1222

October 5, 1973

Prof. William Gould
Stanford Law School
Palo Alto, California

Dear Bill,

Wow! Four million bucks!

Congratulations.

Sincerely yours,

Melvin L. Wulf
Legal Director

Edward J. Ennis, Chairman, Board of Directors • Ramsey Clark, Chairman, National Advisory Council • Aryeh Neier, Executive Director • Osmond K. Fraenkel, Norman Dorsen, Marvin M. Karpatkin, General Counsel

Legal Department: Melvin L. Wulf, Legal Director; Sanford Jay Rosen, Assistant Legal Director • Staff Counsel: Joel M. Gora • Marilyn G. Haft • John H. F. Shattuck • Brenda Feigen Fasteau • Rena K. Uviller

Figure 0.4: Letter from ACLU Director Mel Wulf in response to the news of the *Detroit Edison* 1973 decree.

In tandem with all this, I wrote articles about racial discrimination in employment,[vii] racial seniority disputes,[viii] and the ways in which labor arbitration (this process and my apprenticeship with it are developed in chapter 5) and the right to protest employment conditions could be woven into antidiscrimination strictures.[ix] Acting as an arbitrator, I heard one of the first of the cases presenting arbitration procedures where the parties had tailored contract provisions to both arbitral principles as well as fair employment practice requirements.[x] As employment discrimination law developed in the 1970s, so also did my first book, *Black Workers in White Unions: Job Discrimination in the United States* (1977). I continued with my work on this subject in this century[xi] and I accepted San Francisco Mayor London Breed's invitation to assess racial inequities in the city workforce and thus provide the first post-George Floyd "reckoning" (described in chapter 12) in 2021.[xii] Much of my writing[xiii] and lecturing has involved me in the related subject of South Africa (described in chapter 8).

But, of course, I am a law professor as well as a lawyer. After seven years in the real world of private practice and junior status government service, I was called into the world of law teaching—fifty-three of those years at Stanford Law School as of this writing. I had been publishing contributions since the 1950s, craving the time available to reflect and put pen to paper. And yet in an academic world into which I stumbled accidentally, I have attempted to develop my thoughts—through the written word as well as the teaching of thousands of students—to illuminate the way in which the law and its assumptions frequently do not relate to the real world around them. I have been helped in this quest, not only by my occasional roles as expert witness or as a third-party impartial arbitrator hearing numerous cases through my appointment by labor and management, but also through government service itself. In the important arbitration process, I have analyzed and resolved disputes since 1965 (chapter 5)—and some of my scholarly writing has focused on this process.[xiv]

Amongst labor law academics, there has been a tendency to assume that the law's content necessarily shapes the behavior of labor and management—a tendency that diminishes and sometimes ignores other factors in the labor–management universe. As this book emphasizes, I have been attacking this view since my early years in labor law, though I cannot claim complete consistency in adherence (or lack thereof) to this conventional wisdom.[xv] My book *Agenda for Reform*,[xvi] the object of conservative attacks in my 1993 Senate confirmation hearings, properly emphasizes the law. The law has been deeply enmeshed in gig economy labor disputes over whether workers are employees—protected by the law—or independent contractors.[xvii] The role of law has been similarly dominant in the world of professional athletes[xviii] and now so-called "amateurs" as well—and, for me, this was a fortunate byproduct of my long love affairs with the Boston Red Sox and Boston Celtics, both of which had begun in childhood.[xix]

But, as I have noted in recent commentary,[xx] suddenly in 2023, the United Auto Workers, the International Brotherhood of Teamsters, the Hollywood writers' and actors' unions, hotel and casino workers, and others have seen an upsurge in protests and strikes, a phenomenon obtained without the realization of any element of the law reform sought over more than seven decades.[xxi] Whether this will endure or, equally important, translate into union organizing in Tesla, the foreign automobile transplants, or joint ventures—or in the case of the Teamsters, through organization of Amazon and Federal Express—remains to be seen.[xxii]

In essence, my work has sought to emphasize the reality of considerations beyond the law, about, that is, a balance between law and its background. In 1962 (chapter 3) as well as in 2022,[xxiii] I wrote about the relevance and yet subordinate nature of law in labor relations. Today, as in the years when I started out as a labor lawyer, the infusion of a youthful cadre as a prerequisite to union organizing is once again vital.[xxiv] The springboard for some of my writing and thinking in this regard was articulated in the 1980s, after my examination of the impact of American labor law in other cultural contexts (chapters 4, 7, 8, and 9).[xxv] In the wake of my tumultuous ride as chairman of the NLRB (chapter 10), I noted organized labor's continued decline simultaneous with the pro-collective-bargaining policies of my Clinton Board[xxvi] and, ultimately, the Obama Board as well.

My second governmental assignment was as chairman of the California Agricultural Labor Relations Board in Sacramento (chapter 11). The Agricultural Labor Relations Act had been born out of a dream, often called "a dream statute," created by United Farmworkers' leader Cesar Chavez and Governor Jerry Brown during his first term in the 1970s. But as my own work and numerous discussions with Governor Brown revealed, the dream had become a nightmare. The UFW had become moribund, with no interest in organizing the unorganized, for reasons well developed by Miriam Pawell.[xxvii] Here, because of this kind of behavior, the law did not matter.

The law can be a factor in labor–management relations, but only a factor. Its relevance is why I have developed a scholarly focus upon Supreme Court labor jurisprudence (chapter 9).[xxviii] And, even more important, that is why I wrote one of my early books, *A Primer on American Labor Law*, as the result of many speeches before foreign audiences and other nonspecialists or nonlawyers. An abiding theme of my work has been an attempt to distill the mysteries of the law and to make it accessible to a wide range of individuals.

Finally, there is the political process. Both my Washington and Sacramento assignments brought me near to it and, in some measure, involved me in the process itself, though I always maintained my independence from politics, whether my agency was independent (as in Washington with the NLRB) or part of a department of state government (as in Sacramento with the ALRB).

My role in politics has been on the periphery, perhaps best illustrated not only by my federal and state contacts with all three branches of government, but also by my role as cochairman of the California State Bar Committee on Wrongful Discharge, where I and colleagues provided extensive recommendations relating to workers who are not protected by a collective bargaining agreement or other forms of protection.[xxix] At the same time, I became more directly involved through such ventures as my San Francisco Union Square speech in 2000, protesting Justice Scalia's injunction against Broward County in Florida. The closest I have come to political deliberations themselves has been modest access through (1) my work as a delegate at both the 1962 Michigan Democratic Convention and the 1974 interim Democratic Conference in Kansas

City; (2) the 1996 access to the Democratic Convention in Chicago given to me by my former student, Michigan Democratic Chairman Mark Brewer; and (3) my selection as an alternate without floor privileges to the Democratic Convention in Boston in 2004.

But, in the end, my most substantial political involvement has been my analysis of recent Supreme Court decisions, that is, journal articles emanating from my UAW and London School of Economics days on the relationship between unions and the political process.[xxx]

Those Who Travail is a story of my work in labor law, employment discrimination law, and other arenas. To this work I have tried to put my shoulder to the wheel, like so many who have gone before me. But this book is more than a recounting of my efforts. It is a testament to the values instilled in me by my family, values shaped in a life three generations removed from slavery.

Figure 0.5: William Benjamin Gould, in about the late 1870s or early 1880s.

Figure 0.6: Cornelia Williams Read Gould, around 1890.

Figure 0.7: William Benjamin Gould (1837–1923) c. 1900, when Commander of the Grand Army of the Republic (GAR) in Dedham, Massachusetts.

Figure 0.8: WBG with his six sons in service. This photograph of all of the Gould veterans originally appeared in the NAACP's magazine, *Crisis*, in December 1917 and in *Diary of a Contraband: The Civil War Passage of a Black Sailor*. All of the sons are veterans of World War I except WBG Jr., a Spanish-American War veteran. Standing behind WBG are, from left to right: Lawrence Wheeler Gould, James Edward Gould, William Benjamin Gould Jr., Ernest Moore Gould, Herbert Richardson Gould, and Frederick Crawford Gould.

Figure 0.9: Plaque and road marker established for William B. Gould in Wilmington, North Carolina, November 2017.

Figure 0.10: William Benjamin Gould IV (1936–) delivering a speech about William B. Gould at the establishment of a park named for the latter, Dedham, Massachusetts, September 23, 2021. (Courtesy of Getty Images.)

Figure 0.11: Gould family at William B. Gould Park on September 23, 2021, Dedham, Massachusetts. First row, left to right, grandchildren: Timothy Samuel Jr.; Joseph Jeremy; William Benjamin VI; Alina Emma. Second row, left to right, sons: Edward Blair; Timothy Samuel Sr.; William Benjamin V; author's wife, Hilda Elizabeth; William Benjamin Gould IV; daughter-in-law, Dorena Rodriguez.

NOTES

[i] William B. Gould IV, *Diary of a Contraband* (Stanford, CA: Stanford University Press, 2002), 47, 186; from a diary entry dated May 6, 1864.

[ii] "Come unto me all that travail and are heavy laden, and I will refresh you." Matthew 11:28. For this specific phrasing, see the Church of England, *The Book of Common Prayer* (London: Oxford University Press, 1928), 235.

[iii] William B. Gould IV, "Right to Travel and National Security," *Washington University Law Quarterly* no. 4 (1961).

[iv] William B. Gould IV, "The Seattle Building Trades Order: The First Comprehensive Relief Against Employment Discrimination in the Construction Industry," *Stanford Law Review* 26 (1974).

[v] William B. Gould IV, "The Negro Revolution and the Law of Collective Bargaining," *Fordham Law Review* 34 (1965); William B. Gould, "Labor Law and the Negro," *New Leader*, October 12, 1964, 10; William B. Gould IV, "Race and the Unions: The Negro and Organized Labor by Ray Marshall," *New Leader*, July 5, 1965, 20–21; William B. Gould IV, "Discrimination and the Unions," *Dissent* 14 (1967); William B. Gould IV, "Discrimination and the Unions," in *Poverty: Views from the Left*, eds. Jeremy Larner and Irving Howe (New York: Morrow, 1968).

[vi] Stamps v. Detroit Edison Co., 365 F. Supp. 87 (E.D. Mich. 1973), rev'd sub nom. EEOC v. Detroit Edison Co., 515 F.2d 310 (6th Cir. 1975), vacated, 431 U.S. 951 (1977) (remanding for further consideration in light of Supreme Court's decision in *International Brotherhood of Teamsters v. United States* [citation omitted]). Cf. William Wong, "Lawyer William Gould Prods Courts to End Job Bias; His Activism Sometimes Irks Peers," *Wall Street Journal*, August 21, 1974 (chapter 6, n56); Louis Heldman, "Black Employees Win $4 Million: Edison Is Found Guilty of Bias," *Detroit Free Press*, October 3, 1973 (chapter 6, n48).

[vii] William B. Gould IV, "Racial Equality in Jobs and Unions, Collective Bargaining, and the Burger Court," *Michigan Law Review* 68 (1969); William B. Gould IV, "Black Workers and the General Lockout," *New York Times*, July 17, 1971.

[viii] William B. Gould, "Employment Security, Seniority and Race: The Role of Title VII of the Civil Rights Act of 1964," *Howard Law Journal* 13 (1967); William B. Gould IV, "Seniority and the Black Worker: Reflections on Quarles and Its Implications," *Texas Law Review* 47 (1969).

[ix] William B. Gould IV, "Labor Arbitration of Grievances Involving Racial Discrimination," *University of Pennsylvania Law Review* 118 (1969); William B. Gould IV, "Black Power in the Unions: The Impact upon Collective Bargaining Relationships," *Yale Law Journal* 79 (1969).

[x] *Basic Vegetable Products, Inc.*, 64 Lab. Arb. Reports 620 (1975); *Weyerhauser Co.*, 78 Lab. Arb. Reports 1109 (1982).

[xi] William B. Gould IV, "Title VII of the Civil Rights Act at Fifty: Ruminations on Past, Present, and Future," *Santa Clara Law Review* 54 (2014).

[xii] William B. Gould IV, "Report of San Francisco Independent Reviewer for Mayor London Breed," June 16, 2021, https://sfdhr.org/sites/default/files/documents/Reports/Report-SF-Independent-Reviewer-Mayor-Breed.pdf.

[xiii] William B. Gould IV, "Black Unions in South Africa: Labor Law Reform and Apartheid," *Stanford Journal of International Law* 17 (1981).

xiv William B. Gould IV, "The Supreme Court and Labor Arbitration," *Labor Law Journal* 12 (1961); William B. Gould IV, "On Labor Injunctions, Unions, and the Judges: The Boys Markets Case," *Supreme Court Review* (1970); William B. Gould IV, "On Labor Injunctions Pending Arbitration: Recasting Buffalo Forge," *Stanford Law Review* 30 (1978); William B. Gould IV, "Judicial Review of Labor Arbitration Awards—Thirty Years of the Steelworkers Trilogy: The Aftermath of AT&T and Misco," *Notre Dame Law Review* 64 (1989); William B. Gould IV, "Steelworkers Trilogy After a Half Century," keynote address given at the annual meeting of the National Academy of Arbitrators, May 27, 2010; William B. Gould IV, review of *Labor and the Legal Process*, by Harry Wellington, *Wayne Law Review* 16 (1969).

xv Some of my early writings assumed that the law could do much. William B. Gould IV, "The Question of Union Activity on Company Property," *Vanderbilt Law Review* 18 (1964); William B. Gould IV, "Union Organizational Rights and the Concept of 'Quasi-Public' Property," *Minnesota Law Review* 49 (1965).

xvi William B. Gould IV, *Agenda for Reform: The Future of Employment Relationships and the Law* (Cambridge: MIT Press, 1993).

xvii William B. Gould IV, "Dynamex Is Dynamite, but Epic Systems Is Its Foil—Chamber of Commerce: The Sleeper in the Trilogy," 83 *Missouri Law Review* 989, 1008 n. 130 (2018); William B. Gould IV, "The Future of the Gig Economy, Labor Law, and the Role of Unions: How Will They Look Going Forward?," in *Annual Proceedings of National Academy of Arbitrators, Stanford Public Law* (2017). Cf. *Dial-A-Mattress* 326 NLRB 884, 894 (1998) (Gould, Chairman, dissenting); *Roadway Package System, Inc.*, 326 NLRB 842, 854 (1998) (Gould, Chairman, concurring).

xviii William B. Gould IV, *Bargaining with Baseball: Labor Relations in an Age of Prosperous Turmoil* (Jefferson, NC: McFarland, 2011); William B. Gould IV, Robert C. Berry, and Paul D. Staudohar, *Labor Relations in Professional Sports* (Dover, MA: Auburn House, 1986); Robert C. Berry and William B. Gould IV, "A Long Deep Drive to Collective Bargaining: Of Players, Owners, Brawls, and Strikes," *Case Western Reserve Law Review* 31 (1981); William B. Gould IV, "Players and Owners Mix It Up," *California Lawyer*, August 1988; William B. Gould IV, "Football, Concussions, and Preemption: The Gridiron of National Football League Litigation," *Florida International University Law Review* 8 (2012); William B. Gould IV, "Labor Issues in Professional Sports: Reflections on Baseball, Labor, and Antitrust Law," *Stanford Law and Policy Review* 15 (2004).

xix NCAA v. Alston, 141 S. Ct. 2141 (2021); William B. Gould IV, "In the Wake of Alston: The Future of 'Amateur' Athletics," speech given to the VI in Palo Alto, CA, October 2021; William B. Gould IV, Glenn M. Wong, and Eric Weitz, "Full Court Press: Northwestern University, A New Challenge to the NCAA," *Loyola of Los Angeles Entertainment Law Review* 35 (2015); William B. Gould IV, *A Primer on American Labor Law* (Cambridge: Cambridge University Press, 2019), 491–531. See, e.g., William B. Gould IV, "'87 Red Sox: Que Sera Sera," *San Francisco Chronicle*, April 28, 1987; William B. Gould IV, "The Agony of Following the Sox," *San Francisco Chronicle*, September 11, 1986; William B. Gould IV, "New Players Are Helping Red Sox Challenge for A.L. Pennant," *The Tribune* (Oakland), August 28, 1988; William B. Gould IV, "Truth of Baseball Faces a Changeup," *San Jose Mercury News*, April 5, 1993; William B. Gould IV, "Life with the Red Sox: Ups and Downs," *San Jose Mercury News*, October 9, 1988; William B. Gould IV, "Baseball: The Sweet and the

Sour," *The Tribune* (Oakland), April 4, 1988; William B. Gould IV, "A Two-Strike Swing at Affirmative Action," *San Jose Mercury News*, June 15, 1987.

[xx] "We've seen this leadership style before: William B. Gould IV, a professor emeritus at Stanford University who began his labor law career working at Solidarity House in Detroit when Reuther was in charge, said Fain is channeling the legendary union leader. 'This is a revised update on the tactics that Reuther employed in the 1940s, bringing pressure to bear on those who will not bargain with you effectively while you spare those employers who are providing progress, as they are with Ford,' said Gould, who played a critical role in ending the baseball strike of the 1990s as chairman of the National Labor Relations Board.

'The membership composition of the union has changed from when I was at Solidarity House between 1961–62, and they're trying to find sustenance through new membership and new industries,' said Gould, who wrote *For Labor to Build Upon: Wars, Depression and Pandemic*, (Cambridge University Press, Spring 2022).

'Shawn Fain represents a revival, of sorts,' said Gould, who said he first saw Reuther speak at his alma mater, Cornell University Law School in 1959. 'Reuther would be proud of him if he were with us today. Fain represents a revival of that aggressiveness which existed in the 1940s . . . before diminished union organizing and legal hostility brought the movement to a grinding halt.'

'Reuther was fiery. Reuther was inspirational,' said Gould, the first Black faculty member at Stanford Law. 'Fain's success lies in his ability to reach the workers in much the same way Reuther did. There's no demarcation line between politics and economic activism. The two go hand in hand.'" Phoebe Wall Howard, "Fain's Biting Style Creates Momentum: Gains Could Grow Union, Set Stronger Footing for Future," *Detroit Free Press*, September 25, 2023. See also William B. Gould IV, "SLS's William Gould Discusses the 'Hot Labor Summer' and Why More Strikes Likely Are Coming," *Legal Aggregate*, July 25, 2023; William B. Gould IV, "William Gould on the UAW Strike and the Summer of Red-Hot Labor Unrest Extending into Fall," *Legal Aggregate*, September 18, 2023.

[xxi] William B. Gould IV, "New Labor Law Reform Variations on an Old Theme: Is the Employee Free Choice Act the Answer?" *Louisiana Law Review* 70 (2009); William B. Gould IV, "The Employee Free Choice Act of 2009, Labor Law Reform, and What Can Be Done About the Broken System of Labor–Management Relations Law in the United States," *University of San Francisco Law Review* 43 (2008).

[xxii] Christopher Otts, "UAW Leader's Expansion Drive Struggles," *Wall Street Journal*, November 15, 2024. This difficulty may be compounded in a new Trump era. See Ian Kullgren, "Battered Unions Brace for Years of Clashes Under Trump, Musk (1)," *Bloomberg Law*, November 25, 2024; Chris Bohner and Eric Blanc, "Labor's Resurgence Can Continue Despite Trump," *Radish Research*, November 18, 2024. Cf. Victor Reklatis, "Trump's Labor-Secretary Pick Backs Unions, but Here's Why They Aren't Celebrating Just Yet," *Market Watch*, November 26, 2024; Max Kutner, "Trump Picks Teamsters-Backed Ore. Rep. For Labor Secretary," *Law360*, November 25, 2024.

xxiii William B. Gould IV, *For Labor to Build Upon* (Cambridge: Cambridge University Press, 2022), 3; William B. Gould IV, "America's Latest Union Push Needs Teeth," *Boston Globe*, July 25, 2022; William B. Gould IV, "Those Were the Days; These Are the Days: Some Reflections on the Limits of Law," review of *Beaten Down, Worked Up: The Past, Present, and Future of American Labor* by Steven Greenhouse, *University of San Francisco Law Review* 54 (2019–2020); William B. Gould IV, "Mistaken Opposition to the N.L.R.B.," *New York Times*, June 20, 1985; William B. Gould IV, "Labor Takes Look at Itself, Finds Unsettling Things," *Los Angeles Times*, March 29, 1985; William B. Gould IV, "Taft-Hartley Revisited: The Contrariety of the Collective Bargaining Agreement and the Plight of the Unorganized," *Labor Law Journal* 13 (1962).

xxiv Nora Eckert and Mike Colias, "Activists Helped Get Huge UAW Win," *Wall Street Journal*, November 1, 2023; Nora Eckert, "UAW Urges Honda, Subaru Workers to Join Union," *Wall Street Journal*, November 11–12, 2023.

xxv William B. Gould IV, *Japan's Reshaping of American Labor Law* (Cambridge: MIT Press, 1984); William B. Gould IV, "Taft-Hartley Comes to Great Britain: Observations on the Industrial Relations Act of 1971," *Yale Law Journal* 81 (1972).

xxvi William B. Gould IV, *Labored Relations: Law, Politics, and the NLRB—A Memoir* (Cambridge: MIT Press, 2000).

xxvii Miriam Pawell, *The Crusades of Cesar Chavez: A Biography* (New York: Bloomsbury Press, 2014).

xxviii William B. Gould IV, "The Supreme Court and Labor Law: An Analysis of Recent Trends and Developments," *Case Western Law Review* 16 (1965); William B. Gould IV, "The Supreme Court and Labor Law: The October 1978 Term," *Arizona Law Review* 21 (1979); William B. Gould IV, "The Supreme Court's Labor and Employment Docket in the 1980 Term: Justice Brennan's Term," *University of Colorado Law Review* 53 (1981); William B. Gould IV, "The Burger Court and Labor Law: The Beat Goes on—Marcato," *San Diego Law Review* 24 (1987); William B. Gould IV, "The Supreme Court, Job Discrimination, Affirmative Action, Globalization and Class Actions: Justice Ginsburg's Term," *University of Hawai'i Law Review* 36 (2014) (based on a speech delivered to the Labor & Employment Section of the State Bar of Hawai'i in Honolulu, Hawai'i on October 11, 2013); William B. Gould IV, "Crippling the Right to Organize," *New York Times*, December 17, 2011. Cf. William B. Gould, "Solidarity Forever – Or Hardly Ever," *Cornell Law Review* 66 (1980); William B. Gould IV, "Status of Unauthorized and 'Wildcat' Strikes Under the National Labor Relations Act," *Cornell Law Quarterly* 52 (1966–1967).

xxix William B. Gould IV, "Protection From Wrongful Dismissal," *New York Times*, October 22, 1984; William B. Gould IV, "Wrongful Discharge Litigation: Should There Be Unfair Dismissal Legislation?," statement to the Assembly Labor and Employment Committee of the California Legislature, October 15, 1984.

xxx William B. Gould IV, "Organized Labor, the Supreme Court, and Harris v. Quinn: Déjà Vu All Over Again?," *Supreme Court Review* (2014); William B. Gould IV, "Politics and the Effect on the National Labor Relations Board's Adjudicative and Rulemaking Processes," *Emory Law Journal* 64 (2015); William B. Gould IV, "How Five Young Men Channeled Nine Old Men: Janus and the High Court's Anti-Labor Policymaking," *University of San Francisco Law Review* 53 (2019).

ACKNOWLEDGMENTS

I have been thinking about this book for a number of years, particularly after a trilogy of my books, which involved my work, and which also appeared in this century: *Diary of a Contraband: The Civil War Passage of a Black Sailor* (Stanford: Stanford University Press, 2002); *Labored Relations: Law, Politics, and the NLRB – A Memoir* (Cambridge: MIT Press, 2000); and *Bargaining with Baseball: Labor Relations in an Age of Prosperous Turmoil* (Jefferson, NC: McFarland, 2011).

Though the major focus of this book is my professional work, it also relates to my early, formative years. This aspect of it became more difficult given the deaths of all who had the most direct first-hand information, aside from myself—first, my father, William B. Gould III, in 1983; then, my mother, Leah Felts Gould, in 2008; and finally, my baby sister, Dorothy Leah, in 2019. In the decade between the deaths of my mother and my sister, Dorothy and I had many more frequent conversations about childhood, as we attempted to pull memories together without our parents, who were now both gone. Now she, too, has been gone for five years and with her, necessarily, some of those memories.

I have been fortunate because the Goulds were diarists. This has been clear since the first William B. Gould wrote extensively during the War of the Rebellion, or Civil War, between 1862 and 1865, along with his many written contributions to the *Anglo-African* in

New York City—and then composed his recollections in 1911, the fiftieth anniversary of the Civil War, and gave speeches in Dedham, recorded by the *Dedham Transcript*. I edited, commented upon, and discussed this diary in 2002.

That diarist tradition was passed on to my father, and I possess and have read most of his diaries from the thirties, forties, and fifties. I myself have kept diaries, both as a child and particularly during my United Auto Worker days in the early sixties and my NLRB tenure in the nineties. A strength and weakness in my life lies in my retention of a good deal of paper from the past.

Gabrielle Jacquelynn Braxton, Stanford Law School '25, has done everything: research, administrative organization, typing, and a liaison with numerous publishers who granted us permission to reprint as well. One of the most extraordinary research students I have had over many years, she did it all. She had an interest in *Those Who Travail* and she possessed not only a first-rate mind (after all, this is true of most Stanford Law students), but also enormous energy, unflappability, and a steady and stable temperament in the midst of tumult. She has done it all.

Gabrielle also organized a kind of "Gould team" inside the Law School: the extraordinarily resourceful and able David (Davey) Conand; Sergio Stone; and Alba Holgado. And there have been other valuable research assistants as well: Michael Thorburn and Elizabeth Spaeth. At the beginning of this project, Leeann Park accepted the challenge of typing some of the earlier drafts with good cheer.

A number of people read earlier versions of the manuscript. Professor Michael Klarman of Harvard Law School, our student here at Stanford Law School in the early eighties, not only read the first eight or nine chapters carefully but provided the most detailed editorial advice which I have ever encountered. I accepted most of it. I could not have made it without the Braxton-Klarman duo and the other above-mentioned people, as well as the first-rate Stanford

Law Library. George Wilson and Taryn Marks come to mind in particular, but there are so many in our outstanding library who have been extremely helpful to me.

Beyond Professor Klarman, others read earlier versions of the manuscript as well, and I am grateful to them, too: William Wong, author of *Sons of Chinatown*, as well as an excellent article dealing with my litigation in the seventies (William Wong, "Lawyer William Gould Prods Courts to End Job Bias; His Activism Sometimes Irks Peers," *Wall Street Journal*, August 21, 1974); Professor Michael Wald of Stanford Law School; Sir J. Keith Stuart of London; William Abrams of Seattle; and Richard Morningstar of Marion, Massachusetts.

I was helped substantially by the fine editorial work of Claire Mowbray Golding. Her skillful contributions helped me considerably. Also, I am grateful to Hilary Claggett of Georgetown University Press, who read the manuscript and presented ideas as well.

I am forever grateful to so many in Massachusetts who helped me trace my father's work and accomplishments: Anna Gold and Arthur Carlson, both of Worcester Polytechnic Institute in Worcester, Massachusetts, which my father attended; Bill Ballou of the *Worcester Telegraph and Gazette* filled me in with research and articles about my father's work at Worcester Tech and his life in Worcester, Massachusetts. Ms. Gold and Mr. Carlson organized a wonderful posthumous tribute to my father in May 2023, attended by the president of Worcester Tech as well as Mr. Ballou and many others, commemorating my father through the naming of the Unity Hall entrance in Worcester Tech in his memory. And finally, in Massachusetts, I am grateful to Donna Halper, who pulled together much information about William B. Gould III's professional work in Massachusetts. In New Jersey, I thank Fred M. Carl and John Dilks for their research of my father's work at Fort Monmouth and Camp Evans.

William B. Gould III '25 Entrance

William B. Gould III was among the early African American graduates of WPI. He was active in the early days of the WPI Wireless Association and went on to a distinguished career in electrical engineering. At Fort Monmouth, N.J., he was responsible for the installation and operation of early warning radar systems on the West Coast of the U.S. During the 1950s, he directed research involving instrumentation of long-range guided missiles at Cape Canaveral. He retired as section chief in the Electronic Warfare Laboratory. This gift courtesy of Drs. Laurie Leshin and Jon Morse.

Figure FM.1: In this century, Worcester Polytechnic Institute dedicated a hall of one of their new buildings, Unity Hall, in memory of my father.

ACKNOWLEDGMENTS

Louis Jones of the Walter Reuther Library of Labor and Urban Affairs (to which I donated my *Stamps v. Detroit Edison* papers) was of great assistance to me, and in Detroit, as well, Marshall Widick, now assistant general counsel of the UAW (the post that I held in '61–'62), helped me pull together papers relating to the wage arbitration that I did in 1989 involving the Detroit Federation of Teachers and the Detroit Board of Education. Mr. Widick helped me with the retrieval of UAW memories as well.

As the first William B. Gould was rediscovered in Dedham, Massachusetts, and Wilmington, North Carolina, I encountered many people to whom I am grateful for discussions about him and the Gould family: Brian Kearney; Tom Sullivan; Dan Hart; and Beverley Tetterton. All of these people have been helpful, and I am grateful to them.

I am especially grateful to my wife, Hilda Elizabeth, for her love and support over many years and many books, particularly this one, *Those Who Travail*. She has stood with me throughout and I could not have made it without her.

I owe my family here in Stanford, California, as well as my parents from Massachusetts and New Jersey, the deepest gratitude. It has been my good fortune to benefit from these relationships. Without them, I could not have obtained whatever success has come my way.

William B. Gould IV
December 1, 2024

1

SONG FOR MY FATHER: THE GOULDS I KNEW AND DISCOVERED

On September 8, 1934, my father, William B. Gould III, wed my mother, Leah Jeronia Felts. The ceremony was conducted by the Cowley Fathers at St. John the Evangelist Episcopal Church on Bowdoin Street, behind the Massachusetts State House in Boston.[1] Their first residence was 180 Dana Street, where they could hear the crowd's roar at Fenway Park.[2]

As my mother explained it, my father told her that getting married in the Episcopal Church was important because that way it would "take." It certainly did. Though hardly strait-laced in demeanor, I never heard my father raise his voice to my mother in any discussion. I never heard him utter a swear word, either—not even hell or damn—in contrast to many of his good pals. Indeed, my view always was that theirs was a marriage made in heaven. And I have always felt that their relationship, and the environment fostered by it, gave me a chance in life. Throughout my life, I have always thought of my father as "the man," to use the words of jazz pianist Horace Silver's "Song for My Father."[2]

MY FATHER'S EARLY LIFE

My father—hereafter known as WBG III—was born on March 14, 1902, in Cambridge, Massachusetts. His mother, Hannah Jordan Gould, and father, William B. Gould Jr., a Boston department store clerk and local Republican Party leader in Dedham, resided at 84

Stoughton Street in Readville, Massachusetts, in a house that sat on the boundary line between Dedham and Boston. My father was the oldest of four—his siblings being Ernest, Marjorie, and Robert.

Church, Sports, Radio

From childhood, WBG III was an active parishioner in the Episcopal Church of the Good Shepherd in East Dedham—the parish founded by my great-grandfather, and the one in which the first four William B. Goulds were all baptized. Here, my father served both as a choirboy and an acolyte under the highly regarded Father William Cheney, trudging the long distance from his home to church every Sunday—and often twice a Sunday during Lent. WBG III was also involved with the Boy Scouts, led by Franz Kudlidge, who enjoyed an icon-like status along with Father Cheney and the high school football coach. My father often recounted his experiences in church and the Boy Scouts; football got much less attention.

WBG III appears to have taken advanced math and science courses in school, and read voraciously, as he did throughout his life, but perhaps especially during a bout of rheumatic fever, which kept him out of school for an entire year and caused him to graduate in 1921, a year behind his class in Hyde Park High School. While at Hyde Park, he was the chief operator at the Hyde Park amateur radio station and radio club.

Notwithstanding his illness and other activities, WBG III played football at Hyde Park High. This was a time when eleven men played the entire game, and signals were called out for each play without a huddle. He didn't talk much about those games or his role at right halfback, except for the occasional unflattering story. For instance, he would talk about a 1920 Hyde Park–Fitchburg game, described in the press as one in which "Hyde Park had several opportunities to score but lost thru [sic] fumbling."[3] In this game, as he recounted, Hyde Park was near the goal line. My father said that he was given the ball—perhaps a handoff or a direct snap from center—and "the line opened up a hole big enough for a Mack truck to go through." Upon being given the ball, he fumbled.

A year or two later he was at a dance, having a wonderful time with a very attractive girl until she looked at him carefully and said, "Wait a minute—aren't you the guy who fumbled at Fitchburg?" My father always said that the evening went "downhill from that point onward." But he never spoke of the next week's game, when Hyde Park's fortunes were reversed in a 28–0 victory, and the *Boston Globe* said: "In the fourth period, Killilea went over for a touchdown after bringing the ball down the field with Fellows, Gould and Roman doing most of the rushing."[4] My father's understated personality, like that of my great-grandfather, was modest and self-effacing. He was inherently skeptical of big and loud egos.

Though my father claimed that he was slow moving in his youth, he also ran cross-country. He often spoke of a race when a top competitor had crossed the finish line well before him and a number of people said, "Bill Gould will never cross the finish line." A friend of his contradicted them: "Bill Gould will always finish. He will make it even if he finishes in last place." And he did make it, finishing long after the victors, at the end of the pack. This is a story that I have often reflected upon when confronted with difficulties of my own.

Like many of today's scientists, whose careers began in what has been called the "Age of Information," my father's emerged during the "Age of Marconi," which brought the wireless radio to millions. My father was one of the first thirteen-year-olds to obtain a ham radio license.

In the fall of 1921, WBG III entered Worcester Polytechnic Institute (WPI) on a scholarship. A member and officer of its Wireless Association, he took radio lessons and led WPI's involvement in transatlantic communications. But in 1922 he was compelled to withdraw because, in the words of President Ira Hollis, "It was a matter of great regret to me that we could not give him a scholarship this year. The State scholarships ran out this year and we lost forty scholarships giving free tuition to students."[5]

So he withdrew. But apparently he reentered WPI at least once, and perhaps more than once, as he appears in some of the 1923 and 1924 publications, sometimes identified as a member of the class of

'26. He was an active chief of the college's Wireless Association in '23. In 1924, he represented WPI at the annual convention of the New England division of the American Radio Relay League, held in Springfield, Massachusetts, and he was elected to the executive board of that organization. He also served as a reporter for WPI's Tech News.

And he remained loyal to WPI long after he completed his work at the college. This relationship may have been strengthened by the fact that he remained in Worcester for some years thereafter, and worked at its first radio station, now known as WTAG. Then called WDBH (before its affiliation with the Worcester *Telegram and Gazette* newspaper), my father became its chief when his lifelong friend, Charles Butler, received a promotion: "exigencies of daily and evening broadcasts again demanded an addition to the staff, with a result that William B. Gould, 3d, was secured."[6]

These were years when WBG III seems to have connected with friends of all ages and backgrounds, as he did throughout his entire life. I remember him saying that during this period his substantial group of friends were always asking: "What does Bill want to do? Where does Bill want to go?" He was the center of activity.

Setbacks, the Sea, and Mayor Curley

Although he subsequently took courses at both MIT and Boston University, my father did not find professional employment for much of the twenties and thirties. He was hired at Western Electric in Kearney, New Jersey, but not immediately discerned to be Black. When the company discovered that he was Black, he was told that it was "against corporate policy to hire Negroes."

In the aftermath of this setback, he became involved with the Navy and the sea. The Quincy *Patriot-Ledger* wrote:

> *Gould enlisted in Class V-3 of the Naval Communication Reserve in 1925 as Radioman First Class, and since his enlistment he has performed training periods with the Naval radio compass stations at Deer Island and North Truro,*

> *and on USS Eagle No. 19 and 46, the excellent performance of these duties winning for him promotion to chief radioman. Gould's ultimate transfer to the Third Naval District is a distinct loss to First District Communication Reserve.*[7]

Thus he was part of the U.S. Naval Reserve in the twenties as radioman (and ultimately chief radioman) and served with the Merchant Marines, putting out to sea on the USS *Edith* in the Caribbean and Florida. But even as a seaman, he soon encountered difficulties. In 1928, for example, he disembarked in Jacksonville, Florida, and walked its streets, minding his own business. During the walk he observed another Black man being stopped and arrested by the police for no apparent reason. Soon, he was similarly detained, arrested, and spent the night in jail. The following morning, he and the other fellow appeared before a judge, who sentenced the other detainee to three months of hard labor. My father, having witnessed what appeared to be the innocence of the other fellow, feared for the worst. But when he told the judge his story, explaining that he was simply walking the streets, he was released. He had been in the white part of Jacksonville, the wrong part of town for him to be walking. To this day, I cannot understand how he avoided criminal sanctions, other than through the persuasive quality of his personality.

Even before these terrible incidents, my father, from his post at sea, was looking elsewhere for opportunity. On August 2, 1930, he wrote to W.E.B. Du Bois, the renowned civil rights leader of the NAACP, editor of its magazine, *Crisis*, and frequent opponent of Booker T. Washington, as follows:

> *My uncle, Dr. Ernest M. Gould, of Washington, has told me that he understands that the Government of Abyssinia, is desirous of securing a number of Engineers as part of a development program they are undertaking. He suggested that I write you, since you might be able to give me the necessary information.*

I have had three years of Electrical Engineering at Worcester Polytechnic Institute, and one semester at Massachusetts Institute of Technology. For four years, I was employed as Radio Engineer at Radio Station WTAG in Worcester, Mass. My next work was three months as Telephone Equipment Engineer for the Western Electric Co., Kearny, N.J. Since October 1929, I have been out at sea as a Radio Operator. I am 28 years old.

Any Engineering work in Abyssinia along communication lines, telephone, telegraph or radio, would be of interest to me, and I believe I am well qualified to handle such. My home address is, 84 Stoughton Ave., Hyde Park, Mass., and will you please address me there.

Respectfully Yours, William B. Gould III[8]

Du Bois, who may have known my great uncle Ernest, a World War I veteran, through the former's interest in the Black veterans of World War I[9], responded quickly but rather vaguely.[10] My father did not receive the letter for more than two months, being at sea.[11]

At some point in the thirties my grandmother intervened in my father's fortunes. Somehow, my family seems to have arranged for Mayor James Michael Curley, one of Boston's leading Democratic Party bosses,[12] to speak to the Dedham Sons of Union Veterans of the Civil War. My father was hired as an architect by Mayor Curley—this was valuable work in the desperate circumstances of the Great Depression. But my father's functions were not only the professional work of a draftsman, but also of the ward-heeler variety for the Curley machine. WBG III always spoke of the mayor with considerable fondness, characterizing him as a kind of Robin Hood who helped both the poor and sometimes himself. And he always took care to point out the mayor's shamrock-studded home in Jamaica Plain as we drove by on our summer visits to Massachusetts.

My father enthusiastically described the speeches with which Curley enthralled a wide variety of audiences. Curley would gain the support of the most hostile or indifferent crowds, my father said, by telling them basic facts about their own organization and thus flattering them in the most effective manner. At the same time, he was aware of the mayor's shortcomings, commenting frequently on Curley's ambition to be appointed by the Roosevelt administration—which expressed considerable skepticism about him—as Ambassador to the Vatican.

Boston's Mayor Curley served time in jail while in office on more than one occasion—for example, he was reelected to Congress while in prison for taking a civil service examination for a constituent—but he helped the Gould family when it needed help. My father liked to describe his work distributing Curley campaign literature in the Irish section of Boston. In a fine imitation of the accent, he would relate how the Irish ladies would ask him, in their thick brogue, "Are you a good Catholic bye [boy]?" "Oh yes, ma'am," Episcopalian WBG III would quickly answer, knowing full well that the inevitable response would be, "Well, come right in then, me bye."[13]

MY MOTHER AND OUR EARLY BOSTON YEARS

My mother was born in Attleboro, Massachusetts on July 6, 1914, to Nellie Nash Felts and Cethe Felts Jr. She had four sisters. The oldest was Mary, who died as a young woman from tuberculosis—the scourge at that time—and the others were Jeanette, Naomi, and Ruth. She also had a brother, Cethe Jr. After graduating from Attleboro High School, where she always had the very best grades, my mother enrolled in Boston University and had completed one year when she and my father met at a dance in Boston.

Even prior to her eventual acquisition of a bachelor's degree in the 1940s, my mother began to teach at Red Bank Catholic High School in New Jersey, and then in the public schools in Eatontown. She liked the challenge of this work and was very good at it. In an age before two-income families were common, my father was cautiously supportive. He always wanted the best for my mother, but I think he held the traditional view that earning was the man's responsibility. Notwithstanding this view, I never heard him express anything short of approval of my mother's work.

I was the first of their two children, born July 16, 1936, in Boston at Lying-in Hospital.[14] My first home was a small, modest dwelling at 75 Harvard Avenue in the Hyde Park section of Boston.

I remember very little about those early Boston years. By the time I was born, my father was employed with the Metropolitan Police Radio Department in Boston, and I can remember the lights of the police car flashing when it brought him home at the end of every workday. I also recall that we—and most people in Massachusetts in those days—called the front of the house the *piazza*, because of the large Italian population in Boston. When we arrived in New Jersey in 1940, that portion of the house was called the *porch*.

My only other recollection is of my mother advising me that there would soon be a new addition to the family. My sister, Dorothy Leah, was born on July 18, 1940, also in Boston, shortly before our departure to Long Branch, New Jersey.

A MOVE TO NEW JERSEY

We left Hyde Park when my father obtained a position as an engineer with the United States Signal Corps of the United States Army in Fort Monmouth, New Jersey. Prior to the move, at the time of Dorothy's birth, my parents arranged for me to stay in Maplewood, New Jersey, with one of my father's best friends, Karl Wohlers and his wife Doris. Karl, the son of German immigrants and a graduate of Rensselaer Polytechnic Institute (RPI), had been very close friends with my father since their college days working as summer laborers on the railroad in upstate New York. Doris, Karl's wife, was British.

During my visit I recall that Karl and Doris set up a group of toy soldiers for me, which every morning when I came downstairs had been mysteriously moved from one place to another. This was part of the excitement in a pleasant stay as I waited for both the appearance of Dorothy and the move from Hyde Park to Long Branch, New Jersey. It was the eve of World War II, and the demand for more war production personnel resulted in my father's employment as one of the first Black professionals in Fort Monmouth, which was just a few miles from our new home: 458 Bath Avenue in Long Branch.

On Radar's Cutting Edge

My father's position at Fort Monmouth as a radio engineer for the Signal Corps enabled him to develop expertise in radar, which was advancing rapidly at the beginning of World War II. Indeed, he spent a number of months in California in 1942 installing the early warning radar system that would constitute a barrier against potential Japanese incursions. He was away for so long that, when he returned, my two-year-old sister cried, frightened to see a strange man in the house.

This World War II work resulted in my father being called upon again to perform some of the same functions at the beginning of the Korean War, in Alaska and the Aleutian Islands. His primary workstation shifted from Fort Monmouth to Camp Evans in Belmar, New Jersey. This new round of work began in September 1950, and the weather was already so wintry at his destinations that plane travel to those remote areas was downright scary. So scary, in fact, that my father decided to come back across the country from California by train. There would be no more blinding sleet and snowstorms and consequent air pockets for him when he traveled by train—a mode of travel, in any event, that he always enjoyed.

In the 1950s, WBG III would once again be involved in the pioneering aspects of radar equipment: He directed research involving the installation of long-range guided missiles at Cape Canaveral. His picture appeared in the Asbury Park Press around the time that Sputnik, the earth's first artificial satellite, was launched by the Soviet Union on October 4, 1957. My father had listened to the launch on his ham radio. He was part of the Countermeasures group that spent weeks and months tracking Sputnik to determine its orbits and make predictions about its course. Dr. Harold Zahl, director of research at Camp Evans, had this to say about my father and others involved with Sputnik:

> *But perhaps most important of all during these early hours on October 5 were the efforts of a few of our Countermeasures people operating an experimental direction finding station at Collingswood, N.J. In the open, and in freezing weather, Bill Gould, Harold Jaffe and associates, day after day, all through the long nights, week after week, gave out bearing information—information vitally needed by the Vanguard Computing Center at NRL to determine orbits and make predictions. Yet, the Soviet had kicked off, but before we could really play in the game, we had to find the ball.*[15]

Ultimately, my father was to become a section chief in the Electronics Warfare Laboratory, focusing on both counterintelligence and the use of radio and radar for meteorological purposes. Retiring in 1969, he was honored posthumously by InfoAge at Camp Evans as one of the early Black electronic engineers at Fort Monmouth.

Figure 1.1: "Engineers in the Countermeasures Division, U.S. Army Signal Engineering Laboratories have been pinpointing the satellite orbit with radio direction finders. Picture shows William B. Gould III of Elberon (right) who has been directing the operation, and seated, Walter T.J. Day of Neptune, at the oscilloscopes which record the flights." Asbury Park Sunday Press, October 13, 1957. © by the Asbury Park Press – USA TODAY NETWORK.

Figure 1.2: "William B. Gould (left), Long Branch, can tell almost to the minute when rain will fall. Chief of the radar weather section, at Evans Signal Laboratory, he can see storm clouds as far away as 100 nautical miles thru [sic] this radar equipment. Standing is John J. Slattery, Spring Lake, chief of the radar section, who holds many secrets." *Asbury Park Press,* July 27, 1947. © by the Asbury Park Press – USA TODAY NETWORK.

Figure 1.3: Plaque provided to Gould family of WBG III at ceremony honoring the latter, June 4, 2016.

Childhood Joys and Challenges

I cannot recall the actual move to our home in Long Branch, but I know we lived next door to our landlords, Mr. and Mrs. Maggs, on Bath Avenue in the white part of town. My recollection is that the Maggs were rather dour, forbidding, but not particularly unpleasant. I don't know how they managed to rent their house to us, given the unchallenged segregation existing in 1940.

One of my earliest memories of Long Branch is my father's purchase of a 1937 Plymouth with a large running board, on which a passenger could stand outside of the car. The forties were a period that may seem archaic to many today. For example, during World War II, our milk deliveries were made by a horse-drawn truck. In the winter, I remember seeing drivers signaling their horses to move along by throwing snowballs at them. Another memory is of a new neighbor, Harry Levin of Long Branch, who lived less than a block away from us on the other side of Bath Avenue. A few days after our arrival, Harry pressed his nose against the screen door and looked into our living room. His vivid imagination was impressive—he told my father that he had a job on the railroad at the age of four. Years later, this story still brought smiles to my parents' faces. Harry and I went through public school together and were teammates in football.

Harry and I began kindergarten that year of our arrival, when I also remember meeting Harvey Stein. Harvey was one of my first friends in school, telling me that the way to evade teacher detection and punishment for laughing in class was to put my hand over my mouth. I can recall giggling with Harvey, thinking we were deceiving the teacher by covering our mouths. Aside from Harry and Harvey, I remember only one other student, Alice Zigenfuss, standing on a chair, twirling her long braids through the air when the teacher was out of the room.

From kindergarten through fourth grade, I attended the Broadway School, about a ten-minute walk uptown from our house via Pearl Street. I remember walking down that street one day, wondering who I was—this person I saw in the mirror at home, who acted and spoke a particular way. Who was I?

From the very beginning of my life in Long Branch, there was the problem of accent. All the kids I met made fun of my silent "Rs," my Massachusetts manner of speech. I, therefore, quickly switched to a New Jersey accent, with its sharp "Rs," and I retain it to this day. Contrarily, my parents never lost their Massachusetts accents throughout their lives.

Some of my abiding recollections about the early New Jersey years relate to illness. Twice I was home in bed for substantial periods, felled by pneumonia. The first bout, when penicillin may not yet have been available to us in Long Branch, lasted seven weeks. The second bout ran for four weeks; by then penicillin and perhaps other vital drugs were available. In addition to my bouts of pneumonia, I was asthmatic and in the summer months went through exhausting hay fever sessions accompanied by asthma, and the wheezing and shortness of breath associated with it. To combat all these ailments, I took weekly allergy injections and pills that made me sleepy—probably Benadryl.

Much to my mother's consternation, when I was home ill during the day, I acquired the practice of listening to country music on Newark's radio station, WAAT. This was well before my involvement in jazz, as I recall my mother insisting that I turn off that "terrible music," a view to which I now subscribe.

All my illnesses meant long absences from the early years of school, and from my teachers: Miss Biggio in first grade, Miss Lepow in second, and Mrs. Bresett in third. During those periods, my mother read to me about the enchanting Ichabod Crane, as well as other stories by James Fenimore Cooper, who dramatized those exciting rides through upstate New York. And in the process she taught me how to read so successfully that, returning to Miss Lepow's second grade class after a multi-month absence, I was the best reader in the class! This is just one special illustration of what my watchful, caring parents did for me.

During this time, I can recall reading Thornton Burgess's books and his columns in the New York *Herald Tribune* discussing anthropomorphic animals and birds with colorful, indelible names like Joe Otter, Jimmy Skunk, Reddy Fox, and Paddy Beaver. I could hardly wait for the next day's newspaper.

In those years of sickness, my father did his best to make life easier for me. He created a primitive walkie-talkie "telephone" that I could use to communicate with him and my mother in the event of an emergency during the night. At this time, long before the modern cell phone, only the military had walkie-talkies. As I lay in bed, dispirited, he would often come into my bedroom and dance in front of me with a self-important expression on his face. As he and my mother described it, he was imitating one of my mother's suitors from the time when he first met her. My mother would always respond to this act by saying, "Oh Bill!" His dance and the expression on his face left me in gales of laughter, as it was designed to do, taking my mind off my illness. I can see that dance and his expression to this day, and I still laugh.

Another of my physical problems was eyesight. In third grade I complained to my parents that my teacher, Mrs. Bresett, was writing on the blackboard in a fuzzy, unclear script. I can still remember how my father's and mother's eyes met, looking at one another knowingly. I was soon wearing glasses for nearsightedness. In those days, kids ridiculed anybody with glasses as "four eyes," and even some adults assumed that athletic activity was inconsistent with a bespectacled state.

I recall that in the 1940s my father critiqued my school's textbook lessons dealing with Reconstruction after the Civil War. The books said that Reconstruction was run by "carpetbaggers"—corrupt whites from the North—who joined forces with "scalawags"—whites who supported the Republican Party and were thus viewed as traitors to their race—and ignorant Blacks to create havoc in the South. My father told me not to believe this kind of lesson, as Reconstruction was the South's first encounter with democracy. But his view wasn't recognized widely until the revisionists of the sixties made changes in the nation's textbooks.

Similarly, he spoke disapprovingly of the Thomas Jefferson Memorial in Washington, noting long before the Sally Hemings scandal had been revealed that Jefferson was a slaveholder. In much the same manner, he often pointed out that not only had George Washington held slaves, but he also actively pursued those who escaped enslavement on his property, arguing that the British should return slaves who had crossed battles lines to escape.[16] My father's perspective made me more skeptical and cautious about accepting pronouncements from on high. And with each passing year, new scholarly emphasis upon the Founding Fathers as slaveholders both ratified and magnified my father's knowledge and wisdom.

Music, Chores, Rituals

At St. James's Episcopal Church in Long Branch, my participation in the choir put me in church at least one day during the week for rehearsals, normal attendance on Sunday, and twice on Sunday during Lent. I was in the choir from 1943 through 1949, first for a few months with Mrs. Mapps, the organist and choir leader who was soon succeeded by Larry Dilsner. The dynamic Mr. Dilsner taught me classical piano for five years and directed the high school choir in which I sang. (I remember the football coach praising me once for a good, sharp tackle, stating: "Are you still in the choir?" Of course, he perceived some inconsistency between these two activities.)

Our work in the choir placed the music of the church in my bones. The music and hymns of the Episcopal Church were part of St. James's essence. The Easter hymns "Welcome Happy Morning" and "All Glory, Laud and Honor to Thee Redeemer King" were joyous and celebratory. My father and I would look at one another as we sang "Now the Day is Over" during Lent and Sunday Evensong, he singing bass, I still singing my boyish soprano. I think often of that hymn and his booming voice as it descended profoundly with the words describing the day's end, when "shadows steal across the sky."

In a lighter vein, my sister Dorothy and I "played church" at home where, of course, I was the priest and Dot was one of the congregants. Only years later, after she had become a music teacher, did she make me aware of how much she had chafed at the all-male composition of the choir, let alone the acolytes or altar boys, whose ranks I joined later. Dot's inability to be part of the choir was particularly hurtful, given her love—and our collective love—of the music. This exclusion was a terrible wrong to her.

In Sunday School at St. James's I met one of my best friends in Long Branch: Harry Bowie, whom I came to know later in the college course in high school. We were the only Blacks in that stream, with students being divided into college preparation, commercial (secretarial-like work), and general categories before entry into the world of work. Harry, who was to graduate from New York City's General Theological Seminary and become an Episcopal priest, was very active in our St. James's parish, where our families were the only Black parishioners. A few years after I met him, he became active in the church basketball league, and he unsuccessfully lobbied my father, a Sunday School teacher, to allow me to play weeknight basketball games. "It's for the church," Harry would always say to my father, as the latter smiled skeptically. My father kept me away from those weeknight games, whether they were for the church or not.

My father was a Renaissance man, interested in so many aspects of life. With help from my mother, and occasionally myself and Dorothy, he kept a garden—during World War II, a "victory garden"—and kept up his gardening practice well into his seventies. As I got older, my assignments morphed from the garden into the entire yard, where I cut the grass (later I was to do this work for others, for cash) and raked the leaves. My father, having lived in Boston prior to our move, preached the idea that we had a great advantage in relatively countrified Long Branch—we had fresh, clean air, trees, and birds. I'm afraid, however, that I did a poor job at yard chores; they were not always things that I wanted to do, and my father was frequently dissatisfied with my performance. Years later, when President Clinton appointed me to be chairman of the National

Labor Relations Board, I remember telling my chief counsel, Bill Stewart—to his considerable amusement—that I had sworn that if I ever "got free" in adulthood I would swear off the yard work I'd been assigned to perform as a child.

Another important element of my childhood was ornithology—my parents enthusiastically took us into wooded areas at dawn and dusk in search of birds. I will always recall being startled by the sudden thunder of seemingly hundreds of ruffed grouse rising to the sky when we stepped into their midst. Our house at Bath Avenue was filled with all kinds of bird books, supplemented by Thornton Burgess.

My father was also a philatelist, encouraging Dot and me to develop our own stamp collections—and coin collections, too. First day covers for newly minted stamps were always a big event and part of our collections. And WBG III's love of music extended to other art forms, like poetry. He loved to read aloud to us the well-known Lewis Carroll poem, "You Are Old, Father William."[17] We never stopped laughing at these readings—nor did he!

My parents were avid bridge players, and I loved to listen to the conversations around the bridge table, sometimes after I was supposed to be sleeping. I can still hear the laughter booming through the house—particularly that of Father Robert Anderson, our parish curate, who became a close friend of the family. I never learned to play bridge, or cards of any kind. Instead, my summers were full of Hide-and-Go-Seek (I've thought of this often listening to jazz baritone saxophonist Gerry Mulligan's "Come Out, Wherever You Are") and Kick the Can with other kids in the neighborhood. We also became addicted to games of croquet. All four of us and others, like our neighbors the Hessleins, participated. I recall that Dot got upset when I took the opportunity to send her ball far away from the rest of the players—and I was irritated by the Hessleins when they did the same thing!

The barbershop on Third Avenue, down beyond Monmouth Memorial Hospital near the Station Field where my pals and I played sandlot baseball, was a place my father and I visited every week or two. Mr. Caligori was in charge of the shop, and my parents formed a friendship with him and his family at his Westwood Avenue home. The barbershop usually displayed the *New York Daily News*, a tabloid that we children were forbidden to read, more for its raciness than its reactionary politics. But the conversations at the barbershop were always interesting: Sports and Yankee fandom were ever-present, and the shop's right-wing commentators—both barbers and customers—yearned for General Douglas MacArthur, the "man on the horse"; more than once someone voiced the idea that the United States should A-bomb China. In addition to Mr. Caligori, I remember Jimmy Barbari, who often threatened to inscribe the logo of the hated New York Yankees on the back of my head as he cut my hair.

Two other memories of this period are somewhat at odds with one another. Because my parents had been young people during the Depression, they were terribly conscious of every penny and nickel. Tested by both a dreadful economy and racial discrimination, they lived from hand to mouth during my early childhood in a way I could not appreciate in the more prosperous late forties and fifties. As their diaries of this period reflect—and as I recollect—my parents kept careful records of their expenditures. And later, when I had graduated from high school and lived at home during college and law school summers, my father pounded into me the idea that he should really be charging me rent, even though he never did so.

But there is another subject that seems somewhat incompatible with this first point: the abundance of food in our household. My parents carefully itemized the crops they grew in their New Jersey garden, and the Goulds, perhaps to the detriment of our metabolism and weight, did not go hungry. If I was picking at my meal my mother would say, "Eat your food, the children in Europe are starving." Such was the case during World War II and its immediate aftermath, until the Marshall Plan was well underway.

My mother made delicious strawberry shortcake—a special treat—as well as gingerbread boys, which we found particularly tempting. And Sundays after church, the noon meal was the main meal of the day. Meat (often beef) and rice (Dorothy and I said that my father would do well if captured by the Japanese because of his love for rice) were a regular staple. We did not want for food as children.

FAMILY VISITS

Though gasoline was rationed between the war years of 1942 and 1945, we were always able to take summer trips in my parents' 1937 Plymouth, in part because my father was allocated gas for work. Trips to Dedham and Attleboro, Massachusetts, the land of my forebears, were frequent throughout the forties and fifties.

Before each trip, my father would rouse my sister and me from early morning slumber, shouting, "Rise and shine you lazy loafers, hit the deck!" And the morning call before those long trips would invariably include an imitation of a long, shrill boatswain's whistle. Did this performance stem from my father's service in the Naval Reserve or Merchant Marine, or was it based on what he had heard as a boy, living next door to my great-grandfather,[18] who must have heard this frequently while serving in the Civil War? I am not sure.

Those 300-mile car trips from Long Branch to Dedham could be boring for children—no video games or movies in those days! Sitting in the back seat, my sister or I would place a finger behind my father's ear, and as he drove he would say: "I think that mouse is here," or "It's that mouse again!" Dorothy and I had so much fun giggling at my father's reaction.

But arriving in Dedham was another matter altogether. Dorothy would often say Dedham had been misspelled: it should be "Deadham," to reflect accurately the amount of activity going on there.

In Dedham: My Father's Family

We would stay at the house of Great Uncle Ed (James Edward) Gould and Great Aunt Isabel, his wife, a gym teacher from Charleston, South Carolina. Ed and Isabel were childless, as were the other two great uncles who married, but Aunt Isabel was warm and friendly, relatively tolerant of small children. I always found the great uncles to be rather severe, humorless, "old" (they were much younger then than I am now!), and forbidding people who had little interest in young kids like my sister Dot and me.

Great Aunt Dora (Medora), as well as Great Uncles Lorry (Lawrence) and Fred (Frederick), resided in the house adjacent to Ed and Isabel's on Milton Street at the borderline between Dedham and Boston. Dora, born in 1866 in Nantucket, was also rather forbidding, occasionally irritable with me, and rather cross when I accidentally spilled all the water in the bird bath. She was a literate woman who did not suffer fools gladly, and did not work or marry. Long after my childhood I discovered that Aunt Dora was a dutiful reader of *Crisis*, the NAACP magazine, and had corresponded with W. E. B. Du Bois.

Only my grandfather, William B. Gould Jr. (born in Taunton, Massachusetts in 1869, one of my great-grandfather's six boys), was not part of this Milton Street group. When he married he had established a separate household on Stoughton Avenue[19], and he had died in 1931. Two of his brothers, Herbert and Ernest, did not live in Dedham during the time of our visits from New Jersey, but I met Herbert on a number of his vacations there. Uncle Ernest lived in Washington DC; Herbert resided in Readville, Massachusetts.

During our many visits to Dedham, I don't recall an instance in which we ever spoke of my great uncles' parents or where their parents had been born. This was part of a mystical haze upon which I began to focus only after all of them were gone. And as I became a teenager during Joseph R. McCarthy's time as a U.S. senator, my father and I engaged ourselves in fruitless debate with the great uncles about McCarthy and the right wing of the Republican Party. None of the uncles could extricate themselves from the Republican Party, to which they had adhered rigidly since the time—in the previous century and through the days of Teddy Roosevelt—when it had been supportive of Blacks, while the Democrats were still locked into the segregationist South. Now, both my father and I thought, they followed uncritically every twist and turn of Senators Taft and McCarthy.

When we were not discussing politics, my father approached his uncles with an almost reverential respect. He knew of and was respectful regarding their service in World War I, singing the songs of that war even more often than his renditions of the Civil War's

"Marching Through Georgia." His favorite songs, which he sang frequently, were "There's a Long Trail Unwinding" and "Keep the Home Fires Burning."[20] And he would recite these words from a marching song: "Left, left, I had a good job when I left; I left my wife and two fat babies, left, left."

All five great uncles were in service in the United States Army in World War I, serving in France during the conflict there.[21] Edward and Herbert were stationed initially in Des Moines, Iowa, the special training school for Black officers. Uncle Edward wrote home frequently, beginning on June 12, 1917:

> *Maj. Sturtevant gave a short talk this evening on the general plan of the work. As he always says we are all on trial, he and the other regular army officers who wanted the camp and the candidates, so we must all work together. Tattoo is now blowing and there is only 15 minutes to bed time.*[22]

Uncle Edward spoke of attending NAACP meetings in Des Moines, and the fact that he and his colleagues were able to go to the movies at the local YMCA.

> *The meeting in the evening was small but interesting. The speakers who were all members of the Training Camp spoke of the need of the association and mentioned briefly the work of their local branches. A local lawyer told of the high esteem the authorities of Des Moines hold for the members of the Training Camp, especially when comparing them with the soldiers from Camp Dodge. During our 3.5 months here there has only been one member of the 17th Regiment arrested. He was a Regular and was immediately shipped back to his outfit.*[23]

According to another of his letters, his performance in Des Moines was highly regarded:

> *The Major made a speech to this effect in class Friday and called for Herbert R. Gould. Bert was questioned as to his previous experience in soldiering. My name was called and I also was questioned. When I replied that I had had no*

> *previous experience the Major said that although I hadn't been taken by surprise any more than the others I had made 98% and then added that Bert also had made 98%.*
>
> *You can imagine that this made us both feel pretty good and it is also safe to say that we will not come home this week.*[24]

There is another feature of the great uncles' lives of which I was unaware as a child: All had been outstanding football players for Dedham High School. Ernest and Edward were renowned as the "Gould boys," playing at each end, with Lawrence and Herbert sometimes playing against them for the alumni, positioned as hard-hitting linemen in the interior.[25]

Uncle Ernest, part of the Field Artillery, was a graduate of Tufts University, where he studied dentistry, serving later in the 1920s on the faculty of the Howard University Dental School in Washington, DC. Our family sometimes traveled from New Jersey to Washington to visit his wife, Fannie Butler Gould, but I recall seeing Ernest there only once. He was ill and confined to bed by then, and in 1945 was the second of the brothers, after William Jr., to die. Most of our visits to 1626 S Street NW, where he and his wife resided, took place in the midst of that city's hot and unbearably humid summers, which left us breathless.

In the forties and fifties, when my father was in Washington for his government work, he often stayed at 1626 rather than risk humiliation in Washington's hotels, which were largely segregated. Aunt Fannie was an interesting and extremely smart woman with whom we had many conversations and a good deal of fun. We had frequent contact with her during my two years as a lawyer in Washington, shortly after the March on Washington in 1963, in which she participated. Although she was already in her 70s at that time, I can recall her playing down on the floor with our oldest son when he was a baby.

The only Gould brother I never met was my grandfather, William B. Gould Jr. He had served in the Black Boston unit,

Company L, in the Spanish-American War. He had entered military service as a sergeant in the 6th Massachusetts regiment, which was reconstituted in early 1898 as a unit of volunteers who were deployed to battle. The year following his service, William wrote of it in the Dedham High School Bulletin. He said that he arrived in Cuba as the surrender was "being formed" and that from Santiago they went to Guantanamo Bay where he said that he "saw the largest fleet of US vessels that I think that I shall ever see."[26] He was landed at Guánica, Puerto Rico, on July 27 and encountered "very slight resistance." His Company L, along with Company M, were sent out to picket on July 27:

> [We] struck the Spanish outpost. There was more or less firing back and forth all night. We met the Spaniards in force next day at day break and had an exciting skirmish. July 30, we marched to Yauco. July 31, Co. L. was left to garrison the town.[27]

He then described moving across streams and the problems of procuring food. He wrote of the mud "up to our knees" and the sun as "extremely oppressive, there being no shade." He then wrote of proceeding to the sea, which they had not seen for months. He was ordered to San Juan to proceed home:

> We were rather sorry to leave as this was the best part of the island and has very little rain.[28]

The Boston *Evening Transcript* said this when the regiment returned home to Massachusetts:

> The 6th looked solid, serviceable, and soldierly as it marched through the streets of Boston yesterday. Officers and men appeared to be in excellent physical condition as a whole. Some faces looked worn and pale, but many more were so tanned that the Caucassians [sic] of old Middlesex could scarcely be detected at a glance from the "smoked Yankees" of Company L. The personnel of the regiment is remarkably fine. In few countries could a thousand young men be drawn together without the aid of conscription who

would average as tall, well-formed, and active as the mass of the 6th. They are fully as stalwart as the English linesman, and have a nervous force that Tommy Atkins, with all his good qualities, lacks. Such a regiment in Paris would be regarded as the advance guard of an army of giants. The march of yesterday gave evidence of a home-coming from foreign service by the parrots and game cocks perched on the shoulders of the men, and the Spanish cockades worn in their hats, souvenirs that smacked of the soil of Porto Rico [sic]. Nor was the "mascot" missing, a little white dog born in Porto Rico, who wagged a willing allegiance to the colors of the 6th. The regiment gave evidence also of the benefits a volunteer corps receives from being commanded by a "regular" who has among his associates at least two officers who have either served in the regulars or been educated at West Point.[29]

The regiment had a near "bloodless experience" in the war.[30] Only one member of Company L was lost and they suffered no casualties, notwithstanding exhaustion, hunger, excessive heat, and tropical fever.

In Attleboro: My Mother's Family

I knew both of my mother's parents, my grandparents, and all of her sisters, except Mary. They hailed from Attleboro, in southern Massachusetts near the Rhode Island border, a poor jewelry- and textile-producing part of the Bay State. I can recall the day during World War II when my mother received a telegram advising her of my grandfather's death.

I also recall my mother's grandmother on her mother's side of the family, my great-grandmother, on our visits to Attleboro. We called her "Gami," and I remember her second husband, Charles Lloyd, whom we called "Tudie." She would always call him Lloyd. An extremely warm and personable man, bent over due to his work as a laborer in a lumberyard, he would tickle my sister and myself with his whiskers. We loved it!

Gami could recall Civil War Union troops coming through her yard in Virginia where she hailed, presumably at that time enslaved. My parents held that couple in very high regard and were extremely close to them over the years. They would "people watch" with both Gami and Tudie as they sat outside the Howard Johnson ice cream parlor.

Some of my mother's people (on my grandfather's side) lived in southern New Jersey below the Mason-Dixon line, near Bridgeton in a town called Gouldtown (no relation to the Massachusetts Goulds on my father's side) and in Trenton, the New Jersey state capital. The residents of Gouldtown (that I met as a child) and Trenton were fair-skinned and isolated from both Blacks and whites. Our parents took us to Trenton frequently. After both my sister and I had left home, I recall my parents visiting Gouldtown for festive events on, for instance, Independence Day. Subsequent to their deaths, I became aware that one of my mother's relatives there, Harold Gould, had played baseball in the Negro Leagues.[31]

UNCOVERING MY GREAT-GRANDFATHER'S STORY

The family member (on my father's side) of whom I was almost completely unaware in the forties and fifties was eventually to loom the largest for me: William B. Gould, my great-grandfather, hereafter known as WBG. As a child, I recall my father speaking of him in just two contexts. One was a story about a phone call that my father had received at home, from a rather gruff-voiced person who said, "Bill Gould?" My father responded, "Speaking." The person on the line then said, "The hell it is!" Three William B. Goulds lived near one another, and the call was probably from one of my great-grandfather's Civil War comrades, a fellow member of the Grand Army of the Republic (GAR).

The other story involved his work as a plasterer and mason, as he was commissioned to work on St. Mary's cathedral-like Roman

Catholic church in Dedham in the mid-1880s. Said the *New York Times*, years later:

> Gould picked up his trade skills where he left them before the war, working as a plasterer and eventually as a contractor. While helping to oversee the construction of St. Mary's Church in Dedham, he noticed that a few of his employees had fallen asleep while laying cement, which dried incorrectly. Gould knew that the mistake would likely go unnoticed, but that it could also lead to serious damage years in the future. He had the work torn down and redone, a costly decision that almost bankrupted his business but, as word about it spread, won him significant esteem around town.[32]

From that moment on, my father said, the name Gould was something special in Dedham, as the community knew what WBG *could* have done, and how instead he did the job honestly and properly.

The Diary

My great uncle Lawrence was the only son to take up the plastering trade of his father. When Uncle Lawrence died in 1958, he bequeathed his property to my father, who was a favorite of his. (Lawrence had employed my father when he was young, though my father maintained that Lawrence had been so dissatisfied with my father's work that he had used swear words never uttered indoors by any of the Goulds.) Within a day or so of Lawrence's death, my father went to his home in Dedham; workmen were already there, throwing things out. My father went up to the attic and retrieved a diary consisting of two volumes, which he brought home to New Jersey.

In the summers of '58 and '59, and during recess periods when I was at home from Cornell Law School, I recall my father reading and studying his grandfather's diary carefully in our living room. He encouraged me to do so as well. At that point, all I knew about William B. Gould, apart from the above-referenced couple of stories,[33] was my mother's comment that she thought he was from Wilmington, North Carolina.

When I began to read the diary for the first time, there was still much that none of us knew. Was WBG a free man or a slave? How did he come to be a seaman on the USS *Cambridge* and the USS *Niagara*, the Union ships on which he penned his diary? How did he meet my great-grandmother?

At the point of the diary's discovery, there was no one alive from the period of WBG's service in the U.S. Navy. But there were still people alive who knew others from that period, and who knew people like the Goulds. Soon after the diary's discovery, my father and I planned to meet such an individual in Philadelphia. We thought that we would coauthor and edit the diary and add something about the circumstances during which it was written. But there was always something else in the way, something more pressing, and we never managed to work on the diary together.

Around 1970, while teaching at Wayne State Law School in Detroit, I obtained WBG's pension records from the Department of the Interior in Washington. This acquisition helped unravel one of the mysteries: how he had met my great-grandmother, Cornelia Read. In one of his applications for a veteran's pension, he said that he had known her as a child in Wilmington, North Carolina. How could this be? She was born in Charleston, South Carolina, a considerable distance from Wilmington. Years later I traveled to Nantucket, where she had gone in 1857 when purchased out of slavery from Wilmington. There I discovered the circumstances that brought them together in Wilmington: a second marriage by one of Cornelia's mistresses, to John Maffitt of Wilmington, later to be a Confederate officer in charge of the CSS *Florida*—which William B. Gould's USS *Niagara* attempted to find and destroy during the Civil War in 1864.

The diary displayed a real literary flair, as well as knowledge about the Civil War and world events, which made me skeptical. Could WBG have really been a slave, considering that North Carolina, like the other Confederate states, prohibited slaves from being taught to read and write?

A Breakthrough at the National Archives

In 1988, long after I moved to California, I arranged for the eminent Black historian John Hope Franklin to visit Stanford Law School. Professor Franklin was a friend of my great-aunt, Fannie Gould, and I had introduced myself to him when I was a student at the London School of Economics in 1963, at the conclusion of a lecture he gave there. When Professor Franklin came to Stanford, he discussed the diary with me and wrote a memorandum about it. For many of the reasons noted previously, he believed that WBG was free, and not a slave. But in 1989, while a Visiting Professor of Law at Howard Law School, I had an opportunity to examine documents in the National Archives and to follow WBG's trail more closely. National Archives staff provided me with the log of his ship, the USS *Cambridge*. The log dated September 22, 1862, stated, "strange sail and at 10:30, picked up a boat with eight Contrabands from Wilmington, N.C."

I knew that "contraband" was a term used by the U.S. military in 1862 to identify escaped slaves. The log listed the names of the eight contrabands and their "masters." I knew also that the Union recognized that it was self-defeating to return escaping Blacks to the South, as they would be put to work as laborers aiding the Confederacy. Thus, realpolitik mandated the view that they were contraband—seized property—and therefore could properly join the armed forces, fighting for the United States against the Confederate rebellion. At last, the issue was resolved: I knew that WBG had been a slave. But I still did not know how he and his comrades had escaped Wilmington and approached the USS *Cambridge* in the Atlantic.

Shortly thereafter I returned to Massachusetts, looked at census and church records, and met with the rector of the Church of the Good Shepherd in Dedham, in which WBG had been baptized. On this visit, I found his death certificate, as well as his obituary, published in the Dedham *Transcript*. In the certificate, it said: "Place of birth mother, Wilmington, North Carolina; place of birth father, England." I had never heard anything like this in all my years of discussion with my mother, father, relatives, and friends. My father was gone, having died on August 15, 1983. I am still searching for this English relative.

Exploring Wilmington

My classes at Howard Law School being over for the year, I had a chance to visit Wilmington to find out more. I drove down through Virginia, noting the town of Weldon, as WBG had written about the Weldon–Wilmington railroad. And, most importantly, I spent the night at John Hope Franklin's home at Duke University. At breakfast the following morning, he said, "I wish that I could go with you. I wish that I could walk the streets with you as you look for him." That farewell comment left me with a tingly feeling as I packed my bags.

I arrived in Wilmington in the chill of December weather. I didn't know a soul. Where had WBG lived? What were the route and circumstances of his escape? I remember seeing the name of his master on a street sign: Nixon. Knowing that WBG had been one of the founders of the Good Shepherd, I attended the services at Wilmington's Episcopal parish, St. James. But I met no one, and encountered nothing in particular, before I set off for New Orleans for a visit with friends.

Within a few years, President Clinton's appointment of me as National Labor Relations Board chairman brought me back to Washington, placing me again within driving distance of North Carolina. On my next visit to Wilmington, I attended a Civil War seminar at the Bellamy Mansion, one of the grandest antebellum mansions on Market Street, the city's main drag. I particularly appreciated the elegant and tasteful plastering work done in the mansion. A few weeks later, on my return to Stanford, I received an excited telephone call from the mansion's curator. They had recently opened the slave quarters, he said, and found plasterwork with the initials WBG on it. This meant that WBG had helped to build the house in which I attended the seminar, and actually did the work that I admired. Like the log of the USS *Cambridge*, this confirmed that he had performed the work as a slave.

I visited Wilmington on two or three occasions while based in Washington, and local historian Beverly Tetterton became an organizer of these visits. She arranged for historians David Cecelski and

Chris Fonvielle to meet with me, review the diary, and look at maps of the Wilmington area so that we could interpret WBG's writings. At one point in 1862, when his ship was near Rich Inlet, WBG wrote, "I had a pretty good look at the place that I came from." I went to the area; he was looking at the Nixon plantation. So, step by step, some doors began to open in my quest to discover him.

Finding "Oley"

In what turned out to be a thirty-year search for my great-grandfather, I had two particularly talented research assistants; one was Diana Buttu. WBG had identified many of his comrades by initials in his diary, and Diana, through examination of recent publications, was able to match up the initials with the actual people—many of whom became prominent in Reconstruction! Sarah Preston, another assistant, noting WBG's involvement with a Black abolitionist newspaper called *The Anglo-African*, suggested that we look at all the issues published during his time in service with the United States Navy. This led to a discussion of an *Anglo-African* correspondent who wrote under the nom de plume "Oley," who happened to be in all the places that WBG had been, and who used many of his expressions and manner of speech.

But, equally important, Oley wrote an essay entitled "An Interesting and Romantic Narrative," which described his escape along with seven other comrades. No portion of WBG's diary had described this story—nor the fact that one of his comrades' fiancée was so upset that the eight had left without her that she boarded the ship herself![34] I examined the muster rolls on both the ships to which he was attached and found that WBG was the only individual in all these places during the relevant period of time!

Finally, I could tell my great-grandfather's story.

On the night of September 21, 1862, eight men in a small boat pushed off from Wilmington, North Carolina's Orange Street dock. One of those men was the first William Benjamin Gould. He and his companions hoped to take the boat down the Cape Fear River toward the Atlantic Ocean—and freedom.

As the boat silently set out from Orange Street, the men knew that they must move quickly, in the cover of darkness, for the alarm would soon be sounded for eight missing slaves. The word would go out promptly to the sentries posted along the Cape Fear River: Be on the watch for these fugitives.

They descended the river southward, toward the Atlantic, bending ever so slightly to the west at Smithville before their final dash down toward the Cape itself. Though their boat possessed a sail, they dared not hoist it until they were in the Atlantic's swell. Thus, the eight men had to take turns at the oars on this twenty-eight-mile journey to, in WBG's words, "leave the land of chivalry and seek protection under the banner of the free."[35] It took them the entire night to proceed beyond the river and avoid inevitable detection at daybreak.[36]

On the morning of September 22 their boat was spotted by the USS *Cambridge*, a Union ship patrolling the waters of the southeastern seceding Confederate states. Along with his comrades, William B. Gould was taken onboard and became part of a Black exodus from slavery into the Union's military ranks, nearly 8,000 strong. He took the Oath of Allegiance to "Uncle Samuel" and served in the United States Navy for three years.

William B. Gould's second vessel, the USS *Niagara*, took him to Europe in pursuit of warships built in Great Britain and France to assist the Confederacy and help satiate Europe's thirst for cotton. Ultimately, it was the *Niagara* that brought him to the Charlestown Naval Shipyard in Massachusetts, where he received his discharge papers in September 1865. He then married my great-grandmother, Cornelia Read, in Nantucket. Soon thereafter they settled in Dedham, just south of Boston.

In Dedham William B. Gould, born into slavery in Wilmington in 1837, became a leading citizen. In 1871 he helped found the Episcopal Church of the Good Shepherd. In 1900 he rose to commander of Dedham's Civil War veterans' organization, the Grand Army of the Republic. But perhaps his most lasting contribution to Dedham was through his work as a plasterer and mason.

In 2021, at the ceremony officially establishing William B. Gould Memorial Park, Father Wayne Belschner of St. Mary's Roman Catholic Church in Dedham said the following:

> *As the church was being built, there was one individual who came forward and took on the task of plastering the entirety of the church walls and ceiling. And when the job was done, he was not pleased with what he saw. And so, he redid it at a personal expense to himself. I am told it almost brought him to the brink of bankruptcy.*
>
> *But, that was just one small example of what he did and when he did it, he did it with every ounce of his being. He did it with great dedication. And he did it with honor and distinction. And so, I bring with me over 150 years of gratitude of St. Mary of the Assumption Parish here in Dedham to William Gould for the work that he did.*
>
> *As the church was being repaired several years ago, I remember being up on the scaffolding and touching the ceiling, never realizing that his hands touched that same ceiling. His hands touched those walls. Every part of that church, he is a part of.*
>
> *Every wall, every ceiling, everything in there, he left his mark, and for this we are grateful.*[37]

The search for the truth about my great-grandfather's life turned out to be an extremely significant development in my own life. Reminding me of the temperament and manner of speech of my own father, WBG's diary gave me the strength to see that the conflicts I experienced in Washington (which I describe in chapters 10 and 11) were second in importance to those my great-grandfather experienced long ago. And during a formative period in my professional life, the diary's contents, along with the Supreme Court's landmark *Brown v. Board of Education* ruling,[38] focused my mind more clearly on the road ahead of me. While it did not directly spark my professional career, it validated it and provided perspective at critical junctures. And it solidified the overriding idea that I had begun to develop since childhood at St. James's Church in Long Branch: that my life should somehow connect with the despised, the rejected, and those who "travail and are heavy laden."³⁹

Figure 1.4: A patriotic young William B. Gould III with his younger brother, Ernest, in 1906.

Figure 1.5: William Benjamin Gould III (1902–1983) as a student member of the Wireless Association at Worcester Polytechnic Institute, c. 1922 or 1923. (Courtesy of Worcester Polytechnic Institute.)

Figure 1.6: WBG IV in front of the house occupied by the Gould family at 75 Harvard Avenue, Hyde Park, Boston, Massachusetts (1936–1940). (Photo taken by Trinh Nguyen in 2012.)

Figure 1.7: WBG IV with mother, Leah Felts Gould, and grandmother, Hannah Jordan Gould, c. 1937 or 1938.

Figure 1.8: William B. Gould III with his wife, Leah Felts Gould, and their children, Dorothy and WBG IV, 1940 or 1941.

Figure 1.9: My mother and father, c. late 1940s or 1950s.

WBG's Entry in the *African American National Biography*, authored by WBG IV

GOULD, William B. (18 Nov. 1837–23 May 1923), Union navy sailor in the Civil War and journalist, was presumably born into slavery, in Wilmington, North Carolina, to Elizabeth "Betsy" Moore of Wilmington, a slave, and Alexander Gould, who was white. William had at least one sibling, Eliza Mabson, who acquired her last name by virtue of a publicly acknowledged relationship with George Mabson, a white man in Wilmington. She eventually became the mother of five children by Mabson, including her son GEORGE L. MABSON, the first black lawyer in North Carolina.

Little is known about William B. Gould's early life. As a young man he acquired skills as a plasterer or mason, and he learned how to read and write, although those skills were forbidden by law to slaves. His initials are in the plaster of one of the Confederacy's most elegant mansions, the Bellamy Mansion in Wilmington. Among his young friends were GEORGE WASHINGTON PRICE JR., eventually to represent New Hanover County in the state house of representatives and the senate at the conclusion of the Civil War, and ABRAHAM HANKINS GALLOWAY, the black "Scarlet Pimpernel" of North Carolina who escaped from slavery in 1857 and returned during the war as a spy for Union forces. Galloway also served in the North Carolina legislature after the war.

On 21 September 1862 Gould and seven other "contraband" (as escaping slaves were characterized during the Civil War) from Wilmington made a dramatic dash to freedom, departing from the dock at Orange Street and rowing down to the Atlantic Ocean at the mouth of the Cape Fear River. The eight "contraband" were picked up by USS *Cambridge*, part of the North Atlantic Blockading Squadron. Five days later, Gould began keeping a diary—apparently the only diary of any former slave who joined the United States Navy. On 3 October 1862 the eight contraband joined the navy by "takeing [sic] the Oath of Allegiance to the Government of Uncle Samuel" (Gould, Diary, October 3, 1862). Classified as a "boy," the lowest occupation—and the only one then open to blacks—in the navy, Gould would ultimately progress to wardroom steward.

In the fall of 1862, the *Cambridge* was assigned to inshore blockade duties. Gould described the shots coming from Fort Fisher on the North Carolina shore as "too close to be at all agreeable" (Gould, Diary, January 17, 1863). There were other engagements. "In a brief five days [in November–December '62], she [the *Cambridge*] and two other ships in company took four blockade runners and chased a fifth ashore" (Navy Department, *Dictionary of American Naval Fighting Ships*, 2 [1963]). In the spring of 1863, the *Cambridge* was given a respite and came north to dock at Newport News in Virginia, New York, and Boston.

From the beginning of his service Gould corresponded with a wide variety of colleagues from North Carolina: Galloway, Price, Eliza Mabson, and her son George Mabson, who would serve in both the army and the navy. He also wrote to his future wife, Cornelia Williams Read, whom he had known since childhood in Wilmington. She had been purchased out of slavery in 1857 by JAMES CRAWFORD. Gould eventually reunited with her in Nantucket.

In Massachusetts, Gould, ill with the measles, left the *Cambridge*, and in October 1863 joined USS *Niagara*, one of the navy's most formidable wooden frigates. The *Niagara* proceeded first to Nova Scotia to recapture the steamer USS *Chesapeake*, which had been taken by the Confederates off Cape Cod and was being held by the British authorities in Canada. On 11 December the *Niagara* departed Gloucester, Massachusetts, in search of the *Chesapeake*, following it into Le Havre and Halifax, Nova Scotia. The *Chesapeake* was taken by USS *Ella* and *Annie*. The *Niagara* returned to New York on 20 December. It remained there for approximately six months, during which there was a dramatic rescue of the Italian ship *Galantoumo*, in which the crewmen of the *Niagara* delivered the Italian crew and passengers from "the very jaws of death" ("Perilous Voyage of the *Niagara*," *New York Times*, April 5, 1864).

During this stay in New York City, Gould reunited with Abraham Galloway, attended meetings on the future suffrage of North Carolina, and in June 1864 became a correspondent for the *Anglo-African*, describing his escape in that paper. Meanwhile he began a correspondence with the *Anglo-African*'s editor, ROBERT HAMILTON. Finally, Gould encountered rank discrimination against a Maryland black regiment that boarded his ship and was treated roughly by the crew. Gould characterized the crew as "scoundrels" who treated blacks "shamefully" (Gould, Diary, 18 May 1864).

On 1 June Gould departed for Europe, looking for CSS *Florida* and other ships, and on 24 June, while running up the English Channel, they learned of the sinking of CSS *Alabama*. The crew were as "proud of the deed as if they had done it themselves" (Gould, A Portion of the Cruise of the U.S. Steam Frigate "Niagara," 1911). Active engagements followed in Spain and Portugal.

After returning to Wilmington, another of his contributions to the *Anglo-African* observed that the local black citizens were "well satisfied" with the Thirty-seventh and Thirty-ninth regiments of Colored Troops and that "the Anglo-African takes well" (*Anglo-African*, 1865). He also wrote an article, "Our Noble Tars Speak – How They Feel for the Freedman," which was published on 29 July 1865, in which he recounted donations by the sailors on the *Niagara* and said that they "see the necessities of thousands of our own people liberated by the victorious march of the armies of the Union through the would be Confederacy." Gould returned to Nantucket, Massachusetts, to marry Cornelia Read on 22 November 1865 in the African Baptist Church.

The couple had eight children—six boys and two girls—and made their home in Dedham, Massachusetts. There, Gould became a tradesman and contractor who worked on the construction of St. Mary's Roman Catholic Church. He was also active in the Union veterans' organization, the Grand Army of the Republic (where he served as commander of the Dedham chapter), and in the 1870s was a founder of the Episcopal Church of the Good Shepherd in Dedham, where four generations of Goulds were baptized. One son, William B. Gould Jr., served in the Spanish-American War, and five others served in World War I. In June 1918 the *Dedham Transcript* quoted a speech by William B. Gould in which he commented on his sons' service in World War I: "I have ever tried to set them a good example... and I expect to hear some good things from those boys."

William B. Gould died on 23 May 1923, predeceased by Cornelia in 1906. The following headline appeared in the *Dedham Transcript* on 26 May 1923: "East Dedham Mourns Faithful Soldier and Always Loyal Citizen: Death Came Very Suddenly to William B. Gould, Veteran of the Civil War."[40]

NOTES

[1] The Cowley Fathers, an Episcopal order of monks, were initially founded in Cowley, near Oxford, England—a product of the Oxford Movement emphasizing Anglo Catholicism in the worldwide Anglican Communion in the early nineteenth century.

[2] Horace Silver, "Song for My Father," *Song for My Father* (1965).

[3] "Fitchburg High Plays Rings around Hyde Park," *Worcester Sunday Telegram*, October 17, 1920.

[4] *Boston Globe*, October 27, 1920.

[5] Ira N. Hollis (President), letter to Mrs. W. B. Gould, October 16, 1922.

[6] *Worcester Evening Gazette*, November 26, 1928.

[7] *Quincy Patriot-Ledger*, August 10, 1929.

[8] William B. Gould III, letter to Dr. W. E. Burghardt Du Bois, August 2, 1930.

[9] Chad L. Williams, *The Wounded World: W. E. B. Du Bois and the First World War* (New York: Farrar, Straus and Giroux, 2023). James T. Campbell, "'A Last Great Crusade for Humanity': W.E.B. Du Bois and the Pan-African Congress," in *Making the American Century: Essays on the Political Culture of Twentieth Century America*, ed. Bruce J. Schulman (New York: Oxford University Press, 2014).

[10] Dr. W. E. Burghardt Du Bois, letter to William B. Gould III, August 5, 1930. "I have had a good many interesting reports from Abyssinia but I have no exact information and I do not know where to get it. Recently, there were rumors of a commission of Abyssinians coming here which was to visit me but I have seen nothing of it. The colored newspapers have carried a notice that Dr. West of Washington is going to Abyssinia as King's physician and Health Officer. I am writing him and if I can get from him or anyone else any further information. I shall be glad to pass it on. I am sure that if you can get the right entrée that Abyssinia would be delighted to have you. But everything depends upon the right approach. There is a good deal of international political intrigue in Abyssinia just now."

[11] William B. Gould III, letter to Dr. W. E. Burghardt Du Bois, October 17, 1930: "Thank you for your letter of August 5th which was just received today. I am looking forward with interest to any other information you may be able to obtain for me."

[12] Jack Beatty, *The Rascal King: The Life and Times of James Michael Curley* (1874–1958) (Reading, MA: Addison-Wesley Publishing Company, 1992). My father and I both read and enjoyed the novel by Edwin O'Connor, *The Last Hurrah* (1956), generally assumed to be based upon the life of James Curley.

13 These three paragraphs are taken from Gould, *Diary of Contraband: The Civil War Passage of a Black Sailor* (Stanford: Stanford University Press, 2002), 291.

14 Lying-in Hospital was eventually absorbed into the expanded Peter Bent Brigham Hospital, that was merged into Massachusetts General.

15 "William B. Gould – K2NP – Silent Key," Quarter Century Wireless Association, Inc., August 15, 1983, https://www.qcwa.org/k2np-02217-sk.htm.

16 See Edward J. Larson, *American Inheritance: Liberty and Slavery in the Birth of a Nation, 1765–1795* (New York: W. W. Norton & Company, 2023), 153, 231, 234, 251–257. Larson addresses Washington's extraordinary interest in recapturing his escaped slaves. General Washington insisted, to no avail, that the British in New York return slaves who had escaped and fought with that country against the United States: "New York then harbored a remnant of the most loyal and useful Black soldiers to join the British side during the Revolution, numbering perhaps 3,000 persons. [Guy] Carleton [the British commander for North America in New York] refused to renege on the vows made to them by his predecessors. He unilaterally interpreted the clause in the treaty about not carrying away enslaved Blacks as to exclude those freed by serving or seeking refuge with the British prior to the treaty's execution . . . they stood by us."

17 Lewis Carroll, "You Are Old, Father William," in *Alice's Adventures in Wonderland* (London: Macmillan, 1865).

> "You are old, Father William," the young man said, "And your hair has become very white;
> And yet you incessantly stand on your head – Do you think, at your age, it is right?"
> "In my youth," Father William replied to his son, "I feared it might injure the brain;
> But, now that I'm perfectly sure I have none, Why, I do it again and again."
> "You are old," said the youth, "as I mentioned before, And have grown most uncommonly fat;
> Yet you turned a back-somersault in at the door – Pray, what is the reason of that?"
> "In my youth," said the sage, as he shook his grey locks, "I kept all my limbs very supple
> By the use of this ointment—one shilling the box— Allow me to sell you a couple?"
> "You are old," said the youth, "and your jaws are too weak For anything tougher than suet;
> Yet you finished the goose, with the bones and the beak – Pray how did you manage to do it?"
> "In my youth," said his father, "I took to the law, And argued each case with my wife;
> And the muscular strength, which it gave to my jaw, Has lasted the rest of my life."
> "You are old," said the youth, "one would hardly suppose That your eye was as steady as ever;
> Yet you balanced an eel on the end of your nose – What made you so awfully clever?"

"I have answered three questions, and that is enough," Said his father; "don't give yourself airs!
Do you think I can listen all day to such stuff? Be off, or I'll kick you down stairs!"

[18] Gould, *Diary of a Contraband*, 289–290.
[19] I never met another living great aunt, Luetta Ball, who had moved to New York and separated herself from the rest of the Gould family, apparently so that she could "pass" as white.
[20] Zo Elliott, Oscar Seagle, Columbia Stellar Quartette, and Stoddard King, "There's a Long, Long Trail," 1917, https://www.loc.gov/item/jukebox-817436/.

Nights are growing very lonely, Days are very long;
I'm a-growing weary only List'ning for your song.
Old remembrances are thronging Thro' my memory
Till it seems the world is full of dreams Just to call you back to me.
There's a long, long trail a-winding Into the land of my dreams,
Where the nightingales are singing And the white moon beams.
There's a long, long night of waiting Until my dreams all come true;
Till the day when I'll be going down That long, long trail with you.
All night long I hear you calling, Calling sweet and low;
Seem to hear your footsteps falling, Ev'ry where I go.
Tho' the road between us stretches Many a weary mile,
I forget that you're not with me yet When I think I see you smile.
There's a long, long trail a-winding Into the land of my dreams,
Where the nightingales are singing And the white moon beams.
There's a long, long night of waiting Until my dreams all come true;
Till the day when I'll be going down That long, long trail with you.

Ivor Novello and Lena Guilbert Ford, "Keep the Homes Fires Burning," 1915, https://lccn.loc.gov/2023794362.

They were summoned from the hillside, They were called in from the glen,
And the country found them ready, At the stirring call for men;
Let no tears add to their hardship, As the soldiers pass along,
And although your heart is breaking,
Make it sing this cheery song
Keep the home fires burning, While your hearts are yearning,
Though your lads are far away, They dream of home;
There's a silver lining,
Through the dark cloud shining, Turn the dark cloud inside out, Till the boys come home.

Brigadier General Edmund Louis "Snitz" Gruber, "The Caissons Go Rolling Along," 1908, https://www.loc.gov/item/ihas.200000019/.

Over hill, over dale
As we hit the dusty trail,
And those caissons go rolling along.
In and out, hear them shout,
Counter march and right about,
And those caissons go rolling along.

Then it's hi! hi! hee! In the field artillery,
Shout out your numbers loud and strong, For where e'er you go,
You will always know
That those caissons go rolling along.

[21] Chad L. Williams, *Torchbearers of Democracy: African American Soldiers in the World War I Era* (Chapel Hill: University of North Carolina Press, 2010); Emmett J. Scott, *Scott's Official History of the American Negro in the World War* (Washington DC: Negro Historical Publishing Company, 1919).

[22] J. Edward Gould, letter to Dedham relatives, June 12, 1917.

[23] J. Edward Gould, letter to Dedham relatives, August 5, 1917.

[24] J. Edward Gould, letter to Dedham relatives, September 29, 1917.

[25] *Dedham Transcript*, 1898.

[26] *The High School Bulletin*, Dedham, Massachusetts VI, no. 9 (May 1899).

[27] *The High School Bulletin*.

[28] *The High School Bulletin*.

[29] *Boston Evening Transcript*, October 30, 1898.

[30] Frank E. Edwards, *The '98 Campaign of the 6th Massachusetts, U.S.V.* (Boston: Little, Brown, 1899): xi.

[31] See Harold Gould, *He Came from Gouldtown, to Become a Philadelphia Star of the Negro Baseball Leagues* (United States: Harold Gould Family, 2009).

[32] Clay Risen, "Overlooked No More: William B. Gould, Escaped Slave and Civil War Diarist," *New York Times*, June 17, 2022.

[33] Gould, *Diary of a Contraband*, 293.

[34] Gould, *Diary of a Contraband*, 51–53.

[35] William B. Gould used these words in his "An Interesting and Romantic Narrative," *The Anglo-African*, June 11, 1864.

[36] Gould, *Diary of a Contraband*, 15.

[37] Pamphlet, "Dedication of the William B. Gould Park," September 23, 2021, 6.

[38] *Brown v. Board of Education of Topeka*, 347 U.S. 483 (1954).

[39] Matt. 11:28.

[40] Reprinted, with permission, from Henry Louis Gates and Evelyn Brooks Higginbotham, eds., *African American National Biography* (Oxford: Oxford University Press, 2013), 568–569.

2

MY PATH TO LABOR LAW: MCCARTHYISM, CIVIL RIGHTS, AND *BROWN V. BOARD OF EDUCATION*

While I can trace my interest in labor law and labor arbitration back to the early 1950s, when I was developing a focus on both politics and the civil rights movement, I must confess that my earlier political expressions could fairly be described as confused. In 1944, when I was eight, most of the St. James's Church choirboys strongly supported Republican Thomas Dewey and his running mate John Bricker over Democrats Franklin D. Roosevelt and Harry S. Truman. To prove their commitment to the cause, the choirboys ran around hitting dissenters over the head with hymnals. I'm not sure I joined in this activity, but I certainly didn't present an opposing view.

At the time of the '44 election I was home, ill, and as my father left I asked him to vote for Dewey. To please me, he said he would. But when he returned, I asked him if he had voted for Dewey and he said no. He was a very sensible man who was compassionate to me and my mistaken views, prompted as they were by those St. James's choirboys.

NEW DEAL DEMOCRATS AND THE 1952 ELECTION

The first political campaign in which I felt a real and reasoned involvement was the 1952 contest between Illinois Governor Adlai Stevenson and General Dwight D. Eisenhower. I was sixteen years old.

The previous presidential race in 1948, between incumbent President Harry Truman and Thomas E. Dewey, had helped cement a growing allegiance between the Democratic Party and northern big city Black residents. Between 1935 and 1948, Democrats Franklin D. Roosevelt (FDR) and his successor, Harry Truman, had tried to establish fairer working conditions for whites and sometimes Blacks alike. In 1935 FDR signed both the Social Security Act, which created an unemployment compensation program and guaranteed retiring workers a continuing income after age sixty-five, and the National Labor Relations Act, which granted workers the right to organize unions, take collective action, and seek arbitration. FDR also supported minimum wage principles and protections through the Fair Labor Standards Act of 1938, and in 1941 established the Fair Employment Practices Committee (FEPC) to eradicate discriminatory employment practices in defense industries and government.[1]

President Truman's acceptance of fair employment practices legislation was clearly stated in the Democratic Party platform. In 1949, after he had won the election, Truman pressed for FEPC enactments but was stymied by the filibuster maintained by Southern Democrats.

My father's understanding was that the New Deal Democrats were for the "little guy," and he had the sense that Democrats— even the relatively cautious Adlai Stevenson—promoted at least a tepid adherence to civil rights. That was enough to bring me on board and get me more interested in and committed to politics. My father loved Stevenson's wit and literary flair, and although he had supported the Republican Party of our forebears through the 1920s, he never cast a vote for that party after Herbert Hoover's defeat of Al Smith in 1928.

In the 1950s I began to align myself with a relatively small group of northern Democrats, principally senators, such as Hubert Humphrey of Minnesota[2] and Paul Douglas of Illinois, who were aggressive in championing civil rights legislation. Long before the mass demonstrations and rallies of the sixties, Roy Wilkins of the NAACP— calm, well-reasoned, and sensible—was among my models.

My involvement, while not that of a full-fledged activist, extended not only to tuning in avidly to radio broadcasts (we had no television) and reading the *New York Times* (which supported Eisenhower), but also to examining opposition positions. For example, I attended Senator Robert Taft's speech at the Asbury Park Convention Center on behalf of "Ike," to whom he had lost the GOP nomination. I repeatedly expressed my views and submitted requests for documentation to our congressional district's representative, Republican James Auchincloss of Rumson, who would faithfully respond, "It's good to hear from you again, Mr. Gould."

The 1952 election got me focused; along with my parents, I espoused the Stevenson candidacy. And there were other good reasons to fortify my support for Stevenson. One was the increasing visibility of Republican Senator Joe McCarthy—in many respects the perfect demagogue and precursor to Donald Trump—to whom I had direct exposure as a result of my father's employment at Fort Monmouth. McCarthy was interested in Monmouth because Julius Rosenberg (executed for espionage in 1953) had been employed there during World War II.

JOE MCCARTHY'S RISE AND FALL

Some family friends lost jobs in the wake of McCarthy's widespread accusations of Communism. My father, however, managed to dodge the largest McCarthy-era bullet that came his way. In 1948 he strayed from the Democratic ticket to vote for Progressive Party candidate Henry Wallace, and during the campaign he attended a Paul Robeson rally in support of Wallace. The Robeson name was venerated in our household. An outstanding college and professional football player, bass-baritone concert artist, and stage and film actor, Robeson was larger than life, an extraordinary man by any standard. He graduated from Columbia Law School as a lawyer, but gravitated toward sports and the arts because, as a Black man, he could not find work in the law at that time. His politics had taken him to the left; his admiration of the Soviet Union ensnarled him in passport litigation, a matter to which I adverted in my first law review article, which addressed the right to travel.[3]

At the Wallace rally, the FBI recorded all attendees' license plates. But my father had traveled in a friend's car and thus avoided detection. When I was nominated for the NLRB in the 1990s, I learned that my FBI report stated, "His father was investigated for Un-American activities, but nothing was found." The political atmosphere during this period might best be described by FBI questions put to a white friend of our family: "You are white. Why would you be interested in civil rights for Blacks? You must be a Communist."

My interest in the law and civil rights was furthered by the Army-McCarthy hearings in April of 1954, which were triggered by Joe McCarthy's bullying and abuse of those he accused of Communist sympathies, as well as similar conduct at Fort Dix, in western New Jersey. I recall reading James Wechsler's autobiography, *The Age of Suspicion*,[4] at this time; it summed up the period well.

During this same period I recall a brief and somewhat inexplicable flirtation with the idea of becoming an archaeologist. I was heavily influenced by a book called *Gods, Graves, and Scholars*.[5] That fascination quickly passed, however. Most of my high school course interests were in American history and civics. I was particularly taken by Miss Wilson's American History course, especially her discussions of the economic reasons for America's entry into World War I, and of Woodrow Wilson—regrettably without mention of his racial bias, which was talked about frequently in our household. Years later, in my Stanford Labor Law class, I frequently quoted Miss Wilson's words about organized labor: she "opined that the deaths of Phillip Murray and William Green (leaders of the major labor federations), shortly after Eisenhower's election, were triggered by broken hearts."[6] In labor law, I sometimes connected those comments with the conservative appointments President Eisenhower made to the National Labor Relations Board, which confirmed her viewpoint in my mind.[7]

At the end of my senior year in high school, the McCarthy hearings were on television, and I watched them at school every afternoon. The only other person in daily or near daily attendance was the school principal, Mr. Shoemaker. These dramatic infusions of politics and law, coupled with the personal connection to Monmouth, kept me glued to the television set every afternoon and created a belated and temporary bond between me and Mr. Shoemaker. One day he said to me, "I wish I had known you earlier—I would have taken you under my wing." I could have used that kind of help as I floundered aimlessly through most of high school, excelling only in history, politics, and the Latin class taught by Mrs. Lorena van Breece—a friend of my parents who I knew would tell my parents if I did not perform well!

The Army '54 hearings were inconclusive. McCarthy blustered and evaded censure for his accusatory smears and insults,[8] upstaged only by Boston lawyer Joseph Welch.[9] Welch, after a surprise attack by McCarthy on a young law associate who belonged to the National Lawyers Guild, an organization McCarthy labeled "an arm of the Communist Party," responded memorably: "Until this moment Senator, I think I never really gauged your cruelty or your recklessness . . . Let us not assassinate this lad further, Senator. You've done enough. Have you no sense of decency, sir? At long last, have you left no sense of decency?"[10]

That fall, however, while visiting my great-aunt Fannie on S Street in Washington, I walked to the Capitol to attend a new set of hearings chaired by Senator Arthur Watkins, Republican of Utah. Here I observed firsthand McCarthy's able counsel, Edward Bennett Williams, attempting to fend off Republican dissatisfaction with the Wisconsin senator which had not been visible during the previous spring's proceedings. The Watkins hearings proved to be the more significant ones, concluding with McCarthy's censure by the Senate and what is generally seen as the inflection point for his demise.

A MOMENTOUS RULING, RACE, AND VALUES

Perhaps an even more important development for me took place concurrently with the Army-McCarthy hearings: the Supreme Court's unanimous ruling on May 17, 1954, in *Brown v. Board of Education*,[11] in which "separate but equal" in public school systems was held to be unconstitutional under the Equal Protection Clause of the Fourteenth Amendment, and, as applicable to D.C., the Due Process Clause of the Fifth Amendment.

Although *Brown* did not expressly overrule the 1896 *Plessy v. Ferguson* decision,[12] which had held public transportation segregation to be constitutional, and although Chief Justice Warren's opinion was rooted in facts peculiar to segregation and education, it nonetheless ratified a trend already discernable in government and sports. Examples include President Truman's support of fair employment, his desegregation of the Armed Forces and federal civil service, and Jackie Robinson's 1947 appearance as the first Black major league player in twentieth century baseball, with the Brooklyn Dodgers. And so *Brown*'s reasoning spelled doom for *Plessy* in areas outside of education.

The symbolism of Chief Justice Warren's *Brown* opinion—appreciably impaired through the "with all deliberate speed" 1955 ruling addressing the implementation of the decree[13]—made the law attractive to me, and nurtured my hope that law could indeed produce change. Thurgood Marshall's success before the high tribunal gave him stature throughout the country and the world, placing him on the cover of *Time*[14] and producing other good publicity. He and *Brown* became part of many of my family's dinner conversations.

The *Brown* ruling in 1954 connected me directly to the values my parents held and had attempted to instill in me as a child. Many related memories stick with me still. For example, when my father's good friend Bill Andriotti was at our house for dinner, he said to my father, "Do you know, Mr. Gould, my supervisor held against me the fact that I'm Italian?" My father replied, "Not nearly as much as he would have if you were a Negro." I can still see Bill Andriotti nodding in agreement. The reality of racial discrimination has now come under attack in American politics and law,[15] leading to abstract, contorted constitutional and statutory interpretations by the contemporary Supreme Court on issues such as affirmative action.[16]

My father would not speak of discrimination—that is, discrimination practiced against himself. But he was keenly aware of the world around him and hardly inhibited in expressing a viewpoint. For instance, in 1944 he wrote in his diary: "In Brooklyn, I am surprised and pleased to see a number of colored women 'motormen' on the trolley."[17] On another occasion, as we drove by a Black worker who had been stopped by white police in rural New Jersey, he said, "I really fear what the result of this will be." He loved Eleanor Roosevelt, journalist and activist Dorothy Day, and Frank Sinatra because of their support of civil rights and equality.

Long Branch, where we had moved to from Boston in 1940, had a substantial Black population,[18] but no Black professionals, lawyers, or doctors. Most Blacks had come to Long Branch in its fancier, more prosperous days (at least six presidents summered there) when there was substantial demand for unskilled work in the hotels. The Black part of town was on the northeastern side of the city, toward the Atlantic Ocean. Our home at 458 Bath Avenue was in the white part of town, and only years later did my friend Harry Bowie reveal that many of my Black classmates in the public school system resented the fact that we lived in the white section.

Swedish scholar Gunnar Myrdal has written of race in the United States as the "American dilemma."[19] Perhaps our location in Long Branch highlighted our own "dilemma." But until I was nine or ten, when I first started playing intense daily baseball, I'm not sure that I was conscious of being Black. When the schools in Long Branch desegregated in the 1940s, my parents told me to stick up for the Black kids who were being transferred to our school. I did so. But when they told me that I was Black myself, it was an entirely different matter—I cried because I knew, perhaps better than most, the raw racial realities and the way in which Blacks were regarded by whites. Very few people have had this experience of and exposure to both sides of the race experience in America.

When my mother—who could never be discerned as Black—suggested that I could always be a "fifth columnist" by passing as white, I was left confused and perplexed. When we moved to a new house in Elberon, on the south side of town, in 1950, my father arranged for my mother to appear for us at the public meeting where house lots could be purchased. He correctly assumed that if my light-skinned mother was the buyer, we would evade the color bar then in place throughout the country. She made the successful bid for our family, and we built a house on the property she purchased.

This was a necessary accommodation that we made to purchase property; we had "passed" through that one purchase. But relatives on both sides of the family "passed" permanently and became white. My father was hurt by the fact that his own brothers, Ernest and Robert, did not want him to be present at certain social events, fearing that his presence would reveal their own racial origins. Robert did not want my father to appear at his daughter's wedding reception for the same reason.

Ernest's daughter, my cousin Betty, was visiting us in New Jersey when I was about to graduate from high school, and she noticed the large number of Blacks in my high school yearbook. She said, "I guess they're alright, aren't they?" I responded affirmatively.

In this century, after the publication of my book about my great-grandfather's escape from slavery and service in the United States Navy, I learned that Ernest's children and grandchildren were now questioning their parents about their racial origins. When Father Noble Scheepers, the rector of Dedham's Church of the Good Shepherd, held a grand ceremony at that parish in 2012 to honor the first William B. Gould, my cousin Ernie, Betty's brother, said to me, "I never knew about this"—meaning both our great-grandfather and our racial origins. Yet in Ernest's Naval records from the early 1950s, discovered by his own descendants, he was classified as "Negro."

I "passed" at some points in my life, too. At a swimming pool in Long Branch when I was still a child, the pool attendant said to me: "White or colored?" I said, "White," and I was admitted. If I didn't know it already, Sinclair Lewis's novel *Kingsblood Royal* and the movie and book *Lost Boundaries* quickly informed me of the vivid consequences of being on the wrong side of the color line. After social exclusion in both high school and university, and as the sole Black American student at Cornell Law School, I was often silent about my own racial origins. I recall a conservative law student saying to me, "Why should you be so concerned about support for liberal causes and those of the NAACP?" Again, I was silent. The environment and attitudes of the forties and fifties are captured dramatically by what my British friend, Inge Neufeld, told me years after the fact: that a number of American white women in our residence hall at Cornell had urged her to discontinue our long conversations in the dormitory lounge, inasmuch as that was not regarded as "appropriate" in our country.

Sometimes I felt that my silent posture was akin to Peter's betrayal of Christ. But in one discussion with my father during this period, he said that even he had done something like this on occasions when it was possible for him to be confused with Cubans or Puerto Ricans.

Despite these ambiguities, my father always drummed this instruction into me: "You must be better!" Blacks, he said, must be better than whites to compete and succeed. (Yet he noted, paradoxically, that there would be some whites who would be on "our side" and would support us and our positions. And I have found this to be true for me as an adult.)

Eventually, I connected the stories about racial discrimination that I'd heard in my childhood, and my early experiences and willingness to confront others on this issue, with the values of the Episcopal Church, so significant for our entire family. St. James's seemed to provide as strong a foundation for me as the Church of the Good Shepherd in Dedham did for my forebears. The liturgy of the Church, the vestments, the incense, the Sanctus bell, and the language of the Book of Common Prayer are in my bones as the result of this heritage. Nothing is embedded within me more deeply. As an adult, when I told St. James's rector, Father Herbert Linley, that I'd been to churches all over the world and seen none as beautiful as St. James's, he replied, "Billy, that's because there aren't any." I have often written and spoken about life's eternal verities, characterizing them—for me—as the NAACP, the Democratic Party, the Episcopal Church, and the Modern Jazz Quartet.

As my childhood went on, my father, from his seat on the men's side of the choir across from us boys, would always look knowingly at me when the priest read Christ's Comfortable Words: "Come unto me all that travail and are heavy laden, and I will refresh you."[20] I began to understand how important these words were to my father's view of the Episcopal Church, religion, and life itself. These words soon became integrated into my view of the Church, and the need to protect the masses, our people, and all who were "heavy laden." And subsequently they fused, in my mind, with the Court's *Brown* ruling condemning segregation. If I have been able to make any contribution to workplace fairness, its origin and impetus are to be found in these experiences.[21]

Figure 2.1: Boy and Men's choir of the family parish, St. James Episcopal Church in Long Branch, New Jersey, 1949. WBG IV is second row, second from the right (WBG III was ill and therefore absent that day).

Figure 2.2: WBG III with WBG IV in the early 1940s.

Figure 2.3: My father in Chicago during World War II.

But how did my focus on the Episcopal Church, desegregation, inequality, and the politics that supported my views translate into the work that I would do in life? In high school, I was lost—not a well-directed or purposeful student, despite the urgings of my parents. My father had even taken me to football games at Princeton—when they played Harvard, Brown, and Penn—to stimulate my interest in those universities. But none of this translated into disciplined study, the obvious prerequisite.

On the day of my high school graduation, I found myself walking alone around the athletic track at the conclusion of ceremonies, musing about the fact that at this point in my life I had accomplished nothing whatsoever, academically, or athletically. I was, as my mother frequently said, playing off the title of a popular musical at that time, "The Most Unhappy Fella."[22] I was bored with high school and with the doings of Long Branch; I sought escape at the earliest point possible.

My closest friend in high school—and in my recollection the only other Black student in the college course—was Harry Bowie.[23] He was enrolled in Hobart College in upstate New York and planned to became an Episcopal priest. Harry urged me to room with him there and perhaps pursue the priesthood as a vocation. In retrospect, I was hardly suited for this, and my parents, notwithstanding my admission to Hobart, strongly dissuaded me from attending. Not having the grades even to apply to Ivy League colleges, I then wound up going to the University of Rhode Island, the result of no more than a vague assumption that this made sense because of my New England heritage. All I really knew about Rhode Island—aside from my parents' close friendship with a Pawtucket family—was that Ernie Caverley had won the basketball National Invitational Tournament (NIT) for Rhode Island with a more than seventy-foot shot at the last second against Bowling Green to win the championship.

AT THE UNIVERSITY OF RHODE ISLAND

At Rhode Island, after an underwhelming and inauspicious freshman year, I became a major in history and minor in political science, with some emphasis on constitutional law courses. Some professors were particularly stimulating: Donald Smith, in political theory; John Stitely, teaching political parties; Warren Smith, in both Elizabethan literature and modern drama; the history department's warhorses Donald Tilton on English history and Donald Thomas on Europe, as well as William Metz on America. These gentlemen played a big role in my intellectual growth. Meanwhile, I served regularly as an altar boy or acolyte as I had in St. James's parish in Long Branch. And the idea that my work should have something to do with race persisted.

Of the couple of thousand students at Rhode Island, only five of us were Black—and the four who were in residence at the freshmen dormitory, Butterfield Hall, were segregated. Then a fraternity-dominated university, practically all the fraternities—and sororities too, for that matter—excluded Blacks. This was at a taxpayer-funded university in New England in the mid-fifties—yet no one questioned the matter.

In the spring of '55 I pledged to one of the two open fraternities that didn't exclude Blacks and wound up living in a frat house for three years. Ultimately I became a relatively purposeful student, but I probably imbibed more alcohol in this period than was appropriate. Meanwhile, the issue of race was never explicitly addressed in the university or my fraternity, Phi Mu Delta, until a visit by Thurgood Marshall, who came to campus to speak in my senior year.

Figure 2.4: Phi Mu Delta members, c. 1955 or 1956. First row, left to right: James Warren, Kurt Krause, others unidentified. Second row, left to right: Gary Aznavarian, George Kent, William B. Gould IV, Bill Fall.

Marshall, whom I met during his visit—a highlight of my college experience—spoke of how civil rights litigation in voting, transportation, and schools was progressing. Shortly after his visit, I wrote an article for a university magazine saying that, though the student body had applauded Mr. Marshall, it seemed to me that there was something superficial about the applause, given that there was no campus opposition to the fact that "some fraternities and sororities discriminate against Negroes and Jews through open or hidden clauses."[24] I was subsequently told that the Dean of Men, John Quinn, made a speech characterizing my article as "irresponsible journalism."

Another memorable moment at URI was a brief conversation I had off campus with John F. Kennedy. As I came through a receiving line during the 1956 Presidential campaign, I questioned then-Senator Kennedy about the jury-trial amendment to what became the Civil Rights Act of 1957, designed to protect Black voting rights. The jury-trial amendment, proposed by southern senators and supported by Senator Kennedy, would have nullified that protection in an era when Blacks were still systematically excluded from southern juries. Kennedy responded vaguely but politely to my question, which was undoubtedly inappropriate in the context of a receiving line. (A side note: Although I was initially conflicted about JFK because of his voting rights rapprochement with the South and his family's friendship with Joe McCarthy, ultimately I became a big supporter. As the 1960 presidential election unfolded, my father—who had viewed Al Smith's brand of Roman Catholicism distrustfully—said when we discussed JFK's posture on civil rights, "I think that he will be on our side." Kennedy's understated humor and wit also appealed to my father.)

One of the most memorable political events in the '56 presidential campaign arose when I and a fellow Phi Mu brother, Ray Deveraux, campaigned for the Stevenson-Kefauver ticket. Ray and I drove around the campus with a megaphone, promoting the ticket as well as state candidates. Later, we were told by university administrators that if we did that again we would be expelled. The Warren Court jurisprudence on free speech had yet to emerge or take root.

Throughout this period, my great Aunt Fannie Gould was an abiding presence, through my occasional Washington visits and conversations about her with my parents. Fannie was a strong, wise, and witty woman. Extremely light in complexion, in the 1960s she would say to me, "Billy, don't call me Black," when that word had come into style. Indeed, she was not black in color, but she was an educated woman, a teacher, and a participant in the March on Washington in 1963, when she was well into her sixties, if not her seventies. It was Fannie who introduced me to Julian Cook and Carol Dibble, when Julian was studying at Georgetown Law School in Washington; Julian and Carol were to be the only people I knew when I first went to Detroit in 1960. It was Fannie who took me to a commencement at Howard University sometime in the fifties, when a rising young minister named Martin Luther King Jr. was the commencement speaker, having recently led the successful Montgomery, Alabama, bus boycott. And, along with my parents, she attended my graduation from the University of Rhode Island in 1958.

MOMENTUM TOWARD THE LAW

At this point in my education, I began to read assiduously. I had no idea what was involved in the law, but had been advised—correctly, I think—that a good lawyer should read widely and increase his knowledge of human affairs. I dove into Richard Wright, James Baldwin, Theodore Dreiser, Sinclair Lewis, Dostoevsky, Tolstoy, Joseph Conrad, and even Howard Fast. Fast's book on Reconstruction, *Freedom Road*, like Count Basie's band which I had heard on the Asbury Park boardwalk, excited me so much that I wanted to sprint as fast as I could (an impulse I quickly repressed!).

I became passionate about the Loyalist cause in Spain, reading Claude Bowers' *My Mission to Spain*, Ernest Hemingway's *For Whom the Bell Tolls*, and George Orwell's *Homage to Catalonia*.[25] I was even reading the Loyalist anti-Franco magazine *Iberica*.[26] At about this time, at the age of nineteen, I became friendly with Gene Angrist during a summer job on that same boardwalk at Asbury Park. Through the summers of '56 through '59 the two of us read everything—politics, history, poetry, novels, all of them voraciously—and we discussed these books together all summer long. I recall reading James Agee's *A Death in the Family* after one of our discussions about death had shaken me profoundly. I hadn't thought hard about death since I was a small child, when my parents advised me, much to my dismay, that there would be a day when I would die.

These discussions sometimes included our parents as well. As my father said during one of our conversations, "There are three things worth discussing: politics, religion, and—what was that other thing?" Gene and I spoke a lot about "that other thing," too. When I was reading *The Decameron*, my father walked into the living room where I was reading and stood there, left, and then returned and said, "I understand that the best parts have been removed from that edition." Whatever his demeanor and temperament, straight-laced he was not.

All these readings and discussions pushed me toward the law. The Episcopal priesthood was now in the rearview mirror, perhaps because I favored an attitude about personal morality akin to St. Augustine's sentiments about chastity, that is, make me moral, "but not now." It was at this point that I began to write more, inspired initially by the breezy style of the 1940s *New York Times* sports section, then by what I was reading with Gene Angrist. I soon participated in an essay contest sponsored by the Jesuit magazine *Social Order*, which rewarded me with a rich $100 prize on the theme "The Alert Citizen and Civil Liberties."

After an initial year or so of stumbling, my university grades had eventually gone through the roof. I applied to law school and was accepted at Cornell, Michigan, and Georgetown. I didn't really know anyone who had been to Cornell Law School, and I was to learn later that Cornell was really aimed at those who sought either a Wall Street practice in corporate law or a general practitioner career in upstate New York. In retrospect, Michigan probably had the best reputation as a law school, but my parents and I agreed that Cornell would be the best place for me, and I accepted their offer.

CORNELL LAW SCHOOL

Going to Ithaca, which I soon discovered to be in the high-precipitation belt of the United States, was both a mistake and an opportunity. During that dreary, bleary, and unhappy first year, which bore no relationship to my aspirations, there was only one course remotely connected to my purpose and motivation for law school: Constitutional Law. I loved the reading assignments in the beautiful casebook that I carefully outlined from cover to cover (it sits in my law school office here at Stanford to this very day). Despite the rambling, disorganized lectures delivered by a professor who, I was to learn, had suffered personal tragedy, I was stimulated by this one course and no others—and my grades showed it!

Yet notwithstanding the poor quality of those constitutional law lectures, there was one statement made in them which I shall never forget: "Boys and girls," that professor said, "the greatest constitutional decision ever made took place when Pickett's Charge failed at Gettysburg," referencing the last battle there which sealed the victory for the Union. Years later, when I visited Gettysburg and the landmark location of Pickett's Charge, I reflected anew upon that comment, my great-grandfather's contribution, the sacrifice made by him and his comrades, and his sword, now in my possession in California, taken from the hallowed ground of Gettysburg itself.[27]

But in the midst of all my general disappointment with the offered curriculum, there was also another opportunity. In the first year, all students were required to take a course entitled Legal Research. Our course was taught by a young law professor in his first year out of the legal staff of the United Auto Workers (UAW) in Detroit. He devised a research problem aimed at the confluence and tension between labor law and antidiscrimination principles, such as they were at the time.

The problem Kurt Hanslowe devised for us first-year law students related to a 1944 Supreme Court decision holding that a union, which had sought to exclude Black railway workers from both their membership and the most desirable jobs in the industry, and which refused to fairly represent them, owed those workers a duty of fair representation.[28] The 1944 Court held that the union owed a duty of fair representation to all employees and was prohibited from hostile, in this case racial, discrimination. The issue left unresolved was whether the duty of fair representation obliged the union to drop its racially exclusionary membership policy. The ultimate judicial answer, supplied by a circuit court ruling that the Supreme Court declined to review, was that a union was not required to open its ranks on a nondiscriminatory basis—a position from which I dissented in my paper. Writing this paper interested me immensely, and my work on it brought me to Kurt Hanslowe's attention. From that moment onward, I had a very loyal friend and supporter at Cornell Law School.

At this point, a number of factors combined to alter the focus of my legal career. First, I became aware that there were only four people on Thurgood Marshall's NAACP legal staff in New York; it was therefore unlikely that I could attain a position there, had I applied for one. This reality, coupled with my membership in CIO unions[29] during the '57 and '58 summers, helped me develop labor law interests. I had worked in supermarkets stocking shelves, lifting boxes over my head (my boss would frequently say, "There's a week's wages up there in that box over your head"); patrolled the Asbury Park Boardwalk amusement park machines; and been a member of the Utility Workers Union when employed with the local water company, breaking up roads with my pick and shovel. A few years earlier, I had worked in the open fields about a mile from our house in Elberon, cutting high grass with a scythe near the Hollywood Hotel (just as Hawaiian boxer Bobo Olson was training there for a fight against one of my favorites, Sugar Ray Robinson). The fact that CIO unions supported civil rights made me interested in labor law.

The strong industrial unions, which had come on the scene in the 1930s,[30] contrasted sharply with the traditional craft unions, which were hesitant to support Blacks in the Taft-Hartley era of anti-union policies and the Republican comeback based on this hostility.[31] I nonetheless saw the UAW, with which Kurt Hanslowe[32] had been affiliated, as one of the best—if not the best—unions on civil rights issues. My view, as it emerged, came to be that the workplace was critical to issues of racial justice; my contact with Hanslowe turned my interest to labor law and its complexities.

Figure 2.5: Before my paid work as a laborer, I dug the path from our house to the water line on the adjacent street.

Figure 2.6: The author in more formal attire around the same period.

"A Big Break"

During my second year in Ithaca, Walter Reuther, the fiery red-headed president of the United Auto Workers and innovator responsible for the idea of a guaranteed annual wage,[33] delivered an inspiring, table-thumping speech to the Cornell student body.[34] Kurt Hanslowe had set the table for the Reuther appearances with an introductory talk on the UAW, Reuther, and Detroit.

At the same time, I was now enrolled in Professor Bertram Wilcox's Labor Law class. I found it absolutely fascinating, not only because of the National Labor Relations Act's promotion of collective bargaining and freedom of association—a kind of Bill of Rights for organized labor and workers—but also because of the intellectual challenge posed by the technical complexity and symmetry of the statute and its related interpretations. And Kurt Hanslowe, fortunately, hadn't forgotten my work in his class, recommending me to his former boss, UAW General Counsel Harold Cranefield, for a summer job in the spring of 1960. Soon thereafter, a letter arrived with an invitation to join the legal staff for a summer clerkship at eighty dollars a week. Beyond the inspiration provided me in childhood by my parents, this was to be the most important development in my professional life.

As I wrote in my diary on April 28, 1960, the day the letter arrived at 109 Williams Street in Ithaca:

> *On this day a big break came my way. The United Automobile Workers has offered me a summer job as a law clerk in Detroit. . . . I am extremely elated about the whole thing. It is the opening that I have hoped for. Professor Hanslowe's letter did the trick – he has been so kind! Called home to convey the good news.*

WORKPLACE FAIRNESS LEGISLATION

This was to be the turning point in my professional career. Yet in order to see this next step more clearly, it is important to comprehend something of the content of the field of labor law. My interests, as they emerged, were devoted to three areas that would be central to my future work: (1) the rights of workers to speak up and, if necessary, protest employment conditions which they deemed to be unfair, to organize into labor unions, and to engage in collective bargaining with their employers; (2) the rights of workers to obtain resolution of disputes about discrimination in employment, particularly racial discrimination; and (3) the promotion of an impartial dispute resolution process for labor–management relations. The broad theme in all these areas was fairness in the workplace.

This work has involved me in two of the five or six most transformative and consequential laws enacted in the United States in more than a century, and—aside from the great post-Civil War constitutional amendments—arguably the most significant legislative initiatives since the beginning of the Republic itself. These two laws are the National Labor Relations Act (NLRA), and Title VII of the Civil Rights Act of 1964.

The National Labor Relations Act

The NLRA is applicable to most of the private sector (although it has been copied by many states and municipalities for application to the public sector) and has endured longer than any comparable legal framework in any other industrialized country. Enacted in 1935, and promoted by Senator Robert Wagner of New York (it was frequently called the "Wagner Act" until the enactment of a number of amendments), the NLRA served as a departure from one-sided and anti-union common law and frequently inexpert statutory adjudication by courts of general jurisdiction and, in its place, substituted a specialized, presumptively expert administrative agency.[35] The law ushered in a new National Labor Relations Board (NLRB), an agency whose rulings were not self-enforceable if a party resisted its orders. Thus, in the absence of judicial intervention, NLRB decrees were appealable to the federal judiciary and sometimes the Supreme Court. The bulk of my scholarly and hands-on practical work has been concerned with this agency.

The functions of the NLRB were, and are today, twofold: (1) to conduct secret ballot representation elections to determine whether a majority of workers choose to select a labor organization for the purpose of bargaining collectively with their employer about wages, hours, and conditions of employment; and (2) statutory interpretations to elaborate on the meaning of "unfair labor practice" prohibitions contained in the NLRA itself. Through this mechanism, the NLRB determines whether, for instance, surveillance of union activities, interrogation of employees about union activities, or prohibitions against employee union activities on employer property are unfair, and establishes the circumstances under which discharge or discipline of workers could be deemed unlawful.

The unfair labor practice prohibitions, coupled with representational elections, are designed to promote the policies of freedom of association for workers and the collective bargaining process itself; these rules are necessary because of the inherent inequality in the labor market between the single worker acting on his/her own initiative on the one hand, and capital on the other. Though the Taft-Hartley amendments of 1947 and the Landrum-Griffin amendments of 1959 imposed new obligations upon labor—unfair labor practices in 1935 were solely applicable to the employer—the basic policy remains that set forth in the preamble of the NLRA itself, that is, the promotion of freedom of association and collective bargaining.

To sum up, the policy principles since 1935 of both representation elections and unfair labor practices contain a kind of trinity of principles. The first is that the NLRB, usually through representation elections, determines the appropriate grouping or "unit" of employees who can cast their ballot or express their view in favor of union representation and collective bargaining. The second part of the trinity is that, once the election is conducted, the majority of the unit or grouping of the workers rules in determining whether there will be union representation and collective bargaining or none at all. The third principle is that a union, if chosen by the employees, acts as an independent and exclusive bargaining representative for all employees within the bargaining unit. This process, when completed, obligates both employer and union to bargain in good faith, that is, a good faith intent to enter into a collective bargaining agreement even though, paradoxically, there is no obligation on either side to actually consummate an agreement.

Title VII of the Civil Rights Act

Title VII of the Civil Rights Act of 1964 and its related legal instruments prohibit discrimination in employment (in both private and public sectors) on the basis of race, color, sex, national origin, religion, and—subsequent to 1964—age, sexual orientation (through statutory interpretation),[36] and disability. Initially designed with the NLRA as a model,[37] the legislation created the Equal Employment Opportunity Commission (EEOC) which was given the authority to investigate complaints of discrimination, to attempt to conciliate these matters and, since 1972, the power to sue companies and unions in federal district court for alleged discrimination subsequent to the administrative process.

One of the basic issues arising under this statute and related laws aimed at discrimination relates to proof, that is, how does one prove discrimination? Probably the most important case on this point was *Griggs v. Duke Power Co.*,[38] in which a unanimous Supreme Court held that it is not necessary to show an intent to discriminate in order to prove that employment discrimination law has been violated in some circumstances. As much as any other ruling, *Griggs* put Title VII on the map and, for me, led to books, articles, pathbreaking litigation, and my creation of new seminars at law schools where I taught in the late sixties and early seventies.

REMARKS GIVEN AT STANFORD LAW SCHOOL[39]

Twenty years ago this May, the Supreme Court ruled in Brown v. Board of Education *that separate but equal was unconstitutional in public education. This pronouncement was heard round the world—and it was the first definitive answer provided by our government to what the world knew to be the shame of this country, that is, the caste system, which imposed the badge of inferiority upon Negroes throughout the United States.*

I recall vividly May 17, 1954, and the reports of it contained in the following day's edition of the New York Times. *I was seventeen years old then, a high school senior in a small New Jersey town. At that time I had little knowledge about plaintiff's petition for writ of prohibition lodged with the Supreme Court in 1896 against segregation* in public transportation in which petition he "averred that he was seven eighths Caucasian and one eighth African blood; that the mixture of colored blood was not discernible in him, and that he was entitled to every right, privilege, and immunity secured to citizens to the United States of the white race; and that upon such theory he took possession of a vacant seat in a coach" reserved to whites.

Although I did not know much about Plessy v. Ferguson *in 1954, I knew full well the low esteem in which Black people were held by most white citizens of this country—a point made dramatically by President John F. Kennedy in 1963 when he said: "Who among us would be content to have the color of his skin changed and stand in his [the Negro's] place?" I knew from personal experience the truth of what the first Mr. Justice Harlan had said in eloquent dissent in* Plessy, *that is, that segregation was simply formalization of the master race theory. And I was also well acquainted with the debilitating impact of such attitudes upon the willingness of the oppressed to identify with one another so as to effectively stand up against the oppressor. In this connection it is to be recalled that the plaintiff in* Plessy v. Ferguson *predicated part of his prayer for relief upon the ground that African blood in his veins was "not discernible."*

I am extremely proud to be on the same podium with you, Mr. Chief Justice. For there is nothing which was more important in my decision to become a lawyer than that event of May 17, 1954— your opinion in Brown v. Board of Education. *That decision gave me and other blacks the hope and belief that the law could address itself to racial injustices in this country and that I as a lawyer could make some contribution to end the old order against which my parents had struggled. In their day the struggle was against hopeless odds—hopeless because all who possessed African blood were isolated, ridiculed, despised, and thus regarded as unfit for occupations and work that the white man was willing to perform.*

Brown *changed that. Regardless of the contemporary debate about issues like community control, self-determination, and integration,* Brown *was important to all black people because it gave us hope that we would have our day in court—both literally and figuratively.* Brown *turned us as a nation away from the path of South Africa and made the principle of racial equality a respectable one amongst many educated people. It encouraged civil rights advocates to protest through the courts and elsewhere and to fight back against injustice in all forms. It prompted Congress to move on its own initiative and to pass, amongst other important statutes, comprehensive fair employment practices legislation such as Title VII of the Civil Rights Act of 1964.*

It was May 17, 1954, that set the stage for these developments and others, and it is that decision and the difficult experience with the implementation of its principles which had been a teacher to the courts charged with the interpretation of Title VII. This is so because Brown *and its judicial progeny taught us that the past of racial inequality is inseparable from judicial consideration of the present—and that the affirmative dismantling of segregated institutions is a prerequisite to equal opportunity. And so it is in employment cases, where in the past decade independent federal judges appointed for life have struck down segregated seniority lines and discriminatory no transfer policies which held blacks down in less desirable and low-level jobs. These same judges have laid siege to hiring preference for the sons of white workers and their friends and relatives, where the effect of such preference is to perpetuate an all-white workforce or job classification.*

Brown *also opened the way for the very important decision of the Supreme Court of March 1971,* Griggs v. Duke Power, *where the Court, unanimous as it was in 1954, held that discrimination can be found even when there is no intent to discriminate. The Court was able to arrive at this conclusion in* Griggs *in part because its involvement with the issues in* Brown *and in other civil rights areas had made it clear that blacks as a group were not receiving educational benefits in our country equal to those obtained by whites. From here it was a short step to conclude that employment practices such as written examination, educational qualifications, and apprenticeship programs which reflected societal inequities and which were not related and necessary to the job that a black applicant sought, were discriminatory under federal law.*

And finally, the experience with Brown—*especially between 1954 and 1968—made it clear that centuries of racism would not easily disappear and that delay therefore could no longer be tolerated. All of this prompted the Court to say that segregation must be eliminated both "here and now" and "root and branch." The federal courts, in dealing with employment cases, have learned well from this history, and have therefore not been content to merely slap offenders on the wrist, but at a relatively early stage of the development of the law have imposed goals and timetables for hiring and promotion of blacks and other minorities when there was no other way to remedy discrimination, slapped back pay awards upon defendants and, most recently, awarded millions of dollars of punitive damages against those who flagrantly violate the law.*

Mr. Chief Justice, I am pleased that you could be with us today to commemorate this historic decision. Brown *was and is the first step in our journey of a thousand miles. I do not believe that there can be a turning back from the new era of morality ushered in by that decision.*

For that reason alone, I, and all who believe in equality of the races, pay tribute to you and the Brown *decision today. For me, Mr. Chief Justice, and people of all colors throughout the world, you are a man for the ages. You have given us the hope that we dared not have previously—the hope that our children will become adults in an age of equality—an age in which fate denied our parents the right to live.*

NOTES

[1] All these actions helped establish the basic landscape for the world of work in which I was to be involved, but it was a period during which FDR and Democrats refused to even tiptoe toward anti-lynching legislation for fear of losing the Solid South: Alabama, Arkansas, Florida, Georgia, Louisiana, Mississippi, North Carolina, South Carolina, Tennessee, Texas, Virginia, Oklahoma, and Kentucky. Moreover, even the above-referenced social and welfare legislation was frequently applied discriminatorily toward Blacks. See also note 30.

[2] Samuel G. Freedman, *Into the Bright Sunshine: Young Hubert Humphrey and the Fight for Civil Rights* (Oxford: Oxford University Press, 2023).
[3] William B. Gould IV, "The Right to Travel and National Security," *Washington University Law Quarterly* 4, 349n73 (1961).
[4] James A. Wechsler, *The Age of Suspicion* (New York: Random House, 1953).
[5] C. W. Ceram, *Gods Graves and Scholars: The Story of Archaeology* (New York: Alfred A. Knopf, 1951).
[6] William B. Gould IV, *For Labor to Build Upon: Wars, Depression and Pandemic* (Cambridge: Cambridge University Press, 2022), 5.
[7] William B. Gould IV, "Politics and the Effect on the National Labor Relations Board's Adjudicative and Rulemaking Processes," *Emory Law Journal* 64 (2015).
[8] Larry Tye, *Demagogue: The Life and Long Shadow of Senator Joe McCarthy* (Boston: Houghton Mifflin Harcourt, 2020); "McCarthy and His Men: Cohn & Schine – The Army Got Its Orders," *Time*, March 22, 1954, 21–27.
[9] W. H. Lawrence, "Welch Questions the Authenticity of McCarthy Data," *New York Times*, June 2, 1954; W. H. Lawrence, "Exchange Bitter; Counsel is Near Tears as Crowd Applauds Him at Finish," *New York Times*, June 10, 1954.
[10] Tye, *Demagogue*, 436.
[11] *Brown v. Board of Education of Topeka*, 347 U.S. 483 (1954).
[12] *Plessy v. Ferguson*, 163 U.S. 537 (1896).
[13] *Brown v. Board of Education of Topeka*, 349 U.S. 294 (1955). The vagueness of the decree gave the white South hope that Brown itself would be delayed and ultimately not be implemented if violent opposition and resistance were frequently employed.
[14] "Thurgood Marshall," *Time*, September 19, 1955, cover.
[15] "My father came to this country when he was a teenager. Not only had he never profited from the sweat of any black man's brow, I don't think he had ever seen a black man. There are, of course, many white ethnic groups that came to this country in great numbers relatively late in its history—Italians, Jews, Irish, Poles—who not only took no part in, and derived no profit from, the major historic suppression of the currently acknowledged minority groups, but were, in fact, themselves the object of discrimination by the dominant Anglo Saxon majority." Antonin Scalia, "The Disease as Cure: 'In Order to Get Beyond Racism, We Must First Take Account of Race,'" *Washington University Law Quarterly* 1979 (1979): 147, 152.
[16] Emily Bazelon, "The Undoing of Affirmative Action: How the Landmark 1978 Supreme Court Decision That Upheld the Practice May Ultimately Have Set It on a Path to Being Outlawed," *New York Times* Magazine, February 19, 2023, 29.
[17] William B. Gould III, Diary, July 26, 1944.
[18] Federal Writers' Project of the Works Progress Administration of the State of New Jersey and Federal Writers' Project, Entertaining a Nation; the Career of Long Branch (1940).
[19] Gunnar Myrdal, *An American Dilemma* (New York: McGraw-Hill, 1944).
[20] Matthew 11:28. For this specific phrasing, see the Church of England, *The Book of Common Prayer* (London: Oxford University Press, 1928), 235.
[21] Fortifying this connection was our involvement in the "Anglo-Catholic" wing of the Episcopal Church which had emerged in the nineteenth century through the Oxford Movement in England, embracing traditions and liturgy diminished or lost in the wake

of the Reformation. And connected to this was the movement's immersion in the problems of inner cities in London and New York and the plight of the poor. I participated with groups of acolytes or altar boys and convocations of them in Solemn Processions at the Church of St. Mary the Virgin in New York City, the leading Anglo-Catholic parish in the New York-New Jersey area.

22 Frank Loesser, "The Most Happy Fella," 1956.

23 Subsequent to writing a draft of this passage, my classmate Joseph Asch advised me that there was a Black woman, Euland Whitfield, in our college stream. Regrettably, I have no recollection of Ms. Whitfield.

24 William B. Gould IV, "On Fraternities and Discrimination," *The Puritan*, 1958, 15.

25 However, when I discovered "The Tragic Era" denigrating Blacks during Reconstruction, I developed a different view of him.

26 In this period, I was critical of the Eisenhower administration's relationship with Franco and Spain: "The United States and Spain have signed a twenty-year military pact. Eight years ago we helped keep Spain out of the United Nations because we realized that Franco had definitely been in sympathy with the Axis powers. Can it be that Americans have such short memories? This 'treaty' has not helped America's reputation any." William B. Gould IV, "Treaty with Spain," *New York Herald Tribune*, October 4, 1953.

27 Abraham Lincoln, "Gettysburg Address," Speech, Gettysburg, PA, November 19, 1863.

28 Steele v. Louisville Nashville & N.R. Co., 323 U.S. 192 (1944). The case pending at the time of my paper which triggered the question posed by Professor Hanslowe was Oliphant v. Brotherhood of Locomotive Firemen and Enginemen, 262 F.2d 359 (6th Cir. 1958), cert. denied 359 U.S. 935 (1959).

29 I spoke in favor of the position of Walter Reuther and James Carey of the IUE when they said that they would meet with Soviet President Khrushchev on his first visit to America in 1959: "Walter Reuther and James Carey are to be commended for their dissent to George Meany's refusal to meet with Khrushchev. Their forthright and intelligent position is not only indicative of their own vigor but also is a re-manifestation of the deep division that still exists in the merged labor movement. The A.F.L. unions have clung rather rigidly to the idea that labor's business did not ever go much farther than the collective bargaining process. The C.I.O. position has been a vision of much broader scope. Thus, the C.I.O. unions have emphasized political action and have been particularly helpful in the field of civil rights. The Soviet Union is a part of this world and as such she must be dealt with. It is this somber truth that has influenced Messrs. Reuther and Carey. The Meany attitude seems to indicate a tendency to ignore reality." William B. Gould IV, "Labor's Division," *New York Herald Tribune*, September 5, 1959.

30 See generally Walter Galenson, *The CIO Challenge to the AFL: A History of the American Labor Movement, 1935–1941* (Cambridge: Harvard University Press, 1960).

31 Ira Katznelson, *When Affirmative Action Was White: An Untold History of Racial Inequality in Twentieth-Century America* (New York: W.W. Norton, 2005), 53–79. See also to the same effect, Richard Rothstein, *The Color of Law: A Forgotten History of How Our Government Segregated America* (New York: Liveright, 2017).

32 Professor Kurt Hanslowe was the first member of his Harvard Law School class to argue a case before the United States Supreme Court when he did so in Auto Workers v. Wisconsin Board, 351 U.S. 266 (1956).

33 "The G.A.W. Man," *Time*, June 20, 1955, 20–22.
34 "AFL-CIO Leader Reuther to Present Baily Lecture," *Cornell Daily Sun*, March 3, 1960; "Reuther to Speak in Bailey On 'Priorities in Survival,'" *Cornell Daily Sun*, March 18, 1960. In the speech itself, Reuther said that "we must demonstrate the moral courage to bridge the moral gap between American democracy's noble promises and its ugly practices." Milton R. Newman, "Reuther Asks National Unity Toward Peace," *Cornell Daily Sun*, March 21, 1960.
35 William B. Gould IV, *A Primer on American Labor Law*, 6th ed. (Cambridge: Cambridge University Press, 2019), 9–28.
36 Bostock v. Clayton County, 590 U.S. 644 (2020).
37 William B. Gould IV, "Title VII of the Civil Rights Act at Fifty: Ruminations on Past, Present, and Future," *Santa Clara Law Review* 54 (2014).
38 Griggs v. Duke Power Co., 401 U.S. 424 (1971).
39 William B. Gould IV, 120 Cong. Rec. 16229-30, May 22, 1974.

3
DETROIT AND UNITED AUTO WORKERS: MY LABOR LAW BEGINNINGS

On June 18, 1960, my father drove me to Newark Airport from our Elberon home to catch a flight to Detroit. During that ride, we spoke about the quickly passing years; I noted that I was about to turn twenty-four. At nineteen and twenty, I could hardly wait to be twenty-one. But now, on the eve of twenty-four, everything suddenly seemed to be speeding up. My father said, "You will find that feeling increasing as life moves on." Somehow, I think that we both sensed that this day marked a new and important passage in my life.

My father also spoke about Detroit. I was filled with excitement about my move, but both my parents were extremely uneasy about my upcoming trip to the Motor City. My father's apprehension was rooted in the World War II riots in Detroit that had been triggered by white resentment against a recent migration of Black workers who sought wartime employment opportunities. One leading historian has called Detroit's 1943 riot ". . . one of the worst riots in twentieth-century America."[1] The riots were so destructive, and consequent damage so extensive, that Adolf Hitler had used them as propaganda, denouncing American hypocrisy on the issue of racial equality.

The air flight from Newark to Detroit, in one of the last of the propeller-driven domestic flights in this period, took three hours. I arrived at Willow Row Airport, a defense facility during World

War II, and took a bus to the Hannan YMCA on East Jefferson Avenue, a block or two off the Detroit River and about a mile from the United Auto Workers' headquarters, Solidarity House, at 8000 East Jefferson Avenue.

MY SUMMER CLERKSHIP BEGINS

On Monday, June 20, I walked that mile to begin my summer clerkship (internship, in modern parlance). As I had anticipated in April when I received the offer, this turned out to be the first and most consequential development of my professional life. And—unbeknownst to me as I walked down East Jefferson Avenue—that same day the United States Supreme Court in the *Steelworkers Trilogy*[2] held that the Taft-Hartley amendments to the National Labor Relations Act promoted arbitration and the enforcement of arbitration awards in the courts. This too was to have a major impact on my future work in labor law and labor–management relations, as the arbitration process became increasingly important in the resolution of labor–management disputes, and I was quickly involved in much of it.[3]

When I arrived, the only people I knew in Detroit were Julian Cook and his wife, Carol Cook (née Dibble), whom I had met in Washington through my Aunt Fannie. Julian—or "Buddy," as we called him—whom President Carter later named to the federal judiciary, had moved to Detroit after his graduation from Georgetown Law School and become a member of a newly formed Black law firm composed of outstanding lawyers and politicians. Early that summer I visited Buddy and his colleagues in downtown Detroit. I went with him to functions at the law firm, and I recall meeting Black attorneys like Hobart Taylor, and others from the firm, who would soon join the Kennedy and Johnson administrations.

In those early days and, indeed, when I returned to Detroit after my law school graduation in 1961, I was to spend many Sundays visiting with the Cooks at their apartment or taking the bus down to Grand Circus Park at Woodward Avenue in downtown Detroit, where I would stop at a coffee shop and read the *New York Times* and Detroit newspapers before proceeding to their apartment.

The early 1960s offered interesting background music for a young law student in the heart of Detroit, as some observers thought they could hear the distant strains of organized labor's decline. Union density had reached its zenith, representing about 35 percent of the eligible workforce in 1955, and was now just beginning to diminish. Some observers were issuing Cassandra-like warnings of danger that union bureaucracy had become too bloated, and that union efforts to organize, particularly in the South and rural parts of the West, were meeting resistance. This spelled trouble, they said.[4]

Any such trends were well disguised in Detroit. The UAW, after the recession of the fifties, was on the cusp of new growth, which would continue unabated through the late seventies. Still, the Teamsters were enviously admired for their organizational energy and activity in recruiting nonunion workers. We often said, if anything moved, the Teamsters would be there to organize. Profound decline was still on the distant horizon for the UAW itself.[5]

Colleagues, Responsibilities, Surprises

My clerkship immediately involved me with members of the UAW legal team. UAW General Counsel Harold Cranefield, John Fillion, Gordon Gregory, and "Red" Roche all involved me in writing a series of memos that summer. I wrote about the National Labor Relations Act statute of limitations, duty of fair representation for unions, union dues payment requirements, unemployment compensation, labor arbitration remedies and, for Roche, a series of complicated memos involving obscure issues of federal jurisdiction on which I spent many hours and days.

One memorable case that summer involved a motion for a temporary injunction to restrain a company from relocating its facility from Michigan to Georgia. I accompanied John Fillion as we went to the office of federal District Court Judge Fred Kaess to obtain the order ex parte, meaning without the participation of opposing counsel. The judge, appointed by President Eisenhower, was not in his office when we first arrived, but when he returned he examined our papers rather quickly and said, "You fellows will back me up on this, won't you?" Neither Fillion nor I knew what the judge meant by this, but Fillion quickly said, "Yes, your honor," and I, for what it was worth, nodded approvingly. Judge Kaess then said, "Well, that's good, because they just had a luncheon party for me which I'm returning from, and I'm flying kind of high right now." "Yes, your honor, we will back you up." Fillion said. The order was signed right away.

This was rather heady stuff for a law student previously confined to classroom instruction—most of which, aside from labor and constitutional law, I had found uninspiring. Indeed, the entire summer was the most exciting professional or personal period of my life to that point—at least until the following year, when I joined the UAW legal staff in a permanent position.

That summer I also established friendships with UAW political people like Millie Jeffrey and Bill Dodd as well as other staffers, including Horace Sheffield, Oscar Paskal, and B. J. Widick—all of whom I remained friendly with for the rest of their lives. Widick was the author of many interesting books, the most prominent of them being *The UAW and Walter Reuther*. Sheffield, originally a foundry worker, had been with the UAW since 1940, and had been deeply involved in a major 1941 strike at the River Rouge Plant in Dearborn. He was also committed to the civil rights movement.

I watched part of the 1960 Democratic Party convention in the downtown Detroit Lafayette apartment of Congressman Jim O'Hara, a member of the Education and Labor Committee, and felt the same anguish as many of those present that night. When Lyndon Johnson—a Southern Democrat—received the nomination for vice president on the Kennedy ticket, many regarded JFK's act as a betrayal of the party's values (Robert F. Kennedy was outraged too!). Later that summer I attended a few other Detroit political functions, the most prominent in the Cadillac Hotel where, as an observer, I found myself standing just a few feet away from JFK and Michigan Senator Pat McNamara, a champion of civil rights. Though I had met JFK earlier, in Rhode Island, I was thrilled to be standing proximate to him.

I had another thrill that summer: I won a second essay contest. This time it was one conducted by the National Lawyers Guild, an organization of left-wing lawyers more radical than I or the UAW. My topic—important in labor law to this day—was preemption,[6] the authority of higher levels of government over lower levels. The morning I was informed of my prize I was so giddy and happily excited that a service employee in the Hannan YMCA cafeteria said to me, "Enjoy yourself to the hilt, because there will be other sorrowful days ahead." For me, at the age of twenty-four, those were especially wise words indeed, which I would comprehend more fully much later.

My essay contest award facilitated contact with many in the Detroit National Lawyers Guild. For example, I established a lifelong friendship with Richard Goodman, who lived near my place of work at Solidarity House. Though at this point Goodman was a general practitioner with a burgeoning product liability specialty and tort practice, he knew a lot about labor and the UAW as his father, Ernest[7], was a renowned civil rights lawyer. The elder Goodman had represented the left-wing UAW leadership which Walter Reuther's slate of more right-wing candidates had confronted, attacked, and prevailed over in the late 1940s. (Long after Reuther's 1970 death[8], the Administration Board, or Reuther Caucus, remained successful until a direct membership vote in 2023—reversing the traditional indirect convention style vote—would drive incumbents from power for the first time since the Reuther slate had ascended in the late forties.[9])

Ernest (Ernie) Goodman had represented some of this group and others in litigation under the Smith Act, when left-wing and Communist defendants were prosecuted for their unacceptable political views and conduct. Goodman had also argued an early and important First Amendment case, *Thomas v. Collins*,[10] in which the Supreme Court established the constitutional right to distribute union authorization cards, conduct deemed to be constitutionally protected against state interference. Ernest Goodman described to me the transaction that took place, how he had instructed R. J. Thomas, a CIO vice president, to provide a card to a potential union member when state authorities were in the vicinity, so that the issue would be clearly joined. Like his son, Dick, he was an extremely careful and able lawyer.

On Labor Day, as the summer was winding down, I marched down Woodward Avenue with labor union representatives in the Labor Day parade. Somehow Dick Goodman and I connected later in the day to attend the Labor Day rally in Cadillac Square (now Kennedy Square) in downtown Detroit, where we listened to then-Senator John F. Kennedy, Reuther, outgoing Governor G. Mennen "Soapy" Williams (*Time* magazine had marked his relationship with labor when it coined the phrase "the CIO and Soapy too"[11]), and the soon-to-be elected, one-term Governor John Swainson. Perhaps I was too critical when I wrote in my diary on September 5 that day:

> *Reuther gave the only decent speech—he knows how to catch the fire and the imagination of the crowd. Swainson was horrible. Kennedy, in a disorganized rambling speech had nothing to say.*

That evening at the Goodman firm, I looked through files from the thirties and forties and read about some of the civil rights and labor struggles that had taken place earlier in Michigan. But there was immediate excitement in the air about the day's events in Cadillac Square. After two terms of Eisenhower and consecutive losses by Adlai Stevenson in '52 and '56, the prospect of victory, and a "New Frontier" of social and economic reforms via JFK, seemed certain to us.

Summer's End

The week after Labor Day was to be my last one in Detroit in 1960. On Sunday, September 11, I spent the afternoon with Julian and Carol Cook and in the evening I attended a farewell party thrown for me at UAW colleague Gordon Gregory's house in St. Claire Shores, a Detroit suburb. The Fillions, Win Livingston (who represented some of the UAW locals), and Victoria Cafferty, a senior secretary in the office, were all in attendance. The following day was a long representation hearing in Detroit which didn't end until 7 p.m. And on Tuesday, September 13, I had my first tête-à-tête with Walter Reuther, whom my boss, General Counsel Harold Cranefield, took me to meet. I noted in my diary on September 13:

> *I had a rather lengthy 'audience' by Reuther's standards [according to Cranefield]—about 10 to 15 minutes. We really did not talk to each other—Reuther did most of the talking. It was as though he ripped off a prepared speech. He talked of Red China, American devotion to materialism, the anti-Catholic campaign against Kennedy* [he was particularly anguished about this and spoke about the dangerous appeals made by ministers like Norman Vincent Peale].

The following day, September 14, I was in Lansing, the state capital, and visited the State House, where I met with "Soapy" Williams and chatted for a few minutes. Afterward, I got together with his special assistant Vic Navasky, who later became editor of *The Nation*. I have often reflected on an uproarious barroom confrontation we had with a guy that night whom I characterized in my diary as a "Gross Pointe fascist," anti-Black to the core, who apparently did not realize with whom he was speaking. Back and forth the vituperative exchange went, with no fisticuffs or the threat thereof from either of us. Long after, Navasky frequently reminded me of that evening. In other instances, I had walked away from such talk. But not that night. It lived on in my memory; it was the first of several confrontations during which I mustered the courage to fight back.

MY FINAL YEAR AT CORNELL LAW

Then it was back to Cornell. My last year there ('60-'61) had ups and downs. The highlight was more courses on labor and constitutional policy, content much more to my liking than other Cornell Law offerings available to me at the time. Kurt Hanslowe taught some of these courses. He and I also had numerous meetings, which often took the form of my going to his house for lunch, and which often included his wife and children. He and I also saw a number of movies together. As I said in a eulogy for him after his untimely death in 1982:

> *And in an age of more distant professor–student relationships than that which presently exists, I recall viewing and discussing the British movie "I'm All Right, Jack" with him in a downtown Ithaca theatre, discussing his oral argument before the Supreme Court in* UAW v. Wisconsin Employment Relations Board,[12] *and a lovely evening at his home with Nan and the children, at the conclusion of which he gave me a book on the Scottsboro Boys.*[13]

And, ultimately, on my graduation day in June 1961, there was a warm, generous, wonderful meeting between Kurt Hanslowe and my parents.

A Student for Kennedy

During the fall of 1960, particularly in October, I had become involved with Students for Kennedy. None of us anticipated how difficult a contest this would turn out to be. I sweated out the long night of Election Day, and with a result close and uncertain, I wrote in my diary:

> *I sat right in front of the T.V. this evening and watched Senator Kennedy pile up a lead in the East which began to dwindle after midnight. At this point he had almost enough to win the electoral college, but Nixon showed tremendous strength in the West and Kennedy couldn't get the one state needed although he was leading in many—Michigan, Minnesota, California, Illinois.*

I sacked out at 5:30 a.m. with victory just beyond Kennedy's grasp.

The following day, November 9, I wrote:

> *I woke up at 1:00 p.m. had breakfast and got to the T.V. set just after Nixon conceded. Minnesota put Kennedy across, and Michigan and Illinois went for him also—California*

is in doubt. The popular vote is just slightly in Kennedy's favor. But it is a triumph for liberals and the Kennedy Administration promises to be an exciting one. Humphrey, Douglas, and McNamara were all returning to the Senate. Swainson won the State House in Michigan . . . as for me, I'm completely exhausted.

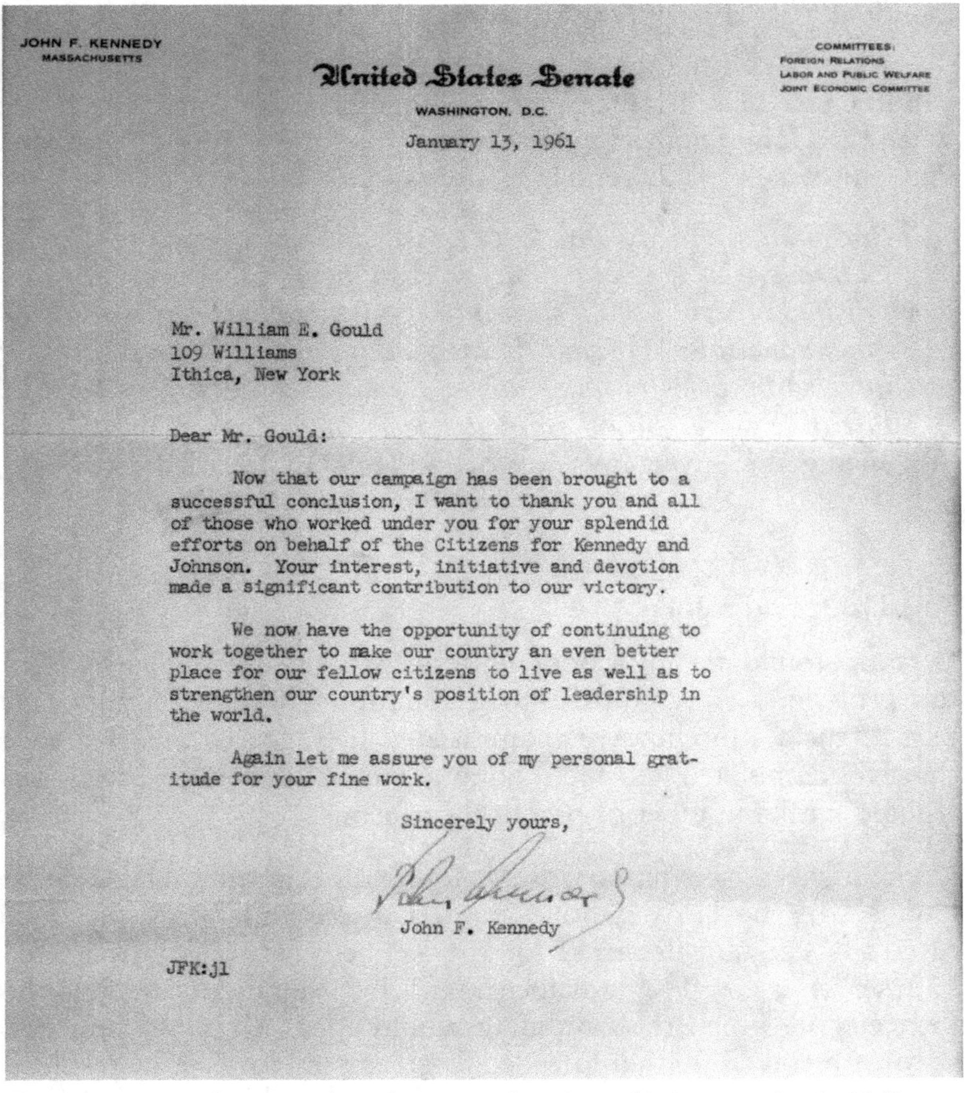

Figure 3.1: Letter from President Elect Kennedy, prior to his inauguration in 1961.

From Ithaca, I watched the unfolding of the Kennedy administration in 1961 with mixed emotions. I was encouraged by the Justice Department's staunch stand on some civil rights issues. On May 7, 1961, I wrote:

> *Attorney General Robert Kennedy said yesterday, in Georgia, that the Justice Department would move vigorously in the area of civil rights. His language was unequivocal. Makes me quite proud of my vote last November.*

But Cuba was another matter altogether. On April 20, 1961, when the United States launched its ill-fated invasion of the Bay of Pigs, this was my diary entry:

> *President Kennedy gave a televised address today on the Cuban crisis. He said that the dispute in Cuba was not finished and that the restraint of the United States was not "inexhaustible." He said that we would not be lectured on interventionism by those who had marked themselves for history by the "blood-stained streets of Budapest"* [referencing the Soviet invasion of Hungary in 1956]. *I think that this Cuban policy is a mistaken one.*

The Draft and a Job

On more mundane law school matters, I struggled with a law school tax problem—a prerequisite to graduation—that regrettably was part of the comprehensive examination. It staggered me. But once that was completed and I had obtained my LLB in June, I was confronted with a number of practical problems.

The first was the military draft in place at that time. The General Counsel of the UAW, who expressed interest in hiring me once "Red" Roche had departed for the Kennedy administration (Red had served as a JFK "advance man" in 1960, scouting out the next city in which the candidate would speak to avoid unnecessary problems), said that I needed to get my military status resolved as soon as possible. On May 29 one of my childhood physicians,

Dr. Frank Altschul, reviewed my records. He had treated me in the past for pneumonia, asthma, and hay fever. He said that he would write a medical letter to my draft board, though he pointed out to me that I had not had asthma recently. Nonetheless, he thought that since there was no international crisis at present, the Select Service Board might well classify me as 4-F. On June 1, the board doctor said that I would not have to take a physical as the board would defer to Dr. Altschul's judgment. The letter came through from the board on June 3 classifying me as 4-F. (Perhaps deservedly, that summer in Detroit I suffered badly from asthma for the first time in years—and had much trouble with it in the years to come!)

The UAW called me on June 7 with a job offer "Subject to Reuther's Approval," and on June 9 I accepted their offer of $6,500 per year, which translated into slightly more than my Cornell colleagues who went to Wall Street. They were paid $7,000, but given that I was provided a lease-free American Motors Rambler with reasonable expenses for gas as well, I was ahead of the game financially.

Figure 3.2: WBG IV, when hired by the UAW in 1961.

RETURN TO UAW

In July, after a few days at our New Jersey home where I enjoyed delightful swims in the Atlantic, it was off to Detroit again. On July 22 my parents took me to Newark Airport. I wrote that day:

> *Mom and Dad took me to the Newark Airport where I caught a 10:15 flight for Detroit. Said farewell to the people who had brought me this far. Nothing that I ever do can possibly compensate them.*

Big Three Negotiations, the Reuthers, and Civil Rights

The following Monday, I was back at Solidarity House, where I began work on a variety of assignments and the already-commenced State Bar course—a schedule which I thought would constitute "an ordeal." But such concerns were more than outweighed by what I saw as my good fortune working for General Counsel Harold Cranefield, a man I regarded as "intellectually superior and human."[14]

Within a week I was involved in representation proceedings arising out of a petition for an election so that UAW workers could vote for or against collective bargaining. Soon thereafter, I plunged into a brief arising out of that year's Big Three automakers negotiations, that is, General Motors' contention that UAW demands were "inflationary," and the question of whether the company was legally obliged to verify its position or open its books on the theory that it was pleading an inability to pay.[15] At best, the answer was a tentative yes. In any event, the UAW was always reluctant to litigate unfair labor practice cases with the Big Three—especially General Motors and Ford.

At the end of August, I was able to sit in on the internal discussions about which company in the Big Three would be selected for a strike, if necessary. (At that point the discussions were truly staged, as the arguments, positions taken, and strategy votes had already been rehearsed and positions taken.) Walter Reuther presided over the deliberations. On August 30, I sat in at the so-called "big table" where contract negotiations were conducted between GM and UAW. I wrote:

> Sat in on negotiations with General Motors—the strike target. Reuther was there. He and [Leonard] Woodcock engaged in verbal fisticuffs with [Louis] Seaton of GM. At the morning break, Reuther came over and spoke to me—[he said] he was glad to have me with the UAW and remarked that I came at an exciting time.

Though this brief Reuther encounter was exciting to a young fledging, I had met his brother, Roy Reuther, also prominent in

UAW leadership, when I first arrived at the UAW Solidarity House headquarters that summer, and he had greeted me with far more effusiveness, and considerable warmth. He said, "Welcome to Solidarity House!" with a big smile on his face. Roy's authenticity was unforgettable. I also had a number of conversations with a third Reuther brother, Victor, who, like Walter, had been shot and lost an eye in the 1940s, almost certainly as a result of his passionate union work. Far more reserved than Roy, Victor[16] was the director of the international relations department, and was to play a role in my life's next chapter, after Detroit.

Meanwhile I was faced during this period with some practical problems. The Hannan YMCA address seemed no longer suitable to a law graduate working as house counsel. But where to live? On August 19 of that same year, I wrote about an upsetting encounter:

> *I was rudely insulted this day by Detroit style racial discrimination. I was in the process of looking for an apartment in the Wayne area and was asked (1) . . . my "nationality" and when I responded I was informed that apartments weren't rented to "colored" and (2) told that in seeking a roommate for a large apartment not to get a Negro—that was the only restriction. Quite hurtful. After the bar examination, a legislative proposal to Governor Swainson may be in order.*

In fact, I wrote to Governor Swainson on September 29, 1961, and advised him that "I was refused the opportunity to lease apartments in the Detroit area solely upon racial grounds."[17] Subsequently, I showed the letter to UAW Washington counsel Joe Rauh and, while he expressed sympathy, neither he nor others provided any help or support.

Civil rights wasn't yet on the agenda in Detroit. True, walking down Woodward Avenue in downtown Detroit, I encountered picketers and leafletters at retail department stores, advising the public of the refusal of those establishments to serve customers in the South on an integrated basis. But southern Democrats and Republicans had stopped proposals for fair employment and housing equality, notwithstanding President Truman's support for such legislation in 1949. (The "Dixiecrats" had walked out of the '48 Democratic convention in support of Strom Thurmond when Truman embraced a strong civil rights platform.) The police dogs and hoses in Birmingham, the March on Washington, and other protests were still years away.

And only in the wake of that upheaval, in 1964, would fair employment be adopted, housing at the federal level still in the distant future of 1968. In 1961, however, a young Black UAW lawyer in Detroit had little or no recourse.

A Busy Schedule

Eventually I was able to find an apartment on Second Avenue in the same area where I had been declined a rental. I moved there after a three-day bar examination which I took in Ann Arbor in September. (An unforgettable feature of that day was standing in line next to the near-seven-foot-tall Walt Dukes, whom my father and I had watched play basketball at Fort Monmouth when I was in eighth grade. Now he was taking the bar exam with me!)

When the bar was completed, I dove into brief writing, in a series of unemployment compensation cases; on September 18, it was off to Benton Harbor and St. Joseph, on the western side of Michigan, traveling through the rolling hills near Traverse City in my Rambler for another series of representation cases. Meeting union organizers in Benton Harbor I wrote in my diary: "had a few drinks with the organizer in this case. He is quite along in years as are most of the organizers—which is, I think, generally unfortunate." While some may view this comment as ageist, I have written about the need for the labor movement to use more young, dedicated, and principled people, unencumbered by responsibilities, as was more frequently the case in the 1930s. I developed the view that the lack of young people negatively affects unions' ability to organize the unorganized. I held this view in the sixties—and I still do today.[18]

A week later I began my most challenging assignment of that period: unfair labor proceedings before a trial examiner (in 1972 they became known as administrative law judges) in the *Cross Company* hearings. The critical question in these proceedings involved replacement of strikers and whether they were entitled to reinstatement by virtue of company unfair labor practices. (Unfair labor strikers, whose strikes are caused or prolonged by the employers' commission of an unfair labor practice, are entitled to reinstatement—in contrast to "economic" strikers, who may be permanently replaced.) My role was to assist UAW-retained union lawyer Winston Livingston, while also writing more unemployment compensation briefs when I returned to the office on East Jefferson Avenue in the late afternoon or evening. Ultimately, the *Cross* hearings concluded after several weeks, and I was advised by Livingston at that point that the brief was my responsibility. I finally finished it, after an extension (in my diary I called an extension "the lawyer's worst enemy"), on November 10.

Almost as a kind of reward for my hard work, when I came up for air after sustained writing, Cranefield sent me off to Wisconsin to see if I could monitor or perhaps promote the back pay proceedings arising out of the highly publicized Kohler Company strike which had begun during my high school senior year and now continued more than seven years later.[19] The employer was, as Cranefield frequently said, an old-school German owner (only much later did the company morph into a multinational conglomerate) which held the view that the union did not belong on "company property." The dispute was complicated by UAW misconduct on the picket line, some of Secretary Treasurer Emil Mazey's staffers figuring prominently in this activity. Before departing from Detroit, I was at lunch with one of the Mazey staffers, Don Rand, who had been photographed engaging in "back to belly" picketing at Kohler, which made it impossible for anyone to cross the picket line. Upon learning of my assignment when I met him in the Solidarity House cafeteria, he declared to me, "You'll never be as famous as me."

I flew to Milwaukee on November 20, booking into Schroeder's Hotel. I spent the following day at the UAW regional headquarters there, examining, discussing, and attempting to digest compliance reports. And then the next morning, I was on an 8:30 a.m. bus off to Sheboygan and its flat farmland. Here I met with representatives of Local UAW 833 (the local Kohler representatives for the workers) and then with local counsel David Rabinowitz—and then a visit to Kohler Village itself. Rabinowitz, who had established a relationship with the Kennedys during the McClellan hearings[20] involving improper union behavior, must have been annoyed by the sudden appearance of a young kid from Detroit looking over his shoulder. Still, we had a cordial meeting. (Rabinowitz would later be nominated by JFK to the federal bench—a nomination withdrawn by LBJ.)

Returning to Milwaukee that evening I met and had dinner with UAW counsel Leonard Zubrensky and his wife, Ruth Zubrensky. "Wonderful people," I wrote in my diary, and they became friends for decades, their son Michael eventually attending Stanford Law School as my student.

On Thanksgiving Day, I took the train from Milwaukee to Chicago, my first visit to the Windy City. Here I met my friend Dick Goodman with his wife, Maria, and Dick's brother, Bill, still a student at the University of Chicago Law School. We had Thanksgiving dinner at Bill's girlfriend's apartment with Dick, Maria, and I taking in downtown Chicago. I characterized the city that day as a "swinging town—and beautiful women." The following day—no holidays then on the Friday after Thanksgiving—I was at the NLRB Chicago regional office meeting with board lawyer Don Squillicate, who had been on the Kohler case "most of the way." I wrote, "probably the most helpful talk of my entire trip."

And then it was on to meet another UAW lawyer, Harold Katz. I had dinner with him, his wife, and others at his Glencoe, Illinois home. I found Katz "intelligent and very easygoing." And the following day I was at the University of Chicago Law School for lunch with Professor Bernard Meltzer, that school's conservative labor law academic, an event that must have been arranged through his former student, my friend Dick Goodman. I wrote in my diary in a November 25 entry:

> *A most interesting discussion and sometimes debate with him on labor–management problems. Dick Goodman had forewarned him of my displeasure with his views so that when I met him his first words were "I hear you don't like me."*

But from my perspective it was a good meeting. And then on Sunday it was back to Detroit in a long drive with Dick and Maria. "Oh, I love Chicago!" I said upon my return.

Fully Fledged

In December I became a lawyer in fact and law. On Sunday, December 10, I recall sleeping very late, until almost noon, as young people can do. Then the following:

> *Carol Cook phoned me this morning to inform me that I had passed the Michigan bar exam and am now a lawyer. I had suspected that the results would be out this weekend but gave up hope last night after calling the newspaper. Called home and Mom was quite happy—Dad is away on travel in Massachusetts. Spent the day with the Cooks musing over ... future plans.*

I received congratulations and celebrated at Solidarity House the following day. On December 12, one of those (perhaps too frequent) Legal Department parties took place, starting at noon and lasting until midnight. On this one, my bar success became the excuse that the others could offer to their respective spouses.

From the middle of December onward, events developed rapidly. On December 16, I was deeply involved in devising contractual language for a bargaining agreement with Cardinal Manufacturing. I also attended my first Trade Union Leadership Council (TULC) meeting on Grand River Avenue, on the far west side of Detroit. I was immediately attracted to TULC because, while committed to organized labor, it spoke independently on trade union failings in the racial discrimination arena. Given Horace Sheffield's leadership in TULC, I was all the more drawn to the organization of which he was the principal leader in Detroit. My friend B. J. Widick summed up TULC's importance when he said:

> *During World War II there had been much 'upgrading' into skilled jobs, but afterward the restrictive policy of 'journeymen only' was adopted by unions, including the UAW, and the black workers went back to their assembly line and other menial jobs. Out of resentment over this policy, and a keen desire to make the UAW and other unions live up to their repeated professions of equality for all members, a number of prominent black unionists in auto, steel, and other unions formed the Trade Union Leadership Council in Detroit. It was a forerunner of the National American Labor Council, which was organized by A. Philip Randolph in 1960 over the objections of George Meany, president of the AFL-CIO. The Detroit organizers were Horace Sheffield, a talented UAW staff man and long-time personal friend and political supporter of Walter P. Reuther, and Robert "Buddy" Battle III, the rugged and undisputed leader of the foundry workers in Ford Local 600.*
>
> *Unlike many "black caucuses" in the union movement, TULC adopted an integrationist policy and invited white unionists to join.... The unpopularity of TULC within the union movement increased its prestige in the Negro community, and soon white politicians hoping to win the support of black voters would eagerly seek its endorsement.*[21]

At the Detroit TULC facilities on Grand River Avenue that day in December, I conversed with Sheffield, who was to become one of my best friends in Detroit. On this occasion, Mayor-elect Jerry Cavanagh spoke. He had been endorsed by TULC the previous month. Contrarily, the UAW and the rest of the Detroit labor movement endorsed incumbent Mayor Louis Miriani, and a tension emerged between Black trade unionists and labor leadership on this issue as well as others.

With my bar examination in the rearview mirror, 1961 ended on a positive note. I was now involved in labor law, the Democratic Party, and TULC, as well as attending meetings of the Young Democrats in the 15th Congressional District on Detroit's west side, represented then by John Dingell and later, in a redistricted new 1st District, by one of my new friends, John Conyers Jr., the son of a UAW staffer. John Conyers told me that he wanted to establish a law firm with me. His idea was that I would represent UAW and other union locals, particularly unions with substantial Black membership. (Nothing ever came of this idea, although we renewed our friendship a couple of years later when I did the first of my two NLRB Washington stints, connecting when John came to Washington in January 1965 to serve his first term in Congress. His tenure in the House of Representatives lasted more than a half century.)

"I want Europe next fall..."

In Detroit, on December 31, as 1961 expired, I wrote with excitement:

> *The year is gone. It was quite a year for me and in the end it was highly successful.... Now everything is before me. I want Europe next fall—preferably the London School of Economics. Now is the time to make my mark as an excellent labor lawyer, writer, and eventually statesman—now, while the slate is still clear and fresh. 1961 has turned out well.*

As if to demonstrate what I had written the day before, January 1, 1962, found me in Solidarity House writing a book review for *The New Leader*, a periodical published by the American Labor Conference on International Affairs in New York. My work for the UAW waited until the following day.

The idea of going to Europe, and specifically to London and the London School of Economics (LSE), had come to me in large part via a British friend I made at Cornell, Inge Neufeld (later Hyman). At Cornell, and after graduation, she and I had had long conversations. Her pitch to me about Britain and the LSE triggered deep feelings about my next steps in life. I felt that my law school experience had made me unable to write as well as I had before Cornell. I sensed a kind of stultification and rigidity which I associated with legal writing. I wanted to write in a manner akin to the way I did when I entered law school in 1958; I wanted to recapture the fluidity that I perceived to be part of my writing style. In spite of my enthusiasm for my work at the UAW, I felt I needed a year to recharge my batteries and start afresh. My many conversations with Inge helped to fortify my view that a year was necessary to do this, and that LSE was the best place to accomplish it. The chance to see other countries would be another valuable part of my education. So I applied to LSE, and waited to hear the outcome.

Politics—National and Personal

On January 9, I was sworn in as a member of the bar—a day that was noteworthy in a number of respects. For one thing, I was in attendance at one of my Young Democrats meetings and we congregated after the meeting at Lou Walker's, which had become one of my favorite Detroit watering holes. The day was also important because over the course of it I formed fast friendships with some of the other Democrats, and even a Goldwater Republican, Mary Jo Walsh, to whom I soon became very close and who later became a feminist founder and leader in the National Organization of Women (NOW).

My friendship with Horace Sheffield involved me in producing memos for him on subjects as diverse as (1) advice on the propriety of right-to-work prohibitions to be adopted in the Michigan Constitutional Convention—a topic which became considerably more relevant in this century as right-to-work legislation was actually enacted in Michigan and then repealed; (2) mechanisms to enforce a Detroit fair housing ordinance (I had my own exposure and experience with that issue!) by the new Cavanagh administration; and (3) ideas about attacking Urban Renewal, which caused so much housing displacement for the Black population that we called it "Negro Removal" instead.

Another matter in early '62 brought me into more direct contact with the new Cavanagh administration, and particularly Police Commissioner George Edwards, who had resigned a state court judgeship to become Cavanagh's police commissioner. (He was later appointed to the United States Court of Appeals for the Sixth Circuit.) The matter which produced the contact is best explained by my February 20, 1962, letter to Commissioner Edwards, in which I wrote:

> *At 12:00 a.m., February 20, I was returning to my apartment (which is at the corner of Second and Canfield). As I approached that corner in a southerly direction on the east side of Second, I saw two men in the road in front of me. One of them was a policeman, the other a young Negro. As I came nearer I observed the Negro lying prostrate in the street and the policeman standing over him shouting, "Get up." It appears as though the Negro could have been intoxicated, exhausted, or he could have been beaten. Two police cars approached this scene as I did. Three policemen pushed the Negro into a car and as they did, one of them shouted, "Get in you rotten f****** nigger."*
>
> *I then returned to my apartment and called the police headquarters at Hancock and Woodward. I asked to speak with the officers who had made the arrest that I observed. I was eventually referred to Patrolman William Weis. I asked him if he was one of the two officers who participated in this arrest. He answered affirmatively. This conversation took place at 1:25 this day.*
>
> *It would be difficult for me to identify the policeman who made the remarks that I have set forth. He stood in the middle of the three policemen and, as I recall, he was the tallest and his hair may have been light. However, Patrolman Weis could identify this person easily as he has admitted that he took part in the arrest.*[22]

Commissioner Edwards called me and came to my office in Solidarity House to discuss this matter. He was both courteous and solicitous. But the upshot of our discussion was his insistence that I look at a series of lineups through which I could identify the offending officer or officers. But I could not identify them, even though I was shown two or three lineups. As I had indicated in my letter, the only way to get to the bottom of this was to speak to William Weis. Surely, I said, Weis could identify the officer in question. But the blue curtain meant he would not do so, and there was no adequate way at that time to provide a remedy.

EXPLORING NEW TERRITORY

Most of my time was now taken up with involvement in unfair labor practice charge filings and representation petitions. One particularly memorable representation case took me up to Lapeer, Michigan, to work with our UAW organizers. When I arrived, they told me that they had already just submitted all the signed union authorization cards of the workers to the company—with all the workers' signatures on them. Immediately, I was both perplexed and uneasy, because I feared that this exposure would lead to retaliation by the company. But the organizers advised me that, in their view, this publicity was worthwhile in that it would best protect workers from retaliation and, specifically, the employer's first defense against the charge that the dismissal or the discipline was unlawful, that is, a lack of knowledge of union activity. Now if the employer considered asserting that he did not know that the worker was a union member, the employer was deprived of this oft-used line of defense. This approach appeared to protect the workers at Lapeer and in other cases.

In March, shortly after my Lapeer visit, at the invitation of Kurt Hanslowe I delivered my first professional paper at a conference held by the Cornell Industrial and Labor Relations School conference at the Sherry Netherlands Hotel in New York City. I was so impressed by my Lapeer experience that I included reference to it in my presentation and in the paper I published afterward.[23]

The conference was a great occasion. I renewed my friendships with Professor Hanslowe and Jack Sheinkman, then general counsel for the Amalgamated Clothing Workers Union in New York City. Mary Jo Walsh, of Port Huron, Michigan, whom I had met on January 9, made the trip also and came to New Jersey to meet my parents. (My father was extremely concerned about this connection because of [1] the unacceptability of interracial marriage, which he thought would be harmful to me and [2] the requirement at that time that any future children adopt Roman Catholicism. He subsequently wrote me a lengthy letter to this effect.)

My connection to Mary Jo took me down another avenue of legal work in Detroit: An introduction to Father (later Msgr.) Clement Kern led to my doing weekly pro bono legal work for workers who were gathered in his parish, Most Holy Trinity, in the Corktown section of Detroit. I would meet with Father Kern on a weekly basis for dinner and then proceed to provide legal advice to workers who came for help. Father Kern was a tower of strength and compassion. Only much later, through a book by Harvard Law School professor Jack Goldsmith, did I learn that some of Father Kern's contacts consisted of a number of Teamster representatives close to Jimmy Hoffa[24] who had quite a bit of "difficulty" with criminal law.[25] Some of the close connections were taking place at the exact same time that I was working with and for Father Kern.

Years later my friend Dick Goodman, who did some of the same work at Most Holy Trinity, told me a very revealing story about Father Kern. Dick's father was the renowned Detroit lawyer who had represented the UAW before Reuther. He said that on one occasion Father Kern had said to Dick, "Isn't your father a Communist?" Dick replied angrily, "If that's the way you feel I'm afraid our friendship can't continue." Father Kern replied, "No, Dick, you don't understand, *I'm* a Communist." That was Father Kern.

Meanwhile, my work at the UAW involved me in providing advice on union organizing and representation petitions (usually involving Michigan area locals), advice on arbitration precedent on matters such as employee privacy issues relating to employer searches of employee lockers, enforcement of union security agreements, and duty to bargain charges arising out of employer refusals to provide information about merit ratings in the collective bargaining process. I also wrote an extensive memorandum on attempts by Florida to license union representatives and business agents examining First Amendment and preemption case law, both of which could render such licensing requirements unconstitutional.[26]

Finally, in February 1962, with a memo, I became involved in identifying steps the UAW could and should take prior to federal employment discrimination law to dismantle segregated locals and their facilities operated by Local 28724 in Muncie, Indiana. Again, the world of legal intervention was still quite different from the one that would emerge later in the sixties, when marches, demonstrations, and boycotts would usher in a civil rights revolution of sorts. There was no law addressing segregated local unions in 1962, and even the progressive UAW still had them—and was complicit in other discriminatory practices as well.[27]

An added difficulty was that I was working with UAW Secretary Treasurer Emil Mazey's staff on the segregation of unions. Mazey was hardly the best person to take on a civil rights issue, in my judgment—and I got an even better insight into Mazey's thinking when I dealt with him later in the sixties in connection with my work for the EEOC on seniority and discrimination. Through his language and body language Mazey indicated a less-than-sympathetic position vis-à-vis Black workers in the seniority dispute. (See chapter 5 for more detail on this issue.)

An Eventful Convention

Then, as the spring unfolded, I headed back to the East Coast: the UAW convention was being held in Atlantic City, New Jersey. Here, Horace Sheffield led the charge, which resulted in the election of Nelson "Jack" Edwards, the first Black representative on the UAW executive board.

Horace had quickly become my best friend and ally inside the UAW. He was the principal organizer in this cause—and indeed had been for the previous two decades, but for some time I hadn't known the important role that he had played prior to our friendship. For instance, at the 1943 Buffalo convention, as a delegate of Local 600, he played a leadership role in opposing the so-called "minority report" introduced by Communist leader Nat Ganley (whom I had also met at his home in the summer of 1960). Said Sheffield in 1943:

> *There are those who have sent this resolution to the Constitution Committee who have no interest and no*

> *desire to see the minority problem worked out. I am sure everyone in Detroit knows that.*
>
> *Brother Chairman, I submit to you the problems we have had are due to the fact that we are making progress on this issue. My theory is that if we remain stagnant we wouldn't have an issue, but we are making progress.*[28]

But in 1959, in nominating the extraordinarily talented Willoughby Abner, Sheffield had said:

> *In the state of Michigan the UAW took the leadership and insisted that Negroes be represented on all levels of government, in the city council, on the bench, and just recently on the state level.*
>
> *However, the Negro people are asking, those outside the labor movement, "What about the UAW? What is wrong with the UAW? They don't do the same thing within their organization as they do in so far as other organizations are concerned."*
>
> *We as Negroes can no longer duck the issue.*[29]

In 1962, Horace and I had hoped that Horace would be the one elected, but he paid the price for being the first to lead the charge. Edwards, who had not been as militant and outspoken, was to be the beneficiary of Horace Sheffield's hard work. (Willoughby Abner played a role in the 1959 convention, dramatizing the absence and exclusion of Blacks in the UAW. I met Abner in the late sixties when I was working in New York City and he had left the UAW to become director of the Federal Mediation and Conciliation Service. He possessed a first-rate intellect and was one of the most impressive people I ever met.[30])

At the convention, I met *New York Post* columnist Murray Kempton, expressed to him my enthusiasm for what Sheffield had done, and extolled Horace's successes along with those of TULC—not only inside the UAW but also through their support for Mayor Cavanagh in his upset of Mayor Miriani. Kempton, I think, was cautiously skeptical of what I had to say, and I'm not sure one word that I provided in that meeting ever made it into print in any of his writings.

The major convention event was the appearance and address of President Kennedy. I sat next to Harold Katz and his wife as the delegates greeted the president with unbounded applause and cheers. I shall never forget his opening line: "Last week, after speaking to the Chamber of Commerce and the presidents of the American Medical Association, I began to wonder how I got elected. And now I remember."[31] It brought down the house! Kennedy had that very special touch to which the UAW and Reuther responded. I responded to it, too.

The Curtis-Wright Case

After returning from the convention, it was back to the East Coast for another unfair labor practice case involving me, this time with UAW Local 300, which had been rebuffed in its request for information about job classifications, descriptions, and rates of pay involving employees whom the local believed were improperly excluded from the bargaining unit at the Curtis-Wright Company in New Jersey. The point of our charge, filed in June 1962, was that it was impossible for the union to determine whether work was properly within the bargaining unit when the company was excluding workers on the grounds that they were "confidential and administrative" jobs, unless the union knew what those excluded workers were doing and what they were being paid.

I prepared a lengthy letter, setting forth our theory and the cases that we relied upon, for union president Tom Lazzio. I met with the union in Newark, New Jersey, and subsequently the NLRB regional representatives in the same city. Ultimately, the board issued a complaint in September, just as I had departed for London. The board in Washington and the Court of Appeals for the Third Circuit in Philadelphia held in our favor.[32]

On this visit—most of which was taken up with successful urging of the region to issue a complaint—I can recall staying at a

New York City hotel and when my meetings were complete, realizing that my Red Sox, whom I had supported faithfully since 1946, were in town. I jumped into a cab in midtown Manhattan and said to the driver, "Take me to Yankee stadium!" Being paid a handsome salary—by my standards—I felt as free as the wind. The Red Sox, however, were still wallowing in mediocrity or worse (quite similar to the recent years of this century). I can recall the Red Sox center fielder, Gary Geiger, dropping a line drive hit right at him, and Yankee catcher Ellie Howard hitting a drive so straight and hard that it arrived at the bullpen gate low enough to have been caught if the left fielder, Carl Yastrzemski, had had time to get there.[33]

INTO THE HOME STRETCH IN DETROIT

Another excursion in June was a command performance: to see my sister Dorothy marry her childhood sweetheart, Hermann Gerber. This was a great ceremony in our lovely hometown parish, St. James's Episcopal Church, on Broadway in Long Branch. Officiating was Father Robert Anderson, a good friend of our family who had been the curate at St. James's when we were children. My Uncle Ed, the last living Gould from that generation, attended with his wife, my wonderful Aunt Isabel. Ed was Calvin Coolidge-like in his clipped, short speech. When I said to him that day, "Uncle Ed, how do you like New Jersey?" he replied: "Nice to visit." That was his honest and direct assessment; I will never forget it.

Back in Detroit, it was the home stretch in this phase of my life. But I still found time to venture out to Tiger Stadium with Mary Jo one weekend to see hard-throwing Earl Wilson defeat the Tigers, 4-2. It was a brilliant performance, marred only by the two runs, both products of Rocky Colavito home runs with the bases empty. Little did I know that Wilson was just two starts away from the West Coast, where he would no-hit the California Angels.[34]

Much of my work that summer of 1962 involved writing memoranda to local union officials on matters as diverse as recent rulings by the Kennedy Board; unfair labor practice charge filings against, for instance, Nicholson Machine Products in Trenton, Michigan, arising out of an organizational drive; advice on the extent to which arbitrators could protect UAW represented workers; and memoranda to local union officials explaining the agency shop requiring dues payments under collective bargaining agreements.

During the same summer period, I somehow managed to achieve my most direct involvement in the political process to date, running for precinct delegate in downtown Detroit. I won my election and attended and participated in the Democratic State Convention in Grand Rapids, Michigan.

The River Rouge Case

As my time in Detroit wound down to its last month—September—I handled one of the most challenging cases of my then-young career, involving UAW Local 600 at the River Rouge in Dearborn. The Rouge is a massive facility where all aspects of auto production and maintenance are performed; during World War II and well after, the plant had employed more than 100,000 workers, and it had grown immensely during the war, producing tanks as part of the war effort.

> *The Rouge, it is to be recalled, included a manmade harbor for Great Lakes coal and iron barges, the largest foundry in the world, and ninety-two miles of railroad track. In 1933, Mexican muralist Diego Rivera captured the monumentality of automobile production at the Rouge. His frescoes at the Detroit Institute of Arts depict workers dwarfed by furnaces belching fire, engaged in seemingly mortal combat with machinery so overwhelming that it called forth herculean labors. These powerful images of Detroit conveyed the sense that the city was the very essence of American industry.*[35]

Local 600 was one of the centers of opposition to the Reuther caucus, its president during this period being Carl Stellato. But divisiveness between Solidarity House and Local 600, the bargaining representative at the Rouge, was not on display during any parts of my case. The case that day in September '62 involved Ford Motor Company's discontinuance of operations in the Dearborn tool and die departments. About 300 workers had lost their jobs as a result of the company's action. I met with a number of workers at Solidarity House and at Dearborn, and filed an extensive pre-hearing brief, arguing that judicial and arbitral precedent established and implied limitation or prohibition of the contracting-out of work to other facilities which had been previously performed by Local 600 represented workers.[36]

The hearing, conducted on one of my last days in Detroit before departing for London, lasted a full day, during which I produced numerous witnesses and exhibits. The day also included one of my most thrilling memories. As I departed at the hearing's conclusion, all the workers in attendance stood up and shook my hand, one of those enduring high points when one feels that one's work is truly appreciated. I shall never forget their look of enthusiasm.

However, much to my regret, a few months later I received arbitrator Harry Platt's award, which ruled against our position.[37] That day left me rather surprised and demoralized: The contracting-out of work had begun to challenge and undermine unionized worker job security, and this, along with the fact that I had been buoyed by worker enthusiasm, made the loss a tough pill to swallow. I confused the moment's emotions with the detached, dispassionate objectivity about the probability of success which a lawyer should always possess.[38]

One other matter remained at the end of that September. I was called upon to file exceptions from the trial examiner's decision rendered in the Cross Company case on which I had cut my teeth in the summer of '61, when I first started with the UAW. Thus, in the main, these exceptions filed with the board in Washington "excepted" to very little because we had won on most of the matters in dispute before the trial examiner. I urged the board to affirm most of which he decided, providing for the reinstatement of unfair labor strikers.

A Fond Farewell

With my work on the River Rouge facility at Ford and the Cross Company completed, it was time for me to return to New Jersey, where I would gather my belongings prior to leaving for London. I had been accepted, as I'd hoped, at the London School of Economics, to work as a research student. I would not be studying for a formal degree; instead, I would take politics and economics courses for a year, and study under Otto Kahn Freund, the leading British and European labor lawyer of that era. I would read widely again and write. In retrospect—given the fact that I loved my UAW job, was dependent upon the savings I had acquired from my handsome UAW salary, and knew no one in London except Inge Neufeld, whose thinking had sent me down this path—this may not have been my best-thought-out decision. Yet, as chapter 4 and those that follow demonstrate, I was lucky indeed. Living in London proved fortunate for a rather wrong-headed and impetuous twenty-six-year-old.

My last night in Detroit was at Most Holy Trinity, advising workers in the clinic that I frequented on a weekly or near-weekly basis. Father Kern blessed me before my departure and, with my UAW colleague Joe Guggenheim driving, we made the 700-mile trek from Detroit to Elberon. I was somewhat the worse for wear when Joe deposited me there, before driving on to his mother's home in New York. But I quickly packed, and my parents, along with Mary Jo, took me to JFK airport for the long propeller-driven flight for London on September 30.

Thus ended a phase of my life which could never be replicated. I was passionate about my job and its related political processes—these were activities for which I had waited much of my life. My social life was unprecedented, with many friends. I'd driven around Detroit in my Rambler for social and work events, including regular visits to my favorite spots—the Hellas Café in Greektown (Gus's, as we called it, named after the owner); frequent visits to jazz clubs like the Minor Key on Dexter Avenue; hanging out at Lou Walker's, to which I could walk in ten minutes from my apartment, and, when at work, with the associates there; frequenting Sinbad's, on the Detroit River. To this day, at least a plurality of my close friends are or have been from my Detroit days. My father described his life in the early 1920s in Worcester, Massachusetts, as a time when he felt like the center of everything. My UAW life in Detroit in the early sixties never fully replicated his Worcester experiences, but perhaps they came close.

"IN MEMORY OF WALTER PHILIP REUTHER"

Along with Hillman, Lewis, Murray, Randolph, and Bridges, he walked across the stage of history in a bygone time of turbulence, success, and stability for the American labor movement. The name of Walter Philip Reuther was synonymous with what was regarded as both dynamic and aggressive in the labor movement, and he stood second to none as a proponent of what is authentic, innovative, and robust in trade unions.

My first impression and recollections of Walter Reuther are based upon Detroit in the 1940s and, specifically, the riots of 1943 during World War II. Twenty years before the March on Washington, the labor movement was hardly seen as a friend of civil rights. But Walter Reuther's support for racial equality and civil rights laws cut against the grain of traditional union leadership and American society at that time.

The policies promoted by Mr. Reuther and other UAW leaders put the union on the side of fair employment practices legislation well in advance of its time. And, most important, in the tumult of Detroit in the forties, when white auto workers refused to work alongside of Blacks on the production line and both threatened and engaged in violence as a response, Reuther insisted that all union members work together and faced his opponents down on this and related issues.

As a student at Cornell Law School during the winter of '59–'60, I was exposed to the podium-thumping inspirational speech that the "Redhead" could give so often. I vividly recall a variation on some of those same themes later at the Cadillac Square 1960 Presidential Campaign Labor Day rally addressed by Mr. Reuther, Senator John Kennedy, Governor G. Mennen Williams, and Lt. Governor John Swainson.

As the most junior of the UAW legal staff, I had very little direct contact with Mr. Reuther. The most memorable of these was early September 1960, as I was about to complete my summer clerkship with the union and return to Cornell. The UAW General Counsel, Harold Cranefield, ushered me into the president's office at Solidarity

House. I recall that most of the discussion was about the 1960 presidential campaign. Norman Vincent Peale had just attacked Senator Kennedy on the ground that his Roman Catholicism disqualified him to be president. I believe that our meeting took place prior to JFK's spirited and eloquent defense in Houston in response to a similar line of attack by a group of Protestant ministers in Texas.

I recall Reuther speaking at length about his hopes for a Kennedy presidency and his lamentations about and dismay with Peale's criticism in particular. He expressed profound disappointment with Peale and likened the religious criticism of Kennedy to other forms of bigotry present in so much of the country.

Most of his other remarks were focused upon public policy issues like Medicare, federal aid to education, and foreign policy. It was left to me to offer some views on the role of labor law at the end of a conversation of about twenty to thirty minutes—an "unusually long meeting," General Counsel Cranefield commented to me as we left Reuther's office.

The Walter Reuther that I knew was an exemplary labor leader and more. He was a unique player on the world stage at a critical time in the development of industrial democracies. Industry representatives who faced him across the bargaining table considered him a master negotiator. But his vision of his role and that of trade unionism in an industrial democratic society was infinitely broader than that of most of his union contemporaries and captains of industry as well.

Reuther, more than any other individual, built the UAW into a fine and first-rate industrial union and developed the UAW's whipsawing or pattern bargaining strategy and used it to win wages and innovative benefit programs and contract provisions that frequently set the pattern throughout industry.

Reuther was one of the first and strongest supporters of cooperation with the introduction of new technology and improved productivity so long as resulting benefits were shared with the auto workers. The bargaining was hard, but the relationship evolved in the 1950s and 1960s into one based on mutual respect and trust on both sides and, ultimately into experiments like Saturn and the GM–Toyota joint venture—both of which, had he lived, I suspect Reuther would have approved.

As president of the CIO, Reuther was largely responsible with AFL President Meany for the merged federation in 1955. At a time when there was a great deal of opposition to the merger, Reuther saw the wisdom of it. Subsequently, he presided over the newly created Industrial Union Department (IUD).

The UAW was never touched by the corruption that for many years tainted other major unions. Under Reuther, the UAW established a Public Review Board composed of eminent academics and citizens outside the union to provide an independent avenue of appeal for members of decisions by union officers which they considered unfair.

As my conversation with him those thirty-five years ago this month made clear to me, Walter Reuther's vision was much broader than his union and the U.S. auto industry. He had a great interest in politics and foreign policy. He campaigned for Norman Thomas in 1932 and later for Roosevelt, Truman, and Kennedy.

He was an early and strong supporter of the Marshall Plan. He forged links with established and nascent industrial unions around the world. As a founder of the International Confederation of Free Trade Unions and head of the World Automotive Department of the International Metal Workers Federation, he anticipated by many years the need which is so apparent today for worldwide trade union communications and unity to assure that worker rights and interests are not forgotten in the developing global market. He was a drum major for procedures which would effectively develop and implement international labor standards.

Mr. Reuther was an early supporter and an active participant in the civil rights movement.

He walked arm in arm with Martin Luther King, Roy Wilkins, and so many other civil rights leaders in the August 1963 March on Washington. His vision for industrial democracy realized in the UAW and CIO still serves as a model mechanism for peacefully accomplishing the myriad adjustments essential in emerging free democratic industrial nations.

Walter Reuther was one of those rare individuals whose every action in life embodied his philosophy. He tied it all together—his austere morality, democratic ideals, his faith in progress, his belief in civil rights and equal opportunity, internationalism, and of course his belief in a strong, independent, democratic trade union movement.

His was a life of action dedicated to furthering these beliefs. At the core of his philosophy was an unwavering sense of justice and fairness that is possessed by our greatest leaders. And he possessed a sense of duty to help the have-nots, the weak, the common man. This was the side he was on and for which he fought. Reuther's untimely death deprived us of a visionary labor leader. All of us here today were touched by his life. His beliefs influenced our own. Our country benefited from his good works. It is meet and right that we honor him here today.[39]

NOTES

[1] Thomas J. Sugrue, *The Origins of the Urban Crisis: Race and Inequality in Postwar Detroit* (Princeton: Princeton University Press, 2005), 29.

[2] William B. Gould IV, "The Steelworkers Trilogy at 50," in *Proceedings of the Sixty-Third Annual Meeting, National Academy of Arbitrators, Philadelphia, Pennsylvania, May 26–29, 2010*, ed. Paul D. Staudohar and Mark I. Lurie (Arlington: BNA, 2011).

[3] That very night of June 20, I took the bus to downtown Detroit's Woodward Avenue, in the center of the downtown area, and listened to a broadcast beamed on the street of Floyd Patterson's defeat of Swedish heavyweight Ingemar Johansson. In a few years, as it turned out, very few people walked that street at that time of night. But that night, a large crowd, both Black and white, stood with me on the street, intensely involved in this combat.

[4] A. H. Raskin, "The Squeeze on Unions," *The Atlantic*, April 1, 1961; Paul Jacobs, *Old Before Its Time: Collective Bargaining at 28* (Santa Barbara: Center for the Study of Democratic Institutions, 1963); Solomon Barkin, *The Decline of the Labor Movement and What Can Be Done About It* (Santa Barbara: Center for the Study of Democratic Institutions, 1961).

⁵ "UAW Membership Hasn't Recovered Great Recession Losses," 2023, U.S. Department of Labor LM-2 Filings.
⁶ This was subsequently published in William B. Gould IV, "The Garmon Case: Decline and Threshold of Litigating Elucidation," *University of Detroit Law Journal* 39 (1962).
⁷ Steve Babson, Dave Riddle, and David Elsila, *The Color of Law: Ernie Goodman, Detroit, and the Struggle for Labor and Civil Rights* (Detroit: Wayne State University Press, 2010).
⁸ I subsequently chronicled my exposure to Reuther when I was at the UAW and discussed his life. William B. Gould IV, "In Memory of Walter Philip Reuther," speech, Orchestra Hall, Detroit, MI, September 8, 1995.
⁹ Neal E. Boudette, "United Auto Workers Usher In a New Era of Union Leadership, Eager to Fight for Contract Gains," *New York Times* Business, March 28, 2023. For an update on the most recent UAW presidential election, see Steven Greenhouse, "IT'S OFFICIAL: Reformer Shawn Fain Wins the UAW Presidency," *In These Times*, March 17, 2023.
¹⁰ Thomas v. Collins, 323 U.S. 516 (1945). Some of what he told me is contained in Babson et al., *The Color of Law* (see note 7).
¹¹ "Big Mistake," *Time*, September 15, 1952.
¹² Auto Workers v. Wisconsin Board, 351 U.S. 266 (1956). In arguing this case, Kurt Hanslowe, Harvard Law School 1951, became the first member of his class to argue before the United States Supreme Court.
¹³ William B. Gould IV, "Recollections of Kurt Hanslowe," *Cornell Law Review* 69 (1984).
¹⁴ Diary, July 25, 1961.
¹⁵ NLRB v. Truitt Manufacturing Co., 351 U.S. 149 (1956). The court held that an employer which pleads poverty or inability to pay may be required to open its books.
¹⁶ See generally, Victor Reuther, *The Brothers Reuther and the Story of the UAW: A Memoir* (Boston: Houghton Mifflin & Co., 1976).
¹⁷ William B. Gould IV, letter to Honorable John B. Swainson, September 29, 1961.
¹⁸ William B. Gould IV, *For Labor to Build Upon* (Cambridge: Cambridge University Press, 2022), 139–148.
¹⁹ William B. Gould IV, "Book Review: Test of Strength, Kohler on Strike by Walter H. Upoff," *Commonweal* 18 (1962).
²⁰ Robert F. Kennedy and Arthur Krock, *The Enemy Within* (New York: Harper & Row, 1960), 226–230.
²¹ B. J. Widick, *Detroit: City of Race and Class Violence* (Detroit: Wayne State University Press, 1989), 150. August Meier and Elliott Rudwick, *Black Detroit and the Rise of the UAW* (New York: Oxford University Press, 1979).
²² William B. Gould IV, letter to Police Commissioner George Edwards, February 20, 1962.
²³ William B. Gould IV, "Taft-Hartley Revisited: The Contrariety of the Collective Bargaining Agreement and the Plight of the Unorganized," *Labor Law Journal* 13 (1962), 351: "Workers are often spread out over rural communities miles away from any common location and thus it is difficult for them to attend meetings and for organizers to visit with them. I can tell you that the hazard of snowy roads in rural Michigan during the past winter has not made travel an inviting prospect."

24 William B. Gould IV, "Book Review: Hoffa and the Teamsters by Ralph & Estelle James and Tentacles of Power by Clark R. Mollenhoff," *Commonweal* 14 (1965).
25 Jack Goldsmith, *In Hoffa's Shadow: A Stepfather, A Disappearance in Detroit, and My Search for Truth* (New York: Farrar, Straus and Giroux, 2019), 276. Speaking about his father-in-law, who was Jimmy Hoffa's right-hand man, Professor Goldsmith said: "Chuckie occasionally attended this church as a boy and used to listen, mesmerized, to Father Clement Kern, the famous 'labor priest.' When he took the alabaster statute of St. Theresa from the customhouse that landed him an indictment in 1963, he donated it to Kern at this church."
26 Despite my memorandum, as I subsequently discovered through memoranda from Regional Director Raymond Berendt to Larry Gettlinger in Reuther's office five years later, the matter was still unresolved. Bernard F. Ashe, letter to Don Rand Regarding Local 287 and the Eastern Indiana Labor Center, Inc., November 16, 1966, Walter P. Reuther Library at Wayne State University, UAW President's Office: Walter P. Reuther Records, Box 239, Folder 44. Raymond H. Berndt, inter-office communication to Larry Gettlinger, July 6, 1966, Walter P. Reuther Library at Wayne State University, UAW President's Office: Walter P. Reuther Records, Box 239, Folder 44.
27 Kevin Boyle, *The UAW and the Heyday of American Liberalism 1945–1968* (Ithaca: Cornell University Press, 1995), 107–131.
28 International Union United Automobile, Aircraft, and Agricultural Implement Workers of America, 8th Constitutional Convention Proceedings, October 4–10, 1943, 380–381.
29 International Union United Automobile, Aircraft, and Agricultural Implement Workers of America, 17th Constitutional Convention Proceedings, October 9–16, 1959, 360–362.
30 Widick, Detroit, 149: "Sheffield became a controversial figure in the UAW and in Detroit politics, since his independent stance on issues jeopardized the trade unions' traditional modes of operation. In 1959 Sheffield had the temerity at the UAW convention to nominate Willoughby Abner—a Chicago black unionist of outstanding ability—for a post on the international executive board of the union. By publicly raising the question of Negro participation at policy-making levels, Sheffield earned many enemies. Emil Mazey, the secretary-treasurer of the UAW, demanded that Reuther fire him."
31 John F. Kennedy, Address in Atlantic City at the Convention of the United Auto Workers, May 8, 1962.
32 Curtiss-Wright Corporation v. International Union (UAW), Local 300, 145 N.L.R.B. 19 (1963); Curtiss-Wright Corporation, Wright Aeronautical Division v. National Labor Relations Board, 347 F.2d 61 (3d Cir. 1965).
33 John Drebinger, "Yankees, Hitless Until 7th, Score 4-to-1 Victory Over Red Sox at Stadium," *New York Times*, May 10, 1962.
34 "Tigers Drop 7th in Row," *New York Times*, June 16, 1962.
35 Sugrue, *The Origins of the Urban Crisis*, 17.
36 In contrast to my case, where I was representing the Local 600 workers on behalf of the International Union UAW in Detroit, Local 600 had failed a decade earlier to successfully challenge the "decentralization" of Rouge operations, resulting in the layoffs of thousands of workers. In both that case and mine, the union grievance was predicated upon the theory that the employer had an implied contractual obligation not to contract out the work in question. Local Union No. 600 v. Ford Motor Co. 113 F. Supp.834 (1953). In that case, brought with Ernest Goodman as lead counsel for

Local 600, the court, relying on the management prerogatives clause in ruling for the company, said "it is . . . a matter of some significance to this Court that the contract was executed on behalf of the International Union . . . yet this group has not joined as a party plaintiff in complaining. . . . the nonappearance in this action of the group who signed the contract allegedly induced by fraud practiced upon it renders doubtful the weight of said allegations" Id at 843. In my case, the International Union UAW was a party to the arbitration and we worked together with Local 600.

[37] *Ford Motor Co.*, 39 BNA LA 1236 (1962).

[38] Harry H. Platt, "The Relationship Between Arbitration and Title VII of the Civil Rights Act of 1964," *Georgia Law Review* 3 (1969), 399: "It is the arbitrator's use of public law which is of current interest and which poses problems. The frequency of disputes containing public law considerations is on the upswing. This is particularly true in regard to Title VII of the Civil Rights Act of 1964, the most far-reaching anti-discrimination legislation in recent years . . . considering the important role played by labor arbitration in the collective bargaining process, it is surprising that arbitration's potential for dealing with racial discrimination has to date received so little attention. In fact, commentary on the law evolving both from administrative agencies and the courts has thus far obscured the role of arbitration. Instead, the focus of discussion has been on public law (such as the National Labor Relations Act, with its duty of fair representation doctrine, and title VII) as a vehicle to deal with racial discrimination in employment"; William B. Gould, "Labor Arbitration of Grievances Involving Racial Discrimination," *University of Pennsylvania Law Review* 118 (1969), 41.

[39] Speech delivered at the Walter P. Reuther 25th commemorative tribute, September 8, 1995 at Orchestra Hall in Detroit, Michigan.

4
"TOO MUCH LABOR LAW": THE LSE AND A LABOUR PARTY PERSPECTIVE

My first international flight was not an easy one—especially by today's standards. The propeller-driven, transatlantic Icelandic Airlines flight, from New York to London via Reykjavík and Glasgow, took twenty-four hours, and was a long, wearying journey. For years afterward, I wanted to propose a new motto for the airline: "Icelandic skims the waves."

I got a good look at Newfoundland before we stopped in Reykjavík, and then we went on to Glasgow. I recall thinking as we neared London that these skies had been filled with war planes not too long before. I remembered reading articles about the German Blitz during World War II, and the valiant defense of Britain by Spitfire fighter planes, which challenged the Germans through the availability of radar—a new technology in which my father was deeply involved at the time. Radar had permitted the Spitfires to meet any incoming attack promptly.

I had many memories of the war, but they were all based on reading and listening to the radio as a young boy—I had little understanding of the firsthand nightmares endured by the British.

MEMORIES OF WARTIME

My most distinctive World War II memory is of the day Japan bombed Pearl Harbor—December 7, 1941—when I was little more than five years old. Willie Goldberg, who worked with my father at Fort Monmouth, and his wife Molly were at our house. My parents must have said something about contemporary events, to which Molly replied, "Don't you know that we're at war with Japan? The Japanese bombed Pearl Harbor this morning." Neither of my parents knew.

In the months following, I recall listening to the large radio in our living room and hearing that Wake Island and Guam had fallen to Japan. "Do you think we will win the war?" I would ask my father. His reply was always uncertain: "I don't know."

Although we were a patriotic family, with deep military service roots in the Civil War, Spanish American War, and World War I, my father took note of the early Japanese successes in the Pacific with this critique of U.S. and European military commanders: "They thought the Japanese couldn't even fly planes, that they were like monkeys in the trees—they found out differently."

For a child like me, removed from the direct horror of war, the conflict had a near romantic quality. I joined children donning war helmets and camouflage as we "fought" against the Japanese in the heavily overgrown "jungle" behind our house. Our next-door neighbor Robbie Hesslein made toy battleships for me out of scraps of wood, with nails signifying the artillery guns on deck. With Robbie's kind assistance, I floated ships in the bathtub and dreamed of the naval war effort. I had models of our P (Pursuit) 38s (later F-38s) and imagined them chasing German Messerschmitts and Japanese Zeros. I read books filled with pictures and silhouettes of all the war planes of the Allies and Axis powers. I also had a special book that revealed the silhouettes of enemy planes, allowing me to distinguish friendly aircraft from enemy planes in case of an air attack. To my mother's embarrassment, I proclaimed to my first-grade teacher, "Isn't the war wonderful!"

Though anti-aircraft guns were placed on New Jersey beaches not far from Long Branch, no attack ever came. But we had air raid drills, and nights when all the lights had to be turned off in preparation for a possible attack. I also saw obvious manifestations of the war on our trips to the beach in Long Branch where, from time to time, the water was filled with oil—direct evidence of the sinking of Allied and Axis ships in the Atlantic. On one of our beach excursions, a great wind came up off the Atlantic and my sister cried out, "Oh, Germany has hit me in the face!"

Another clear sign of the war was the presence of Italian prisoners of war in our town. They were bused to Long Branch from Fort Monmouth to go to the Paramount and the Strand movie theaters near the ocean. They seemed quite happy and content, notwithstanding their drab POW clothes—the United States was simply trying to keep them occupied. And the Italians' status reminded us of what we had heard about German POWs: that they were frequently treated better by Americans than Black American military men ever were.

One of the first movies I saw downtown was 1943's *Bataan*. Japan won the actual Battle of Bataan in 1942, with the fall of the Philippines. The movie version ended with advancing Japanese soldiers being shot down again and again by American machine gunners, but as the last scene dimmed, every viewer knew that the Americans would eventually run out of ammunition and be overwhelmed.

My father, who turned forty a few months after Pearl Harbor, had wanted to enlist, feeling strongly that he should continue the Gould military service tradition, but his age and two children exempted him from the draft—and my mother strongly discouraged him from volunteering. Instead, he made a significant contribution to the war effort through his radar work with the Signal Corps at Fort Monmouth.

Toward the war's end, in 1944 and 1945, I recall being alarmed by the difficulties and casualties suffered by our country, both in Europe and the Pacific. My father, with access to information that the civilian population did not have and he could not share, said more than once, "They are not telling us what is really happening in Okinawa, Tarawa, and Iwo Jima." Moreover, in late '44 and '45 the newspapers were filled with news about the German advances in the Ardennes. Every day, journalists would report that the Germans had advanced ten miles, twenty miles, or even more. The advance ultimately covered sixty miles and before it was brought to a halt. I was absolutely terrified, no longer filled with the romantic visions of a few years ago. My father remained circumspect and noncommittal about the war's likely outcome, in spite of my many questions about it. In short, the war was something I experienced indirectly. My closest contact took place when I heard the church bells ring at the time of the June 6, 1944, Normandy invasion, and as I watched the VJ Day celebrations in August 1945, open cars careening down our street, crowds boisterously happy at Japan's defeat.

Seventeen years later, as my flight descended into London, I realized I was about to get a lot closer to a world from which I had been sheltered. I was soon to see buildings, damaged by German bombing, that still had not been reconstructed.

ARRIVAL IN LONDON

My arrival in London on October 1, 1962, after my long flight across the Atlantic, did not go well. I arrived—in the pouring rain—at the downtown London YMCA as planned, but I hadn't made a reservation, not anticipating that my arrival would coincide with a railway strike. All of London's hotels were filled with workers who commuted from homes on the outskirts of the city or beyond. I began to walk the streets with my luggage in hand, feeling more than a measure of despair at the young and foolish age of twenty-six.

Somehow, I did find a vacancy at a bed and breakfast, where I stayed for much of the following week. My first social contact was with my law school friend, Inge Neufeld (later Hyman), who had inspired me to come to London in the first place. Inge and I had dinner on one of my first evenings in London, and she immediately described in detail what I'd missed while I'd been flying: the enormous conflagration that had surrounded James Meredith, the first Black student admitted to the University of Mississippi. His attempt to enter the university had resulted in violent clashes between Mississippi citizens, National Guard troops, and U.S. marshals; the Kennedy Administration had intervened. That evening, I was left with the distinct impression that the civil rights debate had now reached a new level, possessing an ever-greater potential for confrontation, conflict, and violence.

An Introduction to the Labour Party

My first UK initiative was to attend the British Labour Party Conference in Brighton. "Brighton is so bracing," said *The New Statesman* which, like *The Economist*, I began to read regularly and assiduously. I took a fast-moving (by American standards) train from London to Brighton and happened to strike up a conversation with a young man named Keith Stuart, an official with Britain's Coal Board, who was also proceeding to the conference. Keith gave me some sage advice about British politics, and we connected in Brighton one day during the conference: We were standing in front of a stylish holiday hotel just as British Labour Party leader Hugh Gaitskell arrived to have breakfast.

Keith became a lifelong friend, eventually serving as chairman of Associated British Ports; he was also knighted by Queen Elizabeth. Keith's political views changed over time, in my judgment, and he principally supported the Conservatives in later years. His initial disillusionment with Labour was prompted by the refusal of Prime Minister Harold Wilson's Labour government to accept the trade union reforms advocated by Wilson's Minister of Labour, Barbara Castle. These reforms were laid out in Mrs. Castle's late 1960s white paper, "In Place of Strife," but they were never passed into law. Instead, in Keith's view, the Labour government capitulated to the excesses of the trade union movement, which harmed the economy.[1] Then came the leftward movement of the Labour Party in the 1980s, and in this century in particular, largely through the actions of Michael Foot and Jeremy Corbyn, its left-wing leaders during these periods. The friendship between Keith and myself—involving numerous political discussions in both countries—and our respective families was to exceed more than six decades, to the very date of this writing.

In Brighton, I heard Hugh Gaitskell deliver his "Thousand Years of History"[2] speech, a policy argument against what was then known as the Common Market, the European Union's predecessor, in which he invoked English tradition dating back to the time of William the Conqueror. For a short time, I fell in line with this kind of thinking—which ultimately was revived through Brexit in 2016—arguing about it in correspondence with my mentor, Kurt Hanslowe.

At the conference's conclusion, Keith and I stood as everyone sang "The Red Flag," the anthem of the British Labour Party.[3] Neither of us knew the words; it was the first time I had even heard it. Keith whispered to me that he hoped the CIA did not have a record of my participation in this event—"The Red Flag" is a socialist song, with longstanding ties to international labor and anarchy.

ADJUSTMENTS AND CONTRASTS

Back in London, I settled into a room on Regent's Park Road, near the Underground's Chalk Farm station on the Northern line. (The Underground—or the Tube—is what Londoners call the city's subway system.) I traveled often on the Northern line, reading Graham Greene's *The End of the Affair*; as much of Greene's captivating story takes place in that area, the route remains emblazoned in my mind. As I tried to get used to my new life, I was reminded of something my father had said to me before I left New Jersey: "You are going to be surprised by the way people live there. It's going to be much more difficult for you than it is here." Almost immediately, the absence of central heating made me recall those wise words. I came to depend upon small heaters that warmed one side of my leg or body at a time. Showers were unknown, so I was forced to renew my acquaintance with the soggy, uninspiring bathtubs we had lived with in Bath Avenue, before moving to Elberon. (Ironically, only in Germany, bombed so intensely, were there showers in most of the hotels in the early sixties.) Railway engines, as I observed from the bridge near my room on the way to Chalk Farm station, were still largely steam-driven. I was surprised that there weren't more diesel trains, but I learned that wide adoption of diesel engines was slowed by the economic challenges of the postwar period.

London's gloom was quite an adjustment for me, too. I don't think I saw the sun for more than a month after my arrival. Coupled with homesickness for Detroit, the weather weighed on me considerably. And long before the city's pollution was diminished by environmental policies, London fog was a revelation to me. A few months into my stay, we had a classic bout with fog: I could not see a pedestrian on the sidewalk until he or she was immediately in front of me. This might seem romantic at first, but ultimately I found it rather depressing to have to wipe thick soot off my face after a long city walk.

Of course, London not only lacked sunshine, but its position on the map also conspired to keep the sun in short supply. Many Americans are unaware of Britain's far north location, warmed only by the Gulf Stream. On Sundays in October and November I would walk over to Hyde Park on the weekend to read *The Observer* or *Sunday Times*. But by three o'clock or so, even in October, it was so dark that reading outdoors was extremely difficult. The Northern position of the British Isles provided for very early sunsets—but it also meant that outdoor theater the following June could last until well after nine o'clock at night!

I found the food almost as depressing as the weather. Except for the Indian restaurants, which I habituated whenever I found them, most establishments offered a drab, uninteresting menu consisting of cucumber sandwiches and the like. London's current status as a vibrant international city, full of international and multiracial residents and visitors, was still a few years away. During my initial tenure, even the Italian pizza restaurants in Soho seemed bland and uninspiring.

In December of 1962, Truman's former Secretary of State Dean Acheson delivered an address at West Point asserting that Britain, deprived of its colonies, must now find a new role or mission in the world.[4] Britain seemed adrift to me, too: An evening or two with the locals in London pubs, comparing the thwarted British invasion of Suez Canal with President Kennedy's embargo against Cuba, produced downright British resentment.

COMPARING LABOR ISSUES

The British world I entered that fall appeared to me to be one of economic hardship, instability, and decline. As it happened, the British unions were right in the middle of this discussion.

Unions in the UK had a low dues structure, and they financed all their functions through payments provided by their members. This structure had two important consequences: (1) the unions were pushed out of plant-level representation and necessarily ceded leadership to frequently militant and strike-prone shop steward committees; and (2) there was excessive competition between the dominant and numerous craft unions, which were established in the nineteenth century, and the larger and more general unions, such as the Transport and General Workers Union (somewhat comparable to the Teamsters in the United States). The result was a kind of vacuum at the workplace itself and numerous strikes, with a more militant and sometimes left-wing representative system. The labor movement was historically related to the Labour Party, with the top leadership more moderate or right-wing (by British standards) than the shop stewards.

In these circumstances, the contrast between the United States and Britain was an exciting one for a young labor lawyer from Detroit. In retrospect, my assumptions about the virtues of the National Labor Relations Act and the arbitration system may have made me rather rigid and unbearable for my new British friends. Looking back now, I hope my overly optimistic assumptions about the American system didn't lump me in with the stereotypical "ugly American," about whom the British and Europeans often complained. (I would joke with my British friends about the loud, rich Texans at the American Express bank on Haymarket Square, complaining in their unmistakable drawls about the relationship between the American dollar and other countries, and displaying considerable arrogance in the process.)

In fact, I was wrong about both American labor features—law, and to a lesser extent, the arbitration process. Those weaknesses in the American labor system became more visible a decade later. But I was quite on point about the British system: Not only did it play a role in the country's economic problems of the sixties and seventies, when Mrs. Castle's white paper, "In Place of Strife," was rejected by the Labour government because the unions would not accept its recommendations, but it also provided a calamitous defeat for the Labour Party in 1979's "winter of discontent" and the election of a right-wing Conservative, Margaret Thatcher, as prime minister that year.

The upheavals of this period reminded me of the 1959 British movie *I'm Alright Jack*, which I had watched with Kurt Hanslowe, and Alan Sillitoe's *Saturday Night and Sunday Morning*, a classic British novel about working class grievances and lifestyle in the 1950s, which I read soon after my arrival in London. I was to travel south of the Thames to visit with and interview the representatives of the Amalgamated Engineering Union (AEU), whose leadership seemed to reflect the attitudes and behavior contained in Sillitoe and *I'm Alright Jack*. At the same time I connected with the more right-wing Electrical Trades Union at their modern suburban headquarters, where I noted less focus upon rigid class conflict.

CLASSES, MEETINGS, AND NEW ACQUAINTANCES

Of course, my basic focus and mission during my London stay was my work at the London School of Economics. I attended labor law lectures given by Otto Kahn-Freund, the doyen of British and European labor lawyers. In lectures, he would call on me about all things American, and in our tutor–pupil relationship I met with him regularly to discuss the papers I was writing.[5] Kahn-Freund gave me a new perspective, declaring, "You Americans have too much labor law." He made me drill down and reassess my assumptions about a system of which I had been unduly uncritical at that time.

I also attended Phelps Brown's history of labor economics class but had little personal contact with him. I listened in on many LSE politics classes, which tied into much of what I was reading in the British newspapers. (American news accounts at this time were not filled with opinions and subjective commentary of the kind so prevalent in Britain.)

And, thanks largely to Victor Reuther, I had the opportunity to meet with politicians and trade unionists, principally in London. Victor had arranged most of the introductions; within weeks of my arrival I was in Parliament, having tea with Jennie Lee, the widow of Aneurin "Nye" Bevan, Minister of Health in the postwar government of Clement Atlee and widely known as the father of Britain's National Health Service. After our meeting, I attended the opening session of the House of Commons and heard the Queen's speech about the legislative agenda. Jennie Lee, ever gracious and friendly, was quite critical of Walter Reuther's decision to bring the UAW into an alliance with the Democratic Party; she favored pursuing a more traditionally socialist model, as practiced in Britain and much of Europe. Her disapproval of the UAW's direction was expressed through both her facial expressions and her words, and I think that she saw me as a UAW representative, however young and uninitiated I may have been at the time. The only Conservative Party representative I met was Sir Keith Joseph, who looked at me and said, "Oh! I had expected a much older man."

I was soon in touch with most of the Labour Party's "shadow" or opposition cabinet, that is, the presumed cabinet which formulated policy to which a future Labour government would theoretically adhere. I recall meeting with C. A. R. (Anthony) Crosland, whose books—which addressed how Labour should modify its rigid socialistic adherence to nationalized industries and the like—I had read assiduously.[6] Around this time I also had a lively, wide-ranging discussion with R. H. S. (Richard) Crossman, a rather acerbic member of Parliament—or MP, as they are commonly known—who was considerably further to the left than someone like Crosland.

Labour MP George Brown, whom I met at his deputy leader of the opposition office late one mild spring afternoon in 1963, just as Big Ben struck six, offered me a scotch as I sat down. (I declined it—it wasn't yet my drink of choice.) Brown, sipping his own scotch, aggressively self-confident and peppering every sentence with plentiful f***s, was a memorable person to meet. I met a number of other members of the shadow Labour bench as well, including Michael Stewart (my MP at my second address in London's Fulham area), who was to become foreign secretary when Harold Wilson's Labour Party defeated Alec Douglas-Home's Tories in 1964; Ray Gunter, who was to be minister of labour in 1964; defense specialist Fred Mulley, who held a number of defense positions, and with whom I corresponded years afterward; and Denis Healey, who ultimately became minister of defense as well as chancellor of the exchequer under Harold Wilson and Jim Callaghan. At Stanford in the 1990s I arranged for Healey to give a talk at the law school, though he had no recollection of our brief meeting in my LSE days.[7] I was scheduled and prepared to meet John Strachey, a former Labour minister of food and leftist thinker whose books I had also read,[8] but, regrettably, two days before our meeting date I was advised that Strachey had died.

Around this same time I met with George Woodcock, the general secretary of the Trades Union Congress (TUC) on Russell Street. The TUC is roughly equivalent to our AFL-CIO, a federation formed to bring unions together. Woodcock was a distinguished man with large gray eyebrows. "Welcome to the TUC!" he said to me warmly, a greeting I was to receive from all of his successors in the six decades to follow, though none as special as the one that day in 1962, coming as it did from that thoughtful-looking and acting man. He was attempting to make the British labor movement relevant to the workplace through centralized voluntarism in the pay restraint area, which had begun to emerge in the fifties and sixties—a considerable task given the rise of a more autonomous shop steward movement in the plants. John Cole, the labor correspondent of the *Manchester Guardian*, was his interlocutor; after I initiated correspondence with John, he became a good friend whom I was to see many times on subsequent London visits and in the late 1960s and 1970s in New York, Detroit, and California.[9] These many contacts, a rarity for young people without an extensive record of accomplishments, were made possible by my UAW connection and Victor Reuther's generous letters of introduction.

TRAVELS ABROAD, A COLD WINTER, AND A LIFE-CHANGING DEBATE

As 1962's fall quarter moved into winter, I reconnected at LSE with a fellow I had met in Detroit—Joseph "Jay" Featherstone, a former editor of the Harvard *Crimson* who had been working for the *Detroit Free Press* just after graduating from Harvard. In December, after LSE classes recessed, the two of us went to Paris together and immediately experienced blissful, sunny weather, a sudden change, and particularly welcome after London's nonstop clouds and rain. We stayed in Saint-Germain-des-Prés, an active and interesting part of the city. Though I had studied French in high school, I had not practiced conversation and was immediately out of favor with the impatient French. (On a subsequent visit I greeted someone in the Charles de Gaulle airport by saying, "*Parlez-vous anglais* [Do you speak English]?" He replied, "*Oui. Je préfère français* [Yes. I prefer French].") Jay, however, was conversant and acted as an interpreter when we met—again through Victor Reuther—the Socialist Party leader, Guy Mollet. Most of our conversation concerned the European Common Market, Charles DeGaulle, and his hostility toward Britain—"perfidious Albion" in the parlance of the day.

After a few days in Paris, I set off on my own on the Paris–Rome train, stopping briefly in Bologna and spending Christmas in Rome, where spring-like weather once again provided contrast to the Britain I had temporarily left behind.

Back in London in the New Year of 1963, I moved to Rostrevor Road, near the Fulham Broadway tube stop in the south of the city, near the Thames, where I shared a flat with Jay Featherstone. The Fulham area, in this century quite chic and fashionable, presented a sharp contrast to my previous residence on Regent's Park Road, near lovely Primrose Hill. The Fulham of 1963 was working class through and through, and the popular tabloid *News of the Day* was on virtually every doorstep. (I dropped into one of the local pubs one night, and when I woke up with a cold the following day, I went to the local National Health Service. There were many of the people who had been in the same pub the previous night.) And it was the bitterest January in more than a century: The cold was so severe that the pipes froze in much of British housing, given the relatively moderate climate the country usually enjoys.

Labour Party leader Hugh Gaitskell, whom I had seen in Brighton in October, became seriously ill and was hospitalized toward the end of the month. I was shocked to read that shortly thereafter he had died![10] I had admired the National Health Service established by Clement Atlee's Labour government after World War II and had been pleasantly surprised to see anti-smoking billboards advertising the cancer connection—at that time such signs were completely absent from the U.S. Nonetheless, LSE politics professor Dorothy Pickles (the wife of William Pickles on the same faculty) said to me, "If he was in America this wouldn't have happened." This comment was from a considerably left-of-center Labour Party adherent who was nonetheless critical of the highly respected British healthcare system. But it reflected the widely held view that what America lacked in universal care, it made up for with a higher quality for those fortunate enough to have it. (I recall seeing a dentist who advised me that he could not see me for three or four months, unless my tooth was infected or in need of immediate surgery.)

Notwithstanding the intense cold, January began on a positive note for me personally. At the beginning of the quarter in the student lounge, some British students invited us Americans to share a coffee table with them. There we became involved in a rather animated discussion about the Common Market and I—in contrast to my earlier views at the time of Gaitskell's "Thousand Years" speech at the Labour Party Conference in Brighton—supported it, lock, stock, and barrel. But a young woman who had just finished her graduate degree at LSE opposed my position, and we had an amicable debate—but a debate nonetheless! This young woman was Hilda Fitter, currently a teacher of foreign graduate students. Hilda was to introduce me to much of Britain that year, first through her knowledge of London, and subsequently as we began to travel through northern England.

Figure 4.1: My wife, Hilda Elizabeth, and I, on our wedding day at St. Anne's Anglican Church in London, 1963.

During that spring, Hilda introduced me to the Lake District, and to Manchester and Liverpool from which she hailed, and I began to see a different, cheerier, and warmer side of Britain—quite different from the reserved and relatively stiff London to which I had previously been exposed. As we drove in her Renault, there seemed to be an endless series of Beatles-type groups singing joyfully on the radio. The Beatles themselves were yet to emerge in Britain, let alone internationally. And when they did, of course, they created a great splash, landing in New York City and Washington the following year.

In the summer of 1963, Hilda and I were married at St. Anne's Anglican Church, near her sister's residence in northwest London. My parents remained uneasy about an interracial marriage, still unusual and the object of ostracism in those days. This time, however, there was no religious barrier. Though Hilda was and is antagonistic to organized religion, I was raised as an Episcopalian. And I remembered my father's words to my mother in 1934, when he told her that marrying in the Episcopal Church (the American branch of the Anglican Communion) was an assurance that it would "take." Over six decades after our union at St. Anne's, with sons born in Washington, New York, and Detroit, and four grandchildren in California, the point seems to have been proved again, emphatically. And the debates, which began that January day in 1963, have not ceased.

MUSINGS: WHERE NEXT?

Right around this time I had my first connection with the International Labour Organization (ILO) in Switzerland through their director, David Morse, a friend of Harold Cranefield from the thirties. The ILO flew me from London to Geneva to talk about working for them, and I had a good look at Geneva itself. I liked the ILO and the city, and I think that Hilda would have been interested in it, given its proximity to Britain. But they could not guarantee me an immediate slot in their Labour Law Division, though they expressed confidence about a future position when a vacancy opened. That wasn't good enough for me—I wanted to go into the Labour Law Division right away, and so I declined their offer. From time to time, I've wondered whether and how my life would have been different if I had taken that step toward the ILO and a Geneva residence.

Later, back in London, I recall reading a *New York International Herald Tribune* article about a college classmate, Parker Cramer, who had been killed in Vietnam. This was well before the fighting intensified, and I was struck by the fact that Parker, a person I had known, was now gone from this world, a casualty of a conflict that was just beginning. Reading the newspaper that day left me both sad and troubled.

Missing Home

Letters to Detroit friends and to my parents in New Jersey were my primary means of communication with the United States. The post was delivered in London three times a day, and I remember receiving a New York City letter the very next day after it was sent! Two or three times during my year in London, I telephoned the United States. To accomplish this, I had to go to an underground office in Trafalgar Square and wait about an hour before my name was called to use the phone. The connections were not always the best! (To be fair, there were different standards of communication in America as well: In the 1950s, all local calls we made from Long Branch 6-1219J were shared with one or two other households on a so-called "party line," and any third party could hear your conversation if they picked up their handset.)

As spring unfolded, I read of the civil rights upheavals throughout America, particularly the dramatic confrontations in Birmingham, Alabama, and felt as if I was on the sidelines, thousands of miles away during this critical period. Although I had no television in Rostrevor Road, the *International Herald Tribune* and British papers made me keenly aware of what I was missing: Birmingham, the hoses and police dogs confronting demonstrations lead by Martin Luther King. But I would remain on the sidelines until later in the sixties, when I would begin my work on job discrimination cases in New York City.

Vignettes: Britain and Europe

In Britain, ideas about fair employment and civil rights law remained undiscussed—off the table, so to speak—in the early sixties. Still, there were a substantial number of Black and Asian migrants in the country at that time, and none were members of Parliament, or part of the political process as yet. And I could see signs of possible strife ahead. Within the first few weeks of my arrival in London, I was on a bus where a white customer became irate with the Black conductor and shouted, "You Black bastard!" I was stunned. Though I knew these kinds of things happened frequently in my own country, I had never actually heard a white man speak like that in the United States. I rushed to the conductor's side. "Don't worry," he said, "It's nothing." That wasn't the way I saw it.

Around that same time, my friend Keith Stuart, an official on the Coal Board whom I had met in Brighton, invited me and Jay Featherstone to visit a Welsh coal mine in the Rhymney Valley near Cardiff. Here I became involved in a lively discussion with a coal miner about Aneurin "Nye" Bevan, who had hailed from that part of the country and whose widow I had met earlier in Parliament.

The descent into the mine's considerable depth was memorable: I crawled on my hands and knees for approximately a mile, unable to stand straight because of the low level of the roof. I had been reading *The Road to Wigan Pier*, and Orwell's descriptions of the hard labor required in all kinds of industries resonated clearly, even though I hadn't been working at all that day! Simply crawling left me sore and bruised for almost a week afterward, even at the tender age of twenty-six.

We finished our visit with a tour of the Cardiff dockland suburbs, Tiger Bay, the multi-ethnic home for incoming seafarers. The workers I saw that day in Wales appeared to be Middle Eastern and African, still relatively unusual for 1963 Britain.

I recall attending Robert MacKenzie's politics classes in the middle of Labour Party opposition leader Harold Wilson's challenge to Harold Macmillan, the British prime minister, in the spring of 1963. I was reading Norman Shrapnel's *Guardian* commentary on parliamentary debate, which was vividly described on a daily basis. Then, as the summer months brought an end to classes, the Profumo scandal broke. John Profumo, a Conservative cabinet minister, had been sleeping with one Christine Keeler, who also had a sexual relationship with a Soviet spy in London. As I walked up the stairs of the Bond Street tube station, the newspaper vendor shouted to me, "Sensational, governor . . . read all about it!" Profumo was soon to resign in disgrace—not because of his relationship with Christine Keeler, but rather because he had lied to Parliament about it. Harold Macmillan, who was to resign and make way for Sir Alec Douglas-Home, defended himself by saying that he was unaware of these events because "I do not mix with young people."

I ended my London year with one last tour of the Continent. I vividly recall speaking to young Germans on the train to Berlin who were visibly excited by JFK's memorable "Ich bin ein Berliner" speech, which he had given just a few weeks earlier. They seemed to be on the top of the world, reflecting the unforgettable roar of the Berlin crowd when JFK spoke those words. I've never heard anything like it in America.

I visited the Berlin Wall, made my way across Checkpoint Charlie, and had a meal in East Berlin—at the conclusion of which I had to walk to the Checkpoint to pay with the right money. In East Berlin, bombed-out buildings had been preserved as reminders of the war, in sharp contrast to what I saw in modernized West Berlin.

Beyond Germany, my final stops were in Norway and Sweden, where I benefited yet again from Victor Reuther's contacts—particularly Haoklen Lie, a Norwegian trade unionist who had fought in the insurgency against the occupying Germans during World War II. I recall that we spoke of this and matters related to collective bargaining when he took me out sailing in one of Oslo's beautiful fjords. A brief visit to Stockholm allowed me to connect with another of Victor's contacts, Gunnar Myrdal, author of *An American Dilemma*; I had an hour-long discussion with him about race in America. His book, written in 1944, was a landmark examination of the profound tension between America's espousal of democracy and the second-class segregated status provided to Black Americans. I can still recall an embassy official in Stockholm asking me if, as a Black American, I intended to become part of the civil rights struggle in America. I responded affirmatively.

No Return to Detroit

I headed back to London to get ready for an August return to the United States for Hilda and me. But there was only one problem: Harold Cranefield had retired from his general counsel position and the UAW had brought in Joe Rauh of Washington, who had his own people. There would be no return to Detroit for me, much as I wanted it. I had already turned down the ILO. What was I to do?

In this period of melancholy, I recall being lifted by James Baldwin's *Go Tell It on the Mountain*. Somehow, this book sent my spirits soaring, and I made my plans. I would return to New Jersey, get my work prospects sorted out, and Hilda would then follow.

HOME AGAIN

All I can recollect about my flight back to New York and the reunion with my parents was the sight of New York itself: It looked very dirty indeed compared to London. Once I was home again in Long Branch, and back on the other side of the Atlantic Ocean, my father expressed concern that my accent had too much of a British flavor. But it was good to be back in the USA, and reading James Baldwin's *Another Country* convinced me of how fundamentally American I was. I was sure that my future work would—and should—be undertaken in the United States.

Meanwhile, however, the basic mission had been accomplished: My intellectual horizons were broadened. I had read more widely in politics and history. And I was about to commence not only law journal writing but also writing for publications that reached more diverse audiences: *The Economist* and the *New York Times*, as well as more boutique journals such as *Commonweal, The New Leader,* and *The Nation*. My year in Britain and at the LSE with Kahn-Freund was a turning point—and my marriage to Hilda the most important turning point for my future.

NOTES

[1] Barbara Castle, "In Place of Strife: A Policy for Industrial Relations," LAB 44/288 (1969).
[2] Hugh Gaitskell, speech against UK membership of the Common Market (October 3, 1962).
[3] Jim Connel, "The Red Flag," 1889, https://www.marxists.org/subject/art/music/lyrics/en/red-flag.htm.

> The people's flag is deepest red,
> It shrouded oft our martyred dead,
> And ere their limbs grew stiff and cold,
> Their hearts' blood dyed its ev'ry fold.
> Then raise the scarlet standard high.
> Within its shade we'll live and die,
> Though cowards flinch and traitors sneer,
> We'll keep the red flag flying here.

[4] Dean Acheson, "Our Atlantic Alliance," *Vital Speeches of the Day* XXIX, no. 6, January 1, 1963.

[5] One of my principal papers at this time was discussion of the relationship between unions and political parties. But regrettably, I did not publish anything on this subject until much later. William B. Gould IV, "Organized Labor, the Supreme Court, and *Harris v. Quinn*: Déjà Vu All Over Again?" *Supreme Court Review* 2014 (2014).

[6] C. A. R. Crosland, *The Future of Socialism* (London: J. Cape, 1956); C. A. R. Crosland, *The Conservative Enemy* (New York: Schocken Books, 1962).

[7] The meeting actually took place at the end of a lecture he gave in South Kensington.

[8] John Strachey, *The Coming Struggle for Power* (New York: Modern Library, 1935).

[9] John Cole reviewed one of my post- Washington books, *Labored Relations: Law, Politics, and the NLRB – A Memoir*, and expressed his view there, and in our private conversations, containing disagreement with me about arbitration and the law. John always felt that they were less important in labor relations than I did.
John Cole, "A Quiet American," *The Guardian*, Feb. 26, 2001.

[10] Gaitskell appeared to have a heart condition and may have suffered from lupus, which affected his heart and kidneys. Molli Mitchell, "The Crown: What Really Happened to Hugh Gaitskell Amid KGB Poison Plot?" *UK Express*, November 19, 2019; "1963: Labour Leader Hugh Gaitskell Dies," *The Guardian*, January 18, 1963.

5

ARBITRATION AND MEDIATION: LABOR DISPUTES IN WASHINGTON, DC, AND NEW YORK CITY

With Detroit now closed off to me, where would I go to continue my work? Almost immediately I was in touch with Jacob "Jack" Sheinkman, the general counsel of the Amalgamated Clothing Workers Union in New York City. While I was still a student at Cornell, I had written to a number of house counsel, that is, permanent staff of the organization, in search of labor law job opportunities with unions. One of those unions had been the Amalgamated Clothing Workers. Jack had taken an immediate interest in my letter because I was living in the very same boarding house—109 Williams Street, Ithaca—with the same landlady, as the one he had lived in as a student at Cornell Law School a decade earlier. A serendipitous coincidence!

OFF TO WASHINGTON

I called Jack when I returned from London, and he immediately called National Labor Relations Board Chairman Frank McCulloch in Washington. I was hired on the spot, to begin on September 16, 1963. My Washington great-aunt, Fannie Gould, knew of a place to live about a block away from her S Street residence: the top floor of 1723 S Street, the home of Dr. Carnot Evans, a retired Howard faculty member. Hilda was to arrive by boat from London in October, and this would be our home for the next twenty-two months.

Early Days at the NLRB

Each workday I made the twenty-five-minute walk from S Street, through Dupont Circle to the south, and down Connecticut Avenue to my office at NLRB headquarters, 1717 Pennsylvania Avenue, catty-cornered from the White House. Frank McCulloch, appointed chairman by President Kennedy, was a genteel and kindly gentleman from Chicago, a former aide to Illinois Senator Paul Douglas. McCulloch's NLRB had enjoyed a three-to-two majority of Democrats since shortly after JFK's inauguration in 1961.

I was anxious to join the NLRB in part because of its new direction: away from the conservative cast of the Eisenhower Board. Decisions by that board giving unilateral managerial authority to contract out work[1] and prohibiting picketing of nonunion employers under some circumstances[2] had been or would be reversed. The Kennedy Board was moving the country away from these reversals and limitations.

At the NLRB I shared an office with someone who would become very important to me thirty years later, when I became chairman: Bill Stewart of Indiana, who had just completed some work with the Atomic Energy Commission. Bill became a social friend as well as a professional colleague in those first Washington days.

I relished the chance to witness board agenda meetings, during which each board member, as well as their chief counsel, would discuss and frequently debate competing positions, as the NLRB in Washington generally received the more important, divisive, or policy-implicated cases. Frank McCulloch presided at these sessions, prodding and pulling in an attempt to reason and obtain consensus. Eisenhower appointee Boyd Leedom was gentle and circumspect in his opposition. Gerald Brown, an ex-San Francisco regional director, was voluble, unyielding, and clearly, in my view, the most knowledgeable and expert of the board members at that time. (Brown would be subsequently named by Governor Jerry Brown as chairman of the California Agricultural Labor Relations Board during the governor's first two terms in the seventies—and he and I would be the only two to have served on both boards, I as chairman of both.)

A Very Personal Loss

The most remarkable, tragic—indeed, cataclysmic—development at 1717 Pennsylvania Avenue during my tenure was President Kennedy's assassination on November 22. I still vividly recall of one of the NLRB lawyers coming into my office to tell me he'd heard on the radio that President Kennedy had been shot—and indeed had died. Hastily, I walked from the 1717 building across the street to the White House, where helicopters were flying in and out from the front lawn, and crowds were gathering. More than one person was speculating about the potential for an immediate nuclear attack by the Soviet Union. That day I witnessed what was assuredly the most traumatic public event of my life to date. Any professional or personal concerns immediately faded and, like the rest of Washington, the country, and the world, we were paralyzed, watching the developments from our television on S Street.

President Kennedy's sudden death was an enormous loss for me personally. I had been part of Students for Kennedy in 1960, had met him briefly in a Rhode Island receiving line in 1956, when he was campaigning for Stevenson, and I had engaged him briefly on the jury trial amendments to what became the Civil Rights Act of 1957. Standing so near him at the Detroit Cadillac Hotel in 1960, and within a stone's throw of his open limousine as he and Eamon DeValera, the Irish president, drove past me and my Cornell graduate pal Nat Pierson, coupled with his 1963 support for a fair employment practices law, made JFK almost iconic to me.

With the birth of our first son just a few weeks away, both Hilda and I were numbed by the idea that one man was leaving this earth so violently, as another was entering, almost simultaneously. In death, JFK had become larger than life to me—and to much of the world as well.

AT NLRB: CONSEQUENTIAL CASES, WRITING, AND CONSTRAINTS

Along with the more day-to-day professional problems in which I was directly involved, I had the good fortune to be assigned several consequential cases involving a matter which I regarded (and still do today) as an issue of basic rights: the matter of union conduct and activity on employer property, whether engaged in by workers or nonemployee union organizers. I was so involved in the issue in my review of the cases assigned to me that, in my spare time, I started to write extensively on it, eventually producing an elaborately footnoted article for a law review.[3] Regrettably, when I became NLRB's chairman thirty years later, some of these principles were difficult for me to implement because of views expressed in a 1992 Supreme Court ruling.[4]

In retrospect, I see that this kind of job in Washington was probably pushing me inexorably toward law teaching, but at this time I had not the slightest intention of pursuing such a career. I was deeply involved in my work and writing, not to mention the obligations of new parenthood: Our first son, William Benjamin V, was born in December of 1963. When my high school pal and fellow St. James's Church parishioner Harry Bowie came through Washington, en route to Mississippi and the Freedom Summer of 1964, he urged me to come with him. I begged off, citing both my writing and little Bill. Such a daring initiative—traveling to Mississippi to assist with voter registration, at great personal risk—just didn't seem feasible, though I suffered pangs of regret as I watched the civil rights struggle gain force without my participation.

The most important labor law writing, of course, was not for law reviews, which are read by very few—and certainly not the public, whose ideas one seeks to influence. More significant from my perspective were a couple of pieces I wrote for *The Economist* through the invitation of its assistant editor, Nancy Balfour, whom I met at LSE. I commented on the state of the labor movement in the United States[5]—a subject which I have continued to write about as recently as 2024 in the *Washington Post*[6]—and major Supreme Court rulings on the compatibility between antitrust and labor law.[7] In the first article, I warned of an unfolding labor union decline, a subject that was to consume much of my writing attention in the years to come. Submitting these pieces to *The Economist* in London was an intriguing act in and of itself: I had to walk to a telegram office next to the White House where, one hundred years earlier,

President Lincoln used to come to receive news of the outcomes of major Civil War battles. Faxes, emails, and texts were beyond the wildest workings of our imaginations at that point.

My interest in writing on such topics pulled me away from the McCulloch staff and over to the staff of the NLRB's first Black member, Republican Howard Jenkins Jr., where I acted as a speechwriter as well as a legal assistant. But whichever staff I was on, I found Washington bureaucracy constricted and frustrating. Even speechwriting, attractive to someone who liked to write, could be difficult when Jenkins and I disagreed. Overall, the work took place in a rarified world where one dealt exclusively with paper—to the exclusion of people. The chance to act independently and to have regular, dynamic contact with shop stewards, union representatives, and employer labor relations staff, as I'd had with the UAW in Detroit, was nonexistent. I badly wanted to return to that relatively nonbureaucratic environment, and an opportunity soon came my way.

NEW YORK: ANSWERING TO THREE LAWYERS

In 1965 Samuel Pierce, a former state court judge and one of Cornell University and Cornell Law School's first Black graduates, was a partner at the New York law firm Battle, Fowler, Stokes, and Kheel (referred to hereafter as the Kheel firm). After my friend and NLRB trial examiner Arthur Christopher connected us, Pierce interviewed me, and in the spring of '65 I was invited to come to work as an associate at the firm, located at 280 Park Avenue at 48th Street, near both the Chrysler building to the south and Saint Bartholomew's Episcopal Church to the northeast. My assignment was to assist Pierce, Theodore Kheel, and Morris Lasker on labor law matters.

Samuel Pierce later served as HUD Secretary in the Reagan administration—he was the only Black member of Reagan's Cabinet—and Reagan notoriously mistook him at a public occasion for a Black big city mayor. After Pierce's death in 2000, it was reported that J. Edgar Hoover's FBI hoped to substitute Pierce for Martin Luther

King Jr. as a national Black leader during the civil rights unrest of the sixties.[8] Morris Lasker was later to become a well-respected federal district court judge, appointed by President Johnson.

My parents were delighted that we would now be so close to New Jersey, but my father was concerned that answering to three different lawyers was inherently unstable and difficult. Fortunately, it didn't work out that way in practice, and the job possessed a feature which I found especially attractive and unusual, that is, the ability to represent both employers and unions (most labor lawyers are limited to one side or the other) and to become involved as an impartial arbitrator and mediator, principally when working with Ted Kheel. Kheel was the most prominent third-party labor dispute resolution expert in New York City at that time, the "go-to guy" for Mayor Robert Wagner, the son of New York Senator Robert Wagner, who had authored the 1935 National Labor Relations Act, also known as the Wagner Act. I thought that this unusual combination of assignments would give me just the right balance and understanding of the labor–management relationship.

My one concern was that my work for management would involve me in representation proceedings in which the employer was attempting to convince workers that they should not join a union or other entity that would represent them. This I did not want to do. My view was and is that workers should resolve the matter of representation for themselves, and that employer involvement offers businesses excessive power and advantage. Fortunately, and to my great satisfaction, we were rarely, if ever, involved in any kind of anti-union campaign. My work involved bargaining and arbitration, as well as appearances before the NLRB regional offices representing employers who had established relationships with unions. This role expanded my understanding of collective bargaining systems and better prepared me for work that was to come my way more frequently, that is, third party resolution of disputes in the labor management process itself.

ARBITRATION AND MEDIATION

A Ferry Strike and Its Consequences

I arrived in New York on July 7, 1965, and settled into an apartment on 875 West End Avenue. Hilda, pregnant with our second child, Timothy Samuel, would join me with our son, Bill, a few weeks later.

Almost from the day I arrived, I was involved in a series of interesting matters. A strike by ferry boat operators was my first notable assignment. Ted Kheel was appointed as a hearing officer by Mayor Wagner and acted on behalf of New York City. The issue was whether these public sector employees had engaged in a "strike" within the meaning of the Civil Service Law, commonly known as the Condon-Wadlin Act, which imposed automatic penalties on workers for any exercise of the right to strike. This statute preceded and acted as a kind of warm-up for an independent debate then raging in New York and across the country. The debate centered on whether public employees should have collective bargaining rights comparable to those provided in the private sector under the NLRA, and whether that collective bargaining should include the right to strike or, alternatively, some other dispute resolution mechanism in the event that the parties couldn't resolve their differences.

In New York, the ferry boat dispute, as well as a twelve-day New York City transit strike in 1966 and other public employee union activism, resulted in the enactment of the 1967 Taylor Law (also known as the Public Employees' Fair Employment Act), which prohibited such strikes and provided for fact-finding with recommendations by an impartial third party in the event that labor and the public employer were unable to resolve their differences about the terms of a new collective bargaining agreement. The transit strike, in particular, concentrated the minds of Governor Nelson Rockefeller and the legislature around the need for legal intervention in some form. The fiery Transit Workers Union leader Mike Quill snarled loudly and pugnaciously at the legal sanctions aimed at him and his union under the Condon-Wadlin Law of 1947, which forbade and penalized strikes by government employees. Quill and others rightly viewed Republican Mayor John Lindsay, who succeeded Wagner in 1966, with a mixture of caution and scorn and perceived him as an uninformed amateur. Lindsay, for his part, thought that Mayor Wagner had negotiated improper labor deals. Quill came to despise Lindsay and said: "If Mayor Lindsay gets up to leave the bargaining table to go to the toilet, we will follow him to the toilet."

Kheel and I were not involved in this dispute, as Lindsay saw Kheel as part of the brokered arrangements problem for which he was advocating a new public approach. The dispute produced considerable strife, shutting down the subways, but allowing the privately held buses to operate, as they were covered by federal labor law. I grew to know the streets of Manhattan during the strike, walking to work across the island from West 103rd down to Park and 48th every day. And two years later, in 1968, I was named to the very first fact-finding board the Public Employment Relations Board created under the Taylor Law in New York. The board's first case involved the Mount Vernon police.[9]

An Apprentice Arbitrator

The ferry boat dispute, which antedated Taylor, was my first assignment in New York City. But within a month or so of my arrival, I was hearing cases for Kheel in the pocketbook and transit industries, and drafting opinions for his signature even when he had not heard the case himself. In short, I was a kind of apprentice arbitrator, and this exposed me not only to a wide variety of practical labor problems but also to a legal issue I had not confronted at either the UAW or the NLRB: the authority of an arbitrator to issue cease-and-desist orders against a union which had violated a no-strike clause in the collective bargaining agreement. At the same time, while I would represent Teamster Union locals, particularly Locals 818 and 852 (led by Pat Sullivan and Dennis Crotty, respectively), I also represented employers like Diners Club, Proctor & Gamble (at its large Staten Island facility; it was New York City's largest employer at that time), and U.S. Industries, a major government contractor. I daresay that this combination of responsibilities existed in very few other labor law firms in the country—perhaps none at all.

I got a practical introduction not only to a wide variety of disputes but also to a jurisdictional conflict, both before the NLRB and as a permanent umpire or arbitrator established under one of two relevant collective bargaining agreements. The issues, particularly those which were brought before the NLRB, were intellectually interesting and challenging and exposed me to legal complexities which I had not previously confronted. In the jurisdictional case I represented Western Transport, a freight carrier. My first hearing was before George Mintzer, the arbitrator and impartial permanent umpire (an individual designated to hear disputes for the duration of the collective bargaining agreement) under an agreement applicable to the union and many employers with which the union, Local 102, had bargaining relationships. Local 102 claimed Western Transport work performed by the union with which the employer bargained, the Brotherhood of Railway Clerks. In this case I also got a real introduction to the practical reality of some arbitrations: When I appeared before Mintzer, he began the hearing with, "Mr. Gould, why is your client violating the collective bargaining agreement?"

No evidence had been taken or arguments heard. But my client was one of many covered by this agreement, and Local 102, the union signatory, was the only party on the union side. In a sense, institutionally, Mintzer's attitude was unsurprising, given the fact that my client was a stranger to him, and the union was a permanent customer, the only labor organization dealing with a multitude of employers. Most of the employers—certainly Western Transport—made infrequent appearances before the arbitrator. I saw the arbitrator's role and comments to be improper and the system to be inequitable in this respect, though hardly startling given these power dynamics.

Right around this time, Judge Paul Hays of the Court of Appeals for the Second Circuit, an ex-arbitrator and Columbia Law professor, wrote an article and a book suggesting that many labor arbitration awards were "rigged," that is, opinions were drafted and prepared by the union and employer, frequently without the knowledge of the testifying or involved employees, with the arbitrator simply signing the document that was presented by the union and employer, sometimes completely over the heads of the workers.[10]

In a sense, my experience with Mintzer that day was even worse than what Hays described, and suggested to me that either the power dynamics of the agreement's signatories, or information provided to the arbitrator ex parte, had already resolved the matter for the arbitrator before anything on the record could be presented with all counsel or party representatives present.[11] True, the broad sweep of my arbitration experience before and since that day has been appreciably better. But the warning signals set off in that case are still with me today.

Forays into Collective Bargaining

As 1965 spun to a close, two other matters of significance appeared on my scene; both were to affect my work in years to come. One involved U.S. Industries and its successful bid under the Johnson administration Job Corps for the Custer Job Corps training center (named for the general at Fort Custer) in Michigan near Battle Creek and its Kellogg plants. The second was to get me deeply involved in fair employment matters. In the first one, Teamsters Local 34 demanded recognition for a unit of workers. Rather than contest the matter through the NLRB, I prepared a recognition agreement on behalf of this government contractor to resolve any questions about Local 34's majority status. On the basis of authorization cards, with my old Detroit friend Father Clement Kern acting as the arbitrator, recognition was provided expeditiously to Local 34.

Though I had not anticipated it at the time, this case would involve me in considerable collective bargaining in Battle Creek and was to be a factor in my return to Detroit a couple of years down the road. I spent a number of days negotiating a collective bargaining agreement, the first one consummated between Local 34 Teamsters and U.S. Industries. Although some of my earlier work for Diners Club was of a similar nature, this was a kind of baptism for me. While at the UAW, I had rarely negotiated agreements because of that union's historic suspicion of lawyers—a leftover from the days of internal divisions with the anti-Reuther left, whose lawyers were particularly prominent. In my time with the UAW, we were generally confined to providing legal opinions when called for and not engaging in bargaining itself. But in my early days and months with the Kheel firm, I was thrown into bargaining sessions on a series of fronts in New York City and in Michigan.

In my UAW days, Reuther's view was that, in the main, lawyers should not be in collective bargaining unless a discrete legal issue arose which required counsel's technical advice. That was why I was immediately at the GM bargaining table when I joined the staff in the summer of '61: I was to advise on the question of whether it was unlawful for the company to refuse to open the books when it claimed that UAW demands would be inflationary. The UAW contrasted its approach to lawyers with that of the United Steel Workers: The USW's lawyers, particularly its general counsel, Arthur Goldberg, and later David Feller, were dominant personalities in the union, assuming de facto leadership positions even though they were unelected. The UAW wanted none of this—it took pride in the subordinate role it gave its lawyers—and in fact there was a rivalry between the two unions regarding not only who was actually the innovator in bargaining, but also between the legal staffs themselves on the question of whether more effective representation was provided by one union's lawyers, who offered technical advice (UAW), or the other's, who were in control (USW).

In my new position with the Kheel firm, I was allowed to become deeply involved in all aspects of negotiations, proposing contract clauses, determining strategy, and so on. Though I possessed a basic labor law background before arriving in New York, the experience I obtained at the bargaining table itself was a new frontier for me.

My work at Fort Custer, where I wrote memoranda and traveled frequently to Battle Creek to negotiate, took up my time in New York as well, both at my office and at home. From time to time, I gave telephonic advice so substantively detailed that on one Saturday, when I was supposed to go down the hill to Riverside Park with Hilda and our two boys (Timothy Samuel was born in New York City on the same day I produced a detailed legal memo), I waved her off and said that I would catch them up later at the park. Some three hours later, when they returned, I was still on the phone!

Most of my work in New York did not take me to court, though there were frequent proceedings and appearances before the NLRB regional offices in New York, Brooklyn, and Newark, New Jersey. I traveled by air frequently to Detroit for U.S. Industries, a practice that made me somewhat uneasy, as airplane travel at that time was still viewed by many (including myself) as potentially dangerous. U.S. Industries vice president Fred Anger and I used to discuss this quite often. Around the same time, I remember running into Walter Reuther with his assistants and bodyguards at the Detroit airport and reassuring myself that since Reuther flew far more frequently than I did, there must be nothing to fear. Ironically, a few years later, in 1970, Reuther was killed in the crash of a UAW-chartered jet traveling in fog out of Detroit.

For other clients, such as Diners Club and Proctor & Gamble, I handled arbitrations, as I had done for the UAW. I had a pretty good track record in these arbitration matters—but I lost one, representing a Teamsters local, which was rather spectacular, right out of Victor Hugo, I thought at the time. This was a matter before New York State arbitrator Louis Yagoda, in which a worker possessing ten years of seniority, with no prior offenses on his record, was dismissed for stealing an apple. Arbitral case law generally dictates that the employer has an obligation to counsel and discipline a worker charged with misbehavior before dismissal (so-called progressive discipline) unless it consists of fundamentally offensive misbehavior that interferes with the enterprise's integrity, that is, theft or violence in the workplace. Though the worker in this case was charged with theft, it was one apple, allegedly stolen after ten years of unblemished service. Nonetheless, the arbitrator (said to be formerly or presently a Socialist Party member) upheld the discharge and, some said, may have fashioned such hard justice because he thought the worker was not telling the truth when he denied under oath that he had taken the apple. Whatever the arbitrator's real thinking, the result was more than disappointing to me and to the worker.

Dealing with the Teamster local presidents was often just as interesting as some of their cases. Pat Sullivan of Local 818 was very much the gentleman, proper to the point of fastidiousness, and extremely disapproving of his counterpart at Local 852, Dennis Crotty. Dennis may have warranted some of this disapproval, as his conduct could be both profane and combustible. He was something of a maverick, the only person I ever met who, when we had a breakfast meeting, would have two or three glasses of scotch with his eggs.

The Diners Club labor relations representative, Al Del Guercio, was fun to work with. I argued and wrote a brief for Diners Club in a case where the Office Employees Union was trying to restrict the company's flexibility—and we won. It occurred just a month or so shy of my thirtieth birthday. "We'll grow old gracefully," Al said at the time, as we savored that victory together.

Somehow, in the midst of all this activity, I began to write book reviews, as well as the occasional article addressing labor, race, and politics—frequently British politics—for periodicals like *Commonweal*[12] and *The New Leader*.[13] I even wrote a law review piece on "wildcat" or unauthorized strikes,[14] a subject through which I brushed up against the received wisdom at the NLRB.[15] Years later, the Court of Appeals for the Eighth Circuit expressed agreement with my views and instructed the board to follow my "sound advice."[16] This wasn't the first time that a board majority had been told by a circuit court that my view was the correct one![17]

THE EEOC AND TITLE VII

The most significant endeavor I undertook around this time, however, was to act as a consultant and conciliator for the Equal Employment Opportunity Commission (EEOC). This came about as the result of an interview with that agency when I was still in Washington, in the year between its creation (1964) and its effective date of operation (1965). I had spoken to two of the EEOC's original members: Aileen Hernandez, an ex-union official and later not only a good friend but also a NOW leader from California, and Samuel C. Jackson, a Black Republican lawyer from Kansas. I had an article coming out at that time addressing the seniority clash between Black and white workers in unionized facilities,[18] and suggesting that the leading ruling on that subject needed to be revisited. Hernandez and Jackson were interested in my views and the possible use of them in interpreting the newly enacted statute Title VII of the

Civil Rights Act of 1964. I hit it off with both of them. In '65, I had met the new EEOC chairman, Franklin Delano Roosevelt Jr., and was struck by his carbon-copy resemblance to FDR himself.

But the offer from the Kheel firm had come through first, and, in any event, while I wanted to be involved with job discrimination issues, I wanted to retain my overriding identity as a labor lawyer who worked with employment discrimination matters alongside labor law matters. After I'd moved to New York City, in the spring of '66, Hernandez and Jackson contacted me again, asking me to write a report with recommendations on the seniority issue for the EEOC. In that connection, they wanted me to take up a few assignments as a conciliator so that (1) I could see how the process actually worked and, perhaps, obtain more of a sense of how my recommendations would be applied as a practical matter as I gained exposure to the South; and (2) I could enhance my review of the seniority issue in the process.

An Illuminating Trip South

Except for family trips to Washington, I had never been to the South. My father had had no interest in traveling there, given what he knew about practices and behavior in that part of the country, as well as his own horrific experience in Jacksonville, Florida. At the age of thirty, I had seen much more of Europe than the United States. But in the summer of '66 I interrupted a family vacation with my parents in Manasquan, New Jersey, and took a sleeper to Washington to meet with the EEOC.

It was a memorable night, as I got little sleep on the train, feeling the tracks and rails beneath me throughout the entire trip. The next day, I began a series of meetings in Washington and signed on to the job proposed to me. Hernandez and Jackson were the prime movers, setting up a number of conciliations as well as the seniority paper itself. And my first case involved the General Telephone Company at Myrtle Beach, South Carolina, where I went shortly after my meetings in Washington.

As a child and young man, I had observed that many or most Black workers performed low-level jobs in Long Branch. But in Myrtle Beach, all the unskilled jobs were held by Blacks and all the higher-echelon jobs were filled exclusively by whites. And Myrtle Beach left me with some unforgettable moments. For instance, I had scheduled an interview at my small motel with a Black worker who had filed a complaint in Myrtle Beach against the General Telephone Company. At the appointed hour, I paced around in front of the motel where we were to connect, but no one appeared. Ten or fifteen minutes later, a couple of big, burly white guys got out of a pickup truck and came walking straight for me. My heart was in my mouth.

At this point, it had been only two years since the brutal torture and murder of Andrew Goodman, Michael Schwerner, and James Chaney during Mississippi's Freedom Summer—not to mention countless other acts of violence against Blacks since the fifties. At the last moment, these two fellows veered off toward another motel room. A few minutes later the complainant appeared, and all was well. Hardly surprisingly, I had assumed the very worst that day!

After interviewing people in Myrtle Beach and preparing a draft report in the event that the matter could not be conciliated (conciliation being the only tool available to the EEOC at that point), I moved on to Birmingham, Alabama, and met with civil rights leaders there. The tension was even more considerable. Steel was big in Alabama, and the seniority disputes between Black and white workers were numerous. And it wasn't only steel—paper and tobacco were also at the forefront, along with the dismantling of segregated local unions, particularly in those industries.

The theme in all these cases was the same: hiring Black workers into the less desirable, lower-paying jobs was now seen as unlawful, given the effective date of Title VII in 1965.[19] But the gist of the problem was that Blacks were at a competitive disadvantage: Seniority was only computed on a departmental or job basis, and only within the good jobs or departments from which Blacks had been excluded. Therefore, Blacks would always have less seniority if they transferred. The dispute was about the exercise of seniority *as vacancies became available*—never was it seriously suggested that a remedy to the problem would involve the actual ouster of white workers from their current jobs or departments. Yet, in addition to the competition for future vacancies on the basis of seniority in these plants, the seniority that Black workers had not been able to accumulate in the past due to exclusionary hiring policies placed Black workers at a disadvantage now. They were *able* to transfer now but discouraged from doing so because of the unequal seniority treatment. And so the fight under Title VII was about whether Black workers would be at a disadvantage in promotion and more vulnerable to layoffs under widespread "last hired-first fired" policies, which perpetuated past hiring discrimination practices, disadvantaging Blacks who sought to move upward and take their accumulated seniority with them.

The framers of Title VII had amended the administration's bill (the so-called Case-Clark amendments) to provide that a "bona fide" seniority system was not unlawful; subsequently it was known as the bona fide seniority proviso. This proviso recognized that there was nothing inherently discriminatory about such a seniority arrangement—unless, that is, it was infected by discrimination. The fight that emerged in '65 and '66 was over the question of which systems were infected by discrimination, and which were not. Most of the labor movement was unalterably opposed to any reform of past discrimination, which infected the present system and was therefore enmeshed in future promotions or layoffs.

Early on in my assignment, I met with Don Slaiman, a civil rights director for the AFL-CIO and a defender of the present systems which were under attack, and also with Emil Mazey, the UAW secretary-treasurer, whom I had known from my UAW days. Mazey was hostile, belligerent, and downright nasty to me. It understates the matter to say that the discussion with Messrs. Slaiman and Mazey did not go well that day.

The Steel Workers were prominent defendants in most of the filed cases, and although my meetings with people like General Counsel Bernie Kleiman, arbitration expert Ben Fischer, and civil rights department head Alex Fuller were pleasant and courteous, the response was just as implacable and unyielding as it had been with Slaiman and Mazey. I attended the 1966 Steel Workers convention in Atlantic City and the conversations were convivial, but they produced the same defense of white workers' seniority rights that I'd seen elsewhere.

Another problem was the involvement of John Dunlop, an economics professor at Harvard, who was very close to AFL-CIO president George Meany and the building trades and was involved in construction disputes over discrimination. Dunlop appeared to encourage the view that attacks on the construction unions' exclusionary practices throughout the so-called critical crafts—including sheet metal and iron workers, and electricians—which have excluded Blacks altogether, were inevitably intertwined with the Steel Workers' issues present in manufacturing and elsewhere. This ignored the fact that hiring and promotion were the sine qua non for a statutory violation in the latter cases. Hiring itself was the principal problem in construction, where access was the issue. Closely connected to this line of argument was the view that industrial unions in manufacturing shouldn't throw stones at the construction unions, given the fact that the seniority cases made clear that the former's houses were made of glass.

The building trades' position was that the bona fide seniority proviso was necessary to guard against so-called preferential treatment for Black workers when they were hired from the street. The Steel Workers took much the same view, but only in regard to Blacks who were employed in the enterprise itself, whereas in construction Blacks had been consigned to nonunion jobs uncovered by the collective bargaining agreement. This was distinguishable from manufacturing industries like steel and paper, where Blacks had been hired into the inferior jobs and where the negotiated seniority system carried forward past discriminatory hiring by the very same employer. Dunlop, close to and seemingly sympathetic with the construction unions, dispatched a young Harvard economics professor, Peter Doeringer, to the EEOC. He sat in on some of my meetings and met with some of the same people I did.

Despite my concerns that some kind of joint report was being promoted through Dunlop, I was ultimately able to submit a report to the commission in late '66, advancing seniority credits for Black workers locked into lesser jobs, predicated on my view that the denied seniority credits would have been accumulated but for the previous hiring discrimination that had placed Blacks at a disadvantage. Of course, my proposals related solely to future vacancies and protection against layoffs—and they protected incumbent white workers' seniority, notwithstanding the fact that it had been accumulated under conditions which were now unlawful. Subsequently, every circuit court of appeals in the country agreed with this position[20]—until, that is, a 1977 Supreme Court seven-to-two ruling which upended this position in a flawed opinion from Justice Potter Stewart, with Justices Thurgood Marshall and William Brennan writing in support of my position in a dissent.[21]

In any event, the upshot was that, subsequent to the report, upward progression in employment was available to Black workers for a decade. What happened thereafter is addressed in chapter 6. Meanwhile, notwithstanding the unpopularity of my views on this conflict—I differed with most of the labor movement and much of the labor law world—I fostered some great friendships. Winn Newman, whom I had first met at the International Union of Electricians (IUE) and other unions like the American Federation of State and Municipal Employees (AFSME), became a great friend after much argumentation. Winn actually approached me on a Washington sidewalk and apologized for the position he had taken in the seniority conflict. We became good friends and allies in the Title VII arena and other matters. His premature death saddened me very much.

Across the Atlantic in Great Britain, fair employment problems and mechanisms, which I wrote about after a 1967 visit to that country,[22] were also starting to gain new attention. Britain's Race Relations Board, designed, like our EEOC, to address racial discrimination, came into existence in London in 1965; its formation coincided with a couple of my trips there in the late sixties. While in London, I met with its first chairman, Mark Bonham-Carter. Subsequently, its leading staffer, John Lyttle, and lawyers Anthony

Lester and Geoffrey Bindman came to New York to discuss my EEOC work with me—the first of a number of meetings with people concerned with this issue on the other side of the Atlantic.

ARBITRATION ON MY OWN

As 1966 blended into 1967, I began to do more arbitration of two kinds. First, there were numerous substitutions for Ted Kheel; in February and April 1967 I issued cease and desist orders obliging the National Maritime Union (NMU) not to engage in strikes in violation of their voluntarily negotiated no-strike clause. My unproven suspicion was that some of Ted's absences and my consequent opportunity were due to the unpopularity of this issue with the NMU. Nevertheless, this was a great chance for me, and I had no hesitation whatsoever in issuing the orders which, in my view, were provided by the collective bargaining agreement and an integral part of the arbitral dispute resolution process.

These cases presented not only issues of labor arbitration but also of labor law. At the time of my opinions and awards, the Supreme Court had held that the federal courts could not issue injunctions remedying no-strike violations because of the broad prohibitions against injunctions contained in an earlier statute, the Norris-LaGuardia Act of 1932.[23] But the Court had not addressed the question of whether an arbitrator could perform the same function through a voluntarily agreed-upon arbitration award which could be enforced in court—and the maritime cases before me produced litigation on this issue in which the NMU prevailed at the district courts level.[24] Ultimately, the Supreme Court reversed itself and made injunctions (as well as arbitral orders such as mine) available when the no-strike clause was violated and the underlying matter giving rise to the strike could be arbitrated.[25] So, the Supreme Court ruling ultimately upheld the ruling that I made as an arbitrator—in contrast to the seniority discrimination victories which were reversed by the court.

I began to arbitrate cases where I was chosen as arbitrator on my own, through the lists of organizations like the American Arbitration Association and the Federal Mediation and Conciliation Service, rather than simply as a substitute for Kheel. One of my very first cases, in which I was appointed by the New Jersey Mediation Board, involved the Steel Workers and the National Lead Company;[26] others followed soon thereafter. These appointments began to come about through contacts and exposure that I acquired in Ted Kheel's office as well as from my UAW days.

Another important part of my work at this time was my selection as a neutral in the rapidly growing public sector labor market. The sixties witnessed belated but rapid union growth amongst public employees. State and municipal workers are covered by state and local laws, in contrast to the private sector where labor law, for the most part, is federal law. As I've noted, the right to strike, generally considered to be a fundamental part of the collective bargaining process in the private sector, has been hotly debated in the public sector.

My Mount Vernon dispute was the first in New York[27] after the formation of the three-person fact-finding board by the Public Employment Relations Board. James McFadden, Mayor Wagner's labor commissioner and a confidante of Ted Kheel, was the chairman of the board. I think that McFadden knew the labyrinthian political aspects of the matter. I wrote the board's report and both sides seemed to find it acceptable. This was the first of a number of appointments for me as fact finder in New York, Michigan, California, Nevada, Florida, Arkansas, and elsewhere which, coupled with conventional arbitrations usually involving grievance issues and the interpretation of collective bargaining agreements, as well as "interest" disputes over new contract terms, opened up admission to the blue-ribbon organization of arbitrators, the National Academy of Arbitrators (see also chapter 6).

Through my third boss, Morris Lasker, I represented *Scientific American* in their labor matters. Lasker, ever public spirited, was also involved with the American Civil Liberties Union and he assigned to me the task of writing an amicus, or friend of the court, brief for the ACLU to the United States Supreme Court in *Dennis v. United States*.[28] This case involved the constitutionality of the non-Communist affidavit or oath which union officers were required to execute as a condition for obtaining access to the procedures of the National

ARBITRATION AND MEDIATION

Labor Relations Board. I wrote the brief, which was signed onto by people such as my friend Jack Sheinkman, Gerhard Van Arkel, the NLRB general counsel who resigned in 1947 over Taft-Hartley, and Mel Wulf, the ACLU legal director. I really became involved because Lasker assigned this to me. We prevailed in *Dennis* in 1966—and equally important, I developed a friendship with Mel Wulf that was to be instrumental in the employment litigation in which I would be involved in subsequent years.

Labor Work and RFK

Beyond this EEOC and ACLU work, my other major public policy contributions consisted of a series of initiatives which I undertook on behalf of New York Senator Robert F. Kennedy shortly after his election in 1964. The first of these was an extensive memo that I wrote for him through his legislative aide, Peter Edelman, proposing reform in the national emergency labor disputes arena.[29] Emergency strikes involved matters such as strikes and walkouts in longshore or docks in which the president and Congress had intervened on an ad hoc basis, as well as airline disputes in which the rank and file had rejected union leadership-negotiated agreements. The prospect of a national dispute in trucking was on the mind of many, given the strength of Jimmy Hoffa, RFK's nemesis, at that time.

A second piece of work for Senator Kennedy involved Black worker participation in the construction of the Franklin D. Roosevelt Post Office in Manhattan. Here I spent some time representing the senator in an attempt to increase the number of Black workers in construction in the so-called critical crafts. Meetings took place in New York City on May 25, 1967, at the offices of John Tishman, the realty magnate, on Fifth Avenue. I reported to Senator Kennedy as follows:

> *Throughout the entire discussion Tishman assumed a very offended attitude. Although the number of minority group employees working on the Franklin D Roosevelt project does not indicate that he has done so much about the problem, Tishman seemed to think that he had done more than others in construction. Tishman specifically requested*

that I remind Senator Kennedy that he, Tishman, and James Scheur, had requested President Kennedy to sign the Executive Order dealing with racial discrimination and government contractors before it was signed.[30]

Both Hilda and I had some in-person contact with RFK at the end of 1967. His Christmas card hinted that Vietnam and the consequent declining interest in and support for anti-poverty programs by the Johnson administration made RFK a potential candidate for the presidency. We briefly chatted with him at a Rockefeller Center skating party for campaign volunteers and spouses in early January '68. I met with him and a group of other volunteers in his Manhattan apartment shortly thereafter, but I was not involved in the campaign itself, which commenced in earnest after Eugene McCarthy's strong New Hampshire primary showing against Lyndon Johnson.

Figures 5.1, 5.2, 5.3: Continued.

ARBITRATION AND MEDIATION 153

Figures 5.1, 5.2, 5.3: Christmas card sent to us along with other RFK supporters, with a hint of a 1968 presidential candidacy.

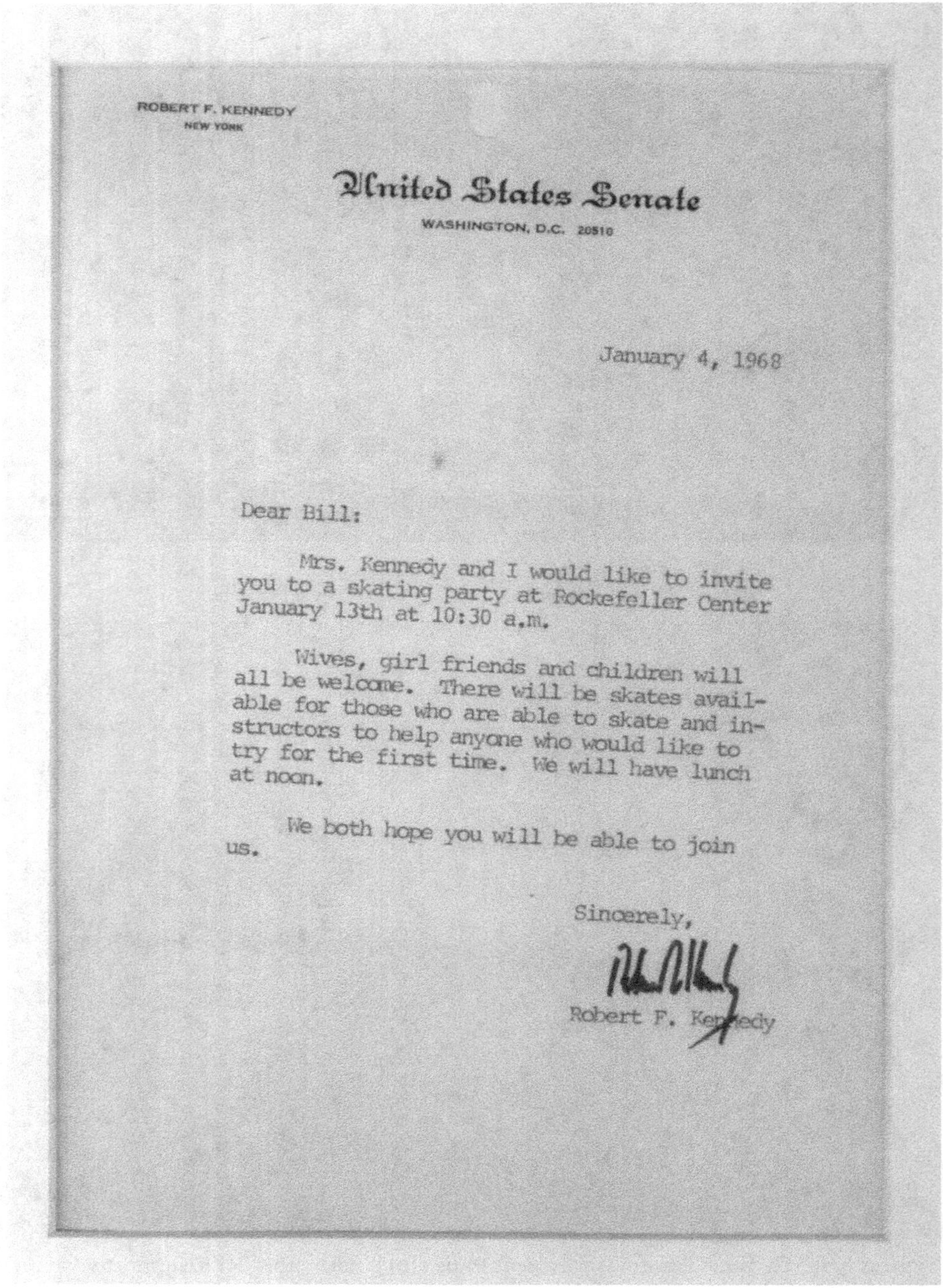

ROBERT F. KENNEDY
NEW YORK

United States Senate
WASHINGTON, D.C. 20510

January 4, 1968

Dear Bill:

Mrs. Kennedy and I would like to invite you to a skating party at Rockefeller Center January 13th at 10:30 a.m.

Wives, girl friends and children will all be welcome. There will be skates available for those who are able to skate and instructors to help anyone who would like to try for the first time. We will have lunch at noon.

We both hope you will be able to join us.

Sincerely,

Robert F. Kennedy

Figure 5.4: The invitation to the Rockefeller Center skating party in January 1968.

The first Hilda and I knew of RFK's tragic assassination in Los Angeles on June 4, 1968, was when we were awakened in our West End Avenue apartment by a radio blaring the horrible news through an open window. This was the second horrific experience that we and the country had endured in a matter of months, the first having been Martin Luther King Jr.'s murder in Memphis on April 4. On the night of that tragedy, after returning from work, I looked north from 103rd Street, where we lived, and could see Harlem's fires raging brightly against the night sky. The assassination of these men, along with JFK in '63, created an aura of profound sadness, instability, and the sense across the country that peaceable reform was literally cut down.

U.S. INDUSTRIES, AND A DETROIT REUNION

Nineteen sixty-seven had already witnessed violent racial upheaval in Newark and Detroit, and I'd been brought closer to it in the wake of my EEOC assignment, as I returned to Battle Creek for more U.S. Industries negotiations. This round of sessions took place with the Michigan Federation of Teachers about staff at the Custer Job Corps. As a result, I began to drive more frequently to Detroit to see old friends and make some new ones. I also had the dubious pleasure of watching my Boston Red Sox lose three out of four games to the Tigers. I saw those three losing games and experienced their Dunkirk moment with them, as they fell about seven games behind on the cusp of the All-Star Game. But that was before their relentless march to the pennant and what became known as the Impossible Dream, on the last day of baseball season!

Sometime during this series of visits to Michigan, I reconnected with University of Michigan professor Ted St. Antoine and his wife Lloyd at their Ann Arbor home; we had met in Washington at his law firm shortly before we moved to New York City. Our renewed connection prompted him to recommend me to his ex-colleague, Wayne State Law School's new Dean, Charlie Joiner. It was St. Antoine's contact with Joiner, I later learned, that prompted a phone call inviting me to come back to Detroit for interviews at Wayne

State Law School. As I discussed this with Hilda, before flying to Detroit from New York, I assured her that this trip would probably be just a chance to see and reconnect with my old pals from UAW days. I was enjoying my work in hearings, courtroom and arbitral appearances, and contract negotiations, and I wasn't even sure that I wanted to go into teaching at all, let alone accept a job at Wayne State, which as I remembered consisted of only a small, modest building for classes and a library just a few blocks from the apartment I'd lived in when I was with the UAW in 1961.

But when I arrived in Detroit, I experienced a number of very pleasant surprises. First was the law school itself: a new, modern building had taken the place of the one I remembered. And when I sat down to talk with the faculty and staff, they offered what I wanted in all respects, and more! I could teach both labor and constitutional law, and they suggested the possibility of an employment discrimination seminar, which had never been taught there. Moreover, as the frequency of my arbitration cases in New York had begun to expand, they welcomed my continued work in that area, as well as (1) in the new fact-finding cases that I had begun to be involved with in New York and (2) my involvement in providing advice, legal memoranda, and briefs for the NAACP Legal Defense Fund on Title VII job discrimination cases.

When I disembarked from my flight back to New York, Hilda and I quickly agreed that the Wayne State job made sense. It seemed reasonable to assume that I would have some relief from the unrelenting hours demanded by a New York City law firm and thus be able to devote more time to family matters—but that assumption turned out to be delusional. I was soon to discover that my research, writing, and litigation placed no bounds on time commitments when I was working alone, for myself. But the sweetener was that, in contrast to the past, when higher education was less well financed, Wayne State actually offered me a raise in pay from my modest associate's salary in New York. I accepted their offer.[31]

Hilda and I flew to Detroit in March of 1968 to look for a house. We purchased a rather grand and spacious one at 17364 Fairfield, just a few blocks north of the University of Detroit at Six Mile and

Livernois on the west side. That weekend was momentous not only personally, as we planned a new home, but also because President Johnson announced that he would not seek another term. And, after having watched my Boston Celtics beat the Detroit Pistons on television, we went to the Detroit airport and there, right before us (this was prior to the days of private team jets), a cadre of enormously tall men walked by. It was the Celtics themselves, arriving to continue the series in Detroit! I had first witnessed the Celtics win in 1953, before the days of Bill Russell, at Madison Square Garden, and I'd subsequently traveled through the snows of upstate New York to see them in Syracuse while I was a student at Cornell. More recently I'd marveled at Sam Jones's bank shots at Madison Square Garden. Now, in one of those dreamlike, surreal moments, I met Bill Russell, Sam Jones, and Bailey Howell, and observed K. C. Jones and John Havlicek nearby. We returned to New York on an absolute high.

WRAPPING UP IN NEW YORK

But there was still much work to do at my New York firm. I represented Proctor & Gamble in more arbitrations, which took me on the New York ferry over to Staten Island, where the company was located. (The ferry in those days cost a nickel!) In another case that occupied much of my time in '67 and '68, I represented the New Jersey-based General Gravure Company, working often at the NLRB's Newark office. The General Gravure case involved me personally in negotiating a second collective bargaining agreement with the New Jersey Lithographer and Photoengraver Local 205. General Gravure's vice president, William Donohue, and I had a series of negotiations with the local on a wide variety of issues, reaching agreement on some of them, but getting absolutely stuck on the union's insistence that the agreement provide the union with a veto over the introduction of new equipment or technological innovations.

Throughout the negotiations our client, Donohue, kept asking me how long bargaining would take and what the end game was, so to speak. I advised him that the company couldn't act unilaterally and implement its own position on any conditions of employment until either an agreement was reached—but there is no statutory requirement that either side enter into an agreement, I told him—or until the parties deadlocked or reached an impasse in negotiations. When deadlock or impasse are reached, he (and my students, in future years) would often ask how both of these terms could be defined. And I stressed then, as I have with my students in labor law, that the answer is frequently difficult to discern or provide.

Bargaining between the parties had commenced in early 1967, and after a lengthy session on a snowy St Patrick's Day morning in the Kheel firm offices, the union reiterated its veto demand over any technological change. When I rejected it on behalf of the company, the union representatives said that there was nothing more to talk about, stood up as they gathered their papers, and promptly walked out. "Now," Bill Donohue said to me after they had departed, "Can't we go ahead and implement our position on all employment conditions?" The discussions had taken place on a Friday morning; Friday afternoon and the weekend were still in front of us. I told Bill that we should sit tight, let the dust settle, and keep our cards close to the vest.

The weekend passed with no action. Then, on Monday morning, the telephone rang. It was the union representative, asking, "When is our next meeting?" Had I jumped the gun and advised the company to go ahead with the changes it wanted to make, I'm confident that the NLRB would have rebuked us, holding that we had refused to bargain in good faith and, most importantly, making any strike the union might initiate an unfair labor practice strike. (A holding that the strike had been caused or prolonged by unfair labor practices entitles the strikers not only to reinstatement, but also to back pay under some circumstances.)

Ultimately, as spring moved into summer and no agreement was reached, the union filed refusal to bargain unfair labor practice charges with the NLRB against the company, but after an extensive investigation, the charges were dismissed by the NLRB regional office.

Then a new chapter developed in the story, the backdrop of which was a Supreme Court ruling rendered a few months after the St. Patrick's Day conflict and its aftermath. *NLRB v. Allis-Chalmers* held five to four that a union could impose fines on members who crossed their picket lines and thus undermined a strike.[32] When an agreement between General Gravure and the local was not concluded, the local had a meeting at which it determined that its members should not accept overtime assignments, and that a picket line would be established without calling for a full-blown strike. Union members who did not adhere to the union's no-overtime policy would be fined.

In the five-to-four *Allis-Chalmers* ruling, a closely divided High Court held that the union could impose fines upon workers who crossed the union's picket line on the grounds that this conduct was inconsistent with union membership or "unbecoming a union member." The heart of the majority opinion authored by Justice William Brennan was that the authority to impose fines or sanctions was predicated not only upon the statutory promotion of a union's right to strike but also was rooted in contract—the contract that the member and union had entered into through acceptance of membership. The obvious and logical conclusion that flowed from this was that if there was no membership, there was no contract and, logically, no authority to impose fines.

My own view was that *Allis-Chalmers* heralded the importance of a right to resign as part of a right not to participate in concerted activities—although I also held the view that a union could impose reasonable restrictions on this right to resign when it was implemented to promote the solidarity that the strike requires, an interest that was at the heart of the court's reasoning in *Allis-Chalmers*. I later expressed this view in some law review articles which I authored[33], and on a cold, rainy day in December during my first year at Stanford in 1972, I eagerly tore open the December 7 advance sheets of a Supreme Court ruling on a case that I thought might undercut me.[34] But it didn't, in the final analysis. Nonetheless, the court soon did so subsequently, when it said that the right to resign was absolute.[35]

However, in my General Gravure case, my client, Bill Donohue, called to tell me of his concern that he would lose key workers who wouldn't cross the picket line; he asked for advice on what to do.

I had examined the union's constitution, which placed no restriction upon resignation. My advice to Donohue was to tell the workers that they could resign if they wished to avoid the fine, stressing that the company was in no way encouraging the workers to do so. The union, which later took the position that resignation could be exercised under the union's constitution only through either leaving the industry or death itself, persisted with fines against those who crossed the picket line.

I prepared and filed unfair labor practice charges against the union with the Newark region of the NLRB which argued, as did my briefs, that the right to resign through leaving the industry or through death effectively barred resignation altogether and was therefore unlawfully restricting and coercing employees under the Act. Since, I argued, *Allis-Chalmers* was predicated upon a contract that required an agreement between member and union, its holding that the union could impose fines under some circumstances disappeared when the right to resign was lawfully exercised. Amazingly, the NLRB region refused to issue a complaint, which is the prerequisite for an unfair labor practice proceeding—the standard for issuance being that there must be "cause" to believe that an unfair labor practice had been committed. When I was rejected in Newark, I filed an appeal inside the NLRB General Counsel's offices in Washington. They reversed Newark and the case went to trial before a trial examiner who dismissed the complaint, putting me right back where I started, just as I was packing my bags to leave New York for Detroit in the summer of '68.

Ultimately, I was vindicated when, two years after my New York departure, the NLRB held that the charge by General Gravure and the complaint of the general counsel contained merit, and that the union had engaged in unfair labor practice conduct which "restrained" or "coerced" the workers who objected to their fines.[36] At this point I took satisfaction in the victory, obtained though it was when I was far away.

A Controversial Speech, and the Joys of Baseball

As the last months wound down in New York City's hot summer of '68, I gave a speech to the Tri-County Long Island Labor–Management Institute. My topic was one that I would reiterate in the years to come, and it continuously ruffled feathers:

> *Let me be frank about where I think the blame lies for the current racial tensions. While it is true that most industrial unions have little if anything to say about hiring policies— and that racial discrimination in employment generally preceded the advent of the labor movement, the national labor movement—both the craft and industrial unions— must shoulder a very major portion of the responsibility for the white racism, which, according to the Kerner Report, lies at the heart of the ever-increasing and self-destructive polarization of the races which we witness today.*[37]

Now, speech and New York work completed, I flew to Detroit to join Hilda and our two boys (a third boy, Edward Blair, was to be born in Detroit shortly thereafter) to begin my work at Wayne State Law School. But it wasn't long before I found myself at Tiger Stadium with my friend Julian Cook, watching the Sox drop two, the second one in extra innings on a homer by Gates Brown off Lee Stange. My enthusiasm for my Red Sox, while in Detroit, remained so solid that I started to be recognized around town. For example, when I went to one of my favorite Detroit pizza places—Buddy's, at Six Mile and Conant—a little girl turned to her father and said, "Daddy, there is the man who roots for the Red Sox." Nothing like that could have happened in New York.

Back in 1960, when I was clerking for the UAW, I leaped to my feet cheering a bases-loaded single by Frank Malzone—but the rest of the crowd was so quiet that you could hear the footsteps of the runners. To prove the point emphatically, in a period when there was a three-way competition between the Red Sox, Tigers, and

Baltimore Orioles, a neighbor's son said to his parents, "Mr. Gould is a law professor? I thought he was the manager of the Baltimore Orioles." In New York City, my enthusiasm was similarly discernable: I rushed to Yankee Stadium in September of '66 to watch the Red Sox squeeze out a ninth-place finish over the Yankees, who finished tenth or last. The year after, I returned to our West Side apartment at 3 a.m. after witnessing a twilight doubleheader between the same teams, the nightcap lasting until the twenty-first inning!

But now, in Detroit, I settled into what was to be a new career inflection point: a teaching job at Wayne State Law School, and an assortment of litigation and dispute resolution assignments that would present new and exciting challenges.

NOTES

[1] Fibreboard Paper Products Corp. v. NLRB, 379 U.S. 203 (1964).
[2] *International Hod Carriers, Local No. 41*, 133 N.L.R.B. 512 (1961); *Houston Building and Construction Trades Council*, 136 N.L.R.B. 321 (1962); Local 259, UAW, 133 N.L.R.B. 1468 (1961).
[3] William B. Gould IV, "The Question of Union Activity on Company Property," *Vanderbilt Law Review* 18 (1964); William B. Gould IV, "Union Organizational Rights and the Concept of 'Quasi-Public' Property," *Minnesota Law Review* 49 (1965).
[4] Lechmere v. N.L.R.B., 502 U.S. 527 (1992); NLRB cases involving Lechmere in which Gould concurred with Republican appointees.
[5] "Labour and the Law," *The Economist*, October 10, 1964, 153.
[6] William B. Gould IV, "Unions are scoring big wins for workers. Why isn't membership surging?," *Washington Post*, February 28, 2024.
[7] "Bargaining in Court," *The Economist*, June 12, 1965, 1279.
[8] Jonathan Eig, *King: A Life* (New York: Farrar, Straus and Giroux, 2023), 356.
[9] *City of Mount Vernon and Mount Vernon Police Ass'n*, 49 BNA LA 1229 (1968) (McFadden, Gould, and Karow, Fact-Finders).
[10] Paul R. Hays, *Labor Arbitration: A Dissenting View* (New Haven: Yale University Press, 1966); Paul R. Hays, "The Future of Labor Arbitration," *Yale Law Journal* 74 (1965).
[11] Commentators have suggested that tripartite or trilateral arbitration might answer this power dynamic problem. Edgar A. Jones Jr., "Autobiography of a Decision: The Function of Innovation in Labor Arbitration, and the National Steel Orders of Joinder and Interpleader," *UCLA Law Review* 10 (1963); Edgar A. Jones Jr., "An Arbitral Answer to a Judicial Dilemma: The Carey Decision and Trilateral Arbitration of Jurisdictional Disputes," *UCLA Law Review* 11 (1964); Merton Bernstein, "Nudging and Shoving All Parties to a Jurisdictional Dispute into Arbitration: The Dubious

Procedure of National Steel," *Harvard Law Review* 78 (1965); Edgar A. Jones Jr., "On Nudging and Shoving the National Steel Arbitration into A Dubious Procedure," *Harvard Law Review* 79 (1965). P&A Constr. Inc. v. Int'l Union of Operating Engineers Loc. 825, 19 F.4th 217 (3d Cir. 2021).

[12] William B. Gould IV, "Expanding Opportunities," *Commonweal* 81 (December 4, 1964); William B. Gould IV, review of *Portrait of a Decade*, by Anthony Lewis, *Commonweal* 81 (March 12, 1963); William B. Gould IV, review of *Unfinished Revolution*, by C. L. Sulzberger, *Commonweal* 82 (September 24, 1965); William B. Gould IV, review of *British Politics in the Collectivist Age*, by Samuel H. Beer, *Commonweal* 84 (April 22, 1966); William B. Gould IV, review of *Hoffa and the Teamsters*, by Ralph James and Estelle James, and *Tentacles of Power*, by Clark R. Mollenhoff, *Commonweal* 84 (June 24, 1966); William B. Gould IV, review of *The Politics of Socialism*, by R. H. S. Crossman, *Commonweal* 85 (November 25, 1966); William B. Gould IV, review of *The Limits of American Capitalism*, by Robert L. Heilbroner, *Commonweal* 86 (June 9, 1967); William B. Gould IV, review of *The Labor Revolution*, by Gus Tyler, *Commonweal* 87 (February 9, 1968); William B. Gould IV, review of *A Constitutional Faith*, by Hugo Lafayette Black, and *Disobedience and Democracy*, by Howard Zinn, *Commonweal* 90 (April 25, 1969).

[13] William B. Gould IV, "Labor Law & The Negro," *New Leader* 47, no. 21 (1964): 10; William B. Gould IV, "Managing Emergency Strikes," *New Leader* 49, no. 6 (1966): 14; William B. Gould IV, "Labor Law for the Future," *New Leader* 44, no. 7 (1961): 27 (reviewing *Law and the National Labor Policy* by Archibald Cox); William B. Gould IV, "Race and the Unions," *New Leader* 48, no. 14 (1965): 20 (reviewing T*he Negro and Organized Labor* by Ray Marshall); William B. Gould IV, "Test of Strength," *New Leader* 49, no. 18 (1966): 22 (reviewing *Kohler on Strike* by Walter H. Uphoff).

[14] William B. Gould IV, "The Status of Unauthorized and 'Wildcat' Strikes Under the National Labor Relations Act," *Cornell Law Quarterly* 52 (1967).

[15] *Silver State Disposal Serv., Inc.*, 326 N.L.R.B. 84, 88–90 (1998) (Chairman Gould, concurring).

[16] NLRB v. Noah's Ark Processors, *LLC*, 31 F.4th 1097, 1104-06 (8th Cir. 2022). The Court of Appeals wrote: In the nearly fifty years since *Emporium Capwell* was decided, the Board and reviewing courts have agreed that decision did not "strip the NLRA's protection from all wildcat strikes." CC1 Ltd. P'ship v. NLRB, 898 F.3d 26, 34 (D.C. Cir. 2018). Rather, a case-by-case analysis is needed to determine whether a particular concerted work stoppage is protected by Section 7. See, e.g., E. Chicago Rehab. Ctr., Inc. v. NLRB, 710 F.2d 397, 400-03 (7th Cir. 1983), cert. denied, 465 U.S. 1065 . . . (1984); NLRB v. Bridgeport Ambulance Serv., 966 F.2d 725, 729 (2d Cir. 1992). The Board addressed this issue in *Silver State*, though only the concurring member discussed *Emporium Capwell* in detail. 326 N.L.R.B. at 85 n8, 103–104. *Silver State* involved a work stoppage that allegedly violated the no-strike clause of an unexpired CBA, but its analysis has been extended to other contexts, including unauthorized work stoppages. See, e.g., CC1 Ltd. P'ship, 898 F.3d at 30. In *Silver State*, the employer terminated a garbage truck driver who had served as president of an employee committee that picketed the employer's headquarters to demonstrate dissatisfaction with the employer and their union. A few days later, the truck driver arrived to pick up his last paycheck and began speaking about his termination. A crowd of employees gathered

outside the facility, refused to begin their shift, and gathered in a nearby vacant lot when police arrived and directed them to leave the facility. When a supervisor appealed to them to return to work, the employees attempted to comply but were turned away by the employer's security staff; 71 were then terminated for an unauthorized work stoppage. The employees grieved their termination; the union met with the employer to urge their reinstatement. After a hearing, the ALJ concluded that *Emporium Capwell* did not apply because, while the committee's earlier picketing was inconsistent with the union's exclusive representation, the later work stoppage was "exclusively related to the termination of Crockett and the processing of his grievance." 326 NLRB at 104. The ALJ found the work stoppage unprotected under the CBA's no-strike clause but condoned by the employer. Therefore, the termination violated Section 8(a)(1). Reaching the same result by a different path, the board found that the employer "has not established that the work stoppage violated the no-strike clause" and therefore "the employees did not lose the protection of the Act." Id. at 85. The panel majority adopted the ALJ's *Emporium Capwell* analysis in a footnote. Id. at 85 n8. Chairman Gould, concurring, addressed this issue at length:

> "[Prior Board decisions] proceed on the assumption that, if there is an identity or similarity of objectives between the union and individual employees, an unauthorized stoppage is protected under the Act. . . . This approach . . . is both naive and misguided. . . . The fact of the matter is that, generally speaking, union and employee goals . . . both before and during negotiations and indeed right through the eleventh hour, are going to be nearly identical if not synonymous. Both . . . want to improve the living standards and protect the job security of the employees. This is as it should be. . . . The Board should discard the thesis that disagreement or agreement about the substantive goals of the strike is relevant to the protected status of the worker's conduct. The key consideration in determining whether the worker's conduct undermines or derogates the exclusive bargaining representative concept is whether there is some consistency or accord between the union and the strikers on the question of strategy and timing. . . . It is consensus about strategy that the Board should look to, not identity of substantive goals as it has in the past. . . . If, for instance, a union wants to delay use of the strike weapon to a time that it deems to be more propitious, it is hard to imagine something that is more inconsistent with the exclusivity concept than a strike at another time. Yet, under the Board's present approach, so long as identity of substantive goals is found to exist, the activity is protected. This approach creates havoc with union policy, good industrial relations, and the sound administration of our Act. . . . And it promotes the balkanization with which Emporium is at war." Id. at 89–90.

Unfortunately, the Board has not followed Chairman Gould's sound advice regarding the Supreme Court's controlling interpretation of the relationship between Section 7, Section 8(a)(1), and Section 9(a) in *Emporium Capwell*. In this case, for example, both the panel majority and dissent stated that the Board determines whether an unauthorized work stoppage is protected "by considering (1) whether the employees were attempting to bypass their union and bargain directly with the employer, and (2) whether the employees' position was inconsistent with the union's position." Dec. & Order p.2.6. Here, the ten employees questioned management whether *Noah's Ark* was complying with terms and conditions of the holdover CBA. Without question, as Chairman Gould explained, the Union would share the employees' substantive position on this issue. Indeed, the Union's duty as exclusive representative arguably required it to pursue the employees' position, by grievance or otherwise. Thus, if the Board had held that the employees' work stoppage was protected concerted activity *merely because* it was not inconsistent with the Union's unstated position on this issue, we would decline to enforce this part of the Board's order as inconsistent with the Supreme Court's decision in *Emporium Capwell*.

[17] TCI W, Inc. v. NLRB, 145 F.3d 1113 (9th Cir. 1998).

[18] William B. Gould IV, "The Negro Revolution and the Law of Collective Bargaining," *Fordham Law Review* 34 (1965); Cf. Whitfield v. United Steel Workers of America, 263 F.2d 546, 551 (5th Cir. 1959) (Wisdom, J.) ("Angels could do no more.").

[19] William B. Gould IV, "Title VII of the Civil Rights Act at Fifty: Ruminations on Past, Present, and Future," *Santa Clara Law Review* 54 (2014).

[20] Teamsters v. United States, 431 U.S. 324, 378 (1977) (Marshall, J., concurring) ("Without a single dissent, six Courts of Appeals have so held in over 30 cases") (citing Acha v. Beame, 531 F.2d 648 (2d Cir. 1976); United States v. Bethlehem Steel Corp., 446 F.2d 652 (2d Cir. 1971); Nance v. Union Carbide Corp., 540 F.2d 718 (4th Cir. 1976); Patterson v. American Tobacco Co., 535 F.2d 257 (4th Cir. 1976); Russell v. American Tobacco Co., 528 F.2d 357 (4th Cir. 1975); Hairston v. McLean Trucking Co., 520 F.2d 226 (4th Cir. 1975); United States v. Chesapeake & Ohio R. Co., 471 F.2d 582 (4th Cir. 1972); Robinson v. Lorillard Corp., 444 F.2d 791 (4th Cir. 1971); Griggs v. Duke Power Co., 420 F.2d 1225 (4th Cir. 1970); Swint v. Pullman-Standard, 539 F.2d 77 (5th Cir. 1976); Sagers v. Yellow Freight System, 529 F.2d 721 (5th Cir. 1976); Sabala v. Western Gillette, Inc., 516 F.2d 1251 (5th Cir. 1975); Gamble v. Birmingham Southern R. Co., 514 F.2d 678 (5th Cir. 1975); Resendis v. Lee Way Motor Freight, Inc., 505 F.2d 69 (5th Cir. 1974); Herrera v. Yellow Freight System, Inc., 505 F.2d 66 (5th Cir. 1974); Carey v. Greyhound Bus Co., 500 F.2d 1372 (5th Cir. 1974); Pettway v. American Cast Iron Pipe Co., 494 F.2d 211 (5th Cir. 1974); Johnson v. Goodyear Tire & Rubber Co., 491 F.2d 1364 (5th Cir. 1974); Bing v. Roadway Express, Inc., 485 F.2d 441 (5th Cir. 1973); United States v. Georgia Power Co., 474 F.2d 906 (5th Cir. 1973); United States v. Jacksonville Terminal Co., 451 F.2d 418 (5th Cir. 1971); Long v. Georgia Kraft Co., 450 F.2d 557 (5th Cir. 1971); Taylor v. Armco Steel Corp., 429 F.2d 498 (5th Cir. 1970); Local 189, United Papermakers & Paperworkers v. United States, 416 F.2d 980 (5th Cir. 1969); EEOC v. Detroit Edison Co., 515 F.2d 301 (6th Cir. 1975); Palmer v. General Mills, Inc., 513 F.2d 1040 (6th Cir. 1975); Head v. Timken Roller Bearing Co., 486 F.2d 870 (6th Cir. 1973); Bailey v. American Tobacco Co., 462 F.2d 160 (6th Cir. 1972); Rogers v. International Paper Co., 510 F.2d 1340 (8th Cir. 1975); United States v. N. L. Industries, Inc., 479 F.2d 354 (8th Cir. 1973); Gibson v. Longshoremen, 543 F.2d 1259 (9th Cir. 1976); United States v. Navajo Freight Lines, Inc., 525 F.2d 1318 (9th Cir. 1975).

[21] Teamsters v. United States, 431 U.S. 324 (1977); William B. Gould IV, "Seniority and the Black Worker: Reflections on Quarles and its Implications," *Texas Law Review* 47 (1969).

[22] William B. Gould IV, "No Coloured Need Apply," *Commonweal* 88 (March 22, 1968).

[23] Atkinson v. Sinclair Refining Co., 370 U.S. 238 (1962).

[24] I issued an arbitration award in *In Re Arbitration* between *Nat'l Maritime Union of Am. and Marine Transport Lines, Inc.* (February 17, 1967). The employer brought a petition to confirm and enforce the arbitral award in the New York County Supreme Court and the case was removed by the union to the Southern District of New York. The district court decided the case along with a parallel petition for enforcement of an award issued by Ted Kheel that raised substantially the same issues. Marine Transport Lines, Inc. v. Curran, of National Maritime Union, AFL-CIO, No. 67-727, 1967 BL 114 (S.D.N.Y. February 27, 1967) (declining to enforce Ted Kheel's arbitral award); *In re Marine Transport Lines, Inc. v. Curran, of National Maritime Union, AFL-CIO*, No. 67-726 (S.D.N.Y. February 27, 1967) (declining to enforce my award). The employer appealed both district court decisions to the Second Circuit, but appeals were dismissed on consent of the parties. Marine Transport Lines, Inc. v. Joseph Curran as President of Nat'l Maritime Union, AFL-CIO, Nos. 31162 and 31163 (2d Cir. May 22, 1967) (dismissing appeal on consent).
Both my and Ted Kheel's arbitral awards are reprinted in the Appellant's Appendix to the Second Circuit in Marine Transport Lines, Inc. v. Joseph Curran as President of Nat'l Maritime Union, AFL-CIO, Nos. 31162 and 31163, (2d Cir. May 1, 1967). In overruling my award, the district court relied on Gulf & S. Am. S. S. Co. v. Nat'l Mar. Union of Am., AFL-CIO, 360 F.2d 63 (5th Cir. 1966) (holding that *Atkinson v. Sinclair*, supra, dictated that the unenforceability of an arbitration award requiring a union to cease and desist from the violation of a no-strike clause in a collective bargaining agreement); accord New Orleans S.S. Ass'n v. Local 1418, Longshore Workers, 389 F.2d 369 (5th Cir.), cert. denied, 393 U.S. 828 (1968). My award reversed by the Southern District of New York was one of a number to the same effect that I rendered in early 1967. *See In Re Arbitration between Nat'l Maritime Union of Am. and Marine Transport Lines, Inc.* (February 20, 1967) (on file with author); *In re Arbitration Between Nat'l Maritime Union of Am., AFL-CIO and States Marine Lines, Inc.* (April 24, 1967) (on file with author); *In re Arbitration Between Nat'l Maritime Union of Am., AFL-CIO and States Marine Lines, Inc.* (April 27, 1967) (on file with author).

[25] Boys Markets, Inc. v. Retail Clerks Union, Local 770, 398 U.S. 235 (1970); William B. Gould IV, "On Labor Injunctions, Unions, and the Judges: The Boys Market Case," *Supreme Court Review* 1970 (1970).

[26] *Nat'l Lead Co. and United Steel Workers of Am., Local 7036*, 48 BNA LA 1161 (May 8, 1967) (Gould, Arbitrator).

[27] *City of Mount Vernon and Mount Vernon Police Ass'n*, 49 BNA LA 1229 (January 10, 1968).

[28] Dennis v. United States, 384 U.S. 855 (1966).

[29] My memorandum was quite similar to the proposals that I set forth in William B. Gould IV, "Managing Emergency Strikes," *The New Leader*, March 14, 1966, 14.

[30] William B. Gould IV, "Memorandum to The Honorable Robert F. Kennedy Regarding Franklin D. Roosevelt Post Office Building Construction: Minority Participation in Construction," May 25, 1967, 5 (on file with author).

31 Somewhere in this period a New York City management labor lawyer, Evan Spelfogel, told me that he thought I had made too many job changes in these years and, though I took his comment to heart, I would make yet another one a few years down the road.
32 N.L.R.B v. Allis-Chalmers Mfg. Co., 388 U.S. 175, 192 (1967) (discussing the "contract theory" of the union–member relationship).
33 William B. Gould IV, "Some Limitations Upon Union Discipline Under the National Labor Relations Act: The Radiations of Allis-Chalmers," *Duke Law Journal* 1970 (1970); William B. Gould IV, "Solidarity Forever – or Hardly Ever: Union Discipline, Taft-Hartley, and the Right of Union Members to Resign," *Cornell Law Review* 66 (1980); William B. Gould IV, "Organized Labor, The Supreme Court, and Harris v. Quinn: Déjà Vu All Over Again?," *Supreme Court Review* 2014 (2014): 133–173.
34 NLRB. v. Granite State Joint Board, Textile Workers Union, Local 1029, 405 U.S. 987 (1972).
35 Pattern Makers v. N.L.R.B., 473 U.S. 95 (1985); William B. Gould IV, "The Burger Court and Labor Law: The Beat Goes On," *San Diego Law Review* 24 (1987).
36 *General Gravure Service Co.*, 186 N.L.R.B. 454 (1970).
37 William B. Gould IV, "The Negro Revolution and the Trade Unionism," speech to the Tri-County Long Island Labor Management Institute, June 23, 1968. Congressman William F. Ryan reprinted my speech in the *Congressional Record* 114. Cong. Rec. 24872 (1968). I also wrote "Having said this, however, I also believe that it is important to take note of the role which certain labor leaders and unions have played in improving the lot of black workingmen and, most significantly, the impact that their efforts have had within the unions and at the workplace over which the unions have jurisdiction."

6

BACK TO DETROIT: WAYNE STATE, PUBLIC EMPLOYEES, AND DETROIT EDISON

The fall of 1968 in Detroit brought for me a flurry of activity. Not only did I have to prepare for and teach two brand-new law school classes, but I also had a busy "extracurricular" life. My New York Taylor Law experience drew me quickly and naturally into the upheavals and new developments in the public employee sector then taking place in Michigan. Coordinating my teaching, writing, and public sector arbitration cases could be daunting at times, but I was eager to be involved in all of it.

JUMPING INTO TEACHING

My first full-time teaching position did not begin with the "light load" that law schools today often offer new faculty. At Wayne State I immediately began to teach two courses: Labor Law and Constitutional Law. Constitutional law was my primary interest and first love in the law (notwithstanding the fact that the overwhelming percentage of my practice had been in labor law), but teaching it was to present multiple and considerable challenges. Fortunately for the country—but, as a practical matter, unfortunately for me—a substantial number of the key decisions in my old Constitutional Law Dowling casebook from Cornell Law School had been overturned by the Warren Court in the 1960s. This meant a frantic scramble on my part to prepare for my classes that fall. Sometimes my discoveries were so belated that I had to appreciably alter what I planned to say on the eve of my lecture. On more than one occasion I called Hilda before class, saying, "I don't know what I'm going to say." Hilda would always respond, "I have confidence in you." In retrospect I wonder: Was this evidence of her confidence in my ability, or an assessment of my garrulous tendencies? There wasn't time to ask.

In fact, no one taught me or provided guidance about how to teach. All I can recall is the sage advice of Wayne State Law Dean Charlie Joiner: "Always tell it to them twice."

No Mr. Chips

The classroom processes of the sixties contrasted sharply with my Cornell student days. Back then, students wore ties and jackets to every class—not in 1968. The so-called Socratic method, whereby professors asked questions and called on students by name to answer them, now seemed less popular or uniform. While I asked questions of my students, I rarely called on them. At Cornell, the opposite had been true, and it produced some cruel consequences. On one occasion, a professor called on a student who was particularly diligent in preparation. That day he was not. The professor said, "You better make sure to be prepared next time. Because one rotten apple in the barrel will spoil all the rest." The impact was devastating.

Throughout my years of teaching, I have become quite close to a number of students, particularly my research assistants. I have watched them and attempted to promote them as their careers unfolded. But I have never been a Mr. Chips,[1] and I have never been the best of teachers. In truth, I came into the law school world because I had ideas about my field that I wanted to put on paper. And I thought—and think—that I write well. That skill, plus my real-world connection to arbitration and labor contract negotiation—and my belief in the possibility of greater fairness through the law, were the driving considerations behind my decision to take up teaching, not the process of teaching itself. In those early years of teaching, in fact, my wife often said that she hoped our sons would not have me as a professor.

PUBLIC EDUCATION ARBITRATION

The Michigan Employment Relations Commission (MERC) possesses jurisdiction over public sector labor–management relations. In retrospect, I realize that soon after my return to Detroit I quickly became the commission's "go-to guy" in the public sector. While it is possible that race constituted a factor in my newfound popularity, given the substantial number of Black workers in the public sector—surely the UAW had wanted a Black lawyer, given their large Black membership—in fact, I now had a New York public sector track record. My work with New York's Public Employment Relations Board and the fact-finding board created to administer the Taylor Law, placed me in some demand.

MERC chose me as a fact finder in a number of their employment disputes, which were occurring with increasing frequency, particularly in public education. One of the first such cases was in Inkster, a town with a predominately Black population near Detroit, where the dispute involved differences between teacher demands (set forth via the Michigan Employee Association) and consequent tensions in a district that possessed little revenue, due in part to low property taxes and inadequate resources to tax. That the parties accepted my recommendations seemed to be an achievement: "The report [of the fact finder] is not completely satisfactory to either side," said a spokesman for the association, "so it may do the trick."[2] And Inkster Superintendent Edward Fort praised what he called the "superior fact finding."[3] Thus, the report appeared to be acceptable to both sides, and successful.

But soon thereafter I was plunged into a more formidable dispute between the community of Gibraltar and its school board, and the Education Association. In this case, I issued a report which the Education Association accepted but the community and school board rejected. Said the *Detroit News*: "The threat of a teacher strike in the downriver Gibraltar school district loomed today as school board members balked at a recommended contract settlement."[4] This dispute produced what was, at that time, the longest strike in Michigan school district history.[5] Whatever praise had come my way in Inkster now seemed lost in the acrimony that followed in

Gibraltar. Nonetheless, there were more cases, and frequently they emerged (with some prodding on my part) into mediation. This process and procedure were quite labor intensive, and on more than one occasion I was still working with the parties as we saw the sun rise in the morning.

I traveled to these Michigan school districts—Gibraltar, Saginaw, Swartz Creek, and others—in my very first purchased car, a 1968 Volkswagen. Driving to the suburbs and small towns in that car gave me an awareness of life outside Detroit—and, parenthetically, I noticed that high schools were now playing football on Friday nights, a practice unknown to high school students of my generation in the fifties.

My involvement with education sector arbitration in Michigan had a long arc. Slightly more than two decades later, long after I had taken a position at Stanford, I was called upon to arbitrate a wage dispute between the Detroit Federation of Teachers and the Detroit Board of Education. This was a so-called interest arbitration, a resolution of a dispute about the new contract terms of a collective bargaining agreement. In this Detroit case, I used a process similar to one I had undertaken in an earlier firefighter wage and economics benefit case, arising under a Michigan statute in which I had the authority to bind both sides to an enforceable award, in contrast to the authority simply to make recommendations—something I had done in many public education cases where I was a fact finder.

In the Detroit wage case, I was designated as chairman of a tripartite board: Doug Fraser, a former United Auto Workers president whom I knew from my UAW days, was the union representative on the board, and Roger Allen was the Board of Education's arbitration representative. Both these gentlemen were extremely helpful in coordinating with the parties and assisting through five days of Detroit hearings, several of which spilled over into the evening. We were extremely fortunate to have top-notch legal representatives in the labor law arena on both sides: Ted Sachs for the teachers' union and George Roumell for the Board of Education.

Ultimately, after numerous meetings, we awarded a 5 percent increase which, we said:

> while not compatible with the comparability factor and one which will allow the Detroit teachers' position to erode further, is nonetheless the appropriate one given the financial difficulties confronted by the Employer as well as the need to have additional monies available for education.[6]

WRITING AND PUBLISHING

During my first year back in Detroit, in addition to teaching, fact-finding in the public sector, and hearing occasional arbitration cases, I also wrote a number of law review articles. Fundamentally, most were based on ideas I had developed in private practice before coming to teaching—I had simply lacked the time in which to put pen to paper. One was a direct result of my public sector experiences.[7]

Two articles focused particularly on the relationship between Title VII's employment discrimination prohibitions and the labor–management relations system. In one, for the *Yale Law Journal*, I addressed the ability of Black or other minority workers to engage in self-help without union authorization or in defiance of the union's position in its role as exclusive bargaining representative.[8] Self-help or direct action through the exercise of economic pressure was frequently the only practical way to resolve a dispute, even though the slow-moving legal avenues were available as well. As Chief Justice Stone said in the landmark ruling, *Steele v. Louisville & N.R. Co.*:

> [Industrial peace] would hardly be attained if a substantial minority of the craft were denied the right to have their interests considered at the conference table and if the final result of the bargaining process were to be the sacrifice of the interests of the minority by the action of a representative chosen by the majority. The only recourse of the minority would be to strike, with the attendant interruption of commerce, which the [Railway Labor] Act seeks to avoid.[9]

The other article was concerned with the grievance-arbitration machinery and the tensions and inconsistencies between it and Title VII. Here, I devised proposals about how the machinery could be adapted and accommodated to the problems posed by arbitration, that is, the near absence of Blacks, other minorities, and women from the arbitration ranks; the unwillingness of arbitrators to use antidiscrimination principles in interpreting collective bargaining agreements; and cases which presented racial tensions between the exclusive representative and minority workers.[10] These articles were to have an impact on me and my subsequent career, as well as on the law. Wayne State Law School reviewed my work and writings within one year of my arrival, and in 1969 awarded me tenure—that had an impact on my career. As for my impact on the law, the Supreme Court relied upon my arbitration piece in the following decade.[11]

The article on self-help by protesting Black workers, while ultimately ignored by the Court,[12] was to attract the attention of three individuals whose interest in it and in me would turn out to be important in my future career: Roderick (Rod) Hills, a Los Angeles lawyer and visiting professor at Harvard Law School who became chairman of the Securities and Exchange Commission in 1975, and with whom I had become friendly when I gave talks in L.A. through a mutual pal, labor editor Harry Bernstein of the *Los Angeles Times*; Derrick Bell, the first Black law professor at Harvard Law School; and Dean Derek Bok, also of Harvard Law. At this time, Bell was the *only* Black law professor at Harvard—and most of the leading law school faculties were lily white as well (a matter I discuss in chapter 8). Bell and Bok invited me to preside over a student moot court at Harvard which they had devised in conjunction with some of the Black students interested in labor law. My participation led, some months later, to an offer to be a Visiting Professor of Law at Harvard Law.

My writing portfolio also included briefs: I strengthened my ties with the NAACP Legal Defense Fund through briefs I wrote for them in 1969 and 1970. In the brief for one case, *Taylor v. Armco Steel*,[13] I relied on some of my earlier consulting work for the EEOC, on articles resulting from that work, and on material I had pulled together for my own employment discrimination law seminar,[14] the first such seminar offered at Wayne State Law School.

Taylor, a per curiam-like reversal of the district court denial of Black workers' accumulated seniority rights, was authored by Judge John Minor Wisdom, one of the Fifth Circuit judges who pioneered equality in the civil rights arena. Judge Wisdom, referencing his own earlier opinion in *Whitfield v. United Steel Workers*,[15] where Black workers had been denied retroactive seniority prior to Title VII, wrote:

> *We rested our decision on the National Labor Relations Act . . . [citing* Steele v. Louisville & N.R. Co. 323 U.S. 192 (1944)*]. . . . Within the context of the NLRA and Steele, Whitfield is defensible. Today, however, the Court must reverse and remand this case to the district court for proceedings consistent with Title VII of the Civil Rights Act of 1964.*[16]

Thus, along with the Fifth Circuit, the weight of authority as reflected in decisions of all courts of appeals relied upon my writings at that time, and I used this material in my newly devised seminar, Employment Discrimination Law, during that first year at Wayne State Law School.

Discrimination in the Construction Industry

During this same period, I began to write and speak about discrimination in the construction industry. In both the *New York Times*[17] and the *Detroit Free Press*,[18] I lauded the Philadelphia Plan, issued in 1969, which imposed goals and timetables for nondiscriminatory hiring on construction employers and unions. At the same time, AFL-CIO leader George Meany was criticizing these mechanisms, advocated by the plan's proponents, for their "implacable hostility" to construction unions. I was critical of so-called voluntary "hometown plans" designed to slow the pace of racial integration by placing authority for progress in the hands of the unions and employers; I knew they would devise their own metrics for determining what constituted both the standards and the progress under them for Black workers.[19]

President Nixon, whom I had always equated with Joe McCarthy, was responsible for the Philadelphia Plan as well as for statutory amendments to Title VII in 1972 which strengthened the enforcement process and remedies available. I praised this.[20] But the Nixon Administration's position on "hometown plans" in construction and the resort to a "Southern strategy," along with the appointment of Peter Brennan, a prominent New York construction union leader,[21] convinced me that he was still the same Nixon I knew in the 1950s. Indeed, in retrospect, I see that the Philadelphia Plan itself was designed by the Nixon administration to divide Blacks and unions.

CONSTITUTIONAL LAW ISSUES

Meanwhile, at the end of my first year at Wayne State, I became involved in Detroit litigation—litigation that was usually sponsored by the American Civil Liberties Union. Here I relied on some of my constitutional law materials and the work I had done in New York City with Mel Wulf in *Dennis v. United States*,[22] addressing the non-Communist affidavit then required of labor union officials.

In June of 1970, I joined Wayne State Law graduate and later U.S. attorney James Robinson on a case that we brought before a three-judge panel. The case involved the question of whether public employees' rights to engage in political activity could be constitutionally restrained by the Hatch Act, a 1939 law limiting some political activities by federal workers. We ultimately lost the case, in an opinion authored by Judge Damon Keith.[23]

Then, with near simultaneity, I became involved in another constitutional case. This one involved my colleague and friend, Professor John "Jack" Mogk. Jack had joined the Wayne State faculty with me in the fall of 1968. A civic-minded law professor who had lived on the east side of Detroit most of his life, he would later run for mayor of Detroit against Coleman Young in 1973. In 1970 Jack attempted to register as a candidate for the City of Detroit Charter Commission but was rejected by the city clerk because he did not meet the 1909 adopted city residence requirement, which held that a candidate must reside for three consecutive years in Detroit prior to running for office. Mogk was disqualified because he had been in private law practice in New York City (like me) in the three years before returning to Detroit to teach at Wayne State.

I represented Jack, suing on behalf of both of us (Jack as a candidate; me as a voter) to attack the residency requirement as an unconstitutional denial of the right to run for office and the right to vote. My argument before a three-judge panel[24] went well. But perhaps that was by default. At the end of the city's argument, Jack tugged at my sleeve and whispered: "Don't get up, don't say anything." Whatever we said, Jack reasoned, couldn't help us any more than the defendant's lawyer had already done for us. And, of course, it could possibly hurt rather than help us. Nonetheless, not to be denied this opportunity, I stood up and argued. Apparently it didn't hurt us, despite the risk involved: The three-judge panel, in a unanimous decision authored by Judge Stephen Roth, held for us.[25] Said the court, emphasizing the technological and other changes that had taken place between 1909 and 1970:

> *What may have been a rational and justifiable classification of eligibility for the public office in 1909 may not necessarily be so regarded in the 1970s. In 1909 Marconi's wireless was in its infancy; the vacuum tube and radio had not yet arrived; and, the carriage makers were just turning to making automobiles.*[26]

And the court, via Judge Roth, offered these important words about who was to decide the eligibility of candidates:

> *It is a matter of common knowledge that those who seek public office go to considerable effort and expense to secure exposure, and it may be safely assumed that opponents in an election race will seek out and make known the shortcomings of their opposition and assert their own superior qualification for a particular post. If a short sojourn in the community is considered to be a disqualification, the electorate may voice its sentiment at the ballot box.*[27]

DETROIT EDISON: RUNNING AFOUL OF TITLE VII

As it turned out, Jack lost his primary; he also lost the primary race for mayor in 1973, but he spent many years in unelected public service, and his career over a half century plus was a distinguished one. One of his most ambitious activities was his involvement in New Detroit, a racial justice organization created to redress some of the inequities that had given rise to the 1967 Detroit riots that had preceded our arrival. Jack's work for New Detroit brought him in touch with a wide variety of people, including a number of Black workers at the Detroit Edison Company, a Michigan power company. The workers came to see Jack because of their exposure to various kinds of discrimination at Edison. As it happened, Detroit Edison's board chairman, Walker Cisler, was one of the key figures in New Detroit. According to a *Fortune* article from the time, Cisler had an "international reputation dating from 1944, when he brought public utilities into Paris with the first Allied troops. Since coming to Detroit in 1945, Cisler has served in just about every civic organization from the board of trustees of the art museum to the Citizens Committee for Equal Opportunity."[28] But Jack, knowing of my new seminar and the work I had done for the EEOC and the NAACP Legal Defense Fund, referred the workers to me. As a result, we met at Wayne State Law School in November of 1970.

The group that came to see me consisted of six Black Edison employees: Willie Stamps, Darney Stanfield, John Washington, Simmie Leonard, Ralph Rice, and James Atkinson. For a couple of hours, they all described a series of textbook illustrations of fair employment practice problems and potential infractions which, in my view, ran afoul of Title VII's prohibitions against racial discrimination. In short, they set forth illustrations of word-of-mouth procedures for hiring, which tend to perpetuate the racial composition of the existing workforce, and a willingness to hire Black workers only into so-called "low-opportunity" jobs, from which they found it impossible to transfer or be promoted into better-paying, more desirable work. They also described harassment for filing grievances, and unwillingness on the part of the unions, whether it be the Utility Workers Union or the International Brotherhood of Electrical Workers (IBEW), to attend to the existing divide. Similarly, they described tests which did not appear to be job related and excluded Black workers; the workers had been denied the opportunity to examine the results or know the basis for the tests themselves.

At this point, aside from litigation against the building and construction trades and the Teamsters in trucking,[29] legal relief had been sought for the most part in the South. The southern cases were frequently a direct product of Jim Crow's "separate but equal" doctrine and of the protests against that doctrine, such as the 1963 March on Washington and the Freedom Summer of 1964 in which my pal Harry Bowie had participated, as well as voting discrimination disputes—and none had been heard in the North. Much to my regret, I had not been part of those southern legal actions, despite Bowie's urging. But this was discrimination in Detroit itself, a northern city already composed of a majority or near-majority of Blacks, and it was staring me right in the face. The employees who met with me put together a scenario which, if true, presented just about every legal violation possible!

Indeed, because the relevant unions had ignored them, the workers had put together an organization of their own, the Association for the Betterment of Black Edison Employees. The association had attempted to address these issues but had been unable to get any response, leaving them frustrated. That's why they had come to see me.

Obstacles

I wanted to help the Detroit Edison workers, but my involvement was delayed by a few obstacles, both professional and personal. In the latter category, the gravest crisis of my life had occurred just a few months earlier. Bill V, my oldest son, had fallen out of a tree at my parents' home in New Jersey, suffered a compound fracture in his left arm and, unbeknownst to the doctors at the time of surgery, became infected with clostridium, a dangerous bacterium. A few days beyond the accident, it became apparent that Bill was in deep trouble, and he was helicoptered to Saint Barnabas Hospital in Livingston, New Jersey, and placed in a hyperbaric chamber with massive oxygen to try to quell the gangrene that had developed with the infection. I flew from Detroit to New Jersey to be with him in Livingston.

By then, however, the doctors were afraid that the gangrene could go to his brain, threatening his life itself. They advised that this situation necessitated the drastic measure of amputation of his left arm below the elbow. I gave consent. Though I had been melancholy in my high school days, I recall thinking that if he did not make it, I did not want to live. The amputation done, both Hilda and I stayed in Livingston. When I wasn't with him, I familiarized myself with Sesame Street in the hospital waiting room, which made me laugh. That was my escape valve.

When we returned to Detroit, I remember thinking that there would be no more baseball. I had pitched to Bill since he was three or four, and to his younger brother, Tim, as well. But before all the bandages were removed, Bill stood in the driveway and said, "Pitch to me." And I did, and he swung hard with one arm: His enthusiasm for the game was unchanged. Later, in California, he would join a Little League, and a Babe Ruth League (where he hit .327), with one arm and sometimes a prosthesis as well, and develop an extraordinary, cannon-like throwing arm. Later still, in Cambridge, England, Bill won his school competition for longest throw of a cricket ball. He went on to play the outfield at Occidental College in California, where he matriculated in the 1980s. But, of course, I could not foresee all that in the fall of 1970.

In that same year, I had begun to handle a case or two beyond Mogk's, and through my work in the earlier-described case involving the Hatch Act before Judge Damon Keith, I came to know Keith professionally. When Judge Keith learned of Bill's accident, he had his godson, Detroit Tiger outfielder Willie Horton, come to our house to visit Bill. Neighborhood kids came streaming out of their houses from every direction. The visit was a grand event, and I think it cheered Bill as much as the rest of us.

Shortly before these events, Harvard Law School had invited me to accept a post as Visiting Professor of Law. But Bill's accident created some uncertainty about when I would be in a position to take up this offer. Thus, the accident and the Harvard situation, as well as my responsibilities at Wayne State, were hanging over me as I contemplated what I should do vis-à-vis the Detroit Edison fellows who had come to ask for help.

My scholarly responsibilities were on my mind as well. In 1970 I received a grant from the Ford Foundation to write a book on Black workers, unions, and problems of discrimination. During the months prior to Bill's accident, in the spring and summer of 1970, this research took me across the country to Cleveland, Chicago, and Los Angeles. I also visited Seattle, where I became deeply involved in the Seattle Building Trades Order, an antidiscrimination decree fashioned by Judge William Lindberg. I produced a law review article about it, and it inspired part of my approach on behalf of the Black Edison workers when I met them at Wayne State.[30]

I continued to act as a labor arbitrator, resolving disputes in the Midwest and elsewhere. In the spring of 1970, I had been admitted into the National Academy of Arbitrators, an honorary and professional organization of arbitrators in the United States and Canada. At just thirty-three, I was one of the youngest arbitrators admitted in the NAA's history. And my scholarly writing continued: I wrote a piece for the *Supreme Court Review* in the summer of 1970 on a seminal ruling on arbitration and union obligations under a no-strike clause in the collective bargaining agreement, the precise question being whether a federal court could enjoin a strike conducted in defiance of a no-strike pledge, notwithstanding the 1932 Norris-LaGuardia Act's limitation upon judicial injunctions in labor disputes.[31] In short, I had a rather broad agenda when I first met with the Edison workers in November 1970.

Complaints, Discovery, Conflict

Nonetheless, we met again soon after the New Year, covering some of the same ground, discussing the idea of filing unlawful employment practice charges with both the Equal Employment Opportunity Commission at its Detroit regional office and the Michigan Civil Rights Commission. I contacted people at Edison in the interim and their response to me was, "Do you think you know more about our business than we do?" When no meetings or discussions could be held with the company, I filed the complaints with the federal and state commissions in January 1971. Little happened in the immediate aftermath, so I got back in touch with my old friend Mel Wulf at the ACLU, and we made this agreement: Mel would allow me to control any litigation that took place and would fund it. In return, I would donate any attorneys' fees to the ACLU if I prevailed. All of this was consistent with Mel's wise recognition of the importance of fact-finding determinations made at the trial process level, and the fact that this was the most critical aspect of litigation.[32]

I then drafted a complaint, which I filed in federal district court on May 17, 1971, the seventeenth anniversary of *Brown v. Board of Education*. Now the business of seeking discovery and taking depositions commenced. But, simultaneously, two immediate conflicts arose. The first was an attempt by some within Detroit Edison to obtain "releases" from some Black workers, advising them that they would no longer be "part of the class" if they signed. This action soon stopped after I wrote a blistering letter to one of the Edison lawyers, Leo Franklin. But a second conflict arose when Edison attempted to advertise their fair employment practice achievements at the Urban League's convention in Detroit in July. The Association for the Betterment of Black Edison Employees threatened to picket the Edison exhibit. Both the association and I said that Edison's exhibit should be withdrawn, and Edison did so, stating that it was responding to a request from the Urban League. However, the *Detroit Free Press* quoted them to this effect:

> *When Mr. Gould threatened the Urban League with picketing the Edison Exhibit and Cobo Hall, then the National Urban League requested that we withdraw the exhibit in the interest of maintaining order at the convention. We regret that Mr. Gould has again interfered with our constructive program on behalf of minority employment.*[33]

As I took depositions in the summer of '71, Edison lawyer Leo Franklin picked up on some of the refrains that were being advanced at the time of the Cobo Hall incident. Here is one of our exchanges:

Mr. Franklin: *For the record I would like to say on behalf of the defendant The Detroit Edison Company, as I stated in Judge Keith's chambers, that not only have we been harassed at the instigation of Professor Gould by actions not in accordance with the rules of the Federal Court, false accusations as to intimidating witnesses, but in addition by having a multiplicity of government agencies descend on us. Mr. Gould has stimulated additional action by the Michigan Civil Rights Commission, Federal EEOC, and I believe apart from Professor Gould that we are also being investigated by the General Services Administration. So far as I know there is no connection between the professor and that action.*

Mr. Gould: *There is.*

Mr. Franklin: *There is?*

Mr. Gould: *There is.*[34]

A YEAR AT HARVARD BEGINS

As the summer moved on there were new developments. Though we had deferred my visiting professorship at Harvard due to Bill's accident and my Detroit workload, we decided to take it up and move to Cambridge in the fall of 1971. I would see *Detroit Edison* through but needed help from local counsel in Detroit while I was in Massachusetts. I had met Roger Craig, a Southfield, Michigan lawyer, during the *Gibraltar* school district dispute, as his law firm represented the education association there; he accepted my invitation to come on board as local counsel. Craig's presence would be important, as more action would take place in the coming academic year.

I spent a little time in Cambridge in late August, getting situated before classes began; Hilda and the boys were about to return from a stay in Britain. We reconnected for the drive from Detroit to Cambridge, moving into a rented modern home in nearby Lexington. That fall I began to teach Labor Law as well as my Employment Discrimination Law seminar.

Regrettably, Derek Bok had by then departed the law school for the Harvard presidency, and I don't believe I ever saw him during that year or subsequently. Archibald Cox, whose articles I had read and whose book I'd reviewed for *The New Leader*,[35] was in residence after his solicitor general service in the Kennedy and Johnson administrations. (His role in the landmark Watergate hearings, however, was still over eighteen months away.) Cox, a leading labor law expert, sat down with me once or twice for brief discussions for, as he pointed out, "we were laboring in the same vineyard."

I had some contact with Derrick Bell, though perhaps I missed out on more socializing with him and other colleagues, given my frequent trips out of town. But the overriding attitude of the Harvard faculty was best expressed by law professor Louis Loss, who said: "You should get to know the faculty better." "No," I said, "I'm the visitor; they should get to know me." Obviously, that wasn't part of the conventional wisdom at Harvard. When I met then-professor Ruth Bader Ginsburg of Rutgers Law School, who was also visiting, she affirmed that view: In spite of her connection to Harvard Law, having been a student there until 1958, she was also a bit of a loner that year, a fact that brought us together for the occasional coffee and lunch.

EDISON: ADVANCES AND DISAPPOINTMENTS

Meanwhile, Edison continued to loom large in a number of respects. First, Willie Stamps and the Association for the Betterment of Black Edison Employees and I received an invitation to participate in a hearing conducted by the Equal Employment Opportunity Commission on "underutilization of minority employees" in utilities on November 15, 1971.[36] I flew into Washington from Cambridge and met Willie and some of the other plaintiffs, who had traveled from Detroit.

At the conclusion of the hearing that day, John de J. (Jack) Pemberton, acting general counsel of the EEOC, made a special trip down from the dais, where he had been sitting with the other commissioners, to meet us. Jack was warm, courteous, and sympathetic, and this was to be the beginning of a long, enduring friendship, personal and professional—one that solidified when he left the EEOC a couple of years later and arrived on the West Coast to teach at the University of San Francisco Law School. Jack, whose forebear of the same name had been defeated during the Civil War by Grant at Vicksburg, would eventually join me in the appellate process and other matters in the employment discrimination arena. Willie Stamps and I knew that we had made a good friend that day.

The upshot of the Washington hearing was a good one. Said EEOC Chairman Bill Brown about the utility industry:

> *A common excuse employers use for not hiring is that qualified minorities and women cannot be found. Time and again this claim has been proved false. In the case of the gas and electric utility industry, most of the companies are located in central city locations where the minority workforce is readily available. These companies generally do not hire skilled craftsmen away from other employers. Rather, the specialized nature of their operations requires that utilities train most of their upper-level blue collar employees.*
>
> *This suggests that entry-level occupations can be used effectively as a conduit for the hiring and upgrading of minorities and women.*[37]

Justice Intervenes

But there was another, more immediate development in the Edison case during that year at Harvard. The U.S. Justice Department intervened on our side, filing a complaint that became consolidated with our case. We had sought Justice's intervention for a considerable period of time, inviting the department to come into the case because of its substantial resources. Now that they had joined the case, we had the firepower for extensive discovery—and not simply statistical data relating to hiring, promotion, testing, and so on. Through the use of FBI agents, we obtained statements about the word-of-mouth avenues for hiring that perpetuated a substantially white workforce. The FBI interviewed approximately eighty workers randomly, forty Black and forty white, visiting the selected workers at their homes to obtain information about how they had been hired or promoted. For us private plaintiffs, such methods were obviously out of the question.

The other side of the coin, however, which posed some problems for us, was that the department was silent on a key remedy we sought, obtained, and held onto ultimately at every stage of the litigation, that is, front pay to compensate Black workers who were denied their "rightful place"—a place they should have obtained but which no court of equity could provide where there was no vacancy, without dislodging other workers, a concession we were always unwilling to demand.[38] And on punitive damages, which we also sought, Justice would not support us out of an articulated concern that the statute did not authorize such and, more importantly, that a jury trial might be mandated in the event that such an award was sought. At this point in employment discrimination litigation, the accepted view was that jury trials were to be avoided at all costs—at least until the 1991 amendments to the Civil Rights Act and, more recently, a series of widely accepted jury trials in employment cases.[39]

However, two phenomena helped us, independent of a reliance upon the department: the facts of the case and much of the law. And Edison was not well served through its representation. One problem was a kind of tone deafness. For instance, at one of the early pretrial conferences, Edison lawyer Leo Franklin said to Judge Keith, one of the first Black judges appointed in Detroit, "Now Judge, with regard to the so-called Black workers . . ." I froze with my head down, unable and unwilling to make eye contact with anyone, feeling immensely embarrassed for Franklin and everyone involved! Finally, after a minute or so, Franklin continued, using the same expression again and again. I looked up and very tentatively turned toward Judge Keith to determine his reaction. Judge Keith was looking directly at me to determine *my* reaction! I was absolutely stunned by Franklin's odd and oafish manner of expression.

In fact, the Edison team seemed to know little or nothing about Title VII. In their defense, it was still early days in the development of case law, before the time when many firms found it in their interest to hire or develop specialists in the area. At times, as I would say to some friends, my court appearances during that period were like shooting fish in a barrel.

Money Is Not Enough

In the fall of 1972, Edison appeared to make a last-minute effort to settle. The company retained ex-Judge Ed Bell, a well-known Black Detroit lawyer, who flew to Stanford, California—where Hilda and I and the family had recently moved after our year at Harvard, as I describe in chapter 7—to discuss settlement matters, dangling hundreds of thousands of dollars that he may or not have been authorized to offer. Nothing came of this offer (real or imagined), nor did anything come of a subsequent meeting with Edison's Vice President of Legal Affairs Leon Cohan, which took place at his house. Here, however, I blundered badly and almost destroyed my relationship with our principal plaintiff, Willie Stamps, when I went inside Cohan's house to sit down and talk with him, leaving Stamps sitting in the car! Later I realized that this gauche conduct had been insulting, unsettling, and had left Stamps at that point mistrustful of my relationship with Cohan. Though I don't believe I spoke another word with Cohan after that meeting, Stamps developed a deep and everlasting concern, a resentment that lasted for a half-century afterward.

In any event, as my discussion about this proposed settlement with Stamps and others made clear, money—however important—was not enough. Indeed, it was a subordinate consideration. In the words of the then-popular Motown hit, the plaintiffs "wanted to testify" and at the trial, when it began, testify they did.

Seattle: A Relevant Model?

My team—Roger Craig, and Wayne State Law graduates Raymond Willis and Ethan Vinson—were part of the trial, which commenced in February 1973. However, a few months before its commencement, I made one of my many San Francisco-to-Detroit flights to argue the question of standing to sue for the above-referenced Association for the Betterment of Black Edison Employees as plaintiff. As noted, this small workers' group had been organized by Willie Stamps and other young Black workers at Edison and resolutely maintained since the 1960s. Their efforts reminded me of the Black construction workers confronting discrimination in Seattle, who had organized so they could play a major role in the enforcement and monitoring of the Seattle Building Trades decree[40]—a role enhanced by their appointment to a court advisory committee created by Judge William Lindberg.

Beginning in late 1971, I had made a number of trips to Seattle to interview all those involved with this comprehensive decree. One of my earliest meetings was with Hugh Hafer, the Ironworkers Union lawyer. I asked him: "How is the decree working?" "Fine," he responded. "Are many Blacks getting jobs?" I asked him expectantly. "No," Hafer answered. This was the problem.

Tyree Scott, the leading Black construction worker and organizer in Seattle, continued to protest in the face of these problems. One night, when Scott and EEOC chairman Bill Brown had dinner with Hilda and me at our home in Stanford, Scott told us all how he and his colleagues had raised a drawbridge in Seattle, bringing traffic to a complete halt as a way to publicize the ongoing discrimination. Brown, probably the best chairman the EEOC ever had, was horrified. I can see them now, discussing this in front of our fireplace. But both men were on the same page when it came to objectives, notwithstanding the fact that they were using appreciably different tactics and were very different people indeed!

Figure 6.1: Chairman William Brown III of the EEOC, participating with me at my Stanford Law School Employment Discrimination Law seminar, c. 1973 or 1974.

Black workers in Seattle had engaged in protest whenever, in their view, the decree went unenforced or was enforced in a tardy manner. Thus, using Seattle as a model, I argued for the Association for the Betterment of Black Edison Employees to be a party plaintiff along with the class plaintiffs—but Judge Keith denied my motion. Defendants Edison and the unions properly pointed out that in Seattle the workers' group involvement was in enforcement of the decree—in contrast to *Detroit Edison*, where there was, as yet, no decree at all.

Testimony

Notwithstanding my role as lead counsel, my teaching and other responsibilities in California meant that I could not be present at all trial days. On days when I was not present, I was replaced by Messrs. Craig and Willis—and of course the Justice Department, which, as plaintiff in its own right, was present every day. My major role at this point was to examine Willie Stamps, who provided extremely persuasive and unrebutted evidence of being denied job opportunities. Stamps testified, for example, that he was always rejected for jobs—until he made it known that he would be willing to work as a janitor. When he applied for a job that he had actually performed previously, he was rejected on the grounds that he was "overqualified," and was told that he could not review his test results when he was denied for other jobs on the basis of those tests. Stamps also provided valuable testimony about how he and others had attempted to establish a union human resources or rights committee to redress racial grievances, but was opposed by Pete Johnson, the president of the Utility Workers Union, Local 223.

But, as the testimony of other witnesses over a three-month duration and Judge Keith's subsequent opinion made clear, there was much more discriminatory practice to uncover. One particularly stunning revelation was the company's use of a "black dot" system, under which Edison identified Black applicants on prospective employees' lists by adding black dots beside their names. When this practice was revealed, the company claimed that it was using the system to implement affirmative action. There was only one problem with this contention: the number of successful Black hires and promotions *declined* once the dot system was introduced![41]

Closing Arguments

Our closing argument took place during the entire day of June 5, 1973, before Judge Keith.[42] The Justice Department and private plaintiffs, for whom I argued, were on the same page regarding our theory of liability. Both of us noted the disproportionate assignment of Black workers to so-called "low-opportunity," unskilled, menial jobs, and the inability of incumbent Black workers to obtain skilled or "high-opportunity" jobs. And as I had written in law reviews, EEOC reports, and NAACP Legal Defense Fund briefs, the inability to transfer with accumulated seniority credits in the wake of racially biased hiring was unlawfully discriminatory, in that such practices carried forward past discrimination into the present promotion and seniority system.

In oral argument, I made the following points on this matter:

> Government exhibit 65 shows clearly that a goodly number of Blacks hired into low-opportunity jobs had superior work experience and education as compared to some white employees who were hired into high opportunity jobs.
>
> Statistics are enough, and the courts say, direct proof of racial discrimination seldom occurs. Most employers and unions do not come forward and say, we are guilty of racial discrimination—although many of them, your honor, unlike defendants in this case, are quite frank about saying we discriminated in the past but today we are trying to remedy that discrimination. Defendants, with an unbelievable blandness in this case, say that they have done nothing wrong to anybody at any time during this entire period. And this, I submit, is a fantastic and less than candid assertion on the part of defendants in light of the state of this record.
>
> The retired personnel director who admitted that blacks were not in many jobs and had not been hired for many jobs and that, with regard to meter readers, blacks weren't there because the white community wasn't ready for blacks to be there. His testimony was relatively frank.
>
> Here we have in connection with Mr. Stamps, your honor, Mr. Stamps testified to bidding for jobs that he had actually performed before and there was no rebuttal put on by the company.
>
> No evidence of business necessity has been shown, no attempt to rebut, no attempt to rebut with regard to any of these. As I said, your honor, we showed approximately 30 violations, 30 violations in three days where blacks with qualifications came forward and said, I bid for a job and I didn't get the job. I saw, I had the qualifications, I actually performed the job. I had it in my background. No explanation, no rebuttal.[43]

I referenced the seniority cases I had relied upon and cited to the Fifth Circuit, cases that the court adopted in *Taylor v. Armco*.[44]

In its rebuttal for the company, Richard Ford, Edison's lawyer, when asked why he had not defended against any of the contentions that qualified applicants had been denied jobs, said the following in response to Judge Keith's question about what caused the small number of Black applicants and employees:

> *In the first place, in 1960 and earlier, the black population in the city, of course, was well less and the black population of that time, I think, tended to be fascinated by the glamor industries in town like the automobile companies and similar places which perhaps paid larger wages and attracted them more to it than to a somewhat more sedate kind of employment such as the Edison Company.*[45]

Ford's defense against the argument predicated upon seniority went as follows:

> *This entire seniority matter isn't a complicated thing and I gather from the dispatch that I have from my partner that I don't understand it at all. So I think I have to perhaps better go on hastily to my next topic, and that is with reference to the supposed difficulty that the black man has in getting to be a supervisor.*[46]

In response I said to the court:

> *Now, your honor, Mr. Ford says that blacks . . . didn't get employed by the Detroit Edison but that they went into glamor industries like the automobile, like the glamorous things, showy, the big Cadillacs, and apparently the black people don't recognize that Edison has more job security than does the average automobile factory or most of the other private employers, most of the other private employers in the city can offer and apparently black people are not smart enough to recognize that Edison offers wage rates to plant cleaners that are as good or better than people on the assembly line in the automobile plants. I submit*

> *that this is—this is totally implausible, to use a euphemism in describing Mr. Ford's characterization of why there were no blacks. We know why there were no blacks on it, your honor, and I might in briefly passing this just specifically make reference to the race identification system. It is interesting to note that Mr. Ford does not mention the race identification system and the fact that minority hiring both in terms of numbers and percentages actually declined after the time the race identification system was instituted.*
>
> *You will recall, Edison came forth and said, we are only trying to help black people here and that is why we put the race identification system into existence. We point out in our proposed findings of fact that the numbers automatically go down in the years immediately following the institution of the race identification system.*[47]

Having started at 10 a.m., we concluded that night at 5:15 p.m. I was spent—it had started in 1970, and now, in 1973, it was over. But I was wrong: this case would go on much longer indeed!

A Sweeping Opinion

On October 2, 1973, Judge Keith issued a sweeping opinion holding Edison liable in connection with virtually every finding and theory which we and Justice had urged.[48] The October 3 banner headline of the *Detroit Free Press* said: "Black Employees Win $4 Million: Edison Is Found Guilty of Bias."[49]

In his opinion, Judge Keith wrote:

> *Evidence was overwhelming that invidious racial discrimination in employment practices permeates the corporate entity of The Detroit Edison Company. The Court finds as proven facts that upward mobility of blacks presently employed at Detroit Edison is almost non-existent, and that qualified potential black employees are refused employment or refrain from applying for employment because of the Company's reputation in the black Detroit community for racial discrimination. The Company has taken*

> *the position that if any inequities exist between blacks and whites at Detroit Edison, such inequities have accidentally evolved and have not resulted from deliberate discrimination. While this Court believes that the law would require it to find that Detroit Edison has violated the law if it has, without intent to discriminate, fostered practices which have resulted in a racially discriminatory impact, the evidence in this case demonstrates that the Company's discrimination has been deliberate and by design.*[50]

Judge Keith emphasized that, notwithstanding the many findings of discrimination, the company never admitted to and did not seek to remedy "employment practices [which] perpetuate racial discrimination."[51] Similarly, he noted that the unions had not sought to remedy discrimination and had encouraged Blacks to withdraw or not press grievances involving discrimination. Moreover, the opinion referenced fifteen instances between 1967 and 1972 when Stamps was "denied transfer because of his race."[52] And the court relied heavily upon the law which had evolved on seniority and the "word-of-mouth and friends and relatives" basis for hiring by Edison. Judge Keith said:

> *A study of the Federal Bureau of Investigation in the course of which eighty-six white employees were contacted indicates that forty-three of such employees had friends and acquaintances who were employed by Detroit Edison and discussed job opportunities with such friends and relatives. Since a disproportionate percentage of employees at Detroit Edison Company are white and since the overwhelming percentage of employees in the higher opportunity jobs referred to above are white, such a hiring practice in this instance had the effect of perpetuating the exclusion of black applicants from employment with Detroit Edison Company and from the jobs referred to above.*[53]

Ultimately, beyond goals and timetables for hiring and promotion as well as the award of seniority credits, and so forth, the court caught the attention of the entire country when it assessed punitive damages in the amount of four million dollars, given its judgment that both Edison and Local 223 of the Utility Workers Union had "been extremely obdurate and intransigent in their determination to implement and perpetuate racial discrimination in employment at Detroit Edison."[54] Less attention was given to the court's assessment of so-called front pay for wages and benefits lost before workers obtained the high-opportunity job to which they were entitled.[55] This front pay remedy was left untouched and virtually unmentioned by the Sixth Circuit. The same was true of the publicity provisions in the decree, which obliged Edison to purchase newspaper and radio advertisements with the *Michigan Chronicle* (the Black Detroit newspaper), *The Detroit News,* and/or *The Detroit Free Press* to tell the public the content of the decree and opportunities for applicants to obtain the benefits from it.[56]

News of the decree swept through the country like lightning and was widely praised.[57] At the next meeting of the Association for the Betterment of Black Edison Employees, on Gratiot Avenue in Detroit, the place was packed—not only with those who had been with us from the early days in 1970, but also with considerably more new faces.

Further discussion about the decree's implications followed. Indeed, as I wrote in *The Guardian*:

> *The lesson of Detroit Edison Company is that black employee organisations are becoming part of the struggle against racial oppression—not for the purpose of racial separation, nor with a view toward opting out of the white led unions of America, but rather with the immediate objective of creating a solidarity to which companies and unions must pay heed.*[58]

Appeals

Edison, of course, announced its intention to appeal to the Sixth Circuit Court of Appeals, filing both a notice of appeal and a motion to stay the nonmonetary portions of the decree. (All parties agreed that the monetary portions of the decree, relating to back pay, front pay, punitive damages, and attorneys' fees, would be stayed.) And a new dimension to the litigation emerged: Edison retained the well-resourced New York law firm of Rogers & Wells, with William Rogers—Eisenhower's attorney general and Nixon's secretary of state—being named its lead lawyer.

Once again I returned to Detroit to try to pull everything together in a brief to the Sixth Circuit in Cincinnati—and I prevailed there in early 1974, when Edison failed to prove a "likelihood of success" on appeal on the merits. This ruling meant that suspension of tests, seniority system, denying Black workers the accumulation of seniority credits and low-opportunity jobs, "goals" in hiring and promotion, and publicity to Black media like the *Michigan Chronicle* would go forward and be enforced immediately, during the appeals process. Most importantly, Edison was obliged to file progress reports on the decree's implementation while the appeals process went forward.

Given the unusually generous resources of the Rogers firm, the inequality between our two sides was particularly visible. For example, I received a call from one of that firm's lawyers, requesting a postponement on a filing. I hesitated for a moment, thinking that I might obtain a concession from him in exchange for my willingness to accept his proposal. But before my mind could even focus on what concession I might request, the lawyer said, "If you don't give me the extension, it doesn't matter. I have a couple of our young lawyers here who could work all night on this matter, and we will meet the deadline that way." That was the true resources dynamic. Naturally, I agreed to his request without a murmur.

Fortunately for us, Jack Pemberton, whom we had met during the 1971 EEOC hearing, was available and living in San Francisco, allowing us to respond to this new situation. And as the appellate process unfolded, Jack became very important in a number of aspects of the case. Within weeks of his arrival at the University of San Francisco, he visited with us at our home, 711 Salvatierra, and, although his only real sports interest was tennis, joined in a basketball game in our driveway with my oldest son and me.

As co-counsel, Jack was to prove an invaluable advisor in several respects. In the first place, he dove deeply into Edison's appeal submissions with me. We were able to sit down both in San Francisco and Stanford and bounce ideas off one another. Most importantly, he arranged a moot court for me at the USF Law School—an event that proved to be extremely beneficial, as it constituted a first draft of oral argument, allowing me to become acclimatized to a presentation that would be riddled with questions similar to those that might come from the judges themselves.

On the eve of my flight to Cincinnati for the oral argument, memories of Jack's parting advice stuck in my mind. I had told him that on my trips home to New Jersey to see my parents, my father would often greet me at the door with a Manhattan in hand for my consumption. As I got ready to pack up the filings, some of which were particularly insulting to me, Jack said, "Bill, when you get ready to reread some of the briefs and papers on the plane, take a good stiff Manhattan!"

Jack also told me that the panel I would draw for argument at the Sixth Circuit could well be staffed with people whom Rogers himself had recommended for appointment when he was Attorney General! Jack was wrong about this—but just barely. Nixon appointee Judge Pierce Lively, who appeared to preside and wrote the court's opinion, was nominated when Rogers was no longer attorney general, but rather secretary of state. But the Sixth Circuit was a conservative one, and my heart sank when Judge Wade McCree, to whom I had been introduced early in my UAW days, was absent from the panel. The panel of judges we drew that day was not to our advantage.

Reversal

Judge Lively, still relatively young and ambitious, was quite hostile to the Keith opinion, both in oral argument and in the written opinion itself. From the date of the Lively opinion—March 11, 1975—to this very day, I've often thought that, had Judge Lively been able to write and think more quickly, he would have taken more from us than he did. But the Lively opinion[59] reversed the widely publicized punitive damages award as unauthorized by Title VII. This became the most publicized aspect of the appellate ruling. Curiously, though the Supreme Court held within two months that punitive damages are awardable under the Civil Rights Act of 1866[60]—under which we had sued—as well as under Title VII, neither the Sixth Circuit nor the Supreme Court would reconsider Judge Lively's opinion which, under a subsequent ruling of the Supreme Court, was in error.

In addition to reversing punitive damages, the court also limited the class of Edison workers entitled to relief to employees, rather than to those who had been rejected as applicants, even though we had shown, and Judge Keith had found, numerous instances of unlawful rejection. Here the court's reasoning was that we had not put defendants on notice of such a scope through our pleadings. Said the court:

> *The private plaintiffs in the present case, did not by pleading or proof, sufficiently advise the court for it to define a class represented by these plaintiffs as including anyone but black employees of Edison. . . . While neither the private plaintiffs nor the government introduced the testimony of actual applicants who were ultimately rejected for employment, a great deal of statistical evidence was admitted on the hiring issue. The district court properly considered the claim in the government case that black citizens had been rejected for employment and otherwise denied employment opportunities by Edison because of race.*[61]

This conclusion contradicted the clear facts, shown time and time again, about the actual rejection of applicants which the statistics supplemented. In any event, notwithstanding all of the above, the Keith findings on discrimination in hiring, promotion, denial of seniority credits, and the relief sought for "goals" in hiring and promotion as well as the obligation to file reports showing progress, were all affirmed. Again, front pay was left untouched.

And there was more to come. While motions were being filed by both sides, and petitions for certiorari were pending before the Supreme Court itself, the Court upended other portions of the Keith decree: In another case, it reversed not only the seniority conclusions in this case, but also in every circuit court of appeals which had considered and adjudicated the issue throughout the country. This was its landmark ruling in *Teamsters v. US*,[62] where a seven-to-two majority held, contrary to the district court in *Detroit Edison*, that the seniority system that denied Blacks (and frequently Latinos, other minorities, and women) seniority credits, which they had been unable to accumulate by virtue of past hiring discrimination, was now lawful, protected by the "bona fide seniority system proviso" in Title VII. Moreover, any worker claiming injury through discrimination in a class action or pattern of discrimination case showing employment-wide systemic discrimination (like that in *Detroit Edison*) was entitled to both seniority and back pay only through an individualized showing of entitlement to such.

In some respects, the individual entitlement requirement for back pay was even more pernicious than the harm already done by the Supreme Court's seniority holding itself, however radical the latter might be. For there were hundreds of worker claims for back pay at Edison and, absent a settlement, there would be hundreds of days of hearings. This put Edison in the driver's seat, as they had the resources—through lawyers, paraprofessionals, and papers—to withstand such challenges, and we plaintiffs did not. Moreover, the sudden departure of my old friend Mel Wulf as ACLU legal director deprived me of a generous, always-available bankroll.[63]

A Surprise Settlement

Yet the next phase in the litigation caught Edison (and, I confess, to some extent myself) by surprise. Suddenly, Detroit social justice lawyer Sheldon Stark appeared on the scene. He succeeded in rounding up young and hungry Detroit lawyers looking to cut their teeth on Edison itself.[64] Suddenly, we had the ability to go to the mat on the many hearings that would have to take place. This development, more than anything, led to a settlement.

The settlement concluded was the richest per capita settlement ever established in any Title VII proceedings up through the seventies and eighties: Approximately 400 claimants shared $5 million. My $250K in attorney's fees went to the ACLU, which was pleased to accept it, notwithstanding Mel Wulf's departure and the fact that he (and I) got neither thanks nor attention for the award.[65] Though we had lost $4.25 million in punitive damages, due to the ambitious, lean, and hungry Judge Lively at the Sixth Circuit, the settlement was still an excellent one, though it took a decade to be completed.

In some respects, the worst wrong anyone can commit against another is to raise expectations that then go unrealized. *Detroit Edison* was emblematic of that wrong and exacerbated by the sheer duration of the litigation. So many times during the case my father would say to me, "Bill, when are those guys going to get their money?" Now, after ten long years, they finally had it.[66]

I had filed the *Detroit Edison* complaint on May 17, 1971. Three years later I would organize a Stanford Law School program, with Chief Justice Earl Warren as the major speaker, on May 17, 1974. In my speech that day, I said:

> *That decision* [Brown v. Board of Education] *gave me and other blacks the hope and belief that the law could address itself to racial injustices in this country and that I as a lawyer could make some contribution to end the old order against which my parents had struggled. In their day the struggle was against hopeless odds—hopeless because all who possessed African blood were isolated, ridiculed, despised—and thus regarded as unfit for occupations and work that the white man was willing to perform.*[67]

Figure 6.2: Chief Justice Earl Warren, May 17, 1974, at Stanford Law School: from left to right, Barbara Babcock, Gerry Gunther, Chief Justice Warren, and the author.

Now, Title VII, notwithstanding the duration of its process, had raised hopes and produced results. I felt I had made up the substantial ground I lost while in London during the 1963 civil rights revolution. The *Detroit Edison* conclusion offered some measure of personal compensation for what I judge to be my failure to answer the call to Mississippi in the summer of 1964. The Edison settlement also encouraged me to involve myself in other actions of this nature, in which the merits and attractiveness were considerable, though success might be elusive. These actions would emerge, for the most part, after my arrival at Stanford Law School in 1972.[68]

NOTES

[1] James Hilton, *Good-Bye, Mr. Chips* (London: Hodder & Stoughton, 1934).
[2] Stan Putnam, "55,000 Students Wait, Talks Fail to Open Doors of Schools," *Detroit Free Press*, September 9, 1968.
[3] Harry Salsinger, "$125,000 Pact Ends Inkster School Strike," *The Detroit News*, September 9, 1968.
[4] "Gibraltar Schools Face Strike," *The Detroit News*, November 5, 1968.
[5] Mary Ann Weston, "Downriver Teachers OK Strike," *Detroit Free Press*, November 7, 1968; John Peterson, "Gibraltar School Strike Drags On," *The Detroit News*, December 16, 1968.

6. Detroit Federation of Teachers and School Board of the City of Detroit, *Tripartite Arbitration Panel: Wage Dispute*, November 30, 1989. The award seems to have been received reasonably well. See "Pay Raises: Mayor and Council Now Owe Detroiters Greater Effort," *Detroit Free Press*, December 4, 1989; Brenda J. Gilchrist, "Detroit Teachers Win 5 Percent Pay Raise," *Detroit Free Press*, December 1, 1989.
7. William B. Gould IV, "Public Employment: Mediation, Fact Finding, and Arbitration," *American Bar Association Journal* 55 (1969).
8. William B. Gould IV, "Black Power in the Unions: The Impact upon Collective Bargaining Relationships," *Yale Law Journal* 79 (1969). Earlier, while in private practice, I had developed broad principles relating to this subject matter to which the Yale piece carved out an exception. See also William B. Gould IV, "The Status of Unauthorized and 'Wildcat' Strikes Under the National Labor Relations Act," *Cornell Law Review* 52 (1967).
9. Steele v. Louisville & N.R. Co., 323 U.S. 192, 200 (1944).
10. William B. Gould IV, "Labor Arbitration of Grievances Involving Racial Discrimination," *University of Pennsylvania Law Review* 118 (1969).
11. Alexander v. Gardner-Denver Co., 415 U.S. 36 (1974).
12. Emporium Capwell Co. v. Western Addition, 420 U.S. 50 (1975).
13. Taylor v. Armco Steel Corp., 429 F.2d 498 (5th Cir. 1970).
14. William B. Gould IV, "Seniority and the Black Worker: Reflections on Quarles and Its Implications," *Texas Law Review* 47 (1969).
15. Whitfield v. United Steelworkers of America, 263 F.2d, 546 (5th Cir. 1959), cert. denied, 360 U.S. 902.
16. *Emporium Capwell Co.*, 420 U.S. at 499 n1, citing William B. Gould IV, "Employment Security, Seniority, and Race: The Role of Title VII of the Civil Rights Act of 1964," *Howard Law Journal* 13 (1967); Gould, "Seniority and the Black Worker."
17. William B. Gould IV, "Letter to the Editor: To End Building Bias," *New York Times*, January 2, 1970.
18. William B. Gould IV, "Letter to the Editor: Nixon Praised for Backing the Philadelphia Plan," *Detroit Free Press*, January 1, 1970.
19. William B. Gould IV, "Blacks and the General Lockout," *New York Times*, July 17, 1971; see also William B. Gould IV, "Chicago Fails to End Bias in Trades: Voluntary Plan Flops," *Detroit Sunday News*, July 25, 1971.
20. "Employers who have been getting away with discriminatory employment practices will soon be feeling the effects of new Federal laws which are exacting heavy penalties for those who have been consistently anti-black, anti-female and generally anti-minority in their hiring programs.

    This was predicted yesterday by William B. Gould, visiting professor at Harvard Law School, to more than 100 persons attending an all-day session of the Massachusetts Commission Against Discrimination held at Boston University. 'For too long these violators of Federal laws—violators because of their refusal or reluctance to employ the disadvantaged—have been escaping from any severe punishment at all. At most, perhaps, they'll sustain nothing more painful than a slap on the wrist,' said Gould, a consultant to the Equal Employment Opportunity Commission, a Federal agency.

    But since March 24 of this year, when President Nixon signed into law important amendments to the Civil Rights Act of 1964, there were indeed some changes made

which guaranteed minorities their rights and also gave the EOC authority to sue in Federal Court." Paul F. Kneeland, "Stiff Fines for Hiring Bias Seen," *Boston Sunday Globe*, April 23, 1972.
21. William B. Gould IV, "Labor & Nixon: Moving the Hard-Hats," *The Nation*, January 8, 1973, 41.
22. Dennis v. United States, 384 U.S. 855 (1966).
23. Petersen v. Michigan Employment Security Commission, No. 35-211 (E.D.S.D. July 13, 1971) (unpublished). The other members of the panel were Judge McCree and Judge Kaess.
24. Judge McCree, Judge Thornton, and Judge Roth.
25. Mogk v. City of Detroit, 335 F.Supp. 698 (E.D. Mich. 1971), "William B. Gould is a Wayne State University professor specializing in constitutional law who practices what he teaches - and it may be easier in the future to run for political office in Michigan because of that." Don Ball, Prof scores in suit, Detroit News June 28, 1970, at 26 A; cf. Jeffrey Hadden, "Candidate Residence Rules May be Void," *The Detroit News*, November 24, 1971.
26. *Mogk v. City of Detroit*, 699.
27. *Mogk v. City of Detroit*, 701.
28. Stanley H. Brown, "Detroit: Slow Healing of a Fractured City," *Fortune*, June 1965, 142, 262.
29. I shall discuss this further in chapter 7.
30. William B. Gould IV, "The Seattle Building Trades Order: The First Comprehensive Relief Against Employment Discrimination in the Construction Industry," *Stanford Law Review* 26 (1974). Judge Lindberg's opinion is reported at United States v. Loc. No. 8, Int. Ass'n of Bridge, 315 F. Supp. 1202 (W.D. Wash. 1970).
31. William B. Gould IV, "On Labor Injunctions, Unions, and the Judges: The Boys Market Case," *Supreme Court Review* 1970 (1970).
32. Richard Sandomir, "Melvin Wulf, Transformative Civil Liberties Lawyer, Dies at 95," *New York Times*, July 16, 2023; In this article, Mel's differences with others inside the ACLU on this point are clearly spelled out.
33. Judy Diebolt, "Blacks Make Edison Cancel Jobs Exhibit," *Detroit Free Press*, July 23, 1971.
34. Association for the Betterment of Black Detroit Edison Employees v. The Detroit Edison Company, Carter Dep. 2, July 20, 1971.
35. William B. Gould IV, "Book Review: Labor Law for the Future, Reviewing Law and the National Labor Policy by Archibald Cox," *The New Leader*, February 13, 1961, 27.
36. "Statement by Willie Stamps, November 16, 1971, 179–189," *Hearings Before the United States Equal Employment Opportunity Commission on Utilization of Minority and Women Workers in the Public Utilities Industry: Hearings Held in Washington DC, November 15–17, 1971* (Washington: Supt. of Docs. U.S. Govt. Print. Off.).
37. Chairman Brown of the Equal Employment Opportunity Commission, in Promise vs. Performance: A Study of Equal Employment Opportunity in the Nation's Electric and Gas Utilities (1972), v.
38. "Rightful place" concept which did not provide for so called "freedom now" was set forth in the *Harvard Law Review*. See "Title VII, Seniority Discrimination, and the Incumbent Negro," *Harvard Law Review* 80 (1967).

39 William Gould IV, "The Supreme Court and Employment Discrimination in 1989: Judicial Retreat and Congressional Response," *Tulane Law Review* 64 (1990). See William B. Gould IV, "Letter to the Editor: No Effective Remedy," *New York Times*, October 19, 1991. Noting that, although the Republican members of the Senate Judiciary Committee expressed skepticism about Professor Anita Hill's failure to file a sexual harassment charge with the EEOC, they voted against a damages remedy for sexual harassment prior to the Thomas–Hill Hearings.

40 William B. Gould IV, "The Seattle Building Trades Order: the First Comprehensive Relief Against Employment Discrimination in the Construction Industry," *Stanford Law Review* 26 (1974).

41 A 1973 article in *The Nation* described Judge Keith's decision, concluding in these words: "Never hesitate to apply for a job because you feel you have no chance because of color, sex, age, etc. If you refrain you are not only passing up a chance to collect personal damages but you are in effect acquiescing in the mistreatment of the group to which you belong, and in social injustice generally." "The Black Dot System," *The Nation*, October 29, 1973, 422.

42 Louis Heldman, "Judge Considering Edison Bias Suit," *Detroit Free Press*, June 6, 1973.

43 Transcript of Oral Argument at 65, 74, Stamps v. *Detroit Edison Company*, 365 F. Supp. 87 (E.D. Mich. 1973).

44 *Taylor v. Armco Steel Corporation*, 429 F.2d 498 (5th Cir. 1970).

45 *Taylor v. Armco Steel Corporation*, Ibid., 95–96.

46 *Taylor v. Armco Steel Corporation*, 112.

47 *Taylor v. Armco Steel Corporation*, 156–157.

48 *Stamps v. Detroit Edison Company*, 365 F. Supp. 87 (E.D. Mich. 1973).

49 Louis Heldman, "Black Employees Win $4 Million: Edison Is Found Guilty of Bias," *Detroit Free Press*, October 3, 1973.

50 *Stamps*, 365 F. Supp. at 95.

51 *Stamps*, 96.

52 *Stamps*, 100.

53 *Stamps*, 103.

54 *Stamps*, 124.

55 *Stamps*, 121–122.

56 *Stamps*, 120–121.

57 William K. Stevens, "Detroit Utility Is Ordered to Pay $4 Million to Black Workers," *New York Times*, October 3, 1973; William Wong, "Lawyer William Gould Prods Courts to End Job Bias; His Activism Sometimes Irks Peers," *Wall Street Journal*, August 21, 1974; William K. Stevens, "The New Legal Weapon for Blacks?" *New York Times*, October 7, 1973; Paul Bernstein and Mike Maza, "Edison Plaintiffs Call Ruling a Breakthrough," *The Detroit News*, October 3, 1973; Jeffrey Hadden, "Impact of Edison Ruling Still to Be Assessed," *The Detroit News*, October 3, 1973, 58. Louis Heldman, "A Detroit Janitor's Plea Jolted the Professor into Action," *Detroit Free Press*, April 27, 1975; Don Ball and Jeffrey Hadden, "Edison Ruling a Civil Rights Success," *Detroit Free Press*, October 19, 1973.

58 William B. Gould IV, "Promotion for Blacks," *The Guardian*, May 29, 1972.

59 Equal Employment Op. Comm'n v. Detroit Edison Co., 515 F.2d 301 (6th Cir. 1975).

60 Johnson v. Railway Express, 421 U.S. 454 (1975).

61 *Equal Employment Op. Comm'n*, 515 F.2d at 311.
62 Teamsters v. United States, 431 U.S. 324 (1977); William B. Gould IV, "The High Court Discriminates Between Sex and Race," *New York Times*, June 12, 1977.
63 Tom Goldstein, "Melvin L. Wulf Quits as Legal Director of A.C.L.U.," *New York Times*, January 13, 1977.
64 "Here's the story of my involvement in Edison from my memory and perspective: I was at the time very active in the plaintiff employment discrimination bar with a leadership position at both the National Lawyers Guild and what was then known as the Michigan Trial Lawyers Association. During a meeting of one of these organizations, it came to my attention that the "Edison class action case" had run into a serious hurdle. Bill Gould, according to the story I was told, had achieved significant victories but hundreds of claimants were to be given damage hearings individually and Bill was overwhelmed. Edison, according to the story, was pushing for a small settlement in the light of the lack of back up assistance. If I'm remembering right, there were some 400 claimants and each one could have taken a day or two." Sheldon Stark, email message to author, July 31, 2022.
65 Sheldon M. Lutz, letter to Bruce Ennis of ACLU, July 15, 1981, enclosing payment of $10,000 to local counsel "a check in the amount of $240,000.00 payable to the American Civil Liberties Union . . . representing the payment of attorney's fees."
66 Helen Fogel, "Edison Will Pay $5 Million to Settle Landmark Bias Suit," *Detroit Free Press*, August 17, 1979.
67 William B. Gould IV, *Remarks at Meeting with Chief Justice Earl Warren at Stanford Law School*, May 17, 1974, in 120 CONG. REC. 16229 (1974).
68 One aspect of my work as an expert witness addressed seniority issues in age discrimination in the airlines in San Francisco. See "Pan Am to Pay Retired Pilots In Age Bias Suit," *The New York Times*, February 4, 1988.

7
GO WEST (AND EAST), YOUNG MAN: TEACHING, AFFIRMATIVE ACTION, POLITICS, TRAVEL

My year at Harvard Law School, which extended from the fall of 1971 to the summer of 1972, was hurried and sometimes chaotic. I flew in and out of Cambridge a great deal, handling the *Detroit Edison* case, making speeches, and attending to many other professional matters. But I had been glad to return, as the *Harvard Law Record* put it, "to the town of his birth, Boston, where his family has lived since the Civil War."[1]

I'm inextricably connected to the generations of Goulds who lived in the Boston area before me: My father was born in Cambridge, and during our Harvard year we reunited with his relatives on both sides, reconnecting with many whom I'd met at the much earlier funerals of my great uncles and Aunt Dora. In March of '72 many of my generation were present at my father's surprise seventieth birthday party, celebrated at our Lexington home. To make the party a true surprise, I kept him occupied, taking him to see a fine exhibit on Black lawyers at Harvard Law School.

If, in the fall of 1971, the Law School had extended me an offer to join the permanent faculty, I think I would have accepted it in a heartbeat. Although my colleagues weren't as welcoming as I'd hoped, and I was a little disappointed by Harvard's large—indeed, enormous—classes (my Labor Law class consisted of 180 students; I found myself reading and grading piles of handwritten bluebooks in airplanes, airports, and hotels all over the country), there was a natural pull, for me, toward the land of my forebears. But it was not to be.

No sooner had I sat down at my desk during my very first week of classes at Harvard, than I received a call from Professor Marc Franklin at Stanford Law School, sounding me out on whether Hilda and I could fly to Stanford to talk about an appointment there. I responded affirmatively and we arrived around October 20. I knew absolutely no one at Stanford Law School and had never been there, but I had a very positive impression of it, based on informal discussions with others in the law school world. And I knew my father had visited Stanford during World War II, in the midst of his radar installation trips to California. (Before and after our arrival, however, he would always ask me about William Shockley, Stanford's white supremacist and eugenicist transistor radio innovator.)

VISITING STANFORD

When we arrived, law professor Tom Grey picked us up at the airport and deposited us at the Stanford Faculty Club. First, I met with the dean of the law school, Tom Ehrlich, who was momentarily distracted that morning by the fact that President Nixon had just nominated Stanford Law alumnus William Rehnquist to the Supreme Court. My visit that day and in the days to come were a whirl of activities, meetings, and conversations, highlighted by a dinner with Keith Mann, a labor arbitrator who had taught labor law a few years back, and Stanford Law graduate James (Jim) Danaher, a general and civil rights practitioner with whom I was to become associated in a major job bias case in California. Jim and I hit it off from the start, and he was to become one of my closest friends, personally and professionally. Jim was a wonderful lawyer and a great advertisement for the quality of Stanford Law School. It was many years later, a year or two before his death, that Jim told me he had also been a CIA civilian consultant and advisor.

Tom Ehrlich and I also established a good relationship at our first lunch together. But we were joined by Wayne Barnett, a tax guy on the faculty who was reputed to have possessed one of the two or three top grade point averages (along with Justice Brandeis) in the history of Harvard Law School. At that lunch, Barnett went after me savagely about an article that I had written in 1962 on *Garmon v. San Diego Building Trades*[2] when I was at the UAW.

Barnett had been at the U.S. Solicitor General's office in the early sixties, and *Garmon* was assigned to him. He expressed the view that I really didn't understand the issue at hand in *Garmon* or the basis for the ruling. I don't think I understood his thinking then—and the passage of years hasn't changed that. But at this point during what became a rather heated luncheon conversation, after returning from a visit to the bathroom, I found Tom and Barnett standing up, engaged in an animated discussion. Tom was doing most of the talking, apparently dressing Barnett down. From that moment onward, I knew that Tom was interested in having me come to Stanford Law School, and I had the feeling that he would support me if I joined the faculty. I sensed that an offer from Stanford was likely, and sure enough, I received an invitation shortly after we returned to Cambridge.

Harvard's Dean Al Sacks, who had succeeded Derek Bok at the Law School, had little interest in me from the moment I arrived at Harvard. At a function held within a few days of our arrival, Sacks was so dismissive of ideas I put forward about employment discrimination law that his wife turned to him and said, "Wait a minute, Bill is the expert on this subject." Sacks provided no response. Thus, when I told him of Stanford's offer, he advised me that Harvard would not make an offer of their own at that time. I accepted Stanford's offer and have never looked back. We quickly adopted the reverse version of a common expression at the time, that is, "Harvard is the Stanford of the East." And when my parents came to visit us in California that first Christmas, in December of 1972, they quickly put aside their preliminary skepticism and enjoyed Stanford immensely. One of my most treasured photos is of my father sitting in our backyard at 711 Salvatierra, enjoying the trees, the oranges, and the sunshine.

CAMPUS LIFE AND STRIFE

From 1972 to 1975 the Law School office building was in the midst of the old Stanford campus buildings where Political Science, History, and Communications are now. I loved my office: it looked out over The Oval onto Galvez Street and University Avenue itself, just a stone's throw from the Memorial Church and slightly less than a mile from our home, from which I would usually bike back and forth. My boys, still fairly young at the ages of 8, 6, and 3, were able to travel most places on their bikes or trikes. I would climb into my '68 Volkswagen at the first sign of inclement weather, and that December of 1972 helped me understand those old song lyrics: "It never rains in California . . . it pours, man, it pours." I had experienced a great deal of rain in my life, particularly in Ithaca, New York (when it wasn't snowing), but the incessant, steady rain at Stanford that winter was entirely new to me.

Also a surprise to me was the area's summer weather. When we'd arrived in July of '72, a climatic version of California not revealed by the Chamber of Commerce was visited upon us, that is, intense dry heat. We were staying in what was then the Tiki Motel on Stanford Avenue, near El Camino Real on campus. It felt so hot that I was sure we could fry an egg on the sidewalk if we tried. I wasn't expecting that kind of heat, but I became increasingly accustomed to it in the subsequent era of climate change.

My office was so distant from the building's entrance that sometimes an assistant would telephone, announcing that someone had arrived to see me, but they'd never appear. The hallways were positively labyrinthian. And because my office looked out on the Oval, I could often hear the conversations of campus visitors, particularly during the quiet of workday weekends.

Figure 7.1: My office in the new Crown Quadrangle Law School building, c. late 1970s or 1980s.

Figure 7.2: Walking outside the new Crown Quadrangle Law School building in the late 1970s or 1980s.

Although I don't remember who was immediately adjacent to my office in those early days, during the Watergate hearings in '73 and '74 former Dean Carl Spaeth, whose office adjoined mine, would discuss the hearings' developments with me almost every day. And Bill Cohen, another law professor, was also in the vicinity. I didn't have many conversations with him, but one of them in particular sticks in my mind. One day, early in the semester, Cohen pulled me aside and said, "You know that you were chosen from a special list, don't you?" I think I said something like I hadn't heard specifically of a list—but I had assumed that something akin to this existed. I really didn't *know* that there was such a list, but I was well aware that a big push to seek out and hire Blacks, Latinos, and women had begun after the riots and unrest of 1968 and 1969. Indeed, the Stanford Law School newspaper publicized my hiring as the first Black professor and Barbara Babcock as the first woman when we both arrived in the fall of '72. But in this exchange, it was clear that Cohen wanted me to know that I was on a "special list" and that thus I was at a level beneath him—and wanted to make sure that I understood this. This conversation deepened some of the ambiguity and uncertainty in my mind about the value of affirmative action itself.

Figure 7.3: Though I remained the only Black faculty member at the Stanford Law School for about fifteen years, there were a number of other Black faculty members in other schools. Back row, left to right: James Gibbs (Anthropology) and Kennell Jackson (History). Middle row, left to right: Clayborne Carson (History), Sandra Drake (English), Sandra Richards (Drama), Arnold Rampersad (English), John Gill (Electrical Engineering). Bottom row, left to right: Arthur Walker (Applied Physics), Ewart Thomas (Psychology), Donald Harris (Economics), William B. Gould IV (Law); c. 1980 or 1981.

More than ten years later, in the mid-eighties, Cohen, along with professor of criminal law John Kaplan, was to play a rather pernicious role in the treatment of visiting professor Derrick Bell, just after the completion of Bell's work as dean at the University of Oregon's law school. For a short time, Cohen and Kaplan arranged to provide so-called "remedial" courses for Bell's own course, without his knowledge, because of alleged student complaints about it. This justifiably created an enormous flap.[3]

I had early contact with both Kaplan and Cohen. I criticized Kaplan's comments in a Northwestern article[4] and invited him to defend his anti-affirmative action thesis (the term was hardly known at that point)[5] in my newly devised seminar, Employment Discrimination Law. The students, who were taking the course by choice rather than as a requirement, virtually ate him alive when he made his presentation. At the end of the seminar, Kaplan said, "I will never come to your seminar again."

Another far more explosive event occurred at Stanford in that early period, a story that was later chronicled by the *Wall Street Journal*'s William Wong, who eventually became a great friend of mine.[6] At one of the Board of Visitors meetings of alumni, an elderly looking lawyer (or so he seemed to me at the time) began to pontificate about the inferiority of Blacks and used the N-word. As noted earlier, I have not always been forthcoming or combative in these circumstances, sometimes preferring to duck and dodge controversy and choose discretion over confrontation. But this was not one of those nights. As a result, there was an uproar at our table, and I'm afraid that I was responsible for it.

But Dean Tom Ehrlich, who only a year or so earlier had welcomed me to the Law School, backed me up. As the *Wall Street Journal* wrote:

> Even at Stanford, he [Gould] encountered racism. At a meeting of disgruntled law-school alumni, Mr. Gould heard remarks about "niggers" and similar slurs. The following day . . . he sharply criticized the alumni and won the full support of the law dean and faculty.[7]

All these events helped strengthen my admiration of Tom. Looking back at his professional work, I've often thought that I would have liked to possess his qualifications and standing—he met the standards my father admired and was the kind of person my father wanted me to be. (Regrettably, Tom was succeeded as dean by Charlie Meyers, a staunch Republican from the South—I thought of him as a Texas Dixiecrat—at whose hands I did not fare as well, a subject to which I return in chapter 9.)

Aside from conversations and confrontations like these, my feelings about that old Law School building were good ones. I taught my lecture classes in a room where the podium was behind a swinging gate, which reminded me of the demarcation line between priest and congregation (especially apt when my lectures took on a preaching tone) or the gate between judge and jury in a formal proceeding.

The student–professor ratio at Stanford was, and still is, substantially superior to that at Harvard, more akin to what prevails at Yale. I came to know many students personally over the years and am still in touch with a number of them, as well as with three of my early research assistants from the seventies—Oscar Rosenbloom, Jeremiah Collins, and Gary Williams—all of whom became lifelong friends. Also during this early period, I began to hit and shag baseball flies with three or four students from my class for an hour or so over the weekend, usually on Sundays. This was great exercise and gave me an ability to track fly balls with more skill than I ever had in my youth—and it furthered relations with some students, probably because they were better than I was!

This practice of casual baseball games, with key participants including Collins, Williams, and Jordan Eth, continued well into the mid- and late 1980s. That was up and until President Clinton's appointment of me as chairman of the National Labor Relations Board took me off to the sultry, unpleasant weather of Washington, DC and an agency workforce that was considerably older than my Stanford students—and thus uninterested in this kind of activity. In the late seventies I also began to jog, usually at the Angel Field track and infrequently with Jack Friendenthal, Ken Scott, and Dave Rosenhan for five or six miles around Campus Drive, sometimes in that intense dry heat.

ARBITRATION

During this early period, I continued to arbitrate, frequently in Oakland or Los Angeles, but also in parts of California that were off my beaten track—Stockton, Tracy, Fresno, Chico, Livingston, and, of course, the state's capital, Sacramento. I enjoyed arbitration, particularly because it gave me firsthand contact with the parties in any dispute, and direct involvement with the subject I was teaching and writing about. The issues could be humdrum, but they were always challenging. (In the pandemic era of 2020 and the years that followed, my hearings were by Zoom, thus depriving me of this contact and exposure.)

Sometimes my approaches to arbitration were considered unorthodox. In one case, when a collective bargaining agreement's procedural provisions had been violated, I ordered that the grievant be given back pay without reinstatement; I was convinced that the grievant was unsuitable for the job.[8] This remedy, while uncommon in labor arbitration awards, is frequently adopted in arbitration settlements as well as in decisions arising under the wrongful discharge rubric in the nonunion arena. I thought the world of arbitration should reflect and mirror the commonsense approach of the settlements adopted in lieu of a written award for an adjudicated decision. Apparently the union lawyer was unhappy with me for this somewhat unusual ruling and expressed his view to other union lawyers years later, after President Clinton had nominated me as chairman of the NLRB. It may not have been a consensus or popular position, but in my view it constituted a sensible and appropriate remedy.

While most of my cases over the years involved straightforward credibility issues (nonetheless difficult to resolve, as were our NLRB Administrative Law Judge rulings), some encompassed complex contractual issues. I arbitrated on a topic of my writings,[9] disposing of a discrimination case arising in an area where the contract itself gave the arbitrator authority to address no-discrimination issues—issues triggered by negotiated contract clauses through which labor and management pledge not to discriminate—using the same standards as a federal district court.[10] This procedure—and I arbitrated a second one involving the same issue a few years later[11]—was devised to provide a measure of deference to arbitration, though not finality, in the wake of the Supreme Court's *Gardner-Denver* holding, which decreed that the courts were open to Title VII litigants, notwithstanding an adverse arbitration ruling. About this matter and my views, the same *Wall Street Journal* article said this:

> Mr. Gould also has challenged another sacrosanct industrial-relations practice: arbitration. An arbitrator himself, he maintains that current arbitration machinery isn't equipped to handle job-bias complaints. In his view, arbitrators chosen by the two parties usually accused of job discrimination—employers and labor unions—aren't likely to "bite the hand that feeds them" by ruling against their benefactors.
>
> For this reason, Mr. Gould has argued that an arbitrator's ruling shouldn't be binding in job-bias complaints, because it then virtually closes off an aggrieved employee's option to sue. Earlier this year, citing one of Mr. Gould's articles, the U.S. Supreme Court ruled that workers who lose an arbitrator's award in a job-bias case can still get a full airing of their case in court.[12]

BUILDING RELATIONSHIPS

In these early years at Stanford, I would drive to Berkeley and its Institute of Industrial Relations on a monthly basis to participate in seminars conducted by Lloyd Ulman, and sometimes others. I enjoyed these sessions and Ulman's very friendly and warm personality—aside from the stimulation provided, they introduced me to people like Bob Flanagan from the Stanford Business School, with whom I taught jointly a few courses on discrimination available to both law and business students. I always enjoyed Bob's company and appreciated his droll sense of humor.

Also at this time, I began to frequently attend meetings of the San Francisco Industrial Relations Research Association (later LERA, the Labor and Employment Relations Association), becoming good friends with Magdalena (Maggie) Jacobsen, an active labor mediator, and Walter Slater of the United States Department of Labor. Maggie—one of Dianne Feinstein's favorite mediators when Senator Feinstein was mayor of San Francisco—went on to become a member of the National Mediation Board in the Clinton administration in the 1990s. So I saw a good deal of her at that time, as well as during early Industrial Relations Research Association (IRRA) meetings in San Francisco. Walter, too, became a good friend and, in this century, organized periodic luncheons at Belmont's Iron Gate with trade union and employer representatives.

In the seventies I also became friendly with a number of labor leaders, including Walter Johnson, secretary-treasurer of the San Francisco Labor Council, and Jimmy Herman, president of Local 34, International Longshore and Warehouse Union (ILWU), and eventual successor to Harry Bridges as president of the entire ILWU (West Coast Longshore or dock workers). They participated in some of my early labor law classes in '73 and '74. A few years later I struck up a friendship with Jack Henning, secretary-treasurer of the California AFL-CIO as well. Jack was a natural raconteur, with a great gift for a good story and a sense of history as well. Among the many and memorable meetings I had with him was one that took place at the time of the 1984 convention of the State, County, Municipal Employees Union Convention in San Francisco. I wrote the following in my diary:

> *Henning, the inveterate world traveler and raconteur—we [the British labor attaché, Vic Munns, and the Israeli labor attaché] were treated to conversations with Earl Warren, and Arthur Goldberg that he had had and Warren's glee (which I share) about Nixon's 1962 defeat at the hands of Pat Brown. Of course, as I had known before, Warren never forgave Nixon for his duplicitous betrayal of the former's Presidential candidacy before the '52 Convention in exchange for his own Veep nomination.*
>
> *Henning thinks that Mondale has a good chance (he will speak to the Convention tomorrow) that [Jesse] Jackson's candidacy has been "historic" in involving Blacks. This Israeli displayed his unease about Jackson on the Mideast and speculated that Jackson might "bargain" on this—but*

both Henning and I agreed that this was simply not possible. Nobody seemed to want to do battle with the Israeli, an amiable pudgy little guy...

Much talk about politics. When the conversation turned to union members, voting as their leaders wanted, everyone noted that this frequently doesn't happen in the US, Britain, and Israel. But Henning noted the paradox—any union leader would be devoured in local union politics if he expressed support for Reagan. Hennings said that Gary Hart was "finished" with labor because of his use of the "special interest" issue against the unions.[13]

TITLE VII REVERBERATIONS

Detroit Edison was very much a part of those early Stanford years, but, in part as a result of *Detroit Edison*, I took on a couple of other cases in which the ultimate results were not as favorable. These two cases were quite different from one another. The first involved an attempt to take law which had developed in the Fifth Circuit Court of Appeals[14] to an additional and somewhat new frontier. The second took on parties that had engaged in conduct much more straightforward in its violation of Title VII strictures than even *Detroit Edison* itself. These cases took up a great deal of time over the next four or five years, and involved much stressful work, frequently during both days and evenings.

Notwithstanding their substantive differences, these two cases contrasted sharply with *Edison* because of a shared common denominator: The two trial judges—Baron McCune and Robert Schnacke—were both appointed by President Richard Nixon. Though their hostility to civil rights varied in some measure, both were indeed hostile. Robert Schnacke was aggressively hostile not only to Title VII but also to any of the interpretations adopted and procedures employed in *Detroit Edison*—and he expressed his antipathy to all things Title VII in the course of the litigation itself. (Judge Keith, one of the first Black judges, had been appointed by President Johnson and then, during *Edison*, to the appellate court by President Carter.) The more recent selection of federal judges by President Trump and President Biden have dramatized the significance of this judicial appointment process all the more.

Black Musicians and Segregated Unions

The chronologically first of these two cases commenced before Judge Baron McCune in Pittsburgh, Pennsylvania, when I was still at Harvard. It involved friends and relatives of Harvard's Derrick Bell, all Black musicians in Pittsburgh, including George Childress, Rubeye Young, DeRuyter "Ducky" Kemp, and George Spalding. On their behalf I brought a class action, again on a pro bono basis, serving without fees through my ACLU relationship. The group was warm and forthcoming, perhaps because of Derrick Bell's introduction.

The proceeding arose out of a somewhat unusual—though hardly unprecedented—situation. The American Federation of Musicians (AFM) had maintained two segregated unions in Pittsburgh, as it did in other cities; most of its unions followed the same procedures. When Title VII was passed, the federation realized that it was required to merge these segregated locals throughout the country; in Pittsburgh, the two to be merged were white Local 60 and Black Local 471. Some case law supported the proposition that, where such mergers took place, a transitional agreement was necessary to preserve the interests of both locals—particularly the Black local, which had been disadvantaged in the political process and sometimes through a lack of work opportunities as well.

In Pittsburgh the federation itself, without court orders, put a transitional agreement into place, arguably to protect the minority interest of 200 Black musicians vis-à-vis 2000 white musicians. The merger agreement was transitional and included no specifics or timetables for future progress metrics but provided for the hiring of a Black office employee as well as the election of two Black officeholders—although the key offices of president and secretary-treasurer were to be held by white members of Local 60. Black members complained of the agreement's failure to hire or to promote involvement of Black musicians in the political process. When the agreement was about to expire in 1969, the Black musicians requested that the agreement be carried forward and extended into the 1970s, but they were refused, and all Blacks were ousted from office in an at-large election that took place in 1970. No white union leader provided for any kind of support for any Black member in the 1970 elections. The respective numbers of the two locals, the declining job opportunities for Black musicians, and the lack of a meaningful political presence in the transition had all combined to leave Black musicians empty-handed.

This is where I came in. I traveled to Pittsburgh and stayed at the Holiday Inn at the bottom of the "Hill District," the most visible Black section of Pittsburgh. During some of my visits I would visit the Crawford Bar and Grill near the top of the Hill, which was owned by the same successful Black entrepreneur who owned the Pittsburgh Crawfords, a baseball team in the Negro Leagues. On one occasion Ducky and I listened to "Groove" Holmes play both the piano and the organ at Crawford's, and mused about the sessions he'd played in that landmark jazz restaurant scene.

I had many discussions with the Black musicians on this and subsequent visits. Their complaint was that they were shut out of all political opportunities within the union. Their union hall no longer existed, depriving them of the opportunities they'd had in the past to catch on as sidemen with the big bands and orchestras that came to town. The conundrum here was that integration seemed to be providing them with less than they'd had in the bad old days of segregation. The phenomenon was similar to the decimation of Black baseball through integration: Jackie Robinson left the Negro Leagues, moving to the National League in 1947 and a few months later, Larry Doby and others followed. The same had occurred for Black teachers who were displaced and thus harmed by the integration of schools.

The Black musicians wanted a revival of the transitional program, as the courts had ordered and the federation had provided in 1965, when Title VII became effective. The dilemma was that race consciousness was necessary, though the problem (subsequently addressed by Justice Sandra Day O'Connor in 2003) was left unanswered: When would race consciousness come to an end?[15] Shortly before we filed our action, a vacancy on Pittsburgh's AFM board appeared and the white union leadership supported an inactive Black union member to fill the position. He was opposed by most of the active Black musicians and ultimately viewed himself as "on the outside looking into" the problems of Black members.

We filed an action under Title VII and the Civil Rights Act of 1866, the post-Reconstruction statute prohibiting racial discrimination in employment contracts. I argued that this case exemplified, as did *Detroit Edison*, the present-day consequences of past discrimination and that, had not the 1965 arrangement been entered into, a court might have ordered the parties to do so. Here I relied upon Fifth Circuit authority.[16] I successfully involved government, this time in the form of the EEOC presenting data relating to lost job opportunities for Black members.

Nixon appointee Judge McCune would have none of this. Notwithstanding the facts—that the local unions had been segregated since 1908, Blacks were voted out completely when the transitional agreement expired in 1970, and the court found that Blacks were "frustrated" by the union political process—the court would not provide a remedy. Its argument was that Blacks who did not win elections did not win because they were "inactive" and had boycotted the union—an argument that disregarded the fact that the boycott took place subsequent to 1970, in the teeth of no white support and a long history of segregation. The court appeared to blame the Black musicians for discouraging the one Black member who had been supported by the union around the time of the commencement of litigation. The court claimed that the Black musicians' position was "inconsistent" because they wanted Black representation reinstituted and yet had discouraged the one Black member subsequently chosen by the Local in 1974 from running for office. Said the court:

> The merger has not satisfied everyone. Those concerned could do no less than institute the agreement in 1966, however, and it must be continued. We do not believe we should destroy the concept that the members can engage together

in running the union. We believe the present officers are sincere. The record shows that black members can win elections and that social intercourse and friendship can develop and become commonplace. It will require effort on both sides and a combined effort has been lacking. Hopefully, this litigation has pointed up the lack of interest in this union by a great many of its members, white and black.[17]

The position of the trial judge is key. *Pittsburgh Black Musicians* turned on the importance of this fact, but this time it worked against me, and my clients and I were unable to get the Third Circuit Court of Appeals to reverse Judge McCune, given his numerous findings. In contrast, the findings and positions of Judge Keith in *Detroit Edison* made it impossible for the Sixth Circuit to turn back anything beyond punitive damages and the scope of the class, much as it appeared that it would have liked to go further.

Seniority in Trucking

In the second case, the contrast with the judicial process in *Detroit Edison* was far more graphic. This case arose in trucking, where no-transfer policies precluded minorities from moving into the more lucrative Teamster "over-the-road" trucking jobs—carrying goods substantial distances—and barred them from accumulating seniority. These were even more straightforward and obvious violations of employment discrimination law.

I recall that when I returned to Stanford after filing my complaint in this case in San Francisco in December '73, my colleague John Kaplan asked me which judge I had drawn. When he heard it was Judge Schnacke he immediately said, "I would advise you to return to the San Francisco courthouse and withdraw the complaint." As this litigation, *Jones v. Pacific Intermountain Express*, unfolded in the months and years to come, I frequently thought back to Kaplan's advice and to its wisdom.

My very first appearance before Judge Schnacke, in fact, confirmed John Kaplan's words. The judge called us into chambers and questioned me about *Detroit Edison*, as well as about the procedures and remedies fashioned there. It was not a friendly discussion, and his attitude was hardly congratulatory—quite the opposite. He frowned skeptically as we discussed the case, and I was soon to get a much more bitter taste of Schnacke's disapproval.

Shortly after the complaint was filed, Wesley Fastiff, the San Francisco lawyer representing the employer, Pacific Intermountain Express, telephoned me to meet and discuss a possible resolution or settlement. I readily accepted and invited him to be my guest for lunch at the Stanford Faculty Club. In the course of our discussion, Fastiff expressed curiosity about whether I would be handling this case pro bono, as I had done in both *Detroit Edison* and *Pittsburgh Black Musicians*, with the promise of attorneys' fees to the ACLU in exchange for their reimbursement of costs. I told him that I hadn't yet made a decision, although later I did enter into the same ACLU agreement as in the past.

The early in-chambers meeting with Schnacke and my lunch with Fastiff began to seem ominously related rather quickly, when the latter filed a motion with the court accusing me of unethical solicitation of potential class members by making speeches to minority truck drivers, advising them of the nature of the action filed and that they could obtain remedies, including back and front pay. Arguing in an affidavit that I would become personally enriched through such speeches, which would expand the class and increase the size of the remedy, Fastiff stated to Judge Schnacke that in this case I had told him that I would not be serving pro bono as I had done in the other cases. This, of course, was completely false. But Schnacke either bought it hook, line, and sinker, or found it to be irrelevant: He imposed a gag order on me. Under the order I was required to advise Schnacke when I had spoken to a portion of a class, and to relate what I had said and to whom I had said it. No findings were entered in support of the court's order.

I responded in oral argument by declaring (1) that the "facts" on which the order had been provided were erroneous; (2) that the order was an unconstitutional interference with the First Amendment's protection of speech and freedom of association; and (3) that I could never reveal the audience to which I was speaking as that would deter them from exercising their own First Amendment rights to communicate. This produced no reaction from Judge Schnacke. When I said that I had never engaged in solicitation of any kind on February 15, 1974, this is what transpired, as reported by the *Stanford Daily*:

> Schnacke then lectured Gould on legal ethics and said "I appreciate that the class action concept seemingly has dulled the notion [of legal ethics] in the minds of some counsel."
>
> "There shall be nothing that smacks of solicitation until the further hearing before this court," said Schnacke. When Gould said that he could "not agree not to communicate," Schnacke retorted that he "didn't care whether you [Gould] agree or not. There will be no communications about the case prior to March 15 and until further order of the Court."[18]

The *Wall Street Journal* summed it up this way:

> The class action case has been nettlesome for Mr. Gould because defense attorneys charge that in attempting to communicate with minority workers who may have been discriminated against, Mr. Gould was soliciting clients—unethical conduct for an attorney. The judge apparently agreed, lecturing Mr. Gould from the bench and issuing an order prohibiting communication with members of the class without prior court approval. Mr. Gould, who denies the charge, says the order is an unconstitutional "gag" and has retained a Stanford colleague to appeal it. Of the charges, he says, "It was a very personal blow."[19]

My colleague Anthony (Tony) Amsterdam, a leading constitutional and criminal lawyer who had successfully challenged the constitutionality of the death penalty before the Supreme Court, jumped in to represent me in the "gag order" aspect of the case, since now, through the plaintiff's lawyer, I had become an object of the litigation. A motion to vacate the gag order was summarily rejected by Schnacke and—much to the astonishment of Amsterdam and myself—the Ninth Circuit denied the appeal. At this point Schnacke, who had admitted me for this case earlier, since my bar membership was in Michigan, began to threaten to require both Amsterdam and myself to take the California bar examination before we proceeded further. And ultimately he made good on one of his threats and kicked Tony out of the case!

The more pernicious effect of these machinations was the time taken away from litigating the case's merits. The tactic worked very well, for, as we fought over the gag order, the case became a war of attrition, with discovery motions and interrogatories filed on both sides. More than once I attempted to disqualify Schnacke, but of course he would not abide the thought of that, and accordingly denied my motions. This was his chance to make his work run contrary to Judge Keith's actions in *Detroit Edison*, just as his early in-chamber discussion had revealed.

Paradoxically, in a sense, I thrived on the guns arrayed against me. As in *Detroit Edison*, I had a great legal team with me: Jim Danaher; Thelton Henderson, who was at that time an assistant dean at Stanford Law School assigned to minority recruitment, and was appointed by President Carter in 1980 to the federal bench; Jack Pemberton, my *Detroit Edison* co-counsel; and Mike Gilfix, a Stanford Law student set to graduate in the spring of 1974 who would later become a leading authority on the law of the elderly. Danaher, Henderson, and Pemberton all had considerable trial experience, and Gilfix, who participated in those weekend fly ball exercises, approached litigation the way he approached the baseball field: hungry, energetic, like an unyielding terrier, grinding into discovery issues as avidly as he fielded ground balls on the baseball diamond.

In early 1974, in a motion argued before Schnacke, I was all by myself. On the other side, arrayed against me, were about fifteen lawyers—all on the clock, of course—representing various trucker defendants and the Teamsters. I loved to stand alone against them: I felt a bit like Serpico, the solitary New York policeman, fighting against the forces of corruption. Yet the reality was that in our litigation the Augean Stables challenged by Serpico would not be cleansed. There was simply no way around Schnacke.

I became so deeply involved in the trucking case during this period that not only was I consumed with it throughout many evenings, but I was also shaken by the numerous depositions staring me in the face in the law school mail room every day. Once, I was halfway to San Francisco on Route 101, where I was set to argue a motion, when I suddenly realized I had a class at the law school at the same time! Fortunately, it was one I was co-teaching with my colleague at the Business School, Bob Flanagan, and he generously covered for me.

Around this time, I'd become quite friendly with Gerry Gunther, an eminent constitutional law scholar. Other than the janitors, we were often the only people in the law school in the evening. I can still hear his footsteps coming down the hallway. We would often interrupt our work for a chat, and one night he told me of his childhood in Nazi Germany, how he was bullied by Nazi teachers and students. He told me of listening to the radio in 1938, when Joe Louis fought the German boxer Max Schmeling, and the Nazi dream of white supremacy was shattered by Louis's one-sided demolition of Schmeling in the first round of their second fight. Gerry told me that the German radio announcers said Schmeling was a victim of cheating, claiming that a white substance on Louis's gloves had been placed there to blind Schmeling.

During another one of those nocturnal meetings, I expressed my deep anguish to Gerry about the interrogatories and discovery demands that I was receiving on an almost daily basis. Gerry said: "Look, Bill, I know that you enjoy Walter Cronkite on the evening news. Here's what you do: Go home an hour or so earlier so that you don't miss Cronkite, and pour yourself a scotch on the rocks as you listen to the news. I think that things will look better for you then." I followed his advice. And since that time a half-century ago, I have poured myself a glass (sometimes two) of Johnny Walker Red at 6 p.m. whenever it was possible to do so. On the basis of Gerry's good advice, the world did indeed begin to look better, notwithstanding Judge Schnacke's bulldog-like anger and all the problems he presented for me and my colleagues.

Continuing Frustrations in *Jones*

My motions to disqualify Schnacke in *Jones v. Pacific Intermountain Express* having met with no success, I turned to other avenues. Conflict in the Middle East had led to the energy crisis of 1974 and resulted in layoffs in trucking and elsewhere. I sought to attack "last hired, first fired" through a preliminary injunction, on the grounds that the same kind of seniority discrimination found in *Detroit Edison* was present here as well. But as was the case with the gag order, the Ninth Circuit affirmed Judge Schnacke's denial of this motion, stating that there was no evidence that jobs had been available through which seniority could be acquired, even though white workers hired into those available jobs had been able to accumulate seniority while discrimination was ongoing, and this was in evidence before the trial court and part of the record on appeal.[20] This holding made no sense whatsoever. Thus the Ninth Circuit, refusing to limit Schnacke in both the gag order and the subsequent last hired, first fired litigation, left us with "Schnacke Justice" staring us down on a near-daily basis.

The only other avenue open to us, I felt, was through a previous Justice Department case, *United States v. Trucking Employers*. Justice had initiated litigation against both the truckers and the Teamsters and entered into an agreement purporting to resolve the back pay issue while transfer and seniority issues remain unresolved.[21] Through attacking this tactic, we were finally able to prevail somewhere in this case. The Court of Appeals for the District of Columbia held, as I had argued, that the agreements that Justice had provided for with the truckers (the so-called *Johnson* intervenors, consisting of Black and Latino truckers employed in a variety of other companies), for which they waived their statutory right to sue, were invalid.[22] Our theory on behalf of the so-called *Jones* intervenors was the successful one because we, in contrast to the

Johnson intervenors, argued that the waiver was not a knowing and voluntary one under the standards of earlier Supreme Court authority, and was thus invalid.

There was yet another indignity frustrating our position in this litigation avenue: The Court of Appeals denied us attorneys' fees normally awarded a prevailing party in Title VII litigation. They did so on the grounds that they had not accepted our theory in this case. But, regrettably, the court confused us, the *Jones* intervenors, with the *Johnson* intervenors who had attacked the Justice Department with a broader, more far-flung theory. I had now argued before four circuit courts of appeals—the Sixth Circuit; the Third Circuit; the D.C. Circuit; and the Ninth Circuit. But the D.C. Circuit's denial of attorneys' fees was a bit difficult to accept, given that the theory of *my* clients, the *Jones* intervenors, had been misidentified. This was terribly frustrating and, on balance, induced me to turn my attention back to my scholarly writing and to venture into the political process.

BACK INTO POLITICS

By the time we moved to California I had attended several Democratic conventions, including the one in Atlantic City, New Jersey, in 1964. (An aside: I also attended the San Francisco convention in 1984, when Mario Cuomo made his eloquent keynote speech. The fact that the Red Sox were in Oakland at almost the same time, with pitchers Roger Clemens and "Oil Can" Boyd called up from the minors, made this period particularly memorable.) My first political campaign participation, beyond JFK in '60 at Cornell and my own delegate contest in Michigan, was in my UAW days, in an Eastside Detroit by-election when I knew I was supporting a loser and did so nonetheless. When I told my UAW boss, Harold Cranefield, about my involvement and that I was knowingly supporting a loser, he responded: "Young man, it is never too early to start winning."

My first connection with politics in California arose in rather unusual circumstances. After I gave a speech in San Francisco to Stanford alumni on my job bias litigation and employment discrimination law writings, an alumna by the name of Barbara Porter suggested that my wife and I join her and her husband, lawyer Bill Porter, for a dinner at her house in the Pacific Heights section of San Francisco. At this function we were seated at the same table as *San Francisco Chronicle* columnist Art Hoppe, and Roger Kent, part of Marin County's well-known Kent family, which had established the small community of Kentfield in the late 1800s.

Much of the discussion that night was about Watergate. The drama was just beginning to unfold, and Kent, who had been chairman of Democrat Pat Brown's second gubernatorial campaign against Richard Nixon in 1962, described an issue which had arisen in that Brown–Nixon contest. As Kent described it, literature claiming that Pat Brown was a Communist Party member was distributed during the campaign, and the Brown people traced it directly to Nixon's campaign offices. As the depositions were going up the chain of command to determine responsibility, eventually they came to Nixon himself. And, as Kent described it, at that point the Nixon campaign folded its cards, admitting responsibility rather than allowing Nixon to be deposed. In concluding this story Kent said to all of us sitting at the table, "You mark my words. The same thing is going to happen now in Watergate."

This was early 1973; I often thought about that lively evening during the next year, particularly when Nixon resigned in August 1974 rather than face impeachment for his involvement in the coverup (and perhaps more) of the Watergate burglary. As 1973 went on, I became more involved in the political process, and when in 1974 the Democratic Party created a kind of mini-convention in Kansas City designed to involve party adherents in the formulation of issues, I threw my hat into the ring.

It was my first candidacy since my delegate's race in Michigan. But I was out of town for the ballot itself, so my friend Jim Danaher spoke for me in my absence. Perhaps that should have been a lesson in itself, for I won handily on the basis of Jim's speech and was able to go to Kansas City and participate. And I won despite other seeming disadvantages as well. The *Palo Alto Times* said the following about me and two others who were elected at that time:

> *The three are among the "reform" elements of the party which want stronger affirmative action clauses in the charter. They intend to fight for them. Gould, who specializes in labor law, has been teaching politics for many years, but the convention will be his first active participation in politics. His selection as a delegate might be attributed to luck—first bad, then good. Delegates were chosen by congressional districts in caucus elections Nov. 9. Gould was a candidate in the 12th district, but his name was inadvertently left off a newsletter list sent by the state party headquarters to members of the Palo Alto-Stanford Democratic Association. Gould complained, and the publicity he received from his complaint made him better known to the 185 Democrats who voted in the caucus than any newsletter could have done.*[23]

The article went on to say that I viewed the convention process in Kansas City as "a terrific opportunity to bring politics closer to the people, for them to become involved in the democratic process." Reflecting the same vein of enthusiasm, I received a letter from my old pal and former New York state senator Basil Paterson, who had represented me on New York City's West Side, along with his more populous Harlem constituents. Basil had subsequently been a candidate for lieutenant governor of New York in Arthur Goldberg's ill-fated 1970 campaign against Nelson Rockefeller. Basil wrote:

> *On a flight from Hilton Head Island, South Carolina (site of the Democratic Governors' Conference) to Atlanta, Georgia (en route to New York) I was informed by Alan Baron (Democratic Planning Group) that a Black cat who is a professor at Stanford University Law School had been elected Delegate to the Kansas City Convention. He wondered who you were and where you were coming from. It was great news!*[24]

The convention itself was another matter altogether. I met people, participated in the Black Caucus working on an affirmative action provision for the convention, which was ultimately, as I said, "ambiguous" and "not really satisfactory."[25] Said the *Chicago Tribune*:

> *William Gould is not a household name in black communities thruout [sic] this land, but at this 1974 Conference on Democratic Party Organization and Policy he gave a powerful thrust to the determination of black delegates who refused to compromise on the "quota" debate...*
>
> *The black caucus debate dragged on until attorney Gould began to point out in precise language that...[the Convention provision denying affirmative action] was in defiance of all of the legal decisions rendered in federal courts pertaining to jobs and voting rights over the last 20 years.*[26]

I was successful with others in obtaining a so-called judicial council which would rule on future challenges to delegate selections. But one reform that I backed—returning to the 1972 practice of choosing delegates to national presidential nominating conventions by caucus elections—was beaten back, and perhaps it should have been. The process, while not completely satisfactory, was an educational experience.

I went on to participate in other political matters, but only at the margins. Friends sometimes chuckled about my propensity for picking losers; in 1984, while supporting John Glenn for the Democratic nomination, I mused in my diary about campaigns I had supported in the past:

> *Mondale...about the worst advertisement that a candidate could have in my view... Bob Kennedy in '68, Ed Muskie in '72, Frank Church in '76 and Ted Kennedy in '80—now John Glenn in '84—not exactly a winning record!*[27]

The trend continued in 1988, when I organized a "Stanford Law School for Anna Eshoo" committee when she first ran for Congress that year, against my colleague Tom Campbell. She was defeated. It goes without saying that Tom was hardly pleased with this development. (However, Anna was successful in 1992 and served as my congresswoman for the next thirty years!) And in 1992 Berkeley Law School professor Willy Fletcher—later a Ninth Circuit judge—was chairing California for Clinton and got me to sign on in the campaign. I gave a number of speeches for Governor Clinton in the

Bay Area. In one of them, at the IBEW Convention in San Francisco, I was called in to substitute for Senator Barbara Boxer. I spoke about the failures of and deficiencies in the National Labor Relations Act, particularly as it relates to the rights of employers to permanently replace economic strikers. This speech turned out to be a table thumper for me—and the delegates seemed to like it too, judging by their response.

In 2000 I was a Bill Bradley delegate; I joked with him that I was his token Boston Celtic delegate, as he'd been a star with the New York Knicks. But Bradley wasn't able to compete effectively in California and, though a top vote-getter at the so-called caucus, I wasn't chosen for the convention because the number of Bradley votes in the primary was too small. Probably my most dramatic moment on the political scene took place during the chaotic general election of that year when, at the invitation of San Francisco labor leader Walter Johnson, in December 2000, I spoke in Union Square San Francisco, urging through a bullhorn held by my wife that all votes should be counted in Florida, where the recount had already been enjoined by Justice Scalia. Regrettably, my little speech had no impact on either politics or law, as the Supreme Court brought a halt to the vote count and gave the election to George Bush.[28]

There was a similar scenario in the delegate selection process of 2004. I was a winner in the contest to represent General Wesley Clark in his presidential campaign but, once again, his votes were so low in California that he withdrew; none of his delegates were sent to the convention in Boston. Nonetheless, I was selected as an alternate delegate for the ultimate nominee, John Kerry, and I went to the Boston convention in that capacity. Much to my chagrin, however, alternates have virtually no access to the floor. Indeed, my former student at Stanford, Mark Brewer, when he became chairman of the Michigan Democratic Party, was able to get me far more access at the 1996 convention when I was living in Washington and attended the convention on a private basis.

In the next presidential campaign, in 2008, I was very much taken by Barack Obama, who had impressed me since I'd heard him give a televised speech in Springfield, Illinois, in 2007, as his campaign began. Shortly thereafter, the Clinton administration's personnel director called and asked me to support Hillary Clinton. I told her that I was for Obama. As if to underscore how remote Obama's chances appeared to be, she immediately said, "Oh, but you'll support Hillary after the convention?" "Sure," I said, accepting her premise that Obama would be defeated. I, of course, cast my California primary ballot for Obama, but I didn't meet him until I visited the White House with the 2013 World Champion Red Sox in April of 2014. On that day, I had a very brief exchange with him and said, "We are all so proud of you." He thanked me effusively—though I immediately wondered whether this comment sounded too patronizing.

Figure 7.4: December 2000 speech at Union Square, protesting Justice Scalia's injunction against vote counting in Florida. I am helped by my wife, Hilda, who is holding the bullhorn as I speak.

Figure 7.5: In conjunction with the 2013 Boston Red Sox World Champions, I met with President Obama at the White House in April 2014 to celebrate 2013's accomplishments.

Figure 7.6: At the Boston Zoo, July 2004, as an alternate delegate for John Kerry of Massachusetts.

British Politics

As I've described, my interest in British politics began at the London School of Economics in the early 1960s. During my New York tenure in the late sixties, I had met with the new British Race Relations Board, chaired by Mark Bonham-Carter, and with race relations specialists Messrs. Geoffrey Bindman, Anthony Lester, and John Lytlle. When I moved to Detroit and Stanford, I connected with them there as well. In 1970, in the wake of Prime Minister Edward Heath's election, when discussion of labor law reform in Britain flourished, I met and arranged for labor and management meetings with numerous British experts during my Wayne State tenure. K. W. "Bill" Wedderburn of LSE, Q. C. Geoffrey Howe (later solicitor with the Heath Government and chancellor of the exchequer under Mrs. Thatcher), and one of my former professors at LSE, Cyril Grunfeld, all came to Detroit in 1970.

When Britain, under the Heath Government, enacted the Industrial Relations Act of 1971, I wrote about it sympathetically[29] and returned to Britain in January of 1973 to give a series of lectures on the American arbitration system.[30] The *New York Times* adverted to these lectures that year, writing:

> Gould . . . told a British audience that another contrast [between America and Britain] *was the heavier reliance in the United States on arbitration which, he said, was a "dirty word" in Britain. He noted that 94 percent of labor agreements in America carried arbitration clauses and they reduced the inclination to strike.* "Here they often use strikes as the first resort," he said. "In the United States, with arbitration they often used strikes as the last resort."[31]

Subsequently, after litigation and politics early in my first Stanford year, I was connected with Britain once again: I was awarded a Guggenheim Fellowship and a grant from the Rockefeller Foundation to examine union relationships with multinational corporations. This took the entire family to Churchill College, Cambridge, in the spring of 1975.

A SOJOURN IN CAMBRIDGE

To be back in Britain in 1975 was wonderful for our family, especially Hilda. She and the boys arrived a few weeks ahead of me, in March. Both Churchill College and Cambridge were lovely, and Hilda and I frequently dined with the other fellows, drank sherry, and toasted the Queen. The weather was balmy and the summer unusually hot by British standards.

I was in London often and spent a good deal of time in Sweden, Germany, and Belgium during that period, examining those countries' systems and the potential for both union–management national cooperation and union–multinational cooperation across national boundaries in Europe.[32] At the end of one of those trips back from the Continent to Britain, the British overwhelmingly voted by referendum to join what was then the Common Market, now known as the European Union. On that cheerful, beautiful day in 1975, we could not anticipate the sad 2016 reversal of the agreement through Brexit, and the consequent departure from principles of international cooperation which the EU promoted.

Despite my peripatetic wanderings through Britain and the Continent, I was able to forge new friendships at Cambridge, particularly with Brian Bercusson, the leading European Union labor law specialist, as well as Paul O'Higgins, an eminent lecturer in labor law at Christ's College. And, of course, this was a great chance to reconnect with old friends from LSE days like Keith Stuart and John Cole. John was still at that point a newspaperman, but in 1985 he would embark upon a career as a political commentator for BBC Television, which made him a much more familiar figure, frequently covering Prime Minister Thatcher. During one cab ride, my London cabbie said to me, "Is that fellow you were just talking to John Cole?"

GO WEST (AND EAST), YOUNG MAN 237

TRAVELS AND RESEARCH ABROAD

After concluding my work in Cambridge, we left London for Portugal and three weeks of a true family vacation in a small seaside town south of Lisbon. The trip was enhanced by the absence of American tourists—they had been scared off by the 1974 revolution, through which the Salazar regime had been deposed, and the instability which seemed to emerge in its wake. Indeed, there were soldiers assembled on bridges, heavily armed with machine guns, but they were not pointed at us. In fact, everyone was extremely friendly to us.

The Portuguese revolution meant the end of the Portuguese empire in Africa, and we observed numerous manifestations of the resulting wars. Photos of slain Portuguese soldiers were mounted next to votive candles in almost every church we visited—Portugal had paid a heavy price for its wars in Angola and Mozambique. There were also large numbers of Black Africans in the Lisbon airport, presumably aligned in some way with Portuguese authority and therefore fleeing the newly independent governments. This political change was to be part of a new dynamic for South Africa (more about this in chapter 8) and for the southern portion of the African continent.

Our vacation ended in late August, and I took my last look at Portugal. But the coming years would bring me much more international travel, research, and exchange. The family returned to California, and I flew to Tokyo, as my Rockefeller grant allowed me a research base at the University of Tokyo Faculty of Law, with a few days in Moscow and Leningrad (St. Petersburg) en route. When I arrived at the airport in Moscow, the Russian security staff were distracted, looking at television pictures of the developments in Portugal, where they may have assumed that a radical pro-Moscow government was about to emerge.

My visit to the Soviet Union lasted less than a week, but I was struck by the beauty of Leningrad, its grand buildings and wide streets, the stunning architecture of the Kremlin, and Vladimir Lenin's embalmed body lying in state. I was amused by the little old ladies who sat in each hotel corridor, apparently to monitor any potential improprieties by foreign visitors. While sailing on the Volga, I asked the guide the name of a particularly prominent building. "It's the ministry of peace," he said. "Ministry of peace?" I asked, having never heard of such a thing anywhere. Of course, it was the Ministry of Defense, in the land of George Orwell-like language contortion. As I flew to Tokyo from Moscow, I was aware that we would pass over Vladivostok, a city whose far eastern location had intrigued me since my schoolboy days; I asked the flight attendant whether the pilot could tell us when we were near or over it. She came back and said, "The pilot wants to know why you want to know."

Japan and Its Labor Laws

The enthusiastic greeting I received in Tokyo's Haneda airport entirely dispelled the air of suspicion that had hung over my Soviet visit. Professor Kicheomeon Ishikawa of Tokyo Law School, with whom I had corresponded from both the U.S. and Britain, was there with some of his young scholars and assistants. My introduction to the Far East began with dinner with the Ishikawas; I then began my seven-week stay in Japan, meeting with lawyers, industrial relations specialists, and union and employer representatives, while also giving speeches to Japanese audiences on the American system of labor law and labor–management relations. Within the first couple of weeks I made contact with Japanese baseball as well. The *Hochi Shinbun*, a Japanese tabloid, ran an article about and picture of my meeting with Gail Hopkins, the former Chicago White Sox first baseman who played for Japan's Professional League team, the Hiroshima Toyo Carp. The article reported, "Professor Gould has come to Japan to look at Japanese labor laws—but really he has come here to look at Japanese baseball."

Figure 7.7: With first baseman Gail Hopkins of the Hiroshima Carp in Kawasaki, Japan, September 1975.

Figure 7.8: With my oldest son, William Benjamin V, and American players, including Adrian Garrett (on the right), on the Hiroshima Carp in Hiroshima, 1978.

My first visit to Japan, and the wide scope of friends and contacts I developed as a result of it, was triggered by a simple phone call while I was in Britain. I had called the American Embassy in London to arrange for a meeting with the American labor attaché, Robert Immerman. The individual with whom I spoke said to me, "Too bad we didn't know you were here in Britain. We could have arranged for you to give talks here on the American labor system. We can do that in Japan—and we can arrange in the future to do it in Europe and Africa as well." This conversation led to speaking engagements all over the world.

Assessing Culture and Contrasts

The appeal of Japan was twofold: (1) It was the first nation in the nonwhite world to pose a challenge to the West; I often recalled my father's comments during the war about America's surprise at Japanese proficiency, and this was dramatized anew in the peace that followed World War II; and (2) the Allied occupation, led by General Douglas MacArthur, imposed American labor law on Japan, incorporating much of the Wagner Act prior to the Taft-Hartley amendments. This was part of the reform agenda that the United States deemed necessary for the creation of a democratic Japan, a country that would not repeat the mistakes that resulted in World War II—or the Pacific War, as the Japanese call it.

I was living a comparative law researcher's dream: comparing two countries with innumerable cultural contrasts; afforded contact with the practitioners of the Central Labor Relations Commission, or Churoi (the Japanese NLRB) and its provincial counterparts; and assessing the ways they resolved the disputes before them. But Japan (in contrast to Canada, which mirrors the American system more precisely) has no NLRB election machinery, no concept of exclusive bargaining representative status for unions, and fundamentally different avenues for addressing unfair labor practice issues. No American or Japanese scholar had previously written comparatively about this legal framework. Determining how the Japanese system worked, and how the two systems might be accurately compared, dramatized the cultural divide that hid beneath superficially similar statutes. American and Japanese statutes might both include words like "unfair labor practices," but that phrase has no precise translation in the Japanese language. My job was to determine what these systems and laws really meant, and how they functioned.[33]

I read a number of books and articles about Japanese labor law and was able to supplement this research with interviews I conducted during my seven-week Japanese tour in 1975. In 1978 I returned, this time with my entire family, to live in Japan for half a year. While this long visit plunged me more deeply into the real world of Japan, Japanese labor, and Japanese baseball, it was a challenging time. Our three boys—two in high school and the third in middle school—left their familiar California schools behind to attend the American School in Tokyo. Our lack of proficiency in the Japanese language and our location, far from the city center in Mashashi-Kogenai, a profoundly non-English-speaking section of Tokyo, meant that we struggled to get proper deliveries of milk and bread. The Japanese were continuously astounded by our three boys' ravenous appetites and meat-eating habits. These habits, coupled with our private travel and the dollar's decline against the rising yen, meant that my grants did not stretch as far as I'd anticipated. And we visited so many stadiums, temples, shrines, and museums that the boys, finally, could take it no longer. It was an unforgettable year, but not one, I think, that endeared me to my family. It was a learning experience for all of us.

Nonetheless, I made other return visits to Japan by myself, the first in November of 1978, when I was called upon to arbitrate an American teacher dispute at the U.S. military base in Okinawa. There, interestingly, the dollar seemed to be in greater use than the Japanese yen because of American military predominance. I spent more than a week conducting the hearing, and on weekends watched Japanese bullfighting, which offered a contrast to the bloody Spanish and Latin American use of matadors: in Japan, two bulls fight each other, each aiming to push his opponent out of the ring, sumo style. After the hearing it was back to the mainland once more. I made a number of return visits to Japan through the late 1980s, gathering more information every time.

Another Book Intervenes

My teaching at Stanford, and lectures in Latin America and South Africa (discussed in chapter 8), slowed my progress on the comparative book about Japan and the United States that I had planned to write. And, as I traveled widely between 1975 and 1980, speaking about the American labor system, I was often asked to recommend a good book on American labor law for specialists, one that was not too detailed and aimed at American labor lawyers. My inability to make that recommendation, coupled with encouragement by Hilda to write it myself, produced *A Primer on American Labor Law*, the first edition of which I wrote in 1980 and 1981. It was published in 1982.[34]

Written at Waikiki

In the fall of 1982 my Stanford colleague, Victor Li, invited me to be a fellow at the East–West Center in Honolulu, a center for cooperative research founded to encourage understanding between the U.S., Asia, and the Pacific Islands. This opportunity pushed my book, *Japan's Reshaping of American Labor Law*, forward to conclusion. No one could believe I was in lovely Honolulu, at Waikiki Beach, writing a book, but write it I did, sometimes sitting on the beach itself as I wrote. Like the *Primer* it was published by MIT Press, and overall I was pleased with the finished product. My only major regret was its title. An essay about it in the *Michigan Law Review* was titled "Remade in Japan."[35] *That* should have been the title!

NOTES

[1] Kermit Kubitz, "Visiting Law Professor William Gould Focuses on Civil Rights, Labor Unions," *Harvard Law Record*, May 5, 1972.

[2] San Diego Unions v. Garmon, 359 U.S. 236 (1959). William B. Gould IV, "The Garmon Case: Decline and Threshold of Litigating Elucidation," *University of Detroit Law Journal* 39 (1962).

[3] Dorothy Gilliam, "An Insult to a Law Professor," *Washington Post*, August 4, 1986.

[4] "One may, of course, question whether the society which we hope to build in the future should actually be completely color-blind. The presence of disparate groups in our culture contributes to its interest and productivity, and one may well feel that we lose something when our Chinese restaurants are staffed by Negroes, Puerto Ricans,

and Italians. Nevertheless, the history of the Negro in America is such that for many generations to come, classification of the Negro as a distinct group can only evoke bitter memories. At least with respect to the Negro, the type of society we probably should envision is one where color is completely irrelevant, not only to all governmental, but to all societal purposes. It may be that the only possible way that this can be achieved is through intermarriage so complete that the Negro no longer exists as a Negro." John Kaplan, "Equal Justice in an Unequal World: Equality for the Negro – The Problem of Special Treatment," *Northwestern Law Review* 61 (1966): 380.

Cited in William B. Gould IV, *Black Workers in White Unions: Job Discrimination in the United States* (Ithaca: Cornell University Press, 1977): 117 (emphasis in the Kaplan quote supplied in the Gould book).

[5] Most of the public and indeed, legal profession, is not aware of the fact that the term and concept of affirmative action began in the National Labor Relations Act of 1935: "If upon the preponderance of the testimony taken the Board shall be of the opinion that any person named in the complaint has engaged in or is engaging in any such unfair labor practice, then the Board shall state its findings of fact and shall issue and cause to be served on such person an order requiring such person to cease and desist from such unfair labor practice, and to take such affirmative action including reinstatement of employees with or without backpay, as will effectuate the policies of this Act." National Labor Relations Act of 1935 §10, 29 U.S.C. § 160.

[6] William Wong, "Lawyer William Gould Prods Courts to End Job Bias; His Activism Sometimes Irks Peers," *Wall Street Journal*, August 21, 1974.

[7] Wong, "Lawyer William Gould Prods Courts to End Job Bias."

[8] *Safeway Stores Inc.*, 64 Lab. Arb. 563 (1974).

[9] William B. Gould IV, "Labor Arbitration of Grievances Involving Racial Discrimination," *University of Pennsylvania Law Review* 118 (1969).

[10] *Basic Vegetable Products, Inc.*, 64 Lab. Arb. 620 (1975).

[11] *Weyerhauser Co.*, 78 BNA LA 1109 (1982).

[12] Wong, "Lawyer William Gould Prods Courts to End Job Bias."

[13] William B. Gould IV, Diary, June 18, 1984.

[14] Long v. Georgia Kraft Co., 455 F.2d 331 (5th Cir. 1972).

[15] Grutter v. Bollinger, 539 U.S. 306 (2003). See Justice O'Connor's concurring decision: "We expect that twenty-five years from now, the use of racial preferences will no longer be necessary to further the interest approved today" at 343.

[16] *Long*, 455 F.2d. Other supportive authority existed by virtue of United States v. Jacksonville Terminal Co., 451 F.2d 418 (5th Cir. 1971); Hicks v. Crown Zellerbach Corp., 310 F.Supp. 536 (E.D. La. 1970); Lee v. Macon County, 283 F.Supp. 195 (M.D. Ala. 1968).

[17] Black Musicians of Pittsburgh v. Local 60-471, American Federation of Musicians, 1975 WL 339 (1975). See also, Black Musicians of Pittsburgh v. Local 60-471, American Federation of Musicians, 375 F.Supp. 902 (W.D. Pa. 1974).

[18] Don Cox, "Law Profs Battle Gag Order," *Stanford Daily*, February 26, 1974.

[19] Wong, "Lawyer William Gould Prods Courts to End Job Bias."

[20] Jones v. Pacific Intermountain Exp., 536 F.2d 817 (9th Cir. 1976).

[21] United States v. Trucking Employers, Inc., 561 F.2d 313 (D.C. Cir. 1977).

[22] *United States*, 561 F.2d 313.

[23] John Stanton, "Local Demo reform trio plot fight," *Palo Alto Times*, December 3, 1974.

24 Basil A. Paterson, letter to Bill Gould, November 20, 1974.
25 John Stanton, "Democrats' charter 'something to build on for 1976,'" *Palo Alto Times,* December 10, 1974.
26 Vernon Jarrett, "Quota agreement elusive to Dems," *Chicago Tribune,* December 8, 1974.
27 William B. Gould IV, Diary, January 29, 1984.
28 Bush v. Gore, 531 U.S. 98 (2000).
29 William B. Gould, "Taft-Hartley Comes to Great Britain: Observations on the Industrial Relations Act of 1971," *Yale Law Journal* 81 (July 1972).
30 William B. Gould IV, "Substitutes for the Strike Weapon: The Arbitration Process in the United States," *Arbitration Journal* 28 (June 1973).
31 Alvin Shuster, "British Union Head Retiring with Regret Over Workers' Image," *New York Times,* September 5, 1973.
32 William B. Gould IV, "Multinational Corporations and Multinational Unions: Myths, Reality, and the Law," *International Law* 10 (1976); William B. Gould IV, "The World's Workers May Yet Unite: Growth of Multinationals Gives New Life to the International Labor Movement," *Los Angeles Times,* September 1, 1975.
33 William B. Gould IV, *Japan's Reshaping of American Labor Law* (Cambridge: MIT Press, 1984).
34 A Primer has gone through six editions now and has proved to be more widely read than most of the books I've authored.
35 Jennifer Friesen, "Remade in Japan," *Michigan Law Review* 83 (1985).

8

PROMOTING LABOR RIGHTS AND STANDARDS ABROAD: SOUTH AFRICA, LATIN AMERICA, AND EASTERN EUROPE

As promised, the American Embassy in London helped me arrange speaking engagements all over the world—first to Japan, and then to Korea, Malaysia, Singapore, Indonesia, Australia, and New Zealand. In 1976 and 1978 I gave lectures in India as well, under the auspices of the U.S. State Department. In all these countries, I gave talks about American labor law and met relevant labor specialists, as I had in Japan. The longest of my visits was to Australia, where I was based at the University of Melbourne law faculty; there I reconnected with Colin Howard, a former colleague at Wayne State Law School, and established a friendship with senior lecturer and social justice advocate Julian Phillips. Australia, having elected a Labor government with Prime Minister Gough Whitlam at its head in 1972, was in the process of revising its historically racist policies toward both Aborigines and Asians—policies that certainly needed revision, in my view: I saw signs in Melbourne in 1975 that still said, "Stop the Asian Invasion!"

Figure 8.1: With my wife, ensconced on the top of an elephant, during my '78 lecture tour of India.

SOUTH AFRICA: APARTHEID, LABOR, STRUGGLE

Thanks also largely to the American Embassy's efforts, South Africa was to become a significant feature of my professional life. Embassy staff in London passed my name on to Joe Glazer, an American union balladeer employed as a labor specialist with the United States Information Agency (USIA) and brother of Nathan Glazer, one of the better-known neoconservatives of the 1960s and 1970s. In 1972 I had had a rather sharp exchange with Nathan Glazer, which began when I published a letter in the *New York Times* expressing surprise that the *Times* had supported what I called an "express attack" on the Department of Health, Education, and Welfare (HEW) for devising "goals" in search of minority candidates. I wrote:

> *Only if unqualified minority group applicants are recruited—and there is no evidence that this has been the case—can HEW proposals interfere with "institutional quality" or "the integrity of a university."*

> *It is to be regretted that the* Times *has given respectability to the reckless arguments of Professor Seabury.*[1]

Glazer attacked me in response, stating that there had been no showing of past discrimination in the HEW process and that it "was surprising that a professor of law should be incapable of seeing the distinction."[2] I responded, again in the *Times*, describing how the law of affirmative action had evolved and concluding with this comment:

> *The "affirmative action" obligation—which is not predicated upon a specific finding of discrimination—is recognition of the general pattern of past discrimination by most employers in our society. The pity is that the obligation has not been more vigorously enforced by the Federal Government. But the greater pity is that people like Professor Glazer seem bent upon doing all they can to thwart effective remedies for past discrimination, attributable to both society in general and particular employers.*[3]

When Joe Glazer first called me, in the late summer of 1976, I was struck by his gravelly and humorous-sounding voice—after that, I never mistook his voice for anyone else's. When I remarked that I had had some encounters with his brother, Joe said something to the effect that the two of them were quite different people. And indeed, they were.

Joe told me that in the wake of the June 1976 Soweto "uprising," the U.S. State Department wanted someone with expertise to talk about labor law and fair employment practice law in America.[4] Labor law was as much a concern as fair employment practice law, given the fact that the Black unions had been able to engage in strikes in Durban in 1973; this meant that labor was the one institution left that might be able to combat apartheid, the formal separation of the races fostered by South African law under the Nationalist government.[5]

In the fall of 1976 the unrest and upheaval spread into Cape Town, where demonstrations and protests by the so-called "colored" people resulted in strikes, arrests, and deadly clashes with police. At this time our family was on vacation in British Columbia, where we were able to witness much of what was happening on television. I remember thinking that all of this increased the probability that I would be going to South Africa and made it more probable that I would be involved in some way in the pressure for change that was emerging.

After President Jimmy Carter won the 1976 election, it became clear that American policy toward all of southern Africa would be changing: The Nixon-Kissinger administration's support of colonialism would soon be reversed, if not scrapped altogether. Joe Glazer contacted me again around this time to sound me out on going to South Africa, promising that any of my speeches would be given to integrated audiences. Joe told me that the South African labor relations people with whom the embassy was dealing preferred a guy named Jim Healy, a Harvard Business School professor, but Joe said he doubted that Healy would accept any invitation because he had too many arbitration commitments at that time. This proved to be the case and, in early 1977, the wheels were set in motion for my first trip to South Africa.

A Decades-Old Fascination

The roots of my interest in South Africa go back many years. Nelson Mandela, who was arrested and imprisoned in 1962 on charges of organizing an illegal strike, had arrived in urban South Africa years earlier. As Jonny Steinberg wrote in *Winnie and Nelson*, when Mandela arrived in Johannesburg:

> *In 1941, the city was changing dramatically. World War II had been on the go for nineteen months, and the wartime economy's demand for labor had brought unprecedented numbers of people to the city. Until now, black South Africa had been a largely rural population; as late as 1936, only seventeen percent of black people lived in a city for any part of the year. By 1946, the black urban population of Johannesburg was double what it had been in 1930.... The increased numbers of urban blacks also triggered fear among whites—blacks began to outnumber them in urban*

> South Africa for the first time in 1946—leading to the surprise election in 1948 of the National Party with its doctrine of apartheid.[6]

I can recall my father's deep concern in 1948—ironically the same year that President Truman desegregated our armed forces—with President Daniel Malan and the National Party. In 1950 Malan's government passed the Population Registration Act, racially classifying all South Africans into one of three categories: white, black, or colored. This act identified those whose parents were both white as white; those belonging to a Black race or tribe as black; and all others who were neither white nor black as colored. Thus, Indians and some who considered themselves white were now classified as colored. These classifications triggered innumerable disputes.

My reading about South Africa had begun in the 1950s with Alan Paton's *Cry the Beloved Country* and *Too Late the Phalarope*, which I still consider a good introduction to South Africa, as well as dramatic and captivating writing. My very first published piece, written as a high school student in 1953, was a comparison of Franco Spain with South Africa. In January 1953, I praised British action against Nazi plotters in Germany, referencing South Africa as ideologically involved with the former.[7] Subsequently, I criticized the Eisenhower Administration for its military base pact with Franco.[8]

My very first written publication, in fact, aside from letters to the editor, was a review of Alan Paton's *Hope for South Africa*, which I sent, unsolicited, to *The New Republic*. I wrote of the terror, unrest, and inequality in South Africa.[9] I concluded by writing that "The tragedy is that by the time the white man is able to love, the natives may be able only to hate."

A Wintry Summer of Union Visits

So, with this background and interest, I jumped at the chance the State Department offered me to go to South Africa in our summer (South Africa's winter) of 1977. Meanwhile, the Ford Foundation, which had assisted me financially in writing my recently published book, *Black Workers in White Unions*, gave me a grant to stay in the country for a month after my speaking engagements concluded. The State Department reiterated Joe's assurances that all my audiences would be integrated, notwithstanding South Africa's current law and practices.

Some friends and colleagues questioned my willingness to go to South Africa under these circumstances. The African National Congress was banned, many of their leaders were in exile, and Nelson Mandela was imprisoned for life on Robben Island. But I thought it was important to go, to observe firsthand what was going on. After all, the renowned and respected tennis player Arthur Ashe had rejected similar criticisms in 1973, at the time of his initial visit and speeches before integrated audiences, and I thought I would be well protected by the more aggressive stance of the Carter administration as it confronted apartheid.[10] Moreover, I saw the trip as an opportunity to preach the gospel, so to speak, in South Africa, and subsequently to speak and write about South Africa in the United States and elsewhere. Both Ashe's visit and mine proved to be worthwhile investments, in my judgment.

The first leg of this journey in July 1977 was to Washington, where I was briefed for a day at the State Department. At the time I found these meetings useful— they gave me a broad overview of politics and economics and their intersection with race. Because of ongoing boycotts against South Africa, travel logistics were convoluted, and the trip was a bone-crunching twenty-four hours long: from Washington to Paris, Paris to Kinshasa, and then onto Malawi, the one country with direct connections to Johannesburg. On the plane coming into South Africa, I had the chance to read some South African newspapers and was struck by their criticisms of the South African government. This was even true of the conservative *Johannesburg Star*. My subsequent experience confirmed this surprise—a surprise because there was nothing resembling free speech or a free press in other repressive governments, and Black protest movements in South Africa had resulted in imprisonment for its leaders. But, within limits, the South African press was unexpectedly free.

A Bumpy Arrival

When we disembarked in Johannesburg, I noticed an interracial couple near me quietly separate into different receiving lines, given South African laws prohibiting interracial sex and marriage. (Similar prohibitions had existed in the United States until the Supreme Court's *Loving* decision in 1967.)[11] When I presented myself to the immigration authorities, I became engaged in a very lengthy and tense conversation. When asked about the purpose and nature of my visit, I said I was there "to give speeches on law and engage in research of a comparative nature." The immigration screener said, "Wait a minute—before you come in here, we will want to know what you are going to say and who your audience will be." I told him that I was speaking about American labor and civil rights, and the impact of law and practice on American society. As the conversation became more extended and difficult, I could see Frank Golino, the American labor attaché who was waiting to meet me, looking anxious. I caught a glimpse of him chomping on a big cigar, a sight with which I would become familiar during this visit and on subsequent trips with him in South Africa and Spain.

Amazingly, no one in Washington had prepared me for this conversation, and it ended with this warning from one of the South African immigration staff: "You tell the American Embassy to submit a memo to us within twenty-four hours, advising us of your itinerary and the audiences to which you will speak. Otherwise," he said, "you will be leaving the country." Only after that conversation did I finally connect with Golino, who drove me to my hotel. We agreed that my first appointment would be at the U.S. Embassy in Pretoria.

When I arrived there the next day and met with embassy officials, the response was immediate: My prepared itinerary was thrown into the fireplace. I can see it burning there to this day. There would be no written plan identifying my South African connections or the purpose of my speeches for their government to review, as that would expose my new contacts to possible retaliation. That very day I met with one target of such retaliation: Eric Tyacke, a white

South African aide to the Black unions, who had been recently "banned" by the government. In South African terms, that meant severe restrictions on all his activities, including communications.[12]

Golino, my near-constant companion for the next three weeks, and others in the embassy made multiple appeals to their South African contacts, particularly to a Professor Nic Wiehan, who held a labor committee position and was charged with providing recommendations aimed at reforming aspects of the South African workplace. Wiehan was reputed to be part of the "verlichte," or enlightened, wing of the Nationalists, who advocated some measure of reform—but a "cosmetic" reform, as I later called it.[13] I met Wiehan a number of times during my visit. I was never sure whether he was responsible for my success in entering South Africa but, very quickly, the South African government allowed me to stay, and Wiehan always took credit for it—he appeared to be well connected and illustrative of a narrow group of white South Africans who sought acceptability with America and the West and were thus concerned with smoothing over troubled waters.

Meetings and Speeches

My very first meeting in South Africa was with a small group of Black trade unionists in Johannesburg, at the Anglican mission of the Community of the Resurrection. Years earlier, I had read *Naught for Your Comfort*, an account of forced removals of Blacks from a poor suburb of Johannesburg, by Father Trevor Huddleston, who had been banned from the country and subsequently became a bishop in Great Britain. At this meeting, I spoke informally with a number of trade union people at what would now be called a workshop. I struck up a friendship with Shako Soklome of Soweto; my first visit to Soweto was to his home there—and a few years later I gave him a tour of the San Francisco Coit Tower, when the State Department brought him to California. Shako helped me navigate Soweto and introduced me to his friends, both in the seventies and on my return in the nineties.

PROMOTING LABOR RIGHTS AND STANDARDS ABROAD 253

Figure 8.2: Beyond the Cathedral of St. Mary the Virgin, I had been able to attend this Anglican Mass in Soweto in 1977.

Figure 8.3: Here I am with Shako and other comrades when they made a visit to San Francisco a few months after my departure from South Africa in 1977.

My focus was on the Black unions. But I also connected with management representatives who seemed to be more open to change than most South African businesses. Illustrative of this category were Zac Dubeer of the Anglo-American Corporation, along with young Bobby Godsell, who handled labor matters for the same firm.

Meanwhile, under State Department auspices, I gave a series of speeches in which I was critical of the South African regime—speeches that were covered by the Johannesburg daily newspapers such as the *Star* and the *Daily Mail*. The *Star*, without much commentary, covered my remarks about the *Detroit Edison* case through its headlines, emphasizing the reach and limits of the law.[14] I stressed that the significance of the new independent Black unions needed to be recognized by our own AFL-CIO.[15] In Cape Town, I spoke about the need for the Carter administration to press for change in South Africa. I vividly recall touring Cape Town[16] with USIA official Frank Sussman and looking out at Robben Island, where Nelson Mandela was held and would be held for nearly fifteen years longer.

I had many meetings in South Africa, and I spoke with people who cut across a fairly wide swathe of the political spectrum—Black and white, banned trade unionists and government officials. Some of the most memorable meetings were with individuals who played very different roles in the struggle against the Vorster government policy of repression; some of them were literally on the run from the South African government at the time of our meetings. Despite the variety of views and personalities, there was one common thread to the remarks—a recognition of the critical role that America played in effectuating change in South Africa and a hopefulness about the intentions of the Carter administration in this effort.

I had lunch with Dr. Nthato Motlana, who had been the leader of the so-called Soweto Ten, which attempted unsuccessfully to negotiate with the Nationalist government on effective local government for the Black residents of Soweto. Soon after that lunch in late August, I recall telling an American friend in Johannesburg how fortunate South Africa was to have such a moderate and sensible Black leader in a country where every Black was subjected to daily indignity. Motlana spent much time speaking to me of the Soweto student boycott against Bantu education, a system that provided Blacks with one sixteenth the financial aid given whites and deliberately attempted to cripple them by teaching a tribal vernacular that was ill-suited to the modern industrial centers where English was a prerequisite. Motlana did not speak of Black majority rule—although I had no doubt that he supported this idea—but rather focused on local government as well as education.

Another of my meetings was with Chief Gatsha Buthelezi, the controversial "homeland" leader of five million Zulu peoples, as well as the main force in its "cultural" (actually more political) organization, Inkatha, the only remaining voice of Black opposition which was not then banned.[17] Buthelezi—so fiercely criticized by the new and militant Black Consciousness movement of which Steve Biko was a leader, primarily because he accepted leadership in the Kwazulu government, the "homeland" for Zulus in South Africa—told me that he would "never" accept independence under the government's separate development policy as others had done. (The policy of the South African government was to create tribal "homelands" for the Black majority, who would supply labor for a white-controlled South Africa.) Buthelezi told me that he could not support divestment or other economic sanctions because he had a responsibility for employment opportunities for his people, but he strongly advocated other forms of pressure. At this point, he alone retained a platform on which to speak out to South African Blacks. Said Buthelezi of the government's recent bannings, "It is an admission that the government of this country is by jackboot as far as Blacks are concerned."

Figure 8.4: Here I am with Chief Buthelezi in Kwazulu in August 1977.

Perhaps my most important encounter of all was a discussion I had with Mrs. Winnie Mandela, wife of African National Congress leader Nelson Mandela. Mrs. Mandela had become a civil rights leader in her own right in Soweto before being banned in May of 1977. My meeting with Mrs. Mandela dramatized more than all else the position of Blacks who dared protest government policy. Mrs. Mandela was under house arrest in Brandfort, banished to this remote town deep in the flat and uninteresting countryside of the Orange Free State, the heartland of Afrikanerdom, where the ruling Nationalist Party was strongest.[18] She lived under curfew in a Black township where no one spoke English or Xosha, her two languages.

I drove out to Brandfort alone, in a rented car, in the early afternoon of August 17, 1977, and arrived on time for our two o'clock meeting. I did not know what to expect that day, in a country where government surveillance was commonplace, and in a part of the nation where English—particularly with an American accent—can attract attention. I stood waiting on the sidewalk of a two-horse town that looked like a wild west movie set, but there was no Mrs. Mandela to meet me.

However, the Security Branch of the South African police were there, equipped with earphones that, I was advised, could monitor any conversation within half a mile. A friendly Jewish woman, whose family had come to Brandfort from Lithuania in 1938, helped me in my search for Mrs. Mandela, as the police sat in their car across the street. "Are you a Carter man?" she asked. "Yes," I responded. "Well, he doesn't understand our situation here." And later, when I thanked her for her help, she said, "I hope that you will tell Americans that we are civilized here in South Africa."

An hour or so later, I found Mrs. Mandela. She had received a message stating that our meeting had been postponed. Both of us suspected that the Security Branch, whose officers sat behind us in a parked car during our entire meeting, were responsible.

Figure 8.5: Meeting with Winnie Mandela in Brandfort in August 1977.

For a woman in such isolation and under such duress, she was in remarkably good spirits. She had been jailed frequently, and like Motlana had been imprisoned the previous year, after Soweto, and was being charged with and tried for violations of her banning orders. She told me that the Afrikaner did not believe that Blacks "had evolved" and that a "clash" over Black–white inequities was made more likely by the degradation of Soweto and similar Black townships throughout the country, whose tiny homes were now the living quarters for Blacks of any economic station.

These three individuals—Motlana, Buthelezi, and Mandela—differed in temperament and approaches. But they seemed to me to be in agreement on one point, that is, that the Carter administration had provided some measure of confidence to South African Blacks that was not there previously. "Does Carter really mean it?" said Mrs. Mandela hopefully. "He must keep the pressure up," said Buthelezi of the Carter administration's call for full political participation for nonwhites in South Africa. And I shall never forget Motlana's last comment as we parted: "You Americans must pick the winners for a change."[19]

Advocating for Change

My 1977 work in South Africa concluded in early September in Johannesburg, just as news was released of the government's murder of Black Consciousness leader Steve Biko. I focused my commentary at this point on what I had seen in South Africa, stating that the recognition of Black unions was necessary and that there was no way of denying Black majority rule in South Africa.[20] In a separate article describing a *Rand Daily Mail* interview, I was quoted to this effect after a University of Witwatersrand seminar:

> *While there was considerable emphasis at the Wits seminar on the "urgent need" for change in our labour relations, it was left to a visiting black American professor to point out that any talk of change is glib rhetoric until certain basic things are done. Like bringing blacks into the negotiating system. "Trade unions here," said Prof. William Gould, "don't represent anyone because up to 80% of workers*

> have no unions." And like the introduction of laws which actively prohibit discrimination. Only then, said Prof Gould, would there be enough commitment by firms to see that real, meaningful change was implemented.
>
> The Professor, of course, is right. And we would add a rider to his comments. Which is that industrial strife is most likely when you have an inadequate system of representation for workers. That is when you get your wildcat strikes which usually are only stopped by brute force. And usually leave behind a worse state of conflict than before.
>
> And the simple truth in all labour relations must surely be that it is always better to negotiate than dictate.[21]

En route back to California, I stopped off in London and gave a speech at Chatham House, which houses the Royal Institute of International Affairs, describing what I had seen in South Africa. British correspondent Colin Legum, whom I had met in South Africa, and I met with Foreign Secretary David Owen to deliver an informal report to him about conditions in South Africa, advocating that greater pressure be applied against its government. Though Owen listened respectfully, he did not seem to be particularly interested in what we had to say.

Upon my return to California, I began to write and comment about South Africa in this country. In one of my first articles, written for *Commonweal*, I wrote, "One of the best hopes for change in South Africa is through a viable and ultimately strong labor movement."[22]

Pushback, Turbulence, Progress

I was able to return to South Africa, this time for a Cape Town Human Rights Conference, in January 1979, which resulted in a law review piece on the Black labor movement.[23] After a third visit, in November 1979, I should have realized that the combination of widely published articles abroad, along with quotes in the South African newspapers, had been brewing trouble for me: At this time my visa was restricted to ten consecutive days in the country.

In order to stay longer, I left South Africa for Salisbury (soon to be Harare) in Rhodesia (soon to be Zimbabwe); I calculated that I could start another consecutive ten days in South Africa thereafter, and see Rhodesia in the meantime.

My plane to Salisbury descended very quickly, aiming to evade Rhodesian revolutionary leader Joshua Nkomo's heat-seeking missiles. Taking account of Rhodesia's fortress-like practices and mentality, I realized I could not travel to picturesque Victoria Falls because I'd have to ride shotgun, protected by armed guards against possible attack by Black revolutionaries. And I could not imagine a more ignominious death than being attacked by Black freedom fighters while I was traveling with white settlers protecting Ian Smith, Rhodesia's white government prime minister.

In 1980 I was writing again, arguing that labor law reform in South Africa, while "the most positive and significant development in South African race and relations since the Nationalist Party first came to power in 1948," was nonetheless "problematic" at best, and I concluded by questioning "whether a normal trade-union movement can evolve in an abnormal country. The answer remains in doubt."[24] Soon thereafter, in 1981, I gave testimony to the House Subcommittee on Africa in support of Congressman Stephen Solarz's legislation affirmatively limiting investment in South Africa, as a form of indirect regulation—investment conditioned upon adherence to trade union rights and desegregation of the workplace.[25] In my testimony, I rejected the voluntary and largely cosmetic Sullivan Principles—a set of six guidelines for businesses operating in South Africa, requiring adherence to some desegregation regulations at work and advocating extraterritorial labor legislation for American companies doing business in South Africa—though warning that enforcement by the executive branch of the United States was problematic because "the Reagan administration had thus far failed to appreciate the immoral nature of apartheid."[26]

With my book on Japan completed, as well as *A Primer on American Labor Law*, the way was clear for me to accept an invitation provided by Professor Anthony (Tony) Matthews, with whom I had had considerable contact in both the United States and South Africa, to give a lecture at his university in Durban. But my father had become ill with cancer in late 1979, and had taken a turn for the worse, so I canceled my 1983 trip to be with him (more about this in chapter 9). In 1984, after my father's death, I was invited again. But the visa to come to South Africa, granted the previous year, was denied this time.[27]

I attempted to enlist help from the political world, as well as from Stanford President Don Kennedy, "to support me in what proved to be a futile attempt to get Assistant Secretary of State Crocker to pressure his South African friends. Kennedy was cool, downright hostile: 'Is this university business?' [he asked]."[28] But he ultimately wrote a strong letter to Crocker, stating:

> *I urge you to seek reversal of this decision. . . . Professor Gould is an internationally known scholar in the field of labor law and has made a particular study of labor relations and the labor movement in the Republic of South Africa. As the University of Natal has been looking forward to Professor Gould's visit for several years, it is quite disturbing that the South African government would deny his visa application at the last minute without providing any explanation of the reasons for the denial. I am hopeful that, with your assistance, they can be prevailed upon to reconsider Professor Gould's application and grant his visa.*[29]

Of course, no reversal was made, and this entire incident constituted a great disappointment to me. Nonetheless, when my visa application was rejected in 1983,[30] I kept involved from afar, maintaining as many contacts as I could. One of those contacts had already visited our Stanford home and had lunch with us in the summer of 1982: a young and dedicated union lawyer and labor leader from the South African Black mine workers named Cyril Ramaphosa. During that luncheon I recall that Cyril, who was to become the president of South Africa in this century, emphasized and explained why South Africa was ripe for change. I am much too transparent in personal relations and discussions, so Cyril smiled when he had finished his presentation, apparently reading the skepticism in my face. In truth, I did not see the possibility of significant or real reform at that time and, while I never lost faith—surely the French Revolution and the War of the Rebellion in this country, along with the expansion of the franchise and the demise of colonialism, made it clear that change of this kind was inevitable—I could not see change in the five to ten years that Ramaphosa and others seemed to anticipate. Nonetheless, Ramaphosa and I became friends that day, and five years later I sent him messages of support in his union's first major strike.

In the mid-eighties, South Africa was to erupt into a turbulent caldron, as the Black unions (in a new federation, COSATU) became aggressive, organizing both in the workplace and politically in place of the still-banned African National Congress. In the midst of the tumultuous eighties, the pressure for sanctions grew.[31] President Reagan (along with his ally, Prime Minister Thatcher), however, was receptive to the South African government's assertion that adequate change was taking place.[32] As pressure for sanctions mounted, Secretary of State George Shultz sought delay by claiming that sanctions would not work and that the Reagan administration needed flexibility to "increase pressure in coordination with its allies as the situation evolved."[33] But by then, embarrassing revelations showed that the United States and Britain had "provided South Africa with intelligence about the banned and exiled African National Congress."[34] This increased the pressure on Reagan and ultimately on South Africa as well.

I wrote that "carefully calibrated" sanctions employed against South Africa were warranted, stating that the Reagan position was "morally bankrupt," giving the Botha Government "respectability," and that South Africa would respond well to "the language of sanctions."[35] A bipartisan Senate vote backed economic sanctions against South Africa,[36] Democrats taking the lead in opposing White House resistance,[37] and the Senate ultimately overrode a Reagan veto of sanctions.[38] Ultimately, the Reagan position of "constructive engagement" began to crumble.[39] Assisting the resistance was Nobel Peace Prize winner Archbishop Desmond Tutu of the Anglican Church, with whom I was able to meet at Grace Cathedral in San Francisco during his first visit there in 1989.[40] Then, with the advent of the DeKlerk administration, the pressure of sanctions, and the decline of the Soviet Union between 1989 and 1991, came Nelson Mandela's release from prison. Thus in 1991, the U.S. State Department renewed its Fulbright program, and I became part of the first group of Fulbright scholars to return to South Africa.

Witness to Change

I returned in their winter, June 1991, to take up a visiting professorship at the University of Witwatersrand. My focus was both the changes that had taken place in the labor movement and the constitutional negotiations led by Cyril Ramaphosa toward a constitutional transition. I wrote the following in my diary on June 27, 1991:

> *Here on the eve of the ANC Conference, virtually all my discussions are about politics and labor. My first impression is that white attitudes here remain pretty much the same (as perhaps they do in the US) and that the DeKlerk-Mandela dialogue is more of a top-down venture which is accepted by the whites because the economy is so devastating. Ironically, this has brought more Blacks to the cities and all discussions are preoccupied with crime-violent, retributive crime like that which dominated Detroit when I lived there in the late '60s, early '70s. This, along with the senseless shootings—a gang of thugs randomly shot passengers on a train to Soweto, the* Star *suggests that elements in the Government may be involved—undermining the rationality of political accommodation between the races.*
>
> *Sanctions, the price of gold, perhaps the cost of the homeland policy, the diminution of tensions caused by the events of '89 and '90 in Eastern Europe all seemed to have driven DeKlerk to the table. Before '90, he was regarded as quite right wing.*
>
> *Clearly the country is different. The return of so many exiles proves that—this week Father (now Bishop) Huddleston and Dennis Brutus are two prominent examples.* Naught For Your Comfort *was such an inspiration to me . . .*

The first scene at the airport and again this weekend is 2 or 3 whites (often quite young) gazing with arms folded as Black laborers toil beneath them in a trench. Denis Kuny [my good lawyer friend in Johannesburg] on the standard Van de Merwe joke when witnessing the hustle and bustle of New York construction: "give me 10 kaffirs [the South African equivalent of nigger] and I can do the job myself."

Corporations are moving to chic northern suburbs like Rosebank to escape the advancing Blacks. Notwithstanding the scare stories, students (women included) walk freely at night here in Park Town [a Johannesburg suburb].

The Black unions remain important. Ramaphosa may become General Secretary of the ANC though he was enigmatic in a telephone conversation I had with him last Friday. He is in mine negotiations and a weekend meeting with trade unionists, apparently on this subject.

On Friday (June 28) morning I attended a criminal trial involving alleged kidnapping of a police agent by Jay Naidoo of Cosatu and other union leaders. During the break he and his lawyers explained their position to me. Most of the facts are not in dispute. Union lawyers were successful in introducing testimony about Cosatu's fears about harassment from the state as a basis for grabbing a guy watching their building.

The testimony was a textbook examination of Cosatu, its concerns, goals. The Afrikaner judge . . . obviously impatient about testimony about apartheid ("everyone knows about it") chastised Naidoo and the lawyers for using the trial as a platform.

On that same day I met with trade unionists and labor journalists with the help of John Dinger, Frank Golino's successor on . . . how the unions got from the '70s, where I came in and left, to '91. One of the perplexing questions for the future, the relationship between unions and ANC. The unions have moved fast becoming like Poland's Solidarity, they have a political issue which worked to their advantage. But what happens in a post-Apartheid system?

July 14, 1991 Bastille Day

A lazy day after a raucous labor law conference in Durban ... on Wednesday I gave a speech to a law professors' conference. I don't think that my efforts there, in Pretoria, or in Durban were particularly good. But in Pretoria, I began my speech (after some remarks by the conference chairman in Afrikaans as well as English) by stating that I look forward to the new South Africa where, if more than one language was used, one would be that of one of the Black African groups. The Blacks, sitting together on my right, erupted uncontrollably. The whites were completely silent, never a muscle moved in any of them. I really stumbled onto something.

An Afrikaner law professor drove me to Pretoria. I knew that we were in for trouble when I commented on the Black construction workers on Trematon Place and noted how cold they were that morning. "Yes," he said, they were suffering more than "us" because they couldn't take the cold. It had something to do with the size of the European nostril and how it differed from Blacks. He vigorously opposed DeKlerk's initiatives stating that he had "painted himself in a corner" and "should have gone more slowly."

This week Bush has suspended sanctions against South Africa, producing great joy in the white press and Government, unease in the ANC. Bush, of course, was never for sanctions which have done the job of pushing DeKlerk. Still suspended are IMF loans and one hopes that they will not be provided until the constitutional process has moved along considerably. Some weapons besides civil unrest must remain.

The Durban ANC conference last week was worthwhile. Chatted very briefly with Winnie Mandela who clearly didn't remember me from '77 and was aloof. Sat in on an interview with Father Huddleston. Of course, the most amazing feature was the cast of previously banned characters . . . rode back to my hotel with Allister Sparks, I've just now finished his comprehensive The Mind of South Africa.

I think that Durban helped the ANC. Nelson Mandela was rational and careful and balanced as in America last summer. He promoted the idea of negotiations but emphasized that they are part of a long "struggle."

July 16, 1991 10:59 pm.

This is my 55th birthday. Halfway up the decade up to 60 and senior citizen status . . . now I take a few minutes out to listen to BBC. I rushed downtown this morning to Winnie Mandela's appeal. I had dinner with Justice Richard Goldstone last night and he suggested that I go to the appeal. Although I arrived at 9:55 am, the hearing had begun early at 9:30 am but I arrived just on time to hear the judge grant leave to appeal from the very judge that has ruled against [Winnie Mandela].

After the hearing, I ran into Ismail Ayob. He remembered me immediately from more than a decade ago but said that my gray complexion made me "look like a white man." We had coffee for an hour, then walked on the street where we had seen Winnie. This time—in contrast to Durban—she greeted me with warm enthusiasm.

July 21, 1991

I was at Mass at the Cathedral of St. Mary the Virgin this morning and it was full of majesty and dignity—just like the way I remember it at St. James's in Long Branch. It was a Sung Mass—a Solemn High, I believe and it lifted my spirits enormously. I walked the streets of downtown

Johannesburg with a different spirit from a week ago . . . it was a beautiful warm sunshiny day and that always lifts one's spirits.

The night before I had dinner with Nazeer Cassim in Mayfair, an Indian-dominated community to the west of Johannesburg. It was a lively evening filled with Nazeer's in-laws, all of whom were businessmen, Muslims, who came here as "passengers" after the period of indentured labor.

70% of the Indians will . . . take the ANC's line before the polling place, but they will vote Nationalists behind the ballot's secrecy. It was clear that they would. Nazeer said his son wanted a Coke before a piano lesson. "After the lesson" was the response. "But what if the ANC takes power while I'm having my lesson," said the child, "there might not be any more Cokes." "Good thinking," said Nazeer, who apparently gave him his Coke.

The big news here—the subject of discussion at a party held by Jenny Pogund Friday night—is the Nationalists' secret funding of Inkatha for rallies in '89 and '90. Now the "double agenda" [the idea that the Government was working with the Zulu homeland against the ANC] to which Mandela made continuous reference in the Durban conference is proven.

August 16, 1991

En route from Joburg to Cape Town on the Blue Train.

Luxurious, tasteful accommodations as we move across the country to South Africa's most beautiful land.

During the past 10 days, beginning on August 7 we had been in the eastern regions (Hilda, [her sister] Mary Jonas, and I). 3 lovely vacation days in Kruger National Park. The first day we saw virtually everything—elephants—a herd, some within 10 feet of our car—rhinos, hippos, *springboks, impala, wild hogs, giraffes, zebras, etc., etc. The most memorable day was the last . . . where I could see two cheetahs in the grass after a kill, a leopard run in front of our car and into the grass, and . . . from the observation post, a lion and lioness moving along. The leopard was completely calm, didn't even notice us—and I then went into reverse to watch him disappear in the grass.*

Then drove through Nelspruit . . . in Eastern Transvaal, Piet Retief, and Vryheid (we stayed in the first and last towns). The Conservative Party had just held its Natal Congress in Vryheid and I saw some posters featuring [the extreme right-winger] (Dr. No) everywhere. "There will be another war here," said a white salesgirl—but this time between the whites." I met young enthusiastic Black supporters of the ANC in all of these cities. When I left the Central Hotel in Piet Retief, saying "Viva Mandela" to our waiter, the little, slightly built guy, raised his fist in the ANC salute. . . . But John Copelyn, the leader of the white Clothing and Textile Worker Union, on a breakfast meeting the morning after in Joburg disparaged the representative quality of my contacts, stating that the ANC couldn't obtain more than 50 percent of the vote . . .

After many inquiries about the number of Black managers and young students, . . . [my interviewee] said that Blacks were not qualified to do these jobs because they were not sufficiently confident in either English or Afrikaans but then he told me how Blacks had advanced to shop assistant jobs. But that didn't require language capability? I asked. No reply was provided.

After emerging from Conservative Party territory, we spent 3 interesting days in Durban and Pieter Maritz. I gave lectures at Natal law schools in both cities and I think that they went well. But the highlight was an informal seminar on affirmative action with business, newspaper types. This gave me a better sense of the vitality of this issue.

My best meeting was with Pierre Cronje, the MP from Pieter Maritz. He described the voting there and the correlation between the outward push of the ANC its recruitment and violence, noting that 70 percent of the surrounding area is ANC. [He] . . . thought that Inkatha-gate had induced the government to opt for genuine reconciliation and honest test of the political market.

Before my Cronje meeting, I visited the Anglican Cathedral of the Holy Nativity, another lovely . . . Anglo-Catholic place of worship. Dean Forbes of the Cathedral was my guide.

September 1, 1991 Johannesburg

Returned from the Cape about 5 days ago. The most beautiful part of the country in my view. Took the luxurious Blue Train which I have described. Met with Frank Sussman at the Cape Town station—as with so many others, I hadn't seen him in twelve years. A wonderful, extremely capable guy, he now talks of retirement though he is 3 years younger than me. He arranged for Trevor Wentzel to take us to some of the colored townships and it was an interesting afternoon. The highlight was a visit to the home of Joe Marks, one of the UDF [United Democratic Front] leaders, near Grassy Park. The following day I saw him again when I attended the UDF Disaffiliation meeting [in light of the ANC reappearance] in Mitchell's Plain. Boesak [the most well-known UDF leader] was the highlight with his soaring rhetoric: "We made them change" – "Now is the time" [he said] . . . the crowd was in his hand.

Lectures and meetings at the Western Cape with Kadar Ashmal, the ANC Constitutional expert . . . the weather was not always the best, cold, and rainy.

We then flew to Port Elizabeth where I spent a day at the university—I had actually forgotten my '77 visit there but some reminded me, and I recalled it. There were fewer

Black students then even at Stellenbosch where incidentally I had a fascinating session with a constitutional lawyer who predicted that the law school would accept the English language because the constitution would make it the language of the country. But I was particularly struck by the large number of Black students on all campuses, except for Port Elizabeth.

I had a spectacular flight to East London in a small plane, 500 feet up. Could see the beauteous coastline and bird sanctuary, Bird Island. My day at the Mercedes plant lacked a good deal as the union representatives were caucusing and the industrial relations guy was away. Saw some film of their bitter, lengthy '90 strike which emphasized the ANC involvement in union activity, how they occupied the plant . . .

The most spectacular part of the journey was a drive through the southern Garden Route. The bays were particularly lovely and the Wilderness, where we stayed, truly spectacular . . . as we left the Wilderness, the most impoverished Black people were living in primitive conditions. This is Conservative Party territory and the home of P.W. Botha [the hardline ex-nationalist President].

September 10, 1991

These past few days make one both hopeful and pessimistic. On Friday, September 6, I participated in a Wits ceremony in which Mandela was awarded an honorary LL.D. A brilliant, warm, sunshine-filled day filled with pageantry. The crowd, large, enthusiastic, slightly giddy and foolish in laughing at serious points by Mandela . . . the singing of the choir was magnificent. Mandela's speech was sharp and dignified. He focused on DeKlerk's constitutional proposals—"a recipe for constitutional paralysis and conflict"— and the reasons for his support of . . . hunger strikers . . . I caught a glimpse of Mandela inside after the ceremony— erect, dignified, regal, in appearance.

> But over the weekend there was terrible violence—at this point more than 80 had been killed. It started in Soweto in Mofolo. Ironically, I came by that area enroute to the Church of the Good Shepard Mass at nine. A ceremony filled with dance, signing and joyous communication—and what incense, the thurifer exceeds the one at St. Mary's.
>
> But while this was going on Inkatha in Soweto were ambushed by unknown assailants—later hand grenades were thrown. Tonight it has spread to Alexandra where I saw Spike Lee's Do the Right Thing. This senseless killing is difficult to understand. It jeopardizes this Saturday's Peace Accord which apparently will still be signed. But what will it mean, if it is signed? How will it be implemented?
>
> On Sunday, I saw a Caspar [the South African tank-like military vehicle] go by and the Irish organist who drove me commented that "I don't like it when the Caspars move so quickly."
>
> Tomorrow afternoon I am back in Soweto to meet Shakeo Sokhome, my old friend from the '70s.

My 1991 visit was truly a watershed for me. In describing this visit I made the following observations: (1) Much of the hierarchical relationship between the races was still an "article of faith" in South Africa; (2) there were now a few Black supervisors who had responsibility for all races—but it was still a "relatively rare occurrence"; (3) the "whites only" signs that I saw everywhere in public transportation, hotels, bathrooms, were now completely gone; (4) it was common to see Blacks and whites, and even interracial couples, together, whereas if you saw a Black and a white in the same car in the seventies, you assumed they were part of the state surveillance system; and (5) the crime rate soared as the number of Black squatters released from previously existing "influx control" meant that the impoverished descended on the cities in great numbers; the single-sex hostels in which Black workers lived still existed.[41]

I personally experienced Johannesburg's crime problem, which had reached new dimensions since 1977, when I used to wander alone for miles in the city on weekends. By 1991 security guards, sometimes armed with machine guns, were present only on weekdays, when whites worked; never in the evening or on weekends. My bank couldn't provide me with funds one morning because it had just been robbed. And on another morning, a beautiful, sunny Sunday, I was mugged downtown, two blocks from the Cathedral of St. Mary the Virgin where I had just attended Mass. It happened very quickly. I thought I heard footsteps unusually close behind me and, as I looked at the reflections in one of the downtown's modern buildings, I immediately took note of a young Black teenager looking at me from across the street. Within what seemed like less than five seconds, three or four youngsters came at me from different directions and immediately grabbed my wallet. My natural reaction was to resist, as they tried unsuccessfully to rip off my watch. "Don't fight," one of them said, and indeed a moment's reflection might have shown me the wisdom of that remark. But there wasn't enough time to think.

All this took place in broad daylight on a busy downtown street. Cars passed by, their drivers observing the robbery and shouting advice, but no one dared to aid me. I wasn't physically injured, only shaken, and impaired more psychologically than anything else.

Continuing Contact

After my 1991 Fulbright visit, Stanford Law Dean Paul Brest arranged for me to take a new series of trips back to South Africa during the constitutional negotiations. Due to my friendship with Cyril Ramaphosa, I had a guaranteed seat at all the discussions that took place. I even taught a seminar at Stanford Law School about the constitutional negotiations and began to write about them, noting during a 1992 visit that "DeKlerk and Mandela need each other."[42]

Ramaphosa visited Stanford Law School, gave some talks at the law school and the university, and as a result of his help, in August 1992 I had a ten-minute tête-à-tête with Mr. Mandela in Johannesburg. "How do you call yourself?" he said to me at the beginning of our meeting, the only time I have ever had that question asked as it would be in the French language. We had a short general discussion, during which he talked of his hope for a peaceful constitutional transition. When Ramaphosa and I arranged for him to speak at Stanford Law School, there was considerable excitement and anticipation of his arrival.[43] Unfortunately, the meeting was canceled at the last moment because of a new round of violence between Inkatha and others in the eastern part of the country. It goes without saying that there was considerable disappointment at this turn of events, both in Stanford and in the Bay Area generally.

Figure 8.6: My first introduction to Nelson Mandela in Durban, South Africa in 1991 at the first African National Congress conference, subsequent to his release from prison.

Figure 8.7: In 1992, I was able to have a tête-à-tête with Nelson Mandela in his Johannesburg office.

In 1994, when I was in Washington and chairman of the National Labor Relations Board, I was able to go to the Mandela inauguration as part of the Clinton administration. That spring day was filled with pageantry and pomp, with South African jets flying over the ceremony, showing off the new rainbow colors of the South African flag in their exhaust. It was a day both solemn and joyous, with Mandela finally president of South Africa, and the first true multiracial democracy ever in existence in that country.

I returned again, as part of the Eisenhower People-to-People program, in 2003. During that visit I was able to introduce Americans interested in South Africa to so many whom I had met previously, some of whom were literally on the run from South African security when I first met them in the seventies. Now a number of them were government representatives and the American participants were able to meet them in that capacity.

In the years since then, particularly subsequent to President Mandela's first term, South Africa has stumbled, and the African National Congress has lost credibility and support. It proved itself unable to recognize and late to remedy the widespread HIV/AIDS epidemic. Its efforts to address increasingly rampant crime have been ineffectual. During the past decade, corruption has become rampant, and the government has aligned itself with Russia's criminal and unlawful invasion of Ukraine.[44] All these factors, combined with a general failure to deliver for the average Black South African, have produced considerable dismay and disillusionment amongst South Africa's friends, as well as an increasing percentage of its population.

TRAVELS BEYOND SOUTH AFRICA

Although my work and involvement in South Africa required a lot of my time and attention, I was able to travel widely in other countries in the 1980s and 1990s, generally for lectures. Not all my trips were academic, however: Hilda and I were in San Jose, Costa Rica on the day of Ronald Reagan's inauguration in 1981—a deliberate boycott on our part of that horrible moment in Washington, DC.

Latin America and Eastern Europe

After Costa Rica, it was on to Santo Domingo, Dominican Republic, for an ABA Labor Law Section meeting and a tour of the city, including a local museum which displayed a rather dramatic painting of Sir Francis Drake. The local guide referred to him as "mal hombre," a somewhat different description than those we had heard in Great Britain. After that there was a second round of lectures for the U.S. government in Brazil, Chile, and Argentina. In the first of two visits to Brazil, I met and had a brief discussion with Luiz Inácio Lula da Silva (Lula), then president of the São Paulo Metalworkers Union and subsequently a three-term president of Brazil. In Chile, with the Pinochet regime still in power, I expressed pessimism about future prospects for freedom of association, both for workers and society.[45]

I was also able to travel to Central America, lecturing in Honduras, El Salvador, and Guatemala. There I spoke out against the Reagan administration's policies in that part of the world, arguing that our government was collaborating with oppressors there.[46]

But an even more memorable travel opportunity, during my period of exile from South Africa, was my visit to Poland, where I attended the first-anniversary conference of Solidarity in Gdansk. This was a heady time for the Solidarity union movement and the West: The Reagan administration—anti-union in the United States—was promoting Solidarity, a free union movement. A considerable part of my time was involved in meeting Solidarity representatives and listening to Lech Walesa, Solidarity's leader. This anniversary, just one year after Solidarity's strikes during the summer of 1980, had received international attention. I reconnected with my Cornell professor, Kurt Hanslowe, who had given me my professional start in the world of labor law. Kurt expressed fear that Solidarity's advent would trigger a Soviet invasion. As it turned out, the Soviets did not invade, but Kurt's prediction was not far off the mark, given the imposition of martial law by Polish authorities at Soviet insistence on December 13, 1981. We remarked to one another that, though separated by a few thousand miles from Stanford to Cornell, we had come an appreciably longer distance—to Poland!—to see one another. Tragically, within a year Kurt Hanslowe died of cancer; I returned to Cornell shortly after his death to memorialize my excellent teacher and good friend.[47]

When I returned to Poland six years later, to deliver a series of lectures at the University of Lodz, martial law had been imposed, and a new gray zone had descended over the country. While I pronounced that Solidarity was "still around,"[48] I nonetheless experienced the same kind of surveillance that I had encountered in South Africa in the seventies. In southern Poland, I saw Solidarity banners. But my lecture references to Solidarity were never interpreted unless I insisted upon it. This was a period of something vaguely in between authoritarianism and free expression. Illustrative of my experience was an encounter I had in Warsaw. I described it thus:

> *Wearing Jaruzelski-type sunglasses, jeans and a plaid shirt, a tall and thin gray-haired man sits down at the next table in Warsaw's Europejski Hotel. As I continue talking with a Solidarity intellectual who writes for one of Poland's anti-government Roman Catholic journals, our new neighbor systematically pushes his chair back until it is within inches of ours, turns his head towards us at every few sentences and then gets up to look at the window and to stare directly at us.*[49]

When I traveled to Poland, Hungary, and Germany in 1990, after the demolition of the Berlin Wall in 1989, I was one of the last to go through Checkpoint Charlie, and the first American to lecture at the Humboldt University Law Faculty since the beginning of World War II. When I arrived in Poland, my experience was dramatically different from that which I had described four years earlier. I wrote:

> *The chill of winter's air is still not entirely dispelled. It is an exhilarating, giddy experience this cloudy June 1 day in Warsaw as I walk the halls of the Sejm, the Polish Parliament. The rooms are decorated with Solidarity posters, photos (some quite humorous) of Prime Minister Tadeusz Mazowiecki, Solidarity labor leader Lech Walesa and Solidarity Parliamentary Chairman Bronislaw Geremek, the office doors of MP's festooned with cards carrying the Solidarity logo. Cheerfully obliging parliamentarians and their assistants allow me to photograph it all.*[50]

Though I wrote subsequently of broad themes that I witnessed in Hungary, East Germany, and Poland,[51] on this occasion I wrote of Poland particularly, speaking of my first meeting with Geremek since we had last talked in 1981 and "we laugh[ed] at the gray hair which we had both acquired in the interim." He was expansive but described the almost magical feeling that he and others were experiencing, with new freedom and the challenges that remain on the economic front. Geremek described the great problems with introducing democracy where it had been absent for such a considerable period. In this century I have often thought back to this conversation as I have witnessed Poland's diminution of democracy. But in the eighties and early nineties my access to Poland partially filled the lonely vacuum created by my exclusion from South Africa prior to 1991. Both countries made enormous strides against substantial obstacles, and in both countries today there is evidence of regrettable backsliding. Perhaps Poland has reversed this trend, given the outcome of recent elections.[52] And a new coalition government in South Africa might represent a push in the same direction. Time will tell.

NOTES

[1] William B. Gould IV, "Letter to the Editor," *New York Times*, April 10, 1972.

[2] Nathan Glazer, "Letter to the Editor," *New York Times*, April 20, 1972.

[3] William B. Gould IV, "Letter to the Editor," *New York Times*, May 1, 1972.

[4] For the reaction to Soweto in the United States by representatives of the Carter administration, see, for instance Graham Hovey, "Young Sets Off a Furor by Calling South Africa Regime 'Illegitimate,'" *New York Times*, April 16, 1977; Anthony Lewis, "Rendezvous in Vienna," *New York Times*, May 16, 1977; Norman Kempster, "U.S. Plans Threat of S. Africa Sanctions," *Los Angeles Times*, May 14, 1977; Charles Mohr, "Mondale and Vorster in Daylong Talks in Vienna," *New York Times*, May 20, 1977; Anthony Lewis, "Reckoning in Africa: II," *New York Times*, August 30, 1977. For the Western reaction, see Colin Legum and David Barritt, "Apartheid Reaps the Whirlwind," *The Observer*, June 20, 1976. For the South African reaction, see C. L. Sulzberger, "Opposite Concepts," *New York Times*, May 22, 1977 ("Mr. Vorster was not impressed by this argument and did not consider the United States experience any model for South Africa. He stressed inherent differences between black Americans and black South Africans. The former, once slaves, had given up their original roots and embraced a wholly new culture; he for one always saw them as 'Americans,' quite like their white brothers. But blacks in his country, he said, who had only encountered white settlers 140 years after the first Dutch arrived, belong to tribes and nations with various languages and cultures. Moreover, they were handicapped by the continent's great problem—they could not find jobs. Thousands immigrated to industrialized South Africa in search of work.")

[5] The early Black union struggle in the wake of Soweto is discussed in John F. Burns, "Blacks in South Africa Urged to Strike," *New York Times*, August 23, 1976; Nicholas Ashford, "Glimmer of Hope for Black Unions," *New York Times*, January 15, 1977; "Black Union Struggle," *San Francisco Chronicle*, April 25, 1976; Denis Herbstein and David Blundy, "Apartheid: The Workers Britain Betrayed," *New York Times*, May 16, 1976.

[6] Jonny Steinberg, *Winnie and Nelson: Portrait of a Marriage* (New York: Alfred A. Knopf, 2023), 62.

[7] "With the threat of Soviet Russia on everyone's mind, many forget that we once fought a war against Hitler and Mussolini and some would seek alliances with Fascist-controlled nations. Such alliances would mock the dead, who have fallen so that we may not fall prey to governments such as Spain and South Africa." William Gould IV, "Letter to the Editor," *New York Herald Tribune*, January 26, 1953.

[8] William Gould IV, "Letter to the Editor," *New York Herald Tribune*, October 4, 1953.

[9] William B. Gould IV, "A Road Away from Destruction," *The New Republic*, September 21, 1959, 22. The note on contributors says: "William B. Gould makes his first appearance as a critic in this issue."

[10] John Burns, "Won't Play in S. Africa, Ashe Declares After Visit," *New York Times*, April 10, 1977

[11] Loving v. Virginia, 388 U.S. 1 (1967).

[12] John F. Burns, "South Africa Curbs Activities of Four Whites Who Gave Assistance to Blacks in Organizing Labor Unions," *New York Times*, November 18, 1976.

[13] William B. Gould IV, "South Africa's 'Reform' Is Cosmetic," *Los Angeles Times*, March 8, 1979.

[14] Siegfried Hannig, "'Job Evils Won't Be Ended by New Laws,'" *The Star* (Johannesburg, South Africa), August 1, 1977.

[15] Siegfried Hannig, "US Labour Shows Scant Interest Here," *The Star* (Johannesburg, South Africa), August 4, 1977.

[16] Climatically, I encountered storms in Cape Town so severe that I recall looking out at a building where people, holding onto lampposts, had their feet flying into the air because of the wind gusts. The newspapers featured a major shipwreck off the coast.

[17] John F. Burns, "Southern Africa, Once a Zulu Kingdom," *New York Times*, August 29, 1976; Robert D. McFadden, "Mangosuthu Buthelezi, 95, Zulu Nationalist and a Mandela Rivel, Dies," *New York Times*, September 10, 2023.

[18] John F. Burns, "South Africa, Amid Uproar, Exiles Wife of Imprisoned Black Leader," *New York Times*, May 19, 1977.

[19] Some of the previous material appeared in slightly in different form in: William Gould, "Carter's Efforts Being Recognized," *Stanford Daily*, January 25, 1978.

[20] Clive Emdon, "Give Black Workers Real Unions—Prof," Rand Daily Mail, September 2, 1977.

[21] "Still a Long Way to Go on Labour," *Rand Daily Mail*, September 9, 1977.

[22] William B. Gould IV, "Are Black Unions the Key," *Commonweal* 105 (November 10, 1978).

[23] William B. Gould IV, "Black Unions in South Africa: Labor Law Reform and Apartheid," *Stanford Journal of International Law* 17 (1981).

[24] William B. Gould IV, "Labor Pains," *The Nation*, February 23, 1980, 196. I also questioned whether reform could take place without political participation. William B. Gould IV, "Unions for Blacks in S. Africa?" *Christianity and Crisis*, March 17, 1980, 50.

[25] Statement by William Gould, Professor of Law, Stanford University Law School. U.S. Corporate Activities in South Africa: Hearing on H.R. 3008, H.R. 3597, and H.R. 6393 Before the H. Subcomm. on Int'l Econ. Policy and Trade of the H. Comm. on Foreign Affairs, 97th Cong. 137–152 (1981).

[26] Thomas E. Mullaney, "12 Big U.S. Concerns in South Africa Set Equality in Plants," *New York Times*, March 2, 1977.
[27] Carl Irving, "S. Africa Yanks Welcome Mat for Vocal Black Law Professor," *San Francisco Examiner*, August 8, 1984; Peter Dworkin, "South Africa Denies Stanford Teacher's Visa," SF Chronicle, August 12, 1984.
[28] William B. Gould IV, Diary, September 2, 1984.
[29] Chester Crocker, letter to Donald Kennedy, August 7, 1984.
[30] William B. Gould IV, "Letter to the Editor: Let Black Unions Monitor the Workplace," *New York Times*, July 9, 1983.
[31] Robert I. Rotberg, "What to Do About South Africa," *New York Times*, July 15, 1986; "How America Stands on South Africa," *New York Times*, August 15, 1986.
[32] Anthony Lewis, "Mr. Botha's Poodle," *New York Times*, July 14, 1986; Alan Cowell, "Pretoria Praises Reagan's Speech," *New York Times*, July 24, 1986; Gerald M. Boyd, "President Opposes Additional Steps To Press Pretoria," *New York Times*, July 23, 1986.
[33] Bernard Gwertzman, "Shultz, Seeking Sanctions Delay, Says U.S. and Allies May Act Soon," *New York Times*, July 24, 1986.
[34] Seymour M. Hersh, "U.S. Is Said to Have Given Pretoria Intelligence on Rebel Organizations," *New York Times*, July 23, 1986.
[35] William B. Gould IV, "S. African Sanctions, Carefully Calibrated," *San Jose Mercury*, August 3, 1986.
[36] Steven V. Roberts, "Senate, 84 to 14 Votes Sanctions Against Pretoria," *New York Times*, August 16, 1986.
[37] Jonathan Fuerbringer, "Democrats Push Pretoria Sanctions," *New York Times*, September 11, 1986.
[38] Steven V. Roberts, "Senate, 78 to 21, Overrides Reagan's Veto and Imposes Sanctions on South Africa," *New York Times*, October 3, 1986.
[39] "Ending Real Constructive Engagement," *New York Times*, June 8, 1987.
[40] Serge Schmemann, "Tutu Will be Installed Today as the Archbishop of Cape Town," *New York Times*, September 7, 1986; Serge Schmemann, "Tutu is Installed as Archbishop, Assailing 'Violence of Apartheid,'" *New York Times*, September 8, 1986.
[41] William B. Gould IV, "Amid Astonishing Change S. Africa Future is Troubling," *San Jose Mercury*, October 6, 1991; William B. Gould IV, "The New South Africa," Sacramento Bee, October 27, 1991.
[42] William B. Gould IV, "S. Africa Grinds Toward Reform," *San Jose Mercury*, February 13, 1992.
[43] Mike McDevitt, "Stanford to Honor Mandela," *Peninsula Times Tribune*, October 22, 1992.
[44] Joseph Cotterill, Polina Ivanova, and David Pilling, "South Africa–US Row over Covert Arms Deepens as Putin and Ramaphosa talk," London *Financial Times*, May 13–14, 2023.
[45] William B. Gould IV, "The Junta & the Trade Unions," *Commonweal* 111 (1980).
[46] William B. Gould IV, "The Tragedy and the Pity of Central America," *Stanford Daily*, April 3, 1981; William B. Gould IV, "Putting the Crisis in El Salvador in Perspective," *Stanford Lawyer* 16 (1981).
[47] William B. Gould IV, "Recollections on Kurt Hanslowe," *Cornell Law Review* 69 (1984).

[48] William B. Gould IV, "Solidarity is Still Around," *San Jose Mercury*, October 11, 1987.
[49] Gould, "Solidarity is Still Around."
[50] William B. Gould IV, "Is There Light at the End of Tunnel for Poland?" *San Jose Mercury*, June 10, 1990.
[51] William B. Gould IV, "Now Comes 'the Hard Part' in E. Europe," *San Jose Mercury*, July 22, 1990.
[52] Andrew Higgins, "Lesson from Poland: Reversing Populist Conservative Policies Is Tough," *New York Times*, November 24, 2024.

9
BASEBALL COMES TO STANFORD LAW: SALARY ARBITRATION AND A NEW COURSE IN SPORTS LAW

Travel, as well as continuing litigation related to *Detroit Edison*, made the 1980s nearly as tumultuous for me as the 1970s. There were lectures abroad, scholarly renewal, public service—but the very first and most important consideration in this decade was a private one: my father's illness with cancer, which began in late 1979. Between lectures, litigation, and visits to my parents' home, I was in the San Francisco airport with such frequency that a number of its employees recognized me, particularly those at the gate for the Newark flight.

LOSING MY FATHER

When his oncologist told me that my father might be gone before my return from Durban, I canceled my lectures in South Africa. I remember that day vividly—I felt a deep sense of relief, knowing that I would remain in the United States and that I would be with him soon. I walked over to White Plaza and found Stan Getz—one of my favorite tenor saxophonists, and at that time in residence at Stanford—playing beautifully in the middle of the plaza. I had an extra day before my departure; it was an immense joy just to stand still and listen. Had I realized what lay ahead, however, I would have been on the plane that very day. Given his rapid decline, every day mattered.

Late in 1983 I wrote in my diary:

This year has been a memorable one for me—one full of sadness as well. My father died this year, August 15, 1983. I was fortunate to be with him his last eight days. He was strong as he confronted death—exactly as he had been during all the years that I knew him. He suffered terribly during those last eight days—and indeed much before that time.

I had known that he could not win this fight ever since the summer of '82 when the cancer flared up again. That spring I had toasted him on his 80th birthday at a special party that Mom had arranged for him.

I was unable to capture the man in that toast and I wrote him to that effect later. He was an extremely unusual blend of many characteristics. But I would say that two characteristics immediately come to mind—first, his goodness, inspired no doubt in part by his Christian upbringing . . . second, the extraordinary breadth of his interests. I'm reminded of this as I now read Morris's The Rise of Theodore Roosevelt. *I see many of the same traits—both in interests and manliness—he would say to me in moments of irritation and impatience: "Be a man, Bill." But he was a very gentle man—Roosevelt whom Dad admired greatly does not seem to have had comparable virtues.*

Later I wrote more succinctly the following:

His characteristics, as I recollect them, were those of compassion, wisdom, and an intelligent thoughtfulness. He was possessed of a passion for equality and fairness. And he was a man who loved his family, church, and country— and, above all, life itself.[1]

In the spring [of 1983] . . . things began to go badly. My first clear recollection was during a May speech to the AFL-CIO Professional Employees Dept. in Los Angeles. I had been jogging and discovered MacArthur Park—he was very familiar with the area. He had spent a good deal of time in LA—during World War II especially, I guess. I then went to Dallas to the UAW Convention. While there Mom telephoned to say that he had taken a turn for the worse ... I spoke with him when he was in the hospital in Philly—he sounded very weak, undergoing radiation (again never complaining) ...

Figure 9.1: William B. Gould III in his 70s.

Somehow the summer is a blur. With him at the end, he was always inquiring about the boys and their futures. That was his way.

I read St. John's Gospel on The Good Shepherd at his Memorial Service. For me, he was the good shepherd. He was able to understand and care about people.[2]

ABA ASSIGNMENTS IN FRANCE, BRITAIN, AUSTRALIA

I do not recall a comparable period of reckoning when, to quote the oft-used expression, one could hear the footsteps of the Lord. The early part of the decade had been consumed with what seemed in retrospect so routine and unimportant, that is, a number of labor law assignments, occupying considerable time. The first was my position as secretary of the American Bar Association (ABA) Labor Law Section, a position I was recommended for by section chairman and Los Angeles labor lawyer George Bodle, a Stanford Law School graduate. This work took me to New Orleans a couple of times, the second visit being the ABA Convention, where I delivered a paper I entitled "Justice Brennan's Term"[3] and in which I roundly criticized a number of the court's holdings from which Justice Brennan had dissented. I featured *First National Maintenance v. NLRB*,[4] which held that employers generally had no duty to bargain with the union over a decision to close or partially close its operations. One management labor lawyer remarked that my views would provide as much scope for management prerogatives free from the collective bargaining process as the Israelis wanted to provide Palestine's autonomy—that is, next to nothing! But I didn't see things that way at all, always arguing for a decision that would provide an involvement for the labor movement—just I have argued for involvement and sovereignty for the Palestinians!

After New Orleans and my work for the ABA in that capacity, I undertook another ABA assignment which I combined with visits to France, Britain (the site of the ABA Convention), and Australia, where I gave more lectures under the auspices of the United States Government. I wrote in my diary about this trip, after arriving on July 13, 1981, and witnessing Bastille Day:

> *In the evening I saw fireworks of the sparkler variety as I sat in a café in Place de la Bastille where the notorious prison once stood. Young people snake dancing, children sitting next to me crying, alarmed by all the noise. It is alarming to have sparklers exploding around you at first but one becomes accustomed.*
>
> *Bastille Day itself was overcast, rainy and my camera didn't function well at the parade. The parade is military—paratroopers, tanks, legionnaires and cavalry somewhat similar to what I have seen in newspapers showing Moscow.*
>
> *Went to the reviewing but Mitterrand had left. Told friends of my '62 meeting with French Socialist Party leader Guy Mollet, when DeGaulle was President.*
>
> *In the evening, watched the fireworks which by my standards were spectacular (certainly much better than I saw on July 4 at Anaheim Stadium with Bill and Ed) from a bridge near Notre Dame over the Seine.*

Next day, July 15, I was on my way to London to preside at an ABA Convention panel on labor law: Has Taft-Hartley Come to Britain—The Thatcher Legislative Trilogy.

Checked in at the Great Western Royal Hotel in Paddington where Keith Stuart had booked me.

The week in London went quickly. Attended a few ABA functions . . . celebrated my 49th birthday in London—the first one I've had there since . . . '63—by dining alone at the The Shah on North Gower St—a restaurant that I have been to often with Hilda, Mary and Peter [her sister and brother-in-law] when he was alive.

On July 17, I presided over the ABA panel. Bill Wedderburn canceled out on the day of the session in itself . . . [My former professor] Cyril Grunfeld had a good message but got carried away with rhetoric about "union dictatorship" and began to lose some credibility with American union lawyers.

Spent a couple of evenings with Keith and Kathy Stuart whom it was a delight to see as usual. Keith has gone right to the top of British business and political circles. After picking me up at my hotel on 7/20 I had tea with them at their house. They dropped me at Heathrow, got me situated and I was off on a 24-hour plane journey to Perth!

I was amazed at the large number of very elderly people on this long, exhausting flight. We stopped in Bahrain, in the Gulf, where I had time to mail some cards . . . The next stop was Singapore, which has a new, modern airport since I was there in '75—where we changed aircrafts. Then, finally, on to Perth, where I arrived at 5 A.M. 7/22 on a cold, chilly, but still dark, morning—it's winter down here!

Actually, the weather in Perth was milder than Stanford in February, for the most part. My base here was the University of Western Australia Law School. The Dean and other faculty were most hospitable. There was hardly an evening where I was not invited to dinner.

My first day in Perth, I wandered up to King's Park and had my first encounter with the Australian magpie, a very big black and white bird which swoops down from trees. I became fascinated and wanted a photo. I eventually came up to three or four which seemed tame, and I was able to get very close. I took a photo of one that looked right at me in the camera. When I turned my back, after taking the photo, I heard a noise of the bird jumping toward me—I turned, startled, and the magpie, now closer, did not flinch. I quickly retreated. The bird was tame and cheeky, I noticed that they were building nests and courting, and was told that they become aggressive toward joggers and cyclists whom they perceived to be invading their territory and the nest to be built. . . . I was sufficiently concerned to watch the trees carefully during my first jog up there—the hill is a stiff one for me!

I became particularly friendly with Bill Ford, a labor lawyer there who took me to dinner twice and to an Australian rules Football game. I had seen one in Melbourne in '75, a fast, exciting, young man's game which looks fairly dangerous—a combination of American football, soccer, rugby, and even basketball, given the dribbling of the ball after five meters.

While I was in Perth, the South African government declared a state of emergency and has now detained 1,300 people, France supported sanctions in the U.N., and the Reagan Administration attacked this!

Meanwhile, this seems to have supported U.S. sanctions legislation.[5]

Australia has withdrawn its ambassador. A cartoon in one of the Australian newspapers,

"Botha: But we've always shot our blacks.

Hawke: But you haven't denied them their rights before."

The world seems more interested now and properly so. Chase Manhattan has withdrawn credit to SA companies. The rand has plummeted.

I left Perth, escorted to the railway station by the Dean and Bill Ford, after a lovely, if hurried, dinner at a Vietnamese restaurant on the Indian Express . . . There is not a great deal to see and regrettably, I missed the kangaroos that others observed. But I read most of The Hawke Ascendancy *by Paul Kelly, which is my reintroduction to Australian politics. Haven't followed it closely since I was here in '75 and '76.*

I was able to get off the train in the Outback—Port Augusta, South Australia. Many Aborigines of varied colors who generally stayed to themselves and did not seem to be amongst those employed.

8/1 – what a contrast was Sydney to the . . . miles of a barren desert. I quickly grabbed a cab . . . to the airport without too much time to spare, the train having been almost 2 hours late!

Sydney, 9/9/85: The weeks in Canberra [I was based at the Australian National University] *went by quickly. My memories are jogging in bitter cold and a good deal of hard rain. Only at the end of my stay there did things get lively—a Woody Herman concert, then some visits to jazz places. But one really needs a car to explore Canberra. I am glad that I came to Australia—but not nearly as sure about Canberra.*

[I visited] . . . Cairns, on August 30, where I went to Barrier Reef. A lovely, sunny boat ride and much natural beauty to behold. In Cairns, I went to a small Italian restaurant, and a young fellow asked me if I was Bill Gould. Turned out, that he was a Stanford Law grad, touring Australia after the bar.

Another remarkable incident—met an LSE law prof, Bill Cornish, in Adelaide. Suddenly realized that I had been at an LSE party for ABA people in July—he had spoken, and we chatted —but neither remembered upon being introduced.

When I got to Port Moresby, PNG on 9/1 for a USIA lecture, I was truly exhausted and the laryngitis was still bad. But somehow, I recovered. On Monday, I flew to Bougainville—spent some time at the big copper mine. Very much on the go—lovely island, grand scenery. Returned to PN on Wednesday, but no real sense of the dangers . . . there is now a state of emergency and curfew . . . The country is so isolated and people desperate for communication. The highlight of my communications was a dinner speech which I gave at the Ambassador's residence, where I couldn't fail to get at Reagan on national labor policy. The Ambassador was quick to disassociate himself.

CHALLENGING ASSUMPTIONS IN AMERICAN LABOR LAW

My work in other countries since the 1960s encouraged me in the 1980s to begin to challenge the status quo and the assumptions of American labor law itself. The best immediate illustration of this related to the problem of wrongful discharge law in the United States. Debate about this subject was increasing in the eighties because of a peculiar anomaly in American labor law. This anomaly flowed from the fact that, notwithstanding the enactment of statutory protections infringing on a free labor market through the National Labor Relations Act of 1935 and Title VII of the Civil Rights Act of 1964, the law in the United States was and is that the contract of employment is terminable at will. Thus, absent a restriction like those contained in the above-referenced statutes or the negotiation of a collective bargaining agreement, the employer is free to discharge a worker at any time for any reason. I had long thought that this was a terrible state of affairs. I had advised friends who had been dismissed, feared dismissal, or had been laid off that they had no recourse, and no protection at all, unless the action taken by the employer was attributable to race, sex, sexual orientation, national origin, or union activity, or unless they were covered by a union-negotiated collective bargaining agreement, which generally obliged the employer to have "just cause" to dismiss the worker.

Gradually, however, judicial decisions on the right to terminate at will began to fashion a limited exception to this framework, that is, an exception rooted in common law, not statutes enacted by state legislatures or Congress. Dismissal could violate public policy, said the California Supreme Court in the landmark *Tameny* ruling, and could provide workers with what lawyers call a cause of action.[6] This meant that the employer could be sued for damages where the employer dismissal was inconsistent with public policy. Lower courts subsequently held that an implied contractual obligation, sometimes in the form of promises made in a company handbook, as well as through representations by the employer, could also limit employer discretion.

Cases proceeding on the theory that discharges were wrongful or unfair began to be brought in the nonunion sector at the state level. But the public policy cases were narrow—involving, for instance, protests against illegal behavior by the company of which only a limited number of employees would have knowledge. And the question of contractual protection, and its scope, was unclear. In January 1983, in response to the large amount of litigation that began to emerge under this rubric, the California State Bar Labor and Employment Law Section created an Ad Hoc Committee on Termination at Will and Wrongful Discharge and appointed six members,[7] naming management labor lawyer Howard Hay and me as co-chairmen.

The committee held hearings and conducted meetings with each of the interested parties in San Francisco, Los Angeles, and San Diego, and other parts of both northern and southern California. The assignment was a challenging one. But I found the other panel members to be dedicated and committed to examination of this subject. Wayne Estes, a fellow academic from Pepperdine who had written in this area,[8] was both soft-spoken and balanced in his approach; he proved to be a particularly valuable committee member. Mark Rudy was an extremely able plaintiffs' lawyer; Helena Wise brought the important qualifications of a union lawyer from southern California. Two very sound management labor lawyers provided balance: co-chairs Hay and my former Stanford Law School student, Maureen McLain, whose rise in the labor law world was appropriately meteoric.

In February 1984 a majority of the committee came to the conclusion in California (and indeed, in the nation as well, although we did not say so) that legislation was warranted and needed for a number of reasons. The committee said:

> *Whatever may be said about the kind of legislation which should be enacted in California, it is clear that some legislation should be enacted by the California Legislature, given the tension between the above-referenced California decisions and others and the common law terminable at will doctrine codified in the statute. For reasons which we make clear, we are of the view that California Labor Code 2922 should be repealed and that the terminable at will approach should be banished and consigned to the laissez-faire philosophy of a previous age of which it is a relic.*[9]

We were also of the view that the standard for judicial review, as well as the measure of damages, were vague and uncertain, though we pointed out that legislative proposals by the committee would not eliminate ambiguities and the lack of clarity in both standards for dismissal as well as remedies. We also emphasized that the form of litigation, before judge and jury, produced wild, unpredictable fluctuations in damage amounts and that the forum of general jurisdiction in the courts was inexpert and thus, in our view, second best.

And finally, we took note that the new California rulings, while finding exceptions to the new terminable at-will principle, did not provide for reinstatement where the employer was liable, even if the relationship was capable of repair. This remedy of reinstatement, of course, is available under modern labor law and collective bargaining agreements obliging employers not to dismiss workers for reasons other than just cause.

The committee recommended that just cause, as in negotiated agreements, should be the standard in the nonunion sector. We said:

> We believe that the just cause standard is the appropriate one as it relates to the case of discharge. While some of the cases and jury instructions in California have spoken in terms of a good faith obligation which is to be imposed upon employers, as we note below, employers will reap considerable advantages and benefits from this statute. Accordingly, it would be a rigid and short-sighted, inflexible approach which would simply carry over the case law—whatever it is—that has arisen at common law.
>
> Moreover, if something other than just cause was used, that is, good faith or reasonable basis, the Legislature would be confronted with an insoluble dilemma. One the one hand, failure to address the issue of progressive discipline would indicate that the statute contemplated an anti-progressive discipline approach and an abandonment of the labor arbitration authority to the effect that employers, except in connection with certain kinds of offenses, have an obligation to counsel and, in some instances, to take less severe disciplinary steps than discharge. The just cause standard has become, during this past century, virtually synonymous with the progressive discipline concept.[10]

With regard to reinstatement, we said the following:

> We believe that reinstatement is presumptively an appropriate remedy where a violation of the statute has been found. But we are of the view that reinstatement should not be provided with automaticity as it seems to be under

both the National Labor Relations Act and arbitration proceedings. There may be circumstances in which reinstatement is not appropriate where, for instance, (1) a confidential or executive type relationship is involved and where the employer or employee relationship is both delicate and complex; (2) contact with the public, for instance, is involved and in the employer's judgment the employee presents an image which is not suitable; (3) where evidence of serious misconduct is found to have taken place subsequent to the occurrences which have given rise to an invalid discharge. Under such circumstances it should be not only within the arbitrator's discretion to deny reinstatement, but also, within the boundaries outlined above, to determine the extent of front pay which should be available to the employee. We note that this flexibility is particularly desirable in nonunion situations where the employee, if reinstated, will not have a union available to him or her which can guard against employer behavior which, if it does not constitute recidivism, would at least discourage the employee from retaining the gains of reinstatement.[11]

We proposed that back pay with interest be substituted for compensatory and punitive damages. In a sense, not only would we eliminate the volatility of the present damages which courts were awarding, but also the average employee, who didn't gain from public policy nor from some forms of contract protection, would nonetheless obtain more access to a less expensive, less formal tribunal, creating protection akin to what a collective bargaining agreement would provide—that is, a trade-off.

We also adopted a statutory approach that would apply to employers who employed fifteen or more workers, following the approach taken in statutes like Title VII. In essence, this would be an enticement for employers. To sum up, we thought that the broader, more practical approach was less expensive, more accessible, and more predictable, with arbitration rather than the courts as the forum.

Figure 9.2: I spoke to a wide variety of groups in the wake of our report. This was a speech that I gave to the Center for Democratic Institutions in Santa Barbara, California in 1984.

In the wake of the report, I testified before a California legislative committee,[12] delivered a paper to the National Academy of Arbitrators in Chicago,[13] and wrote an op-ed for the *New York Times*.[14] However, the report, while soundly conceived and balanced in my view, did not become legislation in any state in the union, with the limited exception of Montana.[15] And then the California Supreme Court in *Foley v. Interactive Data* complicated matters further by eliminating some of the employee leverage, holding that tort damages and punitive relief could not be obtained in contract cases on the theory (applicable to insurance companies) that the covenant of good faith and fair dealing had been violated.[16] Indeed, the court improperly relied upon some of my writings to support this conclusion.[17] I had simply noted that the availability of litigation before the judiciary was ephemeral for most workers—I had never adopted the concept and holding articulated by the court. Bob Egelko, then with the Associated Press, spotted this right away and wrote about it. Radio stations picked it up in broadcasts that made my mother uncomfortable one day, as I drove her to the San Francisco airport—she did not like the idea of any controversy surrounding her son.

Foley eliminated any incentive that employers might have had to support legislation that diminished their liability. The public policy cases, while important, were unlikely to arise in most employment disputes. The average worker was not privy to information he could whistle-blow about or advertise. And though long afterward New York City and Philadelphia enacted ordinances to address aspects of the employee dismissal problem—an approach which in my view is critical for all society—most of the action shifted to one-sided, employer-promulgated procedures promoted by the Supreme Court and its genuflection to what it perceived to be the requirements of the Federal Arbitration Act of 1925.[18] All of the action thus shifted to new standards which the employers themselves, rather than the state or anyone else, would devise for employee dismissals and other employment rights already covered by fair employment practice legislation, health and safety protections, and so on.[19] This is what Justice Ruth Bader Ginsburg properly characterized as "unbargained-for" arbitration[20] imposed by the employer unilaterally. But these inequities continue to this very day.

ACADEMIC UPS AND DOWNS

Inside Stanford Law School, there were some positive developments for me. For example, in 1984 I was named the Charles A. Beardsley Professor of Law. Although not financially beneficial, the award was nonetheless prestigious, not to mention nice sounding.

Although I had joined the law school with a reasonable salary, I soon discovered that Dean Charles Meyers had placed me behind some of my colleagues who were junior to me. This policy was not changed by his successor, John Ely, a dean whom I viewed as a flop and who was hardly to my liking either. Yet there was another development which angered me as much, and perhaps even more, in a world where income is primarily psychic.

I had wanted to bring some of my work in South Africa back to the law school. Thus, when a young Indian lawyer whom I'd met in South Africa applied to do graduate work at Stanford Law School, I was advised by the graduate committee that there was no opportunity to do graduate work at Stanford Law School; the application was promptly rejected by committee chairman John Merryman. His reason: Stanford Law had not had graduate students for advanced degrees beyond the three-year juris doctor program.[21] I knew that this was false, based upon my own discussions with graduate students who had been previously enrolled. But Merryman wouldn't accept my protestations. His position was that whatever had happened in the past, current policy was contrary to it. Naturally, I wouldn't accept this and saw it as an ad hoc, seat-of-the-pants, shifting policy designed to exclude the person I wanted to work with at the law school. I appealed the decision to Dean John Ely. To put it simply, Ely affirmed Merryman without any discussion of the matter with me.

At this point, I was outraged! My good friend Miguel Mendez, the first Latino appointment to the faculty in 1977, said I was like Ralph Ellison's Invisible Man to Ely and Merryman. Miguel noted that they would take no more notice of me than the men who emptied their wastepaper baskets or cleaned their toilets. I decided that I wouldn't allow this to go on. I began to write letters to prominent people I knew, such as Anthony Lewis of the *New York Times* (a contact from some of my British trips) and the Episcopal Bishop of California in San Francisco, with whom I had formed a friendship during my Title VII litigation. They expressed interest and surprise. These developments stunned an embarrassed Ely, and he quickly backed down, allowing the student to be admitted. (At one point, he said, "I didn't know the student was not white," suggesting that he would have admitted the student on what's now called "diversity" grounds if he had known—but he did know, and this probably prompted Mendez's Ralph Ellison remark!)

Years later, while I was in Washington, Stanford started a foreign student graduate program—the exact idea I had been fighting for in the eighties. It was well established by the time I returned in

1998, and it felt like a particularly bitter pill to me, given that I was neither part of the new program nor invited to join it upon my return from Washington. I paid a penalty for going first.

Nonetheless, the eighties brought positive developments in other areas. One was a new course I created: Law and Sports. For years, given the prominence of labor law and labor arbitration in sports, particularly baseball, my sons had frequently asked me why I was not involved. The emergence of sports law offered me an opportunity to combine two of my greatest passions.

MY ROOTS IN BASEBALL

The subway train emerges from a darkened tunnel at the Bronx Grand Concourse station in New York City. It all happens so quickly that I am surprised by the brilliant sunshine—and left absolutely breathless by the sudden view into Yankee Stadium, its grand field far below the train and platform, thousands of spectator seats filling gradually with the arriving throng.

The date is August 21, 1946. I am not quite ten years old. It's the first professional baseball game I've ever been to, and getting me there is no small undertaking for my father: New York City is fifty miles north of our home in Long Branch, and the train ride, tickets, and other incidentals add up to a significant investment for a family of modest means. And it's a doubleheader! The Yankees are playing the Chicago White Sox in "The Stadium."

The first game is relatively straightforward and one-sided, with the Yankees routing the White Sox 10–1. Joe DiMaggio hits a long home run to left field, and outfielder Charlie "King Kong" Keller hits a towering shot to deep right. The second game, or "nightcap," as it's called, goes twelve innings. Joe D. hits another one. Mike Tresh, the White Sox backstop, makes a great impression on me—he's so stolid behind the plate. Chicago White Sox manager Ted Lyons disputes a call when one of his players is thrown out, jumping up and down, gesticulating—even kicking some dirt; this was years before instant replay of close calls diminished umpire decisions. My father laughs aloud and notes the similarity between the game of baseball and grand theater.[22] But the Yankees prevail again, 5–4, in the bottom of the twelfth. Yankee Johnny Murphy—who'd be acquired by the Red Sox in '47 in their vain attempt to catch the Yanks—is on the mound in relief and gets the victory. My father calls my attention to some of Murphy's mannerisms: a deep bow before he begins his windup, a profound swing of the arms backward and forward prior to the ball's delivery. Although these theatrics are common in pitchers of the forties and fifties, my father and I don't know that: We're getting our first look at big league pitchers together—it's my father's first professional game, too.

There are features of that doubleheader that will always be with me. The reaction of the cognoscenti when a particular pitcher appears from the bullpen—so many know him just by the way he walks. (In those days, no relief pitcher *ran* in from the bullpen to speed up the game; they walked in a stately, measured, dignified manner.) The crack of the catcher's mitt as he receives the pitcher's warm-up in the bullpen; the echo that resonates from the bullpen's concrete walls. Years later, in Anaheim Stadium before its twenty-first century renovation, those same sounds take me right back to 1946.

I was grateful to my father for taking the time to go with me to that first big game, but I am not sure that I was adequately appreciative of the fact that he got far more than he bargained for—not only a doubleheader, but extra innings as well! It turned out to be a very long excursion, particularly for a man who had little interest in baseball. Perhaps he sensed that that first game would be emblazoned in my consciousness all throughout my life.

Station Field Sandlot Ball

That summer doubleheader in 1946 capped a sweet summer of sandlot baseball for me. After fourth grade let out that June, our mothers packed lunches for us every day before we jumped on our bikes to pedal toward Station Field, proximate to the New York–Long Branch railroad tracks on the Jersey shore. Our Station Field gang consisted of a dozen or so nine- to twelve-year-old boys, classmates at the Broadway School and choirboys from St James's. No uniforms, no umpires, no adult supervision. Sometimes the catcher—always without equipment—was on one's own team, standing far behind home plate as he took the pitch on one bounce. We were so eager to start the game that we often played with our pants half rolled up, forgetting to roll them down once we'd leapt off our bikes.

It was only baseball, all day long. There were makeshift bases established where the grass had worn thin, and no exact rule of measurement from base to base or from our unelevated pitching mound to home plate. We knew nothing about the proper pitching distance of sixty feet and six inches, designated since 1893. And with no umpires—like the nineteenth-century rules, which at one time did not contemplate called strikes and even allowed a batter to call for a high or low pitch (we didn't follow that rule)—only peer pressure could induce a young hitter to swing at a pitch that was not precisely to his liking. Under these circumstances, the pitcher would frequently "groove one" in the middle of the strike zone to tempt a reticent hitter waiting for that perfect pitch. Batting averages could thus soar—and mine did—well above .700, more than double what a good batter could hit in a properly organized game.

With only one or two balls between all of us, it was imperative that they not be lost; black tape had to be available at all times so that the ball would not come apart at the seams—literally! Today it seems unimaginable that, at both the professional and amateur levels in the so-called "dead ball" era before 1920, prior to Babe Ruth, the same ball would be kept in play for much of the game. Under the circumstances of our sandlot ball, it goes without saying that the guy who owned the ball was particularly powerful and popular!

I loved to hit. The hotter the weather became as July turned to August, the better I thought I could hit and the more relaxed I felt at the plate. On the other hand, my Louisville Slugger would often break on inside pitches on the hands—particularly in the cold of March and April, when I did not like to hit—and black tape came in handy there too, thus temporarily rescuing a good piece of lumber from the fireplace. As with the balls, the surgically repaired bats were never quite as good, but they had to do.

Fielding was a less-developed art. Our gloves were positively primitive by today's standards, with neither deep pockets nor elaborate webbing. We were always advised to catch the ball with two hands, not only because that approach was regarded as intrinsically sensible, but also because the gloves made one-handed catches unrealistic unless they were absolutely necessary! Four seasons at the Station Field, grabbing line drives hit by other .700 hitters, wore my mitt and its minimal padding to a frazzle. In 1949 my parents bought me a new one, but it also soon wore out, in spite of less frequent use as the years went on. A few years ago, when Willie Mays came to my office at Stanford Law School before he was to speak in one of my seminars, he looked in horror at my Bobby Bonds glove from the seventies and said, "I'll send you a proper glove!" And its perfect complexity and beauty so exceeded my imagination that I have never dared use it!

Figure 9.3: The beautiful and modern glove given to me by Willie Mays after he appeared in my Sports Law seminar.

Perhaps the gloves also suffered from our practice of leaving them on the field when we departed to bat in our half of the inning. This was the practice in the major leagues as well until 1953, when because of safety concerns Major League Baseball passed Rule

3.14, which prohibited leaving equipment on the field when a team vacated it to come up to bat. In fact, the safety problems then were much less considerable than in today's parks, where bullpens and high pitching mounds and photographic gear create a real hazard for hard-running outfielders and infielders.

I think that all of us Station Field players saw something that was more inexact and uncertain about fielding that wasn't affected by arm and glove: Where you were positioned affected whether you could get to the ball, and when you put a glove on the ball you might be more easily charged with an error. In an age when defensive statistics based upon a player's ability to get to a ball hit to a particular "zone" were unknown, we Station Field kids knew that Yankee shortstop Phil Rizzuto's mobility did not translate into the best fielding average. When in September 2010 Red Sox left fielder Bill Hall fumbled a grounder by an Oakland A's hitter and allowed the run to score, a poor throw on the same play permitted the A's hitter to advance and ultimately score and tie the game. Neither mistake was ever recorded on the scorecard. My Stanford colleague, the late Leonard Koppett, said great statistics (always unrecorded, of course) are the mistakes that you didn't make that you could have made. Speaking of the obverse, jazz composer and pianist Dave Frishberg wrote, "I see where Reggie Jackson made an error/Now, how could they report that any fairer?/The sun must have got in his eyes."[23]

Hitting or pitching were more satisfying arts than fielding: The confrontation was direct and someone won or lost. So we would practice our swings, throws, and set stretch positions as we held an imaginary runner on first—all of this without bat or ball, in our living rooms at home. Long after I'd grown up, I remember watching the 1972 Oakland–Cincinnati World Series on television and being intrigued with "Blue Moon" Odom pitching out of the stretch, holding and watching the runner at first base out of the corner of his eye. That's what we would do when we were away from the field, at home or at the bus stop—a practice rendered infeasible by baseball's new time-rigid rules, limiting the number of pitches that can be thrown to first base.

Since I was a kid, I've only seen practice gestures like ours engaged in by young children in the Tokyo subways—though more recently my grandson Joey (Joseph Jeremy Gould) impressed me with the way he practiced his bat-cocked-high "corkscrew" Kevin Youkilis batting style and throwing motions, in anticipation of his next Little League game. (Subsequently, Joey became a fine high school catcher.)

My near fanatical devotion to baseball had one interesting academic consequence: I was a math phenom! Though it seems strange given my performance in geometry and algebra in subsequent years, in elementary school Bobby Graham and I were a full year ahead of our class in math; I never enjoyed such success again until ninth grade Latin. And my interest and performance in math translated into batting averages and earned run data, which were part of my daily discussion—I was genuinely obsessed with this aspect of the game.

The All-Consuming Game

In 1946 baseball was an understated game, compared to the way it is played today. Understated or not, however, it truly consumed us—and it consumed the entire country as well. To boost morale among the population, FDR had insisted that the game continue during the war, although most of the great stars, including Ted Williams, Joe DiMaggio, Bob Feller, Stan Musial, Bobby Doerr, and Johnny Pesky, had departed to take up their wartime duties in uniform (as Williams did once again during the Korean War in the early fifties). In 1946, the boys came home from World War II. Attendance soared mightily, and the Red Sox–Yankee, Dodger–Cardinal and Dodger–Giant rivalries fostered excitement and pennant fever.

My father had little interest in baseball but took an interest in my involvement because of his interest in me. When he came home from work, I would hold out my right hand to him, asking him to "check in on his home run as he crossed the plate" with what would be called a "low five" today.[24] Occasionally we would have a catch together, and when Father Anderson, our parish's curate, would visit our home, he would don a glove and short-hop bad throws gracefully in the dirt, prompting much applause from my father and neighborhood kids like Harry Levin, who would always wander over to our house when he heard Father Anderson was around. Years later, in the Oakland Coliseum, I would think anew of Father Anderson as I watched A's third sacker Eric Chavez gracefully short-hop difficult grounders that came in his direction.

One time, hearing that Ted Williams had struck out with the bases loaded against the Yankees, my father consoled me by recalling, "It happened to the Babe also." Though he grew concerned about my almost obsessive devotion to baseball, in 1947 my father hooked up a shortwave radio for me in our cellar so I could listen to Jim Britt broadcast the Red Sox games, and hear those of the National League's Boston Braves as well! Many of the Braves' road games were by-telegraph recreations—we could even hear the clickety-clack in the background.

Figure 9.4: At the inaugural meeting of the Red Sox Hall of Fame 1995, leaning over to the right of my boyhood hero, Ted Williams, I told him that he was "the greatest individual on the planet in the 20th century." He exclaimed to teammate shortstop-third baseman Johnny Pesky, seated to his right, "Johnny, listen to what this fellow is saying about me!"

I was forbidden to read the sports section of scandal-filled tabloids like the *New York Daily News*, although I caught a quick read of it when I went to the barbershop, where it was available to all who dared pick it up. But by reading the *New York Times* and various baseball magazines, I knew the hitting and pitching statistics for all twenty-five players on all sixteen clubs. My father confided in Father Anderson that this kind of pursuit of any subject seemed to him to be out of balance—and it probably was!

Amidst all the almost-daily baseball playing, there was also plenty of baseball talk. We discussed what we read in the *New York Times*'s detailed and gracefully written daily descriptions of all games played outside New York, as well as those involving the Dodgers, Giants, and Yankees. These articles consisted of pure descriptive and analytic commentary, in sharp contrast to today's inane, quotation-laden, player "remarks," for example, "I was seeing the ball really good," in response to a question about what a player thought or felt at the time he hit a homer.

When we were not on the field, we could imbibe the radio-shaped images presented through that medium. Mel Allen and Red Barber were the two best announcers in those days, and their personalities permitted them to make the transfer to television in the fifties. The mellifluous Allen was charming and folksy. During one of the Red Sox–Yankee contests that special summer, as Sox reliever Mike Ryba entered the fray, Allen sang the hit tune of that time, "Hey Ba Ba Re Bop," in his melodic baritone, substituting Ryba for "Re Bop."

I enjoyed hearing the big-league games on the radio almost as much as I loved to play and watch the game itself. Although the Yankees' first televised broadcasts began in 1946, no one had television in our neighborhood in those days, and in 1947 only a few wealthy people had it. Only one family on our block had it, and I think I saw my first televised game at that house in 1947. In the 1940s, radio was dominant—though, because it competed with newspapers and magazines and the like for a literate public, it was not as supreme as television became.

All this quickly changed in the 1950s. Jazz and blues singer Dinah Washington would sing that television was "the thing," and that radio, despite its greatness, was "out of date" in the era before the advent of radio broadcasters like Joe Castiglione and Jon Miller, who revitalized the art of announcing. Americans possessed 400,000 television sets in 1948, 10 million by 1950, and 42 million in 1957. As James S. Hirsch has written: "[By the 1950s] the sport itself, as national televised entertainment, had arrived . . . television showcased players in all corners of the country, forged connections with distant fans, and elevated stars to heroic status."[25]

Figure 9.5: With Red Sox announcer Joe Castiglione upon his induction into Baseball's Hall of Fame, July 2024, Cooperstown, New York.

But in the 1940s I could not wait for 6:45 p.m. to hear Stan Lomax on New York's WOR, 710 on the dial. "Good evening," Lomax would intone, "This is Stan Lomax with the day's doings in the world of sports, and today those Boston Red Sox continued to rare and tear. . ." His next words would be drowned out by one boy's exultations at 458 Bath Avenue in Long Branch.

My Red Sox

Those Boston Red Sox. . . . By the time we started playing at Station Field in June 1946, the Red Sox had an insurmountable lead against all comers. Thus, when we began to choose the team that each of us would support, I immediately identified with the Red Sox, who had their backs to the wind the entire summer, leaving the Detroit Tigers and the New York Yankees buried in the dust. (The Sox were to finish twelve games ahead of the Bengals and seventeen up on the Yanks.) As early as May that year the baseball cartoonist Willard Mullin wrote "Break up the Red Sox," a humorous mimic of the "Break up the Yankees" theme that had emerged in the midst of their success from the twenties through the forties. The *New York World Telegram* ran an item containing the pictures of Johnny Pesky, Dom DiMaggio, and Red Sox catcher Hal Wagner, stating, "Stop these men: dangerous characters . . . headed this way . . . armed with powerful clubs . . . a menace to our fair city."

Figure 9.6: Enos (Country) Slaughter, St. Louis Cardinals, slides across home plate with the winning run of the World Series during the 8th inning of the 7th game at Sportsman's Park, St. Louis, Oct. 15, 1946. Marty Marion, the next Cardinal batter, watches, while still holding his bats. Umpire Al Barlick signals the safe sign. On his knees awaiting the throw-in from Johnny Pesky is catcher Roy Partee. Cards won the final game 4–3 to become Baseball's World Champions of 1946.

I had a solid identification with Boston. First of all, I had been born there. Yes, we'd moved to New Jersey when I was four, but we returned at every opportunity to visit my great-uncles and great-aunt in Dedham and to visit other parts of the Bay State as well, including Cape Cod. I had clear memories of my father pointing out the shamrock-laced mansion of his former boss, Mayor James Michael Curley; his declared admiration of William Lloyd Garrison and Boston's abolitionist tradition also strengthened my alliance with Massachusetts and some things Bostonian. All my life I had heard accounts of the area in our New Jersey home. My parents always thought they would ultimately return to "the Hub."

And there was another factor: our next-door neighbors, the Hessleins, continuously blared Yankee games on the radio from their porch. I remember listening to their constant references and fanatical devotion to Joe DiMaggio and Phil Rizzuto during that summer of 1946. Their unqualified support for the Yanks put me off a bit. (So did Mrs. Hesslein's admission that she wanted to see Billy Conn triumph over Joe Louis that summer because "We need a white champion." Much to my pleasure, Louis proceeded to knock him out in the eighth round.) Simply put, I was from Boston—I should be a Red Sox fan! That is how it all began.

Never again after 1946 (except for possibly 2018) would the Red Sox be quite so supreme. Even in the triumphant year of 2004, when the Red Sox obtained their first World Championship in eighty-six years, the club could never catch the Yankees in the regular season Eastern Division race to the wire and thus replicate that sweet summer fifty-eight years earlier. Still, the heroics of David Ortiz and Dave Roberts made me think back to that third Dave: Dave Henderson, whose dramatic 1986 home run against the Angels rescued the Red Sox from playoff oblivion. They went on to a fourth post-World War II American League Championship that year, only to be denied at the altar again in the most excruciating of last-moment snatches of defeat from the jaws of victory.

Other Leagues

Major League Baseball was not the only baseball influence in my life in 1946. With friends and sometimes my parents, I frequently attended so-called City League games on weekday evenings and became a supporter of Cammarano's Bar, a team composed of the Long Branch Acerra Brothers. The Acerra Brothers were a mainstay in the Long Branch tradition and lore, and even when my parents were elderly, one of them delivered mail to their residence.

The weekends often saw our family go on driving excursions into the countryside in our 1937 Plymouth, which my parents had bought secondhand just before World War II. The purpose of those trips was often bird watching, but as we drove through rolling hills in rural New Jersey I could only imagine chasing fly balls up the near-mountainous terrain—an image that was reawakened for me during a spring training game in Vero Beach, Florida, in 1987. The outfield was not fenced off from the hill behind it where spectators sat, and I saw young then-rookie Ellis Burks race up the hill to grab a long drive by Dodger catcher Alex Trevino, scattering sunbathing spectators in his wake.

The Sundays of those weekends in the forties were very special baseball days—after attendance and choir performance at St. James's Episcopal Church, of course. Sunday was the Jersey Shore League, a group of semiprofessional players who were a cut above our Long Branch City League. On most Sundays I was able to see the Long Branch Green Sox play their local rivals from Red Bank and Fair Haven and watch Joe Magill, with his big roundhouse, overhand, over-the-top fastball, stride toward the plate with an ominous straight-legged kick forward. Most of us perceived him to be unhittable. Frequently I would bike over to Fort Monmouth, where my father worked, and watch Black first baseman "Chief" Crump play for a fine military team that knew how to play the game well. Korean War draftee and Yankee ace "Whitey" Ford was on the team briefly—and they played well in competition with the Philadelphia Athletics and Pittsburgh Pirates, teams I also saw at Fort Monmouth in that same time period.

Figure 9.7: Two William B. Goulds witnessing the Red Sox–Angels October 1986 post-season game, when Dave Henderson's home run saved the season.

Figure 9.8: An autographed photo of Dave Henderson (when he was subsequently a member of the Oakland Athletics) rounding the bases after his dramatic homer in the ninth inning.

Baseball, Race, and Me

Race was another aspect of my relationship with baseball. There were no Black players in organized baseball in 1946. I was light-skinned as a youth, and my mother fretted about the dark tan I was acquiring as I played baseball day after day, but my father, in his perennially understated and gentle manner, told her not to worry about it.

When I first started playing baseball at the sandlot that summer, still shy of my tenth birthday, I do not think I knew I was Black, even though I had imbibed my parents' message of racial equality as a small child. But I was immediately confronted with racial epithets when other players at the Station Field got angry with me. Their calls of "Nigger!" and "You are a lot of mulatto!" left me at that point puzzled as well as hurt. Only gradually did the true picture emerge for me personally—and only much later did I begin to understand the racially exclusionary policies of baseball generally, as well as the Red Sox in particular. Every single player on the major league fields that summer of 1946 was white!

The Red Sox were to be the last team to break the color bar, not hiring infielder Pumpsie Green until I was a student at Cornell Law School in 1959. Like all the other teams in baseball during that fateful summer of 1946, the Sox had no Black players. The difference for them was that they were to remain lily-white until even after teams like the racially exclusionary Detroit Tigers and the Washington Senators broke the color bar.

I did not know that when Tommy Harper, the fine outfielder and greatest base stealer in Red Sox history (until Jacoby Ellsbury in this century) came to the Carmine Hose in 1972, he blew the whistle because of Red Sox complicity in the exclusion of Black players from a lily-white Winter Haven, Florida, social club. Later I learned through Red Sox Cy Young winner Jim Lonborg and his teammate Earl Wilson that this practice had existed in the 1960s. (When I wrote an op-ed piece in the *Boston Globe* on Opening Day in 1986 attacking Red Sox management I, in turn, was attacked in the

Globe by the late Will McDonough. He said I knew nothing about the Red Sox and that he had spoken with Red Sox management who assured him that their predecessors had not been racists![26])

I did not know that Jackie Robinson—who would be such an important part of our household discussions in 1947, when he left the Negro Leagues for the majors—had already had a tryout in '45 with the Red Sox at Fenway. By all accounts he tattooed the left-field wall that day, but the Red Sox did not contact him thereafter. Only later did I learn that Pinky Higgins, the third baseman with the pennant winners and one of owner Tom Yawkey's favorites, whom he twice served as manager in the fifties, was an avowed racist. The unvarnished truth would emerge on the basis of more complete information years later.[27]

My Short-Lived Career

Around 1948, in the midst of one of those well-heated pennant races down the stretch in our sandlot league, John Brockriede (later an outstanding center with the Long Branch football team) threw me a fastball over the middle of the plate. I somehow connected with it, tagging it over the creek in center field—the home-run boundary up against which outfielders were afraid to retreat for fear of falling in—onto Third Avenue.[28] I could scarcely believe what had happened as I hurriedly circled the bases, ever fearful that it was somehow all a mistake, Brockriede with his great velocity having supplied most of the power.

Then, a couple of years later at the age of fourteen, when I had hoped to play first or second base for my ninth-grade freshman team, I had my big chance. After what seemed like a solid batting practice session prior to a high school baseball scrimmage, I came to the plate. I worked the count of three and two on a left-handed pitcher who had a sharp slider with some bite to it. He had caught the outside corner twice with pitches that I thought were off the plate outside—but the umpire had called them strikes, and I was convinced that the pitcher thought I didn't know the strike zone. On the next pitch—the "payoff pitch," as it is called—I thought I would swing, expecting another pitch on that same outside corner in an area which had confounded me. But instead the pitch came in as a fastball, almost entirely over my head. I swung wildly and missed, looking very bad in the process. Coach John Hubley, who had seen me earlier in football, cut me from the team almost immediately. Thus, except for shagging fly balls with my Stanford law students and my sons in the seventies and eighties, that was the end of my on-the-field baseball career.

Figure 9.9: In this same period, I was also able to hit and catch fly balls with my Long Branch High School classmate, Joey Asch, during a visit which he made to Stanford.

A Brief Lull—and a Revival

In the 1950s, baseball turned into background music for me. I felt I needed to make a determined effort to catch up on reading all the history, politics, and literature I had missed earlier. Combine that need with my boredom and bitterness over the New York Yankees' hegemony, and the result was a temporary turn away from the boys of summer. In a surprise move, my father reversed course as well, asking me on more than one occasion: "Whatever became of baseball?"

However, in the 1960s both the decline of the Yankees and the rise of the Red Sox were to revive my interest. A real turning point for me was 1967's "Impossible Dream" season, in which Carl Yastrzemski, with his dramatic late-inning home runs, seemed to singlehandedly take the Red Sox to the pennant that September. I called my father on the season's last day as the Red Sox routed Minnesota ace Dean Chance in the sixth inning and said, "Now do you see what I've been waiting for since 1946?" My thoughtful father replied, "Is the game over?" Of course it was not, and only an extraordinary throw by Yaz to second base to cut down Bob Allison sealed the victory.

Yastrzemski, like Williams before him in 1942 and '47, was to be a Triple Crown winner: He led the league in batting average, home runs, and runs batted in, and he was the last hitter to do this in baseball in the twentieth century. As much as anything, that great four-way pennant race of 1967 brought me back to those days in the 1940s when my father cautiously indulged my baseball passion.

There were exciting pennant races that included the Red Sox in the seventies and the eighties, and again at the turn of this new century. In August '74 I watched the Sox take two of three in Oakland from the defending champion A's, with aging star Juan Marichal pitching eight innings of shutout ball, only to see a seven-game lead over the Baltimore Orioles quickly evaporate thereafter. This "left at the altar" experience was to be repeated many times!

Only in 1978 and 2007 did "those Boston Red Sox" possess a lead comparable to the one they'd enjoyed in 1946. In '78, that was to be frittered away in an injury-riddled September collapse from which the Sox revived three and a half games back in the middle of the month, only to be beaten by the homers of Bucky Dent and Reggie Jackson in the second-ever American League regular season playoff game. (The first was played, also by the Sox, thirty years earlier to the very day! I remember listening to the game on the radio in the grammar school locker room: a one-sided 8–3 loss at the hands of the Cleveland Indians, led by manager-player Lou Boudreau, who homered twice in the game!)

In 2007, when the Red Sox achieved yet another World Series sweep (I was able to be at the final game in Denver), the triumph was truly perfect, given the Eastern Division championship as well as postseason success. Then "Red Sox Nation"—as it had come to be called in the past decade or so—could revel in newfound dominance, which replicated in some measure the five out of fourteen world championships the team had obtained in the early part of the twentieth century. Indeed, the club came close to repeating their 2007 success the next year but lost to the Tampa Bay Rays in a hard-fought seven-game American League championship series.

My oldest son and I traveled to St. Louis in 2013 to see three closely played Red Sox–Cardinal World Series games. Outfielder Jonny Gomes tagged a dramatic three-run homer in the sixth inning of the fourth game, allowing the Sox to tie the series at 2–2. In between the top and the bottom of the sixth inning, the canned music was Chuck Berry's Johnny B. Goode, which has the refrain: "Go Johnny go, Johnny B. Goode"—so appropriate, I thought, given what had just happened on the field. (When I met Gomes at the Obama White House in 2014, he said he had not even been aware of the music that night!) We were also witnesses to a dramatic historical moment: Red Sox closer Koji Uehara picked off a Cardinal base runner to end the fifth game—the first postseason game in history to end with a pickoff.

In the lovely seasons between 2013 and 2017 I frequently conversed with Red Sox manager John Farrell about our proximate New Jersey hometowns, as well as what we had witnessed in a particular game—much as I had done with Leonard Koppett, visiting Dusty Baker in the clubhouse in his San Francisco days. And 2018 was the greatest year of all, it seems. We went to Los Angeles for the World Series, and saw the Red Sox defeated 3–2 in game three, an eighteen-inning nailbiter—the longest game in World Series history—in which Nate Eovaldi demonstrated unparalleled valiance, firing off his 100-mile-per-hour fastballs over seven of the extra innings. And we witnessed yet a fourth World Championship in this century! The long, deep, and high home run shot by Jackie Bradley Jr. seemed like it would stay up in the sky forever. (Of course, by 2020 it was the morning after: The Red Sox gave away the extraordinarily talented Mookie Betts as well as other killer B's like Andrew Benintendi and Xander Bogaerts in a manner similar to the sale of Babe Ruth a century earlier, crushing the team's fortunes for years to come.)

I came into the world of baseball a little more than three-quarters of a century after the first openly professional team, the Cincinnati Red Stockings, appeared on the scene. Seventy-nine years have gone by since my days of sandlot baseball. Don Zimmer, Boston Red Sox skipper in the 1970s, summed up my view nicely one day some years ago. Leaning against the back of a batting cage in Candlestick Park, bedecked in a Chicago Cubs uniform, he said, "There were many more good days than bad ones." That's how I feel about my almost eighty seasons with the Red Sox.

Figure 9.10: 1988 with Red Sox coach and former shortstop-third baseman Johnny Pesky, in Anaheim, California.

BASEBALL COMES TO STANFORD LAW

Figure 9.11: At the Babe Ruth 100th birthday celebration, Hofstra Law School, with Yankee former shortstop and broadcaster, Phil Rizzuto.

Figure 9.12: With good friend Dusty Baker in San Francisco, when he was manager of the Washington Nationals, c. 2017.

Figure 9.13: One of my early meetings with Red Sox outfielder Dwight Evans. I told him that we both advanced to the major leagues in the summer of 1972—Evans to the Red Sox, and I to Stanford.

Figure 9.14: Above with Maurice (Mo) Vaughn, the great Red Sox slugger of the '90s. Below with Jimy Williams, Red Sox manager in the '90s and beginning '00s.

TEACHING AND WRITING ABOUT SPORTS LAW

My involvement with baseball and sports took on a different dimension in the 1980s. My former colleague at Wayne State Law School in Detroit, Professor Bob Berry, and I first began to collaborate on and converse about the subject of sports and sports law in the late sixties and seventies, and to write scholarly articles on emerging baseball labor–management relations in the eighties. After each of us departed our Wayne State assignments in Detroit, we shuttled between San Francisco and Boston, producing a lengthy law review article—a piece that was relied upon by some of the courts, particularly the Court of Appeals for the Eighth Circuit in the football cases[29]—and an article in the *New York Times*.[30] Ultimately I contributed to a coauthored book on professional sports and labor, published in 1986.[31] A major impetus toward putting pen to paper took place over the 1980 summer, when Bob and I co-taught a sports law course at Golden Gate Law School. We graded the papers at Lefty O'Doul's and the Washington Square Bar & Grill—but we were very careful!

Figure 9.15: My good friend Bob Berry with me when I received an honorary doctorate at Capital Law School, Columbus, Ohio, c. 1996.

In the late 1980s I began to teach a sports law seminar at Stanford Law School with renowned baseball journalist Leonard Koppett and Alvin Attles, a former player, coach, and general manager of the NBA's Golden State Warriors. With Leonard's encouragement and advice, I began to write newspaper articles for daily papers like the *Boston Globe, San Francisco Chronicle, San Jose Mercury News*, and others in the late eighties and nineties. This work brought me firsthand contact with major league players and officials. Larry Whiteside, a *Boston Globe* writer whom I met in the Red Sox dugout in Anaheim in 1986, opened a lot of doors for me, with the Red Sox and elsewhere. (He later came to Stanford as a Knight Fellow and participated in some classes in the law school.) I conducted a series of interviews, principally with former players in the late 1980s, and the interviews continued throughout this past decade.

Meanwhile, the three of us—Koppett, Attles, and myself—began to discuss, plan, and teach together. We enjoyed each other's company immensely. The students and others remarked about our disparate appearances in the hallways, laughing with one another as we walked toward either my office or the seminar room. Al, also born in 1936 (I referred to him as my twin), was a towering presence with a uniquely deep bass voice, always easily recognizable on the telephone. Leonard was Mr. Five-by-Five, and I suppose I was something in between.

Leonard would frequently arrive at my office an hour or so before class and would sit there quietly as I sketched out the outline for procedure and presentation that day. I had devised materials based upon four major areas of study: (1) contract disputes between players and owners; (2) antitrust law and the history of its exclusion of baseball; (3) comparisons to other sports; and (4) labor law and labor arbitration that had become important in all sports, particularly baseball, given the absence of antitrust. Al would regale the students with his discussions of meetings with Philadelphia Warriors owner Abe Saperstein, and the fact that there were no real negotiations or bargaining in those years, before the advent of agents and unions. In those days, said both Al and Leonard, a player who insisted on being represented by an agent might be traded the next day, given owner hostility. Leonard's contributions, too, involved the "beginning," when unions and agents were not present or just coming in. And, of course, my major contribution was the law itself.

We had an all-star cast of outside speakers, including Willie Mays, Bill Walsh, basketball union leader Larry Fleischman, Gene Orza of the baseball players' union, as well as sports agents like Bill Duffy. Academics like my old pal Bob Berry, who had formulated the first sports law course taught anywhere in the United States (and perhaps the world), dropped in from time to time; Mark Marquess, Stanford's baseball coach, also spoke. Mike Port, the director of baseball umpires, raised many issues and disputes, taking me, at least, back to my childhood and the first games I had ever seen.

When Leonard arranged a visit by Willie Mays to the Law School, the word of his arrival ran through the law school like electricity. Leonard stood, proud as punch, when Willie arrived. My only concern about Willie's presentation was the fact that he began to call one particularly attractive woman in the class "babe"—a transgression that would have resulted in my immediate dismissal if I had said it. But the students adored him! It was a very memorable day for Stanford Law.

Just as our new course began, I became involved with Stanford baseball—not only as a frequent spectator, as I'd been since my arrival at Stanford in the seventies, but also as a good friend of the team's coach, Mark Marquess, third base coach Dean Stotz, and retired pitching coach Tom Dunton. Dunton and I traveled with the team to Oregon and southern California. Coach Marquess always had me seated next to him at the head table of annual baseball dinners, and he would introduce me as a consummate fan, particularly of my beloved Boston Red Sox. I became friendly with a number of the players, too, particularly Jed Lowrie and Dave McCarty, who both played for the Red Sox.[32]

LAW SCHOOL COMMITTEE WORK

As the eighties unfolded there were other positive developments. Stanford Law School deans Tom Ehrlich, and later Paul Brest, were the best deans for me. Paul, who was aware of some of the problems that had emerged with previous deans Charles Meyers and John Ely, wanted to involve me in law school activities. He named me chairman of a committee that brought outside scholars and others to the law school for short visiting professorships, including the Herman Phleger professorship, reserved for particularly prestigious visitors.

One of the most memorable of my appointments was Pierre Trudeau, Canada's outstanding prime minister, who led the country through the difficult upheavals triggered by Quebec's demands for separatism. I selected Trudeau for the Phleger professorship, but Stanford's president, Donald Kennedy, wanted to send the invitation himself. The difficulty was that he could get no response from Trudeau. I told Paul that I thought I knew a way to get Trudeau's attention. I had become acquainted with some British Columbia labor lawyers, particularly Peter Gall in Vancouver and his Montreal partner, Roy Heenan, who had been active in the ABA labor law section when I was secretary. Gall and Heenan were partners of Trudeau; I had attended an opening-day Montreal Expos game with Heenan. Thus, my phone call to the two of them worked like a charm: Trudeau responded promptly and accepted our invitation immediately.

On Trudeau's first day at Stanford, I picked him up at the Faculty Club. He greeted me warmly, as if we had been old friends—reminding me of the way my father spoke of Boston's Mayor Curley. "Bill, it's so good to see you again," Trudeau said. He was one of those rare people who have both a first-rate mind and great charm as well.

We had a wonderful time that evening at one of San Francisco's most posh restaurants. I was fearful that people would recognize him and his privacy would be breached, but there was no problem at all—no one seemed to recognize him that evening. I'm fairly sure that a former American president would not be able to travel to Canada unrecognized, but such was (and is) America's unawareness of Canada.

Trudeau and I hit it off on that visit, and on his last night, after a dinner at the Stanford president's house, I asked Trudeau if he would like to go to a small Palo Alto club, Café Fino, to hear a jazz singer whom I liked. He said that he would, and the result was an evening I can never forget.

As it happened, Café Fino was owned by a Canadian citizen, Freddie Magdalena. When he saw Trudeau enter the club, he greeted him enthusiastically and told his American customers how delighted he was to have Trudeau there. The singer/pianist, Nancy Gilleland, whom I had seen at Café Fino in the past, suited the Prime Minister's tastes perfectly. He requested a number of tunes, which she played and sang. Trudeau left the club when it closed, quite pleased with the evening.

A Love of Jazz Accelerates

Café Fino, the true jazz scene in Palo Alto, regrettably closed in 2007. It was a favorite after-hours place for me when I was returning from a baseball or basketball game in San Francisco or Oakland. My interest in jazz started picking up considerably in the eighties—I even attempted to learn how to play jazz on the piano, but was unsuccessful, hampered by my ignorance of theory, which was omitted from my five years of classical piano as a child.

In truth, I had listened to jazz firsthand since the fifties, when I heard Count Basie and his band at New York City's Birdland, at 52nd and Broadway, and on the Asbury Park, New Jersey, boardwalk, where Sonny Payne's dramatic drumming had made me sprint excitedly toward the ocean at the concert's conclusion. And in this early period, I can still see a young Cornell undergraduate hunched over a nightclub piano near the boardwalk, playing a memorable rendition of Randy Weston's "Hi Fly." That tune and rendition are still in my mind at this writing. I was mesmerized by alto saxophonist Paul Desmond's melodic, swinging version of "Tangerine" and many of his other contributions on my long-playing records (before the days of CDs).

And I had been to Providence's Celebrity Club, near Route 1, to hear Chris Connor and Anita O'Day, catching both the Modern Jazz Quartet and Dave Brubeck at Kingston, Rhode Island. When I was about nineteen, I heard Gerry Mulligan's big deep baritone sax at Boston's Storyville near Copley Square, and, during my UAW period, Dorothy Ashby's jazz harp at the Minor Key on Dexter Avenue in Detroit—a city where I also heard Sonny Rollins's dulcet tenor saxophone at Baker's Keyboard Lounge. New York's Village Vanguard, and Hickory House in midtown Manhattan, which featured British jazz pianist Marian McPartland, had both been favorites in my youth.

On the West Coast, I was too late for The Blackhawk—the telephone information operator said to me in the late sixties, "The Blackhawk? That's been gone for years!"—but there were a number of interesting venues in both San Francisco and Oakland. Yoshi's, based for the most part in Oakland, put me in touch with Stanley Turrentine's incredible tenor saxophone, an instrument through which, in his hands, the Black church and its preaching resonated. During one of my first encounters with Turrentine at the old Yoshi's, I asked him about the classic movie *Round Midnight*, which featured Dexter Gordon and his experiences in Paris. Turrentine said, "Oh, that was Dexter playing Dexter." I saw Turrentine a couple more times, at Washington's Blues Alley and at the new Yoshi's, just a few days before he died.

Also at Yoshi's was Ernestine Anderson, with her classic "I Think You Made Your Move Too Soon." I saw her one night in the now-closed Kimball's in San Francisco, with only a dozen in the audience. At the end of the evening she expressed thanks to each of us, one by one, pointing her finger at each person as she did. Kimball's was also the venue for the greatest group I have ever heard, the Timeless Allstars (Buster Williams, Billy Higgins, Harold Land, Bobby Hutcherson, and Cedar Walton).

Only in the nineties did I discover Eliane Elias on the radio while I was in Washington, as well as Mulgrew Miller, in a dreamlike concert on the banks of the Delaware River in Philadelphia. Herbie Hancock's "Maiden Voyage" from this period still gives me chills.

Much later at Ronnie Scott's, which had opened in London when I was a student at the London School of Economics, I was to see Les McCann with his classic "Compared to What," which I often used in lectures, speeches, and writings around this country and elsewhere. Finally, I loved no one more than trumpeter Lee Morgan and his classic "The Sidewinder," although I never saw him in person. Ditto for Freddie "Mother" Hubbard, whose music still leaves me entranced.

BASEBALL AND RACE RELATIONS

As the eighties wound to a conclusion, I became involved in writing outside my traditional law and scholarship interests. I began to write articles for Bay Area newspapers and others around the country. The loneliness that I felt sitting at baseball parks after my sons had left home was soon dissipated by a new baseball camaraderie that far exceeded anything I had ever experienced among law faculty!

I began to conduct a series of interviews about race relations in baseball, and the absence of Black managers in the game. This put me in touch with such luminaries as Don Baylor in his dignified Red Sox road uniform, a thoughtful and somewhat embittered Larry Doby, whom I had seen play in Yankee Stadium in the forties with my mother, and hard-throwing, plain-speaking Earl Wilson, whom I was able to interview in Boston after the Baseball Writers' Dinner in 1989. These kinds of interviews also account for my friendship with Dusty Baker when he was the hitting coach for the Giants in 1991.

Two people—Leonard Koppett and Larry Whiteside—introduced me to this new world, which I began to experience directly, rather than through the usual avenues of stadium attendance, radio, TV, or newspapers. Leonard really got me started, suggesting ideas for articles. And Larry, whom I met in Anaheim, opened doors and created new friendships with people like Red Sox general manager Lou Gorman and Joe Castiglione, the "Voice of the Red Sox." I became friendly with Lou and Joe at my first spring training in Winter Haven, Florida in 1987. A thrilling upshot of this period was my assignment as the credentialed reporter for the *San Francisco Chronicle-Examiner* at the 1986 World Series, where I attended four games and wrote two articles for the *Chronicle*.

In the early nineties, my involvement grew even more substantial when I was assigned a salary arbitration, an opportunity to examine the system which baseball had created in 1973 as a kind of "final offer" arbitration, frequently used in interest or new contract disputes, like those I had handled in the public sector throughout the country. The attractiveness of this process in baseball was attributable to the fact that only one issue was in dispute, that is, salary. Each side was required to make a final offer on that one issue. Both sides had a genuine incentive to provide a reasonable position in the hope that the arbitrator would select its position rather than that of the other side. By making the parties reasonable, frequently these disputes could be resolved through negotiation without the need for arbitration. All of this had been designed in the wake of litigation initiated by St. Louis Cardinals center fielder Curt Flood. Flood had unsuccessfully attacked the so-called "reserve clause," a system ratified by the Supreme Court since 1922, when it held that baseball was not a business in interstate commerce under antitrust law, and that players could be restricted to one club, seemingly forever, if the club wished it to be so. This meant that baseball had a free hand in controlling players without any need to make them free agents. Salary arbitration obtained through collective bargaining was seen to be a rough substitute.

My very first case involved Luis Polonia of the California Angels. In fact, I had seen Polonia play against Oakland a few times, and emblazoned in my mind was a late start going back on a fly ball to left field. The testimony for Polonia by his representatives relied upon the large number of stolen bases he had accomplished. "How many times was he caught stealing?" I asked. I knew that nothing took a team out of an inning (and sometimes a game) more quickly than being caught stealing. It turned out that the number was almost as high as the stolen bases.

I noted at this hearing a problem with the arbitration process: Players were extremely unhappy with negative comments made about their work. At the end of the hearing, the Angels' representatives rushed to Polonia and were effusive in their praise for him off the record, stating that they looked forward to seeing him in spring training.

I ruled against Polonia, but as the radio broadcast said that day, "Polonia is not going to have to obtain food stamps." The demands of most players were so high that even if they lost, they did not do poorly, prompting some owners to say, "Heads you win, tails I lose."

I had a second case in the '92 round, again involving a player with whom I had had some familiarity, that is, Jerry Brown (the Governor, as he was called) of the Oakland A's. He was a utility player and was comparing himself with the extraordinarily talented Tony Phillips. But Phillips played other positions, hit over .300, and it didn't take me much time to resolve this one in favor of the A's.

I was called back to do this work again in '93; once again, it was both challenging and interesting. The first case involved Dale Sveum, a utility infielder with the Milwaukee Brewers who had had some very bad luck in 1987. He was hitting home runs at an extraordinary clip that year, but after a rookie raced toward him and stepped on his foot, Sveum was not the same player. I ruled against him as well: He hit less than .200 that year, ratifying my initial judgment.

The biggest case of all involved Andy Benes, a hard-throwing top-starting pitcher with the then-lowly San Diego Padres. The owners said to me, "Benes has a very poor won-and-lost record." I replied, "I think that won-and-lost records are the most deceptive statistic in baseball." They were rather downcast about this. But this point was particularly true for Benes in San Diego, as he had a poor defense as well as few hitters who would give him the runs necessary for victory. I ruled for Benes, and this set off a series of rulings for other pitchers, during which the owners blamed my award for the awards or settlements in their cases.[33] Appointed to hear the Atlanta pitcher John Smoltz's case, the dispute settled just before my plane touched down in Chicago en route to the hearing.

I enjoyed these salary arbitrations, and they offered occasional positive personal repercussions, too. For example, for years afterward, Benes always had a big smile for me whenever I met him in other parks, given the fact that I ruled for him. But my salary arbitrations in baseball were to come to an end in 1993, when President Bill Clinton nominated me to be Chairman of NLRB.

REMEMBERING ALVIN ATTLES JR. (1936–2024)

Along with many Stanford Law School students who were part of the first Sports Law course offered here, I grieve the death of my co-teacher and Golden State Warriors great Alvin Attles Jr. Like most basketball fans, I had seen "Al" as a terrific player and coach for the Warriors. But a chance encounter in the mid-eighties in Oakland led to an enduring friendship and the chance to teach together. Lucky for me and our students, I was able to induce Al to serve as a Stanford Law School lecturer for a tour of duty which lasted two decades. Many Stanford Law School students were to become the beneficiaries of Al's experience, wisdom, and wit.

The Stanford Sports Law seminar began in the eighties, after I helped my buddy and co-author Bob Berry with the curriculum for the first such course at Boston College (Bob and I co-authored A Long Deep Drive to Collective Bargaining *[1981] and shortly thereafter* Labor Relations in Professional Sports *and an op-ed in the* New York Times, *which figured in the curriculum). So, the SLS seminar was not quite the first in the country, but it was taught by a fun trio. Al covered the player and coach perspective, our mutual friend the late Leonard Koppett covered the journalist perspective, and me labor and law and a love of sports.*

Al was a graduate of an Historically Black College and had a teaching position in his hometown Newark, New Jersey, public school system when he tried out for a position with the Philadelphia Warriors, before they moved to the West Coast. Every year he would tell our students about his dramatic negotiation with Philadelphia owner Eddie Gottlieb, which had led to his first contract of slightly more than $5,000.00 and a distinguished basketball career—well before the advent of agents, unions, and antitrust and labor law (arbitration too) in sports. Every year the students were surprised to have Al, known more for his defensive abilities, tell them (after *my prodding) that he was the second highest scorer (17 points) when Wilt Chamberlain tallied a stunning 100 points in Hershey, Pennsylvania.*

Al was always a true gentleman and a distinguished ambassador for organized sports, basketball, and his near-lifelong employer, the Golden State Warriors. Stanford Law School and its alumni grieve Al's death. And, like so many others here and throughout the country, we send our condolences to his family as we mourn the loss of this good and decent man.[34]

NOTES

Much of the material in this chapter replicates or is based upon my earlier book, *Bargaining with Baseball: Labor Relations in an Age of Prosperous Turmoil* (Jefferson: McFarland, 2011), 16–30.

[1] William B. Gould IV, *Diary of a Contraband* (Stanford: Stanford University Press, 2002), 1.
[2] William B. Gould IV, Diary, December 25, 1983.
[3] William B. Gould IV, "The Supreme Court's Labor and Employment Docket in the 1980 Term: Justice Brennan's Term," *University of Colorado Law Review* 53 (1981).
[4] First Nat'l Maintenance Corp. v. NLRB, 452 U.S. 666 (1981).
[5] See chapter 8.
[6] Tameny v. Atlantic Richfield Co., 27 Cal.3d 167 (1980).
[7] William B. Gould IV, Howard C. Hay, R. Wayne Estes, Mark S. Rudy, Helena S. Wise, and Maureen McClain, "A Report of the Ad Hoc Committee on Termination at Will and Wrongful Discharge Appointed by the Labor and Employment Law Section of the State Bar of California," *Labor & Employment Law News*, February 8, 1984.
[8] H. Anthony Miller and R. Wayne Estes, "Recent Judicial Limitations on the Right to Discharge: A California Trilogy," *U.C. Davis Law Review* 16 (1982–1983).
[9] Gould et al., "A Report of the Ad Hoc Committee on Termination at Will and Wrongful Discharge," 3–4.
[10] Gould et al., "A Report of the Ad Hoc Committee on Termination at Will and Wrongful Discharge," 11.
[11] Gould et al., "A Report of the Ad Hoc Committee on Termination at Will and Wrongful Discharge," 14.
[12] William B. Gould IV, "Wrongful Discharge Litigation: Should There Be Unfair Dismissal Legislation?," statement to the Assembly Labor and Employment Committee of the California Legislature, October 15, 1984.
[13] William B. Gould IV, "Reflections on Wrongful Discharge Litigation And Legislation," delivered to the National Academy of Arbitrators, 1984.

14. William B. Gould IV, "Protection from Wrongful Dismissal," *New York Times,* October 22, 1984.
15. William B. Gould IV, *A Primer on American Labor Law* (New York: Cambridge University Press, 2019), 482: "See Montana's Wrongful Discharge from Employment Act (§39-2-904), which according to the Montana Supreme Court has limited an employee's discharge to 'good cause' and thus has 'effectively eliminate[d]' at-will employment in Montana. *Whidden v. Nerison,* 981 P.2d 271, 275 (Mont. 1999). The Supreme Court of Montana has held that the question of whether the employee is at-will is one for the arbitrator to decide."
16. Foley v. Interactive Data Corp., 47 Cal. 3d 654 (1988).
17. William B. Gould IV, "Stemming the Wrongful Discharge Tide: A Case for Arbitration," *Employee Relations Law Journal* 13 (1987); William B. Gould IV, "The Idea of the Job as Property in Contemporary America: The Legal and Collective Bargaining Framework," *Brigham Young University Law Review* (1986).
18. Restaurant Law Center v. City of New York, No. 22-491 (2d Cir. 2024).
19. Gould, *A Primer on American Labor Law,* 325–329; Epic Systems v. Lewis, 138 S. Ct. 1612 (2018); Am. Express Co. v. Italian Colors Rest., 570 U.S. 228 (2013); AT&T Mobility LLC v. Concepcion, 563 U.S. 333, 339 (2011); see William B. Gould IV, "The Supreme Court, Job Discrimination, Affirmative Action, Globalization and Class Actions: Justice Ginsburg's Term," *University of Hawaii Law Review* 36 (2014).
20. *Epic Systems Corp.,* 138 S. Ct. at 1648-49 (Ginsburg, J., dissenting). "If these untoward consequences stemmed from legislative choices, I would be obliged to accede to them. But the edict that employees with wage and hours claims may seek relief only one-by-one does not come from Congress. It is the result of take-it-or-leave-it labor contracts harking back to the type called 'yellow dog,' and of the readiness of this Court to enforce those unbargained-for agreements."
21. At some point a few years after my graduation, law schools changed this degree from bachelor of literature and law to a juris doctor because of a concern that medical doctors had more prestige than lawyers by virtue of their doctorate. A by-product of this was that the law schools could raise revenue by charging earlier graduates to change their degree. I refused to pay and thus remain an LLB, as I was in 1961 when I graduated from Cornell Law School.
22. I am not sure that my father would have concurred with the MLB Vice President for Umpiring Mike Port's views when he said: "This [theatrical behavior] is part of the fabric of the game . . . perhaps what leads to arguments and ejections might relate to the number of decisions made by those officials and those competing within the rules."
23. Dave Frishberg, "The Sports Page," *Live at Vine Street* (1985).
24. Only in the late sixties did my friend Dusty Baker devise the "high five," and all of this antedated the ostentatious religiosity that emerged at the turn of this century when players began to point skyward—as if gesturing to God or a deceased family member—as they crossed the plate after a homer. Some even began to do this after a single! And in the past decade or so, teams took to celebrating game-changing or -winning home runs so violently that one player on the Los Angeles Angels was disabled by the celebration for the entire year! The same thing happened to New York Met ace reliever Edwin Diaz in 2023!

[25] James S. Hirsch, *Willie Mays: The Life, the Legend* (New York: Scribner, 2010), 99.
[26] Will McDonough, "Globe Staff, Sox 'Racist': Says Who? Harper Case No Proof," *Boston Globe,* April 17, 1986.
[27] See generally, John Shea, "Red Sox owner reckons with former owner Yawkey's history with race," *San Francisco Chronicle,* August 20, 2017 (referencing my comment about Yawkey: "Not only was his conduct immoral, but also impractical in that it was a primary factor in the losing records of the Sox between 1952 and the early '60s."); John Shea, "Prominent Red Sox fan's call for action; Prominent Red Sox fan William B. Gould IV urges action on slurs," *San Francisco Chronicle,* May 7, 2017 ("Saddened when hearing about the Adam Jones incident at Fenway Park on Monday, Gould sent a letter to Dave Dombrowski, president of the Red Sox, and cc'd Commissioner Rob Manfred, saying the Red Sox and Major League Baseball 'need to think seriously about more serious sanctions for those who engage in racist misconduct at any ballpark.' MLB would be wise to take the advice. Gould wrote that he's 'concerned and angered by what happened' to Jones, the Orioles' outfielder who said that a racial epithet was directed at him a handful of times and that a bag of peanuts was thrown at him. Gould cited a 2005 incident at Fenway in which beer was dumped on Gary Sheffield by a fan who was banned by the Red Sox the rest of the season. That fan deserved a greater penalty, and so would any fan directing racial slurs at players. I asked Gould, who as the NLRB chairman played a big role in ending baseball's 1994-95 player strike, what type of sanctions he'd like to see. 'I would want all clubs to post a code of conduct stating that each requires a harassment-free environment, meaning no racially abusive or profane language - they purport to do the latter already - reserving to the club the right to pursue violators in both criminal or civil court. This should be set forth on the scoreboard and through loudspeaker announcements, as well as on the ticket stub itself - juxtaposed to the language which purports to address the clubs' own liability.'"
[28] In truth, I think the distance over that creek was much shorter than a Memorial Day 2010 homer hit by one of my grandsons, Joey, in Southern California—compared to the prodigious homers and long drives tagged by another grandson, William Gould VI, in Altadena, California, much later.
[29] *Powell v.* NFL, 930 F.2d 1293 (8th Cir. 1989); Robert C. Berry and William B. Gould IV, "A Long Deep Drive to Collective Bargaining; Of Players, Owners, Brawls, and Strikes," *Case Western Reserve Law Review* 31 (1981).
[30] William B. Gould IV and Robert C. Berry, "Views of Sport; Labor Trouble Is Brewing," *New York Times,* August 10, 1986.
[31] William B. Gould IV, Robert C. Berry, and Paul D. Staudohar, *Labor Relations in Professional Sports* (Dover: Auburn House Publishing Company, 1986).
[32] Much, but not all, of this material was taken from *Bargaining with Baseball.*
[33] Ron Thomas, "Benes' Case Set Stage For Burkett's Salary," *San Francisco Chronicle,* August 3, 1993; Mel Antonen, "Arbitrators See Past Flaws, Focus on Strengths," *USA Today,* February 3, 1993; "Owners Lose Big," *San Francisco Examiner,* February 3, 1993; "Fairly Joins Seattle Broadcasting Team," *San Francisco Chronicle,* February 3, 1993; Murray Chass, "Advantage, A's," *New York Times,* February 6, 1993; "Padres Lose Two Cases," *New York Times,* February 3, 1993.
[34] William B. Gould IV, excerpt from a eulogy given at Stanford Law School, 2024.

10

MR. GOULD GOES TO WASHINGTON: THE POLITICS OF THE CONFIRMATION PROCESS

By the early 1990s my work, over a quarter century of teaching and more than three decades as a labor lawyer, had fallen into three basic categories: labor arbitration; the National Labor Relations Act (NLRA) and its interpretation through labor law; and politics.

Regarding labor arbitration and its process, I had been an arbitrator since 1965 and a member of the blue-ribbon National Academy of Arbitrators since 1970. Some of my writing had involved arbitration and the interplay between labor arbitration and labor law.

As for the NLRA, I had worked for the National Labor Relations Board (NLRB) as a junior lawyer in Washington in the early-to-mid-sixties, had practiced labor law involving the act since my first work for the UAW in 1960 and 1961, and for the Battle, Fowler law firm in New York City in the mid-to-late sixties. Much of my other work outside the NLRA flowed from it through my writings, falling into what could be viewed as subcategories of labor law, such as fair employment practices law in the courts, and consulting work with the EEOC, particularly in the sixties and seventies. My work on wrongful discharge involved me in not only a series of articles and papers, but also my chairmanship of the California State Bar Ad Hoc Committee on Wrongful Discharge in the eighties. In a sense I viewed these last two areas, while separate, as derivatives from my work on the NLRA.

Meanwhile, as noted in chapter 7, I had become involved on the periphery of the political process and had given speeches during Bill Clinton's 1992 campaign. As it happened, Jack Sheinkman—by then president of the Amalgamated Clothing Workers Union, after moving up from the general counsel job he'd held in my Cornell and LSE days—was very close to Clinton. His union was the first in Arkansas to support Clinton for governor of that state. Over the course of our acquaintance, Jack and I had discussed the possibility of my serving in Washington in some capacity. For example, during Jimmy Carter's administration in the 1970s, Jack approached me about possibly working in the White House for President Carter. While I was interested in the idea, I turned Jack down because, at the age of forty, with three rambunctious young men in our family, I doubted that I could handle the exhausting, around-the-clock pace that I identified with jobs at the White House—an enclave of young people who had no limits on their time or energy. In 1979, a *New York Times* reporter called me and told me that I was about to be named to a new wage policy board that the Carter people wanted to establish. But as the end of Carter's term rolled around, I was identified as a supporter of Ted Kennedy in his eventually unsuccessful challenge against Carter. There were no more telephone calls from Washington after that.

In 1992, however, shortly after Clinton's defeat of George H. W. Bush, my old friend Jack wrote, saying he wanted to put my name forward for a job in the new Clinton administration.[1] I had not met Bill Clinton, but at the time of the New Hampshire primary in early 1992, when his fortunes seemed to be sinking, I had sent him a small contribution. I also attended a September San Jose rally just as it seemed more likely that his general election lead would *not* disappear, as Mike Dukakis's had done in 1988. And, as noted earlier, I spoke on Clinton's behalf to a San Francisco IBEW convention when Senator Barbara Boxer was not available. My colleague Hank (the Hankster) Greely invited Miguel Mendez, Hilda, and myself to meet Judge Wisdom of the Court of Appeals in New Orleans at his house and to watch the Clinton–Bush debate. Clinton did well, and I remember Miguel exhaling with a profound sense of relief when the debate concluded. Subsequently, on the night of the Clinton victory, Hilda and I went to the San Francisco Fairmont Hotel and thrilled to the campaign's rendition of the "Battle Hymn of the Republic," just as victory appeared to be assured.

So, I told Jack that I was interested in going to Washington, and we met for lunch in mid- December 1992 at San Francisco's St. Francis Hotel. When Jack asked me what position appealed to me, I told him that my principal interest was in the policy-making echelons of the Department of Labor. But Jack thought the chairmanship of the National Labor Relations Board was the place for me, pointing out that I had worked for Frank McCulloch, President Kennedy's NLRB chairman, and that most of my professional practice, writing, and teaching involved the National Labor Relations Act. "That would seem to be a natural," he said enthusiastically.

While Jack was right—and indeed it could be said that I had fallen in love with the structure and symmetry of the National Labor Relations Act from my earliest exposure to it as a student at Cornell Law School—I had never aspired to be on the board. Indeed, truthfully, I didn't have a particularly high regard for a number of the board members I had met over the years. On the other hand, the board career people, particularly those I encountered in New York, Newark, Detroit, San Francisco, and Oakland, impressed me enormously. And Boston Regional Director Bob Fuchs, son of the former Boston Braves owner Judge Victor Fuchs, had been a great friend. He took me and two of my sons to a lovely Red Sox night game—which regrettably ended on a sour note when Detroit's Bill Freehan hit a bases-loaded homer off Bill Lee, reluctantly filling in for the recently traded Sparky Lyle in the ninth inning.

Thus, from the point of view of experience and intellectual investment, Jack's recommendation was a sound one, and I agreed. When we parted that day, he told me he would recommend me directly to President-elect Clinton, and I promised to follow the strategy Jack outlined for me. With considerable prescience, he advised me to review my arbitration experience and to contact both management and union lawyers involved in decisions I had rendered. He was concerned that my views and writings would be characterized as pro-labor—I was, after all, in favor of collective bargaining—and that some senators would be reluctant to confirm me on that basis. Jack thought it would be useful to have management attorneys who had both won and lost arbitration cases before me attest to my fairness. After excavating a number of my files from the bowels of the Stanford Law School, I got in touch with a dozen or so lawyers and employer and union representatives, asking them to send letters to the White House on my behalf.

THE WHEELS TURN SLOWLY

After my luncheon conversation with Sheinkman, things went quiet. Jack informed me that he had spoken to the president-elect prior to the inauguration at the annual New Year's Hilton Head, South Carolina, social event Clinton initiated while governor of Arkansas. In January of 1993, people began telling me they had heard my name mentioned as a possible head of the Labor Board. During my visit to Johannesburg that month, a leader of South Africa's mineworkers told me that American friends had advised him I would be named to the post. And in early February 1993, when I conducted my second annual round of baseball salary arbitration in Los Angeles, attorneys for San Diego Padres pitcher Andy Benes bumped into me at breakfast and said they had heard I would be appointed. A couple of months later, well-known *San Francisco Chronicle* columnist Herb Caen wrote, "You may bet the farm on this: Stanford law professor William Gould as next chairman of the Nat'l Labor Relations Board."[2] But nary a word did I receive from anyone in Washington.

In the meantime, Secretary of Labor-designate Robert Reich invited me to join the Commission on the Future of Worker–Management Relations, which had as its mission the proposal of labor law reforms. When I met with Reich and the other members of the commission in Washington in March, he reminded me that he had reviewed one of my books for the *Harvard Law Review*.[3] At the time he said nothing about the NLRB, and neither did I.

A Call from the White House

Finally, in mid-May 1993, I had a call from Cynthia Metzler of the White House staff inviting me to talk about the chairmanship with administration officials next time I was in town on commission business. This was the first word of an appointment I had received directly from the White House. Metzler informed me matter-of-factly that she had intended to follow through on the subject for some time. As the next commission meeting was on May twenty-fifth, we scheduled the appointment to discuss the NLRB for that day.

Just before 10:00 a.m. on the twenty-fifth, I walked from my room at the Mayflower Hotel down Connecticut Avenue and across Lafayette Park to the Old Executive Office Building next to the White House. Here, I met with Metzler in the first in a series of meetings she had scheduled for me. All of them were convivial and seemed to go well. After my session with Metzler, I met with Reich and with Lane Kirkland, who was then still head of the AFL-CIO. In a Democratic administration elected with labor support, it was generally assumed that the AFL-CIO had to place its imprimatur (or at least its *nihil obstat*, that is, no objections) on any nominee in the labor field—particularly for the sensitive NLRB position, which could affect the power balance between labor and management.

Both Reich and Kirkland seemed to proceed on the assumption that I would be appointed. When we met in his office, Reich assured me, "You know that Lane Kirkland supports you for this position." In fact, I hadn't known. Because so many of my writings in the 1960s and 1970s had been critical of the AFL-CIO, I had worried about possible opposition, or at best damnation through faint praise. But Jack Sheinkman was at the top of his political game in the federation, as well in the Clinton administration; he had done his work well at the AFL-CIO's 16th Street offices, only a couple of blocks from the White House. Everyone seemed supportive.

Reich formally offered me the job that day and, assuaging an anxiety I had had going into the meeting, also asked me to stay on as a member of the Commission on the Future of Worker–Management Relations. From the beginning of these announcements, Republican lawmakers maintained that there was a conflict of interest between proposing law reforms as a member of the commission and interpreting the NLRA as head of the Board—a theme that was to emerge time and time again during my term of office in Washington. That day, as we talked in Reich's office overlooking the Capitol, I reminded him of Attorney General Robert Kennedy's threat to jump from the Capitol Building if Jimmy Hoffa, the Teamsters president, was not convicted in the trial then pending. (Hoffa was acquitted, and RFK was offered a parachute by his critics.) Reich, who is ten years younger than I am, responded blankly and seemed unfamiliar with the story.

When I left Reich's office, I was elated at the prospect of serving as chairman while also continuing to serve on the commission. As I walked into the Department of Labor cafeteria for lunch, two cowboy dancers were twirling to the song "I Feel Lucky"—my exact feelings. Yet, though I had readily accepted Reich's invitation to be head of the Labor Board, I had tacked on one qualification: I would take the short term, which began in 1993 and expired in 1996. That would be a long enough stay in Washington for me, I told him. Reich seemed to agree, although he said nothing in response to my statement. From that day onward, however, everything took much longer than I expected. And there were many occasions over the next five years, after which I had taken the longest term available because of the many delays in the confirmation process, when I felt most unlucky indeed.

Later I found that my commitment to leave Washington at a certain date set me apart from other NLRB appointees and gave me a sense of independence consistent, I believe, with the board's role. Yet it was always a source of tension with other members of the board; their paramount objective seemed to be to retain their government position or its substantive equivalent, or better. Their overriding goal was to hang on in Washington as long as possible.

In this regard, the words of Professor G. Calvin Mackenzie, with which I became familiar only after my Washington arrival, are right on target:

> What is most distressing ultimately is the transcendent loss of purpose in the appointment process. The American model did not always work perfectly, but it was informed by a grand notion. The business of the people would be managed by leaders drawn from the people. Cincinnatus, in-and-outers, noncareer managers—with every election would come a new sweep of the country for high energy and new ideas and fresh visions. The president's team would assume its place and impose the people's wishes on the great agencies of government. Not infrequently, it actually worked that way.
>
> But these days, the model fails on nearly all counts. Most appointees do not come from the countryside, brimming with new energy and ideas. Much more often they come from congressional staffs or think tanks or interest groups—not from across the country but from across the street: interchangeable public elites, engaged in an insider's game.[4]

At the May meetings, Reich and Metzler said that an "intent to nominate" would be issued by the White House within a couple of weeks. But no announcement came until June 28. By late May and early June, however, newspapers like the *Wall Street Journal* were proclaiming my nomination. I have always suspected that these articles were a deliberate trial balloon put up by someone in the administration who was skeptical about my appointment and doubtful that the Senate would confirm me. When the *Wall Street Journal* piece ran on June 17, my telephone in Stanford rang off the hook.[5]

Then the real challenge began—a drumbeat of criticism and a distribution to newspaper columnists of background papers and books aimed at stirring up resistance to my confirmation. The principal opposition was led by two organizations: the National Right to

Work Committee, which gained prominence in the early eighties when the National Labor Relations Act was interpreted by the U.S. Supreme Court as protecting the rights of anti-union workers; and the Labor Policy Association, an extreme right-wing business group I had never heard of until I joined the worker management commission earlier that year. Several management lawyers who had written the White House supporting my nomination that spring were threatened: the management lawyers' business clients, said the threateners, would be advised of their support of me. These groups used late May and most of June, while rumors of my appointment flew around Washington, to gear up their campaign. During the Reagan and Bush administrations they had had it all their own way—exercising, at a minimum, a virtual veto over any nominee to the board—and they seemed to expect to continue playing the role of power broker. Their attacks on me began a stressful period that was to stretch over the next nine months.

Past Confirmation Struggles

In a general sense, my situation was not all that uncommon. Confirmation struggles involving NLRB appointments had occurred regularly from the 1970s onward. At that time, employer resistance to trade unions was stiffening and dissatisfaction with the NLRB's creaky administrative procedures was emerging. The first serious push for labor law reform in almost twenty years—aimed at providing more effective remedies for unfair labor practices and expediting elections and complaint handling—took place in 1977 and 1978.[6] In October 1977, the House of Representatives passed the Labor Reform Bill, which would have allowed the government to cancel and withhold contracts from employers that repeatedly engaged in labor law misconduct. Because of the inadequacy of existing remedies, the bill imposed new sanctions in the form of double damages for unfair labor practices. Inasmuch as most of the cases involved appeals that were essentially factual, it also mandated prompt review by the NLRB in Washington of the rulings of the regional administrative law judges, who acted as trial judges in these cases. But in 1978 virtually the same package of reforms, though favored by a majority in the Senate, could not be voted on because there were not sufficient votes to break the Republican filibuster.

Meanwhile, the fight over labor law reform spilled over into the confirmation process for NLRB members and heated up as labor and management squared off in the halls of Congress.

The first incident involved William Lubbers, President Jimmy Carter's nominee as general counsel of the board. And the second one, in 1979, concerned continuous Washington insider and career politician John Truesdale, formerly the board's executive secretary. In both instances the attack was led by Senator Orrin Hatch (R-Utah). These initiatives changed the way future board nominations were treated by the Senate. Prior to that time, as political scientist Terry Moe explains:

> *The primary rule is deference to the president: he has a right to build his own administration as he sees fit and thus to have his appointees confirmed as long as they are not clearly unqualified. What, then, counts as "unqualified" and therefore is a legitimate reason for voting against confirmation? Here, the basic rule is that there must be a "smoking gun" of some sort—a serious character flaw, criminal conduct, demonstrable bias, or obvious inability to carry on the duties of the job. A candidate's ideology is not a legitimate basis for voting no.*
>
> *For these reasons—and because senators, like presidents, must save their efforts for the bigger fish that they have to fry—senators of all ideological stripes are strongly disposed to vote affirmatively on virtually every presidential nominee.*[7]

While disavowing the threat of filibuster, Lubbers's congressional opponents claimed that his close ties to NLRB Chairman John Fanning—for whom Lubbers had served as chief counsel—should disqualify him. They argued that the earlier connection would prevent the arm's-length relationship between these two officials that is presumed necessary in some circumstances—for example, when the general counsel, acting as the prosecutor, brings unfair labor practice cases to the board for adjudication. The 1947 Taft-Hartley amendments to the act had deemed those respective roles to be separate, and therefore divided the board from the general counsel.

Hatch also focused attention on meetings related to the 1978 Labor Reform Bill that Lubbers had allegedly attended with union officials. Lubbers maintained that he had not participated in lobbying on behalf of the bill. Ultimately, Lubbers was confirmed—over the objections of the U.S. Chamber of Commerce, the National Association of Manufacturers, and other business groups—but not before a cloture petition was filed in April 1980 to break a Republican filibuster. This was the beginning of a series of difficult confirmations, most of which had formerly taken place on a voice vote without a hearing.

The basis of Senator Hatch's attack on Truesdale was more obviously ideological. He claimed that as a member of the NLRB Truesdale had never decided cases "in favor of any position which was considered contrary to those officially representing union interests." During Truesdale's renomination hearing in 1980, Hatch also criticized the declining rate of appellate courts' affirmance of board decisions and suggested that Truesdale's votes had something to do with it. Truesdale's nomination was unsuccessful.

After the Reagan inauguration in 1981, the Democrats in Congress sought an opportunity to pay back the Republicans. President Reagan's first nominee to the NLRB, John Van de Water, ran into immediate trouble. Van de Water, who had been a management consultant, was opposed by organized labor. In response to questions by Senator Edward Kennedy, he admitted that companies had hired him during union organizing campaigns to keep unions out. In 1981, the Senate Labor Committee rejected his nomination, and, though serving on a recess basis, he could not get a favorable recommendation from the Senate.

Ironically, when the Van de Water nomination failed to move forward, President Reagan nominated as Chairman of the Board Donald L. Dotson, who was confirmed by voice vote on February 17, 1983. His relatively easy route to confirmation—the only senators at the hearing were Don Nickles (R-Oklahoma) and Gordon Humphrey (R-New Hampshire)—resulted in part from exhaustion from the struggle over Van de Water. Though labor and the Democrats had won the battle over Van de Water, they lost the war. Under Dotson, the Board quickly shifted ground in a wide variety of policy areas, laying itself open to charges of anti-union bias. Ultimately, Dotson produced a boycott of the board by certain union leaders frustrated by its procedures and decisions. As Moe points out:

> *Reagan imposed on the NLRB a brand of radical anti-unionism that business leaders did not demand and, in fact, had long resisted . . . but, especially in an environment of economic adversity and union decline, some business leaders began to realize over time that the reality of an anti-union NLRB was not to be feared at all—that it proved quite consistent with their own, more confrontational approaches to unions. They were, in effect, dragged kicking and screaming into the brave new world of political anti-unionism by presidential leadership and some saw that what was clearly impossible in earlier decades was now quite possible indeed.*[8]

Thus, Dotson's tenure—adding to the generally hostile labor-management and political climates and to controversies over nominees to other offices—made it clear that from that time forward any nominee to the NLRB, especially as chairman, would be scrutinized carefully.

Complications

During debate over my confirmation in 1993, matters were immensely complicated by the anti-union groups' distribution of excerpts from my *Agenda for Reform*, which MIT Press was to publish later that year. In it, I argued that the National Labor Relations Act was not working effectively and proposed a number of reforms to the statute and to national labor policy, in particular a wide variety of procedural and substantive reforms designed to implement the aims outlined in the preamble to the act. Among other reforms, I recommended obligatory recognition of unions on the basis of employees' signed authorization cards and payment of union dues; more rigorous guidelines encouraging the board to seek prompt injunctive relief against labor law violations; double or triple back-pay awards for certain violations of the statute;

first-contract arbitration when parties cannot reach agreement subsequent to NLRB certification or recognition; requiring employers to bargain with unions about plant closings and to open the firm's books when financial questions are relevant to negotiation issues; use of court injunctions against no-strike violations by unions in all circumstances; amendments to the act to promote and enhance employee-participation programs; elimination of employers' right to permanently replace economic strikers; and a requirement that unions hold a vote before initiating a strike.

Despite numerous amendments to the NLRA in 1947 (Taft-Hartley) and 1959 (Landrum-Griffin), the original preamble has been unamended since the statute's origin in 1935. The preamble states that

> *[it is hereby declared to be the policy of the United States to . . . encourage] . . . the practice and procedure of collective bargaining and [to protect] . . . the exercise by workers of full freedom of association, self-organization, and designation of representatives of their own choosing.*

It was and is my view that the creakiness of the act's administrative procedures was responsible for the newfound loopholes that allowed employers to delay realization of these rights. The lack of effective remedies and substantive decisions, which diminished the effectiveness of concerted activity generally and the right to strike in particular, undermined the statute's preamble.

I had expressed some of these ideas in earlier law review articles, and a number of other scholars had recommended similar changes both prior to and subsequent to publication of *Agenda for Reform*. All in all, the ideas were moderate, the kind of middle-of-the-road positions I had expounded during most of my professional career in labor–management relations. Nonetheless, as the summer of 1993 wore on, the National Right to Work Committee turned up the decibel level of its critical barrage and labeled the book a liberal or union *Mein Kampf*.

Although the Democrats controlled both houses of Congress, strange things had begun to happen at the beginning of the Clinton administration in 1993. The nominations of first Zoe Baird and then Kimba Wood for attorney general were withdrawn after sparking considerable controversy. And only a few weeks before I was offered the chairman's job by Secretary of Labor Reich, President Clinton had withdrawn the nomination of Black Harvard Law School professor Lani Guinier, his nominee for assistant attorney general for civil rights, when some Republicans tagged her a "quota queen" because her writings advocated several new forms of proportional representation. The nomination of yet another Black appointee, Jocelyn Elders, to be surgeon general was then encountering stormy weather. At this point, as articles critical of me and my writings began to circulate, President Clinton's counselor Bruce Lindsay, I later learned, was expressing misgivings about my nomination.

Just before the excerpts from my book began to appear, my chief-counsel-to-be Bill Stewart, who was then working for the general counsel of the NLRB, asked me if there was anything in my book that could cause controversy. I thought long and hard and said, "There is only one thing I can think of. I advocate expanded remedies for undocumented workers, who have already been declared by the Supreme Court to be protected as employees under the act. Aside from that, I really can't think of anything." In fact, believing that its timely appearance would help my nomination, I had asked the publisher to accelerate the book's publication. I didn't anticipate for a moment that it would cause problems for my confirmation. But Lindsay had become uneasy—particularly about my proposal to grant union recognition on a "members only" basis when there was substantial worker support short of a majority. "Was that his view of the act as currently written?" Lindsay asked Cynthia Metzler. "Of course not," I responded when she relayed the question to me. Lindsay's confusion was genuine, but it was a result of a deliberate disinformation campaign designed to confuse my views about how the statute should be rewritten with my understanding of what the act currently said.

This ploy was a harbinger of things to come and introduced a theme my opponents would return to frequently. They argued that I wouldn't be able to distinguish between my two roles: case adjudication by Chairman Gould, on the one hand, and ideas about law reform by Professor Gould, on the other.

Nonetheless, on June 28, President Clinton announced his intention to nominate me:

> *William Gould has a tremendous amount of both practical and scholarly experience in labor law and stands for the principles that I want the NLRB to uphold—the rights of all workers to participate in labor organizations, and the need for labor and management to work together to increase our nation's competitiveness in a global marketplace. I think that he will be an excellent addition to the Labor Relations Board.*

Nomination—and Delay

On June 28, the very first person who called me from Washington to offer congratulations was the Reverend Jesse Jackson. Speaking from a car phone as he left town at the end of the day, he said he looked forward to meeting with me on my next visit. Throughout my tenure, Jackson took a considerable and constructive interest in labor–management relations and the work of the board. Most of the other congratulatory calls that day came from close friends in California and on the East Coast. At that point, none of us had an inkling of the struggle that was about to ensue.

The president's announcement began the planning process. My contacts in the White House advised me to start my leave of absence from Stanford Law School in the fall of 1993, as they expected me to be sworn in as chairman by then. The plan was to nominate me formally once the FBI check was completed, though the intent to nominate was announced prior to its conclusion. Hearings of the Labor Committee would presumably be held early in the summer, and a Senate vote on my confirmation would take place by early fall. However, my formal nomination papers were not completed and signed by President Clinton until August 6 and not forwarded to Capitol Hill until after that. In the meantime, Senator Nancy Kassebaum (R-Kansas), the ranking Republican member of the Senate Labor and Human Resources Committee, pointed out to a news reporter that "they were very late getting the Gould [papers] back up here . . . We can't do anything until the papers get here."[9] On August 8 the Senate recessed for its summer break. At one point, Charlie Buffon—a veteran Washington lawyer the White House and Department of Labor brought in to head my "confirmation team"—thought the hearings might be held in the middle of Washington's sweltering summer heat, but that was not to be. The committee was in no hurry. No hearing was held in August or in September. Finally, in September, the hearing date was set for October 1.

My nomination was not the only one in the Clinton administration to be affected by delay. In 1993, confirmation took an average of 8.53 months per nominee, compared to 8.13 months in the Bush administration. By these standards, the nearly nine months I waited for the Senate to confirm me (seven months from receipt of the nomination papers) was not excessive. But comparisons with the first year of the Reagan administration (5.30 months) and the Kennedy administration's record (2.38 months) is far more dramatic.[10] For instance, President Kennedy's nominee for NLRB chairman, Frank McCulloch, was in office within two months—as was the other board nominee, Gerald Brown, a San Francisco Democrat who had been an NLRB regional director. In those days both nomination and confirmation proceeded expeditiously.

There was yet another factor. President Clinton's election had brought the Democratic party back to the promised land, but in this first Democratic administration in twelve years, inexperience reigned. On the day of my nomination, a Stanford public relations officer who had been trying to pry information about my appointment from the White House for some time said to me, "I wish I could find an adult there." And, although I appeared to be the only person ever seriously considered for the chairmanship, my appointment was affected by the party's long period in the wilderness. In the first weeks and months of 1993, the White House was besieged by the long-pent-up desires of aspiring officeholders. All of this contributed mightily to the holdup.

As the delay became more pronounced, the business groups intensified their attack on my nomination, and then some of my supporters jumped into the fray. One of the many supportive statements was written and organized by Professor Herman Levy of Santa Clara Law School, my friend, colleague, and former member of the Bay Area Labor Law Discussion Group that I had organized in the eighties. Herman rallied nearly a hundred law professors to sign a letter to the Senate Labor and Human Resources Committee characterizing me as "uniquely qualified" to be chairman. Labor leaders and Bill Coday, president of the Pacific Maritime Association, which bargains with the ILWU and other maritime unions, joined in, a fact referred to by Senator Dianne Feinstein (D-California) during the confirmation debate the next year.

The first of many flaps emerged during one of my visits to Washington in connection with the Commission on the Future of Worker–Management Relations. The Republicans on the Senate Labor Committee, probably encouraged by Senator Hatch, the ranking member on that side, asserted that my nomination for the chairmanship was inconsistent with membership on the commission. I, of course, armed with Bob Reich's statement, felt confident that it was entirely appropriate for me to serve in both capacities. When the Republicans objected, however, the view—expressed to me initially by Senate Labor Committee staffers and later by Department of Labor people below Reich—was that I should not participate in commission business until my appointment was confirmed. I was advised that I should then offer to resign from the commission.

I resisted this position fervently. I believed that someone experienced and charged with the responsibility for interpreting the statute would be in a strong position to recommend useful labor law reforms. But the prevailing administration view was that the Republicans should have their way in this matter. After a long and friendly telephone call with Reich from steamy Boca Raton, Florida, where I was attending the annual meeting of the Black National Bar Association, he said: "I can't tell you what to do. It's really up to you." That comment, so different from his earlier affirmative support, convinced me that it was more important for me to move ahead and get confirmed as chairman.

THE RUMOR MILL CRANKS UP

In the wake of the August 6 nomination, two individuals began to assume primary responsibility for preparing me for the confirmation hearing. The first, Charlie Buffon, prepared a voluminous briefing book that analyzed all my writings going back to the 1950s. The British Labour Party intellectual and London School of Economics professor Harold Laski had written so extensively that wags liked to say that he contradicted himself. I was not to be allowed to do this—at least not consciously. The idea was to prepare me for all the many possible lines of attack. The second person working with me was Nestor Davidson, an extraordinarily bright guy in his early twenties who had worked in the Clinton "war room" during the 1992 campaign. In addition to his brain power, he had a lot of good sense.

Just as the three of us began our preparations for the hearing, the first in an extraordinary series of bombshells dropped on me. One morning early in September, as I stepped out of the shower, I received a call from Mark Childress, one of Senator Edward Kennedy's aides and a counsel to the Labor Committee for the Democratic side.

"Are you sitting down?" Childress asked me.

"What is it?" I asked.

"I have to ask you. Do you gamble?"

Someone on the Republican side, he said, was spreading a story that I had disastrously high gambling debts and was accepting bribes in my arbitration cases to pay them off. People who knew something about me and my interest in sports, particularly baseball—as well as my involvement in the baseball salary arbitrations in 1992 and 1993—could easily have seen this as an opportunity to find fire where they claimed to smell smoke. But no one who knew me personally would believe I would gamble—beyond making a few (mistaken!) five-dollar bets on the Super Bowl with friends.

Had I ever been to Nevada? Atlantic City? Childress asked me that morning. "Did you have arbitrations in those places?" I answered affirmatively with regard to Nevada. In the 1960s and 1970s I had attended Democratic party, United Auto Workers, and United Steel Workers conventions in Atlantic City, but I hadn't been back since gambling casinos were set up there in the 1980s. Childress didn't seem completely satisfied, and when I asked him "Who is circulating this?" I got no response.

Instead, he asked, "Have you been to South Africa and Cuba?" In fact, I had been to South Africa eight times and had just returned from giving a series of lectures there in August. I told him I had been going to that country since the 1970s, had given numerous lectures under the auspices of the U.S. government, and had worked with the Black trade unions beginning in 1977. Another story going around, according to Childress, charged that I was connected with the South African Communist party and was visiting both South Africa and Cuba for this reason. "But I have never been to Cuba," I protested.

I told him that although I had met Joe Slovo, the head of the Communist party in South Africa—and undoubtedly others whose party affiliation I was unaware of—I had certainly never attended a Communist party meeting there. When I repeated my question, "Who is circulating this?" Childress seemed to laugh off the stories and said he couldn't say (or, I supposed, wasn't allowed to say) and that I would be visited by an FBI agent, though I had already received my FBI clearance.

When the FBI agent arrived, she posed the same questions Childress had, and I gave the same answers. When she asked why anyone would say these things about me, I could only speculate: "Perhaps the sources of this are the enemies who are opposed to my appointment to the chairmanship." But the strategy behind the rumors soon began to emerge. As a news reporter who called my

Boston College colleague and friend Bob Berry commented. "He's [Gould] known to love sports. He's Black. Therefore, he must be a gambler." Though the formal debate in Congress was framed in terms of the ideas set forth in my books and articles, it became clear that my opponents were now playing the race card—sometimes subtly and sometimes not. This ploy, along with President Clinton's already acrimonious relations with Congress and my fidelity to the objectives of the National Labor Relations Act, fueled their campaign. Later in the fall, following my confirmation hearing, the dirty tricks were to continue. Meanwhile, the gambling/South Africa/Cuba affair seemed to recede into the background, receiving little public attention until the following spring.

MANY MEETINGS

In mid-September it was time to address the hearing process, and I flew to Washington for a series of "courtesy calls." The first sessions took place on September 14 and 15, and they went well. I began with Senator Dave Durenberger (R-Minnesota). We talked a good deal about sports generally, and baseball, in particular the epic 1967 Red Sox–Twins struggle and the Twins' more recent victories. In our conversation, he was effusive about me and my qualifications, stating that the government was "fortunate to have someone as qualified" as me in the chairmanship. Durenberger's praise of me seemed almost too good to be true—and, indeed, it turned out to be too good to be true. When the committee voted in October, Durenberger, along with then-Republican Senator James Jeffords of Vermont, abstained. And, unlike Jeffords, Durenberger did not cast a vote when the nomination came to the full Senate in 1994.

The next visit was with Senator Paul Wellstone (D-Minnesota), a short, wiry, energetic, bubbly fellow, as enthusiastic a man as I've ever met. He asked me about the erosion of the collective-bargaining process through unlawful means and how it could be revived. Questioning me about remedies to problems in first-contract negotiations and arbitration, he displayed a knowledge of issues most politicians—even those conversant with labor–management affairs—know little or nothing about. Wellstone, a former Carleton College political science professor, was both knowledgeable and intellectually alive. I found his enthusiastic interest in the NLRB and my nomination warming. We were to form a close working relationship during my tenure in Washington.

Next came a very brief meeting with another Democratic senator, Paul Simon of Illinois. Like Wellstone, he was quite sympathetic, and he wanted me to return to discuss labor law reform bills he had introduced or planned to introduce in the near future. I gently resisted this idea, because it would conjure up memories of my commission work and invite the Republicans to attack me on the grounds that I was acting as a policy maker and not a judge. I would be glad to work with him, I said, but the timing wasn't good.

Two weeks later, on September 28, I returned to Washington for another round of courtesy calls. These meetings were more challenging than the earlier ones and were complicated by the need to prepare simultaneously for my October 1 hearing. I began the morning of September 29 by meeting with the late William Curtin, a man who would become a good friend. Curtin was a partner at Morgan, Lewis, and Bockius, a law firm that represented employers in labor cases. When I met with him in his M Street office, he was full of encouragement and confidence about my confirmation prospects.

The second meeting that day was with the congressional Black Caucus on Capitol Hill, and here too I met with a warm and supportive response. Bill Clay (D-Missouri), before whom I had testified in 1984 at the House Labor Committee hearings on the inadequacy of labor law, paved the way. He, along with a number of other old friends, was to be at my side throughout the October 1 hearing. Like Senator Wellstone, the Black Caucus was a group I could always turn to for support in the most difficult of circumstances.

Next, I met with Senator Ted Kennedy, chairman of the Labor Committee, its most important Democratic member, and undoubtedly, in my view, one of the most important senators since the founding of the Republic. He, along with Wellstone, Simon, and Tom Harkin of Iowa, as well as my own California senators, Dianne Feinstein and Barbara Boxer, were to be my principal Senate supporters. Kennedy, who was to play a major role in obtaining the Senate confirmation vote scheduling itself, shepherded the nomination through and remained a friend during the Republican-controlled 104th and 105th Congresses, from 1995 through 1999.

The critical meeting that day was with Senator Orrin Hatch, the second-ranking Republican on the Labor and Human Resources Committee and a spokesman for the right wing of his party. Hatch began by asking me why I would ever leave Stanford for a Washington job like chairman of the Labor Board. Curiously enough, a similar theme was articulated a few weeks later in a *Los Angeles Times* article linking me to a controversial appointment to the U.S. Court of Appeals. Wrote journalist Paul Roberts, "The best bet is that Gould will use his powers to stretch the law at his directions. Why else leave the palm trees in pleasant Palo Alto, if not for the pleasure of wielding power?"[11]

I responded to Hatch by saying that my stay in Washington would end a few years early, and afterward I would move back to Stanford and write about it—a comment that left Hatch smiling. He then treated me to a long monologue about the changes that new board appointees brought. "When the Democrats are in," said Hatch, "they rule for the unions. When we are in, we do what is right." Sitting in on the meeting was my friend Betty Southard Murphy, a Washington management lawyer, former head of the NLRB in the Ford administration, and a friend of Hatch's. (She was also a law partner of my outstanding Harvard labor law student, Elliott Azoff.) At this point she offered her opinion that board members shouldn't comment on legislation, but Hatch said, "That hasn't been my experience." I said nothing in response to this little colloquy; whatever I said would be harmful. If I supported Murphy's position, I would be sailing under false colors; if I supported Hatch's version of the ways things usually operated, I would give my opponents additional grounds for voting against me. I already felt badly enough about leaving the Reich Commission. (It later came to be called the Dunlop Commission after its chairman, Professor John Dunlop of Harvard University.) In any event, I did not want to lose my ability to speak out from time to time on issues relating to labor law reform.

I then mentioned to Hatch the 1979 hearings for the confirmation of Bill Lubbers as general counsel during the Carter administration—a particularly contentious set of proceedings. I emphasized that, in contrast to Lubbers, I would not meet with representatives of labor and management in ad hoc strategy sessions on pending labor legislation, as Lubbers appears to have done. Said Hatch: "I am grateful for that."[12]

Toward the end of our meeting, Hatch said, "I'm aware that you don't like my views on Anita Hill." Here, he appeared to be referring to a letter I had written to the *New York Times* in 1991 attacking the Republican treatment of her during the confirmation hearings of Supreme Court Justice Clarence Thomas, in which Hill had accused Thomas of sexual harassment. I smiled and said, "You are aware of that?" Hatch exclaimed, "Do you think I'm stupid?"— and we both laughed. He then plugged in a supportive comment about Thomas and how much he thought of him. I remained silent, trying to avoid entanglement in something that really had nothing to do with my nomination.

It seemed to me that the meeting had concluded on a fairly positive note, but that was not to be the case with my next one. My encounter with Senator Nancy Kassebaum of Kansas— daughter of Alf Landon, the GOP standard-bearer for president in 1936—presented a more formidable and surprising obstacle. She was accompanied by a young right-wing lawyer named Steve Sola who was, I was told, her Svengali. My White House consultant, Nestor Davidson, was also there. Kassebaum was very pleasant and quite intelligent in her discussion of the points raised. She sought out my views, in particular, about the right to strike and employers' right to make permanent replacements. I was hitting on all cylinders that day and happily provided her with a seminar-type exposition of the Act and its provisions that I thought both clear and unassailable. It was later apparent, however, that this meeting—and the detailed articulation of my views that I had given Kassebaum—was a turning point on my learning curve for the confirmation process.

Although she listened quite politely, she didn't like what I had to say in the least. When I asked for her support as I left her office, she said, "At the hearing you will carry the burden of proof." I was absolutely stunned. This was such a marked contrast with the recent hearings on Supreme Court nominations in which Senator Joe Biden (D-Delaware) had told nominees, "Judge, the presumption is with you." Senator Kassebaum was telling me that the presumption was against me—at least as far as she was concerned.

When Davidson and I left her office, we sat down on a park bench near the Senate office building. We were both depressed about the meeting. "This confirmation could get away from us," Davidson asserted disconsolately, reprimanding me for mishandling Kassebaum. He stressed the havoc she could cause for us among so-called Republican moderates.

Hatch and Kassebaum were at the heart of the forces threatening my confirmation. Kassebaum was the ranking Republican on the Labor and Resources Committee, and Hatch, though he had shifted his major focus to the Judiciary Committee, over the years retained his interest in the Labor Board. From my conversation with Hatch, it was clear that he had either not forgotten the Lubbers and Truesdale hearings or had been well briefed on them.

There was one more Republican moderate to see before the hearings. On September 30, I met with Senator James Jeffords of Vermont. He was careful, soft-spoken, and very much a listener. I responded somewhat affirmatively to his view that the board should give priority to strike-replacement cases. He seemed to believe that doing so would help create a middle ground on this issue between the Republicans and liberal Democrats: The Labor Board should expedite the cases but not change the substance of the law that denied economic strikers the right to return to their jobs. His idea was to resolve quickly the question of whether strikers were protesting against unfair labor practices (and so entitled to reinstatement) or economic strikers who could be legitimately ousted from their jobs. Workers and employers could then get on with their work under existing rules, without any change in the law governing the right of economic strikers to return to their jobs. Jeffords seemed, in the main, sympathetic to my nomination, and I came away thinking that this meeting, in contrast to the one with Kassebaum, had gone well.

On September 30, on the eve of my appearance before the Labor Resources Committee, I met with a group of people who put me through my paces with regard to the questions I would be asked the next day. I had found earlier meetings of this kind frustrating, filled with young congressional hotshots all too ready with answers to questions they thought would be posed. At one point, when I had tried to break in with my ideas about an answer, someone said: "Oh, why not let Bill give his idea?"

But the September 30 meeting was particularly helpful. It introduced me to "Washingtonese"—the art of answering questions in an evasive manner rather than displaying one's substantive knowledge. This was the mistake I had made in my dealings with Senator Kassebaum: Instead of providing direct answers to her questions, I should have been far more circumspect. The basic advice—and I followed it fairly successfully on October 1—was to say as little as possible and to offer bland, general responses that were, in essence, nonresponsive. It was not really my style or instinct as an educator, but I became very good at this practice and employed it later when responding to questions about Labor Board decisions. It must have helped me on October 1, for the hearing went far better than that ill-fated meeting with Senator Kassebaum.

THE HEARING

High drama unfolded on October 1, the date of the hearing. As NLRB chief counsel Bill Stewart and I entered the Dirksen Building on Capitol Hill, a voice called out behind us: "Bill, hello Bill, Bill..." It was Ted Kennedy, greeting us in his warm, gregarious fashion and giving me the lift I needed. I had tossed and turned throughout a sleepless night, unable to close my eyes as I thought about the issues discussed in my "prep" meeting. But by the time we arrived at the hearing, I was fully alert and going on adrenaline.

I had a lot going for me that day. Kennedy, chairman of the committee, was on my side, and I was accompanied by Senators Feinstein and Boxer of California, Congressman Bill Clay of Missouri, and the House member from my own district, Representative Anna Eshoo. Though ready for a full-blown attack on me and my writings, my confidence was sustained by the influential and friendly Democrats flanking me at the hearing table.

Kennedy guided the hearing. Kassebaum was not present because of illness. Hatch, who was to be my principal inquisitor, was there in good form, and as nattily attired as he had been at our meeting two days before. The initial discussion consisted of good-natured bantering, mostly between myself and Senators Jeffords and Durenberger.

Then Hatch commenced a systematic cross-examination. He began with an inquiry into my views on *Pattern Makers v. NLRB*.[13] In this decision the Supreme Court, by a five-to-four vote, had deferred to the board's expertise and held that a member could resign from the union at any time, under any circumstances. My own view was that the right to engage in collective activity should be balanced against the right to refrain from it—in this instance by resigning—but that when a union is in the midst of economic conflict, it can turn down a resignation request in the interests of solidarity. Hatch wasn't pleased.

I then began a very delicate verbal dance with Hatch.[14] Aside from Senators Kennedy, Hatch, Durenberger, and Jeffords, only Senator Wellstone played an active role in the hearing. His remarks focused on the deference generally shown to a presidential nomination—a deference that was eroded seriously during Clinton's term of office.

> Senator Wellstone: *I guess my last point, Mr. Chairman, is that once again I follow the questioning of Senator Hatch, it does strike me that the fact that someone has really been out there with a lot of important intellectual work and a lot of important articles is I think very much in the positive.*

> *I once talked to Senator Hatch when I first came here—and this is true; you were my teacher—and I won't use the name, but there was a particular nominee and we had this discussion and I didn't agree with some of the particular issues. And you said to me: "Listen, this President decided to nominate this person and you may not agree, but if you think that that person has integrity and if you think that person is really qualified, that ultimately is what should matter." I feel that is exactly what applies to Bill Gould.*[15]

Back and forth we went for the balance of that October morning. Finally, after some bantering with Senator Kennedy, Senator Hatch said to me, "I've enjoyed chatting with you, I've enjoyed reading your book and reading other matters that you have written and spoken. You are clearly a very, very, brilliant person, and I think you have been a great teacher. I just want you to know that I'm very impressed with you personally and look forward to further dialogue here. Welcome to the Board."

Senator Kennedy interposed that he was "just waiting to hear that last sentence, that you can support the nomination." But Hatch asserted ominously that he had "deliberately withheld" that comment. Yet when the hearing concluded, Senator Hatch rushed down to where I was standing and asked me to autograph a copy of the book (*Agenda for Reform*) he had questioned me about. Soon thereafter he was to announce his opposition to my nomination. But on that day, Ted Kennedy, standing in the background, said to a number of my supporters, "He [Hatch] never laid a glove on him."

The Aftermath

As we left the Dirksen Building on that sunshiny October day, I and my friends thought that we had handled the challenge and triumphed mightily. We were told that Ken McGuinness, the lobbyist in charge of the right-wing Labor Policy Association, which had worked so vigorously against my nomination during the summer months, had been exasperated and angry about the way the hearing had gone. Three days later, in a speech to the AFL-CIO in San Francisco,

President Clinton mentioned my nomination just after a reference to Secretary of Labor Bob Reich: "We have nominated a chair of the National Labor Relations Board in Bill Gould . . . who believe[s] in collective bargaining."

But there were a number of developments that emerged from what seemed to be a great victory on October 1, all of which diminished or limited it. First of all, the dirty tricks evident in the gambling and South Africa-Cuba rumors continued. On October 31 and November 3, two remarkably similar articles commenting on racially inflammatory issues appeared in the *Los Angeles Times* and the *London Evening Standard*. Both sought to link me with the reputed views of Judge Rose-Marie Barkett, Justice of the Florida Supreme Court, who was later confirmed to the U.S. Court of Appeals for the Eleventh Circuit. The piece by Jeremy Campbell in the *Evening Standard* alleged that:

> *In Barkett's view, American juries are full of people with ambivalent opinions on race, but at such a deep level they are not aware of it. These distortions in the unconscious mind surface as a refusal to acknowledge that a person who commits a crime can be simply redressed in the injustices of the class-ridden society. The idea that certain people are not responsible for their actions, but are driven by occult forces beyond their control is a recurring theme among Clinton appointees. It shows up too, in the opinions of William Gould, a law professor chosen by Clinton to head the National Labor Relations Board.*
>
> *In his writings, Professor Gould suggests that a person who chooses not to belong to a trade union is really a misguided victim of years of conservative brainwashing.*[16]

Paul Roberts, a Treasury Department official in the Reagan administration, sounded a very similar note in the *Los Angeles Times*:

> *As one of her colleagues remarked* [about Judge Barkett] *when she voted to vacate one death sentence, she believed the defendant "is a good man, except that he sometimes*

> *kills people." Gould, a Stanford Law Professor, has a similar explanation about why employees reject unions. It is all due to the Reagan "whirlwind" that creates a "hostile environment" that causes workers to foolishly reject labor unions ...*
>
> *Lining up with the judge who finds socially redeeming virtues in racial murders and with an NLRB Chairman who wants to cram unions down the throats of workers and managements without a majority vote, Clinton seems destined to be smitten by his own appointees.*[17]

Both articles appeared designed to draw me into the emotion-laden morass of crime and race. The source of these very similar stories, and the earlier false rumors, never emerged. Mike Weiss, author of an article on my confirmation published in both the *San Jose Mercury News*'s *West Magazine* and *Mother Jones*, later attempted to pin them down and concluded that they came from Mark Dissler of Senator Hatch's staff. Dissler had distributed packets of material about Judge Barkett and urged journalists to stir up a campaign against her. At the time, Hatch, a member of the Judiciary Committee, was busy proclaiming his indecision about her nomination; he later asserted that he had been unaware of Dissler's actions. Despite his proven involvement in the anti-Barkett campaign, Dissler denied being the source of the smears against me.[18]

In Washington, the cheerful aftermath of the October 1 hearing was soon dimmed as well. First, Senator Kassebaum immediately came out against my nomination in a statement issued that afternoon, notwithstanding her absence from the hearing.

More Meetings

In the last week of October 1993, the White House asked me to return to Washington, DC, to speak to more senators and to woo business groups who had expressed hostility to my nomination. The first meetings were more in the nature of touching base with friendly faces. After I met with Senator Carol Mosley-Braun (D-Illinois), the first Black woman senator in America's history, for a few minutes, I wrote in my diary for November 28:

> *She carries herself like an actress, wonderful carriage, and was friendly to me. Jeff Gibbs [of California, the son of a colleague at Stanford] and Nestor sat in.*
>
> *Also met with Heflin [D-Alabama] the same day. But he really had no time to meet. "You'll be alright," he said a number of times* [and he waved to me, leaving the room as he said it.] [But] *the need* [for him] *to say that made me uneasy.*

That same day I had a quite contentious interview with Senator John Chafee (R-Rhode Island)—a meeting I had arranged myself, without White House help. When I said I wanted to extend union voting by postal ballots, he expressed concern. Earlier, he had worried that my proposed reliance on signed authorization cards wouldn't give employers sufficient opportunity to campaign against a new union. This issue, and not the secret ballot box, was his main concern about mail ballots as well. (In subsequent litigation it also proved to be the primary objection to their use.)

Next, I enjoyed meeting with Senator Tom Harkin (D-Iowa), who seemed to promise me an increase in NLRB appropriations. ("You'll be back to me about appropriations.") His parting shot was "You'll be here by Thanksgiving." At that time, I thought that Thanksgiving would be much too late—little did I know. But what Harkin lacked in clairvoyance, he more than made up for with support and commitment to the act once I got to Washington.

THE OPPOSITION RAMPS UP

The opposition, announced by Nancy Kassebaum in the wake of the hearings, had begun to take root. On October 20 she, along with senators Hatch, Strom Thurmond of South Carolina, Judd

Gregg of New Hampshire, and Dan Coats of Indiana, sent a "Dear Colleague" letter to all senators. In a broadside attack on my views, particularly those set forth in *Agenda for Reform*, the letter claimed that I espoused radical labor law reforms that had no place in the shaping of board interpretations, enforcement of national labor law, or decision making. Ignoring the views I expressed in my dialogue with Senator Hatch on October 1, the letter declared the writers' opposition to my views on permanent strike replacements, recognition procedures, union disciplinary authority, and the obligation of employers to disclose confidential information.

Then, on October 29, Kassebaum put on another hat and sent yet another letter, this one cosigned by Jeffords and Durenberger—both of whom had abstained from the vote reporting me out of committee on October 20. This letter asserted that several Republicans would withhold their support for me until President Clinton sent a "complete package of nominees for the remaining open positions on the Board, including the General Counsel position, and consulted with the Committee Republicans and the business community regarding those nominees." Kassebaum was thus identifying herself with Republicans purportedly interested in having a balanced board that would, they argued, redress grievances in a "fair, consistent, and even-handed manner."

This letter was a watershed development. It allowed Kassebaum to claim that she was not attempting to kill my nomination but only to condition it on Republican approval of other NLRB nominations. The truth was that she would have liked to prevent my appointment altogether. But, given the other vacancies—there were two on the board as well as the important general counsel position—she found an alternative strategy, one that gave her the opportunity to influence the selection of these nominees. In August, President Clinton had nominated another Democrat, a union lawyer from Philadelphia named Margaret Browning, for one of the board seats. By tradition, the remaining vacant seat belonged to a Republican. It was this seat that Kassebaum and the moderates were determined to control.

The practice of "batching" appointments was not entirely new to the National Labor Relations Board. In the early 1990s, the Bush administration was being buffeted on the right by an important constituent, the National Right to Work Committee—which was preoccupied with the Beck issue, the expenditure of union dues for political activities[19]—and from the left by Senate Democrats. In an attempt to mollify both sides, it had put together informal "packages" of nominees. Prior to that time, as Matthew Bodah has noted, "the only example of candidates of opposite parties being confirmed at the same time was fifty-one years ago when Democrat Abe Murdock and Republican J. Copeland Gray were sworn in on August 1, 1947. That situation, however, was extraordinary: The board had been expanded from three to five seats by the Taft-Hartley Act."[20]

But something very new was involved in the Kassebaum proposal, and throughout the Clinton administration, it was to haunt the appointment process for regulatory agencies in general and for the board in particular, especially the 1997 group of appointments. Reagan and Bush—indeed all the Democratic and Republican presidents before them—had selected the nominees of the opposition party on their own. Now the Republicans wanted direct involvement in a Democratic president's choice of a Republican nominee. G. Calvin Mackenzie has noted how the previous ability of presidents to shape the policy direction in administrative agencies was now undercut by delay in the appointment process, resulting in more influence by senators in such processes. The result was incoherent and inconsistent policy directions when the Republicans, who did not believe in the statute's purpose, held the advantage in dealing with Democratic presidents.[21]

This state of affairs later became a justification for advising the board not to take action of any kind, because it would be illegitimate to do so when it was not at full strength. Thus, the Kassebaum-Jeffords-Durenberger approach, supposedly reflecting a compromise between complete opposition to my nomination and acquiescence to it, represented the beginnings of real trouble for the functioning of the board and the appointment process, for the reasons articulated by Professor Mackenzie.

Tug of War

In reference to my nomination, President Clinton had made it clear from the start that he would not—as the press termed it—"do a Lani Guinier," whose nomination for assistant attorney general he had withdrawn under Republican pressure. He appeared ready to resist the Kassebaum initiative. On November 12, he responded directly to Senator Kassebaum, stating that he shared her desire for an able and fair-minded board and intended to consult with the Republicans about the remaining open positions. Clinton wrote/said:

> *It is my hope that, once Professor Gould is confirmed, I will be able to turn my full attention to the remaining positions at the NLRB, to move ahead expeditiously and to work with you in filling the positions in which you are interested.*
>
> *It is critical at this juncture that the Board remain functioning, and, therefore, it is important for the Senate to confirm Professor Gould. I know that you share my goal of an NLRB that has the confidence of both employers and employees, and the confirmation of Professor Gould is the first step towards achieving that goal.*[22]

But much to my surprise, and perhaps that of the White House, Kassebaum's response was to throw down the gauntlet and announce her intention to lead a filibuster until the full package was brought forward. Supported by business groups who would lobby both Democrats and Republicans against voting, she would delay confirmation as long as it took. The anti-labor groups rallied their supporters to oppose me until the full package was revealed.

This produced a long, drawn-out delay and fight: It became unclear whether the Republicans would be satisfied with making a deal on the Republican board members or whether they were insistent on torpedoing my nomination altogether. On January 31, 1994, in an article on the confirmation process, *New York Times* columnist Anthony Lewis railed against the abuse to which Clinton nominees such as Lani Guinier were subjected. Lewis wrote:

> *Attacks are made on nominees, for reasons of ideology and politics, with a zealotry that knows no bounds of truth. The attackers are in both the press and the Senate. Nominees are ordered not to reply, and those who should defend them are too often inept or craven.*

Lewis concluded by saying this about my protracted ordeal:

> *A victim of slow confirmation torture is William B. Gould 4th . . . a Stanford law professor who was nominated by President Clinton last June to be chairman of the National Labor Relations Board. More than seven months later, he is still caught in a snarl caused by Republican partisanship and White House ineptitude.*
>
> *The surprising attacker in this case is Senator Nancy Kassebaum—surprising because she is not usually so partisan or unfair. She has called Professor Gould "radical," though in fact he is a moderate labor-law expert respected by both sides.*[23]

Meanwhile, there were a couple of positive developments. The White House brought in Bill Coleman, a distinguished Black Washington lawyer and prominent Republican, to assist. He was very warm and friendly and would greet me frequently by saying: "Hello, friend." When I told him that I had given a speech in Florida in early 1994 without an honorarium, he asked how many nights I had stayed there at Stetson's expense, noting the fact that others would view free lodging as compensation. "I've tried a few cases, Bill," he said. He promised to make some inquiries.[24]

And a second front opened up almost through serendipity. My friend Dusty Baker, then manager of the San Francisco Giants, expressed concern that my confirmation was being delayed. He told me that he had a good deal of social contact with Walter Shorenstein, one of the Giants' owners, and that the two of them were going to a San Francisco Forty-Niner game together on a Monday night. Dusty noted that Shorenstein was one of the leading figures of the Democratic Party; he might be able to help move things forward. Indeed, Shorenstein did, arranging for a February dinner with Senator Kennedy in Portola Valley. I wrote: "In an hour, I go to a dinner at Walter Shorenstein's Portola Valley home for Ted Kennedy and his reelection campaign."[25] The evening was a fundraiser for Ted Kennedy's 1994 campaign, and Kennedy offered words of encouragement to both Hilda and me.

Figure 10.1: Don Baylor, then manager of the Colorado Rockies, on the right, with Dusty Baker of the Giants.

Figure 10.2: Dusty Baker makes the first of a series of appearances at Stanford Law School in 1994.

Figure 10.3: Dusty Baker and the author at the '94 Stanford Law School lecture.

Figure 10.4: With Red Sox outfielder Ellis Burks in his rookie 1987 season in Oakland, California. (Photo taken by Michael Zagaris.)

At this point the wheels began to turn rather quickly. I had a speaking engagement in Chicago the last week of February. But, as I wrote in a later book about my time at the NLRB:

> *On the twenty-eighth when I returned a call from Ted Kennedy in the lobby of the Chicago Hilton, he assured me that the vote would be taken on March 2. In response to my*

question about whether the votes were there, he responded in the affirmative. As I flew back to San Francisco from Chicago the next day, anticipating that I would be confirmed on that date, I composed a statement for the press.

THE VOTE

The debate on my appointment took place, as Kennedy had predicted, the day after my return to the Bay Area. Hilda and I, and Mike Weiss of the *San Jose Mercury News*, gathered around a television set in our home to watch it.[26] After a considerable amount of debate on the Senate floor, the Senate voted fifty-eight to thirty-eight in favor of my nomination. I received the most "no" votes of any of Clinton's nominees. As I later wrote:

> *Every single Democrat in the Senate voted for me, but only five Republicans did so. As the senators and their aides departed from the floor, Senator Kennedy joked to a number of people within earshot: "Let's hope Nancy's right!"—meaning of course, let's hope Bill Gould is as radical as she claims. In a note he sent me the next day he commented with relief, "It's a good thing the Republicans decided not to filibuster!" Exhausted and yet exultant, my feelings and the mood at Stanford were celebratory. The sense of near-regret I had had as I departed Chicago, knowing that I would miss tenor saxophonist Stanley Turrentine, who was due to arrive at the Blackstone the following night, now almost evaporated. I issued the statement I had composed on the plane the night before. In it I described the vote as a "victory over a determined campaign of cynical character assassination . . . by right-wing ideologues," and characterized the Republican tactics as "antidemocratic." I vowed to "return the Board to the center, to promote balance" between labor, management, and employees and to "let workers, union officials and business people know that they will be treated with respect, civility, and fairness.*[27]

And thus began my years as the chairman of the NLRB.

NOTES

Much of the material in this chapter replicates or is based upon my earlier book, William B. Gould IV, *Labored Relations: Law Politics and the NLRB—A Memoir* (Cambridge: MIT Press, 2000).

1. The Amalgamated Clothing Workers Union subsequently merged into UNITE, the Union of Needletrades, Industrial and Textile Employees, AFL-CIO, CLC.
2. Herb Caen, "The Morning Line," *San Francisco Chronicle*, May 4, 1993. Stanford University is often referred to as "The Farm."
3. Robert Reich, "Labor Law, Reform, and the Japanese Model," *Harvard Law Review* 98 (1985): 697.
4. G. Calvin Mackenzie, "Starting Over: The Presidential Appointment Process in 1997" (Washington, DC: Twentieth Century Fund/Century Foundation White Paper, 1997): 39–40.
5. Kevin G. Salwen, "Gould Expected to Be Named Head of NLRB," *Wall Street Journal*, June 17, 1993.
6. No major reform of American labor law had been fashioned since 1959, when new unfair practices by labor unions were defined by a heavily Democratic Congress, largely as a result of the McClellan Committee hearings in which John and Robert Kennedy played an influential role. The result was a bill of rights for workers against unfair union practices.
7. Terry M. Moe, "Interests, Institutions and Positive Theory: The Politics of the NLRB," *Studies in American Political Development: An Annual* 2 (1987): 273.
8. Moe, "Interests, Institutions and Positive Theory," 272.
9. Quoted in Mike Weiss, "Bill Gould's Ordeal: The Anatomy of a Character Assassination," *Sacramento Bee*, July 10, 1994.
10. Paul C. Light and Virginia L. Thomas, *The Merit and Reputation of an Administration's Presidential Appointees on the Appointments Process* (Washington DC: Brookings Institution, 2000).
11. Paul Craig Roberts, "Clinton May Be Term-Limited by Nominees," *Los Angeles Times*, October 31, 1993.
12. In fact, during debates on the Taft-Hartley amendments in 1947, NLRB Chairman Paul Herzog and General Counsel Gerhard Van Arkel both worked with leading senators—Chairman Herzog to help draft the legislation and Van Arkel to write speeches and the Democratic minority report. In the 1960s, too, Chairman McCulloch's special counsel had drafted the Democratic House's report on labor law reform.
13. Pattern Makers v. NLRB, 473 U.S. 95 (1985).
14. Gould, *Labored Relations*, 34–36.
15. Gould, *Labored Relations*, 35.
16. Jeremy Campbell, "Getting Away with Murder," *Evening Standard* (London), November 3, 1993.

[17] Roberts, "Clinton May Be Term-Limited by Nominees"; "Questions for Professor Gould," *Detroit News,* December 5, 1993 (which offers substantially the same viewpoint as the Roberts article); "Blocking the NLRB Nominee," *Sacramento Bee,* December 14, 1993; "Labor Board: Senate Roadblock Holds up an Outstanding Nominee," *Detroit Free Press,* January 23, 1994.
[18] Neil Lewis, "While Senator Deliberated a Top Aide Politicked," *New York Times,* November 5, 1993.
[19] Communications Workers of America v. Beck, 487 U.S. 735 (1988).
[20] Matthew M. Bodah, "Congressional Influence on Labor Policy: How Congress Has Influenced Outcomes Without Changing the Law," paper delivered at the 51st Annual Meeting of the Industrial Relations Research Association, New York, January 5, 1999.
[21] Mackenzie, *Starting Over.*
[22] Gould, *Labored Relations,* 41.
[23] Anthony Lewis, ". . .Running the Gauntlet," *New York Times,* January 31, 1994.
[24] Gould, *Labored Relations,* 47.
[25] Gould, *Labored Relations,* 48.
[26] Gould, *Labored Relations,* 48.
[27] Gould, *Labored Relations,* 49–50.

11
CHAIRMAN OF THE BOARD: THE BASEBALL STRIKE AND THE NLRB

The tumultuous confirmation process was finally behind me; now the true work began. Miguel Mendez, my colleague and very good friend, swore me in at a private ceremony at Stanford Law School on March 7, 1994, thirty-three years to the day after Frank McCulloch, President Kennedy's NLRB chairman and my ex-boss, was sworn in. A day later my friend and former co-counsel in Title VII litigation, Chief Judge Thelton Henderson, swore me in during a public ceremony in San Francisco. Then I was off to Washington to begin work with my soon-to-be chief counsel, Bill Stewart. I was eager to take on the challenges—there were many, and they were considerable.

Figure 11.1: Here I am with my best friend on the Stanford Law School faculty, Miguel Mendez, on the night of March 7, 1994, when Professor Mendez administered the oath of office to me.

Figure 11.2: My friend, Judge Thelton Henderson, provided my first public swearing-in as NLRB chairman in April 1994 in San Francisco.

CHALLENGES FROM THE START

I announced my intention to create a so-called advisory panel composed of labor and management lawyers. Similar task forces had been formed in the past, but the idea here was to solicit viewpoints from all sides and obtain informal inputs. The concept began to create some problems almost immediately: I discovered that my board colleagues were concerned that a special American Bar Association Labor and Employment Law Practice and Procedure Committee might be annoyed by this idea, given that they had had special access to the board over the years. So the idea was well received by the public, commentators, and much of the labor bar, yet there was a sense of unease displayed by insiders who had a traditional relationship with the agency.

During that first week in Washington and my introduction to the hurly-burly of congressional hearings, I became aware of other board members' simmering resentment over my advisory panel proposal. Yet it was another matter—a trivial, harmless joke, really—that provided an indication of future troubles. Through the former chairman, Jim Stephens, Bill Stewart discovered that Stephens or one of his subordinates had attached a photograph of Don Dotson,

Reagan's chairman who had stepped down in 1987, to the toilet seat in the chairman's bathroom. They thought of it as just a joke, and so did I. However, soon after Bill showed it to friends who were management labor lawyers with close connections to the Labor Policy Association, we received word that the *Wall Street Journal* was about to run a small article naming me as the person responsible for placing Dotson's photo on a toilet seat. (Later, the respected *Washington Post* insisted on publishing pieces of gossip about me that were almost as trivial.) Of course, we immediately removed it to avoid controversy, but it was a portent. Time and time again, I would be urged to respond to perceptions that were completely false. The Dotson-Stephens incident was only one particularly bizarre illustration of this phenomenon.[1]

The question of how the president would fill the two remaining vacancies on the 1994 board presented some difficulties from the beginning. The idea of batching—to which President Clinton acceded when it became clear that the Republicans would filibuster unless their demands were met—meant that the Republican party would select only those who promised to disagree with me and to dissent from positions that I took. A moderate Republican academic was rejected immediately when he refused to pledge dissents against any and all of my policy positions. The president ultimately nominated Margaret (Peggy) Browning (D-Pennsylvania) and Charles Cohen (R-Washington, DC). Cohen became known as "Doctor No" by the staff and dissented from virtually everything I did. Like his successor, John Higgins—Cohen's ideological comrade in arms, who took his place in 1996 after much campaigning—Cohen very much wanted reappointment but did not obtain it.[2]

The other board members and I had disagreements even over the more formal swearing-in ceremony, which was to take place in Washington in April. Because my nomination was the only one put forward initially in 1993, it did not occur to me that there would be a joint swearing-in. I had therefore invited Chief Judge Julian Cook, one of my oldest and best friends, and my first friend in Detroit in 1960, to administer the oath to me. Now, although the batching process had changed the situation, I continued to prefer a separate swearing-in. After all, I had been the object of considerable controversy and had done all the heavy lifting in the confirmation process. The others—quite naturally, I suppose—resisted this idea. I can still see them sitting in phalanx-like formation on the couch in my office, all exhibiting disapproval through their facial expressions and body language. Nonetheless, when it became clear that all four of us—General Counsel Fred Feinstein, Peggy, Charles, and myself—would be sworn in on the same day, I insisted on having Judge Cook swear me in. The oath for the others would be administered by Secretary of Labor Reich.

In spite of all the petty controversies, the ceremony on April 11 was a pleasurable event attended by much of official Washington—even some of our erstwhile enemies during the confirmation process. People were friendly and seemed to enjoy themselves. Bill Stewart organized a nice party afterward at an Italian restaurant near the board offices, attended by some of my friends and family, including my mother, my wife, and our three sons. From time to time, though, my mind drifted back to a comment made at a party we had attended a night or two earlier. Zoe, wife of the president's counsel, Abner Mikva, had introduced me as "Bill Gould . . . the last chairman of the National Labor Relations Board"! This remark kept me in mind of the serious challenges that awaited me.[3]

I began my tenure in earnest by giving a series of speeches to present my priorities and establish the tone I wanted to set as chairman. In a speech to the Detroit AFL-CIO, I declared that I would not be deterred by the large number of "no" votes I had received. "This is my badge of honor," I said, and the audience gave me a standing ovation. Shortly after the Detroit speech, I went on to Minneapolis for a luncheon address to the National Academy of Arbitrators, where I attempted to identify and support some of the themes I thought were present in President Nelson Mandela's recent inauguration in Pretoria, which I had attended as a representative of the U.S. government. I emphasized the importance of dialogue, understanding, and reconciliation between old adversaries.

REFORMS

My next task would be to address specific policies. I proposed reforms involving NLRB administrative law judges, advocating for rules that would expedite the processing of cases by eliminating briefs in certain instances, and providing for bench awards within seventy-two hours of the close of the hearing. Justice delayed is justice denied, I thought then and now. I also created a new core of so-called "settlement judges" who could mediate labor disputes—I could not call them mediators because of a peculiar provision of the act that prohibits mediation! These changes were based on my experience as a labor lawyer and academic and were designed to promote both informality and the expeditious resolution of cases. I had relatively little difficulty in obtaining board support for these initiatives, and in 1994 and 1995 the board set records, producing more than a thousand cases in one year.

Moreover, the board used a provision of the NLRA, frequently ignored in the past, that provides the agency with authority to obtain injunctive relief against offending parties where delay will produce irreparable harm and where such relief is "just and proper." We sought and obtained more injunctions than any other board in the entire nearly ninety-year history of the NLRB! So there were some accomplishments at the beginning.

Other reforms, however, ran into heavy sledding. I promoted postal ballots in representation elections, so that more workers could be reached and given an opportunity to vote, and they could do so in a more deliberative manner than plant premises elections generally provide. But employer opposition to this procedure was rooted principally in the fact that mail balloting would take place over a number of days—in contrast to the one day generally required with balloting at the plant or some other facility. The employer has a right to give anti-union "captive audience" speeches to all workers twenty-four hours before the vote; management's fear was that as the vote took place over multiple days, the impact of such tactics would dissipate during that period. Ultimately, the board issued a landmark ruling, *San Diego Gas and Electric*,[4] enhancing the circumstances under which postal ballots could be conducted.

I also tried to streamline procedures relating to the board in Washington itself—but this proved unsuccessful. Indeed, the major cross I bore during my tenure was delay at the Washington level, due to the reluctance of some board members to issue decisions.

UPS AND DOWNS

Occasionally my work could be considered festive. One such occasion sprang up when my friend Jack Sheinkman retired from his position as president of the Amalgamated Clothing Workers when it merged with another union. Jack, as must be clear from so many chapters of this book, was the best friend I had in my professional world and my "rabbi" in the confirmation process. On November 1, 1994, I was one of the speakers at his retirement party in New York City. Governor Mario Cuomo, who was just about to lose a bitterly fought reelection campaign, sent a message praising Jack and saying, with obvious reference to Jack's participation in demonstrations against the Bush NLRB, "Now that Bill Gould is chairman of the NLRB, what can Jack Sheinkman possibly protest against in the future?" It was a convivial and memorable evening. Leaders of the New York labor movement and the Democratic party were present en masse, and many had come from Washington and elsewhere to honor Jack. But his retirement was a real loss for me, for he had continued to be a key player and my close confidante even after my confirmation.[5]

I keenly felt Jack's loss as an important ally when, around the time of his retirement, I became involved in a case arising out of a dispute between the United Mine Workers of America (UMWA) and one of the major mining companies. The dispute involved strike misconduct, violence by the union, mass picketing, and threats of bodily injury. The dispute had been going on for some time; when I arrived in Washington, I was presented with a letter from former Secretary of Labor William Usery, who requested that the NLRB withdraw charges against the UMWA as part of an overall settlement. The NLRB General Counsel wanted us to back away from contempt litigation. I took the position, in opposition to other Democratic appointees, that we would not tolerate violations of this nature from anyone. That same day, in a speech to a labor law conference for management lawyers, I stated that the board would not tolerate lawlessness and repeated misconduct. I pledged "an evenhanded approach against all those who break the law.... We must stand against lawlessness no matter what the source." As our press secretary's release about the contempt action explained clearly, the board was attempting to avoid recurrence of the violation of individual rights.

The UMWA was incensed and called the decision to initiate contempt proceedings "a reactionary ploy to satisfy board critics."[6] Pointing out that mine owners were willing to drop the charges of unfair labor practices, the union alleged that "this is being driven solely by the National Labor Relations Board." My old friend Harry Bernstein, writing in the *Los Angeles Times*, stated:

> Gould ... will have to try harder to overcome the NLRB's pro-management stance of recent years.... One ominous sign was Gould's deciding NLRB vote to seek as much as $1.3 million in contempt fines from the United Mine Workers for alleged picket line misconduct during last year's seven-month strike against twelve coal companies.... With his vote in the Miners' case, Gould went too far to make his point [of neutrality and impartiality].[7]

A couple of weeks later I got a taste of how personal this kind of dispute could become. Steve Tallent, a management labor lawyer, and Elliot Bredhoff, an old friend and union lawyer, cohosted a party at Tallent's house to welcome me to Washington. The angry UMWA threatened to picket the party and to dissuade union lawyers from attending it. Fortunately, through the good offices of Bredhoff, cooler heads prevailed, and UMWA leader Richard Trumka was dissuaded from taking these actions. No pickets appeared.[8] Nonetheless, the UMWA fracas did win me the lasting and rigid enmity of Trumka, previously the UMWA president, and during my Washington tenure the number two guy at the AFL-CIO. Our relationship was distant and cold at best.

THE BASEBALL STRIKE

Another major challenge for the NLRB—and one that got the attention of the entire country—was our involvement in the baseball strike of 1994 and 1995. Major League team owners, confronted with what they perceived to be excessive salaries and other benefits for the players since the advent of free agency in the 1970s, sought to impose a salary cap. The players' union responded by arguing that if the problem was one of economic disparity among teams, the disparity should be reduced by revenue sharing among the clubs, not economic sacrifice by players. But the owners pressed on. With more than thirty players earning three million dollars a year and the average salary in excess of one million, it wasn't hard to convince the public that players' greediness and unwillingness to accept salary caps—as football and basketball players had—was the heart of the problem.

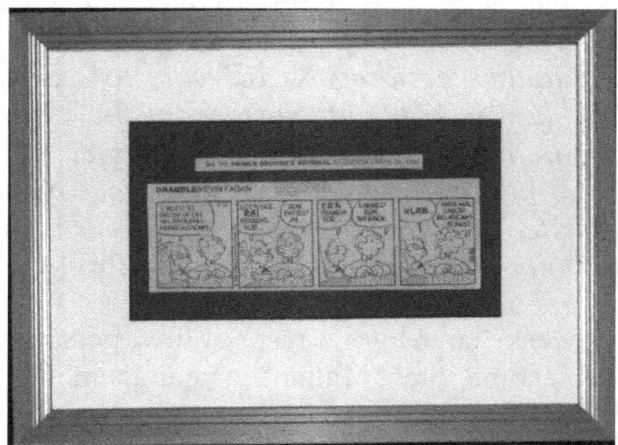

Figure 11.3: The baseball strike and the NLRB involvement in it entered the nation's public consciousness.

Strategy and Posturing

The players set a strike deadline of August 2, 1994, only five months after my term as chairman began. They proceeded on the assumption that they could exert the greatest pressure on owners in the fall, before the lucrative playoffs and World Series. During the winter, by contrast, the owners would be able to impose their last offer unilaterally, after bargaining to impasse—leaving the union with the weak remedy of a strike when it would hurt the owners least. Or, alternatively, owners might risk a lockout in the spring, depriving players of paychecks, again at a time when owners would not feel the pinch.

On the strike deadline, I was at the White House for a social function involving California Democrats. I chatted with President Clinton in the receiving line, remarking that Secretary of Labor Bob Reich and I had been discussing the baseball negotiations. The president expressed dismay at the prospect of a strike. "This is the best year in a long time," he said, referring to the home run records that might be set by Ken Griffey, Mark McGwire, Matt Williams, and others. He remarked that it was hard to have sympathy for either side, given their wealth and "greed." As we parted, he said to me, "If you guys could resolve this, they'd elect me president for life!"

I, too, of course, had a deep personal and professional interest in this issue. I had written a book and taught a course on sports law and had written many newspaper pieces about baseball. I had also arbitrated in salary disputes in 1992 and 1993. In fact, when I left the law school for Washington in the spring of 1994, I told sports journalist Leonard Koppett, my friend and co-teacher, that my deepest regret was giving up my baseball salary arbitrations. Leonard replied, "You'll be more involved now than you ever were in the past. A big conflict is coming between the parties, and the National Labor Relations Board will be right in the middle of it. You'll see." Truer words were never spoken.[9]

At the NLRB we kept a close watch on this dispute. The players established a deadline for resolving the differences between themselves and the owners. Some of the owners believed that either the players would not strike or, if they did strike, would return quickly to the field if they were replaced by minor league players. The dynamics between the parties made the players fear that if they did not strike well in advance of the season's end, the owners would unilaterally institute their own position on free agency during the winter months and open the camps without them, relying, if necessary, on temporary replacements. The players thought that threatening the postseason play that brought owners most of their revenues would give them the maximum amount of leverage. For this reason, they viewed as misguided the proposal Secretary Reich made at Fenway Park in Boston during a game; he wanted the parties to continue talking without resorting to warfare.[10]

On August 12, while I was en route to speaking engagements in Vancouver, B.C., Seattle, and Spokane, the players struck. But their strategy misfired: The owners did not back off from their positions. The Federal Mediation and Conciliation Service—an agency generally operating on a different track from the NLRB, with a focus on informal mediation—regarded it as a victory when, in early September, they were able to induce the parties to return to the bargaining table, the talks having been in recess since late August.[11]

Then the unthinkable transpired. For the first time since 1904, when the National League champions New York Giants refused to play the American League champions Boston Red Sox, the World Series was canceled.

The NLRB Gets Involved

Talks continued after the season's collapse, but with little impetus. On December 22 the owners sought to change the negotiating environment: They unilaterally implemented their salary-cap proposal and eliminated salary arbitration for certain players. Throughout the winter, negotiations dragged on. The NLRB became involved as a result of questions relating to the posture of negotiations and whether the owners had refused to bargain in good faith. The key legal question, thus, was whether there was a prospect of further negotiations, given the players' apparent interest in them. On the theory that the answer to this question was in the affirmative, the players filed a charge of unfair labor practice with the New York City regional offices of the board. For if there was a chance for negotiation when the owners proclaimed a deadlock, their unilateral implementation of the salary cap was an unlawful refusal to bargain in good faith: The owners' conduct unduly choked off a prospect for further negotiations.

Subsequently, the owners stated that they were changing the method of free-agent negotiations so that it would proceed on a centralized basis, rather than club by club. Again, the issue was whether the system of free-agent compensation could be altered when the owners had made a unilateral employment decision. This point—whether proper procedures had been followed—was the question the board considered. The rights, wrongs, or merits of the players' and owners' positions were not the issues before us—and under federal labor policy, those are never the issues before the board. Rather, the question was whether the parties had followed proper procedures and bargained in good faith.

At this point, two fronts of negotiation began to open. One was the litigation before the board; the case was investigated by Dan Silverman, the New York City regional director, acting as prosecutor on behalf of General Counsel Fred Feinstein. The other front was before Congress and in President Clinton's attempts to resolve the matter, either by revising the antitrust exemption—thus allowing players to sue the owners in federal district court for any restrictions imposed on free agency—or through provision of compulsory arbitration.

In January the White House intervened and, late in the month, set a deadline for settlement or progress, appointing as special mediator W. J. Usery, the former secretary of labor in the Ford administration (who was also involved in the Mine Workers' contempt case). His job was to recommend terms for an agreement. Peter Angelos, the outspoken owner of the Baltimore Orioles—who had earlier warned that he would not participate in the 1995 season if temporary replacements were on the field—voiced optimism that a negotiated settlement and real baseball could ensue.[12] Angelos objected to replacement players in part because he thought using replacement players would prevent the Orioles' Cal Ripken from passing Lou Gehrig's consecutive-games record that season, and in part because replacements would harm the game's quality and thus the game itself.[13] In truth, he helped save baseball from disgracing itself with such a debacle.

Figure 11.4: In Baltimore with Cal Ripken, whose consecutive game played record would have been broken if the baseball owners had continued the game by opening the 1995 season with replacement players.

In March, the general counsel issued a complaint, which is a prerequisite for NLRB involvement in unfair labor practice cases. I was in Los Angeles on March 17, 1995, when the general counsel requested that the board issue an injunction. My next stop was Tempe, where I was giving a series of talks at the Arizona State University Law School. When I accepted the invitation, I had hoped to catch a few games of spring training, but given the dispute over the use of temporary replacements, I decided that that was inadvisable.

March 23, 1995

A tumultuous day—the previous evening, just as I arrived back from Arizona, Bill Stewart left a message that Bill Usery, the mediator in the baseball dispute, had left a message stating that he would like the Board to delay its decision in the baseball case and that he would like me to call him. I did so between 8 and 8:30 p.m. last night. Usery stated that he had had two constructive days with the parties on a "confidential" and "fairly quiet" basis. He said that he was trying to establish a meeting with [Acting Commissioner Bud] *Selig and Fehr for Saturday and Sunday and that it might possibly run into Monday. He said that if the parties made an agreement it would be this coming weekend and expressed concern that if we issued an authorization for an injunction that we would run the risk of impeding negotiations and inflaming the relationship between the parties. I asked Usery what the prospects were for a settlement, and he said he could not speak in terms of "odds"—but he stated that this opportunity was better than any other which had existed before. Usery stated that he had talked to fourteen owners that day and said: "We have a group—they have a group" which will meet with the union. He also said that Orza* [Gene Orza, the general counsel of the Players' Association] *had asked him not to interfere with any of the unfair labor practice aspects of this case.*

I then called up Ab Mikva [the president's counsel] *to send him an update about Usery's status, given the criticism that the Players' Union had sent his way. Mikva said that he would check and call me back, and he did and said that while Usery is "technically still our mediator"—he also said "nobody thinks he can reach the players. He has lost his influence."*[14]

Figure 11.5: In the spring of 1995, I was frequently questioned about the status of the proposed baseball injunction. Here I am in my office in Washington in March 1995 answering questions from the press. (Courtesy of Getty Images.)

We then pushed ahead without waiting for further negotiations. The board and general counsel met over the weekend of March 25 and 26, and reporters and television cameras were posted outside our offices. The nightly news reported that this was an unusual example of government employees working over the weekend on a case of considerable national import. I cast my vote to join the other two Democrats and support an injunction requiring the owners to restore conditions of employment to the level at which they were prior to their unilateral changes. A majority of the board, led by John Truesdale, were against the idea of releasing any written opinion to the public or releasing the actual vote of the board. I told Truesdale and others that I would insist on my ability to make my reasoning known to the public, and that I felt the public should know what the actual vote was. This produced a big flap inside the agency.[15]

The board successfully sought an injunction, bringing the longest strike in baseball's history to a conclusion. Then-District Judge Sonia Sotomayor (now Justice Sotomayor of the U.S. Supreme Court), in granting our request for an injunction against unfair labor practices, said the following:

> *The often leisurely game of baseball is filled with many small moments which catch a fan's breath. There is, for*

example, that wonderful second when you see an outfielder backpedaling and jumping up to the wall, and time stops for an instant as he jumps up and you finally figure out whether it is a home run, a double or a single off the wall, or an out.[16]

More than a quarter of a century before this 1995 strike, on a typically warm and humid night in Washington's D.C. Stadium (later RFK Stadium), Red Sox leftie Dick Ellsworth was on the hill against the hometown Washington Senators, and was clearly tiring in the late innings of that 1968 summer night. But Manager Dick Williams had no one in the bullpen effective enough to relieve Ellsworth and thus stayed with him as Hank Allen stepped to the plate with the Senators trailing two to one with two on and two out in the bottom of the ninth. Allen hit a prodigiously long shot to deep left center which Reggie Smith, the then-Sox centerfielder, somehow beautifully tracked down and raced to the wall for—and leaped high against the fence. As he descended to the centerfield grass, we experienced one of those precious moments of which Justice Sotomayor spoke. It was similar to Manny Ramirez, in the September 2004 Yankee Stadium Series, plucking a ball out of the left field stands after it had been hit off the bat of a Yankee second baseman who circled the bases, thinking he'd hit a home run. But as Reggie Smith descended to terra firma, we all pondered the outcome: If the ball was over the fence, the Senators had won the game by two runs on a "walkoff," or what the Japanese called a "sayonara home run." And if it was caught, the game was also over, with the Red Sox the victors.

Only when the Sox bullpen erupted, with players racing down the left field line and onto the field to greet Smith as he held the ball high, was the result apparent. Smith had made a spectacular grab. This was one of those breathless, inescapable moments.[17] Years later, Hank Allen, who had hit the ball Smith caught, joked with me in Baltimore about the possibility that the bullpen had given Smith another ball, so as to feign an out. When I discussed this with Smith at the first Red Sox game in Great Britain in 2019, he was not amused.

Figure 11.6: Conversing with Reggie Smith in London, June 2019, during the first appearance of American baseball in Great Britain, a contest between the Red Sox and Yankees.

Aftereffects

The upshot of all our work at the NLRB between March and April of 1995 was that the players returned to the field and a collective bargaining agreement was consummated in the following year. This produced twenty-seven years of uninterrupted peace, with no strikes or lockouts in an industry that had been riddled with economic warfare from 1972 through 1995. One consequence of this new era was that revenues increased more than tenfold, and players and owners saw their income remarkably enhanced.

But in 2022, it all came to a halt. The owners instituted a lockout during spring training, and the press was interested in my views about how 2022 compared with 1995. The *Boston Globe* said:

> *William Gould IV found nothing surprising as he took stock of baseball's labor battle. "Plus ça change, plus c'est la même chose," he said with a laugh. "The more things change, the more they stay the same."*
>
> *That history gives Gould, a professor emeritus at Stanford Law School, an unusual vantage point from which to view the current labor dispute. Gould found little surprising about a fight between players and owners over money using familiar playbooks.*[18]

I pointed out that this time around the players and owners were arguing principally over money; no basic concepts, such as free agency or salary arbitration, were at stake. I therefore believed it unlikely that this stoppage would have the duration of the 1995 strike. Said the *Boston Globe*:

> "I think of FDR in the 1930s talking about a plague on both your houses," said Gould, referencing President Franklin Delano Roosevelt's reaction to a 1937 steel strike. "It seems so tragic that this game, that is so filled with beauty and grace and skill, is taken away from us by people who have so much more than ninety-nine percent of those who are interested and want to sit in the stands and view it on TV."[19]

The matter was resolved more expeditiously this time around. Said the *San Francisco Chronicle*:

> Bill Gould has seen this ill-fated baseball story before. A labor dispute, an industry shutdown and the cancellation of games.
>
> "It is very much the same kind of divide, the same kind of bitterness," Gould said. "The big difference between then and now is owners have become enormously more wealthy, if it's possible to believe . . .
>
> "Even though the owners are shooting themselves in the foot public relations-wise with this ham-handed lockout," Gould said in a phone interview, "they are squeezing the players more effectively than they were able to in '94–'95 because they're catching the players when they're desperate and most vulnerable."
>
> Nevertheless, Gould expressed optimism that a collective bargaining agreement could be reached within seven to 10 [sic] days because of the movement on some issues before talks in Florida broke down Tuesday and because owners aren't trying to implement a salary cap as they were during the last shutdown.[20]

This was a different day and environment, and notwithstanding the disputatious posture of both sides, I like to think that our 1995 intervention not only produced labor peace and enhanced revenues but also made a more expeditious resolution possible in 2022.

A Baseball Friendship

Orioles' owner Peter Angelos was the only owner who sided with the NLRB throughout the 1995 litigation.[21] We had first become acquainted when he attended a Baltimore speech I gave on the work of the NLRB. From the beginning, Angelos, a labor lawyer who had represented unions and individual workers in substantial class action claims, was a very good friend.

I have developed a number of good baseball friends over the years, principally the quintet of Dusty Baker, then-manager of the San Francisco Giants, *Boston Globe* sportswriter Larry Whiteside, Red Sox radio announcer Joe Castiglione, Stanford Law graduate and Seattle Mariners' president "Chuck" Armstrong (we had met watching the 1987 World Series at my Stanford house), Red Sox impresario Dr. Charles Steinberg, and Stanford coach Mark Marquess. But Angelos, particularly during our clash with the baseball owners in 1995, was as good a friend as any I possessed in baseball during those years.

After the strike ended and baseball resumed in 1995, Angelos invited me to throw out the first pitch when the Red Sox came to town to play the Orioles at Camden Yards. And when the Red Sox returned a couple of years later, he invited me to do it again, but only as we were sitting together in his box before the game. I said, "Peter, I'm not warmed up," so he sent me down to one of the team's subterranean bullpens to let me get loose. When Angelos asked me to do it again in 1998, when the Atlanta Braves were in town, I threw a perfect strike—and the crowd's roar was so loud that it startled me.

The Angelos '95 invite was the most memorable baseball occasion I've experienced, except for Jackie Robinson Day in 2006, when I threw out the opening pitch at Fenway Park in a ceremony orchestrated by Dr. Steinberg, with the first WBG's photo on the scoreboard to commemorate his diary's donation to the Massachusetts Historical Society. The '06 Fenway occasion was grand—but my pitch in '95 was much better!

Figure 11.7: Illustrative of Angelos's friendship with the author, these birthday greetings were presented on the scoreboard at Camden Yards in 1997.

Figure 11.8: The opening ceremonial first pitch in Baltimore after the strike was over in 1995.

Angelos always greeted me effusively at Camden Yards. During the NLRB years, I told him that I had to pay for any ticket because of government regulations. He responded by saying, "Buy the cheapest seat and you will always be my guest here in my box." In 2011 he arranged for me to do a signing of my new baseball book at Camden Yards, and he greeted my grandson Joey with questions and discussion of Joey's own baseball prowess around 2010.[22]

Angelos took the Baltimore Orioles to Cuba in 1999 for an exhibition game, breaking down all the barriers along the way. He also worked with me when I went to Cuba in 2012 to try do it again. I met with the Cuban baseball commissioner (as well as some star players who soon defected), saw fabulous Cuban baseball, and had discussions with Trudeau's labor partner, Roy Heenan, whom I'd met through the ABA. Regrettably, however, my efforts in Cuba came to nothing.

ADVERSARIES AND ALLIES

Harry Truman once famously said, "If you want a friend in Washington, get a dog." I thought often about this as the NLRB was besieged with attacks on our appropriations and rulemaking initiatives and other decisions by numerous luminaries of the so-called Gingrich Revolution (Jay Dickey, "Duke" Cunningham, and Ernest Ishtok are a few prominent examples) who arrived during my first year in Washington. The attacks frequently took the form of straight-out disagreement with our decisions—Senator John Ashcroft was a prominent critic, although Senator Kennedy attempted to tone him down a bit.[23]

Our problems were exacerbated by the fact that the Senate refused to confirm any new board members for three solid years, forcing President Clinton to make numerous "recess" appointments (later declared unconstitutional by a narrowly divided Supreme Court).[24] The immediate practical impact of this was to reinforce an idea long peddled by board insiders: that decisions could not issue unless the board was at full strength. An actual approach or policy of this kind was nowhere to be found in the statute itself.

President Truman's comment notwithstanding, I enjoyed a number of positive experiences in Washington. Each time we had an oral argument before the United States Supreme Court, Justice

Ginsburg would invite me and Chief Counsel Stewart to sit in her box and listen. This was a nice and educational experience for both Bill Stewart and me. I had only attended three or four oral arguments before the Supreme Court prior to my arrival in Washington.

After I departed Washington in this century, my wife and I brought then ten-year-old grandson Joey to the Supreme Court, where I told him of a 1960 oral argument I attended where debate between Justices Frankfurter and Black was so boisterous that counsel could not be heard. As my wife and I led Joey into Justice Ginsburg's chambers, toward the end of their tête-à-tête, she asked him if he had any questions about the Court and he said: "Justice Ginsburg, is it true that sometimes the justices are so loud in their discussions with one another, that the lawyers can't be heard?" "Yes," said Ruth Ginsburg in response, "sometimes that can happen." This did not appear to be the question she wanted.

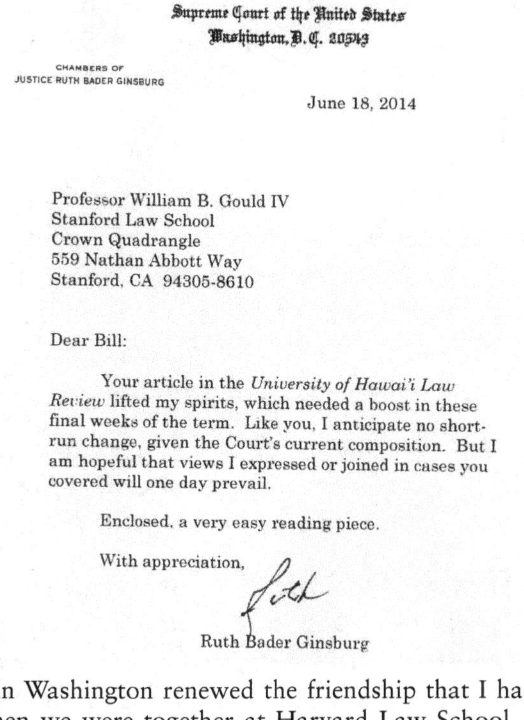

Supreme Court of the United States
Washington, D.C. 20543

CHAMBERS OF
JUSTICE RUTH BADER GINSBURG

June 18, 2014

Professor William B. Gould IV
Stanford Law School
Crown Quadrangle
559 Nathan Abbott Way
Stanford, CA 94305-8610

Dear Bill:

Your article in the *University of Hawai'i Law Review* lifted my spirits, which needed a boost in these final weeks of the term. Like you, I anticipate no short-run change, given the Court's current composition. But I am hopeful that views I expressed or joined in cases you covered will one day prevail.

Enclosed, a very easy reading piece.

With appreciation,

Ruth Bader Ginsburg

Figure 11.9: Being in Washington renewed the friendship that I had first formed with Justice Ginsburg when we were together at Harvard Law School, a friendship which would endure long after my departure from the nation's capital.

Senator Hatfield to the Rescue

The fights over my appropriations and rulemaking initiatives were considerable. Beginning in January 1995, I was testifying before appropriations and oversight committees as much as I was sitting in my office writing and reviewing drafts of opinions. But in the midst of all this, I had one friendship that was not only intrinsically rewarding but also extremely helpful in addressing some of our congressional concerns. That friendship was with Senator Mark Hatfield of Oregon, one of the five Republicans who had voted for me in March 1994.

Hatfield, a former academic himself, had received an advanced degree from Stanford University. Shortly after reading a speech I had given on Abraham Lincoln's birthday, he invited me to lunch in the Senate dining room. This association was a stroke of good fortune for me, personally and professionally, for his Senate Appropriations Committee was critical to the survival of the board. Senator Hatfield, ever a principled and thoughtful gentleman, was a student of President Lincoln and was himself genuinely Lincolnesque in demeanor, thought, and conduct. He was to be a good and valuable friend in the appropriations process during both 1995 and 1996.

The July 27, 1995, entry in my Washington diary read:

> *We [Senator Hatfield and myself] spent four or five minutes talking about the way in which his office is furnished and the shutters. He showed me the very fine craftsmanship involved with the shutters and commented about the desks, one of which had been finished in 1855. (In his office is a painting of President Lincoln) . . .*
>
> *Before I could even begin, Hatfield summarized the precise amount that we had been cut and the consequences that this would pose for us in terms of delays, closing of offices, etc.*
>
> *Senator Hatfield asked me to describe the Section 10(j) process to him, and I did so. I indicated that we had used it more frequently than our predecessors; and I pointed out to him that the opponents of labor law reform had often referred to the existence of Section 10(j) as a basis*

for addressing the delay-in-effective-remedy problem without any [need to amend] . . . the statute. I suggested that we were simply following the approach that had been suggested by the opponents of reform . . . He suggested that we meet with Senator Specter, and I said that we had such a meeting planned for the afternoon. He said that Specter was a real "liberal"—he said "Sometimes I hesitate to use that word, but I think it is important to use it." He said, "I don't like the new word, 'moderate'—it is such a pusillanimous term."

In 1996 Senator Hatfield played a role best described as follows in my diary:

September 11, 1996

Last night I attended a very fine party that Stanford University threw to honor Senator Mark Hatfield [at the Capitol]. When Senator Hatfield arrived, I was the first person that he spotted and he came over to me and said, in his usual gracious and courtly way: "Now we have another bond with one another—Stanford University!" He thanked me profusely for coming to the party, given all the work that we have in front of us. At the end of the evening, he said that he thought that I had done a great job as a "Commissioner."

Ironically, in light of our previous meetings and conversations, he was given a book on President Lincoln that has just been published by the Stanford University Press.

When . . . we were about to part, Senator Hatfield said, "Now there is one thing that I want to change in our relationship. From now, if you are agreeable, I would like it to be Mark and Bill." I mumbled something in a very inarticulate way, I'm sure, concurring with him. And so when he left he said, "Now, good night Bill." And I said, "Good night Mark"—though I felt awkward in doing so because he . . . [and] Bill Coleman are the two people that I am really in awe of in this city.

September 23, 1996

Senator Mark Hatfield telephoned me this morning with some rather somber news. He said that he had run into Senator Specter and that he had asked Specter what the budget would be for the NLRB. Specter said to him that they would have to "bring the Board into line." Hatfield inquired about this and stated that he wondered what the Board had done wrong. All the reports that he had heard were very good. Specter said that the Board was engaging in forum shopping—not his words, mine—but that we were usually looking around for good judges in pursuit of anti-business positions. Hatfield said that he would make another attempt to convince Specter that he was wrong, but he urged me to go in and see Specter and try to use whatever methods I thought would be appropriate. I said to him that I would try to reach people that Specter would listen to.

September 30, 1996

Last Saturday, September 28, I awoke in my apartment to hear the NPR broadcast that a deal had been cut on the budget between 4:00 a.m. and 6:00 a.m. that morning. After a number of phone calls in which I was unsuccessful in finding out how the agency had done, I suddenly remembered that the House was still in session debating the bill that afternoon, and I called Steve Morin in Nancy Pelosi's office. He responded by saying, "Congratulations!" He advised me that we had received $175 million-plus and that apparently this constituted about a three percent increase. He said that we had done "very well" and that we were the "most contentious part of the labor budget."

Along with Fred Feinstein, I met with [Senator Specter] in the Senate Cloakroom. Specter asked, "Why do people complain about the Board so much?" I said that one of the problems was that there had never been a consensus reached about the statute and that the agency had been attacked for years. I stated that the Supreme Court was affirming our positions and deferring to our expertise and that the circuit courts of appeals were acting in a similar fashion. Later on in the conversation, I noted the small number of dissents and reversals of precedent—the very point that I had made in the Senate oversight committee the previous week.

Specter asked us both, Feinstein and myself, whether we had met with the Republicans on the House Appropriations Committee. I told him that I had and I mentioned meetings with Congressman Porter and Congressman Riggs. Specter said, "Have you met with Congressman Dickey?" Feinstein began to laugh and Specter said, "What's so funny?" Feinstein was unable to provide a response, and Specter immediately went after him, saying that he didn't think that this was a funny matter. Feinstein assured him that he didn't think it was funny either. This was a low moment in the entire discussion.

Specter said that he had received a call from Leon Panetta about our budget and that Panetta had been very insistent upon the administration's request.

Perhaps the high point of the meeting was when, during one of the moments in which Specter was raising criticisms and concerns with me, along came Senator Hatfield, who leaned over Specter's shoulder and said, "Good afternoon Mr. Chairman, it's so good to see you!" After shaking my hand in the friendliest way, he then turned to Senator Specter and greeted him and said to me, "He is one of my best subcommittee chairmen." He [Hatfield] then went on his way. The timing couldn't have been better. Both Feinstein and I commented afterward how this had really been helpful to us with Specter.

One bad piece of news was that the rider to the legislation will stay in one single facility [precluding us from rule making which would expedite the resolution of representation cases involving a union petition for a single facility as the unit]. *Since it is an omnibus appropriations bill, apparently this will keep the rider in place and preclude us from engaging in rule making for another year.*

The tradeoff for adequate appropriations was surrender to the Republican Congress on my rule making initiatives to make the Board election process function more expeditiously. The Office of Management and Budget had asked me whether it was acceptable to give this up if we were to be granted appropriations that would permit us to function effectively. This was a no brainer for me and I gladly accepted this deal.

Figure 11.10: Senator Mark Hatfield of Oregon—one of five Republicans who voted to confirm me—proved to be my closest friend in the United States Senate.

Figure 11.11: Senator Edward Kennedy was extremely gracious and helpful to me, both at the confirmation stage as well as during my tenure in Washington.

Figure 11.12: Senator Paul Wellstone of Minnesota was one of my greatest defenders in Washington.

Figure 11.13: Here I am with President Clinton when I met him at the White House shortly after my arrival to Washington in 1994.

DEPARTURES AND DISRUPTION

Miraculously, throughout the political turmoil of 1996, we had somehow continued to issue cases. Yet in retrospect, as the diary extracts make clear, productivity was declining. The political attacks on the agency took their toll internally and were translated into inaction. The high-water mark was fiscal 1995. That year the board produced 935 cases, and we were just beginning to catch our stride. But in fiscal 1996 case production was to show the first of a number of marked declines. The first skid took us down to 709 cases.

The presidentially appointed personnel, of course, were changing. The first to go was the former chairman, James Stephens, who, like Sarah Fox and Fred Feinstein, had been a congressional staffer. When President Clinton's fortunes were lagging before the government shutdown in 1995, I said to Stephens, "If a Republican is elected, you will be chairman again." Stephens replied, "Perhaps. But first I have to get reappointed." But although he was a Washington survivor, Stephens was not able to survive in the Clinton administration. He departed in August 1995 when his term expired.

Charles Cohen's term expired in 1996, and the president replaced him with a recess appointment, Republican John Higgins. Higgins had been a recess appointment during the 1980s too, but his confirmation was blocked by the National Right to Work Committee, which considered him to be less than pure on union security issues. Initially, I thought Higgins's objective was simply to keep the Republican seat warm until his party could find their candidate—much as John Truesdale had done for me between January and March of 1994. I was later disabused of that idea: At the American Bar Association Convention in San Francisco in August 1997 he announced straightforwardly, "Bill Gould has said that the Republicans may have thrown some names across the transom for the vacancy. I hope that mine is one of them."

According to the rankings of the New York City management labor law firm of Nixon, Hargrave, Devans, and Doyle, "During his first Board term in 1988–89, Higgins voted for the union's position 82.1 percent of the time. Approximately a decade later, John Higgins voted for the employers' position 91.4 percent of the time."[25]

Like Stephens and Cohen, Higgins was tied to the rightward drift of his party and its insistence that their nominees possess all the indicia of this trend. He had no hope of Senate confirmation without an unmistakable manifestation of ideological purity. It was a pity, I always thought, that an insufficient number of Republicans were aware of the delight with which he had greeted the 1994 election results. I shall never forget the broad smile on his face when I walked into the board agenda meeting the next morning.

During 1996 the other Democrat serving with me and Margaret Browning was Sarah Fox, a former aide to Ted Kennedy. She was very smart and possessed a fiery temperament, but she also could be a very nice, warm person. For some reason—initially I thought that it was the political environment, but many on the staff believed that it was simply her inability to do the job—she could neither produce decisions nor sign off on them. She was one of the greatest crosses I had to bear while in Washington.

And we were continuously in the Republican crosshairs. The departure of Senator Hatfield from Congress and from the chairmanship of the Appropriations Committee was particularly distressing for the board. There was no one on the Republican side of the aisle who could replace him. As 1996 wound down and 1997 began, therefore, we faced a barrage of interrogatories and investigations. All too frequently, I would hear Mary Ann Sawyer exclaim as if she had been personally assaulted as she opened the most recent document sent to us from some committee chair—perhaps Hoekstra of Michigan or Shays of Connecticut. It was a stressful and trying time for all of us.

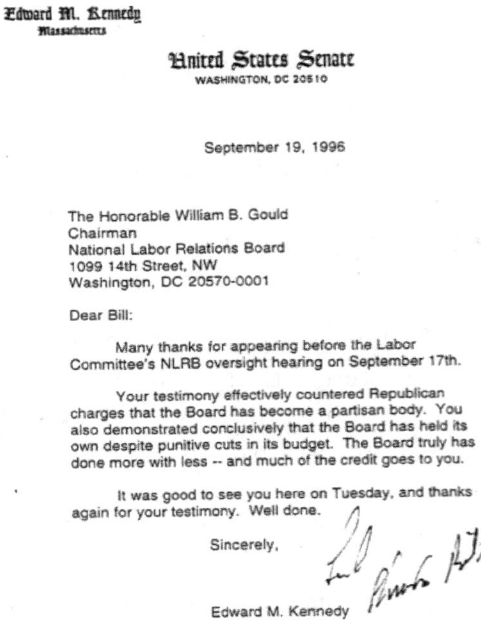

> Edward M. Kennedy
> Massachusetts
>
> United States Senate
> WASHINGTON, DC 20510
>
> September 19, 1996
>
> The Honorable William B. Gould
> Chairman
> National Labor Relations Board
> 1099 14th Street, NW
> Washington, DC 20570-0001
>
> Dear Bill:
>
> Many thanks for appearing before the Labor Committee's NLRB oversight hearing on September 17th.
>
> Your testimony effectively countered Republican charges that the Board has become a partisan body. You also demonstrated conclusively that the Board has held its own despite punitive cuts in its budget. The Board truly has done more with less -- and much of the credit goes to you.
>
> It was good to see you here on Tuesday, and thanks again for your testimony. Well done.
>
> Sincerely,
>
> Edward M. Kennedy

Figure 11.14: Like Senator Mark Hatfield, Senator Ted Kennedy was ever supportive of me and the NLRB throughout my tenure in Washington.

Travel by presidential appointees was a frequent source of Republican ire. Congressman John Boehner of Ohio began the volley in early 1996 with an attack on me and Secretary Reich. Boehner, who headed up the Republican congressional campaign, widely distributed a document entitled "Union Bosses: A Look Behind the Rhetoric." It began with the statement that the AFL-CIO had announced its intention to "steer a considerable amount of union money and resources toward the goal of reestablishing liberal Democrat [sic] control of the U.S. House of Representatives."

The document went on to describe in some detail the intent of the federation to place a hundred union activists in every congressional district in contention; it asserted that the "AFL-CIO has steadily increased the number of Republican House members who are targets for its political activities."

Moreover, on the eve of the 1996 national election, a letter embossed with the American flag—purporting to come from the House Labor Committee, but carrying neither official House letterhead nor committee members' names—excoriated me for my travel, not only leveling Shays's accusations that I attended baseball games while on NLRB business, but also alleging that in May 1994 I had gone "uninvited" to President Nelson Mandela's inauguration in South Africa. In fact, my old friend Cyril Ramaphosa, who represented the African National Congress in the constitutional negotiations that led the 1994 elections, had invited me in 1993, and I also went as an official U.S. government representative. When a formal invitation did not arrive, my staff inquired about it, and the Republicans seized on these communications as a basis for asserting that I engaged in wasteful travel.

This letter, which was distributed a week before the election, caused great concern to Congressman Tom Sawyer of Ohio, the ranking Democrat on the House Labor Oversight Committee and someone with whom I had a good deal of contact. We both saw it as a sign of what was to come after the election. Shays and Hoekstra had sent written interrogatories to all board members asking what they did with their spare time when they were out of town on speaking engagements for the board. This first step in their process seemed to imply that I was in another city simply to attend a baseball game, rather than to fulfill my board functions. Now the Republicans simply would not drop the baseball matter.

My first inclination was to respond that it was none of Congress's business what I did with my free time after my workday ended. But the Office of Management and Budget, which I consulted on all appropriations matters, dissuaded me from taking this position, and I simply avoided answering the question altogether.

The Republicans' next step was more interesting. Both Shays and Hoekstra were fascinated with my connection with Gene Orza and wanted to know all about who had attended a Cleveland–New York game we had gone to in the spring of 1996, after a lecture I gave at St. John's Law School. Their inquiry then moved in a different direction.

> *March 5*
>
> *Today I received a rather insulting and argumentative letter from Shays and Hoekstra requesting yet more information—and I got off a letter to Shays, with whom I had the most discussion about this entire baseball ticket and travel controversy, that will surely get his attention. It looks as though we are in for another battle. Shays and Hoekstra have said that since I have requested a hearing they want to give it to me. I pointed out in my letter of March 5 that they failed to state the basis for my request, their leaking of their communications to me to the* Washington Times *and another publication, which had telephoned me about the communications before I had even received them.*

In their March 4 letter, after surveying my correspondence relating to baseball tickets, Shays and Hoekstra had spent the taxpayers' money by asking the following question: "Please identify 'Dusty' by gender, position, and relationship to the San Francisco Giants, if any." The answer I provided was as follows: "Dusty Baker is a male. He is the manager of the San Francisco Giants and, in that connection, his relationship to the Giants is a prominent and important one." When I related this interrogatory to Dusty at a later point, he said "Bill, they simply wanted to see if you had a girlfriend with the Giants!"

At one point, when Orza had arranged for tickets for me at a Dodgers–Marlins game (which, of course, I paid for), he was so concerned that he considered leaving the tickets in someone else's name. This was an obsession of the Republicans, who sent me unrelenting questions about my attendance at baseball games, both professional and college. What I did with my personal time drew this comment from Major League Players Association General Counsel Gene Orza to Dusty Baker: "Dusty, it would be great to go to a baseball game with Bill Gould. But I'm afraid that if we did it, Congress would subpoena us."

After this turmoil, a great and bittersweet event took place at the board. Bill Stewart, without whom I could have accomplished nothing whatsoever at the board and in Washington, had told me of his wish to retire in early '97. That was the bad news, but it was not a huge surprise: Bill had really intended to leave at the time I came to Washington in '94, and had stayed on because of our friendship, which began when we shared office space at the board in 1963. We held a great party for him in March 1997—the night before the appropriations subcommittee hearing—at a place called "The Mansion," a very nice 1890s-style restaurant. Bill seemed pleased with everything about the party, including funny, witty, roast-like speeches by Bernie Reis and John Ferguson, career NLRB lawyers. My speech was much more straightforward and not as funny, although people seemed to receive it fairly well. There was a great deal of warmth and conviviality throughout the evening.

Figure 11.15: My Chief Counsel, Bill Stewart (whom I first met when we were junior lawyers at the NLRB in 1963), who was my most valuable contributor at the NLRB. Here I am celebrating him along with the NLRB after he received the President's Award for Distinguished Federal Civilian Service award, the greatest honor that a career civil servant can receive in Washington.

In spite of the happiness of the occasion, there is no doubt that Bill's retirement was a tremendous loss for me. When he came in earlier that week, we began going through the whole bonus business for staff, and Bill had really scurried around the agency and found the extra money for it. This is just one of the numerous things that he did besides case handling, responding to congressional inquiries, and fielding attacks on me from other board members. So in early June I was delighted to inform Bill that he had received the President's Award for Distinguished Federal Civilian Service—and he was the first employee in the NLRB's history to do so. It is the highest-ranking and most prestigious award a career federal employee can receive, and he was absolutely overjoyed. We put out a press release about it, and the news just swept through the building. Bill got a beautiful medallion to wear as well as $5,000 and a terrific party.

Few knew the difficulties I encountered with Sarah Fox and John Higgins over this matter. I had wanted to give Bill $25,000, but in order to do that I had to get the permission of Fox and Higgins. They vetoed it. Higgins was very angry about the award, saying his "nose is out of joint" over this, and claiming that the other board members' concurrence was necessary, though this simply wasn't true—I'd researched it fairly carefully. But he was quite unhappy and said, "I would like to see the justification for this."

Around the time of the celebration, I made the following comments about Bill Stewart's work:

> *This is a great day for the National Labor Relations Board—the greatest one, with the possible exception of some of our landmark Supreme Court rulings, that the agency has ever had. Bill Stewart is the finest public servant I have ever known, and I've known plenty. Since he retired in March not a day goes by that I don't think: "I wish Bill were here to help me deal with this." From the distance of his comfortable retirement, I find I appreciate and miss him all the more.*[26]

On the date of the party itself, July 3, 1997, I said:

So many of the good people at the Board were there, and many of his old pals from around Washington, including his brother and sister-in-law and niece and her husband. It really gave me a special pleasure to note again and again that Bill is the very first person in the sixty-two-year history of the agency ever to receive the award. Bill really kept this office and the Board going in the most difficult days of 1994 to 1996.

Subsequently, in October, Bill, his friend and partner Bill Dresser, and I went to the White House to meet with President Clinton. When I introduced them, I said, "Mr. President, I would like you to meet Bill Stewart and Bill Dresser. And so we really have four Bills here." Without missing a beat, President Clinton said, "Well, if we were in a lineup, then we could all say, 'Bill did it.'" We all roared!

THE HOME STRETCH

I began to move into a home stretch of my work as chairman in the late summer of 1997. I promoted Al Wolff, a careful and technically sound lawyer on my staff, to take Bill's place as chief counsel. Kate Dowling—the "wonderful Kate" as Bill Stewart called her—came on board to become deputy chief. The same age as my oldest son, she was extremely able, with plenty of zest and youthful energy. She wrote drafts of numerous important opinions for me in that last year and a half, on a group of election and postal ballot cases about which I felt strongly.

Our growing problem, however, was case production; we had come a long way down from those early days of 1994 and 1995. My last board, filled with compromise appointments negotiated with Senator Trent Lott of Mississippi, was both obstreperous and lethargic. Nevertheless, I had a good feeling about some of the cases that we were able to produce during the entire period, and I appreciated what the Congressional Democrats said about me during hearings in the summer of '97:

Mr. Towns [of New York]: In an effort to eliminate the backlog of cases, Chairman Gould has appointed an advisory panel of pro-labor and pro-management lawyers to recommend ways to improve the processing of cases and improve the agency's service to the public, and I applaud him for that. Additionally, the chairman has instituted speed teams that reduce the time and paperwork involved in hearing a case. These procedures have enabled the Board to reduce its backlog. As the Committee on Government Reform and Oversight, we should also say thank you.

Mr. Barrett [of Wisconsin]: I think you have responded very well and have given a glimmer of hope to what has been otherwise a very sad situation in my district.

Mr. Lantos [of California]: I have been enormously impressed by the Gould chairmanship of the NLRB. . . . I think you have been subjected to unfair criticism from many quarters. I have very carefully looked at and analyzed those bits of criticism and I have found them to be wanting. I think you are performing in a remarkable fashion in an almost untenable situation with only three members of a five-member Board, with two of the three members not having been confirmed. . . . So let me commend you and congratulate you, Mr. Chairman.

Mr. Sanders [of Vermont]: I just want to applaud Mr. Gould for the work that he has been doing, and I hope that this Congress can give him the staff and the associates so that he can do his job adequately.

Mr. Kucinich [of Ohio]: I have to say that Mr. Gould, among all the NLRB chairs that I have been familiar with or have read about, stands out as someone who has fearlessly defended workers' rights.[27]

CHAIRMAN OF THE BOARD   409

Figure 11.16: As this *Washington Post* cartoon indicated, the greatest cross which I had to bear in Washington related to my inability to convince other board members to issue decisions. *Washington Post*, October 31, 1997.

As the clock ticked down at the end of my term, however, there were still major cases that had been pending with us for years, still unproduced. In July 1998, I had begun to transfer some of my books, papers, and furniture back to California as my wife and I took a long drive across the country. One case emerged while I was en route, in South Dakota. This involved a union organizational campaign engaged in by the Service Employees Union. The union had distributed a campaign handbill concerning a sexual harassment investigation that included a statement by a discharged unit employee saying that "black folk have been wrongly touched by whites for over 300 years."[28] The literature was designed to emphasize minority worker solidarity in protest against sexual harassment by whites against Blacks. But all four members of the board, Democrats and Republicans, had circulated a draft invalidating the election on the ground that the union had engaged in a racially inflammatory appeal, an action prohibited by some decisions issued by the board in the sixties, when employers were trying to divide workers against one another on the basis of race.

I said that I would write a blistering dissent absolving the union of wrongdoing and upholding the validity of the election it had won. Immediately the board's unanimity dissolved, and no one voted to invalidate the election. My mission had been to embarrass them through a dissenting opinion, which exposed their outrageous position. But now I wrote a separate concurring opinion, saying:

> *Racial remarks and campaigning which takes race into account involving the employer–employee relationship are part of the reality of the workplace and therefore a legitimate campaign issue. Such appeals are germane to the solidarity and the working conditions of a racial group during an organizing campaign and accordingly are not objectionable regardless of their truth or falsity.*

In my view we reached the right decision, but the transformation of the board's position dramatized the real challenge of working with colleagues during that period of time in Washington.

Pursuing Case Action

Now, after a stay in California, it was back to the East Coast to make one final try on these cases. When I arrived back in Washington on August 17, I received two telephone calls—from representatives David Bonior of Michigan and Bernie Sanders of Vermont. (I had had a good deal of contact with Sanders during the Shays Government Reform Committee hearings the previous summer.) Both calls were very important. In retrospect, I realize that Bonior, who was worried that the *Detroit Newspapers* cases would not issue prior to my departure, had the greatest impact on the board's actions in those last few days. Both Bonior and Sanders reiterated their dissatisfaction with the board's inaction. Sanders had long been concerned about *Telescope Casual*, a lengthy strike involving the International Union of Electrical, Radio and Machine Workers (IUE) in or near his congressional district.

So, as time grew shorter, I did something I should have done much earlier. I revealed to Bonior and Sanders that Fox alone was impeding the issuance of *Detroit Newspapers* (involving a major strike in the two newspapers in that city) and *Telescope Casual*. Both asked whether they could telephone her directly to ask whether she could possibly take action; under the circumstances, I said, I thought such inquiries were completely appropriate. Immediately after their calls, Fox finally began to move and circulated the draft in *Detroit Newspapers* we had been waiting for. It affirmed the employer's duty to bargain about strike replacements. But at this point, with no more than forty-eight to seventy-two hours left in my term, the Republicans balked. They said, with some justification, that they could not respond to Fox's views in such a short period of time. Nonetheless, we reached a consensus allowing the other portions of the case to issue. The other three continuing board members took no position on the issue in her draft and severed it for subsequent adjudication.

Therefore, on August 27, *Detroit Newspapers* was finally issued. The board held, unanimously—both Democrats and Republicans—that the employer had committed unfair labor practices and that, inasmuch as such conduct had caused a prolonged strike, the strikers were unfair labor practice strikers entitled to reinstatement. The majority of the Board also (1) held that the employer's attempt to modify or withdraw from multi-union joint bargaining on one or more particular bargaining subjects was not an unfair labor practice; (2) affirmed the administrative law judge's dismissal of another aspect of the complaint; and (3) unanimously affirmed the administrative law judge's ruling that the employer had refused to bargain in good faith by unilaterally implementing its proposals regarding merit pay and television assignments and by its refusal to furnish the Newspaper Guild with requested information regarding both merit pay and overtime-exemption proposals. Finally, the board, over my dissent, refused to address the employer's duty to bargain with the union with regard to the conditions of employment for strike replacements. It is ironic that when it did so the following spring, the vote was three to two to uphold the employer's position on this issue. Had the work been done—as it should have been—the preceding summer, the vote would have been three to two in favor of my position, inasmuch as both Fox and Liebman dissented from the March 1999 decision.

The burst of activity in that final week made it possible for us to issue forty-seven cases on my last day in office, August 27, and for a good number to go out in the days immediately before. Quite a number of them were "old dogs" that had been pending with us for many years; some were cases involving important policy issues; and some were both old and important. In one, I stood in solitary dissent in favor of concerted activity rights for unorganized workers which were comparable to those enjoyed by their organized counterparts.[29]

One of them was the case Representative Sanders was interested in, *Telescope Casual Furniture, Inc.*[30] In it I joined Hurtgen to dismiss a complaint involving the lawfulness of an employer's bargaining tactic. The employer had made a final offer accompanied by a threat to implement an alternative position containing more onerous terms if the final offer was rejected. Almost two years earlier, I had written a concurring opinion in which I noted that although this employer had utilized the exact same tactic on numerous previous occasions, the parties had then resolved their differences without a strike. I nonetheless viewed the tactic as distasteful:

> *I do not like the employer's tactics in this case and, like Member Liebman [dissenting], I do not find them to be conducive to good industrial relations. Indeed, my personal view is that impasse—a concept inherently vague and thus conducive to perilous litigation for both sides—and unilateral implementation weight the scales against the labor movement improperly in a democratic pluralistic society such as ours. But, we are obliged to subordinate our personal views to the rule of law.*[31]

I am quite confident that Bernie Sanders's union constituents did not like my opinion upholding the employer's position. But, as Sanders had said to me, "I don't care how the decision comes out. I just believe that I'm entitled for it to issue." That was my view too. Moreover, Sanders's intervention, like that of Bonior, was nothing like the incessant attempts of Senate and House Republicans to influence the substance of our decisions. In this respect, they distinguished themselves fundamentally from the House Republicans, who not only advised the board about what to decide but also about when not to decide it.

Meanwhile, however, we were able to issue a number of decisions of consequence. First amongst them would be our rulings on the availability of postal ballots in NLRB-conducted elections, culminating in *San Diego Gas and Electric*.[32] I was also very proud of our ruling in *Novotel New York*,[33] which held that union litigation on matters such as minimum wage and fair employment practices prohibiting discrimination could be engaged in without characterization as a "benefit" which would otherwise interfere with a conduct of an election. I thought that this was particularly important, given the need for unions to show workers what they can do in the employment arena. At the same time, now, more than a quarter of a century later, it seems obvious that unions have not taken advantage of this ruling in many situations.

I was also particularly pleased that we issued rulings on the employment relationship itself, addressing employer attempts to deprive workers of employee status and benefits, as has become frequent in this so-called gig economy. Our rulings were in trucking and created a presumption in favor of employment status.[34]

My board held that private employers that are government contractors are always within the board's jurisdiction and protection.[35] Prior to our ruling, the question of jurisdiction was confusing and case by case. And in a case that had implications for the bargaining process, a board majority held that an employer could not unilaterally implement merit pay proposals, even when bargaining had taken place to the point of impasse. The board said that if the employer was given carte blanche authority over wage increases without regard to time, standards criteria instituted would be "so inherently destructive of the fundamental principles of collective bargaining that it could not be sanctioned as part of a doctrine created to break impasse and restore active collective bargaining." The majority went on to say: "We are preserving an employer's right to bargain to impasse over proposals to retain management discretion over merit pay while, at the same time, maintaining the Guild's opportunity to negotiate terms and conditions of employment."[36]

In another case that the Supreme Court would ultimately reverse in a ruling in this century, we held that because undocumented workers are employees within the meaning of the act, they are entitled to back pay when a violation of the act has been committed.[37] And ultimately, in a case involving the ability of workers to object to dues expenditures for political purposes, we held in a series of decisions that the union must provide information about the obligation to object to such expenditures—but we held that the burden was upon the objecting worker to protest.[38] During my first year or so at the board, this was all or most of what Republican congressmen wanted to address in their hearings. "When are these decisions going to issue?" they would ask. When they finally issued, the Republicans were none too pleased: They didn't agree with placing the burden upon objecting workers to protest, since more protests or the presumption that unions were suppressing worker rights would more easily disrupt union security agreements. Since some employers didn't want such agreements, the Republicans didn't want the burden placed upon workers who would do the employer's bidding.

Finally, I thought that one of our early decisions involving union criticisms of management was particularly important. In *Caterpillar, Inc.*[39] a majority of the board held, in affirming the administrative law judge, that the employer violated Section 8(a)(1) by prohibiting its employees from displaying various union slogans that included a statement—"Permanently Replace Fites"—suggesting that the company president rather than striking workers should be ousted, and violated Section 8(a)(3) by enforcing the rule. The board agreed with the administrative law judge that the slogan was a response to the employer's stated policy of using permanent replacements, rather than an attempt to cause the removal of Fites as the chief executive officer. But, even if they were attempting to remove the chief executive officer, the board's view was that the conduct was protected. I concurred in a separate opinion expressing dissatisfaction with board and court precedent with respect to employee activity which seeks to influence management policy and its protected status. I said:

> *The level of managerial policy or hierarchy protested by the union or employees should have little if anything to do with whether such employee activity is protected. Quite obviously, the level at which managerial representatives are involved in employment conditions will vary from company to company. While I am of the view that concerted activity for the purpose of influencing management policy, which is unrelated to employment conditions, is not protected under the Act, the fact of the matter is that the presence or absence of a particular corporate hierarchical structure or internal organization does not provide the appropriate answer to the question of whether employee activity is protected under Section 7 of the Act.*[40]

Support from the Courts

While the board is the expert agency in labor law matters, ultimately it is dependent upon the courts to obtain enforcement. I was particularly pleased with a number of rulings in which the appellate court either took account of my separate concurring opinion, as the Seventh Circuit did in a successorship ruling,[41] or, as the D.C.[42] and Ninth Circuit[43] did, took my side where I had dissented. In one instance, a D.C. Circuit dissent[44] picked up and supported my own separate opinion, and in a ruling by the Court of Appeals for the Eighth Circuit in a case involving work stoppages which had not been authorized by the exclusive bargaining representative,[45] the court said:

> *Unfortunately, the Board has not followed Chairman Gould's sound advice regarding the Supreme Court's controlling interpretation of the relationship between Section 7, Section 8(a)(1), and Section 9(a) in* Emporium Capwell. *In this case, for example, both the panel majority and dissent stated that the Board determines whether an unauthorized work stoppage is protected "by considering (1) whether the employees were attempting to bypass their union and bargain directly with the employer, and (2) whether the employees' position was inconsistent with the union's position."* [citation omitted] *Here, the ten employees questioned management whether Noah's Ark was complying with terms and conditions of the holdover CBA. Without question, as Chairman Gould explained, the Union would share the employees' substantive position on this issue.*
>
> *Indeed, the Union's duty as exclusive representative arguably required it to pursue the employees' position, by grievance or otherwise. Thus, if the Board had held that the employees' work stoppage was protected concerted activity* merely because *it was not inconsistent with the Union's unstated position on this issue, we would decline to enforce this part of the Board's order as inconsistent with the Supreme Court's decision in* Emporium Capwell.[46]

Rewards

My tenure in Washington was undoubtedly tumultuous, given the tensions of divided government and extreme political polarization, which were mirrored in a frequently dysfunctional administrative agency. Nonetheless, the experience had its rewards. I was particularly proud when, as I was celebrating my fiftieth anniversary at Stanford Law School, President Clinton wrote me and said:

> *I will always be grateful I could convince you to spend four years in Washington as Chairman of the National Labor Relations Board. Your outstanding service brought new vision and purpose to the NLRB at a time of momentous*

economic and social change, and millions are better off today because of it. And perhaps most important of all—you saved baseball![47]

I was able to shape some of our nation's labor jurisprudence. And, as can be seen in some of the final cases I've described, I was able to reach the judiciary itself more effectively than I could have done through writings alone. Moreover, despite the occasional nastiness of the political process, I found some of my contact with the executive and legislative branches to be stimulating and instructive, particularly given my interest in politics since my high school days. Finally, I was able to bring back to Stanford not only new insights and stories for my classes and writings, but also involvement in some key dispute resolution arenas.

NOTES

[1] The two paragraphs are taken from *Labored Relations*.
[2] I've discussed the board personnel in more detail in *Labored Relations*, 55–57.
[3] Gould, *Labored Relations*, 56–57.
[4] *San Diego Gas & Electric*, 325 NLRB 1143, 1146 (1998) (Chairman Gould, concurring).
[5] Gould, *Labored Relations*, 90.
[6] "NLRB Seeks Contempt Citation against UMW for Strike Misconduct," *Daily Labor Report*, May 6, 1994.
[7] Harry Bernstein, "Coal Miners Get the Shaft from the NLRB: The Board's New Chairman, a Liberal, Takes a Tough Stance against Workers," *Los Angeles Times*, July 5, 1994.
[8] Gould, *Labored Relations*, 93.
[9] Gould, *Labored Relations*, 102.
[10] Chass, "Labor Secretary's Plea Is Hardly a Solution," *New York Times*, August 9, 1994.
[11] Chass, "Next Two Weeks Critical for Salvaging Season," *New York Times*, August 29, 1994.
[12] "Selig, Angelos Unite in Praising Clinton," *Washington Post*, January 27, 1995; Claire Smith, "Orioles Say They Won't Play without Regulars," *New York Times*, January 20, 1995; "A Sane Baseball Owner," *New York Times*, January 25, 1995.
[13] Gould, *Labored Relations*, 109–111.
[14] Gould, *Labored Relations*, 114–115.
[15] Gould, *Labored Relations*, 116–117.
[16] *Silverman v. MLB Player Relations Committee, Inc.*, 880 F. Supp. 246 (S.D.N.Y. 1995).
[17] William B. Gould IV, *Bargaining with Baseball: Labor Relations in an Age of Prosperous Turmoil* (Jefferson: McFarland, 2011), 46–47.
[18] Alex Speier, "To Former Labor Board Chair, MLB's Acrimony is Unlike What's Come Before. That's a Good Thing," *Boston Globe*, March 2, 2022.
[19] Speier, "To Former Labor Board Chair."

20. John Shea, "Owners Use More Muscle Than '94: Former NLRB Chief Says Deal not Improbable," *San Francisco Chronicle*, March 6, 2022.
21. Alex Traub and Emmett Lindner, "Peter G. Angelos, Owner of the Baltimore Orioles, Dies at 94," *New York Times*, March 23, 2024.
22. William B. Gould IV, *Bargaining with Baseball: Labor Relations in an Age of Prosperous Turmoil* (Jefferson: McFarland, 2011).
23. Gould, *Labored Relations*, 154–155.
24. NLRB v. Noel Canning, 573 U.S. 513 (2014); NLRB v. New Process Steel, 560 U.S. 674 (2010).
25. Employment & Law Alert, no. 44 (April 1998): 8.
26. Gould, *Labored Relations*, 361.
27. U.S. Congress, House, Hearings of the Government Reform and Oversight Subcommittee on Human Resources, 105th Cong. (1997) (unpublished).
28. *Shepherd Tissue, Inc.*, 326 NLRB 369, 369 (1998) (Chairman Gould, concurring).
29. *Myth, Inc.*, 326 N.L.R.B. 136 (1998).
30. *Telescope Casual Furniture, Inc.*, 326 NLRB 588, 589 (1998) (Chairman Gould, concurring). See also my concurring opinion in White Cap Inc., 325 NLRB 1166, 1170 (1998), pet. for review denied, No. 99-1118, 2000 U.S. App. LEXIS 4686 (D.C. Cir. March 24, 2000), which stressed freedom-of-contract principles.
31. Gould, *Labored Relations*, 592.
32. *San Diego Gas & Electric*, 325 NLRB 218 (1998).
33. *Novotel New York*, 321 NLRB 624 (1996).
34. *Dial-A-Mattress* 326 NLRB 884, 894 (1998) (Chairman Gould, dissenting); *Roadway Package System, Inc.*, 326 NLRB 842, 854 (1998) (Chairman Gould, concurring).
35. *Management Training Corp.*, 317 NLRB 1355 (1995).
36. *McClatchy Newspapers, Inc.*, 321 NLRB 1386 (1996), enfd. den. 1026 (DC Cir. 1997).
37. *A.P.R.A. Fuel Oil Buyers Group, Inc.*, 320 NLRB 308 (1995), enfd. 134 F.3d 50 (2d Cir. 1997).
38. *California Saw & Knife*, 320 NLRB 224 (1995), enfd. sub nom. Assn. of International Machinists v. NLRB, 133 F.3d 1012 (7th Cir. 1998); *Paperworkers Local 1033* (Weyerhaeuser Paper Co.), 320 NLRB 349 (1995).
39. *Caterpillar, Inc.*, 321 NLRB 1178, 1184 (1996) (Chairman Gould, concurring).
40. Gould, *Labored Relations*, 1184.
41. Canteen Corp. v. NLRB, 103 F.3d 1355 (7th Cir. 1997) (Chairman Gould, concurring).
42. Speedrack Products Group, Ltd. v. NLRB, 114 F.3d 1276 (D.C. Cir. 1997) (Chairman Gould, dissenting).
43. TCI W., Inc. v. NLRB, 145 F.3d 1113 (9th Cir. 1998) (Chairman Gould, dissenting).
44. Warshawsky & Co. v. NLRB, 182 F.3d 948 (D.C. Cir. 1999) (Wald, J., dissenting).
45. NLRB v. Noah's Ark Processors, LLC, 31 F.4th 1097 (8th Cir. 2022).
46. Id at 1104–1106.
47. President William Jefferson Clinton, letter to author, October 19, 2023.

12

RETURN TO CALIFORNIA: WRITERS, BUS DRIVERS, FARM WORKERS, AND MORE

As my Washington term was winding down, I telephoned Walter Dellinger, ex-Justice Department Director of the Office of Policy, who had already departed the Clinton administration to return to Duke Law School. Anticipating my return to Stanford, I asked him how he had managed the transition back to the academic world. "It's fine," Dellinger said. "There's only one problem." When I asked him what that was, he said, "On my own, I'm my own administrative assistant."

Except for some very able research assistants at Stanford Law School, I was now on my own, too. In Washington, as chairman of one of FDR's alphabet agencies, it was quite different. With Bill Stewart and Mary Ann Sawyer at my side—and a dynamic young deputy chief, Kate Dowling, coming into one of the top positions after Bill's departure—I had never been so well protected. This was my overriding thought as I made the long drive across the country and returned to Stanford to complete a book about my Washington experience.

Though I was now without Bill and Mary Ann—I miss them both to this very day!—I was fortunate in my selection of a new Stanford research assistant. One of the best of them, he was, the extraordinarily talented William Adams, who responded to my concerns about a particular piece of research by saying, "We can do anything we want!" He always made it seem as though we could.

Returning to Stanford meant returning to writing and teaching. I also began to give a series of papers and speeches about labor law reform, often expressing more skepticism than in the past about what law could do to reform labor–management relations.[1] I can recall my old nemesis, Richard Trumka, in the audience, scowling as I encouraged legislative answers to labor law reform that were more modest than those Trumka himself advocated.[2] My legislative solutions did not square with his idea (and that of many others) that the only problem causing union decline was the law.

But beyond my speeches and scholarly articles, there were new assignments. Most of them tapped directly into my NLRB quasi-adjudicative work. The first of these was an internal dispute involving the Writers Guild of America of the West, based in Los Angeles.

THE 2003 WRITERS GUILD ELECTION DISPUTE

In October 2003, the Writers Guild of America, West, a labor union for professional writers, asked me to provide recommendations in a variety of disputes arising out the conduct of their most recent election. The matter was rather critical, given the fact that the guild was about to commence contract negotiations with the Alliance of Motion Picture and Television Producers, which represents the studio and television networks, and the guild felt the need to resolve outstanding issues before starting those negotiations.

After I accepted their request to provide recommendations, I began to hold hearings arising out of a written protest on October 6, setting forth twelve or thirteen challenges to the election and its procedure on November 7, 2003, concluding on December 1. I took statements or testimony of fifteen witnesses at the guild offices in Los Angeles.

The guild and some of its individual members filed briefs on a variety of issues, but the most prominent of them involved the eligibility of the guild's recently reelected president to stand for that reelection. The president, Victoria Riskin, was a rather prominent person in the movie and television world, as she was "the daughter of Academy Award-winning writer Robert Riskin, whose credits include 'It Happened One Night,' and actress Fay Wray, best known for starring in 'King Kong.' Riskin [was] married to a longtime writer and guild activist, David Rintels."[3] Other issues before me involved (1) procedures established by the guild providing for suggestions through notices mailed to members only in the case of board member elections; (2) the layout in the union newspaper as it related to the election; (3) the propriety of Ms. Riskin's "State of the Union" message; (4) the propriety of endorsements of candidates for union office; (5) the question of whether the Labor–Management Reporting and Disclosure Act (LMRDA) places an affirmative obligation upon a union to inform the membership of their right to inspect the membership lists. All these issues were presented to me, and I concluded that there were no statutory or constitutional violations.

But the big issue involved Ms. Riskin herself and her eligibility to run for reelection. I held that she had not properly maintained her membership status, which required employment prior to the election. I concluded that the plain meaning of the union constitution itself must control, and that Ms. Riskin had not been a member in good standing continuously from September 18, 2002, until September 18, 2003, as required. I said in my opinion:

> *Since she was not a member in good standing during this period of time because of the fact that her current membership lapsed on July 1, as reflected in a failure to submit evidence of compensation by August 4, Ms. Riskin was ineligible for office. Accordingly, the election for President of the Guild on September 19, must be set aside ... With regard to President, this means that under Article V B, Sec. 6, should the Board follow my recommendation and conclude, as I have, that Ms. Riskin was not eligible to be on the ballot on September 19, there would now be a "permanent vacancy in the Presidency of the Guild" and that therefore the "Vice President shall succeed to the Presidency and serve until the next election of officers." My recommendation to the Board is that this take place on January 6 or*

soon thereafter as is practicable so that the Vice President may take up the responsibilities of President at the earliest possible date.[4]

The immediate consequences of my ruling were considerable. It understates the matter to say that Ms. Riskin, and particularly her lawyer, were not pleased with my decision. Riskin resigned, but the union implemented my recommendations and collective bargaining with the alliance commenced subsequent to Ms. Riskin's resignation.[5]

THE FIRSTGROUP INDEPENDENT MONITOR PROGRAM

A second major assignment was of a very different order. In August of 2007, Washington lawyer Joseph Turzi telephoned me to say that a client, FirstGroup, a British transportation company with facilities in the United States employing more than 100,000 workers, was interested in sounding me out on the question of whether I might review labor issues that had arisen inside the company. As a result, I met with company CEO Sir Moir Lockhead in New York City in November. Lockhead, who was the first member of his family to work outside of the mines in Scotland, told me that he wanted me to serve as an independent monitor to resolve issues arising in union organizing in the United States which would involve "freedom of association" matters. Lockhead told me at our New York meeting that, given my work at the NLRB in the 1990s and the independence I had displayed there while promoting freedom of association, he thought that the problems confronting the company were particularly relevant to the assignment that he asked me to accept: the independent resolution of these matters for the company's American operations. After much discussion with him that day, I accepted the assignment. I also eventually enlisted the help of some first-rate Stanford talent: Andrew Oljenik, Lee Goldman, and Regina Petty, my students from a number of years ago, acted as investigators and prepared draft reports for me.

My start date was to be January 1, 2008. I met with Turzi as well as FirstGroup America labor counsel Mary Schotmiller in Palo Alto, at Turzi's law firm's office, and we began to hammer out the procedural details. In the first place, the new FirstGroup policy was designed to contrast sharply with employer arbitration systems created under the Federal Arbitration Act. There would be no attempt to substitute for all or most statutory NLRB procedures, though the idea was to replicate some of its functions. No deference to this system by the NLRB was intended, given the fact that FirstGroup had created the program unilaterally, unlike grievance-arbitration machinery negotiated between unions and employers. There were a number of unions which sought to organize FirstGroup workers and neither the company nor I had any interest in influencing the identity of unions that could or would organize.

The policy and program were, in substantial part, aimed at avoidance of the delay inherent in NLRB-judicial litigation. Simultaneously, the idea was to remove some of the acrimony enmeshed in alleged anti-union behavior by devising a policy of neutrality, in which FirstGroup pledged not to campaign against the unions or to use anti-union campaign material. The program did not purport to devise a new recognition system, such as authorization cards or private elections, and it did not regulate the bargaining process itself, subsequent to recognition. The program was designed to integrate itself into the system of NLRB ballot elections and to more effectively and expeditiously allow employee free choice to be realized within the NLRB system.

The background for this approach is as follows: FirstGroup plc is a British company that claims to be the leading transport operator in the United Kingdom and North America, with revenues of over £6.4 billion.[6] The company employs more than 125,000 staff throughout the U.K. and North America and transports about 2.5 billion passengers each year. The company grew out of the deregulation of bus services in the U.K. In 1989, employees of a municipal bus operator (Grampian Regional Transport) for Aberdeen,

Scotland, bought the company under an Employee Share Ownership Plan. The company acquired several other formerly nationalized bus companies in England and Scotland and merged with the Badgerline Group in June 1995 to form First Bus. First Bus continued to grow by acquiring other English, Welsh, and Scottish nationalized operators and changed its name to FirstGroup plc in 1998, when it acquired railway businesses after the U.K. privatized the railway industry.

In 1999, FirstGroup plc sought to strengthen and diversify its business by acquiring Ryder Public Transportation in the United States. The purchase made FirstGroup America, a wholly owned subsidiary of FirstGroup plc, the second largest operator of school buses in the United States and a leading provider of transit management and vehicle maintenance services. FirstGroup plc viewed the Ryder purchase as a strategic step that would allow it to take advantage of, and apply its public transportation experience and expertise in, the U.S. market. Then, on February 7, 2007, the company agreed to purchase Laidlaw International, Inc. for $3.6 billion. Laidlaw was the largest operator of yellow school buses in the U.S. It also provided transit services and owned and operated Greyhound. The deal closed on September 30, 2007, making FirstGroup America's school bus unit (First Student) the leading student transportation provider in North America, serving more than 1,500 school districts with more than 60,000 buses. The deal also increased operations at the transit management unit (First Transit), which employs 15,500 people and operates 7,000 buses out of 235 locations in 41 states, Canada, and Puerto Rico. FirstGroup retained the Greyhound name and planned to identify strategic opportunities to develop the Greyhound business.

FirstGroup Attracts Labor Union Attention

When FirstGroup plc acquired Ryder in 1999, some of the facilities that it inherited were already organized by several different unions. Those unions were also involved in organizing other former Ryder locations. Shortly after the Ryder purchase, the International Brotherhood of Teamsters contacted colleagues in one of Great Britain's largest trade unions, the Transport and General Workers Union (TGWU)—which represented bus workers at FirstGroup's U.K. facilities—to gather information about FirstGroup. Over the next few years, representatives from the TGWU, the Teamsters, the International Transport Workers' Federation (ITWF), and others met to discuss FirstGroup's business. That business included a Corporate Social Responsibility Policy (CSR Policy), implemented in 2001, which incorporated international standards of corporate governance and individual rights embodied in several different international declarations and codes. One of the many principles in the CSR Policy states:

> *Employees have the rights of freedom of association and collective bargaining. We respect the right of our employees to choose whether or not to join a trade union without influence or interference from management. Furthermore we support the right of our employees to exercise that right through a secret ballot.*

Beginning in 2004, several unions used FirstGroup plc's public commitment to the CSR Policy to exert pressure on the company to alter what the unions considered to be anti-union conduct by managers at FirstGroup America. The Teamsters, the TGWU, and the Service Employees International Union held rallies at FirstGroup offices in the U.K. and the U.S. They worked with a U.K. lobbyist to communicate their positions to members of Parliament, and they hosted a week-long fact-finding mission to the U.S. for three British government officials. They also communicated their complaints about FirstGroup America's anti-union behavior (and about low wages and benefits) directly to FirstGroup plc's shareholders. The Teamsters also commissioned several studies of alleged violations of rights of freedom of association under international human rights law.

Throughout the campaign, FirstGroup plc repeatedly dismissed the unions' allegations as propaganda and accused the unions of bullying its school bus drivers into becoming union members. Meanwhile, in communications to shareholders, the company claimed to be neutral on the issue of unionization, and it went so far as to commission a former member of Parliament to give an independent view on the company's operations. At the same time, it committed in principle to eradicating any alleged anti-union behavior at its U.S. operations.

In 2007, the company issued to its management an internal policy on employee relations that expressed a neutral view on union membership. That policy served as the model for the Freedom of Association (FoA) Policy, which was released to employees in 2008. The FoA Policy stated that the company was committed to supporting the following employee rights: (1) freedom of association, (2) a secret ballot election, (3) an informed choice, and (4) a representative voter turnout. In addition, the FoA Policy expressed management's commitment not to engage in anti-union conduct. It stated: "Management shall not act in any way which is or could reasonably be perceived to be anti-union. This includes refraining from making derisive comments about unions, publishing or posting pamphlets, fliers, letters, posters, or any other communication which should be interpreted as criticism of the union or advises employees to vote 'no' against the union." The FoA Policy also reserved the company's right to provide employees with factual data relevant to election issues. It stated, "We believe that employees should be able to make an informed choice and therefore management may provide balanced factual information to assist its employees in making that choice."

The objective of the FoA Policy was "to manage [the company's] business in support of [its] employees and the above rights and to refrain from management conduct, whether written or verbal, which is intended to influence an employee's view or choice with regard to labor union representation. In particular, during union organizing campaigns, management shall support the employee's individual right to choose whether to vote for or against union representation without influence or interference from management."

But how would the program work as a practical matter? At the time that the program was initiated, it was unclear whether the unions would accept and use this unilaterally implemented Alternative Dispute Resolution (ADR) program and whether employees and front-line managers would know about it.

Prior to January 2008, Lockhead sent a letter to FirstGroup shareholders notifying them of my appointment as the Independent Monitor (IM). He also sent a letter to Teamster president James P. Hoffa Jr., announcing the adoption of the program.

Mr. Hoffa's reply expressed serious concerns regarding FirstGroup's adoption of the IM Program. Although he said that the Teamsters welcomed an Independent Monitor and were pleased with my appointment, he worried that the program would fail (as had previous company monitoring efforts) without "robust" processes in place to ensure implementation and enforcement. Mr. Hoffa also questioned the company's decision to adopt the program unilaterally, without seeking a dialogue with the Teamsters. Later that month, I met with representatives of the Teamsters' Organizing Department to explain the IM Program's procedures. At that meeting, the Teamster representatives raised questions about the program but expressed considerable support for the process.

Although the Teamsters had not yet accepted the IM Program, on January 25, 2008, Lockhead referred two previously received Teamster complaints to the IM Program. Soon thereafter, the Teamsters filed several complaints with the Independent Monitor alleging FoA Policy violations at a number of First Student facilities.

To emphasize to FirstGroup America's senior managers the importance of the IM Program, at a management meeting in February 2008 (in Boston), Lockhead advised these managers that if any of them objected to the FoA Policy or the IM Program, then they could simply resign. To make frontline managers, union organizers, and employees aware of the IM Program, the company and I took the following steps.

On April 25, 2008, the company mailed a letter I wrote to more than 81,000 FirstGroup America employees throughout the U.S. describing the IM Program, the complaint procedure, and the machinery attached to it. This letter was accompanied by a supportive letter from Dean Finch, then Chief Operating Officer for FirstGroup America. Because this communication was brief—just two pages—it seemed to have caught the attention of many employees.

Next, every FirstGroup America facility was outfitted with a glass-enclosed bulletin board on which the FoA Policy and an overview of the IM Program were posted. These documents provided contact information for the IM Program in the event an employee wanted literature about the program or additional information. They also informed employees that this material could be obtained from their local manager.

The company also conducted an internet-based training program for FirstGroup America managers. The training program explained the FoA Policy and IM Program, described what managers could and could not do, recommended actions that managers should take, and advised managers that failure to comply with any aspect of the FoA Policy or IM Program would subject the managers to discipline, up to and including discharge.

Then, in June 2008, the company attached a short letter about the IM Program to employee paychecks. It also added to the employee handbook a copy of the FoA Policy, a description and overview of the IM Program, and a complaint form. The company also created a DVD describing the FoA Policy and the IM Program, which it showed to employees at monthly safety meetings. In the video, Mike Murray, then CEO of Operations for FirstGroup America, explained the FoA Policy and why it was important to the company. I also appeared on the DVD and explained the IM Program's complaint, investigation, and reporting procedures.

Finally, I established a website through which employees and others could: (1) find answers to frequently asked questions about the IM Program, (2) download program documents (including a complaint form), (3) submit a complaint, and (4) learn more about the team of investigators.

I met with senior company representatives and members of the board of directors at a series of meetings in London. I also reported on the program's development to a shareholders meeting in Aberdeen, as the unions had campaigned against the company's labor practice in that forum in the past.

The program continued for three years, until the company terminated it effective December 31, 2010, due to a decrease in the number of complaints filed with the program, a decrease in nonunionized company facilities, national negotiations between the company and the Teamsters, and the retirement of Lockhead. Ultimately, in June 2011, FirstGroup and the Teamsters negotiated a national agreement for school bus drivers.[7]

Overview of the IM Program

After an unsuccessful half century of efforts to reform and revise the NLRA itself, the FirstGroup initiative represented the most comprehensive effort to augment NLRA policies through such measures as employer neutrality and a more expeditious use of the NLRB ballot box. FirstGroup's FoA Policy and IM Program were designed to promote employee rights against the backdrop of public law, including the principles of: (1) the NLRA as defined by the NLRB and the U.S. Supreme Court during the previous 75 years,[8] and (2) international labor law as reflected in Conventions 87 and 98 of the International Labor Organization.[9] A basic premise of the IM Program was that the union recognition process would continue to proceed through the NLRB's secret ballot box election process rather than any form of card check alternative. Matters involving alleged management interference with union organizing and related anti-union conduct would be handled by the IM Program. A key assumption of the IM Program was that resolving freedom of association complaints would reduce or even eliminate impediments to free and fair union elections—and would do so faster and under standards more rigorous than those provided by the NLRA.

Another premise of the IM Program was that the right not to associate was subsumed in the right of association contained in the FoA Policy and the NLRA. Therefore, FirstGroup plc and its subsidiaries were obliged to remain neutral and favor neither side in the union organizing campaign. In addition, because no union was a signatory to the IM Program, the Independent Monitor had jurisdiction over only employer conduct, not union conduct that occurred away from the workplace. (Nonetheless, in some reports and letters, I urged nonemployee union organizers, who in my opinion interfered with the right, to refrain from such conduct.)

IM Program Process

The principal components of FirstGroup's IM Program were the following. Any FirstGroup employee, representative of an employee, or labor union that represented or was seeking to represent the employees could file a complaint—with or without supporting written materials—with the Independent Monitor, alleging one or more violations of the FoA Policy. The complaint form was only two pages long, and it requested basic factual information about the complaining party, the date and location of the incident, a description of the alleged violation, and the names of witnesses. Complaints needed to be submitted within sixty days of the alleged violation, and submitting a complaint did not affect the right to file an unfair labor practice (ULP) charge or to complain to any public agency. A copy of each complaint was furnished to the company, which could respond to the complaint and submit written materials. Complaining parties could file a complaint anonymously or request that their identity be treated as confidential. The Independent Monitor honored such requests after redacting the employee's identity from information submitted to the company.

The Independent Monitor investigated any complaints and reported findings to the company and the complaining party, generally within thirty to sixty days of the filing of the complaint. When a complaint was filed, the Independent Monitor immediately notified senior executives and assigned it to an investigator, who contacted the complaining party to introduce himself or herself. The investigator then described the process and gathered additional information about the complaint. The investigator contacted the complaining party's manager and relevant witnesses to gather information. None of the interviews was taken under oath.

Depending on the scope of the complaint and the factual disputes at issue (if any), the investigator then either scheduled an on-site investigation or continued to conduct the investigation telephonically. Both sides had the opportunity, but were not required, to submit written materials in support of or in opposition to the complaint.

After the investigation and generally within thirty days, the investigator prepared a preliminary report for the Independent Monitor that laid out the facts of the case. The Independent Monitor sometimes requested additional investigation. The IM then analyzed the facts and prepared a final report for the complaining party and the company addressing whether there had been a violation of the FoA Policy. If the Independent Monitor found a violation of the FoA Policy, he made recommendations for actions to be taken by the company to cure the violation.

The company had to decide how to respond to the Independent Monitor's recommendations. It did not have to accept any recommendations. Within thirty days it could adopt, reject, or modify them. It could decide to accept some recommendations and reject the rest from the same report. To provide transparency, the company would send its response to the report to both the Independent Monitor and the complaining party.

Finally, the Independent Monitor periodically reported to the Board of Directors of FirstGroup plc regarding his activities and findings with respect to the FoA Policy and IM Program.

Use of the IM Program

During the IM Program's three-year tenure I, acting as Independent Monitor, received complaints alleging 372 violations of the FoA Policy and issued 143 written reports. Complaints alleged, among other things, that a manager or supervisor discriminated against an employee based on union activity, made anti-union comments, enforced overly broad no talking, solicitation, and distribution rules, or prohibited the wearing of union insignia.

Of the 372 alleged violations, thirty-two were withdrawn prior to the issuance of a report, and seventy-two were found to be outside my IM jurisdiction because they asserted general workplace grievances that did not involve union activity, or were not filed within sixty days of the incident, as required by the program. In those instances, I informed the complaining party of the company's confidential employee hotline.

Slightly over one-half of the complaints were filed by employees, while the rest were filed mainly by unions. Five complaints were referred to the program directly by the company. The vast majority arose from First Student facilities—where the greatest amount of union organizing occurred. However, complaints were also filed with respect to First Transit, First Services, Greyhound, and First Canada facilities.

I found sixty-seven FoA Policy violations and made 152 recommendations. The company adopted 51 percent of those recommendations, modified sixteen percent of them, and rejected 33 percent of them.

Strengths of the Program

The following characteristics of the IM Program contributed to its general success and use by employees and unions alike, increased awareness of freedom of association rights, and led to management training and a modified culture within FirstGroup America.

First, the IM Program provided for an expeditious process. Complaints were promptly investigated and reported on within forty-five days, on average, and 85 percent of the cases were completed in less than ninety days. One of the reasons for the expeditious nature of the process is that it did not require hearings, and, with additional resources, the timetables could be reduced even further. Since the Independent Monitor did not have any subpoena power, the IM Program relied on the cooperation of the parties and a thorough investigation to uncover any inconsistencies and find the facts.

Second, the IM Program was voluntary. Nothing prohibited a party from filing a complaint with the NLRB or any other public agency at any time—even after a complaint was filed.

Third, the IM Program also emphasized transparency by sharing the Independent Monitor's reports and the company's responses with the complaining party. Nothing prohibited either of the parties from further distributing or communicating the findings, conclusions, and recommendations to others.

Fourth, the IM Program was designed to be accessible to employees. The procedures were not overly formalistic. The complaint form was simple and required basic factual information. Complaining parties could submit additional paperwork in support of their allegations, but it was not necessary to initiate an investigation.

Fifth, the FoA Policy and IM Program provided more expansive association rights than were available under the NLRA. One example is the limitation that the FoA Policy placed on the employer's ability to engage in speech that was intended to influence employees' decisions with respect to labor union representation. Another example is that the IM Program provided for publicity of employee rights, while the NLRA does not. The statute does not require any notice advising employees or applicants about the nature of the law. (However, the Obama NLRB proposed rulemaking to reverse this anomaly.)[10] The IM Program was also broader in terms of employee rights than the NLRA in regard to the right to expeditious elections and to be free of discrimination, both of which are discussed as follows.

Limitations of the Program

Several factors threatened the IM Program's effectiveness. First, the program was designed and adopted unilaterally by the company. As a result, unions, employees, and managers were not made aware of it until after the Independent Manager was appointed. Once they were informed of the program, it was uncertain whether they would use the program.

Second, when some union representatives at already unionized FirstGroup facilities learned of the IM Program, they perceived it as a means of undermining their representation of employees. They complained that the FoA Policy had no application where employees were already organized and that the only purpose of informing employees of their freedom of association rights could be to suggest that they could become nonunionized.[11]

Third, acceptance of the FoA Policy and IM Program by senior management and executives of the company was not uniform and unconditional. Acceptance required time. Even so, changes in company leadership generated impediments to the IM Program when the agenda of new leaders conflicted with the FoA Policy.

To a great extent, the company dealt with these problems by publicizing the IM Program and explaining the FoA Policy and the purpose of the Independent Monitor's role to unions, employees, and managers.

But there was one other problem: Due to the unprecedented nature of the IM Program, it created uncertainty and skepticism among some employees and unions. There were several reasons for this. The employees, unions, and company managers had different understandings of what that policy meant and how it should be interpreted. There was no precedent for interpreting the policy. Over the course of the IM Program, the Independent Monitor developed case precedent that provided greater certainty in the application of the FoA Policy. However, the company's ability to reject or modify the Independent Monitor's recommendations undermined that certainty. Furthermore, the company was unwilling to accord any measure of deference to the Independent Monitor's reports.

Overall, the strengths of the IM Program exceeded its limitations, most of which were remediable through publicity and education. This enabled the program to operate for three years. During this time, the standards the Independent Monitor used to interpret the FoA Policy and evaluate alleged violations established the boundaries of appropriate conduct during union organizing campaigns.

Standards of Conduct under the FoA Policy

I primarily relied upon the principles embodied in the NLRA in analyzing alleged violations of the FoA Policy. But, because the IM Program explicitly stated that the scope of protection afforded to employees was broader than the NLRA, I went beyond these principles in certain cases. Here are some examples.

Employer Speech

Although the FoA Policy permitted the company to engage in union-related speech, the FoA Policy circumscribed employer speech more severely than the NLRA does.[12] The NLRA, particularly through Section 8(c) of the Taft-Hartley amendments, allows an employer to use anti-union speech so long as no threats of coercion or promises of benefit are employed.[13] By contrast, the FoA Policy's neutrality policy prohibited the company from using anti-union speech or speech that disparaged the union and its organizational efforts. However, the FoA Policy did not curtail all speech by the company. The company could present balanced facts but not selective data to disparage the union or deliver subjective anti-union propaganda.

Solicitation, Distribution, Talking, and Union Insignia Rules

Freedom of association and free speech rights have been influenced and shaped by First Amendment constitutional principles for more than six decades.[14] However, the NLRA does not prevent an employer "from making and enforcing reasonable rules covering the conduct of employees on company time."[15] Accordingly, under the FoA Policy, a balance had to be struck between employee rights and an employer's right to operate its business and maintain discipline. Disputes commonly arose regarding attempts to solicit and recruit members to the union, attempts to distribute literature about union activity, and the wearing of union insignia. Considerable confusion existed about what conduct was protected and what was prohibited. In other words, where should the line be drawn between employee free speech rights and the employer's right to enforce workplace rules?

NLRB precedent allows employees to talk about the union during both work and nonwork time if the employer does not have a policy (which employers rarely do) prohibiting all conversations about all nonwork-related matters during working time.[16] NLRB precedent also permits employees to wear union insignia, including t-shirts and buttons, during work and nonwork time, unless there are "special circumstances," such as an appearance rule for employees.

However, NLRB precedent regarding solicitation of union membership and distribution of literature is less clear. The U.S. Supreme Court had established relatively clear rules protecting both employee rights during nonworking time, that is, "working time is for work."[17] But, in *Stoddard Quirk Manufacturing Co.*,[18] the NLRB muddied the waters considerably when it held that an employer could prohibit the distribution of literature (but not solicitation) even during nonwork time in work areas. By distinguishing between solicitation and distribution activities in work and nonwork areas, the NLRB complicated the rules and created confusion.[19]

There were practical difficulties in applying NLRB precedent to different forms of union activity and time, manner, and place restrictions. I helped the company prepare clearer rules for employees and managers on solicitation, distribution, and talking rules. In so doing, I provided guidance not available under the NLRA. However, an area of confusion that remained at the end of the IM Program was setting proper boundaries between work and nonwork areas so that employees did not have to guess which speech was protected and which was unprotected.

Expeditious Elections

The FoA Policy offered more protection to employees than the NLRA does when it came to expeditious elections. The company concluded that representation elections should be "held as early as possible," inasmuch as a key concern is delay associated with the erosion of employee free choice. The Independent Monitor concluded that, absent "extraordinary circumstances," appealing the decision of an NLRB regional director to Washington would undercut an expeditious election process and, thus, the right of employees to freely choose whether to unionize. I urged the company to agree to enter into consent election agreements under NLRB rules, which would make the decision of the NLRB regional director final and when confronted with this issue, no appeal application to Washington was filed.

Interrogation of Employees

Under the NLRA, management's questioning of an employee about his or her views on union representation is legitimate only if the employer is attempting to determine whether employee sentiment made it appropriate for the employer to recognize the union on some basis other than a secret ballot box election (for example, a card check procedure) or the likelihood of a union petition to the NLRB for recognition. Because the FoA Policy permitted union recognition only through secret ballot box elections, the Independent

Monitor concluded that no form of interrogation would be permissible under the FoA Policy. As a result, no careful delineation needed to be drawn between interrogation which is precluded and that which is permitted.[20]

Surveillance

Surveillance of union activity by the employer also raises freedom of association issues. In addressing such complaints, the Independent Monitor followed NLRB decisions rendered during the Clinton Administration.[21] These decisions distinguished between observation of open, public union activity, which is allowed, and that which is "out of the ordinary," for example, taking notes of employees who received union handbills, which is not allowed.[22] The Independent Monitor applied NLRB precedent to determine whether the company's observation went beyond the casual and became unduly intrusive.[23]

Discrimination

The FoA Policy also went beyond the NLRA and NLRB precedent in terms of protection from discrimination. The Independent Monitor found unlawful discrimination (and an FoA Policy violation) in any case in which an employee proved by a preponderance of evidence that the company took an adverse action against him or her based in whole or in part on anti-union animus. The company could then show that the adverse action would have occurred in any event, which evidence the Independent Monitor used in determining what recommendations to make to the company. The Independent Monitor based this approach on the Supreme Court's statement in *NLRB v. Transportation Management* that it is "plainly rational and acceptable" to find an unfair labor practice where the adverse action is in any way motivated by a desire to frustrate union activity.[24]

The Issue of Agency Deference to Private ADR Decisions

As is often the case when a private dispute resolution program is implemented for the first time, questions arise as to how that program coexists with existing public law. Should the program be given deference by the NLRB, as is the case with grievance-arbitration under collective bargaining agreements? That is the question posed here with regard to the IM Program.

In *Spielberg Manufacturing Co.*, the NLRB held that it would defer to an arbitration award where: (1) the proceedings appear to have been "fair and regular," (2) "all parties have agreed to be bound," and (3) the arbitral decision "is not clearly repugnant to the purposes and policies of the Act."[25]

Favoring deferral is the fact that the IM Program was designed against the backdrop of the NLRA to constitute a "fair and regular" process (assuming the absence of a hearing does not change this conclusion) in which all relevant facts are considered,[26] and the Independent Monitor's findings and conclusions were grounded in the NLRA so as not to be "clearly repugnant to the purposes and policies of the Act."[27] However, fatal to deferral is the fact that neither the company nor the union or employees agreed to be bound by the Independent Monitor's findings and recommendations. The NLRB has said that "it is patently contrary to the letter and spirit of the Act for the Board to defer its undoubted jurisdiction to decide unfair labor practices to a disputes settlement system established unilaterally by an employer."[28] Thus, the NLRB has looked upon unilateral programs as contrary to public policy. In most cases involving deferral, parties have agreed in a collective bargaining agreement to be bound by the arbitral decision. The IM Program, however, did not contain such an agreement.

If the IM Program were modified so that the program was agreed to by the union and the employees and the employer committed to be bound by decisions of the Independent Monitor, then the program could be said to satisfy the NLRB's requirements for deferral. Extending the NLRB's deferral policy to private programs that adjudicate disputes in a union organizing campaign would be appropriate in light of the strong support and wide acceptance that voluntary arbitration of labor disputes has received in the grievance-arbitration context.

The IM Program fulfilled an exigent need of FirstGroup to resolve union organizing disputes that could disrupt its North American business. Though unilaterally created and implemented, it was cleverly modeled on principles in the NLRA. This enabled unions and employees to view the program as an enhanced surrogate for the statute.

The FoA Policy and IM Program appear to have been well received by both labor and management, notwithstanding the program's nonbinding quality and the fact that numerous violations and criticisms aimed at management were contained in the reports. Unions and employees likely were receptive because in many instances their charges were effectively addressed. Even when they were not, the process likely was cathartic for the parties, since the parties had an opportunity to air their complaints before a neutral third person experienced in labor disputes. This fact made my role as Independent Monitor somewhat different from that of an arbitrator appointed to hear disputes under collective bargaining agreements.[29] I functioned more like a "standing neutral" who is limited to making recommendations to resolve disputes.

Certainly the IM Program process was faster than an administrative proceeding with a formal hearing. And though the company could decide to reject or modify the Independent Monitor's decision on the merits of anti-union activity claims, it no doubt benefited from obtaining a neutral recommendation and probably influenced the company's behavior toward union organizing campaigns. For this reason, I thought that the FirstGroup IM Program could be a model for companies with union organizing disputes to adopt. However, companies that adopt such an initiative must be committed to a faster, more transparent process with greater remedies for workers than under the NLRA. Companies did not appear to adopt these procedures after the FirstGroup program expired in 2010.

The Teamsters, so reticent about the FirstGroup mechanism at that program's initiation, attempted to convince British National Express and its American subsidiary, Durham School Services,[30] to adopt FirstGroup procedures. I testified unsuccessfully at the annual shareholders meeting in London in support of this idea.[31] But it is possible that a different labor–management environment can incentivize such systems in the future.

PROTECTION OF CONSTRUCTION WORKERS' STANDARDS

Within a few weeks of winding up my FirstGroup work, the phone rang at my Salvatierra Street home. It was Ron Sims, the undersecretary of the U.S. Department of Housing and Urban Development (HUD) in Washington, with a request that I help HUD establish "project labor agreements" which establish equitable standards on not only wages, hours, and safety, but also apprenticeship opportunities for young workers. I've been particularly interested in the apprenticeship front since my work in the sixties and seventies to promote Blacks and other minorities, and I readily expressed interest. Moreover, having worked myself out of a job after three years with FirstGroup, Hilda said it best: "One door opens as one door closes."

When one of the HUD staffers called a day or two later to nail down the particulars, she said, "I suppose you know that Bill Lucy recommended you for this." "No," I told her, I hadn't known.

Bill Lucy, then secretary treasurer of the American Federation of State, County and Municipal Employees Union (AFSCMEU), and I had come to know each other in the early seventies when he formed and led the Coalition of Black Trade Unionists, the only independent group of Black trade union leaders on the national scene.[32] Bill had pulled people together to help me when my NLRB confirmation was pending before the Senate. And I had given a keynote speech to the coalition in Philadelphia in the eighties; in 1998 he introduced me again when I spoke at the Atlanta NAACP conference.

When I called Bill to thank him for recommending me to HUD in 2011, he said "Bill, anytime you want praise from me, I'll be glad to give it." And then he laughed and said, "And as LBJ did, anytime you want me to attack you, I'll do that too." He roared with laughter. That was Bill Lucy: thoughtful, principled, and unafraid to stand up to white labor leaders and employers alike.

My work for HUD stemmed from a unanimous 1993 Supreme Court ruling allowing Boston's Big Dig to enforce a negotiated collective bargaining agreement providing for hiring halls and apprenticeship programs.[33] When I wasn't at my Stanford office, I spent part of my regular week working on this out of downtown San Francisco, with my ex-Stanford student John Trasvina, then assistant secretary at HUD in Washington, and meeting with labor, management, and local government in Boston and Los Angeles.

I think the end product—a paper laying out guidelines on how HUD should proceed in the arena of project labor agreements[34]—helped get HUD moving in the Obama years. And it moved HUD directly into the work of promoting Black hiring in the better-paying construction trades.

THE AGRICULTURAL LABOR RELATIONS BOARD

While visiting my sons near Pasadena over the 2013 Thanksgiving holiday, I received a call from one of Governor Jerry Brown's aides, Patrick Henning (ex-California Federation of Labor leader Jack Henning's grandson), asking me about the Agricultural Labor Relations Board (ALRB) chairmanship. The ALRB had come into existence with the enactment of the Agricultural Labor Relations Act (ALRA) of 1975, because farm workers were excluded from federal coverage. This was so because the National Labor Relations Act was enacted in 1935—at that time, many Black workers held farm jobs, particularly in the South, and the Southern Democrats could not accept the idea of a democratic system in the workplace for Blacks. Thus, California had become the only state to provide a farm worker system promoting the right to organize and bargain collectively in the country.

As Patrick was speaking during our call, I expected him to ask me for a recommendation, and I immediately began to think of some of my students who had gone into labor law as possible candidates for the job of chairman. But Patrick had made the call to sound me out on whether I was interested in the job myself. I quickly assured him that I wasn't interested, and the conversation ended before I could provide any recommendations.

I had responded quickly because it was my impression that the board and the Act had fallen on hard times after the early 1980s and the advent of Republican administrations in California. In the heady sixties and seventies, Cesar Chavez's United Farm Workers were successful in organizing farm workers throughout California through the boycott—Hilda and I often said that our sons didn't know the taste of grapes because of that boycott—and through this weapon, Governor Brown had signed the 1975 Agricultural Labor Relations Act as a kind of substitute for self-help—the same rationale as the National Labor Relations Act of 1935 had advanced for the latter's passage.

The statute was modeled on the NLRA structure, but without its weak blemishes in the areas of administrative process and remedies. My friend and colleague, Santa Clara Law School Professor Herman Levy, while working in Sacramento in the early years, wrote the classic article on the statute,[35] a piece of scholarly work cited to this very day. And my research assistant, Gary Williams, was with the board in its very early days.

But those days were now old history in 2013. I knew that the board was, at that point, a shell of itself.

The board's disintegration had begun after Jerry Brown left office at the conclusion of his first two terms and was succeeded by Republican governors George Deukmejian and Pete Wilson. They marched to the tune of the agricultural growers who sought to dismantle this new agency and the "dream" statute, which the ALRA was frequently called. The Republican governors accomplished this, not through statutory amendments, but rather by appointing conservative board members and general counsel who were unsympathetic to collective bargaining.

Despite my knowledge of much of this, and my abrupt rejection of Patrick's proposal, I began to think about the idea. Hilda reminded me that I was often stimulated by challenges of this kind, particularly the turmoil and tension of my NLRB work in the nineties and my consulting for the Equal Employment Opportunity Commission in the sixties. Moreover, the board's Sacramento offices were accessible by car or train, and did not require the kind of lifestyle upheaval involved in my Washington tenure.

So, after a few weeks, near the end of December, I called back and asked Patrick if the job was still available. Though a few people had already been interviewed, Patrick said that it was. The governor's labor secretary, Marty Morgenstern, called me soon thereafter and told me the job was mine if I decided to accept it. I did so.

Comparisons: Sacramento v. Washington

The governor, Jerry Brown, whom I had not yet met personally, announced my appointment as chairman, which would be effective after my return from my near-annual March visit to Red Sox spring training facilities and exhibitions. 2014 was to be a special spring training, as I had just seen the Red Sox World Series road games against the Cardinals in St. Louis, in which they prevailed in two out of three, proceeding to Fenway for the clincher. Thus, as soon as I returned from Florida, I headed to Sacramento for a swearing-in ceremony. For the next three years, I'd be arriving on Monday or Tuesday of most weeks and staying at the Sheraton Hotel across the street from the ALRB offices until Friday afternoon, when I returned to Stanford.

Figure 12.1: My swearing-in ceremony as chairman of the California Agricultural Labor Relations Board, March 18, 2014. Left to right: Sylvia Torres-Guillen (General Counsel), Genevieve Shiroma (Member), William B. Gould IV (Chairman), Cathryn Rivera-Hernandez (Member). (Courtesy of Justin Short Photography.)

I had virtually no personal connection to Jerry Brown. I *had* bumped into his father, Governor Pat Brown, in a Sacramento elevator in the spring of 1976, during the Democratic primaries. Characteristically warm and gregarious, Pat and I were old friends by the time the elevator door opened and the two of us walked out onto the street. Miriam Pawel has written accurately of the first Governor Brown, stating that "Pat's warmth was so genuine, his belly laugh so contagious, he immediately put people at ease and seemed like an old friend after a five-minute conversation."[36] I was a bit embarrassed that day in Sacramento when he saw my '68 Volks with a "Frank Church for President" sticker on it, at the very time that his son Jerry was competing for the same office. Pat said, "Oh, don't worry at all. Jerry wouldn't mind it a bit." As I would soon learn, Pat's personality was fundamentally different from that of his extraordinarily cerebral and capable son. Pawell describes the differences this way: "Pat hugged strangers; Jerry shook hands with his father."[37]

As I began my new assignment, I noticed a number of major differences between Washington and Sacramento. The first was in the identity of appointees. While the ALRB had excellent career civil servants—Tom Sobel and Eduardo Blanco were extremely talented and key people on my staff, and I was able to appoint ex-NLRB administrative law judge William L. Schmidt at the ALRB; Antonio Barbosa ran the ship as executive secretary—its political appointees were quite different. Chapter 10 makes clear how bitterly I complained about political appointees to the NLRB in Washington, but at least they had some experience in labor law. In Sacramento, appointees held office without possessing any kind of background relevant to labor law. Genevieve Shiroma, my predecessor as chairman, who remained on the board and succeeded me three years later, was an intelligent, well-organized individual—but she was trained as an engineer. She knew where the files were and could frequently fill me in on background and personalities. But Genevieve knew nothing whatsoever about law of any kind, and her use of terms like *prima facie* (one of her favorites) was so downright embarrassing that I was fearful of looking at staff as she spoke, concerned that eye contact would produce a giggling fit, embarrassing to all involved.

The general counsel, Sylvia Torres-Guillen, and the other board member, Cathryn Rivera-Hernandez, were lawyers. But they had no knowledge of or background in labor law. Frequently, what they lacked in knowledge they made up for in self-confidence, which was, at times, dispiriting and disconcerting. Even the appointment to the vacancy that my departure created three years later was not even remotely based upon qualifications. This was a problem.

The challenges of the job were considerable. As I said in a speech I gave in Monterey two years after my appointment:

> *When Governor Brown first invited me to take this job . . . in early 2014, I had been told that the farmworkers were living in their cars at the time of the harvest in the Coachella Valley. But what I didn't know—until I saw it with my own eyes—was that in towns like Mecca they are not even able to live in their cars. They must alternate between their cars and mats in the immediate vicinity of their cars since three or four workers often travel in a single car and not all can stretch out in the car to sleep at the same time!*
>
> *At one time we thought we were doing something about this. Just a little more than forty years ago—and we celebrated the fortieth anniversary of the ALRB and the ALRA last summer—the average wage rate for direct hire workers was $2.60 per hour, which translates into a little more than $13.50 per hour in inflation-adjusted dollars. In 2014, California's farmers and ranchers reported an $11.33 per hour figure—that is more than two dollars per hour below what would have been necessary to keep up with inflation during the last four decades.*
>
> *The fact that this decline or failure to raise real wages in a period of labor shortage caused by the sealing of the border to Mexico is truly remarkable! Some employers are apparently embarking upon harvesting robotization of strawberry plants which, as the* Wall Street Journal *noted, "have long required the trained discernment and backbreaking effort of tens of thousands of low-paid workers."*[38]

At the time, I thought that promoting workers' rights possessed legal potential. In June of 2015, at the ALRA fortieth anniversary meeting that we had with the governor at the Leland Stanford Mansion in Sacramento, I spoke about the "path towards justice in the fields . . . [as] a bumpy, evolving, and incomplete process," referencing the five centuries which elapsed from Magna Carta to the evolution of Parliament, and the inspiration of each for the great post-Civil War amendments.[39] On that occasion, I tried to convince Governor Brown that he should make a speech promoting the Agricultural Labor Relations Act at one of the friendly grower locations. He listened politely to me but avoided a direct answer, and nothing was ever heard of this idea again.

Tussles with the GC

My first ALRB crisis involved the considerably more humdrum and boring day-to-day management of the board: the complaint by other board members—and I agreed with them—that the general counsel (GC) had arrogated all day-to-day administrative authority to herself without consultation with anyone. As a result of this complaint, I arranged to meet with Governor Brown on a warm May Saturday morning at the Buttercup, a coffee shop in Oakland that was apparently one of his favorite places to go on weekends away from Sacramento. I had asked the governor for this meeting because the GC had become such a problem for all three board members.

When he arrived, Governor Brown said, "I don't believe that we've met before." I replied, "Actually, Governor, we have met. I was with my oldest son at a 1976 Jimmy Carter campaign dinner in San Francisco and you were there, too. My son asked you for your autograph and you turned him down." Brown was a bit off balance in response, and mumbled something about the fact that he did not believe in "commodification." He then launched into a forty- to fifty-minute discussion about the political scene in both Sacramento and Washington. Since this was my first meeting with him, I recall worrying that he was deliberately talking about broad policy issues to avoid the discussion I wanted to have about the agency. But I learned on that day, and at future such meetings, that this was not true. This was the way Jerry Brown liked to proceed. And I have never had discussions with such a first-rate intellect—not in Washington or at Stanford or at Harvard—not anywhere! There were to be many more discussions like this in the future, arising just as spontaneously as the one that occurred that May morning.

After almost an hour, we began to discuss the general counsel. I told him that there was a double-barreled problem here: her unqualified control over all management matters in the agency, as well as a need to rein her in on future injunction requests made without consultation with the board. In truth, I wanted him to dismiss the general counsel and I told him this. But Brown said that he feared the political consequences, both with Latinos and the United Farm Workers, which liked her and would object. Nonetheless, out of this meeting came a compromise of sorts, which allowed the Labor Department to take over the board's management problems—the GC involvement with litigation without board consultation would be, and was, dealt with later.

Thus, in 2014, I enjoyed a transitory popularity with the other two board members because of what I had accomplished. (People around the governor liked the idea of taking work away from the GC, in part because they did not view the ALRB as independent.) And on case handling itself, in 2015, I would have some measure of success, though I waited until the California Senate confirmed me, this time with a less tumultuous process than that described in chapter 10.[40] In California, the Republicans had only a peripheral role to play, the principal intrigue taking place between Democrats, some of whom were particularly pro-UFW. The Senate Rules Committee, in charge of the confirmation process, was chaired by Senator Kevin de León (later of rather embarrassing fame because of racial comments he made while sitting on the Los Angeles City Council[41]) and the contact between us was careful—almost, I felt, that of cat-and-mouse. The conflict was between de León and the GC (both arguably aligned against me—and in any event, neither of whom were close to me). But I was confirmed easily by a rather lopsided vote, 27–7.

With the confirmation process behind me, I could address the other major GC problem—her insistence on pursuing injunction theories and approaches without consulting the board, which has principal responsibility for shaping the law's direction. We, a unanimous board, took care of this problem by withdrawing her authorization to obtain injunctions without our consent.

The GC was quite angry, and this time around the shoe was on the other foot—she complained to Governor Brown about me! The governor called me in short order and asked how I could introduce a process that would slow the agency down. I assured him that my changes would do no such thing, and that withdrawal of authorization was to make sure that the board spoke with one voice. This call highlighted other issues as well: Unlike the NLRB, the ALRB was not an independent administrative agency. This had resulted from a 2002 reorganization promulgated by the Little Hoover Commission. A discussion of the kind that Governor Brown and I had about the GC would have been impossible in Washington, where, at least in a Democratic administration, all policy people had strict instructions never to speak with us about any matter of substance.[42] The governor had no such compunctions. I always responded to his concerns and worked forcefully to protect any position the board adopted.

Waking up the UFW

But there was another problem as well, about which the governor and I always agreed: the moribund status of the United Farm Workers. In my three years as chairman, with a workforce of as many as 700,000 farm workers in California, the UFW filed one representation petition seeking an election—and this under a statute which, unlike the NLRB, required a petition with the board for a union to obtain recognition as the result of organizing. The UFW did no organizing whatsoever, a lethargy rooted in Cesar Chavez's peculiar behavior, described brilliantly by Miriam Pawel.[43] Jerry Brown, who had viewed the ALRA's enactment as the first major accomplishment of his first administration in the seventies, understood this fact perfectly well and we had countless discussions about it.

The governor told me that in this century, his frustration with the UFW's behavior was such that he had actually met with Jimmy Hoffa Jr. of the Teamsters, as well as the president of the United Food and Commercial Workers, to invite them to come into California's fields and organize the workers, given the UFW refusal to do so. But he was unsuccessful—the large number of undocumented workers, the possibility of UFW conflicts, and the strength of the growers made this task too daunting to others who might be tempted to do the job. So the UFW, while lethargic, faced a challenge that even other, more active unions would not undertake in their place.

The UFW had abandoned the fields from the late eighties and early nineties onward. But it did not abandon Sacramento—quite the contrary. Long before I had taken on my ALRB assignment, during the Gray Davis administration at the century's turn, while driving through Sacramento I unexpectedly ran into traffic so substantial that it was difficult to proceed at all. What caused this? It was a massive rally designed to address a major deficiency in California labor law—and a problem that also exists in federal law under the NLRA. That problem is the inability of workers who had selected a union as their bargaining representative to conclude a collective bargaining agreement or contract that would give them improved wages, benefits, and conditions—the improvements to their working lives that they had really voted for when voting for the union itself. The only obligation thrust upon the growers was to bargain in "good faith" to reach an agreement—not the actual consummation of the agreement itself.

The workers' rally in Sacramento that day was organized by the UFW to address this problem through a statutory amendment. And the UFW was so successful that the Legislature soon enacted, and Governor Davis promptly signed, the so-called Mandatory Mediation and Conciliation Act (MMC), a law which, notwithstanding its misleading title, culminated in arbitration that would impose a contract upon the parties, when they had not negotiated one the first time around, after certification of the union as bargaining representative. These procedures could be triggered when the parties have not negotiated an agreement themselves. This was truly an important step forward, demonstrating a deficiency not only in state law, but in federal law as well.

There was only one problem: the UFW had not invoked the new statutory mechanism providing for arbitration provisions. It did not do so because, as Miriam Pawell vividly chronicled,[44] they had decided to abandon the fields, and with it an attempt to organize the unorganized as well as bargain collectively or negotiate.

When I arrived in Sacramento in 2014 to take up my new assignment, the Mandatory Mediation Act had been on the books for a decade and a half. But the UFW had never invoked it and never sought arbitration to resolve differences where they were unable to obtain a contract. The statute had been used only once, and that was by another union, the United Food and Commercial Workers Union (UFCW). The UFW had been completely moribund. Nonetheless, simultaneous with my arrival, the UFW sought to use the "new" decade-and-a-half-old law—the only problem was that bargaining was a prerequisite to the statute's invocation. So much time had passed since the union had won an election and attempted bargaining that the representatives involved were now gone, either through retirement, moving to another position in another part of the country, or deceased! These factors produced big litigation problems for the UFW in those limited circumstances where they attempted, like Rip Van Winkle, to revive themselves and the bargaining relationship.

So there were some cases before the board during my chairmanship, but for the most part they were meaningless sound and fury. Foremost amongst the cases arising out of union abandonment was *Tri-Fanucchi Farms*, where my board held that "the fact that a labor organization has been inactive or absent, even for an extended period of time, does not represent a defense to the employer's duty to bargain. The board recently reaffirmed its holdings on abandonment and confirmed that, except in cases where the union disclaims interest in representing the bargaining unit or becomes defunct, the union remains certified until removed or replaced through the ALRA's election procedures, regardless of any bargaining hiatus or union inactivity that may have occurred."[45]

Advocating for Prompt Action, and Other Cases

With my NLRB difficulty in getting board members to issue decisions as background, I emphasized, in a concurring opinion, that the problem of agency delay was equally challenging. I said:

> I write separately to emphasize that the need for prompt and expeditious agency action applies not only to the General Counsel of the ALRB—who was alleged in this case not to have met the above-noted standard—but also to the Board itself, and that under other facts showing delay, the Board risks giving up important remedies. The public deserves a vigilant Board, and I intend to meet that standard myself and facilitate its implementation while I serve here in Sacramento.[46]

Closely related to this problem was the question of the extent to which the Agricultural Labor Relations Board should adhere to decisions of the NLRB under a statute that provided for some form of adherence. I wrote a concurring opinion in *Sabor Farms*, stating that the Agricultural Board should not acquiesce in judicial decisions reversing the board unless and until the California Supreme Court had spoken.[47]

I urged a Brandeisian restraint upon the board, taking issue with wide-ranging opinions by my colleagues and quoting Euripides: "Silence is true wisdom's best reply."[48] Advocating similar restraint, I took the view that, in connection with the Mandatory Mediation Act, a requirement to distinguish the mediators' prior reports was unnecessary in the absence of extraordinary circumstances "so long as the mediator adheres to the relevant statutory criteria."[49]

Penultimately, I took the view that a majority of the board articulated an improper rationale to establish union access on private property, emphasizing that (1) great weight and deference should always be given to the vital role of the administrative law judge in the administrative process[50] and (2) the ALJ findings had it made it clear that union access was not at issue.[51]

Finally, in a case that spawned litigation in other contexts, I concurred in *Gerawan Farming*, concluding that the company (which had consumed an appreciable portion of our work time) had violated most prohibitions on an across-the-board basis.[52] These case adjudications were similar to many of the issues with which I had dealt at the NLRB in Washington. But, as noted previously, the contact with the executive branch, in this case the governor himself, was appreciably different. In Washington I had only met with President Clinton and his aides at social occasions, where the matters before the board were not discussed at all except for the president's exclamation that our successful baseball strike resolution might make him "president for life." But the contact with California's governor was different. I spoke with Governor Brown not only at social functions, where my friends said he always sought me out to talk first, but also in long meetings in his office, where we spoke of general public policy matters that dwarfed labor issues considerably.

On one occasion, Hilda and I were at a Portland Red Sox game in Maine with one of our grandsons when I received a call from the governor. I stepped outside the stadium to avoid the noise and to field questions about labor law decisions and issues, principally involving possible changes in the ALRA. I still remember the roar of the crowd in Portland that interfered with our intense and detailed discussion.

These types of contacts with Governor Brown were frequent; I came away from Sacramento viewing him as the most cerebral politician I had ever met, with an intellect that was superior to just about anyone's. This was a lot of fun. But the job itself was frustrating. After an initial flurry of UFW activity, as it tried to revive a select few of the bargaining relationships it had abandoned, the UFW resumed silence—except in the halls of the Legislature, where it attempted to fashion new, mostly meaningless legislative fixes as it had in the past.

In 2015 and 2016, a small number of unfair labor practices were filed at the ALRB, but they had nothing whatsoever to do with the UFW or organizing the unorganized. The trickle of unfair labor practice charges on the docket involved employer retaliation against workers who had protested against what they perceived to be unfair treatment, for example, dismissal or discipline for protesting the refusal to increase wages beyond the minimum wage required by statute. Neither the public nor farm workers are generally aware that this kind of employer response to such protests is unlawful under both the ALRA and the NLRA. The UFW could have used such treatment as an organizing tool—but it was not involved or even aware of these cases that came before us.

The ALRA rules providing for periodic union access to private property had been available since a California Supreme Court holding in the 1970s was affirmed by the United States Supreme Court—the Supreme Court, ironically, relied for its decision upon a number of my articles from the 1960s.[53] The Roberts Court was later to reverse this decision,[54] but it didn't really matter, as the UFW made little use of these procedures.

Worker Education

Meanwhile, in late 2015, I decided to explore the one available avenue to make the statute relevant to farm workers and growers: to hold hearings with a view toward establishing a proposed rule providing for worker education, that is, provision for board representatives to speak with workers about the content of the law during nonworking time under some circumstances. The other board members agreed, and I brought in my former research assistant Karen Snell, a 1981 Stanford Law School graduate, to team up with my staff aces, Eduardo Blanco and Tom Sobell. We made a formidable team, but gaining outside support was another matter altogether.

The UFW president, Art Rodriquez, told me that there was no need for such a rule; the UFW was able to reach workers through Spanish language radio, he said. But my sense was that person-to-person contact is always superior to radio and television broadcast, and broadcast was a weak substitute for the activity the union itself should have been undertaking. Compounding the difficulty was the presence of a large number of indigenous workers who were not fluent in Spanish or English. So, even if Spanish radio could reach some farm workers and provide a poor substitute for direct access to them, the indigenous workers could not understand the radio broadcast at all.

Thus, the board held hearings in Fresno, Salinas, and Santa Maria on the proposed rule to provide worker education. We hired interpreters who were skilled in the indigenous languages and heard from them as well as the Spanish speakers.[55] (Like most Californians, until these hearings I had never heard these languages.) We obtained much interest in these cities, particularly in the most impoverished ones like Santa Maria, where one immediately confronts pawnbroker shops after turning off Route 1 into the city itself.

The idea of a workers education rule was favorably received, but not with the growers—a number of whom participated in our hearings—or the UFW, which saw the rule as a rebuke to them (which it really was). When the rule languished in the bureaucracy for months after we brought it through in September 2016, I decided that this was the last possible thing I could do, and that it would not go forward because we needed the approval of other state agencies, such as finance. The governor, who had authored the act itself, had no interest in supporting what appeared to be a Don Quixote-type campaign against the powerful windmills possessed by the growers, lacking any political muscle in support of the farm workers. Thus, on January 19, 2017, I wrote the governor a letter of resignation, noting that the proposed rule had "languished in the bowels of state bureaucracy" and that part of the problem was that the ALRB, unlike the NLRB, was not an independent administrative agency.

The *Los Angeles Times* ran an article[56] about this immediately, and I surmised that the governor was not pleased. The *Sacramento Bee* also carried a piece written by Dan Moraine, noting the following:[57]

> *To invigorate the Board Gould had proposed sending interpreters into the fields to explain to workers their rights. Simply posting notices wouldn't suffice. Many farmworkers are illiterate and not fluent in Spanish or English, and instead speak indigenous languages.*
>
> *Understandably, farmers, never fond of the Agricultural Labor Relations Act or the Board, would not welcome such an intrusion, and Gould's proposal has stalled.*

> *The letter, first reported by the Los Angeles Times, was not meant to be angry, and Gould certainly didn't mean to offend the governor. Rather, he said by phone and later over coffee, he had become exasperated and frustrated, and the trip from Palo Alto to Sacramento, 3½ hours by train, was taxing. At 80, he figured he could use his time better returning to writing articles and books, and lecturing.*[58]

In the years since 2017 the status quo has been carried forward in the main, notwithstanding a poorly and hastily conceived reform of the law.[59] In a couple of speeches that I have given, I've been asked about the above-referenced Roberts Court's holding that union access provided under the ALRA is unconstitutional and whether that has posed a barrier to organizing. I have always responded: "It makes no difference whatsoever. Nothing was happening before and nothing is happening now." What I said is a sad chapter in a law that once held such promise.

THE CITY OF SAN FRANCISCO: LABOR AND EMPLOYMENT DISCRIMINATION ISSUES

My work for San Francisco really began in 1990, when Mayor Art Agnos selected me to chair a committee examining San Francisco labor law and labor management relations. My good pal, Magdalena Jacobsen, was the top labor person for the mayor and recommended me to him. (I was able to return the favor in 1993 when the White House asked me to recommend someone for the National Mediation Board; Maggie was appointed.) Unfortunately, Mayor Agnos was defeated in his reelection attempt before we could even issue a report. So, while I learned a good deal about San Francisco labor, I was not able to make a written contribution at that time.

Fast forward to 2018 and 2019, when, pursuant to fact-finding procedures of the California Public Employment Relations Act, I was appointed as Impartial Chairman to provide an appeals process for administrative disciplinary proceedings, conducted before the San Francisco Police Commission.[60] I had a number of hearings and meetings with both sides at the San Francisco Police Officers'

Association and at Stanford Law School, where I've often held a number of my arbitration hearings. The critical matter that triggered this proceeding was an appellate court ruling, *Morgado v. City and County of San Francisco*. I wrote:

> Specifically, Morgado *held that the PSOPBRA [Public Safety Officers Procedural Bill of Rights Act]* required a new administrative appeal process be available subsequent to San Francisco Police Commission proceedings. The matter before me is the nature of the process contemplated by Morgado.[61]

The court had held that San Francisco was required to provide a second evidentiary hearing, but one which was not necessarily akin to the existing police commission proceeding. In essence, I was called upon to determine what kind of police disciplinary proceeding complied with the law and was compatible with the parameters established by *Morgado*.

As a result, my opinion held that an administrative law judge from the California Office of Administrative Hearings was to be designated to serve as a hearing officer on all administrative appeals. I rejected the view that the standard of review would be de novo. Thus I said:

> *Accordingly, I therefore opt for an intermediate standard utilized by courts reviewing administrative disciplinary proceedings on petition for writ of administrative mandamus under Code of Civil Procedure section 1094.5. This standard, I believe, would provide a more expansive and appropriate opportunity to reverse findings relating to the falsity of charges and a failure to address mitigating circumstances, as contemplated by* Morgado. *Coupled with the opportunity for the disciplined police officer to introduce evidence excluded because of either an evidentiary ruling or a curtailed process, officers will be able to appropriately present their case for a reversal of the Commission's actions. But I emphasize that my proposal (and rejection of the* de novo *standard) leaves the appeal*

process appropriately circumscribed so as not to needlessly plunge the Hearing Officer deeply into the merits of the Commission proceeding in most or all cases.[62]

This opinion led to a subsequent assignment involving a dispute about the question of whether police officers could examine the videos of others prior to making their own statement about the controversy involving disputes where police had discharged their weapons. Ultimately, the parties agreed that police do not have this right.

THE SAN FRANCISCO INDEPENDENT REVIEWER 2021

Probably the most visible, if not the most important, of my post-Washington work involved an invitation from Mayor London Breed to address alleged issues of racial misconduct inside the San Francisco city workforce. On October 23, 2020, Mayor Breed asked me to accept her appointment as independent reviewer to lead a comprehensive and independent investigation into the equal employment opportunity practices, policies, and procedures of the city and county of San Francisco. I accepted the Mayor's invitation on November 2, 2020, and on November 2, 2020, Mayor Breed commissioned the review.

I was fortunate in retaining two extremely able Stanford Law School students, Cody Kahoe and Colin O'Brien, to join me in this work. With their able assistance, we were able to hold dozens of meetings with Department of Human Resources (DHR) officials and investigators, with the leadership of the city's largest departments, with labor unions, and with employee affinity groups. Given the fact that the investigative process took place at the beginning of the COVID-19 pandemic, practically all our discussions and interviews were conducted by Zoom. We were fortunate in receiving cooperation and were able to engage in a dialogue with city representatives as well as union leaders and many employees in affinity groups. The process took place over a six-month period culminating in the issuance of the report in July 2021 containing numerous findings and recommendations.

The backdrop for all this is best described by some of the introduction in the independent reviewer report which issued in July and was discussed with Mayor Breed in City Hall at that time.

I wrote:

> *San Francisco Mayor London Breed has formulated the first big city "reckoning" in the wake of the George Floyd murder a little more than a year ago through the commission of this report on equal employment opportunity in the City workforce last November. Of course, her initiative, however significant, represents the first effort in what will be a line of proposed policies aimed at the centuries-old practices of racial misconduct in the country. On this eve of Juneteenth, it is an attempt to foster the beginnings of what some have characterized as the Third Reconstruction. This movement has "sparked the biggest civil rights protests in America's history. Some 20m Americans took part, flouting covid-19 restrictions. There were 7,750 protests in over 2,440 places, in every state. Beyond America, Black Lives Matter protests were staged in Brazil, France, Japan, and New Zealand, among others."*
>
> *The first undertaking to redeem our country's promises of 1776 and '87 emerged with our brief interlude of Reconstruction-fashioned democracy which was quickly abandoned in 1877. The second Reconstruction took place with the civil rights movement of the 1960s and the landmark legislation enacted in the form of antibias strictures contained in the landmark trilogy of statutes in '64, '65 and '68. "Despite the gains in legal and political rights made by African-Americans since the civil-rights era, measures of relative poverty and black-white segregation have barely moved for half a century."*
>
> *Thus, we have been here before. More than a half-century ago, the 1967–1968 Nation Advisory Committee on Civil Disorders (more commonly known as the Kerner Commission Report) said: "Our nation is moving toward*

*two societies, one black, one white—separate and unequal."
Incomes and wages, improving ever so slightly so as to
proceed from 55 to 60% for Blacks, as a percentage of
that enjoyed by whites from 1967 through the 1990s has
remained stuck at 60% in recent years. Though there is
considerably more contact between the races than existed
in the sixties, the only relative economic change is in long-
term unemployment and that is attributable to an increase
for whites.*

*In essence, as Robert Putnam has written, we, in the
United States, have taken our "foot off the gas." For a failure to address the past means that it will be left unresolved
and unremedied and thus embedded in the present system.
Since the closing decades of the 20th century, gains in relative life expectancy for Blacks have stagnated; the closing of the Black–white gap in infant mortality rates has
plateaued and in recent years has actually increased for
Blacks; the Black–white ratios in high school and college
degree attainment have shown little or no improvement;
progress toward income equality between the races has
gone into reverse, with the Black–white income gap wid-
ening significantly.*

*Now too, the events—particularly the brutality displayed
in Minneapolis on May 25—of this past pandemic-filled
year have produced what has been called the "Reckoning."
Government at all levels can contribute to providing
answers. San Francisco, an employer of nearly 35,000
workers, can make an important contribution. The Black
exodus from San Francisco during this past half-century
makes initiatives such as those advocated in this report all
the more important, as the City tries to meet the moment
before it and to stimulate a more substantial presence in
the City.*[63]

The report contained numerous findings and recommendations that focused upon the internal procedures of San Francisco, given that "California rightly promotes internal investigative procedures, providing cities like San Francisco with an opportunity to resolve what would otherwise culminate in litigation through both alternative dispute procedure mechanisms as well as investigations."[64] The key findings and recommendations related to a host of issues.

Said Mayor Breed at the time of the report's issuance:

> *I want to thank Professor Gould for all the work he has done to conduct this extensive review. . . . It's critical that we're doing everything we can to protect our workers from workplace discrimination and harassment and creating a welcoming environment for all employees. With the help of Professor Gould's findings, we'll be able to restructure EEO and hiring systems to best serve our city workers.*[65]

The first of my findings and recommendations was that San Francisco's Memoranda of Understanding required employees to choose between filing a complaint about discrimination with the Department of Human Resources (DHR) or, on the other hand, filing a grievance with their union, which could pursue the matter through the collective bargaining agreement. I found that this choice produced confusion about both where to go with a discrimination complaint and about the available remedy. I said that the parties should bargain a revision of this process to allow San Francisco workers to make "an informed decision" about which avenues to pursue. Subsequent to the report, San Francisco and its unions did bargain the revision which the report advocated.

Second, I proposed that remedies consistent with Title VII and the Civil Rights Act amendments of 1991 contained damages remedies such as those included in the 1991 statues. I also recommended that where a conflict between competing employees for, for instance, a job or disputes about sexual and racial harassment, third party representation be allowed for an employee who requested it. This recommendation was not implemented as the city viewed the matter as best handled by the unions themselves through their own internal procedures rather than a collective bargaining agreement between the parties. And on the damages matter, the city viewed this remedy as within the province of the courts and not arbitrators.

However, since the report was issued, the NLRB has held that damages beyond back pay are appropriate under the NLRA and, in my view, it is likely that many arbitrators will now emulate what the board has done.[66]

A third matter on which I made findings and recommendations related to the tardy resolution of discrimination complaints. I noted that the existing policy at the time of the report required the complaint to be resolved within 180 days, but that one quarter of the complaints were not closed within that period, with over two dozen remaining open for over a year. Here I made a number of recommendations, including: (1) that investigation be concluded inside 120 days; (2) that the DHR establish clear benchmarks within that period; (3) that complete authority be given to DHR, rather than contracting out much of it to the city's various departments; and (4) that DHR meet regularly with unions and employee groups in making these changes. Some of these recommendations have been implemented.

The city states that it has now communicated with employee groups and provided more transparency about the process. DHR has initiated an attempt to return the largest department—the Department of Public Health—to the DHR to avoid the confusion arising out of duplicative procedures and inconsistent treatment of complaints in different departments. The significance of this is that nearly 8,000 employees, 22 percent of the city's municipal workforce, and 16 percent of EEO cases are involved. The city also states that it has improved employee communication.

Another recommendation related to the fact that the city had only fifteen investigators for 35,000 workers, each investigator having a burden of 2,000 employees. The city has now hired eight more investigators and states that it has reduced the length of time that cases remain open by 51 percent.

My recommendations focused not only on the need to have clear and expeditious procedure but also to facilitate more effectively the hiring of Black workers. I proposed that the city amend Administrative Code Chapter 12X to allow the city to authorize travel to states that currently impose restrictions on abortion and are hostile to gay workers. The city has now amended the code. This means that now San Francisco can recruit Black graduates from the Deep South, where there are a disproportionate number of Historical Black Colleges and Universities (HBCUs). I also stressed the importance of new procedures to provide opportunities for Black workers to be upgraded into skilled trades jobs.[67] The city now states that it has aligned with recommendations from the Gould report to increase investments in the skilled trades for career progression. The ApprenticeshipSF team leads opportunities to expand apprenticeship programs within the city. These recent efforts include relaunching the Environmental Service Worker 7501 Apprenticeship Program in partnership with the Laborers Union after several years of nonoperation as well as hiring thirteen qualified existing DPW entry-level trainees (Classification 99160) into the new fall 2022 Apprenticeship cohort. The expansion recommends the hiring of a new cohort of twenty Gardener Apprentices in the fall of 2022.[68]

These findings and recommendations—in all consisting of nineteen areas and fifty-seven recommendations to support reform—are just an overview of what the report provided and what San Francisco did as a result of the report. The needle was moved, and I believe that the "basis for positive steps forward in the near future" has been realized, though not with the perfection contemplated by the report.

NOTES

[1] William B. Gould IV, "The Decline and Irrelevance of the NLRB and What Can Be Done About It: Some Reflections on Privately Devised Alternatives," keynote address to the State Bar of California Labor and Employment Law Section Annual Meeting, October 31, 2008 in San Diego, California. William B. Gould IV, "What Would Employee Free Choice Mean in the Workplace?," speech at the 58th Annual Conference of the Association of Labor Relations Agencies: Labor Management Relations and the Global Economic Crisis, July 20, 2009 in Oakland, California.

[2] This took place during my speech at the 61st annual meeting of the Labor and Employment Relations Association in San Francisco, CA on January 4, 2009. William B. Gould IV, "Prospects for Labor Law Reform After the 2008 Election – Law Perspective."

[3] Michael Cieply and James Bates, "Probe Stirs Up Writers Guild," *Los Angeles Times*, January 5, 2004.

[4] In re 2003 WGAW Election Protest, report and recommendations of William B. Gould IV, January 5, 2004.
[5] Michael Cieply and James Bates, "Probe Stirs Up Writers Guild," *Los Angeles Times*, January 5, 2004; Sharon Waxman, "Media Business; Report Backs Overturning Of Election at Writers Guild," *New York Times*, January 6, 2004; James Bates, "Writers Guild Chief Resigns Under Pressure," *Los Angeles Times*, January 7, 2004; James Bates and Michael Cieply, "Plot Thickens at Writers Guild," *Los Angeles Times*, January 6, 2004.
[6] "Our Companies," First Bus, https://www.firstbus.co.uk/about-us/our-companies.
[7] Tim Sharp, "FirstGroup Buries the Hatchet with US Union Teamsters to Pen Bus Driver Deal," *Herald* (Glasgow, Scotland), June 3, 2011. However, wages continue to be negotiated on a local level.
[8] The NLRB is not required to acquiesce in U.S. Court of Appeals interpretations of the NLRA because the NLRB is the expert agency charged to interpret the NLRA. See *Theodore R. Schmidt*, 58 NLRB 1342 (1944).
[9] Harry Arthurs, "Extraterritoriality by Other Means: How Labor Law Sneaks Across Borders, Conquers Minds, and Controls Workplaces Abroad," *Stanford Law and Policy Review* 21 (2010). On differences between U.S. and British labor law, see William B. Gould IV, "Taft Hartley Comes to Great Britain: Observations on the Industrial Relations Act of 1971," *Yale Law Journal* 81 (1972).
[10] Proposed Rules Governing Notification of Employee Rights under the National Labor Relations Act, 29 CFR Part 104 (December 16, 2010). This, along with the board's decision to transmit notices of statutory violations electronically as well as in physical, conspicuous places in the employer's establishment, may assist in making employees aware of the statute and its remedies. *J. Picini Flooring*, 356 NLRB 9 (2010).
[11] Materials were sent to all facilities, union and nonunion, because freedom of association rights apply to both. NLRB v. Magnavox Co., 415 U.S. 322 (1974).
[12] *Eldorado Tool*, 325 NLRB 222, 225 (1997) (Chairman Gould, concurring and dissenting); *Caterpillar, Inc.*, 321NLRB 1178, 1184 (1996) (Chairman Gould, concurring); *Novotel New York*, 321 NLRB 624 (1996); *Shepherd Tissue, Inc.*, 326 NLRB 369 (1998) (Chairman Gould, concurring).
[13] NLRB v. Gissel Packing Co., 395 U.S. 575, 618 (1969); *Eldorado Tool*, 325 NLRB 222.
[14] Thomas v. Collins, 323 U.S. 516 (1945); *Caterpillar, Inc.*, 321 NLRB 1178; *Novotel New York*, 321 NLRB 624.
[15] *Peyton Packing Co., Inc.*, 49 NLRB 828, 843 (1943), enf'd 142 F.2d 1009 (5th Cir.), cert denied, 323 U.S. 730 (1944).
[16] Double Eagle Hotel & Casino v. NLRB, 414 F.3d 1249 (10th Cir. 2005); W.W. Grainger, Inc., 229 NLRB 161, 166 (1977) (no discussion rules should be distinguished from no solicitation rules).
[17] This concept was first adumbrated in *Peyton Packing*, 49 NLRB 828 and accepted by the Supreme Court in Republic Aviation v. NLRB, 324 U.S. 793 (1945).
[18] *Stoddard Quirk Manufacturing Co.*, 138 NLRB 615 (1962).
[19] William B. Gould IV, "The Question of Union Activity on Company Property," *Vanderbilt Law Review* 18 (1964). This confusion was particularly prevalent in the case of FirstGroup's bus operations where the company could not draw a bright line between work and nonwork areas. *Laidlaw Transit, Inc.*, 315 NLRB 79 (1994).

[20] This approach is somewhat akin to the approach taken by the board before the advent of the Eisenhower Administration. *Standard Coosa Thatcher*, 85 NLRB 1358 (1949).
[21] *National Steel & Shipbuilding*, 324 NLRB 499 (1997), enf'd, 156 F.3d 1268 (D.C. Cir. 1998).
[22] *Opryland Hotel*, 323 NLRB 723 (1997).
[23] Local Joint Exec. Bd. of Las Vegas v. NLRB, 515 F.3d 942 (8th Cir. 2008), citing *Kenworth Truck Co., Inc.*, 327 NLRB 497, 501 (1999).
[24] NLRB v. Transportation Mgmt., 462 U.S. 393 (1983); *Frick Paper Co.*, 319 NLRB 9, 10 (1995) (Chairman Gould, concurring).
[25] *Spielberg Manufacturing Co.*, 112 NLRB 1080, 1082 (1955); see also *Olin Corp.*, 268 NLRB 573 (1984); *Mobile Oil Exploration*, 325 NLRB 176, 180 (1997) (Chairman Gould, concurring), enf'd 200 F.3d 230 (5th Cir. 1999). Although there have been many twists and turns and much debate and scholarship regarding the NLRB's deferral policy toward arbitral decisions, these standards still apply.
[26] Although it could be argued that the absence of a hearing causes the procedure not to be "fair and regular," the absence of the hearing makes the process both effective and expeditious. George A. Bermann, "Administrative Delay and Its Control," *American Journal of Compensation Law Support* 30 (1982): 474. ("The path to systemic reform . . . probably lies not only in easing agency workloads and increasing their resources, but also in recognizing that trial-type procedures are not necessarily the best or only fair means of reaching administrative decision.")
[27] Indeed, as one can see from a wide variety of issues discussed previously—the most prominent of them being the company's neutrality policy—the IM Program more effectively protected the basic policies of the NLRA than the statute does itself.
[28] *The American League of Professional Baseball Clubs*, 180 NLRB 190, 191 (1969); see also *Pontiac Osteopathic*, 284 NLRB 442, 466 (1987); *West Maui Resort Partners*, 340 NLRB 846, 850 (2003).
[29] Of course, arbitration itself is therapeutic and not the final step in the process under some circumstances. Carey v. Westinghouse Elec. Co., 375 U.S. 261 (1964).
[30] cf. *Durham Sch. Servs., LP v. N.L.R.B.*, 821 F.3d 52 (D.C. Cir. 2016); *Durham Sch. Servs. LP v. Gen. Drivers Warehousemen & Helpers Loc. Union No 509*, 679 F. App'x 285 (4th Cir. 2017).
[31] "Teamsters, Former NLRB Chair and Community Leaders Lead Symposium on National Express," *International Brotherhood of Teamsters Press Releases*, May 6, 2015; "Institutional investors alarmed at exclusion of shareholder proposal at National Express," Responsible Investor, May 5, 2016.
[32] Sam Roberts, "Bill Lucy, 90, Labor and Civil Rights Leader," *New York Times*, September 30, 2024, A20 (obituary).
[33] Building and Construction Trades Council v. Associated Building et Alia, 507US 218 (1993).
[34] William B. Gould IV, "Draft Guidelines for HUD Contracting Personnel," November 11, 2011 (unpublished, on file with the author).
[35] Herman M. Levy, "The Agricultural Labor Relations Act of 1975 – La Esperanza De California Para El Futuro," *Santa Clara Lawyer* 15 (1975).
[36] Miriam Pawel, *The Browns of California: The Family Dynasty That Transformed a State and Shaped a Nation* (New York: Bloomsbury, 2018), 214.
[37] Pawel, *The Browns of California*.

38 William B. Gould IV, keynote speaker speech, Agricultural Personnel Management Association's 36th Annual Forum, January 28, 2016. Subsequently, the public became aware of substandard farm worker housing, still unaware that many farm workers had and have no housing at all. See Luis Melecio-Zambrano, "Laws Aim to Bolster Farmhand Housing," *San Jose Mercury News*, September 26, 2024, 1, 5. At the time of the tragedy triggering an interest in legislation I wrote: "It's time to provide housing as well as adequate housing. Maybe these killings will wake us up." W. B. Gould IV, Letter to the Editor, *San Francisco Chronicle*, February 1, 2023.

39 William B. Gould IV, speech delivered at the Agricultural Labor Relations Act 40th Anniversary, June 24, 2015.

40 California Senate Rules Committee, 2015 Agricultural Labor Relations Board Confirmation Hearing, February 11, 2015.

41 David Zahniser, Julia Wick, Benjamin Oreskes, Dakota Smith, and Gustavo Arellano, "Racist Remarks in Leaked Audio of L.A. Council Members Spark Outrage, Disgust," *Los Angeles Times*, October 9, 2022.

42 The Republicans have a very different view of this, and it appears that the Roberts Court does as well. William B. Gould IV, "Legal Issues Surrounding Firing of NLRB General Counsel," *Bloomberg Law*, January 28, 2021.

43 Miriam Pawel, *The Crusades of Cesar Chavez* (New York: Bloomsbury Press, 2014).

44 Pawel, *Crusades of Cesar Chavez*.

45 *Tri-Fanucchi Farms*, 40 ALRB 4, 8 (2014) (citations omitted).

46 *Tri-Fanucchi Farms*, 40 ALRB 4, 22-23 (2014) (citations omitted).

47 *Sabor Farms*, 42 ALRB 2, 3 n. 2 (2016).

48 *P&M Vanderpoel Dairy*, 40 ALRB 8, 34 n16 (2014) (Chairman Gould, concurring).

49 *Arnaudo Brothers, Inc.*, 40 ALRB 7, 15 n9 (2014).

50 *P&M Vanderpoel Dairy*, 40 ALRB 8, 33 (2014).

51 *George Amaral Ranches*, Inc., 40 ALRB 10 (2014) (Chairman Gould, concurring).

52 *Gerawan Farming, Inc.*, 42 ALRB 1 (2016) (Chairman Gould, concurring).

53 Agricultural Labor Relations Board v. Superior Court, 16 Cal.3d 392 (1976) (citing William B. Gould IV, Union Organizational Rights and the Concept of "Quasi-Public" Property (1965) 49 MINN. L. REV. 505, 509; William B. Gould IV, The Question of Union Activity on Company Property (1964) 18 VAND. L. REV. 73, 75, 99–100, 102–103).

54 Cedar Point Nursery v. Hassid, 141 S.Ct. 2063 (2021). William B. Gould IV, "Stanford's William Gould on SCOTUS Labor Decision Cedar Point Nursery," *Legal Aggregate*, June 23, 2021.

55 California Agricultural Relations Board, public hearing to receive comment on worksite access, September 9, 2015, Fresno, CA.

56 Geoffrey Mohan, "California Farm Labor Board Chairman Quits in Anger," *Los Angeles Times*, January 13, 2017.

57 Dan Moraine, "Brown Hands out a Plum and Dims his Labor Legacy," *Sacramento Bee*, January 19, 2017.

58 Moraine, "Brown Hands out a Plum," 1-4.

59 Agricultural Labor Relations Voter Choice Act, Assem. Bill 2183, 2021-2022 Reg. Sess. (Cal. 2022). Mathew Miranda and Lindsey Holden, "Biden's Support of California Farmworker Bill Makes It 'Complicated' for Newsom," Sacramento Bee, September 9, 2022.

60 William B. Gould IV (Impartial Chairman), Carol Isen and Gregory Adam, *Public Employment Relations Board Fact Finding Proceedings Between San Francisco Police Officers Association and City and County of San Francisco*, January 28, 2019, 2–3.

61 Gould et al., *Public Employment Relations Board Fact Finding Proceedings*, January 28, 2019, 2–3; Morgado v. City and County of San Francisco et al., 13 Cal App. 5th 1 (2017).

62 Gould et al., *Public Employment Relations Board Fact Finding Proceedings*, January 28, 2019, 6.

63 William B. Gould IV, *Report of San Francisco Independent Reviewer for Mayor London Breed*, June 2021, 2–4.

64 Gould, *Report of San Francisco Independent Reviewer*, 4.

65 City and County of San Francisco, Office of the Mayor, "San Francisco Releases Independent Review of City Workplace Policies and Procedures," news release, July 9, 2021.

66 *Thryv, Inc.*, 372 NLRB No. 22 (2022).

67 This is an important route to better income and security for Black workers who wish to climb the economic ladder but are not inclined to proceed to colleges or universities.

68 Mawuli Tugbenyoh, Deputy Director, Policy and External Affairs to Jacqueline P. Minor, President, Civil Service Commission and Kate Favetti, Vice President, Civil Service Commission, *Status Report on Implementation of Reform Recommendations from the San Francisco Independent Reviewer Report, City and County of San Francisco*, November 23, 2022, 4.

EPILOGUE

Professionally and personally, I have had much good fortune in life. As this book reveals, the springboard for it all was my parents, who provided an environment that allowed me to flourish. As I write this in 2024, at the age of 88, not a day goes by in which I do not recollect some advice or instruction my mother or father provided to me—and which I often ignorantly resisted. My great-grandfather, the first William B. Gould, offered me inspiration, although I never met him. His diary writings echoed the expressions, understated humor, and wisdom of my father, William B. Gould III, whom I've characterized as the greatest man I ever knew.[1] When I encountered and struggled with a variety of difficulties in life, particularly in Washington, reading and reflecting anew on the first WBG's diary gave me both comfort and strength.

But, as I said in the fall of 2023 at the fiftieth anniversary celebration of my tenure at Stanford Law School,[2] I am also lucky due to associations beyond consanguinity. First and foremost, I was very lucky to meet my wife Hilda at the London School of Economics—notwithstanding that it was quite an argumentative meeting, as we debated our differing opinions about the European Common Market! From our enduring relationship emerged three sons and four grandchildren.

Figure 13.1: With my wife, Hilda, at All Saints Episcopal Church in Pasadena, California, at the belated baptism of two of my grandchildren, William Benjamin VI and Alina Emma, c. 2016.

And I was so lucky to have Kurt Hanslowe as my professor during an otherwise dreary, depressing first year at Cornell Law School, to catch his attention by writing one of my best papers for him that year on the confluence between anti-discrimination principles and labor law, and to benefit from his recommendation of me to the United Auto Workers in 1960.

Jack Sheinkman was the second part of the influential Cornell duo. He took a serendipitous interest in me when he discovered that I lived in the same house in Ithaca, 109 Williams Street, that he'd lived in a decade earlier. We met again in New York City in 1962, when I gave my first paper at Kurt Hanslowe's invitation; we corresponded during my time at the London School of Economics; and when I returned to America, Jack's recommendation placed me on Chairman Frank McCullough's staff at the Kennedy administration NLRB. His decision to recommend me to his friend, President Bill Clinton, for a job in which I had not expressed interest, was a major turning point in my career.

One result of the urban riots and unrest of the late 1960s was a push to hire Blacks, Latinos, and women, a development that began to affect academia as the seventies unfolded. I was lucky to appear on the legal scene at that time, when white Americans were temporarily reassessing the relevance of traditional qualifications, even in advance of serious discussions about affirmative action. Although I hadn't been at the very top of my law school class and lacked a judicial clerkship—facts that would have barred me in normal times from recruitment by many law schools—these new social circumstances, combined with my writings, piqued Stanford's interest. I knew no one on the faculty at Stanford Law School until my 1971 interview, but my position there affected my entire career. At Stanford, I was able to write, litigate, consult, and arbitrate without limitation or restriction. My association with so many talented and principled students gave me the sense that my work might last a generation or two beyond my death. As a young lawyer, I had assumed that the law was more important than other factors affecting labor–management relations; my labor law writing at Stanford, as well practical experience obtained as a government official, arbitrator, and civil rights courtroom advocate, broadened and tempered that view.

LABOR AND THE LEGAL WORLD TODAY

As in the 1930s, the first burst of a form of union renewal is now taking place[3] without any law reform whatsoever. Indeed, in the teeth of High Court rulings that constrain the labor movement and employee rights, more militancy has emerged in established labor–management relationships. The legal world looks quite different to me today than it did in the sixties and seventies.

Perhaps now *Brown v. Board of Education* and its progeny provide a similar story about the limitations of law, given the resistance to its implementation, particularly when Black plaintiffs applied to the courts for the elimination of de facto discrimination in the North. Though *Brown* litigation began to sputter, Title VII allowed me to make up for my missing-in-action status in 1963 and 1964, only partially remedied by my work for the Equal Employment

Opportunity Commission in 1966 and 1967. In 2021, as noted in the previous chapter, I was able to fashion extensive recommendations aimed at the road to a "reckoning" for municipal racial misconduct and deficiencies in San Francisco.

My parents, who made my work possible, suffered and persevered under a system which possessed sharp barriers. My father instilled in me a truly accurate sense of American history which, along with *Brown v. Board of Education* and other 1954 developments, turned me toward the law. In the 1980s and 1990s, before I began to actively write and edit the story told in the diary my great-grandfather kept between 1862 and 1865, I had connected the ideas of equality and fairness with law. I observed the significance of the remedial provisions of the National Labor Relations Act in particular and began to focus upon the institutional process devised by Tyree Scott and others in Seattle, attempting to emulate some of what he had done in *Detroit Edison* and in other initiatives.

Now, concepts of reparation, restoration, rehabilitation, and redemption have become increasingly important. The need for a reckoning, which captured the nation's attention through George Floyd and the Black Lives Matter movement, revives the ever-pressing concern with racial inequality. I agree with reparations proponents in their assessment of 2024 and beyond, particularly that articulated by William A. Darity Jr. and A. Kirsten Mullen when they write:

> *Today, black–white racial disparities are real, extensive, and quantifiable. They are attributable to the persistence of racism and discrimination in the United States. The current condition of black Americans is a tragic testament to the nation's brutal racial history.*[4]

But I do not believe that individual payments to the descendants of slavery are the logical or suitable remedy. The process is both under- and over-inclusive, given other alternatives.

Although I am descended from slavery, my good fortune in life makes payment to me—and to others similarly situated—inappropriate. The impoverished, who are disproportionately unable to

EPILOGUE

trace their lineage from slavery or to point to an identifiable forebear in the nineteenth century, need help. Inequality has been and remains part of the American system, tied inevitably to the wrong done and profits obtained through both slavery and its aftermath, in the United States and in the West. And the impoverishment of Blacks and others, disproportionately homeless in the streets, suffering healthcare deficiencies, poor education, and job exclusion, must be addressed. The country desperately needs a domestic Marshall Plan that addresses education, job training, and healthcare inequities.

Of course, the realization of such steps forward is unlikely in the current political environment. But, in my view, it is more likely to be realized than cash payments to individual descendants of slavery, which are also less likely to be effective.

In October 2023, at a colloquium organized at the Los Angeles Public Library, I compared this problem to some of the issues presented in the landmark Supreme Court case *Griggs v. Duke Power*[5] (discussed in chapter 2), where the Court held that neutral practices which are nondiscriminatory on their face could nonetheless violate Title VII because of their adverse disproportionate impact upon Blacks.[6] I pointed out that job relatedness—the relationship between the qualifications for access, and the demands of the work as it is actually performed in the real world—and the standards utilized by companies were not changed only for the group discriminated against. By necessity, they were applied to all employees. *Griggs*, like the California wrongful discharge commission I chaired in the 1980s, was fundamentally a search for fair practices and behavior. This is the legacy provided by these early decisions and, in the case of wrongful discharge, recommendations fashioned in the seventies and eighties. This fairness concept should be appropriate to reparations-type issues. A broad and ambitious plan for the poor and those whose lives have been less fortunate is the best answer. It matters not, it seems to me, that others besides Black workers might also be the recipients.

This general approach, promoting fair practices, is what I have tried to achieve in my life and work. The fundamental motivation was described by the *San Francisco Chronicle* more than two decades ago:

> *On a hot July day three years ago, William B. Gould IV knelt in prayer in Brookdale Cemetery in Dedham, Mass., before the graves of his father, grandfather and great-grandfather, the first William Gould, who had escaped from slavery to fight in the Civil War.*
>
> *As he prayed, Bill Gould could look back on a life of accomplishment. A professor of law at Stanford University, the author of half a dozen books, husband and father of three sons, he had every reason to be proud.*
>
> *While a chairman of the National Labor Relations Board under President Bill Clinton from 1994 to 1998, he didn't back down from political "combat" with conservatives in the nation's capital. He found strength in knowing that "the most withering right-wing Republican attacks were miniscule and of little significance compared to what my great-grandfather endured."*[7]

Since the 1860s, the objective of my family has been to promote the interests of those who "travail and are heavy laden," a lesson I learned in my formative years. It is a lesson and an objective worth carrying forward, in this century and beyond.

NOTES

[1] William B. Gould IV, *Diary of a Contraband: The Civil War Passage of a Black Sailor* (Stanford: Stanford University Press, 2002), 1.

[2] Mirabile dictu, two Stanford Law School 1970 graduates—Richard Morningstar (whom I had met once when he taught a visiting course at the Law School) and Allen Pick (who was unknown to me previously)—organized a fiftieth Stanford Law School anniversary celebration for me in the fall of 2023.

[3] Nora Eckert and Mike Colias, "Activists Helped Get Huge UAW Win," *Wall Street Journal*, November 1, 2023; Nora Eckert, "UAW Urges Honda, Subaru Workers to Join Union," *Wall Street Journal*, November 11–12, 2023.

⁴ William A. Darity and A. Kirsten Mullen, *From Here to Equality: Reparations for Black Americans in the Twenty-First Century* (Chapel Hill: The University of North Carolina Press, 2020), 47.
⁵ Griggs v. Duke Power Co., 401 U.S. 424 (1971).
⁶ Beth Piatote and William B. Gould IV, "Language, the Law, and Restorative Justice: A Conversation with Beth Piatote and William B. Gould," Los Angeles Public Library, October 26, 2023, video recording, https://www.youtube.com/watch?v=bxC4GXzrUCc&ab_channel=LAPublicLibrary.
⁷ Mike Weiss, "Stanford Professor Finds Peace in Publishing Slave Ancestor's Diary," *San Francisco Chronicle*, September 2, 2002.

APPENDIX 1

WILLIAM B. GOULD IV, INTRODUCTION OF REV. JESSE JACKSON, JANUARY 15, 1987 AT STANFORD UNIVERSITY

Accepting the invitation of the Stanford Black Union to introduce the Reverend Jesse Jackson in today's commemoration of Martin Luther King Jr. is a privilege. For it is clear that Reverend Jackson has carried forward into the seventies and eighties the torch held so firmly by Martin Luther King until his death two decades ago. Like Dr. King, Jesse Jackson has preached a social gospel. He has thus linked the good news to the poor, the voiceless, and despised in the Scriptures' teachings to a contemporary world in which the plight of the homeless and the violence of Howard Beach have dramatized anew the need to open up opportunities for all in our country regardless of race, sex, economic status, and other arbitrary considerations.

Dr. King, and others like Reverend Jackson, were on the cutting edge of the movement propelled by these ideas in the sixties. What has arisen in the interim, of course, is the outcome of the '80 and '84 elections, the consequent insensitivity to these concerns now held by the White House's current occupants and the emergence of a vigorous, well-financed fundamentalist religious white right wing. These developments, in turn, have both perverted the Old Testament view of a just God and the New Testament's Comfortable Words to those who travail and are heavy laden and they have also confused in some minds our well-founded adherence to separation of church and state on the one hand with the relationship between politics and religion, the concepts of justice that are properly involved in both.

The Episcopal Church's House of Bishops put it well in the midst of the '84 campaign when it said:

> *If in some sense, a wall of separation is seen to be drawn between the institutions of the church and those of the state, there is no legitimate separation between religious belief and the shaping of public policy. To separate religion from politics is to impoverish both. The prophetic voice adds a vital perspective in the shaping of public policy. Religion serves its proper function when it seeks to speak on behalf of the voiceless the voice of God among the powers of any society. That is an essential element of the people's free expression of religion.*[1]

There are then at least three themes which make manifest the Reverend Jackson's focus upon the principles articulated so forcefully and bravely by Dr. King. The first is the one that has been alluded to a number of times here, the irrelevance of national boundaries to the struggle for justice throughout the world. For like Poland's Solidarity, which broke forth spontaneously more than six years ago, the unceasing campaign of the now 75-year-old African National Congress in South Africa is internationally center stage and properly so. And our speaker has played an important role in putting it there and reaching with his word and deeds to the powerless in that country as well as in this country.

A second theme is especially appropriate for us to reflect on during this 200th anniversary of our Constitution, which belatedly became an imperfect vehicle for the attack upon racial oppression in this century, in this country. The fact is that this struggle is forever hobbled in a society such as ours, which has become increasingly unequal economically. The Reverend Jesse Jackson's Rainbow Coalition focused attention upon this subject early in the '84 campaign.

And third, the Reverend Jackson, by standing for President in '84, made Americans of all races consider seriously the idea of a Black American as President of the United States. And, in so doing, he put the forgotten cause of civil rights back on the agenda of American politics.

We do well to commemorate Martin Luther King's birthday today. But as Lincoln said at Gettysburg, it is for us the living rather to be dedicated here to the unfinished work they have thus far nobly advanced. What Jesse Jackson said to students in the '84 primaries is with us today. Your generation cannot become great just by remembering what that generation did. You must serve your present age.

On behalf of the entire Stanford community, it is a pleasure and privilege to introduce to you the Reverend Jesse Jackson.

APPENDIX 2

"FAIR WINDS AND FOLLOWING SEAS," REMARKS GIVEN AT MEMORIAL SERVICE FOR EUGENE P. ANGRIST, NOVEMBER 5, 2005 IN WASHINGTON, DC

Bookshelves and baseball games . . . that's where it all started. We knew each other during the summer months and would go our separate ways during the academic year, which diminished the potential for independent reading.

The sometimes wheezy hilarity and expressiveness in that uproarious laughter . . . the biggest reclining chairs that I had ever seen in my life—and probably at any point thereafter—addressing ourselves as "counselor" as each of us began to advance through law school . . . and those many, many discussions.

When this year I saw Gene Angrist during two visits to this area, we reflected anew on how we had met fifty years ago and become fast friends in New Jersey during the summer of 1955. I was working at the Asbury Park Boardwalk and met Gene through one of my coworkers who was a good friend of Gene's from high school. Politics and baseball were to be perennials with us and sparked the first of many discussions that we had over the years—particularly those first early years of our friendship. We drove back and forth from our respective homes in Elberon and Belmar and became thoroughly acquainted with and enjoyed each other's parents during that time.

Unlike so many of our generation who found it fashionable to abandon either the Giants or the Dodgers or baseball altogether because both teams had moved west, Gene's loyalty to the Giants remained intact then and extended beyond the frontiers of Coogan's Bluff. Gene had a TV grander than the one in my Elberon home, and I can recall countless occasions in his living room watching his Giants in the midst of memorable events, particularly the Alou brothers' simultaneous outfield appearance for his *Los Gigantes*. Except for 1955 and 1959, those were doleful days for my Red Sox and my recollection is that they nearly always took a backseat to Gene's team.

Politics and baseball . . . not always in that order . . . and then, politics, baseball, and literature. I remember that my father, in his understated way, repeated the well-worn maxim to Gene and myself that there were only three things worth discussing—politics, religion, and, he said, the third was "what was that other one?" Gene and I also often spoke of the "what was that other one?" in those days.

We also spoke of death. I remember that these talks left me so unsettled and unaccepting that Gene suggested that I read about it. Either at his suggestion or my own initiative—I cannot now remember which—I read James Agee's *A Death in the Family* and its description of the "sour and cold, taciturn taste of iron" which must be endured. This week I reread that book as I reflected on my friendship with Gene.

Last March when I returned home to the west coast after what was to be my penultimate meeting with Gene, I wrote to tell him how important our nearly daily discussions of what we had read in those years had been to me. There has never been a time when I read so voraciously . . . Tolstoy, Faulkner, Hemingway, Theodore Dreiser, Richard Wright, Boccaccio, the Greek scholars, the list goes on. And it was because of our friendship, the fact that we could discuss these works together frequently, Gene suggesting a title which would take me down completely unanticipated avenues. In my letter to Gene, I think that I told him that, along with our daily and weekly reading of the *New York Times* and *The New Republic* and the foibles of Eisenhower on civil rights (this year we spoke of how well they compared to Washington in 2005), nothing had influenced my future work and writing so directly.

This year we agreed that we would see a couple of baseball games together. As many here know, Gene, to put it mildly, had become enthused about the advent of the Washington Nationals, lobbying hard for a new franchise in the nation's capital. So we made a deal: We would go to one Washington Nationals game and one of the Baltimore Orioles, presided over by my good friend Peter Angelos, about whose baseball acumen Gene has expressed some skepticism. I had tried to alter Gene's views, in part, because Angelos had become such a good pal.

In late May and early June we went to both parks, Gene being in the best of spirits and form for a remarkably candid discussion with Angelos as we heard his views about his manager and his team while we sat with him in his box. Gene seemed to love every minute of it.

In a day or so we were at RFK together on a lovely afternoon when a disputed home run revealed that the field was not laid out properly. I think that here also Gene had a splendid time—and the fact that he was greeted by colleagues was icing on the cake. At some point during those days he told me that it was his hope to see Opening Day in 2006. If only that had been possible.

On that day, next year, if I should see it, I will think especially of Gene and our memories of this past half century—just as I do when I look at the bookshelves in my home and office and realize that so many of the volumes came into my life by virtue of my friendship with this intellectually curious, remarkable and good man, Gene Angrist.

APPENDIX 3

WILLIAM B. GOULD IV, "ALWAYS AND FOREVER, A RED SOX DEVOTEE," *RED SOX MAGAZINE*, 2008

It all goes back to that sweet summer of 1946. That was the first year our sandlot baseball gang played the game daily, morning and afternoon, on a New Jersey makeshift lot with right-field dimensions more hitter-friendly than those in left field that the Red Sox confronted in the Los Angeles Coliseum in March. The Red Sox had the wind to their backs that summer, sprinting ahead of both the Tigers and Yankees, and I threw in my lot with the Carmine Hose, both because Boston was my birthplace as well as the fact that I found New Jerseybased Yankee fans to be insufferable.

Cocktail chatter about the "Curse of the Bambino" was then unknown, and 1947 left me undeterred. My loyalty was unwavering even through the dolorous 1950s and early 1960s, caused in part by the club's tardiness in dropping the color bar.

For it was the Sox eternal verities which always kept me in the fold, idiosyncratic Fenway Park, the "Green Monster," so comfortable for the likes of Vern Stephens, Jackie Jensen, Jim Rice, and Tony Armas . . . the home white uniforms emblazoned with the beautiful red-lettered "Red Sox," and the dignified, black-lettered, gray road uniform. Meanwhile, I exulted in "Yaz" and the 1967 "Impossible Dream," flying to Boston for the first World Series game I had ever witnessed.

Before and after '67, a mélange of memories sustained me . . . present day Coach Luis Alicea turning an acrobatic-like double play behind Tim Wakefield in 1995 . . . the unbeatable Luis Tiant in the 1972 pennant race until it all fell short on the season's penultimate day. On the other side of the spectrum, the same year I witnessed zany Bill Lee's 9th-inning surrender of a grand slam home run to Bill Freehan over the Green Monster to ruin rookie Lynn McGlothen's earlier flirtation with a no-hitter and then a shutout.

My father took me to my very first Red Sox game in May 1947 when 25-game winner Dave Ferriss was bested by Spud Chandler, 5–0, and Ted Williams went hitless at Yankee Stadium. While a student at the London School of Economics sixteen years later, he regularly mailed me the standings which showed the Johnny Pesky-led BoSox leading the pack with Dick Stuart (Dr. Strangeglove) authoring prodigious homers—but when I returned to America the lead had already vanished!

My mother and I went to Yankee Stadium on Memorial Day 1950 to see the Townies drop a doubleheader (emblematically her pocket was picked), a team on which every single member of the lineup was hitting over .300. That Red Sox club posted the last team .300 batting average ever at a clip of .302. In the seventies, year after year my boys and I sat in the Oakland Coliseum to bid farewell to the team after the conclusion of their last series of the season, regardless of the last game's outcome, until the ushers shooed us out.

At times of near despair, I could almost concur with the comment of a lady sitting next to me during the free agent exodus of Lynn, Fisk, and Burleson of the early eighties when she said, "I don't care whether they win or lose, it's just good to see them out there." But, of course, I always wanted the Red Sox to win. Don Zimmer, manager of the power-laden Sox from '76–'79, encapsulated my perspective when he said to me behind a Candlestick Park batting cage years later: "There were always so many more good days than bad days."

I shall never forget the Fenway sixteen-homer barrage in a June 1977 three-game series—four were tagged off "Catfish" Hunter in the first inning—when the Red Sox swept the Yankees and Billy Martin tussled with Reggie Jackson in the dugout.

But, though Boston born, most of the hundreds of Red Sox games that I have witnessed have been in exile in cities like Washington, Baltimore, New York, Detroit, and now in Oakland and Anaheim, California, since my arrival here thirty-six years ago. In 1960, I leaped to my feet when Frank Malzone hit a bases-loaded single, in the midst of Tiger Stadium silence so profound that one could hear the Sox's footsteps rounding the bases. All of this gave me the chance to appreciate both solitary devotion as well as traits which the home park had undervalued in the past century: speed and defense.

Now, in the twenty-first century, it has all happened. After attending the '03 fifth Oakland A's–Red Sox playoff game in which Derek Lowe somehow pounded out the last two batters in the most tense, hard-fought post-season game that l have seen (since the three that were played in Anaheim in 1986 in which Dave Henderson brought us back from the dead in the fateful game five), I have seen the second coming of Dave (Dave Roberts) with his critical stolen base in the fourth ALCS '04 game.

Now the team, possessing speed, power, pitching, and capacity attendance (my first '51 Fenway game was attended by 5,000), has twice achieved the Holy Grail in this century. As an acquaintance said to me during the late summer of '07 referring to '04: "Now you can die in peace." Anticipating what was to come that year, I said to him: "Oh no, I want many more." And I still do. And I want many, many more. Go Sox!

APPENDIX 4

WILLIAM B. GOULD IV, "MY FIFTY YEARS IN BASEBALL: WAYS IN WHICH THE GAME HAS CHANGED AND STAYED THE SAME," AS THE INAUGURAL SPEAKER OF THE ANNUAL HUGHIE JENNINGS MEMORIAL LECTURE SERIES, APRIL 1, 1996 AT UNIVERSITY OF MARYLAND LAW SCHOOL

A year ago today, Judge Sonya Sotomayor granted the National Labor Relations Board's injunction order that it had voted to seek on March 26, 1995. In the hope that the owners and players could resolve their differences voluntarily without resort to law, I had delayed the board's meeting on this matter—but it quickly became apparent to me that consideration of legal intervention was required. With an order restraining unilateral changes on critical employment conditions in place, the players agreed to return to work. The owners accepted their offer, an abbreviated spring training commenced, free agents were signed out of a new training camp devised by the players association, and thus was born the '95 season. Now, as spring hesitantly attempts to dispel the dolorous memories of the Blizzard of '96 and the senseless government shutdowns that were associated with it, baseball—both sides of the bargaining table—solicits forgiveness from America. Notwithstanding their inability to negotiate a collective bargaining agreement, the NLRB's injunction has pushed the parties back to negotiations with reports of proposals and offers and counterproposals floating through the air.

Young boys and girls—and some not so young—can once again practice their batting stances or hold the runner on base pitching out of the stretch while imagining tense moments, along with the celebrations and glory of the game in their living rooms, while waiting for buses or trains, mimicking Blue Moon Odom's countless throws to first base as he carefully scrutinized each advancing Cincinnati base runner from his eye's corner in the '72 World Series.

Baseball, the world's most elegant game, is back, with spring's renewed hope about life itself—and, in this Holy Week before Easter Day, back for its first full length season since Joe Carter's joyously animated base-circling home run trot drew down the '93 season for the since plummeted Toronto Blue Jays.

Truly, Baltimore is an appropriate venue for this discussion—and not simply because the advent of no-nonsense manager Davey Johnson with a passel of new superstars like Roberto Alomar make the Orioles the game's most promising team on paper since the Boston Red Sox of the late forties and its 1950 version which hit .302—the last team ever to hit .300.

Peter Angelos, the O's executive helmsman, is the one who has brought Mercker, Surhoff, Meyers, McDowell, and Wells here to augment last year's acquisition of the terrible tempered Bobby Bonilla. And, even more importantly, it was Mr. Angelos, along with the sagacious Sparky Anderson—whose last game (hopefully not forever) was managed here in Camden Yards—who refused to accede to the employment of strikebreakers, an idea so silly as to have imperiled baseball's future far beyond anything imagined today.

And it is Cal Ripken, with his grace and selflessness in a sport which indulges individualism, who began the road back with his gracious acceptance of last September's accolades for breaking Lou Gehrig's record. Ripken's next sixty-two games will match the world's consecutive games record held by Sachio Kinegusa of Japan's Hiroshima Carp, with whom I had a clubhouse visit in that country's '78 season.

But it is the University of Maryland Law School's own Hall of Famer, Hughie Jennings, the inspiration for this lecture series, who dramatizes the contemporary paradox. For, like love and life itself, it transcends the immediate, burrowing itself deeply within our inner fabric and psyche. And yet, the fact that baseball was even spelled differently in the time of Jennings—it was the National Base Ball League and National Base Ball Players Association more than 100 years ago—which tells us that the game inevitably changes, even when it appears returning to old themes. Jennings, a member of the previous century's original Baltimore Orioles and, like myself, a graduate of Cornell Law School, employed baseball's most notorious strikebreakers when he managed the Detroit Tigers and the team struck to protest Ty Cobb's suspension for attacking a spectator. The incident, which ended with Commissioner Ban Johnson's $50 fine per game, antedated the National Labor Relations Act by twenty-three years, occurring the same year as baseball's shrine, Fenway Park, was constructed. Thus, the protected status of that 1912 walkout never came to my agency for adjudication.

My fifty years in baseball takes me back almost halfway to Hughie Jennings to our house on 450 Bath Avenue, Long Branch, New Jersey. Our neighbors, the Hessleins, had three kids who were all older than me—and the activities in their house, particularly the radio on their porch, held deep fascination for this kid about to turn 10. In that hot summer of 1946, the radio blared loudly from the Hessleins' porch with Mel Allen's soothing baritone references to a "Ballantine Blast" and a "White Owl Wallop," and his newsy descriptions of the activities of Joe DiMaggio and Phil Rizzuto. (Another of his favorite personalities, Yogi—or Lawrence Peter as he was initially known—Berra would only arrive the following September.)

In 1946 I looked up to Robbie Hesslein who, just a few years before, during World War II, had been so clever and generous in building a couple of wooden battleships for me that I could float in the bathtub, dreaming of the war that I constantly read about with Germany and Japan and how my ships would fare against air attacks from Messerschmitts and Zeros. But, somehow, I could not accept the Hessleins' lead in baseball. Perhaps it was because Mrs. Hesslein confided in me that she really wanted Billy Conn to defeat our beloved "Brown Bomber" Joe Louis in that summer of '46. But I think that it was rooted in events which transpired just a few miles away from our home off the Jersey shore.

Every day that summer my mother packed a lunch for me in the morning and I, and my pals, bicycled to the Station Field near the railroad tracks and played baseball from morning to dusk. Every day, as we biked back and forth to the field, we talked about playing the game and what we had read in the *New York Times* (my parents forbade me to read the *Daily News*) and the dramatic descriptions provided to us at 6:45 p.m. through Stan Lomax's "day's doings in the world of sports."

In the late forties I listened as Stan Lomax said:

> *Good evening everyone, this is Stan Lomax with the "day's doings in the world of sports." And today those Boston Red Sox continued to rare and tear . . .*

Lomax's next sentence or two would sometimes be drowned out by the ensuing eruption. In that sweet summer of 1946, the Red Sox had the wind to their back and, notwithstanding the delay in clinching the pennant until Ted Williams's uncharacteristic inside the park home run to left field of all places in Municipal Stadium (he always defied the "Williams Shift" devised by Lou Boudreau), were never seriously challenged until that fateful seven game series in October in which St. Louis Cardinal slugger Enos Slaughter raced daringly to the plate with the winning run.

Ted Williams socked two beautiful home runs in the American League's route of senior circuit in the All-Star Game held in Fenway Park that year—the second particularly dramatic because it came off the famous "blooper" pitch of the Pittsburgh Pirates' Rip Sewell. Fireballing, Iowa-born Bobby Feller of the Cleveland Indians fanned a record 348 and the multitalented Mel Allen sang, "Hey Baba Reba" as Boston's Mike Ryba entered a game from the Boston bullpen.

APPENDIX 4 491

That summer of '46 was a fateful one in a number of respects. First, it inculcated in our group of sandlot ballplayers an unqualified love and passion for the game itself and, in my case, the Boston Red Sox, with whom I made a lifelong commitment, returning to my birthplace in Boston and ultimately scheduling business trips throughout the country so as to coincide with the arrival of the Carmine Hose. One of the "down" moments with the Red Sox—and, of course, there have been a good many in the many near misses over the past fifty years—was the elimination of the dignified road gray uniform with black-lettered BOSTON and no names on the back in 1990. "I feel like a California Angel," Red Sox perennial right fielder Dwight Evans told me that summer. The front office simply did not really understand how emblazoned that uniform was in the consciousness of this California Red Sox fan in exile.

Yet the distinctive home uniform white with red letters remains. It is still the timeless game which could go on forever, with the real grass, and idiosyncratic ballpark features which we all took for granted suddenly being appreciated anew here in Camden Yards and Cleveland's Jacobs Field. Baseball's exposure to the elements, the potential rain which I feared so much that May 1947 day when my father and I took the train to Yankee Stadium . . . and then the sun broke through the clouds, allowing me to see the Red Sox and the great Ted Williams, the greatest that the game has produced in my lifetime, for the first time ever. The rain delays that plagued us today makes one think back to "Oil Can" Boyd's ability to pitch after an hour of rain delay in Memorial Stadium in 1984. Along with the wind and the location of the sun, they add to elements so uncertain as to be comparable to the contours of life itself.

The immediate post-World War II period of my childhood was important in more fundamental respects and developments, and baseball mirrored them as well. My late father—who had no real interest in the game at that time, announced at the dinner table that Jackie Robinson had knocked one in in the first game of the Yankee–Dodger Subway Series in '47, even before I could read it in *The Times* myself. Robinson's lonely and brave fight to succeed in the face of racial insults from his fellow players, along with the Supreme Court's landmark decisions and the 1960s enactment of employment and voting discrimination legislation, paved the way for people like myself in the legal profession and able managers like my friends Dusty Baker of the San Francisco Giants, and Don Baylor, who was an indispensable element in the '86 Red Sox AL Championship, now mounting the top steps of the Colorado Rockies' dugout. The adoption of Number 42 by MVP Bosox slugger Mo Vaughn is yet another appropriate tribute to Robinson's unique achievement in baseball and American history.

But I only saw Robinson play once in my life in person. I never saw the Great Ted Williams hit one out of the park. My contact with the game was rooted in playing sandlot ball on that much frequented Station Field, and the imagery I fashioned from both radio and newspapers. (There was no television then and in the late forties; it seemed as though only the rich had access to it.)

Figure A.1: Celebrating the dedication of William B. Gould's diary to the Massachusetts Historical Society, the Boston Red Sox invited me to throw the ceremonial first pitch on Jackie Robinson Day, April 15, 2006. (William B. Gould's photos appeared on the scoreboard of Fenway Park that day.)

APPENDIX 4   493

"Do the Red Sox know how much you appreciate them?" said my Aunt Isabel during one of my visits to her Dedham home when I was a visiting professor at Harvard Law School in '71–'72. Only in May 1986 did I first set foot in a big-league dugout when credentialed as a journalist freelancer for the *San Francisco Examiner*. My broadcasts of Stanford baseball games, as well as my work as a salary arbitrator for baseball and my involvement in the game as chairman of the National Labor Relations Board was to come much later, but the roots of it all were in those long idyllic summer days of the forties.

For as we continued our baseball activities in yet another hot summer of 1949, suddenly names with which none of us had been very familiar began to emerge—Mickey Owen, we read, had dropped that famous third strike in the '41 World Series . . . somehow I had been able to recall Pearl Harbor, but not that classic moment. The Cardinal left hander, Max Lanier, whose son was later to climb the dugout steps in President Bush's adopted city of Houston . . . Sal "The Barber" Maglie, who was to figure so prominently in both Brooklyn and New York Giant lore—and the relatively obscure, Danny Gardella, the utility player who struggled to traverse the Mendoza line of a .200 batting average.

All of these people had departed organized baseball for the Mexican League in 1946—and suddenly here they were returning as we played on in '49 in that incredibly tense Red Sox–Yankee pennant race in which the fortunes of each team shifted so dramatically as the months unfolded, the circus-like catch which Al Zarilla made, leaping into the Yankee Stadium right field stands a week before the pennant race ended, the much disputed winning run produced by Johnny Pesky's slide under Ralph Houk's tag— all culminating in the high-noon confrontation on the final day of the season as Tommy Henrich gloved the high-twisting foul ball by Birdie Tebbetts in front of the Yankee first base dugout for the last out.

The players who had left for Mexico that year had violated the terms of the reserve clause and were banned from playing in organized baseball in the Major Leagues. Gardella, of the New York

Giants, brought suit under the Sherman Antitrust Act. The federal district court dismissed Gardella's complaint on the ground that it had no jurisdiction. This conclusion was arrived at because of the United States Supreme Court's holding *in Federal Baseball Club of Baltimore, Inc. v. National League of Professional Baseball Clubs*.[2]

In that case, it is to be recalled that Justice Holmes, like some of the great baseball players of our time, had a bad day, and held that major league baseball clubs were not engaged in interstate commerce or trade, at least within the meaning of antitrust legislation, the issue presented there. Notwithstanding the principle of stare decisis, the U.S. Court of Appeals for the Second Circuit in *Gardella v. Chandler*[3] had sent the case back to trial. Judge Hand, concluding that it was possible for the plaintiff to prove that interstate activities were present in baseball, stated that although: "insufficient before, in conjunction with broadcasting and television—[might] together form a large enough part of the business to impress upon it an interstate character." Judge Frank, who adopted an even more questioning posture toward *Federal Baseball*, noted the "comprehensive sweep" of both the Sherman Antitrust Act and its reliance upon cases construing the National Labor Relations Act and stated that we must, given modern developments: "consider this case as if the only audiences for whom the games are played consists of those persons who, in other states, see, hear, or hear about the games via television and radio."

For the most part, my world was radio—not television. Mel Allen, the Dodgers' Red Barber with his relaxed musings about the "catbird seat," and then Jim Britt of the Red Sox on the shortwave radio that my father had fixed up for me so that I could listen to the developments involving my club firsthand. The *Gardella* case was remanded for trial in light of the court's distinction of and ultimately challenge to the principles of *Federal Baseball*—a distinction based upon radio heard by a ten-year-old, a medium once feared by the owners because they thought it would empty their parks.

Gardella sent a tremor through organized baseball and, thus, it settled with Gardella, Owen, Maglie, Lanier, and others. But the Second Circuit's challenge to *Federal Baseball Club* died aborning

APPENDIX 4   495

in *Toolson v. New York Yankees, Inc.*,[4] and *Flood v. Kuhn*[5] in which the St. Louis Cardinals eminent center fielder who, bad arm and all, threw underhanded from the outfield in the 1967 and 1968 World Series, unsuccessfully sought to have the court reconsider *Federal Baseball*.

Meanwhile, however, another drama was unfolding. My predecessors at the National Labor Relations Board, taking into account the National Labor Relations Act cases to which Judge Frank referred, took jurisdiction over the industry in 1969[6] and set the stage for our involvement in the biggest dispute of them all, the '94–'95 strike of the Major League Baseball Players Association.

In the last weekend of the '95 season, as the Red Sox prepared for their fateful playoff confrontation with the demonstrably superior Cleveland Indians in which old friend Tony Peña put an end to "impossible dream"-type hopes with a home run at 2:15 a.m. Eastern Standard Time, and rumors swirled around the head of Sparky Anderson about his future employment as his team played out the string with the Baltimore Orioles here in this town, the Court of Appeals for the Second Circuit affirmed the position taken by the board and Judge Sotomayor in resounding fashion. The court concluded that free agency, salary arbitration, and other provisions relating to the reserve clause were mandatory subjects of bargaining within the meaning of the act. The court reiterated its view that collective bargaining between professional athletics and leagues raises "numerous problems with little or no precedent in standard industrial relations."[7] The court concluded that the injunction which our agency had sought was "just and proper." Said the court:

> Given the short careers of professional athletics and the deterioration of physical abilities through aging, the irreparable harm requirement has been met.[8]

The board's decision and its affirmance by the district court and in the Second Circuit Court of Appeals was vindication for the public interest and the effective interpretation and administration of the National Labor Relations Act. It was indeed a long deep drive for collective bargaining![9] It brought about the resumption of the 1995 baseball season, and it heralds the chance for baseball to reclaim its status as the nation's game.

Though a new round of hearings is scheduled to begin with an administrative law judge of our agency on April 29, the fact is that the hearing has been postponed on a number of occasions in the past at the request of both sides in order to accommodate the continuing efforts to reach a collective bargaining agreement and to thus settle the unfair labor practice charges which are still outstanding before us. Questions of a payroll tax and revenue sharing are being discussed with the parties, and it is generally anticipated that strikes and lockouts are not part of the plans for the '96 season.

And so it appears that there will be a chance to focus upon the game. "Strike called at the knees" is something that I heard frequently in those broadcasts of the forties and fifties. The new rule changes have brought us full circle. Similarly, the sight of a Brady Anderson triple with the ball ricocheting high off the ledge in Camden Yard's right field brings back special memories of the ball doing the unexpected in Fenway's "Pesky's Corner" and long fly balls which are recorded as putouts in Yankee Stadium's "Death Valley" in left center.

But there is a good deal of change this 1996 Opening Day. Paradoxically, the emergence of the new parks seems to have spelled almost immediate demise of not only Candlestick Park with its winds that come kicking up at 3:00 p.m. every day, but also the shrines like Fenway Park and Tiger Stadium. It can be built and they will come—so said the voters of San Francisco last month!

Notwithstanding the effectiveness of the National Labor Relations Act in producing peace in baseball, the lengthy '94–'95 strike as well as recurrent strikes and lockouts before it indicate that the act may not be relevant to some of the problems which plague America's game. President Clinton proposed compulsory arbitration legislation in early '95 only to have it rejected by the Republican leadership in Congress.

As the Second Circuit has said, the problems with professional sports are different. This is the way the Supreme Court's consideration of *Brown v. Pro Football*,[10] now before the Supreme Court, a dispute between the NFL Players Association and the National Football League over the unilateral imposition of a uniformed salary for so-called developmental players, dramatizes anew the anomalies between the legal treatment of baseball and other sports. This case involves the applicability of antitrust to professional football—an earlier decision did the same for basketball[11]—and the accommodation that must be struck between antitrust and labor law—an accommodation not present in baseball given the continued viability of *Federal Baseball Club*.

In *Brown* the Court of Appeals for the District of Columbia stated that antitrust could only be used where the union and the collective bargaining process were not in existence. On at least three occasions in the past, in both football and basketball, the players associations have used the basic implications of this line of authority to disappear through decertification or something akin to it—and then revive mirable dictu in order to negotiate an agreement which the owners needed desperately to avail themselves of the implied labor exemption immunity to antitrust law which a collective agreement clearly gives them. The difficulty with the position taken by the lower court in *Brown*, however, is that it invites game playing on both sides about the actual existence of the union, promotes an incentive to a false hari-kari or union suicide, and promotes disaffiliation with unions and the collective bargaining process, which is the antithesis of the policy purposes of the National Labor Relations Act for which I have responsibility.

Professional sports are different, and they will see change. Perhaps the Supreme Court's promotion of antitrust at some point subsequent to impasse and the collective bargaining process—but considerably short of the elimination of the process altogether—will invite reexamination of baseball and antitrust. Players will move from team to team with the advent of antitrust [*sic*]—but Cal Ripken is testimony to the fact that players can remain with one team even in today's enhanced free market.

And, of course, the Washington Senators, the Philadelphia Athletics, and the St. Louis Browns always dealt players to other teams—through trades or sales and not free agency. In response to escalating costs associated with players' salaries, as well as antitrust litigation by cities who have been left out of Major League baseball, expansion and even relocation in the future may be inevitable. This will lead to a new focus upon expansion south of the border as well as north of it—a phenomenon which we will hear more about when the San Diego Padres, pushed out of town by the Republican Party this summer, will play games in Mexico. Ultimately, in one form or another there will be formal playoff or a genuine World Series between America and Japan. The advent of Hideo Nomo of the Los Angeles Dodgers as well as the tensions confronting Fidel Castro have made Americans aware that there is a great deal of good talent in the Far East, Latin America, and Australia. All of it will not come to America.

Meanwhile, interleague play advocated by many like Williams, even when I was a small boy in Long Branch, will be good for the game. But baseball should not tinker with the game itself—for there is nothing wrong with it. What baseball needs to do is to advertise its ambiance, to invite, for instance, fans into the stadium when batting practice commences. Then, once again, fans will know the identity of those more mobile players without any concession to limited attention spans and the consequent need to place names on the backs of the uniform in gauche fashion. Somehow baseball must reach the television and Internet generations that may have less time for reflection.

Unless baseball does the unthinkable and introduces aluminum bats at the professional level, nothing will change the sweet sound of the crack of the bat. Nothing can change the beauty of a double-play, the ability of Luis Alicea to somehow release the ball on time to almost shove it at first base for a game ending twin killing with the Baltimore runner barreling down upon him last August. Nothing can change the dumbfounded amazement of father and son looking at one another in wonderment as Dave Henderson's dramatic ninth inning '86 home run disappears over the left field wall beyond the reach of a downcast Brian Downing when all odds seemed to favor doom that brilliant sunshine filled Anaheim Sunday afternoon.

Of course, nothing will ever be like it was. Even the Fenway famed "Green Monster" is different from the one off which the Splendid Splinter played carom shots. Yaz, Rice, and now Greenwell have had an easier time of it since 1976 when the new one—like so much else which is new, it looks like the old one—was built.

But, notwithstanding the foibles of those who play it and own it, the game lives on in 1996—for me like the Democratic Party, the Episcopal Church, NAACP, and the Modern Jazz Quartet, it is truly one of life's eternal verities.

APPENDIX 5

WILLIAM B. GOULD IV, "THE CURSE OF THE BAMBINO," SPEECH DELIVERED AT "BASEBALL AND THE 'SULTAN OF SWAT'": A CONFERENCE COMMEMORATING THE 100TH BIRTHDAY OF BABE RUTH, APRIL 27, 1995 AT HOFSTRA UNIVERSITY

> *Issuing the injunction before opening day is important to insure that the symbolic value of that day is not tainted by an unfair labor practice and the NLRB's inability to take effective steps against its perpetuation.*
>
> Opinion of Judge Sonya Sotomayor, Southern District of New York in *Silverman v. Major League Baseball Players Relations Committee, Inc.*, April 3, 1995.

Like the Constitution, the flag, and "straight ahead" jazz, baseball, to paraphrase President Clinton, is the "glue" which holds the Nation together. Combining the analytical and cerebral with the country's passion for that which is romantic, it is one of life's eternal verities in which the clock stands still forever, transcending all periods of one's life—a game in which there is no buzzer or horn in the form of an arbitrary or predestined time limitation. Like life itself, it gives one the sense and hope that it could go on forever, but in reality, meanders through streams and corners which defy all earthly predictions.

The "Babe" made the dramatic home run central to this game and the expressions associated with the "roundtripper" as well as the game's other aspects have permeated the entire English language, at least on this side of the Atlantic. And it is certainly appropriate in a paper which addresses the "curse of the Bambino" to note that this tradition of grand majestic long drives has lived on in Red Sox lore over the years, first with Jimmy Foxx—and then, in my memory, in the forties, seventies, and early eighties in the form of Williams, Stephens, York, Doerr, Vaz, Tony C., Rice, Lynn, Scott, Evans, and so many others. Canseco, Vaughn, and Whiten carry on this great tradition in the new shining season of 1995 which burst forth this week, like spring itself, full of promise, hope, and fantasy.

On March 31, the day of Judge Sotomayor's oral bench opinion in the baseball case in which the National Labor Relations Board successfully sought an injunction against alleged owner unfair labor practices, she said:

> *The often leisurely game of baseball is filled with many small moments which catch a fan's breath. There is, for example, that wonderful second when you see an outfielder backpedaling and jumping up to the wall, and time stops for an instant as he jumps up and you finally figure out whether it is a home run, a double or a single off the wall, or an out.*

More than a quarter of a century before the 1995 baseball case, on a typically warm, humid night in D.C. (later RFK) Stadium, Dick Ellsworth was on the hill for the Red Sox against the hometown Washington Senators and was tiring in the late innings. But, Dick Williams, the Bosox manager from '67 through '69, had no one in the bullpen to relieve Ellsworth and, thus stayed with him as Hank Allen stepped in at the plate with the Senators trailing by two with two-on and two-out in the bottom of the ninth. Allen hit a long shot to deep left center which Reggie Smith, the then Sox center fielder, tracked down and raced to the wall for—and leaped high against the fence.

As he descended to the center field grass, there was that precious moment of which Judge Sotomayor spoke. But in this case, if the ball was over the fence the Senators had won by one run on what the Japanese call a sayonara home run—and if it was caught, the game was over with the Red Sox the victors.

Only when the Sox bullpen erupted, racing down the left field line and onto the field to greet Smith as he held the ball high, was the result apparent. This was that breathless inescapable moment . . .

And on a brisk Oakland, California, evening twenty years later, a ground ball is hit into the hole between short and third for which Alfredo Griffin ranges far to his right. Griffin turns as if to throw to first base, and the runner from second base advances off the bag, anticipating an effortless capture of the third sack on the throw to first—and in mid-air, with the skill of a ballet dancer, Griffin gracefully twirls and throws to second, eliminating the lead runner from the base paths.

No game is more basic to America's essence than that of baseball. Its elegance and dignity, the big sweep of Burt Blyleven's breaking curve, the heavens opening to the soaring deep fly ball into the distant horizon, the major league pop-up which disappears into the stream of brilliant sunshine, and the virtuosity of the double play or "twin killing." And no player is more associated with it than Babe Ruth, the Bambino.

As a young boy, listening to the radio during the 1946 season I heard Ted Williams strike out with the bases loaded—and my father was able to console me with this comment: "It has happened to the Babe also." And Ruth himself said:

> *I swing big, with everything I've got. I hit big or I miss big. I like to live as big as I can.*

The Babe's early years were in Baltimore where Cal Ripken and Peter Angelos now hold forth. But his major league professional baseball career began with the Red Sox—as a pitcher, who eventually hit twenty-nine homers when he switched to the outfield in 1919. And a very fine pitcher he was—particularly in the 1916 and 1918 World Series, which culminated in the Red Sox last World Championships ever. His ERAs in those two post-seasons of play were 0.64 and 1.06 respectively. In those two Series he pitched 29 2/3 consecutive scoreless innings, a record that was not broken for forty-three years!

The sale of Babe Ruth to the Yankees from the Red Sox in 1919 to finance owner H. Harrison Frazee's Broadway ventures does seem to have placed the "Curse of the Bambino" upon the Red Sox.[12] No world championship has been won by the Townies since then, the ultimate goal having been tantalizingly just missed in the seventh game of the '46, '67, '75 and '86 World Series and in countless other playoffs and tense pennant drives decided on the last day—or, as in 1972, the penultimate day of the season.

I followed every last step of those tense come-from-behind pennant races in '48 and '49 when the Sox, having come back from an enormous deficit, in both seasons, lost the pennant on the last day—in '48 on a playoff date itself, only to be repeated in '78 when, this time around, a double digit lead had been squandered against the Yankees.

Like Ruth's $125,000 sale itself, those just-missed championships remind us not only of Luis Aparicio falling to the ground as he rounded third base in '72, but also the '46 and '49 groundouts of Tom McBride and Tom Wright—and even more important, the deficiencies of the Supreme Court's ruling in 1922 in *Federal Baseball*[13] when Justice Holmes, on one of those bad days that all great baseball players have, concluded that baseball was not a business in interstate commerce within the meaning of the Sherman Antitrust Act. But, of course baseball has always been a business—as the National Labor Relations Board recognized when it took jurisdiction over this sport in 1969.[14]

Accordingly, Denny Gatehouse would not have been on the mound for the Red Sox in the 1948 playoff game if the St. Louis Browns, like the infinitely more successful 1995 Montreal Expos, had not decided to send their players to big market teams for cash and minor leaguers. Mike Torrez would not have been on the hill in that fateful '78 playoff game in which Bucky Dent homered, had not Andy Messersmith and Dave McNally prevailed in the arbitration case which made them free agents and produced the first of a series of collective bargaining agreements allowing major league players to exercise a measure of free agency.

And had not Carlton Fisk, the hero of the sixth World Series game in 1975 by virtue of the extra inning home run that he figuratively willed fair, been able to become a free agent as the result of the Red Sox failure to tender an offer under the '76 collective agreement, he, rather than Rich Gedman, might have been behind the plate in that nightmarish after-midnight (by daylight saving time) final inning of the 1986 sixth game and would have then gloved Bob Stanley's inside wild pitch which produced the tying run—and thus would have made Bill Buckner's infamous error anticlimactic.

Nothing has more directly affected baseball's on-the-field developments than the legal developments off the field. The 1975 *Messersmith* arbitration decision of Peter Seitz, alongside the salary arbitration provisions first negotiated in 1973, provided the Players Association with a surrogate for antitrust law which *Federal Baseball* and its progeny had earlier denied them.[15] This is the first of a number of ironies affecting baseball and modern employment and labor law.

The second lies in the fact that *Federal Baseball* was never followed by the courts in other major league professional sports such as football, basketball, and hockey. These decisions were influential in establishing unions in these sports because the owners could not avail themselves of the non-statutory labor exemption to antitrust law without a collective bargaining agreement and the players could leverage this liability against them. Accordingly, the antitrust decisions initially gave great impetus to unions and an obligation to recognize and bargain collective bargaining agreements because, in the absence of such agreements, which could provide them with a non-statutory labor exemption, the owners would be liable for antitrust violations for unreasonable restrictions upon player mobility in the form of reserve clauses, draft procedures, and the like. By virtue of *Federal Baseball*, and the Supreme Court's affirmance of it in both the *Toolson*[16] and *Curt Flood*[17] decisions, baseball players did not have the same advantage.

But the second phase of the antitrust decisions dealing with the nonstatutory labor exemption has produced a more profound irony. For in at least two circuit courts of appeals—the District of Columbia and the Second Circuit—the courts have said that owners may avail themselves of the labor exemption after having negotiated an agreement, even when unsuccessful in negotiating a subsequent agreement—unless the employment relationship becomes non-union altogether. The result of this is that, as Judge Wald properly noted while dissenting in the recent *Brown v. Pro Football, Inc.*[18] case, the non-statutory labor exemption becomes available only under "bizarre" circumstances, that is, where the union pretends to eliminate itself altogether as the National Football League Players Association did in the wake of the 1987 strike—and as the National Basketball Players Association threatened to do—and then uses the antitrust laws as a vehicle to revive itself for the purpose of negotiating a new agreement and the consequent labor exemption.

The other major result of both *Brown* and *National Basketball Association v. Williams*,[19] decided here in the Second Circuit, is that any kind of balance between the properly competing policies of labor and antitrust laws is eliminated altogether. Thus in football, basketball, and presumably hockey, antitrust law and its treble damages remedy is relegated exclusively to the non-union sector, thereby creating an incentive for the players in the major professional sports to be non-union and for employers to foster unionized relationships regardless of their bona fide origin or status—a result which is hardly compatible with the promotion of freedom of association, collective bargaining, and autonomous labor–management relationships—goals all enshrined in the National Labor Relations Act.

In my judgment the new approach to the non-statutory labor exemption is flawed in another major respect as well. It misconceives the role of the National Labor Relations Act. National labor law does not provide for balance, parity, or equality of power,[20] as the D.C. Circuit said.[21] Illustrative of this point is the rule which establishes the lawfulness of permanent economic replacements of strikers engaged in protected activity of the act.[22] Notwithstanding the court's comment in *American Ship Building* to the effect that the strike and lockout are "correlative," the economic weaponry provided the parties is not equal and, most important, the statute, as interpreted, does not contemplate such equality.

This then is the current backdrop to any discussion about the appropriate relevance of antitrust and labor law to the business of baseball. The Supreme Court, of course, can change both *Brown* and *Williams* and limit the labor exemption to either the point of impasse in the bargaining relationship or, as I have advocated in a book and a couple of articles published during the past fifteen years, at some point subsequent to impasse—perhaps a reasonable period of time transpiring in its wake.[23]

The difficulty with either approach, as Justice Harlan remarked in his separate opinion in the *Borg Wamer*[24] decision about some of the rules relating to impasse, is that it is inherently vague—a point noted by the Court of Appeals in *Brown*. But this limitation is infinitely preferable to the untoward policy consequences involved in eliminating antitrust law from basketball and football as the Courts of Appeals in the District of Columbia and New York have done.

Congress, should it apply antitrust law to baseball—and there is no earthly reason why the same standards should not apply to baseball as other major league professional sports—would have to address the labor exemption issue and establish some kind of demarcation line for availability of the exemption and a balance between it and the good faith bargaining objectives contained in the National Labor Relations Act.

Whatever the outcome of the antitrust debate, it is clear that labor law has been extremely relevant to the 1994–1995 strike. The difficulty with the National Labor Relations Act—and this has made the unions in professional sports all the more interested in using antitrust law—is its ineffective remedies and poor procedures.[25] My agency, the National Labor Relations Board, can do little about the ineffectiveness of our remedies because of limitations which have been established by the Supreme Court or the language of the act itself. It is difficult for the board to level the playing field of any relationship within the parameters of existing law.

But there is much that the board can do within its procedures—particularly with regard to the use of its authority under Section 10(j) to seek temporary injunctive relief against employer and union unfair labor practices. Since I and President Clinton's other NLRB appointees arrived in Washington, DC, almost fourteen months ago, we have used this provision of the law against both employer and union unfair labor practices with unprecedented frequency—a total of 132 times. The purpose is to bypass an unduly time-consuming and burdensome administrative process where, by virtue of delay, the relief fashioned would be too late to effectively implement the statute's objectives.

In *Silverman v. Major League Players Association*,[26] the board voted to authorize the use of temporary injunctive relief to restore the status quo ante in the employment relationship which had been altered by virtue of the owners discontinuance of the free agency and salary arbitration system. On March 26, the board voted to seek injunctive relief against such conduct and, in my view, therefore concluded that there was reasonable cause to believe that this conduct constituted an unfair labor practice and that relief was just and proper—principally because the passage of time would make the remedy, when provided, relatively meaningless.

The board has no authority to oblige the parties to resume or continue the season—or to fashion an agreement for them. Under our system of voluntary collective bargaining, that process is for the parties themselves. The board's only role is to insure adherence to proper procedures to rid the process of unlawful impediments, and to provide for an appropriate framework for future collective bargaining.

If the administrative process was the only avenue available, restored employment conditions might have been realized in the 1997 season. Meanwhile, the 1995 and 1996 seasons might not

APPENDIX 5

have taken place—or under circumstances in which quickly eroding baseball skills could not be compensated under processes established voluntarily by labor and management.

Thus, the use of Section 10(j) so as to preserve the status quo ante can be particularly significant in established bargaining relationships—as well as in the unorganized sector. It was, as Judge Sotomayor said in her opinion, critical to the 1995 baseball season and a back-to-work agreement. The board's remedy provided the proper legal framework for future bargaining.

My own judgment is that my agency's use of labor law in the '95 baseball strike may be yet another instance of baseball constituting a mirror image of other societal developments. The most dramatic example of that proposition in my lifetime is the advent of Jackie Robinson at first base for the Brooklyn Dodgers in 1947—and the hiring of Larry Doby and Dan Bankhead soon thereafter. Robinson, who hit .296 playing at an entirely new position in his rookie year, broke baseball's color barrier before President Truman desegregated the Armed Forces and seven years before the Supreme Court's historic ruling in *Brown v. Board of Education* declaring segregation in education to be unconstitutional. The example and contribution of these brave men against odds truly incalculable can never be forgotten.

The board's reliance upon Section 10(j) injunctions reflects a renewed conviction about our National Labor Relations Act and its purposes, and to the rule of law in the workplace itself. Our weekend work on March 26, and the importance of baseball to our country, made our law and its procedures known to millions who may not have heard of the board or the act previously. It was the mirror image of injunctions sought throughout industry in this country and, like Robinson's contribution, it could conceivably influence other relationships. My hope is that this will trigger more awareness of the law and promote voluntary compliance with its provisions.

In particular, I want to pay tribute here in New York to Regional Director Dan Silverman and his staff who not only played an extremely competent role in investigating the matters brought before us but also presented the case to Judge Sotomayor. The board's prompt intervention is properly seen as the vehicle through which the parties put aside their differences and resumed baseball and began the 1995 season this week. Meanwhile, of course, the board is adjudicating the baseball case on its full merits in its administrative process.

Of course, the owners and players themselves have not yet negotiated a new collective bargaining agreement. It was their failure to do so which triggered the 1994 strike, the longest dispute in the history of professional sports in this country and anywhere in the world! Under our system, these negotiations are for the parties themselves under their own voluntary autonomous system of collective bargaining.

But, what the board and, ultimately the judiciary, have done through the use of Section 10(j) is to create a framework in which the collective bargaining process is fostered. This is the kind of objective that our law was designed to accomplish when first enacted by Congress in 1935 in the form of the Wagner Act. Over the years we have sometimes lost our way because of the failure to use the provisions which give our statute strength.

My belief is that our March 26 determination to seek injunctive relief in the 1995 baseball dispute was consistent with the law, has been good for the game of baseball and its '95 season in particular, and, most significant of all, is important to the effective administration of our statute.

As is true of all of American society, we need to have the game of baseball be one in which the interests of all parties—players, owners and fans—are taken into account. This is consistent with the policies of the National Labor Relations Act which my agency administers. A balanced relationship in which genuine voluntary collective bargaining is encouraged and conflict is diminished is consistent with our national labor policy and with the honor that we appropriately bestow upon Babe Ruth.

This spring of 1995 represents a new season in which a long deep drive was hit for baseball, for effective labor law enforcement, and for so much of what is truly great about our country on this 100th anniversary of the Babe's birth.

APPENDIX 6

WILLIAM B. GOULD IV, "SYMPOSIUM ON SPORTS AND THE LAW: INTRODUCTION," REPRODUCTION OF SPEECH DELIVERED AT LEONARD KOPPETT'S MEMORIAL SERVICE IN LOS ALTOS, CA, JULY 7, 2003, *STANFORD LAW AND POLICY REVIEW* 1 (2004)

I am indeed honored to be selected by the Koppett family to give this talk about my good friend, Leonard Koppett. I give my condolences to the Koppett family and to his many friends who mourn the loss of him.

My last meeting with Leonard Koppett was June 16—six days before his death in San Francisco at the symphony. It was one of our periodic luncheons at the Gordon Biersch Restaurant on Emerson Street in Palo Alto where we would meet with no prearranged agenda to talk about the business of baseball or sports, politics, history, music and, occasionally, our Stanford Law School seminar or other joint ventures.

On that day Leonard—dressed in his trademark navy blue suit—had had the *Official Rules of Baseball* (the 2003 edition) in front of him when I arrived. "Look at this," he said. "Rule 1.01. Baseball is a game between two teams of 9 players each." And he looked up at me and paused. "Oh," I said, "They haven't taken account of the American League designated hitter rule." "Exactly," he responded, as he flipped through the Rules pages, now ready to move the discussion on to new areas.

"You know," Leonard said, "there are many of these rules that are out of date and need careful review." And he then launched into a very detailed discussion of contemporary umpiring—so detailed that when he began to talk about the number of umpires in the 1940s and 1950s and compared them to 2003, the rotation amongst all clubs, the infrequent instances in which each club would now see the same umpire—thus impairing a needed familiarity with the individual umpire, and the consequent difficulties in knowing the umpires' strike zone, I asked him to slow down. I began to take notes on the back of an article he had just provided me. For just a second he seemed bemused by my note-taking and then went on with his lecture-like discourse on the state of umpiring and its impact on disputes about the strike zone.

On the evening of June 22, when I began to call some of Leonard's friends to tell them the sad news of his death, I reached Dusty Baker in Chicago and recounted some of that week's discussion to him. "That's exactly what we were talking about today," said Dusty. "We didn't even know the names of most of the umpires out there," let alone how they would call pitches.

That comment confirmed anew Leonard's baseball sagacity and detailed knowledge of the game as well as its history. I noted the San Francisco Chronicle obituary which described Leonard's involvement going "all the way back" to Joe DiMaggio—you would think it was before the Peloponnesian War, said one of his friends. Leonard had known the game since his mother took him to Yankee Stadium as a small child, where he saw Ruth and Gehrig play.

No discussion of Leonard Koppett can ignore the wide variety of subjects treated in his writings. They were both humorous and serious—sometimes a combination of the two. In a *1969 Sporting News* piece, he wrote about what baseball would look like in 2069, noting that after the 2002 season a global consolidation of teams— no one was using the globalization term then—took place because the "antagonism between East and West, capitalist and communist, Russia and China and the United States, had been worked out"— and then proceeded to allude to a group of colorful characters—like "bruising Boris Borodnitzky, the right-handed slugger who made it fatal to start a left-handed pitcher against the Moscow Bears"; "Show Me How . . . Peiping's [Beijing today] No. 1 hero [Leonard wanted to call this team the Peiping Toms]; Max (Professor) Moriarity of London, who broke all records for stealing bases; Abba Bubba, the Israeli curveballer who pitched the Rome Cardinals to three straight pennants"—who had all produced a "true Golden Age" in the 2010–2060 era.

In this same vein, I particularly liked the less lighthearted piece laced with sarcastic irony last year in the *New York Times* entitled "Business of National Pastime Is Unpatriotic." I read the following lines and others to many a friend. Leonard wrote:

> *Many have scoffed at baseball's claim that 28 of its 30 teams lost money over the last seven years, including $500 million in 2001 alone. But I have no basis for doubting their figures or their sincerity. What shocks me is their utter lack of patriotism. How? By refusing to share, with the rest of the American business community, the secret of their greatest discovery: how to lose millions year after year, stay in business and even double their revenue. Such selfish secrecy can only be called unpatriotic . . . And they won't tell the rest of us how they do it? It's particularly disturbing because President Bush is one of their recent alumni. He deserves their help. This [is] no way for the custodians of Our National Game to behave.*

The name Leonard Koppett was first part of my consciousness from the time that my father and I bought a program for twenty-five cents at our first National Basketball Association game in March 1953 between the pre-Bill Russell Boston Celtics and the New York Knickerbockers. Leonard was with the *New York Herald Tribune* then, and in the program he provided a punchy prose which fused the excitement of previous games between the clubs with solid business analysis of the rise of the Celtic–Knick rivalry, the Boston–New York "population centers" as important to the NBA. "Whoever loses this series," Leonard wrote, "The NBA wins."

In both conversation and the classroom, one of Leonard's central theses was that in order to understand the business, "don't approach it as a fan." However, as the 1953 program showed, this didn't keep him from a genuine love of the game. In language reminiscent of that fifty-year-old program on Opening Day this year in both San Francisco and Oakland, he allowed that he was excited about the possibility of another Bay Bridge World Series.

I began to read his columns in both the *Post* and the *Times* regularly as a young man but had no contact with him until we both moved to the Bay Area in the early 70s. Our first meeting was in '76 or '77 when some of our students had invited him to speak at Stanford Law School. This began a professional and personal relationship with this Renaissance man for the past quarter century which flourished all the more when we began a seminar at the Law School with Al Attles in 1988.

One never worried about a conversation lag with Leonard. Ideas, viewpoints, and arguments flowed nonstop. Through intellect and personality he displayed a feistiness, both obdurate and resilient, which met all my own points and arguments and those of others who discussed and debated with him as well. Sometimes I accused him of taking a position just because I had taken another. He rarely yielded. Sometimes he was wrong and occasionally, as I recall, in a few instances he actually admitted it. But as ex-Yankee catcher Charlie Silvera said to me in discussing Leonard, "You didn't win. You might get a tie."

Leonard Koppett was both classy and classic—in a class by himself among sports writers. The author of sixteen books, he told me that because of its voluminous resource material, his *Koppett's Concise History of Baseball*, published in 1998, was the one that he viewed as essential to publish before his death.

Leonard was the only writer ever to be a member of the Writers' Hall of Fame in both baseball and basketball—elected in '92 and '94 respectively. And he was respected widely by not only his peers, but also by the baseball barons whom he frequently criticized.

APPENDIX 6

The fundamental dimensions of this wonderful man became clear to me only as our association developed in the 1980s.

When Leonard Koppett left this world, I think that many or most with whom he had contact felt that they had some special relationship with him. This is because Leonard was a very giving man, as well as a learned man.

When I first began to write baseball newspaper articles on race and labor in the mid-80s, I turned to Leonard for advice in a number of areas. He was an adviser and counselor, never in the least interested in credit or attribution for himself—notwithstanding the fact that he really prompted the approach that I took to my very first pieces of this kind.

Leonard was one of those unusual people who was really on the level about race. In this respect, as well as in so many others, he was unalterably authentic. Although I did not know him from the 1940s and 1950s, I know that he was one of those people who was outspoken and honest when it was not fashionable to speak of equality between the races.

I always treasured his comments which he wrote on Jackie Robinson in *The Sporting News* piece that he did in 1972:

> *What is so hard to remember now (and completely unknown to younger people) is the devastating fact that until Jackie Robinson, there was no pressure whatever from the "decent" people to break the color line that all accepted. . . . So when all is said and done, as much as Robinson meant directly to his own people—as an example and inspiration and pioneer—he meant even more to the white society. He did more than any other single human being could do to focus their attention on the inequities of a system in which lily-white baseball was only one small symptom. The consequences of the waves his appearance spread far beyond baseball, far beyond sports, far beyond politics, even to the very substance of a culture.*

In 1988, when Leonard, Alvin Attles, and I began to teach our sports law seminar together at the Law School, our contact increased. We looked forward to our meetings, and many said that the hallways were livened with the jocular banter of not only ourselves, but also some of the interesting guests that we brought in—usually through Leonard's efforts. The students were wowed by Leonard's friends like Bill Walsh, Willie Mays, Dusty Baker, the late Larry Fleischer, and the like. Leonard taught at Stanford (he also taught in Communications and Continuing Education at Stanford), and when we took our show on the road to Oregon's Willamette Law School last fall, he was a hit there as well!

This is because Leonard was a fabulous teacher. He created a "timeline" of professional and amateur sports which we distributed with our materials, giving the students a sense of how the major sports had developed. Leonard brought dry case doctrine to life with colorful and sometimes firsthand accounts of the case's background. He dominated the classroom—so much so that Al would turn to me and whisper, "He's taking over the class." And he was! We all benefited from that.

Equally unforgettable was the same giving attitude—that I described earlier—toward the students. The students enjoyed and loved Leonard! So many of them have written to me these past two weeks to express their sadness about his death. I shall always remember the beginning class when I announce office hours. Then I would turn to Leonard and Al, and Leonard would always say to the students, "You can come and see me anytime!" That was the way he was.

We had planned so much for the coming months and years. This week a panel on which we were both participating—"Baseball in 2020" at the Society of American Baseball Research Convention in Denver—then a celebration of the 75th anniversary of his arrival in the United States, a sports law conference here at Stanford, and another one up in Portland, as well as another round of classes this fall.

It may be that the most remarkable feature of Leonard Koppett's distinguished life is its most recent years. No comparable writer continued writing with such fervor and frequency as they moved into their seventies.

It almost seemed as though he was taking it up a notch as he described in one of our last conversations the series of books and projects which he had scheduled. In recent months, he was contributing to the Hall of Fame publications, writing articles for the *Seattle Post Intelligencer* on pitch count, the disputes about the strike zone, and most important of all, his unpublished white paper, entitled "Reorganizing Baseball." And in a piece published two days before his death, he argued that it was futile to attempt obtain "competitive balance" because of market disparity between different major league cities, and he contended that there was a relationship between this subject and the need to contract the number of teams in baseball. He was a great proponent of contraction of teams—but for reasons different than those put forward by the owners. Said Leonard about competitive balance in vintage Leonard Koppett: "The whole history of baseball, if they [the owners] would bother to read it, spells out how and why it [balance] is impossible."

In one of our last discussions he held forth with vigor on the silliness of recent "flavor-of-the-month" books like *Moneyball* which purported to present the significance of on-base percentages and the abilities of players with unorthodox physiques as new ideas. This was but a corollary to one of Leonard's many valid theses, that is, that nothing had fundamentally changed the game since 1903, and that its century-long stability and tradition allowed it to transcend successive generations.

Truly, at the end of his life—with book projects pending (one book on baseball and the press will appear soon), weekly columns in the newspaper, and numerous teaching assignments—Leonard was operating on all cylinders!

The world has lost a great man, and I have lost a very good friend indeed. It is hard for me to accept the reality that I shall never again witness this consummate gentleman's gallant bow when I would introduce him to a friend or acquaintance, or, when the telephone rings, hear that voice say: "Bill!—Koppett!"

I extend my heartfelt condolences to his wife, Suzanne, and to his children, David and Kathy, and the grandchild that he never saw, Lia.

APPENDIX 7

WILLIAM B. GOULD IV, "PROSPECTS FOR LABOR LAW REFORM AFTER THE 2008 ELECTION – LAW PERSPECTIVE," SPEECH GIVEN AT THE 61ST ANNUAL MEETING LABOR AND EMPLOYMENT RELATIONS ASSOCIATION, JANUARY 4, 2009 IN OAKLAND, CALIFORNIA

2009 finds us on the brink of a bitter debate over labor law reform and the best ways in which to amend the National Labor Relations Act of 1935—the basic private sector labor law framework which has not been amended in major respects since 1947 and 1959 in the form of the Taft-Hartley and Landrum-Griffin amendments. The issues are not new. The overarching theme has always been the denial of justice through its delay. If 2009 is to be at the center of a stormy debate between labor and management and Democrats and Republicans, we can see that the clouds were already on the horizon in 1961 when I was a young lawyer with the United Auto Workers in Detroit, fresh out of Cornell Law School.

For it was just at that point that labor observers were beginning to comment upon the fact that a decline from labor's zenith in 1955 had commenced. The intervening years have seen no appreciable reversal of this trend as it galloped onward in the Reagan 1980s and during the presidencies of Bill Clinton and both Bushes. With union representation now at a level of 12 percent in the public and private sector combined and almost down to 7 percent in the private sector, the goal of workplace democracy promised by the National Labor Relations Act seventy-four years ago is more distant than ever.

Of course, this isn't to say that the law has been the primary factor in this trend—it hasn't been. But the 1935 law has played a role, however subordinate it is when other factors are considered, and its creakiness and vulnerability to delays during which employers can engage in anti-union propaganda against union organizational efforts have created a disrespect for the rule of law in the workplace which a democratic society can ill afford. Moreover, labor law reform could reenergize the labor movement as it has not been since the Great Depression when the union organizing slogan was "FDR wants you to join the union!"

The labor law system is broken and badly in need of repair. Sixteen years ago I laid out a comprehensive agenda to accomplish this in a book which I wrote.[27] The principal question in 2009 is whether the Employee Free Choice Act provides the best answer—and the answer to that question is both yes and no.

It is "yes" because of the fact that the delay in the administrative process which has given rise to employer anti-union campaigns, both lawful and unlawful, is fundamentally attributable to the lack of effective remedies. The traditional "cease and desist" order to remedy illegal behavior has been recognized as a mere "slap on the wrist" for decades and, almost a half century ago, back pay was seen by the Pucimski Committee as a "license fee" for misconduct, a problem exacerbated by frequently convoluted controversies about how much was to be deducted from back pay when there was a dispute about the employee's "reasonable diligence" in seeking another job subsequent to unlawful dismissal.

The Employee Free Choice of 2009 will change this by providing for treble damages for statutory violations committed during union organizing campaigns and the period of first contract negotiations, civil fines not to exceed $20,000 for each violation as well—and it will mandate the NLRB to seek prompt injunctive relief against these violations. I can tell you that the major law enforcement tool

APPENDIX 7

that my NLRB had in the 1990s was the injunction—but the law, as now written, gives the board discretion to take such action—in contrast to the NLRB's obligation to address union unfair labor practices in the courts—and the number of such initiatives has diminished rapidly in the recent years of the Bush NLRB. EFCA will change this, and this is very much to the good.

EFCA also provides—properly in my view—a system of so-called first contract arbitration to resolve differences between the parties when they are unable to do so through collective bargaining when the relationship is embryonic in the wake of an NLRB certification of the union as bargaining representative. In the main, this system has worked well in most of the Canadian provinces that have adopted this framework. Too many labor–management relationships perish under the status quo which saddles unions with unsatisfactory and time consuming "duty to bargain" litigation leading all too frequently nowhere. But EFCA, as currently written, simply provides for automatic access to arbitration if bargaining is not successfully concluded in four months—and does not incorporate standards that the arbitrator is to follow. The former could undermine collective bargaining, encouraging the union simply to wait for a third party when they find the employer's offer unsatisfactory. To this problem the Canadians have attempted to devise so-called "screens" to encourage bargaining before resort to arbitration by making the date of access to a third party uncertain. The latter could not only create constitutional infirmities but also, again, undermine bargaining if it is thought that the award will enshrine a pattern of contract terms. The employer's ability to pay (and a consequent obligation to open the books) should be the dominant criterion. In any event, these matters can be addressed during the legislative debate through amendments which will preserve an arbitration process so important because of the ineffectiveness and delay involved in disputes about so-called "surface" bargaining—and yet promote collective bargaining itself.

But the fundamental issue which has received most attention—particularly in the many newspaper editorials that have been written on this subject—is the substitute of card check or authorization cards as a basis for recognition of unions rather than secret ballot box elections which are part of the current law. In my judgment, this is the substitution of one imperfect mechanism for another.

The status quo is unacceptable because employers have all too frequently undermined employee support for unions by delay—the best-case scenario for conduct of an election is 50–60 days subsequent to the filing of a union representation petition—and have used that period of time to propagandize an anti-union message. But EFCA's answer is also unacceptable, because it promotes a form of recognition which is not always deliberative—I have previously advocated that the payment of dues or some monies to the union should be a prerequisite to the counting of the card—and because there have been numerous controversies about misrepresentation, coercion, and the like prior to the cards' signing. British Columbia, when it had card check legislation (most of the Canadian provinces have repudiated this approach in favor of the ballot box), provided that the union certification could be revoked for the falsification of one card! EFCA contains no similar safeguard or anything akin to it—though presumably the NLRB can address this and related issues through regulations pursuant to EFCA.

Thus, I have advocated that the flaws in the system can be fixed by a method other than card check. Representation elections can be conducted within five to ten days of the filing of the petition as both Ontario and British Columbia so provide. This will necessarily postpone the resolution of disputes about who is eligible to vote and sometimes even what unit in which the vote should be conducted. The NLRB adopted a similar approach under some circumstances in the 1990s and the new statute could impose time limits upon the agency to resolve these matters after the vote so that the parties are able to get on with their own affairs promptly.

Of course, it may be said that employers will simply respond with more virulent and expeditious anti-union behavior notwithstanding the short time frame for campaigning. But this highlights a penultimate deficiency in EFCA, that is, its failure to address and to reform the existing system which excludes non-employee organizers in practically all instances from company property. Union organizers ought to have carefully arranged periodic access to company property so as to carry their message and to be able to respond to employer "captive audiences" under which employees lawfully may be compelled to listen to the employer's anti-union speeches and literature. If there is to be a marketplace of ideas in the workplace, that must exist for both sides.

EFCA has focused upon only some of the areas in need of reform. This makes sense because the perfect should not be the enemy of the good on issues such as the permanent replacement of strikers, lack of union and employee protection when a successor employer acquires or purchases another company, the ability of union members to resign membership without some form of reasonable limitation through union constitutions or bylaws, the narrow scope for collective bargaining over closures, relocations, and the like, which are all postponed for another day.

But there are a few issues too critical to be postponed—though one of them will be caught up with the debate about immigration legislative reform. This relates to the rights of undocumented workers. In 1984 the Supreme Court said that such workers are employees within the meaning of the National Labor Relations Act in part, because a contrary ruling would create an incentive for employers to exploit them and all American workers. But in 2002 the Supreme Court reversed my board's 1995 precedent giving such employees the only significant remedy now available, that is, the monetary one in the form of back pay. The *New York Times* had it right when it said last week:

> *If you ignore and undercut the rights of illegal immigrants, you encourage the exploitation that erodes working conditions and job security everywhere. In a time of economic darkness, the stability and dignity of the work force are especially vital.*[28]

EFCA is underinclusive in other respects as well. It fails to address the vital issue of depoliticization of the NLRB, a reform so appropriate to the Obama Administration's focus upon bipartisanship. This concern translates into two basic provisions which should be part of labor law reform. The first is the process of appointment of NLRB members and general counsel, the need to bring representatives of both political parties from diverse backgrounds from all over the country. Washington, DC, New York, and the eastern seaboard have no monopoly upon labor law expertise. And, in order to ensure that we get the very best people coming to Washington for the very best reasons, there should be a limit on the term of office to one term.

Too much of labor law's delay is attributable to the NLRB itself—what Ninth Circuit Judge John Noonan called the "dilatory virus"! One term will encourage board members to focus on the processing of cases before them rather than the prospects for reappointment in a second term. Like Cincinnatus, they can depart the trappings of Washington when their work is done.

The statute should also be altered so that the one term is longer than the present one, that is, eight years rather than five years. In this way, the public gets the benefit of accumulated knowledge of the member, in contrast to the status quo which requires new appointees to reinvent the wheel with each appointment over a relatively brief period of time.

The second way in which the objective of depoliticization can be realized is through the use of rulemaking. Not only is rulemaking—in contrast to adjudication—desirable in that it garners more public input beyond the immediate parties but, even more important, it exalts the principle of stare decisis, that is, adherence to principle which can guide the parties and as a consequence avoid the sharp swings from one side to the other each time a new White House occupant appears on the scene with a new group of appointees.

And there should be timelines not only for the handling of representation petitions, that is, a ballot within five or ten days as the Canadians do and a time period for resolving problems arising out of the election, but also timelines for the board's handling of a wide variety of unfair labor practice issues. EFCA has already recognized the importance of speed in case resolution by mandating the board to go directly to federal court for an injunction. Congress can and should impose time limits for case handling by the agency itself.

Finally, Congress ought to allow, let alone promote, the adoption of private procedures such as those employed by First Group America to attempt to resolve controversies about union organizational disputes before they get to the NLRB. In the case of First Group America, the parties have established an Independent Monitor system wherein such matters can be addressed and resolved through public recommendations to the parties within thirty to sixty days of the filing of the complaint—with the parties free to pursue their NLRB options. A revised EFCA could promote or allow the parties to have their cases resolved by administrative law judges—as we did in the nineties by creating settlement judges who could mediate disputes—or private citizens who have experience as arbitrators, mediators, or fact finders. Again, if the process works well, the dispute can be immediately resolved rather than opening up the wounds inevitably associated with lingering litigation. And if neither party finds the system satisfactory, it may proceed to a newly constituted Obama NLRB just as the parties may do under the First Group America Program.

To sum up, EFCA contains many badly needed reforms that have been proposed since the 1960s and 1970s onward. The emergence of a Democratic president with a Democratic majority in the Congress—the first time that has been a feature of American government since January 1995 presents a great opportunity for reform. My sense is that amendments to the National Labor Relations Act involving recognition and protection of the collective bargaining process in its most fragile first contract form are so vital that we must be sure to get this done correctly. I am of the view that a failure to address the recognition part of the piece properly will inevitably impose excessive strains on collective bargaining subsequent to recognition, even with the availability of first contract arbitration. Failure to address the recognition process sensibly will create an incentive for employers to test the representative nature of unions as bargaining proceeds and suspicions remain that employee sentiment is not supportive of their exclusive bargaining representative.

My sense is that the White House will prefer a bipartisan approach now that the Democrats have close to the sixty votes needed to making legislation filibuster-proof in the Senate and that substantial revisions in the secret ballot box process are more likely to attract moderate Republicans from Pennsylvania and Maine as well as some of the more conservative Democrats.

The great reforms of our country, of which Title VII of the Civil Rights Act of 1964 is a major one, have had the support of both Democrats and Republicans. Contrarily, the Taft-Hartley amendments of 1947 exacerbated a "them and us" divisiveness which has harmed our labor–management relations and our competitive status as a nation.

This time we must get it right. A variation on the EFCA theme such as that outlined previously can realize that goal and, as a consequence, redemption of the promises of the 1935 legislation.

APPENDIX 8

WILLIAM B. GOULD IV, REMARKS GIVEN AT WILMINGTON RIVER WALK WATERMEN SIGN DEDICATION, OCTOBER 21, 2003 IN WILMINGTON, NORTH CAROLINA

Thank you for your invitation to speak at this Riverwalk Watermen Sign Dedication here in Wilmington, North Carolina, the city of William Benjamin Gould's birth in 1837 and his escape from slavery 25 years later. Let me also give special thanks to Beverly Tetterton of the New Hanover Public Library for providing research and resource in my writing of *Diary of a Contraband*, and who has been a key organizer of this event. Also, I wish to acknowledge the members of my family present here today, my wife, Hilda Elizabeth Gould, and my sister, Dorothy Gerber and her husband, Hermann. They and my three sons, William Benjamin V, Timothy Samuel, Edward Blair join in the honor and tribute to the brave men of September 21, 1862, particularly my great-grandfather William Benjamin Gould.

Throughout the South, there is scarcely a word noted about the great struggle for freedom and liberation—undertaken nearly a century and half ago in the War of the Rebellion. And there is little or no mention or acknowledgment of the Black military involvement in this effort, the "holiest of all causes" as WBG called it, to obtain the New World's central political and legal achievement.

As I have traveled through the states of the former "would-be Confederacy," as WBG called it, I have been struck by the abiding omnipresence of Confederate statues and commemorative markers.

Just this past weekend, we passed through Richmond's Monument Avenue to see again the memorials to Jefferson Davis—"would-be King Jeff" as WBG called him—Stonewall Jackson, and Jeb Stuart, and the laud and honor given to their pursuit of "constitutional principles" and the Confederate Navy which WBG and his comrades fought against and defeated.

Thus is it meet and right that Wilmington, North Carolina this day takes note of the perilous journey that William B. Gould and seven other comrades began here at the foot of Orange Street on the night of September 21, 1862—and the wider complement of fourteen others who left Wilmington in concert with those eight who boarded the U.S.S. Cambridge. It is meet and right that we note their names—WBG's comrades being Joseph Hall, Andrew Hall, George Price, John Mackey, Charles Giles, John Mitchell, and William Chanse. These men were to use their knowledge of North Carolina and its waterways on behalf of our country to interdict supplies destined for Lee's army in Virginia.

But as your sign properly notes, the September 21 escape involves others as well—many of them WBG's associates and correspondents—Virgil Richardson (for whom one of WBG's sons may be named) and Ben Greer who boarded the *Penobscot*—and Thomas Cowan, Charles Mallett, and Frank Clinton of the *Monticello*. All of them boarded these North Atlantic Blockading vessels near the mouth of the Cape Fear River for the same purpose—freedom and participation in the war effort against slavery. Many of these men, both literate and skilled, became key players in Reconstruction, the South's first brief nineteenth century interlude with democracy. Many, though not WBG, returned to Wilmington after its liberation in 1865.

These men—part of the 8,000 who fled the Confederacy to fight for freedom in the U.S. Navy—were part of a silent black exodus which transformed the war's nature. They made my life possible. And more than any other event since September 21, 1862, and its aftermath, here and now, 141 years and 1 month later they provide hope for my grandchildren, Timothy Samuel Jr. and Joseph Jeremy and the generations of all mankind yet to come.

APPENDIX 9

WILLIAM B. GOULD IV, REMARKS GIVEN AT THE DEDICATION OF WILLIAM B. GOULD PARK IN EAST DEDHAM, MASSACHUSETTS, SEPTEMBER 23, 2021

It is both an honor and a privilege to be with you today, to return to Massachusetts, the Algonquin word meaning "the people living near the great hills"—the land of the Blue Hills, near Blue Hill itself, which I saw frequently here as a child. Today we celebrate William B. Gould and the dedication of the William B. Gould Park here on the banks of the Mother Brook, selected, as I'm told, with a nod toward his extraordinary escape to freedom down the Cape Fear River at Wilmington, North Carolina.

It is meet and right that this ceremony takes place in the area where my father often spoke of seeing hundreds of Civil War veterans march through the streets of Boston—and many here in Dedham too.

I want to extend my thanks on behalf of the Gould Family to so many of you who made this day possible: Brian Keaney, who, I believe, initially came forward with his "dream" of this project—and others who worked with him, like Dan Hart, Tracey White, and Tom Sullivan from adjacent Hyde Park on the boundary of Dedham where the Goulds resided for more than a century.

I am also grateful to Senator Mike Rush and Representative Paul McMurtry who helped make this day possible as well, and I am pleased to meet Father Wayne Belschner of Saint Mary's Roman Catholic

Church (of which I had heard as a child) as well as to renew my acquaintanceship with Father Noble Scheepers who held a special commemoration in 2012, on the 150th anniversary of WBG's escape to freedom, at the Episcopal Church of the Good Shepherd—where I was baptized, as were the three William B. Goulds who went before me.

When this project's organizers first approached me about this idea, they referenced a theme which has seized more attention with each passing year—the importance of building upon memories which enhance a democratic vision, not simply tearing down what has existed. As statues fall, things appear to fall apart, to paraphrase Yeats;[29] the center cannot hold.

But "What will take its place?" is a question we have discussed as the Robert E. Lee statue in Richmond was dismantled a couple of weeks ago. "What will take its place?" En route to Wilmington, when WBG was first honored there in 2003, we asked this question as we drove through Richmond's avenue of monuments which even had one for the Confederate Secretary of the Navy who fought against the United States and William B. Gould's Navy.

There has been a tearing down all over the world the statues of slavers in Bristol, Great Britain, and Belgium, where Leopold II was responsible, and there too this question is always asked.

It is estimated that there are somewhere in the vicinity of 1,800 Confederate statues and memorials to those who revolted against the duly constituted authority of the United States in 1861. It is estimated, in a 2018 *Smithsonian* article, that American taxpayers have paid over $40 million in the last decade for preservation and upkeep of them.

While I cannot be certain what William B. Gould would say today, I know from his diary that the honor given to Jefferson Davis's Confederacy through national memorializations—"would-be King Jeff," as WBG called him, would be anathema to my great-grandfather. For his support was for the United States before, during, and after those three years at sea for the Navy, pursuing, as he called it, the "holiest of all causes."

APPENDIX 9 531

William B. Gould, born in Wilmington, North Carolina, on November 18, 1837, escaped from slavery in Wilmington on September 21, 1862, to serve "Uncle Samuel" as he called our Uncle Sam, in the United States Navy, as a "contraband," seized human property, as escaping slaves from rebellious states were called prior to the Emancipation Proclamation. Gould first patrolled the southeastern United States aboard the U.S.S. Cambridge as part of the North Atlantic Blockading Squadron, attempting to interdict supplies destined for Lee's army in Virginia. In the spring of '63, his ship moves north and on March 27, 1863, he writes in his diary: "At Boston. We arrived and came to anchor off the Navy Yard about 2 Oclock . . . Set foot on the old Bey state." This was part of the diary which he kept from 1862 through 1865, which indicates some familiarity with this area prior to his arrival.

At that time there were two obvious connections to Massachusetts. The first is through his mother's sister, "Aunt Jones" née Mary Moore, who lived just behind the State House in Boston. I visited her residence there two decades ago.

The second is my great-grandmother, Cornelia Williams Read, whom he would marry at the war's end. She had lived in Nantucket subsequent to her purchase out of slavery in 1857.

When WBG finished his tour of duty with the U.S.S. Cambridge, a second assignment was to place him aboard the U.S.S. Niagara in Gloucester. This involved chasing Confederate vessels across the Atlantic, they being constructed in Britain and France, placing him in a relatively unchronicled portion of the war arena. This effort took him in pursuit of such ships in Britain, Ireland, Spain, Portugal, Belgium, as well as islands in the Atlantic. Before his service was complete, he was to disembark in the Charlestown Naval Shipyard in September 1865 where he received his discharge papers. A couple of months later WBG and his fiancée were married in Nantucket.

But even aboard the U.S.S. Niagara in the Atlantic, his mind was not far away from developments in the Bay State. Listen to what he says in 1864 about events two miles east of 303 Milton Street where he was to settle: "Heard of the departure of one battalion of the 5th [54th] Regiment Massachusetts Cavalry from Camp Meigs for Washington, D.C. May God protect them while defending the holiest of all causes, liberty and Union."

When WBG and Cornelia settled here in Dedham in 1871, the first two of eight Gould children were already born—Medora (or Aunt Dora as I called her) born in 1866 (I have some of her books in my house today) and William B. Gould Jr., my grandfather, a veteran of the Spanish American War, who was born in Taunton, Massachusetts, in 1869 and died before my birth. I knew the other sons, all World War I veterans, from our summer visits to Dedham: Lawrence, Frederick, James Edward—and Ernest, Edward's twin brother, from our visits to Washington, DC, where he taught dentistry at Howard University.

Beyond WBG's own statement, that his home had burned during the War and that his birth had been recorded in a Bible in his home, hardly anything is known about him or Cornelia prior to their respective departures from Wilmington in 1857 and 1862. But subsequent to my 1996 visit to Wilmington's Bellamy Mansion—where I had observed the fine tapestry on display in this most elegant antebellum mansion at a Civil War Seminar—I received an excited telephone call from the mansion's curator, advising me he had found my great-grandfather's initials on some of the plaster lying in the old slave quarters behind the mansion. The work that I had observed was that of my great-grandfather.

And so it was that when WBG came to Dedham he worked as a plasterer and brick mason, ultimately as a contractor employing other men, fulfilling President Lincoln's dream of a fair opportunity for all.

With the help of Morris Rabinowitz, the Dedham librarian, I was to learn of a number of the buildings which had been constructed here through his work.

But there was one building about which I had already known since I was a child, St. Mary's Church in Dedham, a magnificent cathedral-like church, as most of you know, that can be seen for a great distance. As a child, my father had told me that

APPENDIX 9   533

William B. Gould had done the plastering in the construction or renovation of the church in the 1880s when he was a contractor. But, according to my father, some of WBG's workmen fell asleep at a critical time in the process relating to cement. Their failure could not be observed and could have been easily covered up without the defects becoming apparent until years later. My great-grandfather had all the plaster ripped out of the church and had the work done again at such great expense that he was nearly bankrupted. From this moment on, his stature in Dedham was enhanced, as was the name Gould. For even then, well before the disastrous collapses of structures in this century, people knew the results of shoddy workmanship and that William B. Gould would not tolerate it.

The second major Dedham contribution made by WBG flowed directly from his service to Uncle Samuel—his work for the Civil War veterans' association, the Charles W. Caroll Post Chapter 144 of the Grand Army of the Republic, or GAR. WBG was to become commander of this Dedham GAR chapter in 1900 and 1901 and in later years served as adjutant for the organization.

His fervor for the war's mission and objectives is expressed well in much of what he says in his diary. Listen to him speak of the Confederate surrender at Appomattox:

> *On my return on board I heard the Glad Tidings that the Stars and Stripe[s] had been planted over the Capital of the D--nd Confedercy by the invicible Grant. While we honor the living soldiers who have done so much we must not forget to whisper for fear of desturbeing the Glorious sleep of the ma[ny] who have fallen. Mayrters to the cau[se] of Right and Equality.*

This translates directly into his commitment to the United States itself and his judgment about the ideals for which our country stands. In 1865, he writes:

> *We see by the papers that the President in A speech intimates Colinization for the collard people of the United States. This move of his must and shall be resisted. We*

were born under the Flag of the Union and we never will know no other. My sentiment is the sentiment of the people of the States.

His third connection here in Dedham consisted of his role as one of the founders of the Church of the Good Shepherd in 1871. Father William Cheney, the Good Shepherd's Rector in much of the previous century, was spoken of with considerable reverence in the home to which we had moved in New Jersey. My parents, my sister, and I attended the Good Shepherd on our many visits here, from the 1940s, 1950s, and again, when my wife, children, and I lived here for a year in Cambridge in the early seventies. If you go to the Good Shepherd, you will find the Chapel of All Saints dedicated to Father Cheney, which bears the names of those Goulds, beginning with WBG and Cornelia themselves. And thus the Good Shepherd and Dedham are deeply embedded in our fabric.

And so, on behalf of the entire Gould family, we thank you for this dedication. I am not sure how William B. Gould would react if he were here today. I am certain that he would be horrified, as am I, with the recent destruction of the San Francisco monument of General (later President) Grant, whom WBG called the "invincible Grant." (The same would hold true of the attempt to remove Abraham Lincoln's name from one of the San Francisco public schools.)

I feel confident that he could not abide the false argument that dismantling of Confederate statues contravenes a proper examination of past and present or erases history any more than statues honoring Hitler would be appropriate in today's Germany. True, as Santyana has said, "those who cannot remember the past are condemned to repeat it."[30] But in understanding the world today, to what past shall we provide laud and honor?

My judgment is that more than mere iconoclasm is required. In order for history to be preserved, surely the past reflected by Frederick Douglass, Robert Smalls, who seized a Confederate vessel in South Carolina, and yes, William B. Gould provide a narrative too often obscured by the icons of Lee, Stonewall Jackson, and likeminded luminaries who betrayed their pledge of allegiance to our country. Roy Wilkins, the measured secretary of the NAACP in the fifties and sixties, and John Lewis, now so well known for his role in voting rights in the previous century and this one, are more contemporary figures warranting attention. Contrarily, the Confederate legacy is similar to what we witnessed in Washington on January 6 of this year.

Whatever WBG's views of 2021, I know that he would be proud as he was in the previous centuries for the abiding cause of "right" and "equality" and the "reckoning" aimed at its implementation.

My hope is that that is what will take the place of the now falling statues. My sense is that this is what William B. Gould would want, not only in his birthplace of North Carolina, but also here in Massachusetts and indeed the entire United States.

Then our celebration of William B. Gould today and all that he accomplished in the time available can be more full-throated and clearheaded. For this will not only fill the empty pedestals of this past century and a half but strike a chord for the propositions that he stood for so emphatically, that is, preservation of the United States itself and achievement of a more equal society.

APPENDIX 10

WILLIAM B. GOULD IV, REMARKS GIVEN AT THE UNVEILING OF THE STATUE OF WILLIAM B. GOULD AT GOULD PARK IN DEDHAM, MASSACHUSETTS, 169 CONG. REC. E551-52, MAY 28, 2023

On behalf of the entire Gould Family on this 100th commemoration of William B. Gould's death here in Dedham, today I express our thanks to Dedham's citizens who made this day possible. Specifically, Joe Castiglione, Voice of the Boston Red Sox and my friend for nearly forty years, for his kindness in accepting this position as Master of Ceremonies of this event.

And I thank Father Wayne L. Belschner of St. Mary's Roman Catholic Church which William B. Gould helped construct in the 1880s. I shall never forget your eloquent and vivid speech eighteen months ago here in Dedham about him and his work and I thank you for it.

And thank you Father Chitral De Mel, Rector of the Church of the Good Shepard here, where we attended the Eucharist this morning and where the first four of the six William Benjamin Goulds were baptized.

Penultimately, thank you Pablo Eduardo for your fine artistry in sculpting this statue of my great-grandfather.

Finally, I thank Brian Keaney, who along with Dan Hart and so many others here in Dedham discovered William B. Gould three years ago and set in motion a chain of events which have led to this day.

"Bring the good old bugle, boys, we'll sing another song," writes Henry C. Work when he wrote *Marching Through Georgia*, which my father sang to us so often in our New Jersey household.

"Sing it with a spirit that will start the world along—Sing it as we used to sing it, fifty thousand strong, While we were marching through Georgia."[31]

These words, sung with gusto by my father, along with the Battle Hymn of the Republic, have been with me since childhood and throughout my three-decade long search for my great-grandfather, gone from this world thirteen years before my birth.

As we arrived in Boston a few days ago after a visit to Savannah, Georgia, I thought anew about those days, reflecting upon General Sherman's great "march to the sea" when "treason fled before us" as the United States marched through Georgia and presented a Christmas present of Savannah to President Lincoln.

Two decades ago, when some of the Gould Family traveled to Wilmington, North Carolina, William B. Gould's birthplace and the site of his audacious escape from slavery to join the United States Navy in the War of the Rebellion, we noted the absence of any statues for the Black veterans of that conflict.[32]

Contrarily, we noted the many Confederate statues throughout the country, a phenomenon made graphic today as some have been pulled down, relocated or destroyed. In Wilmington in 2003 I said:

> *There is little or no mention or acknowledgment of the black military involvement in this effort, the "holiest of all causes" as William B. Gould called it, to obtain the New World's central political and legal achievement.*[33]

Statues cannot be viewed as neutral, and they do not exist in a vacuum.[34] They project the memories of the past and the values associated with them. Their oldest confirmed examples of stone and portrait are said to be before recorded history, 35,000 to 45,000 years ago. When the time capsules contained within this statue are opened, one hundred and two hundred years from now, it may be that William B. Gould's values, expressed in war and in peace here in Dedham, will in some way shape or promote the discussions of future generations.

Of course, it was my father, William B. Gould III, raised here on the Boston-Dedham boundary line, who truly lit the spark for this day. It was he who bequeathed the cadence of the Civil War, its principles, music, literature, and knowledge of its military battles as part of our upbringing. It was he who found the diary itself here in Dedham. It was he who manifested an ever-courteous reverence toward my great uncles who had fought in France in World War I. It was he who kept the flame alive.

On this Memorial Day weekend, we remember the first William B. Gould's service to the United States and his well-written words at sea in 1865. "We were born under the Flag of the Union and we never will know no other,"[35] he said in response to ideas which abounded before and during the War about Black colonization in Africa, while pursuing Confederate vessels near Southampton, Great Britain. "My sentiment is the sentiment of the people of the states," he said.[36] And for my great grandfather, this flag was the "Flag of Right" and "the Flag of Equality."

This day marks honor for that commitment and for those previously forgotten. For until my father discovered the diary and the citizens of Dedham took notice of it three years ago, William B. Gould had been forgotten. To be forgotten was illustrative of what I described a number of years ago, that is, "the old order against which my parents had struggled. In their day the struggle was against hopeless odds—hopeless because all who possessed African blood were isolated, ridiculed, despised—and thus regarded as unfit for occupations and work that the white man was willing to perform."[37] It was the forgotten who, in the words of the Book of Common Prayer, "travail" and are "heavy laden." This is what William B. Gould had in mind when, in his diary, he railed against the tearing of "benighted Africans" from their "loved homes on the free plains of Africa's shores" to be "transferred to the Wilderness of America so that they would become "the Hewers of the Wood and Drawers of Water to clear their Land, to Build their Cittys and feed their Mouths?"[38]

I cannot speak for what William B. Gould would say about the current discussion and debate on recompense or reparations and what form, if any, they should take. But today we can experience firsthand the exhilaration of victory at sea as well as on land, the conclusion of what, in his Second Inaugural Address, President Lincoln called "the bondman's two hundred and fifty years of unrequited toil" and "every drop of blood drawn with the lash."

In 2023, these wounds still exist in our country today, more than one hundred and sixty years after William B. Gould's service. For his generation of family and war comrades, who were ever devoted to full freedom and equality, surely today he would want us to repair the inequality in our country, as he did through his work, with great care and honesty. As St. Mary's parishioners know today, he was a smart, capable, and practical craftsman who worked with his mind as well as his hands. He would be, as he was then, promoting that which is compatible with Lincoln's overriding goal to "bind up the nation's wounds" so that we may live with equity in dignity with respect for one another.

Thank you, Dedham, Massachusetts, for this honor to William B. Gould. God bless you in your efforts to reflect upon the past and affect the future.

NOTES

[1] A Pastoral Letter from the House of Bishops, Jackson, Mississippi, October 4, 1984, 365.
[2] 259 U.S. 200 (1922).
[3] 172 F.2d 402 (2d Cir. 1949).
[4] 346 U.S. 356 (1953).
[5] 407 U.S. 258 (1971).
[6] The American League of Professional Baseball Clubs, 180 NLRB 190, 191 (1969).
[7] Wood v. National Basketball Association, 809 F.2d 954, 961 (2d Cir. 1987).
[8] Silverman v. Major League Baseball Player Relations Committee, 150 LRRM 2390, 2396 (2d Cir. 1995).

9 See Berry & Gould, *A Long Deep Drive to Collective Bargaining: Of Players, Owners, Brawls, and Strikes*, Case Western Reserve Law Review 31 (1981).

10 Brown v. Pro Football, Inc., __ F.3d __ , 148 LRRM (BNA) 2769 (D.C. Cir. March 21, 1995), cert. granted __ U.S. __ (1995).

11 National Basketball Association v. Williams, 45 F.3d 684 (2d Cir. 1995).

12 This theme has been eloquently chronicled in D. Shaughnessy, *The Curse of the Bambino* (1990). I have found this work to be an informative one, although some of the connections between Ruth and the Red Sox performances in recent years are a bit overdrawn.

13 Federal Baseball Club of Baltimore, Inc. v. National League of Professional Baseball Clubs, 259 U.S. 200 (1922).

14 The American League of Professional Baseball Clubs, 180 NLRB 190, 191 (1969).

15 Professional Baseball Clubs v. Major League Baseball Players Association, 66 Lab. Arb. (BNA) 101 (1975) (Seitz, Arb.).

16 Toolson v. New York Yankees, Inc., 346 U.S. 356 (1953).

17 Flood v. Kuhn, 407 U.S. 258 (1971).

18 Brown v. Pro Football, Inc., _ F.3d _, 148 LRRM (BNA) 2769 (D.C. Cir. March 21, 1995).

19 National Basketball Association v. Williams, 45 F.3d 684 (2d Cir. 1995).

20 In Brown, the court stated that under federal labor policy, there prevails "a delicate balance of countervailing power," which "favors neither party to the collective bargaining process, but instead stocks the arsenals of both unions and employers with economic weapons of roughly equal power." Brown, 148 LRRM (BNA) 2769, 2776.

21 First National Maintenance Corp. v. NLRB, 452 U.S. 666 (1981); American Ship Building v. NLRB, 380 U.S. 300 (1965).

22 NLRB v. Mackay, 304 U.S. 333 (1938). President Clinton recognized that the balance of economic power is tipped heavily in favor or employers under this rule, leading him to issue an Executive Order banning the Federal Government from contracting with companies that hire permanent replacements during strikes. Executive Order 12954, 60 Fed. Reg. 13023 (March 8, 1995). I have often addressed this troublesome issue myself, most recently in a speech which I gave before the Bar Association of San Francisco on February 25, 1995. See 38 DLR
(BNA) AS, February 27, 1995. Of course, in the recently concluded 1994–1995 baseball strike, the owners hired temporary replacements for the striking ballplayers during the spring training exhibition season and have now hired temporary replacements for the umpires during the regular season.

23 See Berry & Gould, "A Long Deep Drive to Collective Bargaining: Of Players, Owners, Brawls, and Strikes," *Case Western Reserve Law Review* 31 (1981), 774; Gould, "Players and Owners Mix It Up," 8 *California Lawyer* 56 (August 1988). See generally, R. Berry, W. Gould, and P. Staudohar, *Labor Relations in Professional Sports* (1986).

24 NLRB v. Borg Warner, 356 U.S. 342, 351 (1958).

25 Gould, *Agenda for Reform: the Future of Employment Relationships and the Law*, (MIT Press: 1993).

26 Silverman v. Major League Baseball Player Relations Committee, __ F. Supp. __, 148 LRRM (BNA) 2922 (D. N.Y. Apr. 3, 1995).

27 Gould, *Agenda for Reform: the Future of Employment Relationships and the Law*, (MIT Press 1993).

28 *New York Times*, December 26, 2008, A24.
29 William Butler Yeats, "The Second Coming," *The Collected Poems of W. B. Yeats* (1989); see also Philippe Sands, "Monumental Injustice," *Financial Times*, September 5, 2021, B7; Alex von Tunzelmann, *Fallen Idols: Twelve Statues That Made History* (2021).
30 George Santyana, *The Life of Reason: Reason In Common Sense*, 284 (Scribner's 1905).
31 Henry C. Work, *Marching Through Georgia* (Boston: Tiknor and Company, 1889).
32 William B. Gould IV, speech at the Wilmington Riverwalk Watermen Sign Dedication (October 21, 2003), 150 *Cong. Rec.* 972 (2004).
33 Gould, speech at Wilmington Riverwalk Watermen Sign.
34 von Tunzelmann, *Fallen Idols* (2021).
35 William B. Gould IV, *Diary of a Contraband: The Civil War Passage of a Black Sailor* (2002), 251.
36 Gould, *Diary of a Contraband*, 251.
37 William B. Gould IV, Remarks at Meeting with Chief Justice Earl Warren at Stanford Law School (May 17, 1974), 120 *Cong. Rec.* 16229 (1974).
38 Gould, Remarks at Meeting with Chief Justice Earl Warren, 18n7.

INDEX

Note: Subentries for persons are chronologically arranged.

Abbreviations:

WBG, William B. Gould
WBG Jr., William B. Gould, Jr.
WBG III, William B. Gould III
WBG IV, William B. Gould IV

Abner, Willoughby, 97, 108n30
Adams, William, 419
affirmative action, 48, 69n16, 70n31, 190, 212, 230–231, 243n5, 247, 268, 330n19
African National Congress, 250, 256, 262, 280n34, 273, 275, 403
AFL-CIO
   See American Federation of Labor-Congress of Industrial Organizations
Agricultural Labor Relations Act (ALRA) of 1975, 441–442, 445– 446, 448, 450 452–453, 455, 465n39
Agricultural Labor Relations Board (ALRB), 441, 444–449, 451–452, 454, 465n38, 465n46
Agenda for Reform, 343–344, 358, 362
Allen, Mel, 305
Allen, Roger, 172
American dilemma, 49, 68n19, 128
   See Gunnar Myrdal
Alternative Dispute Resolution (ADR) program, 426, 437

Amalgamated Clothing Workers Union, 94, 131, 334, 370n1
American Bar Association (ABA), 275, 285–287, 290, 322, 374, 392
American Civil Liberties Union (ACLU), 150–151, 182, 199–200, 203n32, 205n63, 205n65, 214, 223
American Embassy
   in London, 240, 245
   in Pretoria, 251
American Federation of Labor-Congress of Industrial Organizations (AFL-CIO)
   discrimination in the construction industry, 39–40, 175, 202n19
   reaction to nomination for chairman of the National Labor Relations Board, 337, 358
   See George Meany, Walter P. Reuther
American Federation of State and Municipal Employees (AFSME), 148
American Federation of State, County and Municipal Employees Union (AFSCMEU), 440
Amsterdam, Anthony (Tony), 224–225
Anderson, Reverend Robert, 17, 99, 304–305
Angelos, Peter, 383, 390–392, 417n21
Anglo-American Corporation, 254
Angrist, Gene, 57–58
anti-affirmative action, 213

anti-union bias, 343
anti-union campaign, 136, 423
anti-union workers, 340
Anglo-African, 30, 37, 38, 42n35
apartheid, 247, 249, 264–265, 278n6, 279n23, 280n40
    Carter administration and, 248, 250, 278nn4–5; 279n10
    Reagan administration and, 260, 280n26
A Primer on American Labor Law, 63, 71n35, 242, 260, 330n15, 330n19
Arbitration
    approach to, 215
    collective bargaining and, 136, 181
    complex contractual issues and, 216, 243n12
    "final offer", 326
    for salary in sports, 326, 336, 382, 389, 417n19
    grievance arbitration, 174, 423
    in job-bias complaints, 216, 243n12
    in public education, 171–173
    interest arbitration, 172
    labor, 298, 333, 335–336
    lectures in Britain on American system of, 118, 235, 244n31
    National Labor Relations Board and, 382
    provision of compulsory arbitration, 383
    "reserve clause" and, 326
    See United Farm Workers (UFW), *Spielberg Manufacturing Co.*,
Armstrong, Chuck, 390
Ashcroft, John, 392
Ashe, Arthur, 250
Association for the Betterment of Black Edison Employees, 179, 182, 184, 188–189, 195
Attleboro, Mass., 7, 19, 24
Attles, Jr., Alvin, 320, 328
Auchincloss, James, 45
Australian National University, 289
Ayob, Ismail, 266
Azoff, Elliott, 353

Babcock, Barbara, 201, 212
Baker, Dusty, 315, 317, 325, 330n24, 366–368, 390, 404–405
Baldwin, James, 57, 129

Bantu education, 255
Barber, Red, 305
Barbosa, Antonio, 444
Barkett, Rose-Marie, 359–360
Barnett, Wayne, 209
baseball
    American League, 308, 314–315, 382
    Cincinnati Red Stockings, 316
    collective bargaining agreement to settle strike and, 388
    Cuba and, 392
    free-agent negotiations, compensation discussions, 383
    labor-management relations and, 319
    National League, 304, 382
    race relations and, 325
    salary arbitration and, 326, 336, 382, 389, 417n19
    secure injunction against unfair labor practices to settle strike, 386
    strike of 1994 and 1995, 380–389
    the National Labor Relations Board (NLRB) and, 383
    the salary cap and, 380, 382, 389, 418n20
Baseball Writers' Dinner, 325
"batching" appointments, 363
Battle, Robert "Buddy", III, 90
Battle, Fowler, Stokes, and Kheel, 135
    See Kheel firm
Bay Area Labor Law Discussion Group, 348
Bay of Pigs, 82
Baylor, Don, 325, 366
Bell, Derrick, 174, 184, 213, 219
Bell, Ed, 187
Bellamy Mansion, 29, 36
Belschner, Reverend Wayne, 32
Benes, Andy, 327, 336
Bercusson, Brian, 236
Berlin Wall, 128, 277
Bernstein, Harry, 174, 379, 417n7
Berry, Bob, 319, 321, 328, 351
Biden, Joe, 355
Biko, Steve, 255, 258
Bindman, Geoffrey, 149, 235
Black Consciousness movement, 255
"black dot" system, 190, 204n41
Black labor movement, 259, 279n23

INDEX

Black Musicians of Pittsburgh v. Local 60–471, 219–222
Black National Bar Association, 349
Black trade unionists
 in Detroit, 90
 in South Africa, 252
Black Workers in White Unions, 242–243n4, 249
Blanco, Eduardo, 444, 453
blue curtain, 94
Bodle, George, 285
Boehner, John, 402
Bok, Derek, 174, 184, 209
Bonds, Bobby, 301
Bonham-Carter, Mark, 148, 235
Bonior, David, 410–411, 413
Boston Globe, 3, 39n4, 311, 320, 331n26, 388–389, 417nn18–19
Boston Red Sox, 155, 234, 306, 314, 316, 321, 331n32, 382
Botha, P.W., 270
Bowie, Harry, 16, 49, 54, 70n23, 134, 179
Boxer, Barbara, 232, 334, 352, 357
Bradley, Bill, 232
Brandfort, Orange Free State, Afrikanerdom, 256–257
Bredhoff, Elliot, 379
Breed, London, 457–458, 460n63
Brennan, Peter, 176
Brennan, Justice William, 148, 159
Brest, Paul, 272, 322
Brewer, Mark, 232
Brexit, 116, 236
British Labour Party, 115–116, 349
British Race Relations Board, 148, 235
British unions, 118
 Amalgamated Engineering Union (AEU), 119
 Contrast between US and, 118
 Electrical Trades Union, 119
 Transport and General Workers Union, 118, 424
Brockriede, John, 312
Brotherhood of Railway Clerks, 139
Brown, Bill, 185, 188, 203n37
Brown, Gerald, 132, 347
Brown, Jerry, 132, 327, 442–444, 447–448
Brown, Pat, 217, 229, 444

Brown v. Board of Education of Topeka, 32, 42n38, 69n11, 69n13
Buffon, Charlie, 347, 349
Buthelezi, Chief Gatsha, 255–256, 258, 279n17
Buttu, Diana, 30

Caen, Herb, 336, 370n2
Café Fino, 323
California Agricultural Labor Relations Board, 132, 443
California Public Employment Relations Act, 455
Campbell, Jeremy, 359, 370n16
Campbell, Tom, 231
Cape Town, South Africa, 247–248, 254, 267, 269, 279n16
 1979 Human Rights Conference in, 259
Carter, Jimmy, 248, 334, 341, 446
Cassim, Nazeer, 267
Castiglione, Joe, 305–306, 325, 390
Castle, Barbara, 115, 119, 129n1
Caterpillar, Inc., 414, 418n39, 463nn12–13
Chafee, John, 361
Chavez, Cesar, 442, 448, 465nn43–44
Checkpoint Charlie, 128, 277
Cheney, Reverend William, 2
Childress, Mark, 349–350
Christopher, Arthur, 135
Chicago Tribune, 230, 244n26
Churchill College, 235–236
circuit courts of appeal
 arguing before, 228, 397
Civil Rights Act of 1957, 56, 133
civil rights legislation
 See Title VII of the Civil Rights Act of 1964
civil rights movement, 43, 76
Civil Service Law, 137
 See Condon-Wadlin Act, 137
Civil War, 112, 135, 185, 207, 242n1
Clark, General Wesley, 232
class action case, 205n64, 224
Clay, Bill, 352, 357
Clinton, Hillary, 233
Clinton, William, 328, 334–335
 National Labor Relations Board and, 328, 346
cloture petition, 342

Coalition of Black Trade Unionists, 440, 464n32
Coats, Dan, 362
Coday, Bill, 348
Cohan, Leon, 187
Cohen, Bill, 211–213
Cole, John, 121, 130n9, 236
collective bargaining
   Big three automakers and, 84, 95, 100
   public employees' right to strike and, 137, 150, 176
   process, 150, 286, 351
   President Clinton, WBG IV and, 359
   private employees/government contractors and, 413, 418nn34–35
   The 2003 Writers Guild Election Dispute and, 420–422
collective bargaining agreement, 64, 137, 140, 147, 149, 157, 172, 181
   the 1994–1995 Major League Baseball strike and, 388–389
Collins, Jeremiah, 214
colonialism, 248, 262
Commission on the Future of Worker-Management Relations, 336
Common Market, 122–123, 129n2, 236
Commonweal
   WBG IV contributions to, 107n19, 108n24, 129, 163n12, 166n22, 259, 275n45, 279n22
Community of the Resurrection, 252
Cook, Julian and Carol (wife, née Dibble), 56, 74, 161, 375
Condon-Wadlin Act, 137
   See Civil Service Law
congressional Black Caucus, 352
Conyers, John, Jr., 91
Cornell Law School, 131, 135, 169, 335
constitutional law, 54, 58–59, 76, 156, 169, 176, 226
Cornish, Bill, 290
Corporate Social Responsibility Policy (CSR Policy), 425
COSATU, 262, 264
"courtesy calls", 351–352
Cowley Fathers, 1, 39n1
Cox, Archibald, 184, 203n35

Craig, Roger, 183, 188–189
Cranefield, Harold, 62, 75, 79, 84, 87, 103–104, 107nn14,19 125, 128, 228
Crisis, 5, 20
Cronje, Pierre, 269
Crotty, Dennis 138, 142–143
Cry the Beloved Country, 249
Cuomo, Mario, 228, 378
Curley, James Michael, 6, 39n12, 308
Curtin, William, 352
Curtis-Wright case, 98–99
Custer Job Corps, 140, 155

Daily Mail, 254, 259
Danaher, James (Jim), 208, 225, 229
Davidson, Nestor, 349, 354–355
"Dear Colleague" letter, 362
Dedham High School, 22–23
de Klerk, F. W., 262–263, 265, 270, 272, 280n42
de León, Kevin, 447
Dellinger, Walter, 419
Democratic Party, 6, 39n12, 44, 51, 76, 90 120, 229, 231–232, 244n26, 347, 350, 366, 378
Dewey, Thomas, 43–44
Del Guercio, Al, 143
Dennis v. United States, 150–151, 166n28, 176, 203n22
Department of Health, Education, and Welfare (HEW), 246–247, 278n1
Department of Human Resources (DHR), 457, 460–461
Detroit AFL-CIO, 376
Detroit Edison case, 207, 254, 279n14
Detroit Edison Company
   Black employees document racial discrimination practices at, 178, 183
   found guilty of bias, 193–195, 204nn49–50
   file appeal to Sixth Circuit Court of Appeals, 195
   settlement reached and awarded to employees, 200
Detroit Free Press, 122, 175, 182, 195, 204n49, 204n56–57
Detroit National Lawyers Guild, 77
Detroit Newspapers' strike, 411

INDEX 547

Detroit Tigers, 307, 311
Dibble, Carol, 56–57
   See Cook, Carol
Dinger, John, 264
Discrimination
   See employee discrimination, racial discrimination
   black workers and, 185, 186, 204n30
   See Detroit Edison Company
   within the construction industry, 147–148, 175, 178, 188
   See Philadelphia Plan
Dissler, Mark, 360
"diversity" grounds, 297
DiMaggio, Dom, 307
DiMaggio, Joe, 303, 308
Doby, Larry, 220
Dodd, Bill, 76
Doeringer, Peter, 147
Doerr, Bobby, 303
Donohue, William (Bill), 157–160
Dotson, Donald L., 342–343, 374–375
Dotson-Stephens incident, 375, 417n1
Douglas, Paul, 44
Dowling, Kate, 407, 419
Dubeer, Zac, 254
Du Bois, W.E.B., 5–6, 20, 39nn10–11
Dunlop, John, 147–148, 353
Durban, South Africa, 247, 261, 265–268, 273, 284
Durenberger, Dave, 351, 357, 362–363

The Economist, 115, 129, 134, 162n5
Edwards, George, 92–93, 107n22
Edwards, Nelson "Jack", 96–97
Elders, Jocelyn, 345
Ehrlich, Tom, 208–209, 213, 322
Eisenhower, Dwight D., 43, 45–46, 78, 132, 196, 274
   WBG IV critical of Eisenhower administration's relationship with Franco and Spain, 70n26, 249, 279nn7–9
employee dismissal, 296
employment discrimination, 63, 65, 143–144, 455
employment discrimination law, 65, 96, 209, 222

author's consultant work for the Equal Employment Opportunity Commission (EEOC), 143–148
Stanford Law School and Wayne State Law School seminar on, 175, 183, 189, 202n14, 213
See *Title VII of the Civil Rights Act of 1964, Griggs v. Duke Power Co.*
employment relationship rulings, 413, 418n34
Emporium-Capwell Co. v. Western Addition, 163–165n16, 202n16
   NLRB v. Noah's Ark Processors, LLC, 415–416, 418nn45–46
Equal Employment Opportunity Commission (EEOC), 65, 143–148, 202–203n20, 442
   Detroit Edison workers and the, 181
   "underutilization of minority employees" in utilities, 184, 203nn36–37
Eshoo, Anna, 231, 357
Estes, Wayne, 292, 329nn7–8
Eth, Jordan, 214
European Union, 116, 236

Fair Employment Practices Committee (FEPC), 44
fair employment practices law
   JFK support for, 133
   in the courts, 333
fair employment practices legislation, 67, 103
fair housing ordinance
   enforcing of in Detroit, 92
Fair Labor Standards Act of 1938, 44
Fanning, John, 341
Farrell, John, 315
Fastiff, Wesley, 223
Federal Arbitration Act of 1925, 296, 330n18
Federal Bureau of Investigation (FBI), 46, 135, 185, 194, 204n53, 346, 350
Federal Mediation and Conciliation Service, 97, 149, 382
Feinstein, Dianne, 217, 348, 357
Feinstein, Fred, 376, 396–397, 400
Feller, Bob, 303

Felts, Leah Jeronia (wife of WBG III), 1
    Birth of, 7
    Parents and siblings of, 7
    Education of, 7
    Marriage to WBG III, 1
    Children of (WBG IV and Dorothy Leah Gould), 8, 40n14
    Teacher in New Jersey schools, 7
    Family in Attleboro, Mass., 24–25
"fifth columnist", 49
filibuster, 44, 340–342, 364, 369, 371n27
Fillion, John, 75–76
FirstGroup America
    WBG IV serves as independent monitor for labor union organizing, 426–427; reviews labor issues within, 430; develops the Freedom of Association (FoA) Policy strategy, 426
    FirstGroup plc acquires Ryder Public transportation, Laidlaw International, Inc., 424; accuses unions of bullying tactics, 425
    Attracts labor union attention, 425–426
    Teamsters commission studies of alleged violations of FoA rights, 425
    FirstGroup adopts Independent Monitor (IM) Program, 426–427; informs James Hoffa, Jr. (son of Jimmy), Teamsters president, 426; conducts managerial training program on FoP and IM program, 428
    IM program successes, 432–433; limitations, 433–434
    First Group, Teamsters negotiate national agreement for school bus drivers, 429, 463n7
First National Maintenance v. NRLB, 286, 329n4
Flanagan, Bob, 216, 226
Fletcher, Willy, 231
Flood, Curt, 326
Floyd, George, 458, 466n63
Foley v. Interactive Data, 295, 330n16
Ford, Bill, 288–289
Ford Foundation, 181, 249
Fox, Sarah, 400, 402, 406
Franklin, John Hope, 28–29
Franklin, Leo, 182–183, 186, 203n34
Franklin, Marc, 208

Fraser, Doug, 172
Freedom of Association (FoP) Policy, 426–429, 432
    Standards of conduct under the, 434–439
    See First Group America
Freedom Summer of 1964, 134, 179
free-agent compensation, 383
free-agent negotiations, 383
Fuchs, Bob, 335
Fulbright program, 263

gag order, 223–225, 227, 243n18
Gaitskell, Hugh, 115–116, 123, 129n2, 139n10
Ganley, Nat, 96
Garmon v. San Diego Building Trades, 107n6, 209, 242n2
General Gravure Company, 157, 159–160, 167n36
Geremek, Bronislaw, 277
Gerawan Farming, 451, 465n50
Gilfix, Mike, 225
Gingrich Revolution, 392
Ginsburg, Ruth Bader, 184
    and "unbargained-for" arbitration, 296, 330n20
Gladstone, Richard, 266
Glazer, Joe, 246–248
Glazer, Nathan, 246–247, 278nn2–3
Godsell, Bobby, 254
Goldman, Lee, 422
Golino, Frank, 251–252, 264
Gomes, Jonny, 315
Goodman, Ernest (Ernie), 77, 108–109n36
Goodman, Richard and Maria, 77–78, 88, 95
Gorman, Lou, 325
Gould, Alexander and Elizabeth "Betsy" Moore (parents of WBG), 36
Gould, Dorothy Leah (sister of WBG IV)
    Birth of, 8
    Early years of, 8–9, 16, 18–19, 35
    Marriage to Hermann Gerber, 99
Gould, Edward Blair (son of WBG IV), xxv, 161, 527
Gould, Dr. Ernest M. (son of WBG, uncle of WBG III), 2, 5–6, 22, 50
    Fannie Butler Gould, wife of, 22, 28, 131

INDEX   549

Gould, Frederick (son of WBG, uncle of
  WBG III), 20
Gould, Hannah Jordan (mother of WBG III),
  1, 34
Gould, Herbert (son of WBG, uncle of
  WBG III), 20–22
Gould, Hilda Elizabeth (née Fitter) (wife
  of WBG IV), 123, 133, 170, 180,
  233, 236, 242, 275, 335, 366, 369,
  440, 442
  Marriage to WBG IV, 124–125, 129
Gould, James Edward (son of WBG, uncle of
  WBG III) and Isabel Gould (wife), 19
Gould, Joseph Jeremy "Joey" (grandson of
  WBG IV), 303, 313, 331n28, 392–393
Gould, Lawrence (Lorry) (son of WBG,
  uncle of WBG III), 20, 22, 26
Gould, Medora (Dora) (daughter of WBG,
  aunt of WBG III), 20
Gould, Timothy Samuel, Sr. (son of WBG
  IV), xxv, 137, 141, 527
Gould, William B. (WBG)
  Birth of, 36
  Early life, 36
  Diary of, 26, 30, 32, 36–38, 40n13,
    41n18, 42nn33–34, 42n36
  Free man or slave, 27–29, 36
  Member of the Grand Army of the
    Republic (GAR), 35, 38
  Union Navy Sailor, Civil War, 36–37
  Significance of Wilmington, N.C., 26,
    28–31, 36–37
  Designated contraband (escaped slave),
    28, 36, 40n13
  Plasterer and mason, 25, 31
  Oley, *The Anglo-African* correspondent,
    30, 38
  Escape to freedom aboard USS
    Cambridge and USS *Niagara*, 28, 37
  Marriage to former slave Cornelia
    Williams Read, 31; father of eight
    children, 38
  Founder of Episcopal Church of the
    Good Shepherd, 31, 38
  Reputation in Dedham, 26
  Dedication of the William B. Gould
    Memorial Park, 32, 42n37
  Death of, 38

African American National Biography
  entry, 36–39, 42n40
Gould, William B., Jr. (WBG Jr.)
  Birth of, 20
  Spanish-American War service, 22–23,
    38
  Marriage to Hannah Jordan, 20
  Death of, 20
Gould, Wiliam B., III (WBG III)
  Birth of, 1
  Siblings Ernest, Marjorie, and Robert,
    2, 33
  Childhood in Readville, Mass., 2
  Active parishioner of Episcopal Church
    of the Good Shephard, East
    Dedham, Mass., 2
  Joins the Boy Scouts, 2
  Plays football at Hyde Park High
    School, 2–3
  Becomes chief operator of Hyde Park
    High amateur radio stations and
    club, 2
  Obtains ham radio license, 3
  Enters Worcester Polytechnic Institute
    (WPI) on scholarship, 3
  Active in WPI Wireless Association, 3
  Loses scholarship, withdraws, reenters
    WPI, 3
  Radio work at WDBH in Worcester
    after graduation, 4
  Marriage to Leah Jeronia Felts, 1, 35
    See Felts, Leah Jeronia,
    (Mrs. William B. Gould III)
  Employed at Western Electric, Kearney,
    N.J., 4
  Loses job for being Black, 4
  Enlists in U.S. Naval Reserves as
    Radioman, 4–5
  Serves with Merchant Marines, 5
  Impact of Jacksonville, Fla. incidents, 5
  Employment correspondence with
    W.E.B. Du Bois, 5–6, 39nn8,10,11
  Hired as architect for Boston Mayor
    James Michael Curley, 6–7
  Employed by the Boston Metropolitan
    Police Radio Department, 8
  Birth of children, William B. Gould IV
    and Dorothy Leah Gould, 8

Radio engineer, United States Signal
Corps, United States Army stationed
in Fort Monmouth, N.J., 8–10
Develops radar expertise, 9
Work during World War II and Korean
War, 9
Involvement with Countermeasures
group and Sputnik, 9–10
Uses radio and radar for counterintelligence and meteorological
purposes in the Electronics Warfare
Laboratory, 10–11
Retires in 1969, 10
Death in 1983, 283–284, 329nn1,3
Posthumous honor as an early Black
electronic engineer at Fort
Monmouth by InfoAge at Camp
Evans, 11
Gould, William B., IV (WBG IV)
Birth of, 8
Early life in Hyde Park, Mass., 8
Birth of sister, Dorothy Leah, 8
Childhood in Long Branch, N.J., 8–13,
15–16, 49–50, 113, 298–299
And early friends, 12, 16
Attends Broadway School, 12
Deals with illnesses, 13
Develops love for reading, 13
Influence of Thornton Burgess's writing,
13–14
Father's (WBG III) critical views of
Reconstruction and Thomas
Jefferson Memorial, 14–15
Choirboy at St. James Episcopal
Church, Long Branch, 15–16, 52
Describes father as Renaissance
man, 16
Toils in the victory garden at home, 16
Develops interest in ornithology and
philology, 17
Observes abundance of food in home;
careful spending by parents, 18
Visits family in Massachusetts, 19–21, 24
Uncovers WBG diary, 25–28
Explores Wilmington, N.C., for proof
of WBG slavery, 29–30
Finds Oley's (aka WBG) *Anglo-African*
essay on escaping slavery, 30
Impact of WBG on WBG IV, 32–33,
42n39

Passing in Long Branch, N.J., 49–50
Army-McCarthy hearings cause interest
in law, civil rights, 46
Influence of 1954 *Brown v. Board of
Education* ruling and opinion
from Chief Justice Earl Warren,
47–48
Attends University of Rhode Island, 54
See Thurgood Marshall, Phi Mu
Delta
Conversation with JFK about protecting Black voter rights, 55
Entertains joining Episcopalian priesthood, 54
Accepted to Cornell Law School, 58–60
Summer clerkship at the United Auto
Workers (UAW), 62–65, 75–76
Dealing with the military draft, 82–83
Passes bar exam, 89
Works with the Cavanagh administration, 90, 92–93
Delivers first professional paper at
Cornell Industrial and Labor
Relations School conference in
New York City, 94
Handles the Curtis-Wright Case, 98
Named to the Public Employment
Relations Board established under
the New York Taylor Law and the
first fact-finding board, 138, 150,
171
Sister Dorothy's marriage to Harmann
Gerber, 99
Elected Precinct Delegate to 1962
Democratic State Convention in
Grand Rapids, Mich., 100
Seminal work on the River Rouge Case
ends, 100–102
Memories, impact of World War II,
110–114
Adjusting to London, 114–117
Attends the British Labour Party
Conference, 115–116
Examines British Labour Unions, 118
Meets the British Labour Party's opposition cabinet, 120–121
Studies at the London School of
Economics, 91, 102, 119, 235
Meeting, courtship, and marriage to
Hilda Fitter, 123–125

See Gould, Hilda Elizabeth (née Fitter)
Return to America, joins the National Labor Relations Board (NLRB), 131–132
Commences law journal writing; pursues publications to reach diverse audiences, 129
Effect of JFK assassination on, 133
Birth of son William B. Gould V, 134
Move to New York labor law firm of Firm Battle, Fowler, Stokes, and Kheel; studies collective bargaining systems and third-party resolution of disputes in labor management process, 135–138
Manages, hears apprentice arbitrator cases in maritime, transit, and pocketbook industries; also represents Teamsters, Diners Club, Proctor & Gamble, and U.S. Industries, 138
Significance of Western Transport collective bargaining agreement, 139–140
Birth of second son, Timothy Samuel Gould, 141
Consultant and conciliator for the Equal Employment Opportunity Commission (EEOC), 143–149
Solo arbitrating: Steel Workers and the National Lead Company, 149–150
Public policy writings for Senator Robert F. Kennedy, 151–155
Closing General Gravure Company case, 157–160
Teaching Labor Law and Constitutional Law at Wayne State Law School, 155–156, 169–170
Birth of third son, Edward Blair Gould, 161
Fact finder for the Michigan Employment Relations Commission (MERC) public education employment disputes, 171
Involved in constitutional law issues, 176–177
Stamps v. Detroit Edison Company, 178

Workers claim racial discrimination at Michigan power company, 178–183, 190–195, 204n58
Utility found guilty of racial bias, 193, 204n49
Edison ordered to pay $4 million to Black employees, 193, 204n57
Life-altering surgery for eldest son, Bill, 179–180
Admitted to the National Academy of Arbitrators, 181
A year at Harvard Law School, 183–184, 207–208
Friendship with Ruth Bader Ginsburg, 184, 393
Hired as the first Black professor in the Stanford Law School in 1972, 201, 208–212; encounters racism, 213, 243n7
Elected delegate to 1974 Democratic Party convention, 229–231, 243n23, 244nn24–26
Awarded Guggenheim Fellowship and Rockefeller Foundation grant to examine union relationships with multinational corporations; relocates to Churchill College, Cambridge, England in 1975, 235–236
Seminal travels to Portugal, Russia, Japan, and Hawaii, 237–242
Significance of South Africa for, 242
Meeting with Mrs. Winnie Mandela in Brandfort, Orange Free State, Afrikanerdom, 256–258, 279n18
Advocates for Black unions in South Africa, 252, 254, 258–260, 263, 279nn21–26
Witnesses constitutional transition in South Africa in 1991, 263; describes visit as a watershed, 271, 289n41
Attends Nelson Mandela's South African presidential inauguration, 274
Speaks out about Reagan administration, 275–276, 280n46

Travels, lectures in Latin America and Eastern Europe, 275–278
Death of WBG III, 283–284, 329nn1–2
Labor law assignments for the American Bar Association (ABA) in Europe and Australia, 285–290
Appointed co-chairman of California State Bar Labor and Employment Law Section Ad Hoc Committee on Termination at Will and Wrongful Discharge, 291, 329nn7,9–11; recommends repeal of California Labor Code 2922, 292, 329n9
Named the Charles A. Beardsley Professor of Law at Stanford Law School in 1984, 296; proposes foreign student graduate program, 296–298
Teaches significant Law and Sports course, 298, 319–321, 328, 331nn29–31
Tracing baseball roots: Sandlot Ball to the Boston Red Sox, 298–310
Studies relationship between race and baseball in writings, 311, 325, 331nn26–27
Enjoying jazz at Café Fino, 323
President Clinton nominates WBG IV for National Labor Relations Board (NLRB) Chairman, 328, 334, 339, 346–347
Resistance to confirmation expressed, 339–340, 343–345
Mark Childress and the gambling/South Africa/Cuba affair, 349–351
Confirmation hearings postponements, 347–348
Senator Nancy Kassebaum filibuster delay; calls WBG IV a "radical", 356, 361–365, 371n23
Senate approves WBG IV NLRB chairman nomination, 368–369; sworn in, 373–376
Suggests creation of labor and management legal advisory panel, 374
Proposes several reforms to NLRB processes, 377–378
United Mine Workers of America (UMWA) case, 378–379

Baseball strike of 1994–1995, the salary cap, collective bargaining consummated, 380–388
Thoughts on 2022 baseball lockout, 388–390, 417nn18–19, 418n20
Throws first pitch at 1995 Red Sox-Orioles game at Camden Yards, 390–391; and on Jackie Robinson Day in 2006 at Fenway Park, 390
Friendship with Senator Mark Hatfield during 1995–1996 appropriations process, 394–398
NLRB case production slows in 1996; adjusts to personnel changes, 400–403
Attends President Nelson Mandela's 1994 inauguration in South Africa, accused of wasteful travel, 403
Baseball tickets and Dusty Baker commotion, 404–405
Bill Stewart, NLRB Chief Counsel, retires, 405–407, 418n26
Resolves final NLRB cases: Service Employees Union, *Detroit Newspapers*, *Telescope Casual Furniture, Inc.*, *San Diego Gas and Electric* (*Novotel New York*, *Caterpillar, Inc.* issue earlier); 404–413, 418nn30,32–33; 418n39
Letter from President Clinton citing NLRB successes, 416–417, 418n47
Return to California, 419
The 2003 Writers Guild Election Dispute
  Settles outstanding issues before contract negotiations begin with the Alliance of Motion Picture and Television Producers, 420–422, 463nn4–5
Serves as independent monitor for FirstGroup to resolve union organization issues, 422–440
  See First Group America
Develops project labor agreement guidelines for the U.S. Department of Housing and Urban Development (HUD), 440–441

INDEX 553

Accepts Agricultural Labor Relations Board (ALRB) chairmanship, 441–443
Deals with myriad job challenges, concerns in Sacramento, 445, 465n38
Reaches compromise with California Governor Jerry Brown on the General Counsel situation, 447–448
Handles the United Farm Workers (UFW) and outdated arbitration provisions, 448–450
Encourages farm worker education on labor statute, 453–455
Resigns from ALRB position, 454, 465n56
Examines alleged issues of racial misconduct inside San Francisco work force, 457
Appointed Impartial Chairman for the California Public Employment Relations Act for appeals process for administrative discipline proceedings before the San Francisco Police Commission, 455–461, 466n63
Gould, William B., V (son of WBG IV), xxv, 134, 239, 527
Gould, William B., VI (grandson of WBG IV), 331n28
The Great Depression, 6
Greely, Hank (the Hankster), 334
Green, Pumpsie, 311
Gregg, Judd, 361–362
Gregory, Gordon, 75, 78
Grey, Tom, 207
Griggs v. Duke Power Co., 65, 71n38, 165n20
Grunfeld, Cyril, 235, 287
Guinier, Lani, 345, 364–365
Guardian, 195, 204n58
Gunther, Gerry, 201, 226

Hafer, Hugh, 188
Hall, Bill, 302
Hanslowe, Kurt, 59–60, 62, 70n32, 79–80, 94, 107nn12–13, 116, 119, 276, 280n47
Harkin, Tom, 352, 361
Harper, Tommy, 311

Hart, Gary, 218, 243n13
Harvard Business School, 248
Harvard Law School, 70n32, 95, 174, 180, 202–203n20, 207, 209, 345, 392–393
Hatch Act, 176, 180
Hatch, Orrin, 341, 353
Hatfield, Mark, 394–398, 401–402
Hay, Howard, 291–292, 329n7
Healy, Jim, 248
Heath, Edward, 235
Henderson, Thelton, 225, 373–374
Henning, Jack, 217–218, 441
Henning, Patrick, 441–443
Herman, Jimmy, 217
Hernandez, Aileen, 143–144
Higgins, John, 375, 401, 406, 418n25
"high-opportunity" jobs, 190
Hill, Anita, 203–204n39, 354
Hills, Roderick (Rod), 176
HIV/AIDS epidemic, 275
Hoekstra, Pete, 402–404
Hoffa, James, Jr., 426–427, 449
Hoffa, Jimmy, 95, 108nn24–25, 151, 163n12, 338, 426–427, 449
  See Teamsters
Hollis, Ira, 3, 39n5
Hoover, Herbert, 44
Hope for South Africa, 249, 279n9
Hoppe, Art, 229
Horton, Willie, 180
House Subcommittee on Africa, 260, 279n25
House Labor Oversight Committee, 403
Howard, Colin, 245
Howard Law School, 28–29
Howe, Geoffrey, 235
Huddleston, Reverend Trevor, 252, 263, 266
Humboldt University Law Faculty, 277
Humphrey, Hubert, 44, 69n2, 81

Independent Monitor (IM) Program
  overview and process of the, 430
  role of the IM, 431–432, 439
  strengths, successes of the, 432–434; limitations, 433–434
  FirstGroup and the, 422–434
  coexisting within existing public law, 437–440
  See First Group America, Teamsters

Industrial Relations Act of 1971, 235, 244n29
Industrial Relations Research Association (IRRA), 216–217
Inkatha, 255, 267, 269, 271, 273, 279n17
Institute of Industrial Relations, 216
International Brotherhood of Electrical Workers (IBEW), 178, 232, 334
International Brotherhood of Teamsters, 424, 464n31
International Longshore and Warehouse Union (ILWU), 217, 348
International Transport Workers' Federation (ITWF), 425
International Union of Electrical, Radio and Machine Workers (IUE), 148, 411
interracial sex and marriage, laws governing, 251, 279n11

Jacobsen, Magdalena (Maggie), 216–217, 455
Jackie Robinson Day, 390
Jackson, Reverend Jesse, 346
Jackson, Reggie, 302, 314
Jackson, Samuel C., 143–144
Jazz, venues attended by the author, 323–325
Jeffords, James, 351, 355–357, 362–363
Jeffrey, Millie, 76
Jenkins, Jr., Howard, 135
Jersey Shore League, 309
Jim Crow, 179
Johannesburg, 252, 267, 269, 272–274, 336
Johannesburg Star, 250, 254, 263, 279nn14–15
Johnson, Lyndon, 76, 152
Johnson, Pete, 190
Johnson, Walter, 217, 232
Joiner, Charlie, 155, 170
Jones v. Pacific Intermountain Express, 222, 227, 244n20
Juneteenth, 458, 466n63
just cause, 291, 293, 329n10

Kaess, Fred, 75–76
Kahoe, Cody, 457
Kahn-Freund, Otto, 102, 119
Kaplan, John, 213, 222, 242–243n4

Kassebaum, Nancy, 347, 354–357, 360–365, 371n23
Keith, Damon, 176, 180, 203n23
Kennedy, Don, 261, 280nn28–29
Kennedy, Edward "Ted", 342, 349, 352–353, 356–357, 366, 368–369, 371n25, 399, 402
Kennedy, Robert F. (RFK), 76, 82, 151–152, 166n30, 338, 370n6
Kennedy, John F. (JFK), 56, 66, 76, 78–79
    reaction to the 1960 presidential election, 80–82
    addressing the 1962 United Auto Workers (UAW) convention, 98, 108n31
    assassination of, 133
Kent, Roger, 229
Kern, Msgr. Clement, 95, 102, 108n25, 140
Kerry, John, 233–234
Kheel firm, 135, 141
    See Battle, Fowler, Stokes, and Kheel
Kheel, Theodore "Ted", 136–178, 149–150, 166n24
King, Martin Luther, Jr., 57, 105, 126, 135, 155
Kirkland, Lane, 337
Kohler Company strike, 87
Koppett, Leonard, 302, 315, 320, 325, 328, 381
Kruger National Park, 267–268
Kudlidge, Franz, 2
Kuny, Denis, South African lawyer and good friend of the author, 264

Labor and Employment Relations Association, 216–217, 462n2
    See San Francisco Industrial Relations Research Association
labor arbitration, 43, 75, 109n38, 139, 162nn10–11, 202n10, 215, 243n9, 293, 320, 333
labor law
    challenging assumptions to American, 290–296
    reforms, 340–341, 352–353, 394, 420
    disputing reform impacts National Labor Relations Board (NLRB) congressional confirmation hearings, 337–343

INDEX

wrongful discharge, 290–291, 333
labor law reform(s), 336, 420
   in Britain, 235
   in South Africa, 260, 279n24
labor management disputes
   importance of arbitration process in, 74
labor management relations, 74, 238, 319, 344, 346, 420, 455, 462n1
   workplace fairness legislation and, 63
   relationship between Title VII's employment discrimination prohibitions and, 173
   Michigan Employment Relations Commission (MERC) and, 171–173
Labor Management Reporting and Disclosure Act of 1959 (LMRDA), 421
Labor Policy Association, 340, 358, 375
Labor Reform Bill, 340, 342
Landrum-Griffin Amendments of 1959, 64
Lasker, Morris, 135–136, 150–151
Laski, Harold, 349
Lee, Jennie, 120
Lester, Anthony, 148–149, 235
Levin, Harry, 12, 304
Levy, Herman, 348, 442, 464n35
Lewis, Anthony, 297, 365
Lie, Haoklen, 128
Lindsay, Bruce, 345
Lindsay, John, 138
Livingston, Winston "Win", 78, 87
Lockhead, Sir Moir, 422, 426–427, 429
Lomax, Stan, 306
London Evening Standard, 359
London School of Economics, 28, 91, 102, 119, 235
Long Branch Acerra Brothers, 309
Long Branch City League, 309
Long Branch, N.J.
   substantial Black population in 1940, 49, 69n18
   See WBG IV: Childhood, Passing in Long Beach; Tracing baseball roots
Los Angeles Times, 353, 359, 379, 417n7, 454–455, 465n56
Loss, Louis, 184
Loving v. Virginia (1967), 251, 279n11
low-opportunity jobs, 178, 191, 196
Lowrie, Jed, 321, 331n32

Lubbers, William, 341–342, 354–355
Lucy, Bill, 440, 464n32
Lytlle, John, 235

Mabson, Eliza (sister of WBG), 36–37
Mackenzie, G. Calvin, 339, 363, 370n4, 371n21
Major League Baseball safety
   passes equipment Rule 3.14, 301–302
Malan, Daniel, 249
Marks, Joe, 269
Mandatory Mediation and Conciliation Act (MMC), 449
   and the United Farm Workers (UFW), 448–450
Mandela, Nelson, 248, 250, 254, 256, 263, 266, 273–274, 376, 403
Mandela, Winnie (wife of Nelson Mandela), 256–257, 266
Mann, Keith, 208
Marquess, Mark, 321, 390
Marshall, Thurgood, 48, 55, 60, 69n14, 148, 166n21
Matthews, Anthony "Tony", 260
Mays, Willie, 301, 321, 330n25
Mazey, Emil, 87, 96, 108n30, 146–147
McCarty, Dave, 321
McCarthy, Joseph R., 20, 45–47, 56
McCulloch, Frank, 132, 135, 335, 347, 370n12, 373
McCune, Baron, 219–220, 222–223
McDonough, Will, 312, 331n26
McGuinness, Ken, 358
McLain, Maureen, 292
Meany, George, 70n29, 90, 105, 147, 175
Mendez, Miguel, 297, 334, 373
Merryman, John, 297
Metzler, Cynthia, 337, 339, 345
Meyers, Charles (Charlie), 214, 296, 322
Michigan Chronicle, 195–196, 204n56
Michigan Civil Rights Commission, 181, 183, 203n34
Michigan Employment Relations Commission (MERC), 171
Mikva, Abner and Zoe, 376, 385, 417n3, 417n14
Miller, Jon, 305
The Mind of South Africa, 266
Mintzer, George, 139–140

INDEX

Modern Jazz Quartet, 51, 324
modern labor law, 293
    at-will principle, 293
    reinstatement, 87, 101, 158, 215, 293–294, 329n11, 355, 411
    just cause standard, 293, 329n10
    progressive discipline concept, 293, 329n10
Moe, Terry, 341, 343, 370nn7–8
Mogk, John "Jack", 176–178, 180, 203nn25–27
Mollet, Guy, 122, 286
Morgado v. City and County of San Francisco, 456, 466n61
Mosley-Braun, Carol, 361
Mother Jones, 360
Motlana, Nthato, 255, 258
Murphy, Betty Southard, 353
Musial, Stan, 303
Myrdal, Gunnar, 49, 69n19, 128
    See American dilemma

Naidoo, Jay, 264
National Academy of Arbitrators, 106n2, 150, 181, 295, 329n13, 333, 376
National Archives, 28
National American Labor Council, 90
NAACP, 5, 21, 44, 51, 60, 440
NAACP Legal Defense Fund, 156, 174, 178, 190
national labor policy, 163n13, 203n35
    Ronald Reagan and the, 230, 343
National Labor Relations Act (NLRA)
    Agricultural Labor Relations Act and, 441–442, 445–446, 448, 453, 455
    1935 origins, functions of, 63–64
    collective-bargaining agreements under, 64, 137, 449
    1947 and 1959 amendments to the, 344
    FirstGroup initiative to augment NLRA policies, 429
    compared with the Independent Monitor Program, 429–434
National Labor Relations Board (NLRB)
    functions of, 63–64
    case worked assigned from the, 132–136
    President Bill Clinton nominates WBG IV to lead the, 328, 346
    becoming Chairman of the, 369
    NLRB v. Allis-Chalmers ruling, 158
    WBG IV proposes administrative law judges reforms; creates core of "settlement judges" to mediate labor disputes; promotes postal ballots in representation elections, 377
    San Diego Gas and Electric ruling re: postal ballots in elections, 413
    1994–1995 Major League Baseball strike and, 380–387
    FirstGroup Independent Monitor Program and, 422–429, 433
National Lawyers Guild, 47, 76–77, 205n64
National Maritime Union (NMU), 149
National Mediation Board, 217, 455
National Organization of Women (NOW), 92
National Party, 240
National Right to Work Committee, 344, 363, 401
Nationalists, 252, 267
Naught for Your Comfort, 252, 263
Navasky, Vic, 79
"Negro Removal", 92
    See Urban Renewal
Neufeld, Inge, 91, 114
New Detroit, 178
"New Frontier", 78
New Leader, 90, 130, 143, 184, 204n35
New Republic, 13
New York Daily News, 28, 304
New York Herald Tribune, 7
New York Times, 45, 58, 66, 74, 130, 297, 305, 328, 339, 354, 365
New York World Telegram, 307
Newman, Winn, 148
Nixon plantation, 30
Nixon, Richard, 20, 176, 202n18, 202–203n20, 203n21, 208, 217, 219, 222, 230
Novotel New York, 413, 418n32

Obama, Barack, 232–234, 441
O'Brien, Colin, 457
O'Connor, Sandra Day, 220–221, 243n15
O'Higgins, Paul, 236

INDEX 557

The Office of Management and Budget, 398, 403
Oljenik, Andrew, 422
Organized labor, 46, 62, 75, 89, 131n5, 163n13, 167n33, 342
Orza, Gene, 321, 385, 404–405, 417n14
Owen, David, 259

Palo Alto Times, 229–230, 243n23, 244n25
Panetta, Leon, 397
Paskal, Oscar, 76
Paterson, Basil, 230, 244n24
Paton, Alan, 249
Pattern Makers v. NLRB, 357, 370n13
Pawel, Miriam, 444, 448, 450
Pelosi, Nancy, 396
Pemberton, John de J. (Jack), 184–185, 196–197, 225
Pesky, Johnny, 304, 307
Petty, Regina, 422
Phi Mu Delta, 55–56
Philadelphia Plan, 175–176, 202nn17–18
Phillips, Julian, 245
Pierce, Samuel, 135–136, 162n8
Pieter Maritz, South Africa, 268–269
Pittsburgh Black Musicians, 219–223
Plessy v. Ferguson, 48, 66, 69n12
Pogund, Jenny, 267
Polonia, Luis, 326–327
Population Registration Act, 249
Porter, Barbara and Bill, 228–229
Preston, Sarah, 30
Progressive Party, 45
public education arbitration
    Michigan cases in Inkster and Gibraltar school districts, 171–173, 201n4
    Michigan Employment Relations Commission (MERC) and, 171
    wage dispute between Detroit Federation of Teachers and the Detroit Board of Education, 172, 202n6
Public Employees' Fair Employment Act, 137
    See Taylor Law, 1967
Public Employment Relations Board, 138, 150, 171, 466nn60–62
public policy cases, 291, 296
Public Safety Officers Procedural Bill of Rights Act (PSOPBRA), 455, 466n61
public sector labor market, 150

Quill, Mike, 137–138

Race consciousness, 221–222, 244n15
racial discrimination,
    Detroit apartment situation, 88
    Workplace fairness legislation and, 62–63
    TRADE Union Leadership Council (TULC) and, 89–91
    See Detroit Edison case
Racial misconduct
    inside San Francisco city work force, 457–462, 466n63
Ramaphosa, Cyril, 261–264, 272–273, 280n44, 403
Reagan, Ronald, 275–276
    See WBG IV Speaks out about Reagan administration
"The Red Flag", 116, 130n3
"Red Sox Nation," 314
Reich, Robert, 336–339, 345, 348, 353, 359, 370n3
reinstatement
    eligible for due to unfair labor practices, 87, 158, 355, 411
    inappropriate circumstances for, 215, 243n5, 293–294, 329n11
    See modern labor law
Republican Party, 1, 14, 20, 44, 375
Reuther, Roy, 84–85
Reuther, Victor, 85, 107n16, 120–122, 128
Reuther, Walter Philip, 62, 70n29, 71n34, 76–77, 79, 84, 103–106, 142
Rhodesia (now Zimbabwe), 260
right-to-work
    legislation, 92
    prohibitions, 92
Riskin, Victoria, 420–422, 463n4
River Rouge Plant, Dearborn, Mich., 76
    UAW Local 600 case at, 100–101
Rivera-Hernandez, Cathryn, 443–445
Rizzuto, Phil, 308
Robben Island, 250, 254
Roberts, Paul, 353, 370n11
Robeson, Paul, 45
Robinson, Jackie, 48, 221, 312
Robinson, James, 176
Roche, "Red", 75, 82
Rockefeller, Nelson, 137, 230

Rodriquez, Art, 453
Roosevelt, Eleanor, 49
Roosevelt, Franklin Delano (FDR), 44, 68n1, 144, 419
  Baseball during World War II, 303
Roosevelt, Franklin Delano, Jr., 144
Rosenbloom, Oscar, 214
Roth, Stephen, 177, 203nn25–27
Roumell, George, 172
Royal Institute of International Affairs, 259
Rudy, Mark, 292

Sabor Farms, 451, 465n47
Sachs, Ted, 172
Sacks, Al, 209
St. Anne's Anglican Church, London, 124–125
St. Antoine, Ted, and wife, Lloyd, 155
St. James Episcopal Church, Long Branch, N.J., 15, 52, 99, 309
St. John the Evangelist Episcopal Church, Boston, Mass., 1
St. Mary, the Virgin, Cathedral of (Anglican) Johannesburg, South Africa, describing the author's "mugging" near the Cathedral after attending Mass, 271
St. Mary's Roman Catholic Church, Dedham, Mass., 32, 38
salary-cap proposal, 382
San Francisco Chronicle, 229, 320, 336, 370n2
San Francisco Industrial Relations Research Association, 216
  See Labor and Employment Relations Association (LERA)
San Francisco Labor Council, 217
San Jose Mercury News's *West Magazine*, 360
sanctions
  South African economic, 256, 262–265, 280nn31–38
Sanders, Bernie, 408, 410–413
Sawyer, Mary Ann, 402, 419
Sawyer, Tom, 403
Schultz, George, 262, 280n33
Scientific American, 150
Scheepers, Reverend Noble, 50
Schmidt, William L., 444
Schnacke, Robert, 218
Schotmiller, Mary, 423

Seattle Building Trades decree, 188–189, 204n40
Segregation
  Black-white, 458–459, 466n63
  in Washington, D.C., hotels, 16
  in Long Branch, N.J., 12
  on public transportation, 65–66
  in unions, 96, 143–148, 220–221
Selig, Bud, 385, 417n14
Senate Labor and Human Resources Committee, 347–348
Service Employees International Union, 425
Service Employees Union, 409–410, 418n28
Shays, Christopher, 402–404, 410
Sheffield, Horace, 76, 89–90, 92, 96–97
Sheinkman, Jack, 94, 132, 151, 334, 336–337, 378
Shiroma, Genevieve, 443–444
Shockley, William, 366, 371n25
Shorenstein, Walter, c10
Simon, Paul, 352
Sims, Ron, 440
Slaiman, Don, 146–147
Slater, Walter, 217
Smith, Reggie, 387–388
Snell, Karen, 453
Sobell, Tom, 453
Social Security Act, 44
Soklome, Shako, 252, 254
Sola, Steve, 354
Solarz, Stephen, 260, 279n25
Solidarity, free union movement
  Conference of in Gdansk, Poland, 276–277, 281nn48–50
Sotomayor, Sonia, 386–287, 417n16
Soweto, 252–253, 255–256, 258, 271, 278n5
Soweto Ten, 255
Soweto "uprising", 1976, 247–248, 278n4
Spaeth, Carl, 211
Sparks, Allister, 266
Specter, Arlen, 395–397
Spielberg Manufacturing Co., 438, 464n25
sports law, 298, 301, 319–321, 328, 381
Stamps, Willie, 184–185, 188
Stanford Business School, 216
Stanford Daily, 224, 243n18

INDEX

Stanford Law School, 208–209, 212, 296, 301, 320, 322, 328–329, 373, 416, 417n18
Stanford University, 370n2, 394–395
Stark, Sheldon, 199–200, 205n64
Station Field, 17, 299, 301–302, 306, 311
Steele v. Louisville & N.R. Co., 173, 175, 202n9,16
  See Stone, Harlan F.
Steinberg, Charles, 390
Steinberg, Jonny, 248, 278n6
Stevenson, Adlai, 43–45, 56, 78, 183
Stewart, Bill, 17, 132, 345, 356, 373–376, 385, 393, 405–407, 419
Stewart, Potter, 148, 166n21
Stoddard Quirk Manufacturing Co., 435, 463n18
Stone, Harlan F., 173, 202n9
  See *Steele v. Louisville & N.R. Co.*
strike-replacement cases, 355
Stuart, Keith, 115, 127, 236, 287
Sullivan, Pat, 138, 142
Sullivan Principles, 260
Supreme Court Review, 181, 203n31
Sussman, Frank, 254, 269, 279n16
Sveum, Dale, 327
Swainson, John, 78, 81, 85, 103, 107n17

Taft, Robert, 20, 45
Taft-Hartley Act
  amendments of 1947 to the, 64, 341
  amendments to the National Labor Relations Act, 74
  and the National Labor Relations Board, 363, 371n20
  arrives in Great Britain, 244n29, 287
Tallent, Steve, 379
Tameny ruling, 291, 329n6
Taylor v. Armco Steel, 165n20, 174, 192–193, 204nn44–47
Taylor Law, 1967, 137–138, 162n9, 169, 171
  See Public Employees' Fair Employment Act, 137
Teamsters, 75, 140, 179, 338, 424–425, 427, 449
  Teamsters v. US, 199, 204n62
Telescope Casual Furniture, Inc., 412, 418n30
terminate at will,

limited exception to, 291
Thatcher, Margaret, 119, 235, 237, 262, 287
Thomas, Clarence, 354
Thurmond, Strom, 86, 361
Tishman, John, 151–152, 166n30
Title VII of the Civil Rights Act of 1964, 65
  "last hired-first-fired" policies of, 146, 227
  enactment of a bona fide seniority proviso to, 146–147
  grievance-arbitration and, 174, 423, 438
  Detroit Edison Company racial discrimination case and, 178, 183–201
  1991 amendments to, 186
Too Late the Phalarope, 249
Torres-Guillen, Sylvia, 443, 445
trade-off, 294
Trade Union Leadership Council (TULC), 89–91, 98
Trades Union Congress (TUC)
  Meeting with George Woodcock, general secretary, 121
Transport and General Workers Union (TGWU), 424–425
Transit Workers Union, 137
Trasvina, John, 441
Tri-Fanucchi Farms, 450, 465nn45–46
Trudeau, Pierre, 322–323, 392
Truesdale, John, 341–342, 355, 386, 401
Truman, Harry S., 43–44, 48, 86, 249, 392
Trumka, Richard, 379, 420, 462n2
Trump, Donald, 45, 219
Turzi, Joseph, 422–423
Tutu, Archbishop Desmond (Anglican Church), 262, 280n40
Tyacke, Eric, 251–252

Uehara, Koji, 315
Ulman, Lloyd, 216
undocumented workers, 345, 414, 418n37
unfair labor practices, 87, 158, 241, 340
  unfair labor proceedings, 86–87
  Lapeer, Mich. case and, 94
  The *Curtis-Wright* case and, 98
  United Mine Workers of America (UMWA) and, 378–380

Judge Sotomayor grants baseball strike-ending injunction against, 386–387
"Union Bosses: A Look Behind the Rhetoric", 402–403
union-management national cooperation, 236, 244n32
union-multinational corporations, 235–236, 244n32
union voting
    extend through postal ballots, 361
United Auto Workers (UAW)
    addressing dismantling of segregated local unions in Indiana, 96
    advice on union organizing and representation petitions, 95
    employee privacy issues, 95
    and civil rights issues, 60
    merit ratings in the collective bargaining process, 95
    Solidarity House, Detroit headquarters, 74, 77, 84–85, 87, 89, 100–101
    See River Rouge Plant
United Democratic Front (UDF), 269
United Farm Workers (UFW), 442, 447–450, 452–454
United Food and Commercial Workers Union (UFCW), 450
United Mine Workers of America (UMWA)
    dispute with the NLRB over contempt litigation, 378–379, 417n7
United States Information Agency (USIA), 246, 254, 290
U.S. Department of Housing and Urban Development (HUD), 440–441, 464n34
U.S. Justice Department, 82, 185, 189–190, 227–228, 419
U.S. State Department, 245, 247, 249–250, 252, 254, 263
United States v. Trucking Employers, 227, 243n21
University of Lodz, 276
University of Melbourne law faculty, 245
University of Western Australia Law School, 288
University of Witwatersrand, 258, 263
Urban Renewal, 92
    See "Negro Renewal"

Usery, William J., 378, 383, 385, 417n14
Utility Workers Union, 60, 178, 190, 195

Van de Water, John, 342
"verlichte" (enlightened), 252, 279n13
Vinson, Ethan, 188
Vorster government policy of repression, 255

Wagner, Hal, 307
Wagner, Robert (Mayor), 136–138,150
Wagner, Robert (Senator), 63
    Wagner Act and, 63, 240
Wallace, Henry, 45–46
Wall Street Journal, 213, 216, 339, 375
Walsh, Mary Jo, 92, 94–95, 99, 102
Warren, Chief Justice Earl, 48, 56, 169, 200–201, 205n67, 217
    Influence of 1954 *Brown v. Board of Education* ruling and opinion on WBG IV, 47–48
Washington, Booker T., 5
"Washingtonese", 356
Watkins, Arthur, 47
Washington Post, 134, 162n6, 375, 409
Watergate, 184, 211, 229
Wayne State Law School, 27, 155, 161–162, 174–175, 178, 245, 319
    See WBG IV Teaching Labor Law and Constitutional Law at Wayne State Law School
Wedderburn, K. W. "Bill", 235, 287
Weis, William, 93, 107n22
Weiss, Mike, 347, 360, 369, 370n9
Wellstone, Paul, 351–352, 357
Western Transport, 139
Whiteside, Larry, 320, 325, 357–358, 390, 399, 417n15
Whitfield v. United Steel Workers, 143, 165n18, 175, 202n15
Whitlam, Gough, 245
Wiehan, Nic, 252
Widick, B.J., 76, 90, 107n21
Williams, Edward Bennett, 47
Williams, G. Mennen "Soapy", 78, 103
Williams, Gary, 214, 442
Williams, Ted, 303–304
Willis, Raymond, 188–189
Wilson, Earl, 99, 311, 325

INDEX

Wilson, Harold, 115, 121, 127
Winnie and Nelson, 248–249, 278n6
Wise, Helena, 292
Wolff, Al, 407
Wong, William, 204n57, 213, 243nn6–7, 243n12, 243n19
workers education rule, 454
World Series, 302, 307, 314–315, 382, 390, 443
World War I
    Gould family service, 15
    Black veterans, 5
    U.S. Army, 15
Writers Guild of America, West, 420–422
wrongful discharge, 215, 290, 329nn7–13, 330n15, 330n17, 333
Wulf, Mel, 151, 176, 182, 199–200, 203n22, 203n32, 205n63, 205n65

Yale Law Journal, 173, 202n8, 244n29
Yankee Stadium, 99, 162, 298, 325, 387, 484
Yastrzemski, Carl "Yaz", 99, 108n33, 313–314
Yawkey, Tom, 312, 331n27
Youkilis, Kevin, 303
Young Democrats, 91–92

Zimbabwe (formerly Rhodesia), 260
Zimmer, Don, 316
Zubrensky, Leonard and Ruth (wife), 88
Zulu
    homeland, 267
    people, 255

ABOUT THE AUTHOR

William B. Gould IV is Charles A. Beardsley Professor of Law, Emeritus, at Stanford Law School. A prolific scholar of labor and discrimination law, Gould has been an influential voice in worker–management relations for more than fifty years and served as chairman of the National Labor Relations Board (NLRB, 1994–1998) and subsequently chairman of the California Agricultural Labor Relations Board (2014–2017). Professor Gould has been a member of the National Academy of Arbitrators since 1970. As NLRB chairman, he played a critical role in bringing the 1994–1995 baseball strike to its conclusion and has arbitrated and mediated more than three hundred labor disputes, including the 1992 and 1993 salary disputes between the Major League Baseball Players Association and the Major League Baseball Player Relations Committee. He served as secretary, Labor and Employment Law Section, American Bar Association (1980–1981) as well as Independent Monitor for FirstGroup America, addressing freedom-of-association complaints (2008–2010). Shortly after the passage of Title VII of the Civil Rights Act of 1964, Professor Gould served as a consultant to the Equal Employment Opportunity Commission (1966–1967) providing recommendations on seniority disputes and conciliation procedures, and in 1967 he was a member of the very first Fact Finding Board established under the New York Taylor Law. Gould also served as Special Advisor to the U.S. Department of Housing and Urban Development on project labor agreements (2011–2012) and as independent reviewer on Equal Employment Opportunity for the Mayor of San Francisco (2020–2021). A critically acclaimed author of eleven books and more than sixty law review articles, Professor Gould is the recipient of five honorary doctorates for his significant contributions to the fields of labor law and labor relations.

www.ingramcontent.com/pod-product-compliance
Lightning Source LLC
Chambersburg PA
CBHW070357230426
43665CB00012B/1151